THE TORTURE DEBATE IN AMERICA

As a result of the work assembling the documents, memoranda, and reports that constitute the material in *The Torture Papers* questions were raised about the rationale underlying the Bush administration's decision to condone the use of coercive interrogation techniques in the interrogation of detainees suspected of terrorist connections. The condoned use of torture in any society is questionable but its use by the United States, a liberal democracy that champions human rights and is a party to international conventions forbidding torture, has sparked an intense debate within America and across the world. *The Torture Debate in America* captures these arguments with essays from individuals in different disciplines. This volume contains essays covering all sides of the argument, from those who embrace the absolute prohibition of torture to those who see it as a viable option in the war on terror, and with relevant documents complementing the essays.

Karen J. Greenberg is the Executive Director of the Center on Law and Security at New York University School of Law. She is the co-editor of the recently published *The Torture Papers: The Road to Abu Ghraib*, editor of the forthcoming *Al Qaeda Now*, and editor of *The NYU Review of Law and Security*.

THE TORTURE DEBATE IN AMERICA

Edited by

KAREN J. GREENBERG

CENTER ON LAW AND SECURITY
NEW YORK UNIVERSITY SCHOOL OF LAW

CAMBRIDGE
UNIVERSITY PRESS

CAMBRIDGE UNIVERSITY PRESS
Cambridge, New York, Melbourne, Madrid, Cape Town, Singapore, São Paulo

Cambridge University Press
40 West 20th Street, New York, NY 10011-4211, USA

www.cambridge.org
Information on this title: www.cambridge.org/9780521857925

First published 2006

Printed in the United States of America

A catalog record for this publication is available from the British Library.

Library of Congress Cataloging in Publication Data

The torture debate in America / edited by Karen J. Greenberg.
    p.   cm.
Includes bibliographical references and index.
ISBN-13: 978-0-521-85792-5 (hardback)
ISBN-10: 0-521-85792-9 (hardback)
ISBN-13: 978-0-521-67461-4 (pbk.)
ISBN-10: 0-521-67461-1 (pbk.)
1. Human rights – Government policy – United States. 2. Torture.
3. Political prisoners – Abuse of. 4. Military interrogation. 5. War on
Terrorism, 2001– . I. Greenberg, Karen J.
JC599.U5T665 2005
323.4′9–dc22   2005022921

ISBN-13   978-0-521-85792-5 hardback
ISBN-10   0-521-85792-9 hardback

ISBN-13   978-0-521-67461-4 paperback
ISBN-10   0-521-67461-1 paperback

Contents

Acknowledgments

This book could not have been done without the advice and guidance of many. Marty Lederman kept constant and generous vigil on the torture debate that occurred and the documents that appeared around us as we assembled the essays. Francesca Laguardia provided wise counsel on the documents that underlay the debate. Gayle Horn shared her expertise on interrogation manuals and their usage.

Kristin Henderson's and Jonathan Voegele's thoughtful editing made the book come to life. John Berger's patience, encouragement and colleagueship made the work pleasurable as well as viable. The staff at the Center on Law and Security offered editing and assembling help.

Last but by no means least, Stephen Holmes flooded me with ideas and materials, all the while keeping me steadily afloat.

To all of them, my thanks.

Contributors

M. Cherif Bassiouni is Distinguished Research Professor of Law at DePaul University College of Law and President of the International Human Rights Law Institute. He is also President of the International Institute of Higher Studies in Criminal Sciences in Siracusa, Italy, as well as the Honorary President of the International Association of Penal Law, based in Paris, France, after having served as President and previously as Secretary-General for thirty years. Professor Bassiouni is the author of 24 and the editor of 44 books, and the author of 217 articles, mainly on international criminal law, comparative criminal law, and international human rights law.

Richard B. Bilder is the Foley & Lardner-Bascom Emeritus Professor of Law at the University of Wisconsin-Madison where he has taught particularly in the areas of international and foreign relations law. He served for some years as an attorney in the Office of Legal Adviser at the U.S. Department of State. Among other positions, Professor Bilder has served as Vice-President, Honorary Vice-President and Counselor of the American Society of International Law and as a member of the Board of Editors of the *American Journal of International Law*. He served as Chair of the International Courts Committee of the American Bar Association and Committee on Diplomatic Protection of the International Law Association. He was educated at Williams College and Harvard Law School, and was a Fulbright Scholar at England's Cambridge University.

David W. Bowker is a counsel in the international litigation group at Wilmer Cutler Pickering Hale and Dorr LLP in New York. Before joining the firm, Mr. Bowker was an attorney-adviser for the law of armed conflict in the Office of the Legal Adviser at the U.S. Department of State. Mr. Bowker previously worked in the field of counterterrorism as a graduate intern for the National Security Council staff. He is an adjunct professor at the Benjamin N. Cardozo School of Law, where he teaches a course on international humanitarian law and the war on terrorism.

David D. Caron is the C. William Maxeiner Distinguished Professor of Law at the Boalt Hall School of Law at the University of California, Berkeley. He served as a legal assistant to Judges Richard Mosk and Charles Brower at the Iran-United States Claims Tribunal in The Hague. He was a senior research fellow at the Max Planck Institute for Comparative Public and International Law from 1985 to 1986, and served as director of studies (1987) and director of research (1995) at the Hague Academy of International Law. He is a member of the board of editors of the *American Journal of International Law* and received the 1991 Deak Prize of the American Society of International Law for outstanding scholarship by a younger academic. He presently serves as a member of the precedent panel of the U.N. Compensation Commission for claims arising out of the Gulf War and is also a member of the Department of State Advisory Committee on Public International Law.

Lee A. Casey is a partner in the law firm of Baker & Hostetler LLP, and serves as an expert member of the United Nations Sub-Commission on the Promotion and Protection of Human Rights. From 1986 to 1993, he served in various capacities in the federal government, including the Office of Legal Counsel from 1992–93 and the Office of Legal Policy from 1986–90 at the U.S. Department of Justice. He was Deputy Associate General Counsel of the U.S. Department of Energy from 1990 to 1992. Mr. Casey received his J.D. from the University of Michigan School of Law in 1982, and served as law clerk to the Hon. Alex Kozinski from 1984–85.

Michael C. Dorf is the Michael I. Sovern Professor of Law at Columbia University and the author of dozens of scholarly articles on constitutional law and related subjects. He is the editor of and wrote the introduction to the book, *Constitutional Law Stories* (Foundation Press, 2004). With Laurence H. Tribe, Professor Dorf is the co-author of the book *On Reading the Constitution*. His bi-weekly column appears on the website writ.FindLaw.com. Professor Dorf is a graduate of Harvard College and Harvard Law School. Following law school, he was a law clerk for Judge Stephen Reinhardt of the U.S. Court of Appeals for the Ninth Circuit in Los Angeles and then for U.S. Supreme Court Justice Anthony Kennedy.

Joshua Dratel is a practicing attorney in New York City. He is President of the New York State Association of Criminal Defense Lawyers and serves on the Board of Directors of the National Association of Criminal Defense Lawyers. Along with Major Dan Mori, he is assisting in the defense of Australian detainee David Hicks. He also defended al Qaeda member Wadih el Hage after the bombings in Tanzania and Kenya. He has written articles on defending terrorism cases, including *Ethical Issues in Defending a Terrorism Case: How Secrecy and Security Impair the Defense of a Terrorism Case and Ethical Issues in Defending a*

Terrorism Case: Stuck in the Middle. He is co-editor of *The Torture Papers: The Road to Abu Ghraib.* He received his B.A. from Columbia College and his law degree from Harvard Law School.

Joyce S. Dubensky is the Executive Director of the Tanenbaum Center for Inter-religious Understanding. Before joining the Tanenbaum Center, Ms. Dubensky served as the national Director of Communications and, later, the Deputy Executive Director of a regional office of the National Conference for Community and Justice. An attorney, Ms. Dubensky founded the legal department at UJA-Federation of New York and served as its General Counsel for over a decade. Ms. Dubensky holds her J.D. from New York University School of Law, where she graduated with honors, and has her M.A. in American History (with an emphasis on Minority Studies) from Adelphi University. Currently, she serves on the Board of Advisors for the Center Against Violence in the Family.

Noah Feldman is professor of law at New York University School of Law. He served as senior advisor on constitutional law to the Coalition Provisional Authority in Iraq and as advisor to Iraqis involved in the constitutional process there. He is the author of *What We Owe Iraq: War and the Ethics of Nation Building* and *After Jihad: America and the Struggle for Islamic Democracy.* He received his A.B. summa cum laude from Harvard University. Selected as a Rhodes Scholar, he earned a doctorate in Islamic Thought from Oxford University and his J.D. from Yale Law School, after which he served as a law clerk to Justice David H. Souter of the U.S. Supreme Court.

Stephen Gillers is professor of law at New York University School of Law, where he served as Vice Dean from 1999–2004. He now holds the Emily Kempin chair. Professor Gillers has written widely on legal and judicial ethics, including in law reviews and the legal and popular press. He has taught legal ethics as a visitor at other law schools and has spoken on lawyer regulatory issues at federal and state judicial conferences, ABA conventions, state and local bar meetings nationwide, before Congress, at law firms and corporate law departments, and in law school lectureships. He is currently Chair (and since 2002 has been a member) of the American Bar Association's Joint Committee on Lawyer Regulation. Following a clerkship with Chief Judge Gus J. Solomon in Federal District Court in Portland, Oregon, Professor Gillers practiced law in New York City before joining the NYU faculty.

Stephen Holmes is currently Walter E. Meyer Professor of Law at NYU School of Law. From 1979 to 1985 he taught at the Department of Government at Harvard University. From 1985 to 1997, he was Professor of Politics and Law at the Law School and Political Science Department of the University of Chicago. From 1997 to 2000, he was Professor of Politics at Princeton. He was the editor-in-chief of the *East European Constitutional Review* from 1993–2003. In 2003, he was selected as a Carnegie Scholar. His fields of specialization include the history of liberalism, the disappointments of democratization after communism, the Russian criminal justice system, the weaknesses of international criminal law, and the near-impossibility of combating terrorism within the limits of liberal constitutionalism.

Scott Horton is a partner of Patterson, Belknap, Webb and Tyler LLP. He is an Adjunct Professor at Columbia University School of Law and chairs the Committee on International Law of the Association of the Bar of the City of New York. He has served as an advisor for the Central Eurasia Project at the Open Society Institute, and Chair of the Advisory Board for the Eurasia Group. He is a Founding Trustee of the American University in Kyrgyzstan and President of the International League for Human Rights.

Christopher Kutz is Professor of Law in the Jurisprudence and Social Policy Program, Boalt Hall School of Law, U.C. Berkeley. He teaches moral, political, and legal philosophy, as well as criminal law, and is the author of Complicity: Ethics and Law for a Collective Age. His recent work includes articles on democratic theory, reparations, and non-uniformed combatancy.

Rachel Lavery is the Religious Affairs Researcher at the Tanenbaum Center for Interreligious Understanding. She is also a J.D. candidate at the Benjamin N. Cardozo School of Law of Yeshiva University, where she is a member of the Cardozo Law Review. Ms. Lavery holds a B.A. in Religious Studies from New York University, where she wrote her honors thesis on the Church of Jesus Christ of Latter-Day Saints and its relationship with American culture.

Anthony Lewis was a columnist for the New York Times from 1969 to December 2001. He has twice won the Pulitzer Prize and in 2001 he was awarded the Presidential Citizens Medal. From 1956–57 he was a Nieman Fellow and he spent the academic year studying at Harvard Law School. Mr. Lewis was for fifteen years a Lecturer on Law at Harvard Law School, teaching a course on the Constitution and the press. He has taught at a number of other universities as a visitor, among them the Universities of California, Illinois, Oregon, and Arizona. Since 1983 he has held the James Madison Visiting Professorship at Columbia University.

David Luban is the Frederick J. Haas Professor of Law and Philosophy at Georgetown Law School. Previous to his tenure at Georgetown, Professor Luban taught at Kent State University and the University of Maryland. His numerous articles and chapters have focused on a range of topics in legal ethics, the social responsibility of lawyers, law and philosophy, jurisprudence, and social justice. He has been a Woodrow Wilson Graduate Fellow, a Guggenheim Fellow, a Danforth Fellow, a Keck Foundation Distinguished Senior Fellow in Legal Ethics and Professional Culture at Yale Law School, and a Fellow of the Woodrow Wilson International Center for Scholars. He was chosen by the American Bar Foundation for the 1998 Keck Foundation Lecturer Award in Legal Ethics and Professional Responsibility.

Heather MacDonald is a John M. Olin Fellow at the Manhattan Institute and a contributing editor to *City Journal*. Her writings have also appeared in *The Wall Street Journal, Washington Post, New York Times, The New Republic, Partisan Review, The New Criterion, Public Interest*, and *Academic Questions* and she is also a frequent guest on Fox News, CNN, and other television and radio programs. A non-practicing lawyer, Ms. MacDonald has clerked for the Honorable Stephen Reinhardt on the U.S. Court of Appeals for the Ninth Circuit and she was an attorney-advisor in the Office of the General Counsel of the U.S. Environmental Protection Agency. She has testified before the Subcommittee on Civil and Constitutional Rights of the Committee of the Judiciary of the U.S. House of Representatives.

Andrew C. McCarthy was an Assistant U.S. Attorney for the Southern District of New York for eighteen years. He led the 1995 terrorism prosecution against Sheik Omar Abdel Rahman and eleven others, and is currently a senior fellow at the Foundation for the Defense of Democracies. The recipient of numerous awards, including the Justice Department's highest honors: the Attorney General's Exceptional Service Award (1996) and Distinguished Service Award (1988). Mr. McCarthy has also served as an adjunct professor of law at Fordham Law School and New York Law School.

Major Michael (Dan) Mori, United States Marine Corps, currently serves as Military Defense Counsel for Mr. David Hicks, an Australian citizen, before a military commission at Naval Base Guantanamo Bay, Cuba. Major Mori has served as Judge Advocate in the U.S. Marine Corps since 1996 and has performed the duties of Defense Counsel, Prosecutor and Special Assistant U.S. Attorney.

Burt Neuborne is the John Norton Pomeroy Professor of Law at NYU School of Law and the Legal Director of the Brennan Center for Justice. For 30 years, he has been one of the nation's foremost civil liberties lawyers, serving as National Legal Director of the ACLU, Special Counsel to the NOW Legal Defense and Education Fund, and as a member of the New York City Human Rights Commission. He has argued many Supreme Court cases, and litigated literally hundreds of important constitutional cases. He challenged the constitutionality of the Vietnam War, pioneered the flag-burning cases, worked on the Pentagon Papers case, worked with Justice Ruth Bader Ginsburg when she headed the ACLU Women's Rights Project, and anchored the ACLU's legal program during the Reagan years.

Deborah Pearlstein is the Director of the U.S. Law and Security Program at Human Rights First and a visiting lecturer in human rights and national security at Stanford Law School. Before embarking on a career in law, Pearlstein served in the White House as a senior editor and speechwriter for President Clinton. After her graduation from Harvard Law School in 1998, Pearlstein clerked for Judge Michael Boudin of the U.S. Court of Appeals for the First Circuit, and then for Justice John Paul Stevens of the U.S. Supreme Court. In 2002, Pearlstein shared the ACLU's Voting Rights Award for her work on election systems reform in California following the 2000 presidential election.

Dana Priest covers the intelligence community and national security issues for *The Washington Post* and is an analyst for NBC News. Her widely acclaimed 2003 book about the military expanding responsibility and influence won the prestigious New York Public Library Bernstein Book Award and was a finalist for the Pulitzer Prize. In 2004, she was a Pulitzer Prize finalist twice, for her reporting on clandestine intelligence, and for her contribution to the Post's reporting on the Abu Ghraib prison abuse scandal. In 2001, Priest was awarded a MacArthur Foundation Research and Writing grant and was a guest scholar in residence at the U.S. Institute of Peace. The same year, she won the Gerald R. Ford Prize for Distinguished Reporting on the National Defense and the State Department's Excellence in Journalism Award.

Michael Ratner is President of the Center for Constitutional Rights. He was co-counsel in representing the Guantanamo detainees in the Supreme Court, where a major victory was won in June 2004. He and his office have sued two of the private contractors in Iraq, alleging their employees were involved in the abuses and torture at Abu Ghraib. He recently filed a criminal complaint in the courts of Germany against Secretary of Defense Rumsfeld and other U.S. officials seeking the initiation of criminal prosecutions for the Abu Ghraib abuse and torture. Mr. Ratner serves as an Adjunct Professor at Columbia Law School, where he teaches international human rights litigation, and previously as a Lecturer at Yale Law School. He is a former President of the National Lawyers Guild, and has served as Special Counsel to Haitian President Jean-Bertrand Aristide to assist in the prosecution of human rights crimes.

David B. Rivkin, Jr., is a partner in the Washington, D.C., office of Baker & Hostetler LLP. Mr. Rivkin is a Visiting Fellow at the Nixon Center, Member of the UN Sub-Commission on the Promotion and Protection of Human Rights and a contributing editor at the *National Interest* and *National Review*. He served in the White House Counsel's Office and in the Departments of Justice and

Energy during the Reagan and Bush Sr. Administrations. He frequently writes on international and constitutional law matters, as well as foreign and defense policy issues, for a variety of newspapers and magazines including *The Washington Post, Wall Street Journal, New York Times, Financial Times, LA Times, Foreign Affairs*, and *Foreign Policy*, and appears regularly on a number of TV and radio shows.

Jeffrey K. Shapiro is a lawyer in private practice in Washington, D.C. His practice focuses primarily on helping medical device and diagnostic manufacturers comply with U.S. Food and Drug Administration (FDA) regulatory requirements. Mr. Shapiro is the co-author of a book published in April 2005, Combination Products: *How to Develop The Optimal Strategic Path for Approval*, which is a guide for manufacturers seeking FDA approval of groundbreaking new medical products and therapies that combine drug, device or biologic therapies. From 1991 to 1994, he served as an attorney-advisor in the Justice Department's Office of Legal Counsel. He is a graduate of Harvard Law School.

William H. Taft IV is of counsel resident at the Washington D.C. law firm of Fried Frank, Harris, Shriver & Jacobson LLP. In 2001, Mr. Taft was appointed as Legal Adviser to the Department of State, where he served for four years. From 1981 to 1984, Mr. Taft was General Counsel for the Department of Defense. He also served as the Deputy Secretary of Defense from January 1984 to April 1989 and as Acting Secretary of Defense from January to March 1989, as well as the U.S. Permanent Representative to NATO from 1989 to 1992. Prior to his initial appointment to the Department of Defense, Mr. Taft was in private law practice in Washington, D.C., from 1977 to 1981. Mr. Taft received his J.D. in 1969 from Harvard Law School and his B.A. in 1966 from Yale University.

Detlev F. Vagts is the Bemis Professor of International Law at the Harvard Law School and has taught there since 1959. Prior to his academic career, Professor Vagts was associated with Cahill, Gordon, Reindel & Ohl in New York City from 1951–53 and 1956–59, and a Judge Advocate in the United States Air Force from 1953 to 1956. He graduated from Harvard College and Law School, and was an Associate Reporter of the Restatement (Third) of Foreign Relations Law and Counselor on International Law at Department of State.

Peter Weiss is a leading human rights lawyer and Vice President of the Center for Constitutional Rights. He also serves as Vice President, former President, of the International Association of Lawyers Against Nuclear Arms. He litigated the seminal case establishing the right of victims of torture to sue their torturers in U.S. courts (*Filartiga v. Pena-Irala*). Since his retirement in 1996 from Weiss Dawid Fross Zelnick & Lehrman, a leading trademark firm, he has been Senior Intellectual Property Counsel to The Chanel Company Ltd. He is also a founder and former President of the American Committee on Africa and former Chairman of the Board of the Institute for Policy Studies in Washington. He has also long been an activist for peace in the Middle East and is currently a member of the Arab-Jewish Peace Group in New York and of the Executive Committee of Americans for Peace Now, which supports the Peace Now movement in Israel.

The Rule of Law Finds Its Golem: Judicial Torture Then and Now

Karen J. Greenberg

THE MATTER OF TORTURE AT THE HANDS OF AMERICANS HAS BEEN ON public display for more than a year now as this book of essays and documents goes to print. In this past year, 2004–2005, we have learned much. We have learned that, starting in 2002, the abuse of prisoners from Iraq, Afghanistan, and elsewhere took place at more than one American military prison; that ghost prisoners and ghost detention centers exist under American supervision; that the practice of rendition, sending prisoners to countries that torture, is practiced by the United States government; that the Bush administration supported a policy that narrowly defined torture and then declared abusive behavior permissible in the case of suspected terrorists, enemy combatants, and other detainees of the war on terror.

We have learned something else as well. We have learned that very few Americans are eager to engage in a debate about the revival of torture as an overt practice conducted in their name. Despite the appearance of pictures of abuse on television and in the print media, despite the publication of a wealth of documents and government reports attesting to the use of abusive, torturous methods, the public response has remained at best apathetic. It is not that Americans don't care about the introduction of torture into our language and our national identity, it is more that we are confused about how to address the issue. And in that respect, we have had very little guidance. Academic lawyers have conducted a policy debate among themselves, but the wider public has not been privy to the legal debate any more than it has been privy to some of the more thoughtful philosophical and ethical perspectives.

The essays in this volume present the debate that has belatedly but importantly taken place among intellectuals, policymakers, lawyers, journalists and others in the wake of the revelations of the "Torture Memos," previously published in *The Torture Papers: The Road to Abu Ghraib*.[1] Until now, this debate has taken place largely outside of the public view. Together, these pieces are meant to bring these arguments into the public consciousness, to open up to a wider audience learned considerations on what it means for a nation to know that torture is being conducted in its name. Amidst the myriad forms of ethical, moral, political, and strategic considerations, the authors included here have all asked themselves the question, what does the introduction of the fact of torture mean to the United States? Does it make us safer? Was the policy of granting the president unprecedented broad powers important even though it opened the door to the practice of torture? Are there long-term consequences to the use of torture? And finally, where do we as a nation want to go from here?

For some, the mere introduction of torture as an issue to be contemplated and debated has changed the nature of the American experiment; it has taken perhaps the ultimate taboo and made it part of the landscape, both theoretically and in practice. For many, the use of torture threatens to alter the very identity of Americans and their systems of values. David Luban considers the use of torture akin to the "unraveling of liberal ideology." Stephen Holmes takes it one step further: we have, despite ourselves, become our enemies. For others, it is a practice that, ultimately, may save us as a nation. Andrew McCarthy laments the fact that this is the moment to which we have arrived, but nevertheless, we cannot run and hide from a distasteful and dangerous reality.

Many of the essays focus on the Torture Memos themselves. They are concerned with the legal dimensions of the argument as it positions the United States internationally and domestically. Whether or not the United States should be bound by the prisoner of war protections of the Geneva Conventions in the post 9/11 years, the nature and extent of the power that accrued to the president in the wake of 9/11, and how to assess and understand the Torture Memos are central legal questions in the growing debate over the Bush administration's policy towards detainees from Afghanistan and Iraq. On the matter of the Geneva Conventions, the Bush administration concluded that the Geneva Conventions applied neither to the Taliban nor to al Qaeda. The former functioned within a failed state, the latter was a nonstate actor. Not everyone agrees with this conclusion however. Some, like William Taft, IV, who was legal advisor to the secretary of state, and David Bowker who worked for the Office of Legal Counsel (OLC) at the time, disagreed then as they disagree now. Others who worked at the OLC at the time the Torture Memos were written concur with the Bush administration's decision. David Rivkin and Lee Casey point out that there needs to be a rethinking of honoring reciprocity over treaties even when one party is not or does not consider itself to be reciprocally bound, especially now that the United States is engaged in asymmetric warfare. Dana Priest and Major Michael Dan Mori raise an alternative possibility, namely, the use of court martials. Priest maintains that the military would have liked to try the detainees rather than lock them up in unlimited detention without charges.

For still other contributors, torture is an unpleasant means to a necessary end. The authors in this volume consider each one of these issues, and more, in order to try and give readers a broad perspective on the need for change in the wake of 9/11. Heather MacDonald argues that coercive interrogation ultimately serves the nation well. Michael Dorf points out that the August 1, 2002 "Bybee Memo" – which defined torture as pain associated with "serious physical injury so severe that death, organ failure, or permanent damage" results – was revoked with the December 30, 2004 memo from Daniel Levin to James Comey, which declared that "torture is abhorrent both to American law and values" and leaves room for the authorization of torture when necessary. Deborah Pearlstein sums up the fundamental parameters of the debate surrounding torture. And Anthony Lewis points out that, bottom line, the decision to use torture is a decision that feeds power.

A final and more focused discussion that takes place in these pages is over questions of legal ethics and, in particular, how we as readers should assess the role which the lawyers in the Department of Justice played as advisors to the president and the secretary of state. The panel on "Torture: The Road to Abu Ghraib and Beyond"[2] that is printed here raises this question several times and from several different angles. Burt Neuborne defines the philosophical underpinnings of the legal context of torture. Joshua Dratel and Stephen Gillers point to the way in which the OLC lawyers behaved more as corporate lawyers than as public servants. Jeffrey Shapiro disagrees, arguing that in fact, the lawyer's job is to interpret the law with an eye towards wise policy and that in these circumstances, the lawyers behaved responsibly.

Many of the contributors to this volume have chosen to look back in time for answers, for guideposts, in an attempt to formulate a rational response to a situation that is overshadowed by the emotions of victimhood, anger, and the seeming loss of control in the post 9/11 era. The authors look in these pages to Vico, to Hobbes, to the Federalist Papers and to the basic theories of liberalism and war. Joyce Dubensky and Rachel Lavery point to the way in which religious canons – Christian, Jewish, Islamic, and others – have condoned torture. Scott Horton has described the crumbling of law under the National Socialist regime in Germany in the 1930s. Detlev Vagts and Richard Bilder consider the matter of accountability in Germany – as evidenced at Nuremberg, for example – as a backdrop for understanding the American policy of abuse. Michael Ratner turns from the past and explores the way forward through legal remedy and retrospective accountability. And Noah Feldman contributes a trenchant analysis of the philosophical, legal, political, and religious questions that underlie the essays in this volume.

The historical approach reminds us that torture has a subtle relationship to the rule of law; it is the unspoken realm of the forbidden, the unnamed that law represses. It is, in many ways, the ghost in the closet. And like the ghost's relative, the Golem, it always lies in wait to announce itself, unexpectedly, and with the express challenge to remove it before it spreads its destructive impulses too widely.

The numerous references to prior ages in which torture was utilized proves illuminating. Torture was used in Austria, Germany, Italy, Spain, England, and elsewhere, primarily during the 13th–17th centuries. It was used to elicit confessions and to punish those who had broken the law. Then as now, the definition of torture was broad-ranging. It included methods ranging from humiliation – as in the use of the public stocks – to death, which was the intended result of methods such as impalement, or the wheel to which one was tied until one died, or the saw on which one was placed upside down as a wide-toothed implement cut the body in half lengthwise starting between the legs. All of these methods ensured that the suspect would die a slow death. Sometimes, the intended result was merely to maim, as in the cutting out of one's tongue or the use of the "iron boot." Often, the intent was to instill the fear of death, as in the use of water torture. And sometimes, the purpose was merely to inflict intolerable pain, as in the use of thumbscrews, or the tying up of the body into different positions, actions which could result in maiming but which were not specifically intended to cause lasting physical damage.

However wide-ranging the types of torture, they shared a physicality. Torture was about harming the body and involved others to engage physically with the victim to cause that harm. As drawings from the time demonstrate, the medley of implements often required the attention of more than one attendant, particularly in the use of the rack or of other forms of tying a person up to inflict pain, or in flaying a body. The human contact itself conveyed an intimate bond between the tortured and the torturer, which the sounds of pain would have deepened.

A further extension of that physicality was the frequent involvement of a sexual dimension to the torture. Often, the charge itself involved a sexual crime, such as adultery. But the sexual nature of the punishment was present for charges of sexual as well as other criminal behavior. In medieval torture, bodies were often in a naked state. Given the prevalence of accused females, the female body parts were often the subject of the abuse, as in the use of pincers at her breasts, or the pear inside her vagina. For men, the pear was used to pierce through the body's anal openings.

Much of the rationale for medieval torture was religious. In addition to crimes of theft and murder, the accused was often considered guilty of heresy, or of violating the mores of the Christian religion, either by sexual or otherwise immoral behavior. The confession was important to the sanctity of one's soul, both that of the tortured and that of the torturer. The need for a confession was to serve justice, to complete the narrative that the accusation initiated, but justice was largely a reflection of religious doctrine. Before death, it was imperative to elicit the truth.

The imperative to fulfill the judicial narrative via torture attested to the tie between law and torture. Medieval torture was about eliciting information for convicting criminals; it was imperative to gain either two eyewitness accounts or a confession by the accused in order to convict a criminal. As a result, the law was present as a standard bearer. The jurisprudence of torture began in the 13th century and extended until the 18th century and was tied inextricably to the notion of proof. In Europe, the law of torture was reserved for capital crimes. Torture warrants in England and elsewhere relied on legal documentation, beginning with the issuing of a torture warrant, specifying the crime and the nature of the torture. The end result of the specified torture was to serve justice.[3] The kinds of torture were often tied to legal proceedings. For example, evidence gained through water torture was then considered "torture lite" and as a result was valued particularly for not distorting the quality of the information introduced into court. Sometimes, not only the legal system but the authority of the state was given to justify the routine use of torture, as when sovereign authority decreed the need for torture as a customary practice of law.

The similarities across the ages are striking. Today, any American can open up his newspaper and find mention of similar methods of torture, from the infliction of pain to the causing of death. In fact, very little innovation has accompanied the newer methods of torture. Hooding, water torture, short-shackling, and anal and vaginal piercing are prevalent now as they were in the 15th century. Moreover, there is a strong emphasis now as then on sexual humiliation at the hands of interrogators. Today's interrogators smear menstrual blood on male Islamic prisoners and force detainees to wear women's underwear on their heads.

The general impetus to physicality is present today as well. As David Luban reminds us, it is a form of intimate human contact, the opposite of love and affection, but nonetheless an intense emotional entanglement. Beyond the intimacy, there is also the possibility that the appeal of physicality as an expression of anger may be a reaction to the excessively technological practice which modern warfare has become. Perhaps it is a form of longing for an aspect of war that disappeared with the first world war, the mano a mano, one on one, aspect of harm inflicted by one human being onto another. Perhaps the age of technology that we have in our midst has deprived our soldiers and others of the kind of physical release that anger and aggression, the basis of war, find necessary. Torture has without a doubt enabled the act of war to be personal again. Gone are the video game tactics, the explosions from afar, the need to find the satisfaction of conquest on a screen. Torture restores the screams of the victims, the faces of defeat and, albeit ironically and perversely, the human side of warfare. More than that, it tells us that human beings have the capacity for cruelty; it also may tell us that human beings on some very deep level reject the technology of our times and the degree to which it has, as the philosophers of the twentieth century warned, alienated humans from themselves. Torture, seen in this light, restores man to himself.

In thinking about the cycles in which torture appears and disappears, one is struck as much by its disappearance in the past as by its appearance today. Like the Golem, whom many would consign to the imaginations of superstitious times, so images of torture belong to an age before science and reason. Long considered a taboo for Western culture, the reintroduction of the word and the practice of torture has an eerie quality, as if it is returning a spectre from the past. Like the dangerously mystical Golem that is said to haunt Eastern Europe, hidden but reappearing to cause damage from time to time, torture appeared in Roman times, in Medieval times and has reasserted itself today.

The first modern thinkers, the philosophers upon whose ideas the modern state and the age of rights have been fashioned, equated the need for a more enlightened philosophy of rights with the need for the disappearance of both superstition and injustice, most notably torture. The Rule of Reason, the birth of notions of equality and justice, put the passions of men into restraint if not shame and provided a forum for the rationale and impersonal disposition of justice.

With even more precision and impact perhaps, developments in the legal sphere brought the practice of torture to an end. The movement toward a system of law and conviction which no longer required certainty but which rested content with the ability of the judge and/or jury to weigh the evidence and come to a reasonable rather than a certain conclusion brought to an end the need for torture. On the Continent, the law of proof standardized the need for evidence – gathering as opposed to confession as a means of establishing the legal record. In England, the emergence of the prosecutor similarly established the nature of evidence-gathering as a skill to be practiced in lieu of eliciting a confession.

It was, then, the legal process itself that contributed to a way out of the torture policies of yore. And for today's debate on torture, this is a significant point of reference. It was not just that liberal ideology could not tolerate torture; it was that the practice of law could not tolerate torture. Evidence-gathering, judicial standards, and the role of the prosecutor and the jury had made torture unnecessary and in turn were compromised by the fact of torture today. There is the sense that the legal debate has distracted us from the more important policy issues embedded in a torture policy, that the lawyers are splitting hairs rather than addressing the morally abhorrent nature of torture. But this is far from the case. If the history of the eradication of torture offers any example, it is that the abolition of torture is not just about moral outrage or concerns about the diminishing power of liberalism; it is rather a shift in the thinking of an age that enabled law to trump torture. Similarly for religion, as Dubensky and Lavery demonstrate, the universally acknowledged religious assertion is that "common humanity precludes torture." In the religious paradigm, it was the recognition of the shared human experience that led to the atrophy of violence and torture in the name of religion.

To some extent the reappearance of torture as a policy suggests that judicial torture was repressed rather than eradicated, that law exists together with torture in a dance between good and evil. Torture lurks beneath the law, waiting to see the light of day, never destroyed. The trauma of 9/11 seems to have reawakened the power of torture in contradistinction to the law. Similarly, in the religious context, the rebirth of torture indicates a return to a time when the shared humanity of mankind was not a determinative value – a return to a time when differences outweighed commonalities.

If history is our guide, then the dismissal of torture will rely on the discovery of a new way of thinking about our world, not one that is reactive but one that emerges over time, through thought, debate, and the adoption of new ways of understanding in an altered context. Because the Torture Memos were written in the fraternity-like secrecy of the OLC, the public and those professionals with the skills to think about such matters did not engage in a debate over the use of torture and its relationship to law and to the American national security agenda. The secrecy of these discussions led to a quick and violent form of behavior in the name of law. But it is not impossible that a sustained debate about law, values, and the efficacy of violence at the hands of the state would result not in a policy that condoned torture but in one that considered the nuance of current geopolitical circumstances and decided in favor of law, not torture.

In the establishment of the law of proof as a replacement for torture, there was in essence an intellectual paradigm shift that took place; individuals took uncertainty upon themselves. Instead of the "certainty" of confession, they came to value the ability of the judge and the jury to consider reasonable proof. They took it upon themselves to live with uncertainty, to trust their own judgment.

One of the more telling characteristics of the post 9/11 era is the lack of trust in the judgments of the courts and its officers. As the country has engaged in a war on terror, it has to a large extent emasculated and second-guessed its established judicial processes. To date, in the three and a half years following 9/11, there has been but one conviction on the charge of terrorism and insufficient cooperation between American government officials and foreign courts. Instead of civilian or military courts, the U.S. government has established secret military commissions. Along these lines, there has been no talk of bringing the leading terrorists that are in U.S. custody – Khalid Sheik Mohammed, Abu Zabaydeh, and Ramsi bin Al Shibh, for example – to trial. Torture is but one more sign of the possibility that we as a nation are forsaking the judicial system and its ability to effect justice though the trial system, which begins with the attempt to interrogate and find information.

Recent public discussions about the general dilemmas posed by the spectre of terrorism suggest what paradigmatic changes might have to occur to move to a more sophisticated argument for once again repressing torture. First, the judicial system and the American government and public will need to learn once again to trust itself even in the face of uncertainty. Caught off-guard on 9/11 and without the tools of knowing with certitude the players and practices of terrorists, the authorities understandably looked for ready, immediate means to their ends. But torture became the behavior of the flailing and inept. It was meant to find answers in a context where we had lost years of preparation. (By contrast, the European legal system, out of necessity, has been tracking and following terrorist cells for decades.)

A second paradigm shift that is required for a renewed dissociation from torture is a greater tolerance for long-term consequences. Again, the legal dilemma takes its cues from the larger context of the war on terror. Americans are stymied by the need to understand the war on terror as the effect of policies that may be remote in time. Rather than the immediacy of cause and effect, there is a distance between cause and effect. For example, if there has been a growth of new terrorist cells in Iraq and of terrorism worldwide in response to American policies in Iraq and its torture of innocent Muslims in Guantánamo and Abu Ghraib, then it is not an effect that will be felt immediately. Americans who opposed these policies often warn of long-term consequences, but this is a complicated way of thinking, one that, like the court process itself, defies certainty and calls instead for judgment.

Ultimately, what the practice of torture at American hands in the wake of 9/11 tells us is not that human beings are potentially evil, but that they are missing the trust in self, and the intellectual tools of analysis and understanding that lead easily to reason and the rule of law. Many of these essays struggle to find their way back to the law itself, and in so doing, they are a valuable contribution to the debate that must inevitably proceed a reengagement of law as nuanced rather than aggressive, healing rather than harmful, and aimed at peace not war.

In today's context, the use of torture may very well find some explanation in the past. Torture today is not used in an effort to achieve certainty; on the contrary, most experts agree that the information gained through torture is at best unreliable. But the use of torture may indeed reveal a lack of trust in the legal system itself. As medieval torture existed in a vacuum designed to replace the absolute knowledge of God, so contemporary torture looks for an arbiter that is larger than the abilities of human beings who sit in judgment. The war on terror and the prospect of an unknown enemy, viewed by public officials and the media as mythic and outside of known American experience, seems to call for a means of determining facts that supercedes the talents, skills, and professionalism of American lawyers, soldiers, and intelligence officers.

What is instructive here, then, is that the legal reasoning included in the essays in this volume, is important for reasons beyond the ethical responsibility of the OLC, beyond the powers of the executive, and beyond the role of military and covert intelligence agencies. Legal minds may very well be our way out of torture, but not due to moral arguments or to philosophical theorizing or to references to the Constitution. Rather, legal minds can move us forward to rediscovering a comfort with nuance, with uncertainty, and with the abilities of men to determine, without torture, the facts surrounding those who would endanger us as individuals and as a nation.

The documents included in this volume are of several types. They include those memos and pieces of discussion in Washington that occurred after the publication of *The Torture Papers*, among them the long awaited memos drafted in the spring of 2002 by William Taft, IV, one of the unsung heroes of this story.[4]

And last but not least, there is a document from the 1920s written by Roscoe Pound, Felix Frankfurter, and ten other legal minds of that era. In the "Report upon the Illegal Practices of the United States Department of Justice," these men consider what should be done when the Department of Justice overreacts in fear and, in their estimation, misreads the law.

All told, these essays and documents are intended to provide an essential piece of the picture of the United States today. As it confronts the age of terrorism in the years beyond the initial shock and anger of 9/11, the country is poised to consider what, if anything, it chooses to keep sacred as it goes forward. Though it is early yet to assess the full ramifications of the Bush administration's willingness to tinker with the law, it is not too early to begin at least to reflect upon ourselves and our behavior at this moment in time. One of the great lessons of history is that with whatever passion and sense of righteousness we may see ourselves and our choices today, we may at some future point in time, given new facts and subsequent events, see ourselves, our motives, and our judgments in a new light. This volume is intended to help us gain some insight into the nuances of today's public discourse and to provide us in the future with a window onto our time and ourselves.

NOTES

1. Karen J. Greenberg and Joshua L. Dratel, eds., *The Torture Papers* (New York: Cambridge University Press, 2005).
2. *See* p. 13.
3. John H. Langbein, *Torture and the Law of Proof* (University of Chicago Press, 1976), p. 7–17.
4. Taft – Haynes March 22, 2002 Memo Re: President's Decision about Applicability of Geneva Conventions to al Qaeda and Taliban, p. 283.

THE ISSUES

Torture: The Road to Abu Ghraib and Beyond

Burt Neuborne, Dana Priest, Anthony Lewis, Joshua Dratel, Major Michael (Dan) Mori, and Stephen Gillers

ON SEPTEMBER 23, 2004, THE CENTER ON LAW AND SECURITY SPONSORED an open forum at New York University School of Law entitled "Torture: The Legal Road to Abu Ghraib and Beyond." This event brought together noted experts in the fields of law, academia, and journalism to discuss the implications of the recently released memos and reports on the Bush administration's torture policy. The panelists included defense attorney Joshua Dratel, NYU law professor Stephen Gillers, journalist Anthony Lewis, military lawyer Major Michael Dan Mori, journalist Dana Priest. NYU law professor Burt Neuborne served as moderator. Below are the proceedings from the event.

Burt Neuborne: Montesquieu observed that this is a society dominated by law and legalism. There is no stronger proof of Montesquieu's thesis than the enormous role that lawyers have played in the evolution of the policies on torture that have brought us to this place.

Historically, it is an unfortunate truth that there is no inherent relationship between legalism and decency. The sad fact is that law has been placed in the service of barbarity as often as it has been placed in the service of decency. One has only to look at the role of Nazi lawyers and Nazi judges, the finest trained legal minds in Europe. The German legal profession in the 1930s consisted of the most brilliant collection of lawyers that had ever been put together in any place at any one time. And yet, the profession collapsed during the Nazi years and prostituted its talents in ways that now look to us to be inconceivable.

Consider as well the legal profession of South Africa during the apartheid years, clearly the cream of the legal profession on the African continent. In South Africa, one of the great bars of the world allowed its talents to be used to defend apartheid and crush human rights. For every Richard Goldstone, who fought for decency from within the South African judiciary, and Arthur Chaskalson, who fought apartheid from within the South African bar, there were 100 judges and 1,000 lawyers who vigorously enforced manifestly unjust laws without questioning the ends to which law was being put. There, too, is the Indian judiciary during the emergency under Gandhi, and its failure to uphold the principles of the Indian Constitution during that crisis.

The U.S. government lawyers that have brought us these policies on torture are among the best and the brightest; good lawyers doing intensive legal analysis. One of the questions that we need to answer, or begin to answer, is "To what end?" Does the work of the government lawyers who use their talents to build a legal façade for torture differ in any real way from the work of the Nazi lawyers who used their talents to build a legal façade for Nazi racism?

I believe that the American bar has allowed itself to drift into an ethical climate where lawyers believe that when they are called upon to advise a client – whether that client is the President of the United States or the President of Enron – their role is to construct the kind of adversary justification for questionable behavior they would make if their client had been indicted. Lawyers routinely construct arguments during the advice phase of a relationship that would be perfectly appropriate if they were being made in defense of a criminal charge, but which are unjustified as pre-action advice. Lawyers seem to forget that, instead of making arguments at the end of the process, they are making their arguments at the beginning of the process in order to justify the behavior. Is there something that we are doing in American law schools that is allowing the best and the brightest of our profession to drift into a situation where they think that all they have to do is find an argument that will justify their client's goal, that will keep their client out of jail? This question transcends any of the other things we are doing as teachers. It addresses the very soul of the legal profession.

In the matter of torture, if we focus on the future instead of the past, we ought to wise up and stop expressing mere outrage and start saying instead that the rule of law is a deck chair that we take out in sunny weather, and we sit on it, and we enjoy it. But when it starts to rain, we fold it up and we put it away, which is why it has lasted so long, because it has never gotten wet. When things get tough, the law disappears, and lawyers like me are shocked. We cannot believe it, but it is gone.

If you look into our history, it is an ugly history as far as that goes. President Adams suspended the Constitution with the Alien and Sedition Acts. The very first time that there was a serious political debate in this country, the dissenters got locked up. Abraham Lincoln suspended the Writ of Habeas Corpus during the Civil War. Oliver Wendell Holmes voted to put people in jail for opposing the First World War. The Supreme Court upheld the Japanese concentration camps during the Second World War. The Supreme Court never really stopped McCarthyism until long after the hysteria was over. How many times does it take for us as lawyers to realize that paper parchments are paper parchments? And that there is not some extraordinary set of laws, some *deus ex machina* that is going to drop down and save us in times of crisis?

This is just the most recent collapse of the rule of law. It is painful for us, because it was orchestrated by some of the smartest lawyers we know. Now, how do we break out of this? Am I being too cynical? Do we do better than I give us credit for doing in times of crisis?

If we do not do better, how can we build for the future in ways that will stop us the next time there is a national crisis from having another meeting like this where we talk about how terrible it was that we collapsed and how we can do better in the future?

Dana Priest: It is hard to believe that we are sitting here talking about torture. There have been many times in the past year where, following conversations on the telephone, I got off the phone and gulped and said to myself, "Where am I?" I found myself trying to understand the difference between the water-boarding technique and the wash-boarding technique, and how one might be considered torture and the other not! It is a very strange, topsy-turvy time for me, as an American and as a journalist. However, it is also an exciting time because we have made inroads trying to understand what the government tried to keep secret.

Have our views on torture changed? I think they have. They did change after 9/11, and I think they are changing again. I want to go back to 9/11 because that is really where all this starts.

Right after 9/11 the government said, "We are doing things differently." They went to Congress, rather than acting by themselves. They went to the intelligence committees, which I cover, and said "You know, in order to prosecute the war on terror, we think that we need to do things we have not done in this country for a long time. We need to interrogate people in a different way." Eventually, they came to the discussion of having to assassinate people using predator drones.

There was nobody I could find in Congress who was talking both to members of Congress and to their staffs and the people who brief them who said, "Well, wait a minute. Maybe you should not do that." In fact, the context in which the intelligence world and the military, but mainly the intelligence world, came to them and said, "Well, if we can find terrorists, do we have the go-ahead – never, never using the word 'torture' – to use extraordinary interrogation techniques?" They not only got a free hand, but many members of Congress who were on those oversight committees said, "Yes, and make sure that you are pressing as hard as you can. And the gloves are off." So, that is truly the context in which all these things then evolve.

We are now in the situation where the government, having been embarrassed by the memos that came out, has put a hold on all of those interrogation techniques, as far as we can tell. The CIA has pulled back and told its field officers and their interrogators that they cannot do those things anymore. So, we are yet again in the situation where the views of torture are changing. I think the pendulum was swinging one way and right after 9/11 it swung back. I could not predict at all where it is going to end up. It depends upon who is elected and whether there is another terrorist strike.

The go-ahead that the government got to prosecute the war as it saw fit, that it got from your representatives, did quickly evolve into, "Let's bring the lawyers in so that when we get caught, so that if we need to know where our limits are, we need to do it in a legalistic way." And that is what they did. There were lawyers at the CIA, the National Security Council, and at the Department of Defense (DoD). None of the techniques that were okayed, and the techniques that were discussed, were the result of any kind of rogue operations. This was central to how the government agreed to proceed; it needed these techniques, it believed, to prosecute the War on Terrorism.

As we saw in the August 2002 memo from Jay S. Bybee, Assistant Attorney General, U.S. Department of Justice (DOJ) to Alberto R. Gonzales, Counsel to the President],[1] it went all the way up to the White House into the Justice Department's Office of Legal Counsel. The Legal Counsel at DOJ wrote the over-arching legal framework that would be used later by DoD in Guantánamo. When the CIA discovered that it would have these terrorists to detain, they realized that, up until this point, they had not had these sorts of people in their custody. They did not want to put them into any courts, they wanted to keep them out of the courts. They wanted to keep them away from any type of scrutiny whatsoever.

My point is that it was all done, in the government's mind, in a legal way. It was vetted the way that it is supposed to be vetted, and lawyers looked at it. Many lawyers will say that that was a proper thing, and none of this is rogue activity. So, the most interesting debate did not happen in the CIA context because that was really close to 9/11 and everybody was saying, "Go." There were not many people saying, "Put the constraints on."

The interesting debate occurred, though, a year later when, faced with an insurgency they did not expect to be as strong, in a prison system they did not even anticipate having to work in, under conditions that were really awful, they found themselves pushed by their own desire to break the insurgency, yet trying to get intelligence out of people in the prison. The DoD and the Judge Advocate General's Corps (JAG) lawyers in particular have this fierce tussle with one another.

It was mainly the civilians who were running DoD at that time – Secretary of Defense Donald Rumsfeld and William Haynes, General Counsel at DoD. They stood against a lot of military uniformed JAG officers who, steeped in the Geneva Conventions, put the reigns on the government for the first time by saying, "Excuse me, but this will not hold up in terms of the Geneva Convention."

Finally, there is the question, where do you go from here? How do you think of our government's role in torture or interrogation, tough interrogations? One of the members of the intelligence committee, Jane Harmon, has said that everyone has to have a status. The Guantánamo detainees have a status. It was a new status, so it was confusing, and it caused a lot of debate. But, they had a status, and they have access to the International Red Cross, as do other military detainees.

The CIA detainees have no status that no one, except for a very small, covert operation within the CIA, knows of. We do not know where the detention centers are. We do not know what the permitted interrogation methods are or the chain of command that needs to be bought off on that. And we do not know how many people have been exported, or rendered through rendition process to foreign countries for the explicit purpose of interrogating in their facilities at an arm's length distance from the U.S. government.

And, I think that that is one thing that has gained momentum recently. So, where are these people? Let's account for them. The CIA's Inspector General is now trying to do an accounting of it. But, in my view, that has to be shared much more broadly. It has to be shared in Congress which, for the first time, may have the backbone to actually ask the questions that are more detailed than they did before. That is because now they realize the public has many questions about this.

My final point is that, *while there may be a lot of criticism of lawyers who wrote some of these memos, I think it is the legal profession that we have fallen back on and laws that we have fallen back on to say where are we now as a country and what we are doing in this regard.* And, if there is one way that the chain of command at DoD will ever be revealed, it is through, I believe, the discovery method, through the defense of the troops at Abu Ghraib, who have been charged with committing crimes.

So, it is the discovery in our own legal system. It is going back to the very basics that may actually reveal whether or not these people were carrying out orders from above. This is what gives me some hope and comfort that our legal system has actually come back and is working the way it should.

Burt Neuborne: Dana's narrative makes one remarkable point: the inversion here of what we usually believe. We are usually trained to say that it is the civilians that have to ride herd on the military, that civilian control of the military is the essence of maintaining the rule of law.

The narrative here is that the first time anybody really began to speak up and put a brake on this stuff was when the military lawyers tried to control their civilian bosses, who essentially had completely reneged upon the notion of the rule of law. One of the things we have to remember here is the ability of military professionals, both at the level of command and at the level of law, to be an important process. I will confess that, over the years, I have written them off as a group that one could not rely on. And, it turns out that in this crisis, they were one of the strongest forces calling for the return of the rule of law.

Anthony Lewis: I think the military has shown itself to be believers in process. And the people, at least at the top of government, have been believers in something else, which is their own power. That's my notion of it.

I want to begin by recalling an episode which will tell you how I feel about these matters. Many years ago, at least 20, maybe more, I was in Jerusalem and had an interview with Jacobo Timmerman. Timmerman was a prisoner in Argentina who was tortured. Actually, his life was saved by the Carter Administration, which protested strongly enough to keep him from being killed. When Timmerman was finally released, he chose to go to Israel.

Timmerman and I were talking about a lot of things one day, and we got onto the subject of torture. He started asking me questions. Now, remember, this is long ago, ladies and gentlemen, before these matters were in all our minds. He said, "Now suppose you had a prisoner, and you knew that he knew that there was a bomb about to go off in a crowded city." This is the sort of thing we read about now, but I had not thought about it then. And, Timmerman continued, "Say you knew that it was going to happen within two or three hours. And that you thought that if you tortured this man, you could find out where the bomb was, and you could prevent the terrible loss of life. Would you do it?"

I tried to avoid his question. I said, "I am interviewing *you*, you know. Come on." And so on and so on. But, finally, he said, "Answer the question." I said, "Well, I am reluctant, but I guess I would." And he shouted, "**No! You cannot start down that road!**" I have never forgotten that moment. *You cannot start down that road.* That is what I believe about torture.

There are a lot of reasons for my conviction, all of which you are familiar with, among them, these: facts or alleged facts obtained by such methods tend to be unreliable; the torturers are ruined, as are the tortured. We all know this. But I do not think I want to live in a country where torture is accepted or excused as it is excused in the administration's memoranda. The defenses outlined in these memoranda are over the edge, even by the standards of colorful lawyers. The idea that a torturer could argue self-defense, meaning self-defense of the country, is one of the more far-fetched arguments I have ever heard.

I think power is a very strong motivating factor, running through everything the Bush administration has done since 9/11. The starting point has been the sense that we, the administration, have to be in charge. We cannot have any courts, any judges in charge. We cannot have the Constitution waved at us. We have to keep everything secret. We must not let anything out. It is a matter of the power of the Executive Branch and those who run it. That has been evident from the start.

One of the very first things that happened after 9/11, legally speaking, was that President Bush's order for Military Commissions was designed to keep things under control without access to civilian courts. Although, there was a strange moment when the President's Counsel, the White House Counsel, Alberto Gonzales, wrote an op-ed piece for the *New York Times* in which he said, "We have carefully preserved the right of review in civilian courts."[2] It was an absolute falsehood written by him, or by someone at his direction, for the *New York Times*. I thought it was amazing. It occurred a short time after the publication of the text of the order which said explicitly, "This and any judgment of the Military Commission may not be taken to any court anywhere in any country." You could not be more explicit than that. Then, the handling of the prisoners at

Guantánamo I thought was maybe the most dramatic indication of the state of mind of the administration.

The Third Geneva Convention requires that people captured in conflict be given a hearing before a competent tribunal to discover and decide on their status, who they are, whether they are legitimate prisoners of war, spies, terrorists, or others. Hundreds of such hearings were held in the first Gulf War, and a very large percentage of the hearings resulted in findings in favor of the prisoner.

So, it is in our history, it is not unusual. It was Colin Powell, after a life in the military, who objected strongly – passionately really, for a memorandum – to the course that President Bush took. That course was simply to say, "We are not going to allow the Geneva Convention, even though we signed and ratified it. The Geneva Convention and its predecessors have been part of our military culture for many, many years. We are just not going to pay any attention to it."

"We are going to say – without a hearing, without any fact-finding process, simply on the orders of the President – that everybody who is in prison at Guantánamo Bay is an unlawful combatant." This is a phrase which is not found in the Geneva Conventions by the way.

And then of course, there was the refusal – that is the powerful, strong resistance – to any attempt to challenge that finding in the courts, an attempt which failed in the Supreme Court last June. The brief of the Solicitor General in the Supreme Court in that case said that the President has conclusively found that all these prisoners are unlawful combatants, and there can be no review of that. That is that. That is their position. We do not want a judge or anybody else messing around with our findings.

Now, I have not talked about torture. Dana Priest has said very effectively how odd it is to be discussing torture. I want to say just how grateful I am to her and to her colleagues at the *Washington Post* and elsewhere, but especially the *Post*, for unearthing the facts about these matters. A great editor of the *Manchester Guardian* said once, "Comment is cheap. Facts are dear." And it is the facts about torture and about the legal arguments that went into torture that have made an enormous difference. We all owe a debt of gratitude to those in the press who brought them out.

Those memoranda read like the advice of a lawyer for a mafia don on how to stay out of prison without actually changing what you do. I know I am naive about these things. I spent a lot of time covering the Justice Department, and I had an enormous respect for government lawyers. Maybe too much respect. But, to me, it was really unpleasant to read those memoranda and to think that people working for the U.S. government thought that was the way to present the issues.

One of them, John Yoo, who at the time was in the Office of Legal Counsel, was regularly and is again a Professor at Boalt Hall, University of California Law School at Berkeley, wrote a piece for the *Los Angeles Times* saying, "We did not take any policy position. All we did was give advice, as lawyers do, on what would be a defense if you got into trouble."[3]

Well, of course, you know it is easy to say, "We did not take a policy position." But, the purpose of a memoranda was to open the way for the government to do what it wanted to do. That was the point. And so it is hypocrisy of the worst kind for lawyers to say, "Oh, well you know, we are not for torture. We did not take any position on torture. We just told them that if they did torture somebody, well, here were seventeen ways they could not be prosecuted successfully."

One more example away from the torture field, which I think needs to be included as part of this picture, is the Bush administration's legal operation since 9/11. A very, very important issue has been the treatment of the two so-called enemy combatants, American citizens held in prison in this country. Yassir Hamdi has been in detention for nearly three years and in solitary confinement for most of that period without access to a lawyer and without access to the outside world in any way. He had no idea that anybody was acting on his behalf.

Fortunately, someone was. And, if we want to say a good word for the legal profession, we could say it for Frank Dunham, Jr., the U.S. Public Defender in Virginia who volunteered to take on the case of Hamdi when the government was desperate to keep lawyers out of it. With tremendous courage and persistence, he took the case from the beginning right through the Supreme Court of the United States and into the negotiating that led to a decision to release Hamdi. Lawyers can still make a great difference.

Anyway, for Hamdi, as for Jose Padilla, the government's every effort was to keep lawyers and courts away. "Let us do what we want." And, we do not actually know what was done to Hamdi and Padilla in prison. We do not know what kind of pressure was put on them. The only thing we do know is that when a trial judge in New York held that Padilla should be allowed to talk to a lawyer, the government strenuously objected. The government asked for a rehearing on the ground that the decision would interrupt the relationship between the prisoner and his questioners, that it would disrupt the sense of trust and confidence that had built up between them. You can see what that sense of trust and confidence was.

I will close by saying that nearly a year ago a member of the highest court in the United Kingdom, the House of Lords, Lord Steyn, made a speech. A very unusual speech for a sitting judge about Guantánamo in which he said, "Guantánamo was a black hole in the world of Justice."[4] He said he had been brought up to think that the United States was the acme of justice, and its ways of doing things were the right way.

None of us has yet spoken of what this episode, the torture episode, Abu Ghraib, has done to that reputation in the world. But this was a year ago, before Abu Ghraib. Lord Steyn said, "The United States maintains that if a prisoner from Guantánamo came forward and said, 'I am being tortured,' no court could hear his claim." He said that, and I read that and thought, "Well, that is a rather exaggerated way of putting it."

It actually had not occurred to me. That is how out of it I am, or how much I am distorted by my habit of thinking government lawyers do the right thing. It had not occurred to me that people were actually being tortured at Guantánamo or in Iraq. Well, ladies and gentlemen, they were. A significant number were tortured to death. Let us not forget that. It was not just the water-board technique or the wash-board technique. Fortunately, I do not know the difference. They were tortured to death. And, that is what has been done in our name.

Burt Neuborne: I am going to ask you an unpleasant question, Tony. If they had found weapons of mass destruction as a result of this, would we be here now talking about a major change in interrogation technique as appropriate? Are we here now, so confidently speaking out against this, because it apparently failed? It did not generate any important intelligence.

Are you so sure that Timmerman was right? And, that you are right when you say, "I will never start down that road?" Even if I am pretty sure it is going to get me to a place where I would have information that would save enormous numbers of lives?

Anthony Lewis: It is not an easy question, Burt. I think it is not a fair question because most of the time when the government thinks it knows that people know something, it is wrong. They do not know anything. And that is why it has been a failure, because all of the suspicions have been exaggerated.

If I actually believed, if I had credible evidence and if I came to believe that somebody who was a prisoner under my control knew where there were weapons of mass destruction, nuclear weapons (that is what we are talking about) that were going to be used shortly, I might change my view. Yes, I might.

Joshua Dratel: In terms of going forward, what it means to me is: are there sanctions? Is there a penalty that is paid for that kind of conduct? What you have in a military commissions system and in Guantánamo Bay – with respect to the other detainees who are not necessarily in the commission system but have combatant status – is an entire system that is composed of evidence obtained by coercive, abusive interrogation methods.

Most of these people, if not all of them, were apprehended or captured by the Northern Alliance, not by U.S. troops. The circumstances of their capture are unknown. You will not have first hand evidence of that. What they were actually doing in Afghanistan before then or in Pakistan or wherever is unknown. It is all obtained from their statements and the statements of other detainees as a result of this type of treatment.

The concept of torture to me is limited because it does not include coercion. Coercion to me means that you do not have to be tortured very often to have your will overborne. Conditioning is the key. It only has to happen once. It does not even have to happen to you. It can happen to the guy in the cell next to you, and that is all you have to know.

I had a conversation with a CIA station agent who was a witness in a case I was involved in. It was around the time that the Abu Ghraib scandal broke in the news, and we said to him over a lunch break, "So what do you think?

How would you deal with torture?" He said, "They would never get that far. I would speak immediately because why bother? You are going to break. You might as well speak before the pain." This is a professional intelligence officer of many years standing. It was a perfectly reasonable response, and when you get further into the process in terms of dealing with actual persons who have actually been involved in this treatment on the receiving end, it is very clear what is going on. You cannot be isolated in the situation that these people were in and not capitulate.

Are we going to permit a system to continue that is based on this? To me the principle that we have to work on is sanctions. Otherwise it is a no-lose proposition for those who violate the law. Because what they say is, as soon as I am caught, I will stop. But I will enjoy all the fruits of all the illegality I have done up until now. I think the entire commission process is illegitimate as a result of this trove of evidence that is going to be used against each of them, that *is* used against each of them. There exists almost no independent evidence as to any detainee.

With respect to efficacy, torture makes people talk. The threat of torture makes people talk. All these things make people talk but the problem is that you do not know what they are saying. It is not possible to distinguish between the true and the false, or that which is parroted back to an interrogator in these incredibly unrestrained interrogation sessions.

I have sat through an extraordinary number of interrogation sessions in my experience as a criminal defense attorney for 25 years. I know the way a professional U.S. Attorney or District Attorney operates in an interview. Above all, you do not give to the person that you are interviewing the answer that you want.

If they know what you want to hear, that is all you are going to get. They will give you what you want, if they know what you want. In these interrogations that are done unprofessionally and abusively, what you get is a parroting back to the interrogator of what the detainee knows that the interrogator wants to hear, because that is what will relieve the abuse. That is what will get them back to the ordinary minimum standards of living as opposed to the punishment and the substandards of living that is imposed upon them if they resist.

There are jurisdictions where confessions are not allowed because they are assumed to have been obtained by torture, and are therefore assumed to be of questionable reliability. So torture makes people speak, but reliability is a totally separate issue which cannot be answered simply by saying it is okay and there is something out there that somebody knows that we have to find out, because in truth, you do not know.

In essence, this is the corporatization of government lawyering. It is a conversation that I assume has occurred in many board rooms, some of which have ended up in court and some of which have not. The meeting might go something like this: the chief executive, or the chief financial executive, says to a general counsel, "This is what we would like to do." The general counsel says: "Well, you know there is a regulation that says that you cannot do that." So the chief executive officer or the chief financial officer says, "Maybe you did not hear me. This is what we would like to do, and I would like something in the morning from you on this." Now the lawyer has a choice of what to do.

It is a personal choice in that context. It is a professional choice in that context. But it is done. And it is done in the corporate context because the loyalties are very narrow there. The problem with doing it in a governmental context is that the loyalties are not so narrow. They are much broader.

One of the problems with law schools, to me, is that the concept that lawyers are not supposed to examine moral consequences of their actions is, I think, wrong. It does not mean that you always act in a way that you think is moral in a broader sense, because sometimes you have specific roles. But you have to be conscious of what you are doing in terms of what your role is.

As a criminal defense attorney, my obligation is zealous representation of my client regardless of what he has alleged to have done, regardless of what he has done, regardless of who he is or what he is, or what he believes. So I have to put a lot of that aside to fulfill my role in the system. Because if I do not, no one will. And then all his rights will go by the board. But government lawyers have a very different standard. It is a codified different standard.

They are supposed to do justice, they are supposed to uphold the Constitution. And when you get into these narrow areas where they are just assigned to a specific task to get a result, they are missing the boat. Because that is not their job as government lawyers.

So if I were to teach people in law school, I would teach them that you can make moral choices as you wish, but you have to understand that you are making moral choices. If you ignore them, you walk down this road. You walk down the road of Nazi lawyers and Nazi judges following orders. Look at the Hamdi case. The significance of his release is that the government has demonstrated its distrust, its fear, its lack of confidence, and its distaste for our system of justice.

The system of justice was created by the Constitution that they are sworn to uphold. The government does not like this. They have done everything they can to deprive a federal court, an independent judiciary, from exercising its authority. And this is the latest. In the case of Hamdi, the government caved because instead of giving him a day in court with due process, they would prefer to let him go.

There are people in custody who are alleged to have done less than Hamdi, who is alleged to be an American citizen fighting against the United States to the coalition forces under arms, captured on the battlefield, according to the government's allegation.

I am not saying he should not be released. But I am saying that he is being released while other people are languishing there who they cannot prove are guilty in a million years. In these cases, the government, to my mind, is just extraordinarily unAmerican. They are doing everything they can to avoid the American legal system and its core values. And they undermined it on a continual basis with this conduct. It seems like they are only comfortable in a totalitarian context, and that is obviously very dangerous. It is born of panic. It is born of desperation. It is born of ignorance. But that does not make it any less dangerous. This is the practice and the attitude we have to fight.

This is where have to consider sanctions. It is up to the other two branches of government – to Congress and the Judiciary to impose sanctions. And obviously it is up to all of us as lawyers, students, other people – ordinary, good people.

Lawyers need to take it upon themselves to make this a priority, to make sure that those other two branches of government exercise their authority in a way that imposes sanctions to prevent this from occurring again.

Beyond lawyers are the law schools. The first thing I think I learned working was that the obsession in law school with legal precedent is wrong-headed. There is a legal precedent for every position you need to take. You will always find a case to support your side of the argument. You will have no difficulty doing that. What you have to do is find facts. Facts are where cases are won or lost. And you have to apply law to facts. What that requires, above all, is judgment. That is what judges do. That is what judges have to do. And that is what they have been deprived of doing in this context because the Executive has made decisions.

When you combine the corporatization of the law with the rectitude and arrogance of government lawyering, an arrogance and rectitude that is not warranted, and with power and the result-oriented context of the current situation, the result is that everybody is embarrassed and disgraced by this whole process.

Burt Neuborne: Let me ask you one question, Josh. You have used the word "capitulation." You said that the detainees will eventually capitulate. Let me play devil's advocate for a minute. There are people in custody that I think have important information. They have information on the structure of al Qaeda, important information on the operations of terrorism that could assist in making the country safe. So capitulation is exactly what I want. Tell me how I go about getting that capitulation and still stay inside notions of decency and human rights. Is it your position that we provide them all with lawyers, give them Miranda warnings, and then just sit there while they are absolutely silent and then let them go?

Joshua Dratel: Let me first challenge the premise of your question. When I say capitulation, I do not mean telling the truth, I mean responding to interrogation. I will give you a perfect example: the men who were released in England, the "Tipton Three." All admitted to being in a video they were not in. That is capitulation. That is not telling the truth. That is not the information we want. That is purely overbearing one's will.

It is also important to note that we need to distinguish between the battlefield and Guantánamo Bay. I am not saying that you need battlefield Miranda warnings, but once you decide to apprehend someone, capture them, and detain them, you are bound by certain rules, including the rules of the Geneva Conventions, the rules of our military regulations, the rules of the Constitution, and the rules of international law, all of which have been ignored. The government is proud that they have developed a system that meets the standards of none of those systems.

It is just mind-boggling. But let's remember, interrogation is an art. The best ones never lay a finger on people. They get confessions that are legitimate and valid, and that stand up.

Major Michael Dan Mori: I hope everybody here understands that I am not a spokesman for the Department of Defense. I have the privilege to speak out more publicly as a military officer because of my unique role in representing a non-U.S. citizen, David Hicks, who is locked up at Guantánamo Bay. I would never have the opportunity to speak out like this had it not been for this job that I have been assigned to. Needless to say, I have to confine my remarks to my representation and to what that encompasses. I cannot give you my personal opinions. I can give you my personal opinions about my case, but I cannot tell you what I would do if I had to decide whether or not to torture someone.

To give you a perspective on where I am coming from, back when these memos were being written, I was the head prosecutor in the Marines, in Hawaii. I was doing Special Assistant U.S. attorney work. I was focusing on assisting the commands that I was supporting – giving advice and prosecuting marines and sailors who did bad things – used drugs, mostly.

I was in Waikiki Beach, and I started noticing these orders coming up on the creation of the military commissions in the military community, as in the legal community. This would mean military commissions for the first time in 50 years. I began to wonder who was behind the military commission order and the military instructions that were beginning to come out. It did not make any sense. It did not seem like anything I had learned in my experience in the Marine Corps about fairness and justice. It did not seem like anything that I had learned in college or at law school.

The commissions of the forties had served as the military justice system until 1951, when the Uniform Code of Military Justice was established. We evolved. So how could anybody who went to law school support the type of justice system that they were proposing to try my client in? Then these memos came out, and it all made sense. The same people who wrote these memos created the system of military commissions.

I think it is very important that we get the memo from November 6, 2001, on the legality of the use of military commissions. It is the first memo, and it has not been released yet. That memo is going to show the motivations and the reasons we have to resurrect a justice system from 1940. We will then understand what goals it will achieve for us.

I think that it would be very important to see this as well as the December memos that have not been released dealing with the possible jurisdiction over Guantánamo. I mean you could see this was mind-gaming. It was strategic, and there was an end in sight. I think the end was the use of military commissions, because that is the first thing that happened right from September 11. And on November 13, the President wrote his orders approving the use of military commissions. But the issue had already come alive earlier; he had received the persuasive advice on November 6. And I think that after he approved the use of the commissions, they asked, what do we have to change? What do we have to avoid?

When I was looking at the rules, I kept noticing that there were no rules here to suppress statements. "What?" I asked. There had to be. And then, once I got involved in the process, I realized these prisoners did not have any rights. They were not prisoners of war. They did not have protections.

Subsequently, we saw the memo from the Secretary of Defense, which came out on January 22, saying that they did not have prisoner of war status.[5] Why did that memo have to go out? Because the military was doing it as they had always done it. In the military, you capture someone and assume that he is a prisoner of war until you have a hearing that says he is not a prisoner of war. From my experience in the David Hicks case, the military was stopped by the civilian leadership.

Torture is something which I look at in terms of interrogation techniques. You know, obviously, that I am thinking about a criminal case here. And from my experience, I cannot tell you how odd this is, from a traditional military perspective. We are dealing with cases where I found myself arguing with the judge about whether I was on the defense or the prosecution side. In previous military cases, I would say to the judge, "They interrogated him until 11 o'clock at night, your honor. It should be suppressed. You know he missed dinner or he was two hours late for going to chow hall." How abhorrent!

The interrogation of prisoners is a totally different world. This is all an interrogation process, beginning in Afghanistan with their initial capture, and extending to their treatment at Guantánamo Bay. So I kept wondering, when am I going to get the recordings? If this is important testimony, they have got to be documenting it.

Well, do you remember when the U.S. Air Force translator was charged? He was accused of spying. His case was dropped, just dropped. He pled guilty to some minor classified mishandling. But then it came out, and he was arrested. The government said "We are going to go back and review all the transcripts, all the recordings to make sure he did not do anything wrong." And then several months later, General Geoffrey Miller from Guantánamo said, "We never recorded anything because we did not want it to be provided to the detainees because it might have exculpatory evidence." And I asked myself then, as now, "What system am I in?"

There are people talking outside of the system, trying to keep us down, but you know they are trying to get my client, David Hicks, and they are talking out of both sides of their mouths. I think it is very difficult to operate as a legal practitioner coming from experience in a very structured system.

And the recordings are something that I just cannot understand. *If you are interrogating someone who might have such valuable information, and you know the question is posed such that, if they had this information about the location of weapons of mass destruction, how al Qaeda operated, wouldn't you want to record and document the raw data so that other people could review it to make sure that it was accurate?*

The art of interrogation is a science. Above all, the interrogator must speak the language, the dialect even, of the person they are interrogating, otherwise it just does not work. A cop from New York is going to be able to interrogate a suspect from New York better than a cop from Texas can. There are going to be connections made, there are going to be understandings.

So when you are speaking a different language and find yourself in foreign countries, it is even more important. I do not think they wanted to record the interrogations because they might end up documenting what a poor job they were doing. And if the quality of the translation services is anything like those that existed at the first commission hearing, then you know there are definitely some big questions.

I think it is tremendously important to deal fairly with people when they are captured on the battlefield because I want my client to receive a fair trial. But I also think it is very important in terms of getting reciprocal behavior for our service members. We need to address questions about the moral compass of lawyers. Not to brag for the military again, but I think the military justice system has been a little bit ahead on this issue. In 1951 the military said that the accused had a right to remain silent, a right to counsel, before Miranda. If you are going to ask anybody a question that might incriminate him, it does not matter if it is custodial or not, you have got to read him his rights. That is far greater protection than the civilian justice system. I think our Article 32 investigation, which in a way replaces the federal grand jury or the defense, is even present in the civilian code. But in the military, the defense is there and can put in evidence, which I think is a much fairer system.

But in our legal ethics, at least in the Navy and the Marine Corps, we are responsible to provide not only the technical and the legal advice and their obligations, but what might be the morally correct action to take in any given situation. And that is part of our ethical regulations. We can argue over whose morality is correct or not, but I think that was a step in the right direction to raise the awareness for lawyers that they are not just looking at what might be permissible, but at what is right to do.

Stephen Gillers: In Spring 2004, the *Newsweek* website posted the January 9, 2002 memorandum that John Yoo and Robert Delahunty, Justice Department lawyers in the Office of Legal Counsel (OLC), wrote to the general counsel of the

Defense Department.[6] Its subject is the legal protection, if any, for Taliban and al Qaeda members taken prisoner in Afghanistan. Until this memo was made public, I was an interested and concerned observer of the torture and human rights issues raised by Seymour Hersh's *New Yorker* articles.

I should have realized there would be legal memos. We cannot issue stock or mount a hostile takeover in the United States without lawyers. Neither can we wage war without lawyers. And we cannot run an off-shore facility for persons captured in that war without legal advice. I was inclined at first to agree with what Joshua [Dratel, see above] has said about how similar the memo seemed to what corporate lawyers write for their clients, or the officers of their clients, when they are instructed, subtly or otherwise, about the advice the client wants to receive. "Do not tell us it cannot be done. Just tell us how to do it." I initially thought the tone of the memo was of the same ilk, but it is not. It is worse. One has to read it to realize how relentless it is in the pursuit of the advice it gives. How dismissive it is of contrary argument. How absolute it is. How confident it is about the accuracy of its advice.

Once this and other memos began to appear, I shed my observer status. How lawyers work, the responsibility of lawyers, is something I do know something about. And here is one thing I know. When lawyers are asked to provide advice that flirts with the limits of the law, even the most aggressive corporate lawyer will include significant qualifying language. They will qualify their advice simply as a matter of self-protection and self-respect, anticipating that new corporate managers, a regulator, or a plaintiff may later question the failure adequately to explore risks and contrary arguments. But the authors of the January 9 memo would not likely have worried about any second guessing from these sources.

I read the memo several times to be sure I fully appreciated the extremity of its advice. And it is extreme. The authors are telling the government that the members of al Qaeda and the Taliban imprisoned at Guantánamo or elsewhere, or captured in Afghanistan and imprisoned there, live in a lawless world. They are outside the rule of law. The memo says, in effect, that the prisoners enjoy less protection from pain than stray animals in New York City.

Pause to appreciate how remarkable a conclusion that is in the United States of the 21st century. One would think that the need for qualification, the need for caution, would be at its height when the advice is so controversial, when the advice is that the client possesses a degree of power over others that the law has given to no branch of government in the United States, state or federal, in the history of the nation. The two authors, one a law professor then on leave, the other now a law professor, used the form and substance of the law's voice and methodology to destroy law, to create a lawless world for this group of prisoners.

I then tried to dig a little deeper. The memo of January 9 is marked "Draft." Well maybe it is a draft, I thought. Maybe these are two particularly overzealous lawyers whose advice was tempered by their seniors. But it was not. Shortly, there emerged a memorandum signed by the head of OLC, Jay Bybee, now a judge in the Ninth Circuit. The Bybee memorandum, dated January 22, comes to the same conclusions.[7] It adds some paragraphs to the January 9 memo, deletes some, and reorders yet others, but it makes the same arguments and advises that persons taken prisoner in Afghanistan have no legal protection. None. They are owned by their captors.

Further, so far as we can tell based on what has come to light, the United States acted in reliance on the Yoo/Delahunty "draft" even before the final Bybee memo. You can see that in two instances. You can see it in a memorandum from the Secretary of Defense dated January 19,[8] ten days after the Yoo/Delahunty memo and three days before the Bybee memo, which incorporates the Yoo/Delahunty advice in a directive to the Joint Chiefs. And you can see that again in a memorandum from White House counsel Alberto Gonzales to the President dated January 25[9] in which he refers to the President's decision on January 18, again before the Bybee memo, to accept the advice of the Department of Justice. Now, the only advice we have seen from the Department prior to January 18, and perhaps the only advice there is, is the advice of these two mid-level lawyers on the OLC.

Eventually, the press revealed August 1 memos from Mr. Bybee[10] and Mr. Yoo.[11] This is now nearly seven months after the Yoo/Delahunty memo. It turns out that there are legal restraints on the treatment of the Afghanistan prisoners after all, though barely. The August 1 memos explore the requirements of the Convention against Torture and the federal torture statute. The Convention against Torture and the torture statute are not mentioned in the January memos upon which Secretary Rumsfeld and the President relied.[12]

Think about that. Advice was given to the executive branch about the legal limits on the treatment of prisoners without discussing the implications of two bodies of relevant law. For nearly seven months, it appears, the client was making decisions based on the unqualified advice in the original January 9 memo that no law protected its prisoners. Although the Bybee and Yoo memos of August 1, 2002 did find that the Convention against Torture and the federal torture statute protected the prisoners, they offered such little protection against pain that, after they were revealed, the government disowned them.

There is another remarkable aspect of the January 9 memo. Although the memo describes the laws that do not protect Taliban and al Qaeda prisoners, and mentions none that do, nothing in this legal advice tells the client anything at all about risk of error in identifying prisoners. What if the government makes a mistake and imprisons and tortures someone who is in neither group? What legal consequences follow from such an error? We know now that there were significant errors, that people in both groups were swept up not only in Afghanistan but also in Iraq. Nothing in the advice these lawyers gave to their client identified the risk to the client – let alone to the prisoners – of a mistake or how to avoid mistakes. The Bybee memo of January 22 does talk about process for determining whether a prisoner is or is not entitled to Geneva protections. But it does so by way of providing a road map for avoiding the process, and the need for prisoner of war protections. Listen to the tone: "As we understand it, as a matter of practice, prisoners are presumed to have Article Four POW status [and therefore Geneva protection] until a tribunal determines otherwise. Although these provisions seem to contemplate a case by case determination of an individual's detainee status, the President could determine categorically that all Taliban prisoners fall outside Article Four. . . . A Presidential determination of this nature would eliminate any legal doubt. Saying so makes it so as to the prisoner's status as a matter of domestic law and would therefore obviate the need for Article Five tribunals."[13] The memo then goes on to identify the facts that the Department of Defense would have to find in order for the President to deny categorically POW status to members of the Taliban militia. The relentless tone, the assurance, the sanctimony, the "do not worry about it" attitude that permeates the memo also surfaces here.

A few weeks later, in a memo to Mr. Gonzales dated February 7, Mr. Bybee was even clearer in his conclusion.[14] True, the Geneva Convention Relative to the Treatment of Prisoners of War said that prisoners were entitled to certain protections, pending determination by a "competent tribunal," if there was "any doubt" about their status. But the President's power under the U.S. Constitution, Mr. Bybee wrote, entitled him to make a finding "that would eliminate any legal 'doubt' as to the Taliban prisoners' legal status" and thereby "obviate the need" for such tribunals. The gap here is huge: even if the president has this power with regard to the Taliban, how could such a generic finding possibly establish that a particular person was a member of the Taliban and therefore outside the protection of the treaty? That individualized determination is precisely what a tribunal is expected to do. Notwithstanding, on February 7, the President made the "finding" in accordance with Mr. Bybee's advice and similar advice from the Attorney General on February 1.[15]

I think what happened here was not an accident. We are dealing with intelligent lawyers, indeed, the very brightest. I think their memos were written to provide executive branch officials with an advice of counsel defense, either in the court of public opinion or some other court if it ever comes to that. "Our lawyers said it was legal and we relied on them," would be the defense. Indeed, this reliance is explicit in the President's memorandum of February 7, certainly drafted by a lawyer. The President wrote that in reaching the several conclusions in the memo, he was "relying on the opinion of the Department of Justice dated January 22, 2002, and on the legal opinion rendered by the Attorney General on February 1, 2002."[16] Among the memorandum's conclusions are that Geneva did not apply to al Qaeda; that the President had the constitutional authority to suspend Geneva as between the United States and Afghanistan (though he was not then exercising that authority "at this time"); that common Article 3 of Geneva did not apply to either al Qaeda or the Taliban; and that because the Taliban were "unlawful combatants" they did not enjoy prisoner of war status.

We do not know, and may never know, all of the conversations between and among the President and his White House Counsel, on one hand, and the various opining lawyers on the other. But the series of memoranda we do have from this period, written as many detainees were about to arrive at Guantánamo and others were in custody in Afghanistan or elsewhere, strongly suggests that the administration did not want an unfettered investigation of competing legal arguments. Instead, it wanted a green light, and the lawyers realized as much and provided it. In other words, the entire sequence suggests an orchestrated plan.

What the lawyers seem to have forgotten is that those officials are not their clients. They are representatives of the client. The client was the United States and to the extent that the lawyers forgot that, and considered that their job was to provide government officials with the patina of legal authority for already decided objectives, as I believe happened, they failed both their client and the law. If the law means anything, it surely cannot be endlessly malleable. The lawyers had an obligation to treat centuries of human rights law with respect, to reflect in their arguments the subtleties, the nuances, and the uncertainties that we all know exist in this area of law, as experts on human rights law have argued since the various memoranda have become public.

Perhaps nuance and qualification were sacrificed because the government lawyers figured – unlike corporate lawyers, whose opinions would not have been so one-sided – that nothing could happen to them. They were not going to be sued by their client. They may have felt confident that they were immune from any kind of civil liability, criminal liability, and even disciplinary liability.

I suspect we are going to see more memoranda leaked. We are going to get more information about what the lawyers did and did not do. And I fear, in the end, that the news is going to be even worse than it now appears.

NOTES

1. Assistant Attorney General Jay S. Bybee, U.S. Department of Justice, August 1, 2002 Memorandum to Counsel to the President Alberto R. Gonzales, in *The Torture Papers*, ed. Karen J. Greenberg and Joshua L. Dratel (New York: Cambridge University Press, 2005), Memo #14, p. 172.
2. Alberto R. Gonzales, "The Rule of Law and the Rules of War," *New York Times*, May 15, 2004.
3. John C. Yoo, "A Crucial Look at Torture Law," *Los Angeles Times*, 6 July 2004.
4. Johan Steyn, "Guantánamo Bay: The Legal Black Hole," *International Comparative Law Quarterly*, Vol. 53, January 2004, pp. 1–15.
5. Secretary of Defense Donald Rumsfeld, January 19, 2002 Memorandum to Gen. Richard B. Myers, Chairman of the Joint Chiefs of Staff, in *The Torture Papers*, Memo #5, p. 80.
6. Deputy Assistant Attorney General John Yoo, U.S. Department of Justice, and Special Counsel Robert J. Delahunty, U.S. Department of Justice, January 9, 2002 Memorandum

to General Counsel William J. Haynes, II, U.S. Department of Defense, in *The Torture Papers*, Memo #4, p. 134.

7. Assistant Attorney General Jay S. Bybee, U.S. Department of Justice, January 22, 2002 Memorandum to Counsel to the President Alberto R. Gonzales, and General Counsel William J. Haynes, U.S. Department of Defense, in *The Torture Papers*, Memo #6, p. 81.

8. *See* note 4.

9. Counsel to the President Albert R. Gonzales, January 25, 2002 Memorandum to President George W. Bush, in *The Torture Papers*, Memo #7, p. 118.

10. Assistant Attorney General Jay S. Bybee, U.S. Department of Justice, August 1, 2002 Memorandum to Counsel to the President Alberto R. Gonzales, in *The Torture Papers*, Memo #14, p. 172.

11. Deputy Assistant Attorney General John Yoo, U.S. Department of Justice, August 1, 2002 Memorandum to Counsel to the President Alberto R. Gonzales, in *The Torture Papers*, Memo #15, p. 218.

12. *See* note 5.

13. *See* note 7.

14. Assistant Attorney General Jay S. Bybee, U.S. Department of Justice, February 7, 2002 Memorandum to Counsel to the President Alberto R. Gonzales, in *The Torture Papers*, Memo #12, p. 136.

15. President George W. Bush, February 7, 2002 Memorandum to The Vice President, The Secretary of State, The Secretary of Defense, The Attorney General, Chief of Staff to the President, Director of CIA, Assistant to the President for National Security Affairs, Chairman of the Joint Chiefs of Staff, in *The Torture Papers*, Memo #11, p. 134.

16. *Id.*, p. 134.

ESSAYS

1 Liberalism, Torture, and the Ticking Bomb

David Luban

TORTURE USED TO BE INCOMPATIBLE WITH AMERICAN VALUES. OUR BILL
of Rights forbids cruel and unusual punishment, and that has come to include all
forms of corporal punishment except prison and death by methods purported to
be painless. We Americans and our government condemn states that torture; we
grant asylum or refuge to those who fear it. The Senate ratified the Convention
Against Torture, Congress enacted anti-torture legislation, and judicial opinions
spoke of "the dastardly and totally inhuman act of torture."[1]

Then came September 11. Less than a week later, a feature story reported that
a quiz in a university ethics class "gave four choices for the proper U.S. response
to the terrorist attacks: A.) execute the perpetrators on sight; B.) bring them back
for trial in the U.S.; C.) subject the perpetrators to an international tribunal; or
D.) torture and interrogate those involved." Most students chose A and D –
execute them on sight and torture them.[2] A few days later, another news article –
this one about the burden that terrorism places on religious leaders – reported that
clergy thought the question of whether to torture terrorists was one they would
certainly have to guide their congregations through.[3] Six weeks after September
11, news articles reported that frustrated FBI interrogators were considering
harsh interrogation tactics,[4] and the New York Times reported that torture had
become a topic of conversation "in bars, on commuter trains, and at dinner
tables."[5] By mid-November 2001, the Christian Science Monitor found that
32% of surveyed Americans favored torturing terror suspects.[6] Alan Dershowitz
reports that "[d]uring numerous public appearances since September 11, 2001,
I have asked audiences for a show of hands as to how many would support the
use of nonlethal torture in a ticking bomb case. Virtually every hand is raised."[7]
American abhorrence to torture now appears to have extraordinarily shallow
roots.

To an important extent, one's stance on torture runs independent of pro-
gressive or conservative ideology. Alan Dershowitz favors torture, provided it

Reprinted with permission from the *Virginia Law Review*.

is regulated by a judicial warrant requirement;[8] and liberal senator Charles Schumer has publicly poo-pooed the idea "that torture should never, ever be used."[9] He argues that every U.S. senator would back torture to find out where a ticking time-bomb is planted. On the other hand, William Safire, a self-described "conservative and card-carrying hard-liner[]," expresses revulsion at "phony-tough" pro-torture arguments, and forthrightly labels torture "barbarism."[10] Examples like these illustrate how vital it is to avoid a simple left-right reductionism. For the most part, American conservatives belong no less than progressives to liberal culture, broadly understood. Henceforth, when I speak of "liberalism," I mean it in the broad sense used by political philosophers from John Stuart Mill on – a sense that includes conservatives as well as progressives, so long as they believe in limited government and the importance of human dignity and individual rights.

My aim in this paper is threefold. First, I wish to examine the place of torture within liberalism (Sections I and II). I hope to demonstrate that there are reasons that liberals find torture peculiarly abhorrent to their political outlook – but also reasons why liberal revulsion toward torture may be only skin deep. I will argue that within liberalism materials remain to justify torture for interrogational purposes in the face of great danger. These materials allow us to construct a liberal ideology of torture, by which liberals reassure themselves that essential interrogational torture is detached from its illiberal roots. The liberal ideology of torture is expressed perfectly in so-called "ticking bomb hypotheticals" designed to show that even perfectly compassionate liberals (like Senator Schumer) might justify torture to find the ticking bomb.

Second, I criticize the liberal ideology of torture and suggest that ticking bomb stories are built on a set of assumptions that amount to intellectual fraud (Sections III and IV). Ticking bomb stories depict torture as an emergency exception, but use intuitions based on the exceptional case to justify practices and procedures of torture. In short, the ticking bomb begins by denying that torture belongs to liberal culture, and ends by constructing a torture culture.

My third aim in the paper is to illustrate these dialectical adventures of the liberal ideology of torture through a detailed case study: the executive branch lawyers who solicited or wrote memoranda justifying some cases of official torture by the executive branch (Sections V–VII). My discussion focuses on the now notorious memorandum of August, 2002, by the Justice Department's Office of Legal Counsel (OLC), which defined torture extremely narrowly, advised about criminal defenses to charges of torture, and argued that torture authorized by the President is not illegal.[11] For largely political reasons, the Justice Department and eventually the OLC disowned the memo, but it is worth analyzing anyway. In place of conventional legal arguments, the memo substitutes a powerful normative vision, based on the liberal ideology of torture, for dramatically reinterpreting the law. The result, I believe, is a perfect example of how a secretive torture culture emerges from the liberal ideology of torture – a disquieting illustration of how liberalism deals with the unpleasant question of torture.

I. PUTTING CRUELTY FIRST

Unhappily, torture is as old as human history. Montaigne once wrote, "Nature, I fear, attaches to man some instinct for inhumanity."[12] That sounds right. Most children at some point entertain sadistic fantasies, and many act them out. Infantile sadism may actually be an essential stage in the process of differentiating self from other and acquiring physical agency in the external world: "*I* can pinch and I feel nothing, but *you* or *she* or *the cat* yelps in pain; I am not you or her or the cat; and it's fun making you or her or the cat notice me." Causing pain in others allows the child to learn that some of the objects around him are themselves subjects with feelings of their own, and in this way bouts of infantile sadism may be essential to developing adult empathy. The toddler pinches his parent, who exaggeratedly says "Ouch" and "No, you mustn't pinch." The toddler giggles and does it again. It's a learning game. But the third time the parent is genuinely annoyed, and chastises or spanks or sends the child to his room, amidst wails and tears. While infantile sadism may be essential for human development, so is its repression. The process of socialization requires that torture fantasies be driven deep under ground, although in most people they persist for years beyond infancy, often accompanied by experiences of shame at having them.

Not everyone is ashamed, of course. Sadism forms the core of many people's erotic lives, and unacted-upon sadistic fantasies surely belong to the mental furniture of many more – and can be fully compatible with great moral sensitivity. At age 19, C. S. Lewis was still writing to his best friend about his spanking fantasies, fantasies that did not prevent him from maturing into an inspiring moralist.[13] The widespread, perhaps universal, presence of sadistic fantasies, more or less deeply repressed, may help explain what happens in actual torturers: being placed in a situation where the restraints come off may unleash deeply-repressed torture fantasies and translate them into reality – one of the dynamics that surely was at work in Abu Ghraib, where sex, sadism, and the power-rush of having enemies in your total control turned out to be nearly indistinguishable from each other.

It is an important fact about us – us modern liberals, that is – that we find scenes such as the Abu Ghraib photographs, to say nothing of worse forms of abuse and torture, almost viscerally horrifying (and I am convinced that this is just as true for those who believe that torture may be acceptable as for those who do not). That is unusual. As Nietzsche and Foucault remind us, through most of human history there was no taboo on torture in military and juridical contexts, and so no need to repress the infantile sadism that nature has bequeathed us.[14]

Indeed, Judith Shklar notes a remarkable fact, namely that cruelty did not seem to figure in classical moral thought as an important vice.

[O]ne looks in vain for a Platonic dialogue on cruelty. Aristotle discusses only pathological bestiality, not cruelty. Cruelty is not one of the seven deadly sins. . . . The many manifestations of cupidity seem, to Saint Augustine, more important than cruelty.[15]

It is only in relatively modern times, Shklar thinks, that we have come to "put cruelty first," that is, regard it as the most vicious of all vices. She thinks that Montaigne and Montesquieu, both of them proto-liberals, were the first political philosophers to think this way; and, more generally, she holds that "hating cruelty, and putting it first [among vices], remain a powerful part of the liberal consciousness."[16] Shklar also observes that putting cruelty first, as liberals do, incurs genuine moral costs. Cruelty is a wrong done to another creature, not a sin against God, and so ranking cruelty first among vices "place[s] one irrevocably outside the sphere of revealed religion."[17] Furthermore, "[i]t makes political action difficult beyond endurance, may cloud our judgment, and may reduce us to a debilitating misanthropy. . . ."[18]

Perhaps the concern about making political action difficult accounts for the ease with which we abandoned our reluctance to torture in the aftermath of 9/11. But I believe there are indeed reasons why torture and cruelty are particularly incompatible with liberalism. And, as I hope to show, one way this incompatibility manifests itself is through arguments designed to show that torturing terrorists for information is not done out of cruelty.

II. THE FIVE AIMS OF TORTURE

What makes torture, the deliberate infliction of suffering and pain, specially abhorrent to liberals? This may seem like a bizarre question, because the answer seems self-evident: making people suffer is a horrible thing. Pain hurts and bad pain hurts badly. But let me pose the question in different terms. Realistically, the abuses of detainees at Abu Ghraib, Baghram, and Guantanamo pale by comparison with the death, maiming, and suffering in collateral damage during the Afghan and Iraq wars. Bombs crush limbs and burn people's faces off; nothing even remotely as horrifying has been reported in American prisoner abuse. Yet, much as we may regret or in some cases decry the wartime suffering of innocents, we do not seem to regard it with the special abhorrence that we do torture. This seems hypocritical and irrational, almost fetishistic, and it raises the question of what makes torture more illiberal than bombing and killing.[19]

The answer lies in the relationship between torturer and victim. The self-conscious aim of torture is to turn its victim into someone who is isolated, overwhelmed, terrorized, and humiliated. Torture aims, in other words, to strip away from its victim all the qualities of human dignity that liberalism prizes. It does this by the deliberate actions of a torturer, who inflicts pain one-on-one, up close and personal, in order to break the spirit of the victim – in other words, to tyrannize and dominate the victim. The relationship between them becomes a perverse parody of friendship and intimacy: intimacy transformed into its inverse image, where the torturer focuses on the victim's body with the intensity of a lover, except that every bit of that focus is bent to causing pain and tyrannizing the victim's spirit. At bottom all torture is rape, and rape is tyranny.[20]

I am arguing that torture is a microcosm, raised to the highest level of intensity, of the tyrannical political relationships that liberalism hates the most. I have said that torture isolates and privatizes. Pain is an alarm-signal to the brain that the body is being damaged. It is our extremities' way of screaming to the brain *Help! Danger! Do something!* Acute pain is impossible to ignore because pain evolved precisely to be impossible to ignore. Pain forcibly severs our concentration on anything outside of us; it collapses our horizon to our own body and the damage we feel in it. Even much milder sensations of prolonged discomfort can distract us so much that it becomes impossible to pay attention to anything else – as anyone knows who has had to go to the bathroom in a situation where it can't be done. Wittgenstein wrote that the world of the sick man is different from the world of the healthy, and this is not simply a figure of speech when we suffer severe pain. The world of the man or woman in bad pain is a world without relationships or engagements, a world without an exterior. It is a world reduced to a point, a world that makes no sense and in which the human soul finds no home and no repose.[21]

And torture terrorizes. The body in pain winces; it trembles. The muscles themselves register fear. This, too, is rooted in pain's biological function of impelling us in the most urgent way possible to escape from the source of pain – for that impulse is indistinguishable from panic. U.S. interrogators have used the technique of "waterboarding" to break the will of detainees. They are strapped to a board and immersed repeatedly in water, just short of drowning. As anyone knows who has ever come close to drowning or suffocating, the oxygen-starved brain sends panic-signals that overwhelm everything else.

And torture humiliates. It makes the victim scream and beg; the terror makes him lose control of his bowels and bladder.[22] The essence of cruelty is inflicting pain for the purpose of lording it over someone – we sometimes say "breaking" them – and the mechanism of cruelty is making the victim the audience of your own mastery. Cruelty always aims at humiliation. One curious feature of legal procedures in both ancient Greece and Rome was a rule that slaves were permitted to give evidence in a court of law only under torture. Sir Moses Finley's plausible explanation is that the rule served to mark off the absolute difference in status between slaves and even the lowliest freemen.[23] The torture rule reinforces the message that slaves are absolutely subjugated. Humiliation occurs when I am low and you are high and you insist on it.

The predominant setting for torture has always been military victory. The victor captures the enemy and tortures him. I recently saw some spectacular Mayan murals, depicting defeated enemies from a rival city-state having their fingernails torn out before being executed in a ritual reenactment of the battle.

Underneath whatever religious significance attaches to torturing the vanquished, the victor tortures captives for the simplest of motives: to relive the victory, to demonstrate the absoluteness of his mastery, to rub the loser's face in it, to humiliate the loser by making him scream and beg. For the victorious warrior, it's fun; it's entertainment.[24] It prolongs the rush of victory. Montaigne denounced what he called "the uttermost point that cruelty can attain," namely torture "for the sole purpose of enjoying the pleasing spectacle of the pitiful gestures and movements, the lamentable groans and cries, of a man dying in anguish."[25] Even if the torturer's motives do not reach that level of cruelty, the victim's humiliation and subjugation are undeniable.

Already we can see why liberals abhor torture. Liberalism incorporates a vision of engaged, active human beings possessing an inherent dignity regardless of their social stations. The victim of torture is in every respect the opposite of this vision. The torture victim is isolated and reduced instead of engaged and enlarged, terrified instead of active, humiliated instead of dignified. And, in the paradigm case of torture, the victor's torment of defeated captives, liberals perceive the living embodiment of their worst nightmare – tyrannical rulers who take their pleasure from the degradation of those unfortunate enough to be subject to their will.

There are at least four other historically significant reasons for torture besides the victor's cruelty, the paradigm case – and, as we shall see, all but one of them is fundamentally inimical to liberalism.

First, there is torture for the purpose of terrorizing people into submission. Dictators from Hitler to Pinochet to Saddam Hussein tortured their political prisoners so that their enemies would be afraid to oppose them, knowing that they might face a fate far worse than death. Genghis Khan's conquests were made easier because his reputation for cruelty against those who opposed him led cities to surrender without a fight. Terror is a force-magnifier that permits a relatively small number of police to subdue a far larger population than they could if would-be rebels were confident that if they are captured they will be treated humanely. But of course, for liberals a practice that exists to make it easier to subdue and tyrannize people is fundamentally hostile to their political philosophy.

Second, until the last two centuries torture was used as a form of criminal punishment. It was torture as a form of punishment that drew Montaigne's condemnation, and it is noteworthy that the Eighth Amendment to the U.S. Constitution prohibits cruel and unusual *punishment*, rather than cruelty more generally. Beccaria condemns punishments that are more cruel than is absolutely necessary to deter crime, arguing on classical-liberal grounds that people in the state of nature will surrender only the smallest quantum of liberty necessary to secure society – and "[t]he aggregate of these smallest possible portions of individual liberty constitutes the right to punish; everything beyond that is an abuse and not justice, a fact but scarcely a right."[26] Strictly speaking, there is always a possibility that punishment by torture is necessary to deter crime. But Beccaria makes it clear that torture would turn society into "a herd of slaves who constantly exchange timid cruelties with one another."[27] Such punishments, he adds, "would also be contrary to justice and to the nature of the social contract itself" – presumably because turning society into a herd of slaves undermines the liberal understanding of the ends of society. Beccaria was widely read in America during the founding era.

Foucault argues that the abolition of punitive torture had little to do with increased humanitarianism. Instead, it had to do with a change in the distribution of crime in western Europe. As the west grew more prosperous, property crimes became widespread, and eclipsed crimes of passion as a social problem. This led to calls for a milder but more certain system of punishments – milder to ensure that they would actually be administered. The trouble with torture was that when the punishment is so awful, the temptation for mercy becomes too great. Imprisonment, out of sight and out of mind, replaced the public spectacle of torment and "honorable amends."[28]

Be that as it may, it seems equally clear that punitive torture had no place in liberal polities. Torture, as Foucault explains, was a symbolic assertion of the absolute sovereign whose personal prerogatives had been affronted by crime. It was a ritual of royal dominance and royal revenge, acted out in public spectacle to shock and awe the multitude.[29] With the growth of liberal democracy, the ideology of popular sovereignty deflated the purpose of punitive torture: if the people rule, then the responsibility of torture would fall on the people, and the need for a spectacle of suffering by which the people could impress themselves seemed pointless.[30]

Curiously, when Beccaria writes explicitly about the subject of torture, he does not mention torture as punishment. Rather, he polemicizes against judicial torture in order to extract confessions from criminal suspects.[31] This is the third historically-significant use of torture, distinct from punishment, even though judges administer both. The French language has different words for them: *le supplice*, torture as punishment, and *la question*, torture to extract confessions. As John Langbein observes, premodern legal rules required either multiple eye-witnesses or confessions for criminal convictions. At first glance, these were important rights of the accused, but they had the perverse effect of legitimating judicial torture in order to make convictions possible.[32] But once it was accepted that the criminal justice system should base guilty verdicts on evidence of various sorts that rationally establishes facts, rather than insisting on the ritual of confession, then the need for torture to secure convictions vanished. Furthermore, the only crimes for which the primary evidence is the perpetrator's own words were crimes of heretical or seditious belief – and liberalism rejects the criminalization of belief.[33]

These, then, are the four illiberal motives for torture: victor's pleasure, terror, punishment, and extracting confessions. That leaves only one rationale for torture that might conceivably be acceptable to a liberal: torture as a technique of intelligence-gathering from captives who will not talk. This may seem indistinguishable from torture to extract confessions, because in both torture is coupled with interrogation. The crucial difference lies in the fact that the confession is backward-looking – it aims to document and ratify the past for purposes of retribution – while intelligence-gathering is forward-looking – it aims to gain information to forestall future evils like terrorist attacks. It is striking, and in obvious ways reassuring, that this is the only rationale for torture that liberal political culture admits could even possibly be legitimate. To speak in a somewhat perverse and paradoxical way, liberalism's insistence on limited governments that exercise their powers only for instrumental and pragmatic purposes creates the possibility of seeing torture as a civilized, not an atavistic, practice, provided that its sole purpose is preventing future harms. Rejecting torture as victor's spoils, as terror, as punishment, and as a device to force confession drastically limits the amount of torture that a liberal society might conceivably accept. But more than that, the liberal rationale for torture – as intelligence-gathering in gravely dangerous situations – transforms and rationalizes the motivation for torture. Now, for the first time, it becomes possible to think of torture as a last resort of men and women who are profoundly reluctant to torture. And in that way, liberals can for the first time think of torture dissociated from cruelty – torture ordered and administered by decent human beings who abhor what circumstances force them to do. Torture to gather intelligence and save lives seems almost heroic. For the first time, we can think of kindly torturers rather than tyrants.

I shall shortly be arguing that this way of thinking represents a dangerous delusion. But before abandoning the subject of how torture "became civilized," it is important to note one other dimension in which torture has become less cruel.

Readers of Foucault's *Discipline and Punish* will probably never forget its nauseating opening pages, in which Foucault describes in loving detail the gruesome death by torture of the man who assaulted Louis XV.[34] Foucault aims to shock, of course, and he certainly succeeded with me: I closed the book and wouldn't open it again for twenty years. There is a vast difference between the ancient world of torture, with its appalling mutilations, its roastings and flayings, and the tortures that liberals might accept: sleep deprivation, prolonged standing in stress positions, extremes of heat and cold, bright lights and loud music – what some refer to as "torture lite."

I do not mean to diminish how horrible these experiences are, nor do I mean to suggest that American interrogators never go further than torture lite. Waterboarding, withholding of pain medication from wounded captives, putting lit cigarettes in their ears, rape, and beatings all go much further.[35] At least five, and maybe up to twenty captives have been beaten to death by American interrogators.[36] My point is rather that liberals generally draw the line at forms of torture that maim the victim's body. This, like the limitation of torture to intelligence-gathering, marks an undeniable moderation in torture, the world's most immoderate practice. It's almost enough to persuade us that torture lite is not torture at all, or at least that it isn't cruel enough to make liberals wince – not when the stakes are high enough. Indeed, they may even deny that it is torture.

Let me summarize this part of my argument. Liberals, I have said, rank cruelty first among vices – not because liberals are more compassionate than anyone else, but because of the close connection between cruelty and tyranny. Torture is the living manifestation of cruelty, and the peculiar horror of torture within liberalism arises from the fact that torture is tyranny in microcosm, at its highest level of intensity. The history of torture reinforces this horror, because torture has always been bound up with military conquest, regal punishment, dictatorial terror, forced confessions, and the repression of dissident belief – a veritable catalogue of the evils of absolutist government that liberalism abhors. For all these reasons, it should hardly surprise us that liberals wish to ban torture absolutely, a wish that became legislative reality in the Torture Convention's insistence that nothing can justify torture.

But what about torture as intelligence gathering, torture to forestall greater evils? I suspect that throughout history this has been the least common motivation for torture, and thus the one most readily overlooked. And yet it alone bears no essential connection with tyranny. This is not to say that the torture victim experiences it as any less terrifying or humiliating; and so torture will seem no less tyrannical from the victim's point of view. The victim, after all, undergoes abject domination by the torturer. But it will dawn on reluctant liberals that the torturer's goal of forestalling greater evils is one that liberals share. It seems like a rational motivation, far removed from cruelty and power-lust. In fact, the liberal may for the first time find it possible to view torture from the torturer's point of view rather than the victim's.

Thus, even though absolute prohibition remains liberalism's primary teaching about torture, and the basic liberal stance is empathy for the torture victim, a more permissive stance remains as an unspoken possibility, the Achilles heel of absolute prohibitions. As long as the intelligence needs of a liberal society are slight, this possibility within liberalism remains dormant, perhaps even unnoticed. But when a catastrophe like 9/11 happens, liberals may cautiously conclude that, in the words of a well-known *Newsweek* article, it's "Time to Think About Torture."[37]

But the pressure of liberalism will compel them to think about it in a highly stylized and artificial way, what I will call the "liberal ideology of torture." The liberal ideology insists that the sole purpose of torture must be intelligence gathering to prevent a catastrophe; that torture is necessary to prevent the catastrophe; that torturing is the exception, not the rule, so that it has nothing to do with state tyranny; that those who inflict the torture are motivated solely by the looming catastrophe, with no tincture of cruelty; that torture in such circumstances is, in fact, little more than self-defense; and that, because of the associations of torture with the horrors of yesteryear, perhaps one shouldn't even call harsh interrogation "torture."

And the liberal ideology will crystalize all of these ideas in a single, mesmerizing example: the ticking time-bomb.

III. THE TICKING TIME-BOMB

Suppose the bomb is planted somewhere in the crowded heart of an American city, and you have custody of the man who planted it. He won't talk. Surely, the hypothetical suggests, we shouldn't be too squeamish to torture the information out of him and save hundreds of lives. Consequences count, and abstract moral prohibitions must yield to the calculus of consequences.

Everyone argues the pros and cons of torture through the ticking time-bomb. Senator Schumer and Professor Dershowitz, the Israeli Supreme Court, indeed every journalist devoting a think-piece to the unpleasant question of torture begins with the ticking time-bomb and ends there as well. The Schlesinger Report on Abu Ghraib notes that "[f]or the U.S., most cases for permitting harsh treatment of detainees on moral grounds begin with variants of the 'ticking time-bomb' scenario."[38] At this point in my argument, I mean to disarm the ticking time-bomb and argue that it is the wrong thing to think about. If so, then the liberal ideology of torture begins to unravel.

But before beginning these arguments, I want to pause and ask why this jejune example has become the alpha and omega of our thinking about torture. I believe the answer is this. The ticking time-bomb is proffered against liberals who believe in an absolute prohibition against torture. The idea is to force the liberal prohibitionist to admit that yes, even he or even she would agree to torture in at least this one situation. Once the prohibitionist admits that, then she has conceded that her opposition to torture is not based on principle. Now that the prohibitionist has admitted that her moral principles can be breached, all that is left is haggling about the price. No longer can the prohibitionist claim the moral high ground; no longer can she put the burden of proof on her opponents. She's down in the mud with them, and the only question left is how much further down she will go. Dialectically, getting the prohibitionist to address the ticking time-bomb is like getting the vegetarian to eat just one little oyster because it has no nervous system. Once she does that – *gotcha!*

The ticking time-bomb scenario serves a second rhetorical goal, one that is equally important to the proponent of torture. It makes us see the torturer in a different light, one of the essential points in the liberal ideology of torture, because it is the way that liberals can reconcile themselves to torture even while continuing to "put cruelty first." Now, he is not a cruel man or a sadistic man or a coarse, insensitive brutish man. Now, the torturer is a conscientious public servant, heroic the way that New York firefighters were heroic, willing to do desperate things only because the plight is so desperate and so many innocent lives are weighing on the public servant's conscience. The time-bomb scenario clinches the great divorce between torture and cruelty; it placates liberals, who put cruelty first.

Ludwig Wittgenstein once wrote that confusion arises when we become bewitched by a picture. Wittgenstein meant that it is easy to get seduced by simplistic examples that look compelling but actually misrepresent the world we live in. If the subject is the morality of torture, philosophical confusions can have life-or-death consequences. I believe the ticking time-bomb is the picture that bewitches us.

I don't mean that the time-bomb is completely unreal. To take a real-life counterpart: in 1995, an al Qaeda plot to bomb eleven U.S. airliners was thwarted by information tortured out of a Pakistani suspect by the Philippine police. According to journalists Marites Vitug and Glenda Gloria, "For weeks, agents hit him with a chair and a long piece of wood, forced water into his mouth, and crushed lighted cigarettes into his private parts. His ribs were almost totally broken and his captors were surprised he survived."[39] Grisly, to be sure – but if they hadn't done it, thousands of innocent travelers might have died horrible deaths.

But look at the example one more time. The Philippine agents were surprised he survived – in other words, they came close to torturing him to death *before* he talked. And they tortured him *for weeks*, during which time they presumably didn't know about the al Qaeda plot. What if he too didn't know? Or what if there had been no al Qaeda plot? Then they would have tortured him for weeks, possibly tortured him to death, for nothing. For all they knew at the time, that is exactly what they were doing. You can't use the argument that preventing the al Qaeda attack justified the decision to torture, because *at the moment the decision was made* no one knew about the al Qaeda attack.

The ticking time-bomb scenario cheats its way around these difficulties by stipulating that the bomb is there, ticking away, and that officials know it and know they have the man who planted it. Those conditions will seldom be met.[40] Let's try some more realistic hypotheticals and the questions they raise:

1. The authorities know there may be a bomb plot in the offing, and they've captured a man who may know something about it, but may not. Torture him? How much? For weeks? For months? The chances are considerable that you are torturing a man with nothing to tell you. If he doesn't talk, does that mean it's time to stop, or time to ramp up the level of torture? How likely does it have to be that he knows something important? Fifty-fifty? Thirty-seventy? Will one out of a hundred suffice to land him on the water board?

2. Do you really want to make the torture decision by running the numbers? A one percent chance of saving a thousand lives yields ten statistical lives. Does that mean that you can torture up to nine people on a one percent chance of finding crucial information?

3. The authorities think that one out of a group of fifty captives in Guantánamo might know where Osama bin Laden is hiding – but they don't know which captive. Torture them all? That is: torture forty-nine captives with nothing to tell you on the uncertain chance of capturing Osama?

4. For that matter, would capturing Osama bin Laden demonstrably save a single human life? The Bush administration has recently downplayed the importance of capturing Osama because American strategy has succeeded in marginalizing him. Maybe capturing him would save lives – but how certain do you have to be? Or doesn't it matter whether torture is intended to save human lives from a specific threat, as long as it furthers some goal in the war on terror?

   This question is especially important once we realize that the interrogation of al Qaeda suspects will almost never be to find out where the ticking bomb is hidden. We don't know in advance when al Qaeda has launched an operation. Instead, interrogation is a more general fishing expedition for any intelligence that might be used to help "unwind" the terrorist organization. Now one might reply that al Qaeda is itself the ticking time-bomb, so that unwinding the organization meets the formal conditions of the ticking bomb hypothetical. This is equivalent to asserting that any intelligence which promotes victory in the War on Terror justifies torture, precisely because we understand that the enemy in the War on Terror aims to kill American civilians. Presumably, on this argument Japan would have been justified in torturing American captives in World War II on the chance of finding intelligence that would help them shoot down the *Enola Gay*; and I assume that a ticking bomb hard-liner will not flinch from this conclusion. But at this point, we verge on declaring all military threats and adversaries that menace American civilians to be ticking bombs, whose defeat justifies torture. The implied limitation of torture to emergency exceptions, implicit in the ticking bomb story, now threatens to unravel, making torture a legitimate instrument of military policy. And then the question becomes inevitable: Why not torture in pursuit of any worthwhile goal?

5. Indeed, if you're willing to torture forty-nine innocent people to get information from the one who has it, why stop there? If suspects won't break under torture, why not torture their loved ones in front of them? They are no more innocent than the forty-nine you've already shown you are prepared to torture. In fact, if only the numbers matter, torturing the loved ones is almost a no-brainer if you think it will work. Of course, you won't know until you try whether torturing his child will break the suspect. But that just changes the odds, it doesn't alter the argument.

The point of the examples is that in a world of uncertainty and imperfect knowledge, the ticking time-bomb scenario should not form the point of reference. The ticking bomb is the picture that bewitches us. The real debate is not between one guilty man's pain and hundreds of innocent lives. It is the debate between the certainty of anguish and the mere possibility of learning something vital and saving lives. And, above all, it is the question about whether a responsible citizen must unblinkingly think the unthinkable, and accept that the morality of torture should be decided purely by totaling up calculating costs and benefits.[41] Once you accept that only the numbers count, then anything, no matter how gruesome, becomes possible. "Consequentialist rationality," as Bernard Williams notes sardonically, "will have something to say even on the difference between massacring seven million, and massacring seven million and one."[42]

I am inclined to think that the path of wisdom instead lies in Holocaust survivor David Rousset's famous caution that normal human beings do *not* know that everything is possible.[43] As Williams says, "there are certain situations so monstrous that the idea that the processes of moral rationality could yield an answer in them is insane," and "to spend time thinking what one would decide if one were in such a situation is also insane, if not merely frivolous."[44]

IV. TORTURE AS A PRACTICE

There is a second, insidious, error built into the ticking time-bomb hypothetical. It assumes a single, ad hoc decision about whether to torture, by officials who ordinarily would do no such thing except in a desperate emergency. But in the real world of interrogations, decisions are not made one-off. The real world is a world of policies, guidelines, and directives. It is a world of *practices*, not of ad hoc emergency measures. Any responsible discussion of torture therefore needs to address the practice of torture, not the ticking time-bomb hypothetical. I am not saying anything original here; other writers have made exactly this point.[45] But somehow, we always manage to forget it and circle back to the ticking time-bomb. Its rhetorical power has made it indispensable to the sensitive liberal soul, and we would much rather talk about the ticking bomb than about torture as an organized social practice.

Treating torture as a practice rather than as a desperate improvisation in an emergency means changing the subject from the ticking bomb to other issues – issues like these:

Should we create a professional cadre of trained torturers? That means a group of interrogators who know the techniques, who have learned to overcome their instinctive revulsion against causing physical pain, and who acquire the legendary surgeon's arrogance about their own infallibility. It's happened before. Medieval executioners were schooled in the arts of agony as part of the trade: how to break men on the wheel, how to rack them, and even how to surreptitiously strangle them as an act of mercy without the bloodthirsty crowd catching on.[46] In Louis XVI's Paris, torture was a hereditary family trade whose tricks were passed on from father to son.[47]

Of course, in our era, higher education has replaced hereditary family trades. Should universities create an undergraduate major in torture? Or should the major be offered only in police and military academies? Do we want federal grants for research to devise new and better torture techniques? Patents issued on high-tech torture devices? Companies competing to manufacture them? Trade conventions in Las Vegas? Should there be a medical sub-specialty of torture doctors, who ensure that captives don't die before they talk? Consider the chilling words of Sgt. Ivan Fredericks, one of the Abu Ghraib suspects, who recalled a death by CIA interrogation that he witnessed: "They stressed the man out so bad that he passed away."[48] Real pros wouldn't let that happen; it wastes a good source. Who should teach torture-doctoring in medical school?[49]

The questions amount to this: Do we really want to create a torture culture and the kind of people who inhabit it? The ticking time bomb distracts us from the real issue, which is not about emergencies, but about the normalization of torture.

Perhaps the solution is to keep the practice of torture secret in order to avoid the moral corruption that comes from creating a public culture of torture. But this so-called "solution" does not reject the normalization of torture. It accepts it, but layers on top of it the normalization of state secrecy. The result would be a shadow culture of torturers and those who train and support them, operating outside the public eye and accountable only to other insiders of the torture culture.

Just as importantly: who guarantees that case-hardened torturers, inured to levels of violence and pain that would make ordinary people vomit at the sight, will know where to draw the line on when torture should be used? They never have in the past. They didn't in Algeria.[50] They didn't in Israel, where in 1999 the Israeli Supreme Court backpedaled from an earlier permission to engage in torture lite because the interrogators were running amok and torturing two-thirds of their Palestinian captives.[51] In the Argentinean "Dirty War," the tortures began because terrorist cells had a policy of fleeing when one of their members had disappeared for forty-eight hours.[52] Authorities who captured a militant had just two days to wring the information out of the captive. Mark Osiel, who has studied the Argentinean military in the Dirty War, reports that at first many of them had qualms about what they were doing, until their priests reassured them that they were fighting God's fight. By the end of the Dirty War, the qualms were gone, and, as John Simpson and Jana Bennett report, hardened young officers were placing bets on who could kidnap the prettiest girl to rape and torture.[53] Escalation is the rule, not the aberration.[54]

There are two fundamental reasons for this, one rooted in the nature of bureaucracy and the other in social psychology. The first is entirely straightforward. When a prisoner is turned over to interrogators, their assignment is to get as much valuable intelligence as possible from the prisoner, and it is not their job to wonder whether this is a ticking time-bomb case. They will work within the guidelines they are given, whatever those are. But one thing the guidelines will not say is "escalate the harshness depending on how vital the information is." That's not for the grunt-level interrogator to determine.

The liberal ideology of torture presupposes a torturer impelled by the desire to stop a looming catastrophe, not by cruelty. Implicitly, this image presumes that the interrogator and the decision-maker are the same person. But the defining fact about real organizations is the division of labor. The person who decides whether this prisoner presents a genuine ticking bomb case is not the interrogator. The decision about what counts as a ticking bomb case – one where torture is the lesser evil – depends on complex value judgments, and these get made further up the chain of command. The interrogator simply executes decisions made elsewhere.

Interrogators do not inhabit a world of loving kindness, or of equal concern and respect for all human beings. Interrogating resistant prisoners nonviolently and nonabusively still requires a relationship that in any other context would be morally abhorrent. It requires tricking information out of the subject, and the interrogator does this by setting up elaborate scenarios to disorient the subject and propel him into an alternative reality. The subject must be gotten to believe that his high-value intelligence has already been discovered from someone else, so that it is of no value. He must be fooled into thinking that his friends have betrayed him, or that the interrogator is his friend. The interrogator disrupts his sense of time and place, disorients him with sessions that never take place at predictable times or intervals, and manipulates his emotions. The very names of interrogation techniques show this: "Emotional Love," "Emotional Hate," "Fear Up Harsh," "Fear Up Mild," "Reduced Fear," "Pride and Ego Up," "Pride and Ego Down," "Futility."[55] The interrogator may set up a scenario to make the subject think he is in the clutches of a much-feared secret police organization from a different country ("False Flag"). Every bit of the subject's environment is fair game for manipulation and deception, as the interrogator aims to create the total lie that gets the subject talking.[56]

Let me be clear that I'm not objecting to these deceptions. None of this rises to the level of abuse or torture lite, let alone torture heavy, and surely tricking the subject into talking is legitimate if the goals of the interrogation are legitimate. But what I have described is a relationship of totalitarian mind-control more profound than the world of Orwell's *1984*. The interrogator is like Descartes's Evil Deceiver, and the subject lives in a false reality as profound as *The Matrix*. The liberal fiction that interrogation can be done by people who are neither cruel nor tyrannical runs aground on the fact that regardless of the interrogator's character off the job, on the job every fiber of his concentration is devoted to dominating the mind of the subject.

Only one thing prevents this from turning into abuse and torture, and that is a clear set of bright-line rules, drummed into the interrogator with the intensity of a religious indoctrination, complete with warnings of fire and brimstone. American interrogator Chris Mackey reports that warnings about the dire consequences of violating the Geneva Conventions "were repeated so often that by the end of our time at [training school] the three syllables 'Lea-ven-worth' were ringing in our ears."[57]

But what happens when the line is breached? When, as in Afghanistan, he gets mixed messages about whether Geneva applies, or hears rumors of ghost detainees, of high-value captives held for years of interrogation in the top-secret facility known as "Hotel California," located in some nation somewhere? Or when the interrogator observes around him the move from deception to abuse, from abuse to torture lite, from torture lite to beatings and waterboarding? Without clear lines, the tyranny innate in the interrogator's job has nothing to hold it in check.[58] Perhaps someone, somewhere in the chain of command, is wringing hands over whether this interrogation qualifies as a ticking bomb case; but the interrogator knows only that the rules of the road have changed and the posted speed limits no longer apply. The liberal fiction of the conscientious interrogator overlooks a division of moral labor in which the person with the fastidious conscience and the person doing the interrogation are not the same.

The fiction must presume, therefore, that the interrogator operates only under the strictest supervision, in a chain of command where his every move gets vetted and controlled by the superiors who are actually doing the deliberating. The trouble is that this assumption flies in the face of everything that we know about how organizations work. The basic rule in every bureaucratic organization is that operational details and the guilty knowledge that goes with them gets pushed down the chain of command as far as possible. As sociologist Robert Jackall explains,

> It is characteristic...that details are pushed down and credit is pulled up. Superiors do not like to give detailed instructions to subordinates.... [O]ne of the privileges of authority is the divestment of humdrum intricacies....Perhaps more important, pushing details down protects the privilege of authority to declare that a mistake has been made....Moreover, pushing down details relieves superiors of the burden of too much knowledge, particularly guilty knowledge.[59]

We saw this phenomenon at Abu Ghraib, where military intelligence officers gave MPs vague orders like "'Loosen this guy up for us.' 'Make sure he has a bad night.' 'Make sure he gets the treatment.'"[60] Suppose that the 18-year-old guard interprets "Make sure he has a bad night" to mean, simply, "keep him awake all night." How do you do that without physical abuse?[61] Furthermore, personnel at Abu Ghraib witnessed far harsher treatment of prisoners by "other governmental agencies" (OGA), a euphemism for the Central Intelligence Agency.[62] They saw OGA spirit away the dead body of an interrogation subject, and allegedly witnessed a contract employee rape a youthful prisoner.[63] When that's what you see, abuses like those in the Abu Ghraib photos will not look outrageous. Outrageous compared with what?

This brings me to a point of social psychology. Simply stated, it is this: we judge right and wrong against the baseline of whatever we have come to consider "normal" behavior, and if the norm shifts in the direction of violence, we will come to tolerate and accept violence as a normal response. The psychological mechanisms for this re-normalization have been studied for more than half a century, and by now they are reasonably well understood.[64] Rather than detour into psychological theory, however, I will illustrate the point with the most salient example – one that seems so obviously applicable to Abu Ghraib that the Schlesinger Commission discussed it at length in an appendix to their report. This is the famous Stanford Prison Experiment. Male volunteers were divided randomly into two groups, who would simulate the guards and inmates in a mock prison. Within a matter of days, the inmates began acting like actual prison inmates – depressed, enraged, and anxious. And the guards began to abuse the inmates to such an alarming degree that the researchers had to halt the two-week experiment after just seven days. In the words of the experimenters:

> The use of power was self-aggrandizing and self-perpetuating. The guard power, derived initially from an arbitrary label, was intensified whenever there was any perceived threat by the prisoners and this new level subsequently became the baseline from which further hostility and harassment would begin. ... [T]he absolute level of aggression as well as the more subtle and "creative" forms of aggression manifested, increased in a spiraling fashion.[65]

It took only five days before a guard who prior to the experiment described himself as a pacifist was forcing greasy sausages down the throat of a prisoner who refused to eat; and in less than a week, the guards were placing bags over prisoners' heads, making them strip, and sexually humiliating them in ways reminiscent of Abu Ghraib.[66]

My conclusion is very simple. Abu Ghraib is the fully predictable image of what a torture culture looks like. Abu Ghraib is not a few bad apples. It is the apple tree. And you cannot reasonably expect that interrogators in a torture culture will be the fastidious and well-meaning torturers that the liberal ideology fantasizes.

That is why Alan Dershowitz has argued that judges, not torturers, should oversee the permission to torture, which must be regulated by warrants. The irony is that Jay S. Bybee, who signed the Justice Department's highly permissive torture memo, is now a federal judge. Politicians pick judges, and if the politicians accept torture, the judges will as well. Once we create a torture culture, only the naive would suppose that judges will provide a safeguard. Judges don't fight their culture. They reflect it.

For all these reasons, the ticking time-bomb scenario is an intellectual fraud. In its place, we must address the real questions about torture – questions about uncertainty, questions about the morality of consequences, questions about what it does to a culture to introduce the practice of torture, questions about what torturers are like and whether we really want them walking proudly among us.

Once we do so, I suspect that few Americans will be willing to conclude that everything is possible.

V. THE CONSTRUCTION OF A TORTURE CULTURE: THE TORTURE LAWYERS OF WASHINGTON

A skeptic might respond that my dire warnings about a torture culture are exaggerated and overwrought. In what follows, I wish to offer an extended case-study of a torture culture constructed under our noses in Washington. I am referring to the group of lawyers who wrote the highly permissive secret memoranda that came close to legitimizing torture for interrogation purposes. They illustrate as graphically as any group how quickly and easily a secret culture of torture supporters can emerge even in the heart of a liberal culture. They illustrate as well how readily the liberal ideology of torture transforms into something far removed from liberalism.

I am particularly interested in the torture lawyers because of a decades-long interest in the professional ethics of lawyers. But the torture lawyers present an especially interesting case, because lawyers are the last group one thinks of as a potential torture culture. Lawyers are usually sticklers for formality and playing by the book; as Tocqueville suggested, lawyers are instinctive conservatives. When business executives complain about their in-house lawyers, the complaint invariably centers around the fact that the lawyers are the natural enemies of bold, decisive action. Lawyers are supposed to be cautious and, by and large, lawyers are cautious – especially in the face of illegality.

And, on its face, torture is completely illegal. The United States is a party to the Convention Against Torture, a comprehensive anti-torture treaty. We have criminalized torture, created civil remedies for torture victims, and provided safe haven to illegal aliens who face torture if they are sent home. Given this mass of law, it is startling to find groups of lawyers marching in near lock-step into a brave new world of legally sanctioned official torture. It is particularly startling because the legal arguments they use are, in conventional professional terms, awful. This leads me to an obvious conclusion: the torture lawyers were doing something far bolder than conventional legal advising, and they had no use for conventional forms of legality and legal argument. What they were doing, I believe, is self-consciously constructing a torture culture.

By now, the background is well-known, but it may be worthwhile to recapitulate briefly. There were, in reality, over a dozen memoranda going back and forth between the Department of Defense, the State Department, the Justice Department, and the White House that pertained to the interrogation of detainees.[67] The most controversial, though, emerged from a single office: the Office of Legal Counsel (OLC) in the Justice Department. Two OLC memos, written in early 2002, concluded that the Geneva Conventions do not cover al Qaeda or Taliban captives.[68] These set the stage for President Bush's February 7 memo affirming that conclusion, and asserting that prisoners would be treated consistently with Geneva "to the extent appropriate and consistent with military necessity" – a large loophole for intelligence-gathering.[69] In effect, the President, relying on the OLC, proclaimed that if military necessity requires it, Geneva is gone.

Six months later, OLC tendered another memo, this one on the question of whether harsh interrogation tactics violate U.S. obligations under the Torture Convention and its implementing statutes. This memo, signed by OLC chief Jay S. Bybee, reached a series of startling conclusions: that the infliction of pain rises to the level of torture only if the pain is as severe as that accompanying "death, organ failure, or serious impairment of body functions";[70] that the infliction of psychological pain rises to the level of torture only if the interrogator specifically intended it to cause "lasting...damage" such as post-traumatic stress disorder;[71] that it would be unconstitutional to apply anti-torture laws to interrogations authorized by the President in the war on terror;[72] and that, "under current circumstances, necessity or self-defense may justify interrogation methods that violate" the criminal prohibition on torture.[73]

The Bybee Memo, as I will call it, proved to be enormously influential. In January 2003, Defense Secretary Donald Rumsfeld formed a working group on interrogation techniques, which produced its own report in April.[74] Significantly, the working group report based itself substantially on the Bybee Memo, and in fact incorporated large chunks of it verbatim. The working group report, in turn, influenced policy on interrogation tactics.

None of these memoranda and reports was produced in a vacuum. According to Kenneth Roth, the Executive Director of Human Rights Watch, the initial OLC memos on whether the Geneva Conventions apply were written "in response to a request from the CIA to the White House counsel saying please give us guidance on the kind of interrogation we can do."[75] Specifically, the CIA wanted approval to waterboard Abu Zubaydah, the first top Al Qaeda leader in U.S. custody.[76] The Bybee Memorandum "was vetted by a larger number of officials, including lawyers at the National Security Council, the White House counsel's office and Vice President Cheney's office."[77] Apparently, then-White House counsel Alberto Gonzales requested the memorandum.[78] And the DoD working group was formed after the head of an Army interrogation team requested permission to escalate to harsher tactics.[79]

Unsurprisingly, once they were leaked, the OLC memos proved to be incredibly controversial, so much so that in the wake of the Abu Ghraib scandal, the Justice Department repudiated the Bybee Memo. It also turned out that when the Geneva memos were first written, the State Department's legal advisor had vigorously denounced them to the White House.[80] Indeed, former OLC lawyers from past Republican administrations criticized the memos, and Ruth Wedgwood, perhaps the most prominent academic defender of Bush administration legal positions in the war on terror, denounced the torture memos in a blistering *Wall Street Journal* op-ed, which she co-authored with former CIA Director

R. James Woolsey.[81] In December, 2004, shortly before Alberto Gonzales was to face confirmation hearings as Attorney General, the OLC issued a new torture memorandum, repudiating and replacing the Bybee Memo. It was posted unannounced on the Department of Justice's website.[82]

To understand how astonishing it is that the OLC produced a memorandum with such dubious credentials, you must realize that the OLC is one of the most elite groups of lawyers in the federal government. Its charge is to serve as primary legal advisor to the executive branch, and its reputation – at least before Abu Ghraib – has always been stellar and unimpeachable.[83] These are among the best and the brightest in the legal profession. And yet, as we shall see, the Bybee Memorandum was a laughingstock judged by the standards of conventional legal argument.[84] The question is, why?

I believe the Bybee Memo's authors proceeded from the assumption that the law as conventionally understood was simply unsuitable for the post-9/11 world. As an article in the *New York Times* explains,

> The administration's legal approach to terrorism began to emerge in the first turbulent days after Sept. 11, as the officials in charge of key agencies exhorted their aides to confront Al Qaeda's threat with bold imagination.
>
> "Legally, the watchword became 'forward-leaning,'" said a former associate White House counsel, Bradford Berenson, "by which everybody meant: 'We want to be aggressive. We want to take risks.'"

The challenge resounded among young lawyers who were settling into important posts at the White House, the Justice Department and other agencies.[85] As an example of "forward-leaning" legal strategy, the article mentions an OLC memorandum by John Yoo on how to overcome Fourth Amendment objections to the use of military force against terrorists within the United States, for example "'to raid or attack dwellings where terrorists were thought to be, despite risks that third parties could be killed or injured by exchanges of fire.'"[86] This memorandum was written just ten days after September 11. The article explains that "lawyers in the administration took the same 'forward-leaning' approach to making plans for the terrorists they thought would be captured."[87] The most crucial portions of the strategy – which included not just interrogation issues but military tribunals and the applicability of the Geneva Convention as well – were formulated in near-total secrecy, intentionally excluding anticipated dissenting voices in the State Department and the Judge Advocate General (JAG) Corps.[88] And, significantly, the role of the OLC changed dramatically. Where in past administrations OLC weighed in after relevant federal agencies had addressed legal questions, now "the office frequently had a first and final say."[89]

In the Bybee Memo, OLC lawyers simply discarded the project of providing an impartial analysis of the law as mainstream lawyers and judges understand it. Instead, they substituted a rethinking of standard legal doctrines based on the liberal ideology of torture – the idea that torture to obtain information useful for national defense is not impermissible and that those who commit it for inter-rogational reasons have done nothing wrong. If conventional sources of law do not include these conclusions in the doctrines of necessity, self-defense, or *mens rea*, then the analysis should simply ignore them, which it does. In effect, they were writing an advocacy document for a pro-torture conclusion, in order to give those who order or engage in torture legal cover.

Lawyers have a word for a legal opinion that does this. It is called a CYA memorandum – Cover Your Ass. Without the memorandum, the client who wants to push the legal envelope is on his own. But with a CYA memo in hand, he can insist that he cleared it with the lawyers first, and that way he can duck responsibility.

As a CYA memo, the OLC documents have the promise of being spectacu-larly effective. Suppose that some American intelligence officer were to order an interrogator to torture a detainee. And suppose that the interrogator was found out and tried for torture. Her lawyer would certainly recommend a "superior orders" defense. In military law, this defense is available to defendants who did not actually know that the order they were following was unlawful, provided that it was not *manifestly* unlawful. Now, in an egregious case of torture, this defense would almost certainly fail on the ground that torture is manifestly unlawful, that is, in the colorful language of military law, it "flies the black flag of illegality" above it. But now the skilled defense counsel can point to the OLC and DoD memos and offer an ironclad rejoinder. If two high-echelon working groups of skilled lawyers argue that torture can be legally justified, then *even if they are wrong* and torture is unlawful, it cannot be *manifestly* unlawful. Notice that for this argument to succeed, it doesn't matter whether the torturer or her superior knew anything about the memos. The defense here rests on a different argument than that the torturer relied on the memos. The defense here is that the mere existence of these memoranda proves that if torture is illegal, its illegality is subtle and hard to see – the opposite of "manifest." The fact that the Levin Memo replaces and repudiates the Bybee Memo will not matter; indeed, it illus-trates even more graphically that the illegality (or not) of torture lays shrouded in legal obscurity. In other words, from this date forward the mere existence of the Bybee Memo covers the ass of any interrogator who tortures under color of superior orders.[90]

VI. MAKING THE WORLD SAFE FOR TORTURERS

The time has now come to examine the Bybee Memorandum. This may seem like a pointless exercise, given that the Levin Memo has repudiated it. But the analysis is far from pointless. My argument will be that the legal deficiencies of the Bybee Memo are neither careless nor random. Rather, at almost all points they express the vision that I have called the "liberal ideology of torture." In this respect, the Bybee Memo strikes me as a more authentic document than the

Levin Memo, which appears to be an exercise in damage control coupled with the political needs of the Gonzales confirmation.

Examining the Bybee Memo will turn out to be a detailed task, and before undertaking it, I will summarize. I am making a different claim than that the Bybee Memo gets the law wrong. On contentious legal issues, conventional legal materials can always be marshaled to generate recognizably plausible arguments on all sides. Not everyone will agree which are the more plausible, and no generally-accepted technique exists to settle the matter – nothing that corresponds to the way that mathematicians check the steps of a proof or that natural scientists replicate or fail to replicate experimental results. In this sense, law is indeterminate. (A medieval Jewish commentary once declared that nothing in the Law is clear-cut – rather, when the Holy One imparted each clause, He imparted with it forty-nine reasons to interpret it one way and forty-nine reasons to interpret it the other.[91])

My claim is different. What makes the Bybee Memo jarring by conventional legal standards is that in its most controversial sections, it barely goes through the motions of standard legal argument. Instead of addressing and rebutting the obvious arguments against its conclusions, it elects not to mention them; in several of its crucial sections it cites no statutes, regulations, or judicial decisions to support its most controversial conclusions (presumably because there are none); and when it does cite conventional sources of law, it employs them in utterly unconventional ways. I thus disagree entirely with Eric Posner and Adrian Vermeule, who describe the Memo's arguments as "standard lawyerly fare, routine stuff."[92] It is nothing of the kind.

Thus, in its discussion of presidential power, the Bybee Memo never mentions plain constitutional language suggesting a very different conclusion, nor the principal Supreme Court case on the subject.[93] In its discussion of the necessity defense in criminal law, it fails to analyze the effect of the Torture Convention on the necessity defense to charges of torture. The necessity discussion draws on a treatise, but no statutes, regulations, or cases (other than one decision recognizing that the defense exists in federal law). Nor does it mention the awkward fact that the necessity defense never succeeds in federal law, and has never been accepted by a federal court for a crime of violence. The self-defense discussion cites a few cases, but none in support of its main points.[94] And the Memo's analyses of conventional sources of law are bizarre – for example, its argument that because a health-care statute lists severe pain as a possible symptom of a medical emergency, only pain equivalent to that accompanying medical emergencies is severe; or its attempt to show that while the necessity defense applies to torture, it need not apply to life-saving abortions; or its argument that when Congress forbade torture regardless of its purpose, it thereby declined to judge torture worse than whatever good it might do. Despite the Byzantine subtlety of much of the Memo's reasoning, the overall assessment must be that its authors had no desire to engage in legal argument as lawyers conventionally engage in it. The Levin Memo backhandedly says as much about some of these issues. The blunt assessment is that of Peter Brooks: the Bybee Memo "offers a remarkable example of textual interpretation run amok – less 'lawyering as usual' than the work of some bizarre literary deconstructionist."[95]

It follows that the Bybee Memo's authors also had no desire to offer legal advice as conventional legal ethics understands it: informing the client of the state of the law as mainstream lawyers and judges understand it. Its aim, if it was anything more than a CYA memorandum, was to propose a paradigm-shift, cutting across several areas of law, to advance the liberal ideology of torture and make torture acceptable.

The Bybee Memo covers a lot of ground, and much of the immediate reaction to it had to do with its conclusions about presidential power to authorize torture notwithstanding the Torture Convention and the federal statute criminalizing official torture. Strikingly, the Levin Memo never repudiates these conclusions, instead choosing to duck the question with a politician's transparent evasiveness.[96] I will say a few words about the subject of presidential power, which fits in with part of the liberal ideology of torture (its insistence on the "power of the exception"), but mainly I wish to focus on the Memo's treatment of what torture is, and the criminal law defenses to torture charges. These issues go right to the moral core of torture and its ambiguous place in liberal politics; and, as I hope to show, the Bybee Memo relies crucially on the liberal ideology of torture to make its conclusions palatable.

I begin by examining the Bybee Memo as though it were a piece of conventional legal advice by lawyers to their client. I hope to show that, understood in conventional terms, the Memo falls far below minimum standards of professional competence – but, more importantly, that it incorporates the leading ideas of the liberal ideology of torture.

A. "Severe Pain"

Let us begin with the memo's insistence that "severe pain" amounting to torture must be equivalent to the pain of serious injury, organ failure, or death – a standard far stricter than most of the world's law governing torture. Where, one might ask, did the OLC lawyers get this stuff?

The answer is that they scoured the federal laws for anything that used the term "severe pain," and came up with "statutes defining an emergency medical condition for the purpose of providing health benefits."[97] There they learned that an emergency medical condition is one where the person experiences symptoms that might indicate "serious dysfunction of any bodily organ or part."[98] Unsurprisingly, among those symptoms we find severe pain. From this, they concluded that federal law defines 'severe pain' as the kind of pain that indicates possible organ failure.

The problem is that the law does nothing of the sort. The statute they quote is a definition of 'emergency medical condition,' not of 'severe pain.' It neither states nor implies that only pain indicating possible organ failure is severe.[99] It merely lists severe pain as a typical symptom of an emergency medical condition. Imagine a statute offering federal benefits to chemotherapy patients experiencing symptoms such as hair loss. It would be crazy to read the statute as a legal definition of baldness, namely the level of hair loss typical of chemotherapy patients. But that is precisely how the Bybee Memo reads the health benefits statute. Reading the statute as a definition of severe pain would imply the absurd consequence that the pain you experience when a dental drill hits a nerve is not severe, because the average person understands that this sudden moment of agony is not a serious health threat. The OLC's definition would also imply that an interrogator crushing out cigarettes in a detainee's ear is not torture, because its pain is not equivalent to that of a medical emergency.

Besides its frolicsome way with the federal health care statutes, the Bybee Memo makes forays into dictionary definitions of 'severe,' 'prolonged,' and other words from the statute. One legitimately goes to the dictionary in order to deal with ambiguities. It is always possible that one has overlooked an alternative meaning of a word, or that the word has an obsolete meaning, or has acquired a new meaning. But there is a difference between ambiguity and vagueness. A vague word like 'severe' has univocal, even clear, meaning, but indeterminate reference. Here, the interpretive problem is not multiple meanings but fuzzy borders. Any dictionary definition that is worth its salt will be as vague as the word itself – otherwise, it has altered rather than defined the meaning. And any attempt by a lawyer to wring greater specificity of a vague term out of a dictionary definition is, by the very terms of the problem, a cheat.[100] Here, the vagueness of the word 'torture' gets replicated in the dictionary by the equivalent vagueness of the word 'severe' as in 'severe pain.' Recourse to the dictionary does nothing except provide a list of equally vague synonyms, and citing the dictionary serves only to provide a seemingly-objective source for spinning the meaning of a word the way they want it to be spun. Indeed, the OLC appears to have selected its dictionaries carefully, using half-a-dozen dictionaries going back as far as 1935 to cull definitions of various words in the statutes – and, as Peter Brooks observes, relying at one point on a 1935 definition that Brooks's 1979 dictionary describes as "obsolete."[101]

However, the forays into the dictionary and the statute book do serve an important ideological function. Beneath the comedy of legal textualism lies a very clear and serious point: that legal bans on torture are meant to encompass only torture in its most unbearable forms, the forms that modern liberals do not engage in. This is not how most jurists view modern prohibitions on torture; the worldwide trend has been toward expanding the prohibition beyond torture at its most gruesome. In this respect, the Bybee Memo misdescribes the path of the law (as the Levin Memo subsequently concedes[102]). But Bybee's aim is not to describe the path of the law; it is to resist it. Theirs is a normative argument that the prohibition on torture never should have reached pain-infliction in its less devastating forms. The devastating forms are unmistakably cruel; liberals reject cruelty – therefore, the less cruel forms of treatment liberals employ in interrogation should not be regarded as torture. (One could put the syllogism a bit more tendentiously: Torture is wrong. We do not do wrong; but we use techniques X, Y, and Z. Therefore X, Y, and Z are not torture.)

B. Specific Intent

Next, consider the Bybee Memo's lengthy discussion of the specific intent for the crime of torture as defined by the federal anti-torture statute. The statute requires that the perpetrator specifically intend "to inflict severe physical or mental pain or suffering . . . upon a person within his physical custody or control." The phrase "specific intent" is a criminal lawyer's term of art – unfortunately, one that has multiple meanings and that many lawyers find confusing. The Bybee Memo adopts one of these competing meanings, namely that to "specifically intend" some consequence when performing an action means to perform the action for the purpose of achieving that consequence. In other words, achieving the consequence is the goal of the action, not simply a foreseen but unintended byproduct of it. Knowingly inflicting severe pain on someone isn't torture unless your purpose is to inflict severe pain. As the Memo puts it, "the infliction of such pain must be the defendant's precise objective."[103] It goes on to explain that "knowledge alone that a particular result is certain to occur does not constitute specific intent."[104]

The Bybee Memo is on conventional ground in concluding that Congress used the "specific intent" language to narrow the definition of torture to those cases in which the torturer's purpose is to cause pain. Otherwise, the statute would criminalize a host of innocent actions that the actor knows will hurt without that being the actor's purpose – actions like extracting your wisdom teeth or performing a quadruple bypass.[105]

But why does the Bybee Memo belabor this simple point for two densely-written, single-spaced pages, reiterating again and again that knowingly inflicting severe pain is not torture unless inflicting pain is the "precise objective"? After all, the memo is written for interrogators, not people who inflict pain as a mere by-product of their job, such as periodontists or heart surgeons. In interrogation, if you knowingly inflict pain, it's because you are trying to inflict pain. This is one context where specific intent and knowledge empirically coincide. So why get into an elaborate discussion of the subtle differences between intended agony and foreseen-but-unintended agony, when in the interrogation business the latter category consists of the null set? A good legal advisor, it seems to me, would take the opposite tack in explaining the criminal law of torture to an interrogator. The good advisor would say, "Don't get fancy with the words 'specifically intended.' The legal distinction between specific intent and other mental states doesn't matter in your line of work. All you need to know is that under the law, using severely painful interrogation techniques makes you a torturer."[106] The OLC forgot one of the Supreme Court's well-taken admonitions (in a case that the Bybee Memo cites for its own purposes): "The administration of [law] is confided to ordinary mortals.... This system could easily fall of its own weight if courts or scholars become obsessed with hair-splitting distinctions" among mental states.[107]

Unfortunately, I suspect that the authors of the Bybee Memo had a reason for splitting hairs, and not a nice one. The Memo insists, again and again, that to count as torture the infliction of severe pain must be the interrogator's "precise objective," that "even if the [interrogator] knows that severe pain will result from his actions, if causing such harm is not his objective, he lacks the requisite specific intent" and is not guilty of torture. "Well," says the military intelligence officer who reads this, "our *objective* is getting usable intelligence, not making this dude suffer. So I guess the lawyers are telling me that it isn't torture. We can tell the interrogators that they're safe." To see how easy it is to misconstrue the Bybee Memo along these lines, consider a question posed by a reporter to Alberto Gonzales, then White House Counsel, at a press conference on Abu Ghraib in June 2004:

REPORTER: ...I read the memo like, over a week ago, but there were all sorts of things in there, like, if you didn't – if you weren't doing it just to make someone suffer, but for the purposes of gathering information, maybe it wasn't torture then.[108]

Gonzales does not respond "no, no, that's not what the Memo says." Instead, he brushes the question aside:

MR. GONZALES: I haven't looked at that memo closely recently. So in terms of what that memo actually says, I'm not going to comment specifically on it.[109]

Even the chief White House lawyer, giving a public briefing on the Bybee Memo (among others) could not, immediately and off the top of his head, identify the misreading. It is hard to believe that this is not exactly how it was meant to be understood. Remember that the report was written at the behest of intelligence officials who wanted legal clearance for harsh techniques because their interrogators had balked at elevating to the next level.[110]

After the memo, they stopped balking. FBI documents leaked in December 2004 indicate systematic abuse of detainees by Guantanamo interrogators, including stress positions for as much as 24 hours at a time, in which detainees were bombarded with bright lights or strobe lights along with rap songs at ear-splitting volume. They underwent "strangulation, beatings, placement of lit cigarettes into the detainees' ear openings and unauthorized interrogations."[111] One detainee was found the next morning next to a pile of his own hair; in his misery, he had pulled it all out.

Contributing to torture culture at Guantanamo is another memo, by Lieutenant Colonel Diane Beaver, a torture lawyer in the Department of Defense. Beaver offers an analysis of both the torture statute and the prohibition on cruel, inhuman, or degrading treatment ("CID," in lawyers' vernacular) in the Torture Convention. She notes that the United States entered a reservation to the latter article in the Torture Convention, stating that U.S. standards of cruel, inhuman, or degrading treatment would go no further than Eighth Amendment standards prohibiting cruel and unusual punishments. Turning to Supreme Court cases on the Eighth Amendment, she concludes that "[u]ltimately, an Eighth Amendment analysis is based primarily on whether the government has a good faith legitimate governmental interest, and did not act maliciously or sadistically for the very purpose of causing harm."[112] Hence,

> so long as the force used could plausibly be thought necessary in a particular situation to achieve a legitimate governmental objective, and it was applied in a good faith effort and not maliciously or sadistically for the very purpose of causing harm, the proposed techniques are likely to pass constitutional muster. The federal torture statute will not be violated so long as any of the proposed strategies are not specifically intended to cause severe physical pain or suffering or prolonged mental harm.[113]

Notice that Beaver places her statement of the *mens rea* for the crime of torture immediately after her analysis of the *mens rea* for cruel, inhuman, or degrading treatment, with no transition – and that the analysis for cruel, inhuman, and degrading treatment analyzes the *mens rea* exactly along the lines of the misreading of the plausible misreading of the specific intent requirement for torture. If you had a legitimate objective, and weren't being malicious or sadistic, you weren't guilty. Of course it gets the law wrong to conclude that if the objective of inflicting severe pain is getting usable intelligence, it can't be torture. You can intend to get usable intelligence *and*, as a way of doing so, intend to cause severe pain. The latter intention makes it torture regardless of the former intention. To be sure, neither the Bybee Memo or the Beaver Memo ever literally says otherwise – they merely incorporate a discussion that naturally and foreseeably leads to this misreading of the law, in part because otherwise their entire discussion would be pointless.

Taken together with the Bybee Memo's definitions of "severe," the specific intent analysis is lethal. An interrogator who intends to inflict pain, but does not specifically intend it to be as severe as the pain accompanying organ failure, death, or serious bodily injury – even if the pain actually turns out to be severe under this definition – has not specifically intended to commit severe pain, and therefore has not tortured. Nor has the interrogator engaged in cruel, inhuman, or degrading treatment, according to the Beaver Memo, if he or she had a legitimate interrogational purpose.

The Bybee Memo's foray into specific intent serves another function as well, which becomes clear when we turn to their treatment of psychological torture. There, the OLC lawyers construe the federal torture statute's prohibition on "prolonged mental harm" to mean that the psychological damage must be

long-lasting, not merely confined to the interrogation session itself. The infliction of terror, for example, as in threatening a naked, helpless prisoner with an
attack dog, will not amount to torture unless it produces long-lasting psychic
trauma. On top of this controversial conclusion, however, OLC adds that the
interrogator must specifically intend to cause prolonged mental harm to be convicted of psychological torture. Given the analysis we have seen of specific intent,
this means that unless the interrogator's purpose was to traumatize the prisoner
long after the interrogation – which it never is – he has not committed the crime
of torture. Lieutenant Colonel Beaver is quite explicit about this when it comes
to the use of faux-suffocation techniques such as waterboarding: "The use of a
wet towel to induce the misperception of suffocation would also be permissible
if not done with the specific intent to cause prolonged mental harm, and absent
medical evidence that it would."[114] The specific intent requirement exonerates
interrogators who use terror tactics, no matter how intense, provided that the
interrogator has no purpose beyond the interrogation itself.

Notice one last point about this misreading, according to which pain-
infliction for the good purpose of obtaining useful intelligence is not torture
because it is not the specific intent of the interrogator. This is precisely the modern ideology of torture, the ideology that takes the ticking time-bomb hypothetical as its catechism, and insists that the contemporary torturer has left behind
the world of cruelty, that he tortures reluctantly, and only with the purest of
motives. Given the liberal ideology of torture, it is only natural to think that the
law should excuse him.

C. Self-Defense

I turn at this point to the two criminal defenses the Bybee Memo thinks are available to an interrogator accused of torturing a suspected terrorist for information:
self-defense and necessity. The Memo's arguments turn out to be extraordinarily
interesting, both for what they include but also for what they do not.

I begin with self-defense. Alongside the standard criminal defense category
of self-defense, and typically lumped together with it, we find the category of
defense of others. If someone is about to shoot me, I can shoot him in self-
defense. But the same is true if I see him prepared to shoot you, and the only way
I can stop it is by shooting him. Clearly, when the question is whether someone
can torture a terrorist to obtain information vital to forestalling a future terrorist
attack, the torturer herself is seldom in physical jeopardy. The torturer is using
violence in defense of others. It is in this form that the OLC explores the self-
defense justification of torture. And this far, at any rate, the Bybee Memo restates
familiar and accepted legal doctrine.

However, even when we realize that the justification is defense of others
rather than self-defense in the strict sense, the self-defense argument is a giant
departure from standard criminal law. The doctrines of self-defense and defense
of others, which justify the use of force against an assailant when there is no other

reasonable alternative, both presuppose a physical attack by the assailant. But in an interrogation torture case, the person being tortured is attacking no one. He has already been physically subdued and imprisoned. No criminal lawyer would recognize an interrogator giving the third degree to a jailed, shackled detainee as a case of self-defense as the law understands it. Indeed, the paradigms stand on opposite ends of the legal universe. In traditional self-defense, the person against whom one uses defensive violence is dangerous; in the torture case, he is helpless.

Unsurprisingly, the OLC cites no cases, statutes, or regulations to support its radical redefinition of self-defense. The reason is obvious: there is no conventional legal authority to support it. Their sole source, in fact, is a law review article by theorist Michael S. Moore. Moore argues that torturing a terrorist for information about the ticking bomb resembles self-defense in one respect: in both scenarios, Moore writes, one person "has culpably caused a situation in which someone might get hurt. If hurting him is the only means to prevent death or injury of others put at risk by his actions, such torture should be permissible, and on the same basis that self-defense is permissible."[115] These two sentences are the sole authority for OLC's argument that torturing the terrorist can be justified self-defense.

Let us look a bit more closely at Moore's argument. Moore does not purport to be restating the positive law of self-defense in any jurisdiction. Rather, his argument is an intervention in a high-level philosophical debate about self-defense. The doctrine of self-defense may seem obvious to the standpoint of common sense, but it presents an enormous puzzle to theoreticians. Is it grounded in a right to life and limb possessed by the person under attack? That seems plausible until we realize that such a right would also permit us to kill an innocent person to save our own life. Or is the basis of self-defense that the assailant has waived her own right to life and limb through the act of attack? Then why does the waiver end the moment the attack ends? Both these theories have major drawbacks, and providing a ground for self-defense that doesn't prove too much turns out to pose an enormous challenge.[116]

Moore's argument is an intervention into this theoretical debate. He approaches it by noting "that the aggressor creates a situation in which someone must be killed, either he or his intended victim."[117] By assumption, both lives are identical in worth. Therefore, what entitles the victim to substitute the death of the attacker for his own death is not differential worth, but the fact that it is the attacker who bears responsibility for the fatal encounter. "Since he is the one creating such a threat, he in all fairness is the one to be selected when someone has to bear the harm threatened."[118] This argument provides Moore with a principled account of self-defense, grounded in the relative innocence of the two parties.

Moore's argument represents a plausible resolution of a puzzle in criminal law theory. It does not represent anything like a consensus view, however, and

Moore certainly never claims that it does. It is one theory among several in a complex philosophical debate, but that is all it is.

This takes us to the application of the theory to torture. In the passage that OLC quotes, Moore argues that the principle of relative innocence suggests that if someone has to suffer violence, either the victims of terrorism or the terrorist, it should be the terrorist. Moore does not claim that torturing the terrorist represents an application of the law of self-defense – his claim is one of analogy, namely that his principle of relative innocence justifies both self-defense and torture of the terrorist. Thus, not only does Moore not claim that his account of self-defense is accepted in positive law, he does not even claim that his account of torture is an instance of self-defense as lawyers understand it. By suggesting otherwise, OLC misrepresents the status of Moore's argument as legal authority.

Furthermore, OLC misrepresents Moore. Lifting two sentences out of context, they neglect to mention the primary point of his article, which is to defend an absolute prohibition on torture.[119] Moore utterly rejects the consequentialist view of morality, and the cost-benefit reasoning it implies. His concession to torture is simply that even absolute prohibitions must have exceptions for catastrophic situations – and his argument about relative innocence is simply an attempt to specify the basis for an exception. Nothing that Moore says is compatible with OLC's conclusion that self-defense is always available for presidentially-authorized torture of suspected terrorists.

Finally, it is also important to understand that even on its own ground, Moore's argument runs into the same objections as the ticking bomb case. Moore stipulates a situation in which either the attacker or the victim must suffer physical violence, in order to argue that in that instance it should be the attacker. But what if the victim, or rather the victim's agent, the interrogator, doesn't know with certainty whether a terrorist strike is in motion? Or whether torturing the detainee will actually prevent it? Moore's self-defense analogy, like the ticking bomb, derives its moral principle from a hypothetical in which the victim knows he is being attacked, and in which disabling the attacker offers him safety. So far as I can determine, the argument has nothing whatever to say in cases where either of these is doubtful.

Where does that leave the OLC's self-defense argument? It leaves it unsupported by any legal authority, even the one nonbinding authority it cites.

The Bybee Memo offers one additional self-defense argument, namely that when it is a question of a presidentially-authorized interrogator torturing a detainee to obtain intelligence vital to the war on terror, national self-defense blends with criminal law self-defense. But, in the traditional law of war, it doesn't. The most basic distinction in military law and ethics is that between *jus ad bellum* – the justice of going to war – and *jus in bello* – the justice of how one fights the war.[120] In modern doctrine, aggressive wars are unjust *(ad bellum)*, and wars of self-defense are just *(ad bellum)*. But the fact that the U.S. is waging a war in self-defense (if it is, in fact) does not justify war crimes on grounds of self-defense.

To say otherwise collapses the entire distinction between *jus ad bellum* and *jus in bello*. The two doctrines of self-defense – national and criminal – have no legal connection except the name.

Again, however, conflating national self-defense with criminal self-defense makes perfect sense within the liberal ideology of torture. Criminal self-defense, including defense of others, represents an emergency exception to the normal rule forbidding the use of deadly force – an emergency exception that is almost universally recognized as morally legitimate. By identifying national self-defense with criminal self-defense, the Bybee Memo in effect represents every use of force in national self-defense, even uses of force forbidden by the law of war, as a justifiable emergency measure that rational, normal people would rightly undertake if they were in the same circumstance.

D. The Necessity Defense

From a moral point of view, it seems clear that the most compelling criminal defense to an accusation of torture is the necessity defense – the claim that the criminal act is justified because it was necessary to prevent a greater evil. The Bybee Memo indeed discusses the necessity defense and agrees that it offers a legal justification for torture. This should form the heart of the argument. Is torture an absolute evil that trumps any good that may come of it? Or is it merely a presumptive evil that can be outweighed by dire necessities like the ticking bomb? The Bybee Memo argues, plausibly, that the necessity defense in criminal law encapsulates the second answer. Because the criminal law recognizes the necessity defense, torture is not an absolute evil that trumps any resulting good. To be sure, all the concerns raised earlier about uncertainty (that interrogators have the right detainee, that the detainee knows something valuable, that the valuable information is necessary to prevent a greater evil) remain. But the Bybee Memo agrees that the necessity defense may not apply in cases of uncertainty. In this respect, it reads the necessity defense as a perfect embodiment of the liberal ideology of torture.

However, its conclusion that the necessity defense applies to cases of official torture reasonably believed to be necessary to avert a greater evil is very far from a slam-dunk. For one thing, the defense has only the most tenuous toehold in federal common law, the only law that matters in cases of federal government agents engaging in torture.[121] Although federal courts have acknowledged the existence of a necessity defense, I have been unable to find any federal case in which the defense actually succeeded. The appellate decisions recognize necessity in theory but deny it in the case at bar. Furthermore, while in theory the defense can apply to crimes of violence, none of the federal cases involves a crime of violence. Necessity has been pled (unsuccessfully) in medical marijuana cases,[122] prison-break cases in the face of prison rape or abuse,[123] antinuclear protests on military bases,[124] wire and mail fraud in order to obtain emergency care,[125] and even driving a car in a protected part of a national park after the defendant became lost.[126] Obviously, none of these come anywhere near a necessity defense for torture. One court has held that the necessity defense is closely related to the defense of duress, and held that duress is not a valid defense to first-degree murder.[127] Judged as a piece of legal advice, the Bybee Memorandum fails dismally in that it never mentions what most clients would take to be central facts about the law as it currently stands: that the defense invariably fails in federal courts, and that it is not even pled in defending crimes of violence. The proposition that federal law might recognize the necessity defense in a torture case has no visible means of support in current law.

Furthermore, federal cases enumerating the elements of the necessity defense agree that it cannot succeed unless the danger that the crime forestalls is imminent, and no lawful alternative means exists for avoiding that danger.[128] It would work, if anywhere, in the ticking bomb case – but nowhere else.

Lastly, the United States is a party to the Torture Convention, and Article 2(2) of the Torture Convention declares that "[n]o exceptional circumstances whatsoever, whether a state of war or a threat of war, internal political instability or any other public emergency, may be invoked as a justification of torture." On its face, Article 2(2) abolishes the necessity defense for the crime of torture.[129] However, this Article of the Torture Convention is non-self-executing, and – as the OLC observes – when Congress implemented the Torture Convention it omitted Article 2(2) from the implementing legislation. "Given that Congress omitted CAT's effort to bar a necessity or wartime defense, we read section 2340 as permitting the defense."[130]

OLC's interpretation sounds plausible, but, as elsewhere in the Memo, it is far weaker than it appears. Even though Article 2(2) of the Torture Convention is not part of U.S. law, it remains an international obligation of the United States not to engage in official torture even under the strong necessities of war or public emergency. The United States entered no reservations to Article 2(2) when it ratified the Torture Convention. International legal obligations, whether or not they are self-executing, affect the interpretation of U.S. law. Under the *Charming Betsy* canon, federal statutes are interpreted to minimize conflicts with international legal obligation.[131] The necessity defense is not even federal statutory law – it is a judicially-created defense. It is hardly obvious that courts confronting a case of torture can instruct on a necessity defense if doing so would place the United States in default of international legal obligations, since no federal statute creates the defense in the first place. Nor is it clear that the *Charming Betsy* canon would allow the reading that OLC gives to section 2340. Absent the international obligation created by U.S. ratification of the Torture Convention, the Bybee Memo may be right that Congress's omission of Article 2(2) could be read as an attempt to leave the necessity defense intact and available in torture cases. But, given the international obligation, *Charming Betsy* precludes reading Congressional silence about the necessity defense as an affirmative intention to make the defense available. There is room for debate here. The problem is that the Bybee Memo never engages in it, and seems to assume that international legal obligations are largely irrelevant.

To discuss the necessity defense to torture charges without raising the argument – even for purpose of rejecting it – that America's international legal obligations affect the interpretation of section 2340 or judicially-created rules such as the necessity defense begs the most crucial question that liberal arguments about torture raise. That is the question of whether or not liberal societies have "put cruelty first" in the strong sense of agreeing that nothing justifies torture. That is what the Torture Convention says, and the question is whether our ratification really meant it. The Bybee Memo seems so bent on validating every possible defense of torture that it overlooks the central legal and moral question confronting us.

At one point only, the Bybee Memo registers a quiver of doubt about the necessity defense, because an untrammeled defense of necessity might justify abortion to save a woman's life. The memo responds that there would be an exception to the necessity defense in an abortion case if the legislature had specified that fetal life is more important than maternal life. The memo then notes, with almost palpable relief, that this exception does not apply in the torture case, because Congress "has not explicitly made a determination of values vis-à-vis torture. In fact, Congress explicitly removed efforts to remove torture from the weighing of values permitted by the necessity defense."[132]

I think it is unnecessary to comment on the overall weirdness of the OLC plunging into a sea of dialectical subtleties in order to fashion a necessity defense that permits torture but not life-saving abortion. More to the point is that the statutory analysis OLC supplies to back its conclusion makes very little sense. OLC observes that when Congress defined 'torture' it removed a clause in the Torture Convention limiting the definition to torture "for such purpose [ ] as obtaining . . . information or a confession."[133] In other words, Congress adopted a broad definition of torture, prohibiting it without regard to its purpose. But OLC instead understands Congress's action as "evidencing an intention to remove any fixing of values by statute," such as the value of information as compared with the evils of torture. On OLC's analysis, when Congress broadened the definition of torture to ensure that *no* purpose, interrogation or anything else, suffices to justify torture, they were really narrowing it to allow for the possibility that interrogation might justify torture.

E. Presidential Power

I shall spare only a few words on the Bybee Memo's argument that the President's Commander-in-Chief power allows him to authorize interrogation by torture regardless of the Torture Convention and the federal criminal statute against official torture – not because it isn't important, but because others have already argued, more ably than I could, that it is a constitutional distortion.[134] Astonishingly, when it argues that the Constitution vests complete discretion over interrogation to the Commander-in-Chief, the Memo does not discuss *Youngstown Sheet & Tube*, the major Supreme Court case on the limits of presidential power.[135] Nor does it so much as mention Congress's Article I authority to "make rules concerning captures on land and water" and "to make rules for the government and regulation of the land and naval forces."[136] And what of the President's constitutional duty to "take care that the laws be faithfully executed"?[137] Doesn't the "Take Care" clause straightforwardly entail that the President has no constitutional authority to override federal statutes? OLC never raises this question, let alone answers it.[138] The Memo's only mention of the Take Care clause is an argument that the clause can never require the President to prosecute illegal executive branch actions, because then Congress "could control the President's authority through manipulation of federal criminal law."[139] Given that only the executive branch can prosecute crimes, this argument effectively places the executive branch above the law. The Memo cites no legal authority to support its constitutional argument other than one of its own previous opinions backing the Reagan administration in a fight over executive privilege.[140]

VII. THE LAWYER AS ABSOLVER

At this point, I wish to examine the Bybee Memo from the standpoint of conventional legal ethics. Is there anything wrong with writing a CYA memo for a client? Aren't lawyers supposed to spin the law to their clients' advantage? The traditional answer in the legal profession is: when you're advising your client, absolutely not. The distinction between lawyers in their roles as advisors and advocates is fundamental to the ethics of the legal profession.[141]

The distinction between the roles of advocate and advisor was incorporated into the ABA's Code of Professional Responsibility, the bar's model code until it was replaced in 1983. The Code states that "the two roles are essentially different.... While serving as advocate, a lawyer should resolve in favor of his client doubts as to the bounds of the law. In serving a client as adviser, a lawyer ... should give his professional opinion as to what the ultimate decisions of the courts would likely be as to the applicable law."[142] The current Model Rules of Professional Conduct likewise distinguish the roles of advocate and advisor, and the rule for advisors calls for "independent professional judgment" and "candid advice."[143] A comment to this rule explains that the lawyer should provide independent and candid advice even if "the advice will be unpalatable to the client."[144]

Perhaps the clearest explanation of this traditional conception of the legal advisor's role appears in a classic report on professional responsibility issued by a joint conference of the ABA and the Association of American Law Schools nearly half a century ago. Co-authored by Lon Fuller, the greatest jurisprudentialist of the time, and John Randall, a prominent bar leader, the report argues that the two roles of advocate and counselor

> must be sharply distinguished. The man who has been called into court to answer for his own actions is entitled to a fair hearing. Partisan advocacy plays its essential part in such a hearing, and the lawyer pleading his client's case may properly present it in the most favorable light. A similar resolution of doubts in one direction becomes inappropriate when the lawyer acts as counselor. The reasons that justify and even require partisan advocacy in the trial of a cause do not grant any license to the lawyer to participate as legal adviser in a line of conduct that is immoral, unfair, or of doubtful legality. In saving himself from this unworthy involvement, the lawyer cannot be guided solely by an unreflective inner sense of good faith; he must be at pains to preserve a sufficient detachment from his client's interests so that he remains capable of a sound and objective appraisal of the propriety of what his client proposes to do.[145]

Notice the argument here. The Joint Conference Report begins with the assumption that it is one-sided partisan advocacy, not impartial advising, that stands in need of special justification. Among writers on legal ethics, this point is fundamental. Legal ethics is at its most troubling when a lawyer adopts a wholly partisan point of view on behalf of a client, because that viewpoint discounts to zero the interests of everyone but the client, and no real-life system of ethical thought, secular or religious, countenances writing off all interests but one. Legal ethicists usually go on to provide a special justification of partisan advocacy, often based on the requirements of the adversary system. The Joint Conference Report offers several arguments along these lines, and its authors ultimately defend partisan advocacy in the adversary system against the charge of amoralism.[146]

To be sure, there has never been a case of a lawyer disciplined for violating MR 2.1. But that has nothing to do with the validity of the standard. It has to do with the fact that the cases seldom come to light, and when they do no one has an incentive to litigate them. Attorney–client advice is shrouded in the privilege; clients are seldom in a position to know when their lawyer's advice has not been candid; aggrieved clients are more interested in obtaining malpractice damages than filing grievances; and in the rare case when a lawyer's bad advice becomes an issue – for example, when a receiver takes over a bankrupt corporation and goes after the lawyers that colluded with the old management – there are almost always easier to prove and more serious charges to file.

But that hardly means that the "independent and candid advice" standard is unimportant. As a matter of the theory of legal ethics, MR 2.1 is far from marginal. Without it, the duty of confidentiality crumbles. One of the major puzzles in legal ethics has always been how to justify the linchpin of professional ethics, the lawyer's duty of confidentiality. After all, on utilitarian grounds it's a bad bet for society because it allows crooked clients to hide the evidence so frequently – as witness the 40-year history of Big Tobacco stonewalling the facts via their lawyers.[147] Given this embarrassing fact, how does the profession justify its sacred norm of confidentiality? It does so by arguing that the lawyer needs confidential information

> to advise the client to refrain from wrongful conduct. Almost without exception, clients come to lawyers in order to determine their rights and what is, in the complex of laws and regulations, deemed to be legal and correct. Based upon experience, lawyers know that almost all clients follow the advice given, and the law is upheld.[148]

In other words: confidentiality is a good bet for society *only* because we can count on lawyers to give good advice on compliance (and clients to take that advice). If the lawyer doesn't give independent, candid advice, this entire argument, and indeed the whole edifice of confidentiality, comes tumbling down. The bar has long regarded confidentiality as its most sacred norm.[149]

But what happens when the client doesn't want candid advice? When the client comes to the lawyer and says, in effect, "Give me an opinion that lets me do what I want to do"? The answer is that the lawyer cannot do this – or rather, that if the lawyer does it, she has crossed the fatal line from legal advisor to moral or legal accomplice.

Obviously, it happens all the time. Journalist Martin Mayer, writing about the 1980s savings-and-loan collapse, quoted a source who said that for half a million dollars you could buy a legal opinion saying anything you wanted from any big law firm in Manhattan.[150] In the Enron case, we saw Enron's lawyers writing opinion letters that koshered the creation of illegal "Special Purpose Entities," even though they knew that they were skating on thin ice. I assume the same thing happens in government all the time – that when the State Department's legal advisor's office is asked to opine on the legality of use of force, its mission is to come up with an opinion that says it is okay, not an opinion that says it isn't. But this is unethical unless the opinion represents candid advice. In white-collar criminal cases, some courts in some contexts will accept a defense of good-faith reliance on the advice of counsel. But when the client tells the lawyer what advice he wants, the good faith vanishes, and under the criminal law of accomplice liability, both lawyer and client should go down.

Giving the client skewed advice because the client wants it is a different role from either advocate or advisor. One might call it the Lawyer As Absolver, or, less nicely, the Lawyer As Indulgence Seller.[151] Luther began the Reformation in part because the early Renaissance popes were selling papal dispensations to violate law, along with indulgences sparing sinners the flames of hell or a few years of purgatory. Rodrigo Borgia once brokered a papal dispensation for a French count to sleep with his own sister. It was a good career move: Rodrigo later became Pope Alexander VI.[152] Jay Bybee merely ended up on the Ninth Circuit Court of Appeals.

The important thing to notice is that the role of Absolver, unlike the roles of Advocate and Advisor, is totally illegitimate. The advocate is supposed to – in the words of the old ABA Code of Professional Responsibility – "resolve in favor of his client doubts as to the bounds of the law."[153] The advisor, by contrast, owes the client independent and candid advice, even if it's "unpalatable to the client." In conventional legal ethics, the advocate's arguments follow only the permissive nonfrivolity standard; the advisor must honor the more demanding candid, best-judgment standard. The advocate's biased presentation will get countered by the adversary in a public hearing. The advisor's presentation will not. In the courtroom, the adversary is supposed to check the advocate's excesses. In the lawyer's office, advising the client, the lawyer is supposed to check the client's excesses. Conflating the two roles moves the lawyer out of the limited role-based immunity that advocates enjoy (although I think that the profession exaggerates the immunity there, too) into the world of the indulgence seller.

In December, 2004, nineteen former lawyers in the OLC drafted a set of principles for the office reaffirming its commitment to this standard conception of the independent legal advisor.[154] Apparently, this is not how the current OLC conceives of its job, for none of its lawyers was willing to sign.[155] It has emerged that OLC provided an opinion justifying the Central Intelligence Agency in removing prisoners from Iraq for interrogation elsewhere, a likely grave breach of the Geneva Conventions.[156] Reportedly, OLC's opinion was written after it had provided an earlier opinion stating that a ghost detainee named Hiwa Abdul Rahman Rashul could not be removed from Iraq.[157] According to an intelligence source, "'That case started the CIA yammering to Justice to get a better memo.'"[158] The purpose of Rule 2.1 is to insure that lawyers do not back off from candid legal advice when their clients start yammering to give them a better memo.

Defenders of the Bybee Memorandum may offer a response to the argument that they were not functioning in the proper legal advisor's role. In good legal realist fashion, the passage quoted above from the ABA's Code of Professional Responsibility equates advice about the law with predictions about how courts will ultimately resolve legal issues. Perhaps the OLC authors believed that, ultimately, courts will go along with torture. In other words, they may have believed that if an American interrogator claims, credibly, that she tortured a detainee in order to obtain information vital to the global war on terror, judges will buy the arguments of necessity and self-defense offered in the Memo, even though they have little or no support in conventional legal argument.[159]

If so, it illustrates my central point: the torture lawyers aim to construct a judicially-endorsed practice of permissible torture. They are banking the legitimacy of their memorandum as a piece of legal advice on the prospect that its arguments will succeed in reconstituting American law along the lines of the liberal ideology of torture. If they fail, then their advice will probably do as much political damage to their clients as the revelation of the Memo did in the wake of Abu Ghraib. If they succeed, they will have created a torture culture in the law.

VIII. CONCLUSION

What do we make of this? Not much, some might say. The Justice Department has disowned the memo, Mr. Bybee has been promoted out of the OLC to the federal appellate bench, and Professor Yoo has left government service. One way to understand the Bybee Memo is that it represents an odd moment when several stars and planets fell into an unusual alignment and the moonshine threw the Office of Legal Counsel into a peculiarly aggressive mood. Now, the OLC has officially rescinded the Bybee Memo and replaced it with a document that begins with a ringing affirmation of U.S. opposition to torture.[160]

But the lawyers' torture culture is not just the Office of Legal Counsel in an isolated period of time, now past. Remember that the Bybee Memo was vetted by lawyers throughout the upper echelons of the Bush administration, and quickly taken up by the Defense Department working group charged with devising interrogation guidelines. As Seymour Hersh observes, "the senior legal officers in the White House and the Justice Department seemed to be in virtual competition to determine who could produce the most tough-minded memorandum about the lack of prisoner rights."[161] Furthermore, it would be a mistake to suppose that the Justice Department has abandoned its views merely because it has disowned the Bybee Memo. Although the Levin Memo condemns torture and repudiates the Bybee Memo's narrow definition of "severe pain," it does not broaden it substantially: stunningly, all its illustrative examples of "the nature of the extreme conduct that falls within the statutory definition" of torture are on the upper end of the scale of barbarism. They include, for example, "severe beatings to the genitals, head, and other parts of the body with metal pipes, brass knuckles, batons, a baseball bat, and various other items; removal of teeth with pliers . . . cutting off . . . fingers, pulling out . . . fingernails" and similar atrocities.[162] Levin includes no indication that torture lite, or even torture medium, is prohibited by the statute. Nor does Levin retract the Bybee Memo's analyses of self-defense or necessity; it simply declines to discuss defenses. And, as we have seen, it evades the question of whether the president can authorize torture. The Levin Memo is perhaps the minimum possible retraction of the Bybee Memo: it retracts only the portions that journalists had criticized harshly (the "organ failure" definition of torture and the specific intent analysis), and retains a conception of torture as atrocity fully in line with the liberal ideology.

Indeed, OLC prepared other memoranda at the same time as the Bybee Memo, never released, which approves specific interrogation techniques – and there is no indication that these approvals have ever been rescinded. In December 2004, the Bush administration fought off restrictions (passed by a 96-to-2 Senate vote) which "would have explicitly extended to intelligence officers a prohibition against torture or inhumane treatment, and would have required the CIA as well as the Pentagon to report to Congress about the methods they were using."[163] When asked why at their confirmation hearings, both Alberto Gonzales and Condaleezza Rice replied that it was to deny protection to people who do not deserve protection. Neither finished the sentence: "... protection from cruel, inhuman, or degrading treatment."

Mr. Gonzales also told the U.S. Senate that cruel, inhuman, and degrading treatment of detainees is forbidden to interrogators only within U.S. territory. The legal basis for this opinion was another piece of loophole lawyering on a par with the Bybee Memo. When the U.S. ratified the Torture Convention, it attached a reservation interpreting "cruel, inhuman, and degrading" treatment to mean treatment violative of the Fifth, Eighth, or Fourteenth Amendments.[164] Because these amendments do not apply extraterritorially, Mr. Gonzales argued, the prohibition on CID does not bind U.S. interrogators abroad. Clearly, however, the Senate's reservation was referring to the substantive standards in the three amendments, not their jurisdictional scope. Similarly, as mentioned earlier, in March 2004, OLC prepared a draft memorandum loopholing the Geneva Convention's prohibition on removing captives from the country of their capture and authorizing brief transfers of Iraqi captives out of Iraq for interrogation.[165]

The only reasonable inference to draw from these recent efforts is that the torture culture is still firmly in place, notwithstanding official condemnation of torture. At most, torture has given way to CID. The persistence of torture (or CID) should surprise no one, because the Bybee Memo represents a normative vision powerfully in tune with the liberal ideology of torture. The memos illustrates the ease with which arguments that pretend that torture can exist in liberal society, but only as an exception, quickly lead to erecting a torture culture – a network of institutions and practices that regularize the exception and make it standard operating procedure. And once a practice becomes standard operating procedure, it too will develop its exceptions, more extreme than those that have now become the rule.

Arguably, the "ghost detainees" are the next set of exceptions.[166] According to Seymour Hersh, they are in the hands of a "special access program" (an SAP) – a top-secret "black" unit created by the Secretary of Defense out of frustration with the excessive legalism that prevented the launching of a missile that might have killed Mullah Omar during the Afghanistan War – that operates outside of legal limits (and that may have been the "Other Governemental Agency" (OGA) involved at Abu Ghraib.[167]) Torture cultures invariably overflow their own boundaries; for the reasons we have explored, that is their nature.

For this reason, the liberal ideology of torture, which assumes that torture can be neatly confined to exceptional ticking time-bomb cases and surgically severed from cruelty and tyranny, represents a dangerous delusion. It becomes more dangerous still coupled with an endless war on terror, a permanent emergency in which the White House eagerly insists that its emergency powers rise above the

limiting power of statutes and treaties. Claims to long-term emergency powers
that entail the power to torture should send chills through liberals of the right
as well as the left, and no one should still think that liberal torture has nothing
to do with tyranny.

NOTES

1. *Filartiga v. Pena-Irala*, 630 F.2d 876, 883 (2nd Cir. 1980).
2. Amy Argetsinger, "At Colleges, Students are Facing a Big Test," *Washington Post*, Sept. 17, 2001, at B1.
3. John Blake, "How to React to Enemies Raises Tough Issues for People of Faith," *Atlanta Constitution*, Sept. 22, 2001, at 1B.
4. Walter Pincus, "Silence of 4 Terror Probe Suspects Poses Dilemma for FBI," *Washington Post*, Oct. 21, 2001, at A6.
5. Jim Rutenberg, "Torture Seeps into Discussion by News Media," *New York Times*, Nov. 5, 2001, at C1.
6. Andrew McLaughlin, "How Far Americans Would Go to Fight Terror," *Christian Science Monitor*, Nov. 14, 2001, at 1.
7. Alan M. Dershowitz, *Why Terrorism Works* 150 (2002).
8. *Id.* at 158–61.
9. Senate Judiciary Subcommittee, "U.S. Senator Orrin G. Hatch (R-UT) Holds a Hearing on the Federal Government's Counterterrorism Efforts," *FDCH Political Transcripts*, June 8, 2004.
10. William Safire, "Seizing Dictatorial Power," *New York Times*, Nov. 15, 2001, at A31.
11. Most of the memoranda, Abu-Ghraib related reports, and other essential documents dealing with U.S. interrogation policy, torture, and treatment of detainees have been assembled in *The Torture Papers: The Road to Abu Ghraib* [henceforth: *The Torture Papers*] (Karen J. Greenberg & Joshua L. Dratel eds., 2005). The August memorandum, which I shall refer to as the "Bybee Memorandum" or "Bybee Memo" (because it went out over the signature of Jay S. Bybee, although its principal author was apparently John Yoo), is included in *The Torture Papers* at 172–217.
12. Michel de Montaigne, "Of Cruelty," *The Complete Essays of Montaigne* 316 (Donald M. Frame trans., 1958).
13. A. N. Wilson, *C. S. Lewis: A Biography* 49–50 (1990).
14. Both Nietzsche and Foucault describe torture as a festive occasion. See Friederich Nietzsche, "On the Genealogy of Morals," in *Basic Writings of Nietzsche* 501, 503 (Walter Kaufmann ed. & trans., 1968) ("Without cruelty there is no festival"); Michel Foucault, *Discipline and Punish: The Birth of the Prison* 8 (Alan Sheridan trans., 1977)("the gloomy festival of punishment").
15. Judith Shklar, "Putting Cruelty First," in *Ordinary Vices* 7 (1984).
16. *Id.* at 43.
17. *Id.* at 9.
18. *Id.* at 43.
19. I have heard this argument from several people, but Paul Kahn and Mike Seidman have pressed it on me most compellingly.
20. My point here is somewhat different from that of Henry Shue, "Torture," 7 *Phil. & Pub. Aff.* 124 (1978), which considers the argument that since killing is worse than torture, and killing is permitted in warfare, torture might be as well. Shue argues that in warfare,

there is a kind of reciprocity between combatants, who place each other mutually at risk, whereas torture is more like killing the defenseless. I am arguing that torture is like tyrannizing the defenseless rather than killing them.

21. This is one of Elaine Scarry's chief points in *The Body in Pain: The Making and Unmaking of the World* (1985). "As in dying and death, so in serious pain the claims of the body utterly nullify the claims of the world." *Id.* at 33. Scarry offers perhaps the most famous phenomenology of torture. However, as will soon become apparent, I differ from Scarry because she thinks that torture exists only in the context of interrogation. *Id.* at 28 ("Torture consists of a primary physical act, the infliction of pain, and a primary verbal act, the interrogation."); 29 ("Pain and interrogation inevitably occur together...."). I subsequently argue that coupling torture with interrogation is only one historically significant motivations for torture.

22. The Fay–Jones Report on Abu Ghraib mentions "an alleged contest between the two Army dog handlers to see who could make the internees urinate or defecate in the presence of the dogs." LTG Anthony R. Jones & MG George R. Fay, Investigation of Intelligence Activities at Abu Ghraib (Aug. 26, 2004), in *The Torture Papers, supra* note 11, at 1070.

23. M. I. Finley, *Ancient Slavery and Modern Ideology* 93–97 (1980); *see especially id.* at 94–95. I suppose that the rationale was that if a slave were permitted to testify against his own master freely, then the society would be admitting that property can freely betray its owner – a dangerous thought in slaveholding societies. Hence, the slave can only be permitted to testify under compulsion. Hannah Arendt claimed it was because the ancients believed that "nobody can invent a lie under torture," but this speculation does nothing to explain why slaves and only slaves had to be tortured. Hannah Arendt, *The Human Condition* 129n (1958).

24. Nietzsche, *supra* note 14, at 507–08; *see also id.* at 501, describing "the pleasure of being allowed to vent his power freely upon one who is powerless, the voluptuous pleasure *'de faire le mal pour le plaisir de le faire,'* the enjoyment of violation."

25. Montaigne, *supra* note 12, at 316.

26. Cesare Beccaria, *On Crimes and Punishments* 8–9 (David Young trans., 1986).

27. *Id.* at 10.

28. Foucault, *supra* note 14, at 82–89.

29. *Id.* at 48–49 ("It is a ceremonial by which a momentarily injured sovereignty is reconstituted. It restores that sovereignty by manifesting it at its most spectacular.... [T]his practice of torture was ... a policy of terror: to make everyone aware, through the body of the criminal, of the unrestrained presence of the sovereign.")

30. Though it certainly persisted in the American practice of lynching.

31. Foucault, *supra* note 14, at 29–33.

32. John H. Langbein, "Torture and Plea Bargaining," 46 *U. Chi. L. Rev.* 3 (1978); Langbein, *Torture and the Law of Proof: Europe and England in the Ancien Régime* (1977).

33. See Alan Donagan, "The Right Not to Incriminate Oneself," 1 *Soc. Phil. & Policy* 137 (1984).

34. Foucault, *supra* note 14, at 3–6.

35. The Fay–Jones Report mentions incidents of alleged rape and alleged sodomy of a detainee with a police stick. Fay–Jones report, *supra* note 12, at 1059, 1070, 1077. Placing lit cigarettes in detainees' ears were reported by FBI officers at Guantanamo. Neil A. Lewis & David Johnston, "New F.B.I. Memos Describe Abuses of Iraq Inmates," *New York Times*, Dec. 21, 2004, A1.

36. In July 2004, an investigation of detainee operations in Iraq and Afghanistan by the Army's inspector general, Lt. Gen. Paul T. Mikolashek, disclosed 94 cases of alleged abuse, including 39 deaths in U.S. custody – 20 of them suspected homicides. Craig Pyes, "U.S. Probing Alleged Abuse of Afghans," *Los Angeles Times*, Sept. 21, 2004. The

military has reportedly investigated, or is investigating, 58 deaths in Iraq, which include nine cases of justifiable homicide, seven homicides, and 21 deaths from natural or undetermined causes. Demetri Sevastopulo, "Two more soldiers charged with homicide Iraq Deaths," *Financial Times*, Sept. 29, 2004.

Though several soldiers have been charged with abuse in cases where detainees died, prosecutors have not found enough evidence to charge them with homicide. Eric Schmitt, "Navy Charges 3 Commandos with Beating of Prisoners," *New York Times*, Sept. 25, 2004. Army investigators have, however, recommended that negligent homicide charges be filed against at least three Army Reserve soldiers, including reserve military police soldier Captain James P. Boland, for their roles in beating to death two prisoners in Bagram detention facility outside of Kabul. Tom Bowman, "Charges Urged in Deaths of Detainees," *Baltimore Sun*, Sept. 16, 2004. Two Marines, Lance Cpl. Christian Hernandez and Maj. Clarke A. Paulus, were charged with negligent homicide in relation to the death of Nagem Sadoon Hatab in the Camp Whitehorse detention center outside Nasiriyah. The charges against Hernandez were eventually dropped. "Iraq POW Death Remains a Mystery," *The Times Union* (Albany, NY), Aug. 1, 2004.

According to the Schlesinger Report on Abu Ghraib, there have been "five cases of detainee deaths as a result of abuse by U.S. personnel during interrogations" already substantiated. *Final Report of the Independent Panel To Review DoD Detention Operations,* Aug. 2004 [hereinafter: Schlesinger Report], at 13.

37. Jonathan Alter, "Time to Think About Torture," *Newsweek* (Nov. 5, 2001).

38. Schlesinger Report, *supra* note 36, Appendix H, at 2.

39. Marites Danguilan Vitug & Glenda M. Gloria, *Under the Crescent Moon: Rebellion in Mindanao* (2000), quoted in Doug Struck et al., "Borderless Network of Terror; Bin Laden Followers Reach Across Globe," *Washington Post*, Sept. 23, 2001, at A1.

40. See Oren Gross, "Are Torture Warrants Warranted? Pragmatic Absolutism and Official Disobedience," 88 *Minn. L. Rev.* 1481, 1501–03 (2004). Gross reminds us, however, that the catastrophic case can actually occur. *Id.* at 1503–04. The ticking bomb case might occur if a government has extremely good intelligence about a terrorist group – good enough to know that it has dispatched operatives to carry out an operation, and good enough to identify and capture someone in the group that knows the details – but not good enough to know the details without getting them from the captive. Israel seems like a setting in which cases like this might arise; and indeed, Mark Bowden reports on just such a case. Mark Bowden, "The Dark Art of Interrogation," *The Atlantic Monthly* 51 (Oct. 2003). Importantly, however, the Israeli interrogator got the information through trickery, not torture.

41. For a powerful version of the consequentialist argument, which acknowledges these consequences and accepts them (at least for dialectical purposes), see Michael Seidman, "Torture's Truth," *U. Chi. L. Rev.* (forthcoming).

42. Bernard Williams, "A Critique of Utilitarianism," in J. J. C. Smart & Bernard Williams, *Utilitarianism: For and Against* 93 (1973).

43. Quoted in Hannah Arendt, *The Origins of Totalitarianism* 303 (rev. ed. 1973).

44. Williams, *supra* note 42, at 92. Williams suggests "that the *unthinkable* was itself a moral category. . . ." *Id.*

45. Bowden, *supra* note 40; and see especially Michael Ignatieff, "The Torture Wars," *The New Republic*, April 22, 2002, at 40, 43; Marcy Strauss, "Torture," 48 *N.Y. Law Sch. L. Rev.* 203 (2004).

46. Arthur Isak Applbaum, "Professional Detachment: The Executioner of Paris," 109 *Harv. L. Rev.* 458, 459–60, 475 (1995).

47. *Id.* at 459–60.

48. Quoted in Seymour M. Hersh, *Chain of Command* 45 (2004).

49. Summarizing extensive studies by researchers, Jean Maria Arrigo notes medical partic-ipation in 20% to 40% of torture cases. One study, a random survey of 4,000 mem-bers of the Indian Medical Association (of whom 800 responded), revealed that "58% believed torture interrogation was permissible; 71% had come across a case of probable torture; 18% knew of health professionals who had participated in torture; 16% had witnessed torture themselves; and 10% agreed that false medical and autopsy reports were sometimes justified." Jean Maria Arrigo, *A Consequentialist Argument Against Torture Interrogation of Terrorists* (unpublished manuscript presented at Joint Services Conference on Professional Ethics, 2003), available at <http://www.usafa.af.mil/jscope/JSCOPE03/Arrigo03.html>, summarizing Jagdish C. Sobti et al., *Knowledge, Attitude and Practice of Physicians in India Concerning Medical Aspects of Torture* (n.d., c. 1996).

50. This is the conclusion Michael Ignatieff draws from the memoirs of French torturer Paul Aussaresses, *The Battle of the Casbah: Terrorism and Counter-Terrorism in Algeria, 1955–1957*, who remains completely unapologetic for torturing and killing numerous Algerian terrorists. Ignatieff, *supra* note 45.

51. Bowden, *supra* note 40.

52. Mark Osiel, *Mass Atrocity, Ordinary Evil*, and Hannah Arendt: *Criminal Consciousness in Argentina's Dirty War* (2002).

53. John Simpson & Jana Bennett, *The Disappeared and the Mothers of the Plaza: The Story of the 11,000 Argentinians Who Vanished* 109 (1985).

54. Ignatieff, *supra* note 45.

55. Schlesinger Report, *supra* note 36, Appendix E. *See also* Chris Mackey & Greg Miller, *The Interrogators: Inside the Secret War Against Al Qaeda* 479–83 (2004).

56. *See generally* Bowden, *supra* note 40.

57. Mackey & Miller, *supra* note 55, at 31.

58. This point gets made in the Fay–Jones Report on Abu Ghraib. After noting that conflicting directives about stripping prisoners and using dogs were floating around simultaneously, the Report adds, "Furthermore, some military intelligence personnel executing their inter-rogation duties at Abu Ghraib had previously served as interrogators in other theaters of operation, primarily Afghanistan and GTMO. These prior interrogation experiences complicated understanding at the interrogator level. The extent of 'word of mouth' tech-niques that were passed to the interrogators in Abu Ghraib by assistance teams from Guantanamo, Fort Huachuca, or amongst themselves due to prior assignments is unclear and likely impossible to definitively determine. The clear thread in the CJTF-7 policy memos and published doctrine is the humane treatment of detainees and the applicabil-ity of the Geneva Conventions. Experienced interrogators will confirm that interrogation is an art, not a science, and knowing the limits of authority is crucial. Therefore, the existence of confusing and inconsistent interrogation technique policies contributed to the belief that additional interrogation techniques were condoned in order to gain intel-ligence." LTG Anthony R. Jones & MG George R. Fay, Investigation of Intelligence Activities at Abu Ghraib 21 (Aug. 26, 2004).

59. Robert Jackall, *Moral Mazes: The World of Corporate Managers* 20 (1987).

60. Hersh, *supra* note 48, at 30.

61. As a military police captain told Hersh, "when you ask an eighteen-year-old kid to keep someone awake, and he doesn't know how to do it, he's going to get creative." *Id.* at 34.

62. "Working alongside non-DoD organizations/agencies in detention facilities proved com-plex and demanding. The perception that non-DoD agencies had different rules regard-ing interrogation and detention operations was evident.... The appointing authority and investigating officers made a specific finding regarding the issue of 'ghost detainees' within Abu Ghraib. It is clear that the interrogation practices of other government agencies led to a loss of accountability at Abu Ghraib." Fay–Jones Report, *supra* note 58, at 5.

63. Hersh, *supra* note 48, at 44–45.
64. For details, *see* David Luban, "Integrity: Its Causes and Cures," 72 *Fordham L. Rev.* 279 (2003); David Luban, "The Ethics of Wrongful Obedience," in *Ethics in Practice* 94 (Deborah L. Rhode ed. 2000).
65. Craig Haney et al., "Interpersonal Dynamics of a Simulated Prison," 1 *Int'l. J. Criminology & Penology* 69 (1973), quoted in Schlesinger Report, *supra* note 36, Appendix G at 2–3. *See also* Philip Zimbardo et al., "The Mind is a Formidable Jailer: A Pirandellian Prison," *New York. Times*, Apr. 8, 1973, §6 (Magazine), at 41; and the remarkable internet slide-show of the experiment, Zimbardo, *Stanford Prison Experiment: A Simulation Study of the Psychology of Imprisonment Conducted at Stanford University* (1999), at <http://www.prisonexp.org>.
66. John Schwartz, "Simulated Prison in '71 Showed a Fine Line Between 'Normal' and 'Monster,'" *New York Times*, May 6, 2004, at A20; Zimbardo, *supra* note 65, at slides 8, 18, 21, 28, 33.
67. Many are included in *The Torture Papers*, *supra* note 11. But they are still coming out – thus, *The New Yorker* posted several new memoranda on February 8, 2005 in conjunction with an article on the "outsourcing" of torture. Memos posted at <http://www.newyorker.com/online/content/?050214on_onlineonly02>. The article is Jane Mayer, "Outsourcing Torture," *The New Yorker*, Feb. 14 & 21, 2005, at 106.
68. These are reproduced in *The Torture Papers*, *supra* note 11, at 38 and 81.
69. Memorandum from President Bush, February 7, 2002, *id.* at 135.
70. Office of Legal Counsel, Dep't of Justice, Memorandum for Alberto R. Gonzales, Counsel to the President Re: Standards of Conduct for Interrogation under 18 U.S.C. §§2340-2340A, Aug. 1, 2002 [hereinafter: Bybee Memo], at 6.
71. *Id.* at 7, 8.
72. *Id.* at 2.
73. *Id.*
74. Reproduced in *The Torture Papers*, *supra* note 11, at 286.
75. *Lehrer News Hour* (PBS television broadcast, June 21, 2004, transcript #7655).
76. Douglas Jehl & David Johnston, "White House Fought New Curbs on Interrogations, Officials Say," *New York Times*, Jan. 13, 2005, A1, at A16.
77. Dana Priest, "CIA Puts Harsh Tactics On Hold; Memo on Methods Of Interrogation Had Wide Review," *Washington Post*, June 27, 2004, at A1.
78. David Johnston & Neil A. Lewis, "Bush's Counsel Sought Ruling About Torture," *New York Times*, Jan. 5, 2004, at A1; R. Jeffrey Smith & Dan Eggen, "Gonzales Helped Set the Course for Detainees," *Washington Post*, Jan. 5, 2004, at A1.
79. *White House Briefing: U.S. Treatment of Prisoners of War*, Federal News Service, June 22, 2004.
80. Memorandum from William Howard Taft, IV to Alberto Gonzales, Feb. 2, 2002, available at <http://www.fas.org/sgp/othergov/taft.pdf> (visited October 5, 2004).
81. Ruth Wedgwood & R. James Woolsey, "Law and Torture," *Wall Street Journal,* June 28, 2004.
82. Memo for James B. Comey, Deputy Attorney General, Re: Legal Standards Applicable Under 18 U.S.C. §§2340-2340A, Dec. 30, 2004, from Daniel Levin <http://www.usdoj.gov/olc/dagmemo.pdf> [hereinafter: Levin Memo]. *See* p. 361.
83. For useful discussion of the OLC, *see* Nina Pillard, "The Unfulfilled Promise of the Constitution in Executive Hands," *Mich. L. Rev.* (forthcoming).
84. This is not true, I believe, of Professor Yoo's Geneva memorandum which, as its author concedes, takes an extreme position that most international lawyers would disagree with, but does not engage in the solecisms and bad lawyering of the Bybee Memorandum.

85. Tim Golden, "After Terror, a Secret Rewriting of Military Law," *New York Times*, Oct. 24, 2004, A1, at A12. The lawyers were political conservatives, mostly veterans of the Federalist Society and clerkships with Justices Scalia and Thomas, and Judge Laurence Silberman. Some sources for the article stated that their "strategy was also shaped by long-standing political agendas that had relatively little to do with fighting terrorism," such as strengthening executive power and halting U.S. submission to international law. *Id.*

86. *Id.*

87. *Id.*

88. *Id.* at 12–13.

89. *Id.*

90. This is not to say that the defendant will succeed in offering the superior orders defense. Higher-ups will always deny that any such order was given, and the prosecution will fight hard to prevent the defense from questioning or subpoenaing high-ranking officers. In some cases, perhaps, the torturer will decide (maybe willingly, maybe under veiled threats and promises) to "take one for the team" and claim that she was acting on her own.

91. Midrash Psalms 12, in *The Jewish Political Tradition: Volume One: Authority* 317 (Michael Walzer et al. eds. & trans., 2000).

92. Eric Posner & Adrian Vermeule, "A 'Torture Memo' and Its Tortuous Critics," *Wall Street Journal*, July 6, 2004.

93. *Youngstown Sheet & Tube v. Sawyer*, 343 U.S. 579 (1952)

94. The five cases it cites in its self-defense section do not bear on its principal arguments. One is cited simply to show that federal law recognizes self-defense, three are cited to show that the President has the constitutional authority to authorize force, and one is cited to show that the use of force in self-defense can be part of a federal officer's official duties.

95. Peter Brooks, "The Plain Meaning of Torture?" *Slate*, Feb. 9, 2005, at <http://www.slate.com/id/2113314>.

96. "Because the discussion in that memorandum [the Bybee Memo] concerning the President's Commander-in-Chief power and the potential defenses to liability was – and remains – unnecessary, it has been eliminated from the analysis that follows. Considerations of the bounds of any such authority would be inconsistent with the President's unequivocal directive that United States personnel not engage in torture." Levin Memo, *supra* note 82, at 2. This is the equivalent of the politician's standard evasion of the question "What would you do if...?": "I'm not going to debate hypotheticals."

97. Bybee Memo, *supra* note 70, at 5.

98. *Id.*, quoting 42 USC §1395w-22(d)(3)(B).

99. The statute refers to "acute symptoms of sufficient severity (including severe pain) such that a prudent lay person, who possesses an average knowledge of health and medicine could reasonably expect the absence of immediate medical attention to result in – placing the health of the individual...(i) in serious jeopardy, (ii) serious impairment to bodily functions, or (iii) serious dysfunction of any bodily organ or part."

100. *See generally* Craig Hoffman, "Parse the Sentence First: Curbing the Urge to Resort to the Dictionary When Interpreting Legal Texts," 6 *N.Y.U.J. Legis. & Pub. Pol'y* 401 (2002/03).

101. Brooks, *supra* note 95.

102. Levin Memo, *supra* note 82, at 8 and 8, n. 17.

103. Bybee Memo, *supra* note 70, at 3.

104. *Id.* at 4. This is not the only meaning lawyers have given to 'specific intent'; for example, in obstruction-of-justice cases most courts hold that specific intent to obstruct justice means intent to perform actions that the actor should have reasonably foreseen will naturally and probably obstruct justice. *See* the sources cited in Julie R. O'Sullivan, Federal White

Collar Crime 407 (2nd ed. 2003), at note 4. In these cases, "knowledge alone that a particular result is certain to occur" *does* constitute specific intent. Interestingly, the Levin Memo acknowledges this second meaning, supporting it with a citation from LaFave's treatise on substantive criminal law (which the Bybee Memo chose to ignore, although it cites the treatise in its discussion of the necessity defense). Levin Memo, *supra* note 82, at 16.

105. In these cases, the physician performs surgery knowing that it will cause severe pain, but causing pain is not the aim of the surgery. The physician would do the surgery even if it didn't cause pain; presumably, she would be delighted if it caused no pain. By contrast, the torturer would not whip the victim unless it hurt, and that is how we know that hurting the victim was the purpose of the whipping. That's why whipping is torture and surgery is not; and drawing this vital distinction was Congress's aim in including the specific intent requirement.

It might be thought that the statutory limitation to torture performed by official state actors would already safeguard the periodontists and heart surgeons. But of course periodontists and heart surgeons can and do work for the federal government. Furthermore, consider the paradigm of an official state actor: a soldier or federal law enforcement officer. When a soldier shoots an enemy, she probably knows that gunshot wounds are severely painful. The specific intent requirement is essential to insulate her from the charge of torture. She isn't a torturer because she does not specifically intend to cause pain. Her purpose is to incapacitate the enemy, not to make him scream.

106. The closest the Bybee Memo comes to this sort of advice is its acknowledgment that juries may have a hard time differentiating between techniques known to be painful and techniques specifically intended to be painful. Bybee Memo, *supra* note 70, at 4. But this is a watered-down warning: it implies that, ignorant juries aside, the law is really on the interrogator's side – and that will very likely be sufficient reassurance for real-life interrogators, who know that the chances are minuscule that they will find themselves before a jury.

107. *U.S. v. Bailey*, 444 U.S. 394, 406–7 (1980). The Bybee Memo cites this decision twice, but seems to have overlooked the quoted passage.

108. Special White House Briefing (as released by the White House) – Subject: U.S. Treatment of Prisoners of War, Federal News Service, June 22, 2004 [hereinafter: Gonzales Briefing].

109. *Id.*

110. *Id.*

111. Quoted from the memoranda in Neil A. Lewis & David Johnston, "New F.B.I. Memos Describe Abuses of Iraq Inmates," *New York Times*, Dec. 21, 2004, A1; *see also* Dan Eggen & R. Jeffrey Smith, "FBI Agents Allege Abuse of Detainees at Guantanamo Bay," *Washington Post*, Dec. 21, 2004, at A1 (detailing additional abuses).

112. Dep't of Defense Memorandum for Commander, United States Southern Command – Subject: Counter-Resistance Strategies, Oct. 11, 2002 [henceforth: Beaver Memo]. This conclusion by no means represents a straightforward reading of the cases.

113. *Id.*

114. Beaver Memo, *supra* note 112.

115. Michael S. Moore, "Torture and the Balance of Evils," 23 *Israel L. Rev.* 280, 323 (1989).

116. *See, e.g.,* David Rodin, *War and Self-Defense* (2003); Jeff McMahan, "Self-Defense and the Problem of the Innocent Attacker," 104 *Ethics* 252 (1994); David Wasserman, "Justifying Self-Defense," 16 *Phil. & Pub. Aff.* 356 (1987); Philip Montague, "The Morality of Self-Defense: A Reply to Wasserman," 18 *Phil. & Pub. Aff.* 81 (1988); Judith Jarvis Thomson, "Self-Defense and Rights," in *Rights, Restitution, and Risk: Essays in Moral Theory* 33 (William Parent ed., 1986).

117. Moore, *supra* note 115, at 321.

118. *Id.* at 322.
119. *Id.* at 332–33.
120. For a textbook articulation of this distinction, see the *JAG School's Law of War Workshop Deskbook* 10-11 (CDR Brian J. Bill ed., 2000), available at <http://64.233.161.104/search?q=cache:SXTUauXdafcJ:www.jagcnet.army.mil/JAGCNETInternet/Homepages/AC/TJAGSAWeb.nsf/8f7edfd448e0ec6c8525694b0064ba51/9dc02ec45aba401d852569ad007c79df/%24FILE/LOWW%2520Master%2520Document.pdf+army+law+of+war+desk+book&hl=en>.
121. The Bybee Memorandum relies on treatise discussions of the necessity defense, but these state the contours of the defense in general common law, not specifically the federal common law. No federal statute or regulation establishes the necessity defense, and – of course – since *Erie*, American law rejects the notion that there is a "general common law." For discussion, see, e.g., Curtis A. Bradley & Jack L. Goldsmith, "Customary International Law as Federal Common Law: A Critique of the Modern Position," 110 *Harv. L. Rev.* 815, 821, 827 (1997)(observing that *Erie* abrogated general common law). I cite the Bradley/Goldsmith article in connection with *Erie* only because Professor Goldsmith worked in the OLC, and his famous *Erie* argument was well-known to Professor Yoo and, I suspect, to other lawyers working on the Bybee Memo.
122. *E.g., U.S. v. Oakland Cannabis Buyers' Co-op,* 532 U.S. 483 (2001).
123. *E.g., U.S. v. Bailey,* 444 U.S. 394 (1979).
124. *U.S. v. Quilty,* 741 F.2d 1031, 1033–34 (7th Cir.1984).
125. *U.S. v. Milligan,* 17 F.3d 177 (6th Cir. 1994).
126. *U. S. v. Unser,* 165 F.3d 755, 765 (10th Cir.).
127. *U.S. v. LaFleur,* 971 F.2d 200 (9th Cir. 1991).
128. *See, e.g., U.S. v. Meraz Valeta,* 26 F.3d 992, 995 (10th Cir. 1994)(citing *U.S. v. Seward,* 687 F.2d 1270, 1276 (10th Cir. 1982)(en banc)); *U.S. v. Unser,* 165 F.3d 755, 765 (10th Cori. 1999); *U.S. v. Sued-Jimenez,* 275 F.3d 1, 6 (1st Cir. 2001); *U.S. v. Nelson-Rodriguez,* 319 F.3d 12, 40 (1st Cir. 2003); *U.S. v. Newcomb,* 6 F.3d 1129 (6th Cir. 1993); *U.S. v. Singleton,* 902 F.2d 471 (6th Cir. 1990).
129. The Bybee Memorandum notices this point in a section discussing an Israeli Supreme Court opinion that permits the necessity defense to torture. "Moreover, the Israeli Supreme Court concluded that in certain circumstances GSS officers could assert a necessity defense. CAT, however, expressly provides that '[n]o exceptional circumstances whatsoever, whether a state of war or a threat of war, internal political instability or any other public emergency, may be invoked as a justification of torture.' Art. 2(2). Had the court been of the view that the GSS actions constituted torture, the Court could not permit this affirmative defense under CAT." Bybee Memo, *supra* note 70, at 31.
130. Bybee Memorandum, *supra* note 70, at 40, n. 23. 18 U.S.C. §§ 2340–2340A are the criminal prohibition on torture that implements the Torture Convention. The non-self-executing character of Articles 1–16 of the Torture Convention was a condition of Senate approval. See U.S. RUDs, Convention against Torture and Other Cruel, Inhuman or Degrading Treatment or Punishment, 136 Cong. Rec. 36194 (1990).
131. *Murray v. The Schooner Charming Betsy,* 6 U.S. (2 Cranch) 64, 118 (1804). See Restatement (Third) of the Foreign Relations Law of the United States, §114. For discussion, see Curtis A. Bradley, "The Charming Betsy Canon and Separation of Powers: Rethinking the Interpretive Role of International Law," 86 *Geo. L.J.* 479 (1998).
132. Bybee Memo, *supra* note 70, at 41.
133. *Id.* at 41 note 23.
134. Kathleen Clark & Julie Mertus, "Torturing the Law: The Justice Department's Legal Contortions on Interrogation," *Washington Post,* June 20, 2004, at B3; Wedgwood & Woolsey, *supra* note 81.

135. *Youngstown Sheet & Tube v. Sawyer*, 343 U.S. 579 (1952).
136. Article I, sec. 8.
137. Article II, sec. 3.
138. Perhaps this is because the Bybee Memo adopts a different strategy, arguing that because statutes should be interpreted to minimize their clashes with the Constitution, the federal torture statute should be read not to apply to the President or to interrogators authorized by the President. Bybee Memo, *supra* note 70, at 33–35. But this argument presupposes that the President's power to authorize violations of federal law is not limited by the Take Care clause – and that makes the question of how properly to interpret the Take Care clause even more important, not less important.
139. *Id.* at 36.
140. *Id.* at 35.
141. *See* Clark & Mertus, *supra* note 134.
142. *ABA Model Code of Professional Responsibility*, EC 7-3 (1969).
143. *ABA Model Rules of Professional Conduct*, Rule 2.1.
144. *Id.*, Cmt [1]. According to Geoffrey Hazard's and William Hodes's standard treatise on the Model Rules, a lawyer who counsels a client uncandidly, because of the lawyer's political agenda, has violated the rule. 1 Geoffrey C. Hazard, Jr. & W. William Hodes, *The Law of Lawyering* (3rd ed. 2001), §23-4–23-5.
145. Lon L. Fuller & John D. Randall, "Professional Responsibility: Report of the Joint Conference of the ABA/AALS," 44 *A.B.A. J.* 1159, 1161 (1958).
146. I, on the other hand, disagree with their arguments. *See* David Luban, "The Adversary System Excuse," in *The Good Lawyer: Lawyers' Roles and Lawyers' Ethics* 95–97 (David Luban ed., 1983); Luban, "Rediscovering Fuller's Legal Ethics," 11 *Geo. J. Legal Eth.* 801, 819–26 (1998). For a thoroughgoing critique of standard views of advocacy, see William Simon, "The Ideology of Advocacy: Procedural Justice and Professional Ethics," 1978 *Wisc. L. Rev.* 29.
147. This point has been argued for more than a century, beginning with Jeremy Bentham's classic 5 *Rationale of Judicial Evidence, Specially Applied to English Practice* 302–11 (1827), and most recently and effectively in Daniel Fischel, "Lawyers and Confidentiality," 65 *U. Chi. L. Rev.* 1 (1998).
148. Comment [2] to Model Rule 1.6.
149. Susan Koniak, "The Law Between the Bar and the State," 70 *N.C.L. Rev.* 1389 (1992).
150. Martin Mayer, *The Greatest-Ever Bank Robbery: The Collapse of the Savings and Loan Industry* 20 (Collier Books 1992).
151. See David Luban, "Selling Indulgences," *Slate*, Feb. 14, 2005, available at <http://www.slate.com/Default.aspx?id=2113447&>.
152. Ivan Cloulas, *The Borgias* 38 (trans. Gilda Roberts, 1989).
153. *ABA Code of Professional Responsibility*, EC 7-3 (1969).
154. The principles may be found at <http://www.acslaw.org/OLCGuidelinesMemo.pdf)>.
155. Private communication from Martin Lederman, one of the signers of the Guidelines.
156. This memo is included in *The Torture Papers*, *supra* note 11, at 366.
157. Dana Priest, "Memo Lets CIA Take Detainees Out of Iraq," *Washington Post*, Oct. 24, 2004, A1, A21.
158. *Id.* at A21.
159. I focus on judges rather than juries because juries do not settle legal issues, even if they engage in nullification and acquit. Before juries retire to deliberate, the judge must first instruct them on defenses such as necessity, self-defense, and lack of specific intent; and that is where legal argument matters.
160. The Levin Memo begins: "Torture is abhorrent both to American law and values and to international norms." Levin Memo, *supra* note 82, at 1.

161. Hersh, *supra* note 48, at 4.

162. Levin Memo, *supra* note 82, at 10.

163. Jehl & Johnston, *supra* note 76, at A1, A19.

164. Sen. Exec. Rpt. 101–30, *Resolution of Advice and Consent to Ratification* (1990), at I.(2).

165. Draft Memorandum for Alberto R. Gonzales, Permissibility of Relocating Certain "Protected Persons" from Occupied Iraq, March 19, 2004, reprinted in *The Torture Papers, supra* note 11, at 366.

166. When asked by Senator John Warner about the approximate number of ghost detainees, General Kern testified, "I can't give you a precise volume, Chairman, because there is no documentation of the numbers. We believe, and I would ask General Fay to perhaps add to this, that the number is in the dozens to perhaps up to 100. I cannot give you a precise number." Hearing of the Senate Armed Services Committee, Federal News Service, September 9, 2004. Senator Leahy has emphasized this quote from General Kern's testimony in subsequent statements about the abuses in Iraq. Statement of Senator Patrick Leahy on Abuse of Foreign Detainees, States News Service, October 1, 2004.

167. Hersh, *supra* note 48, 16–17, 20, 47–60.

2 How to Interrogate Terrorists

Heather MacDonald

IT DIDN'T TAKE LONG FOR INTERROGATORS IN THE WAR ON TERROR TO
realize that their part was not going according to script. Pentagon doctrine,
honed over decades of cold-war planning, held that 95 percent of prisoners
would break upon straightforward questioning. Interrogators in Afghanistan,
and later in Cuba and Iraq, found just the opposite: virtually none of the terror
detainees was giving up information – not in response to direct questioning, and
not in response to army-approved psychological gambits for prisoners of war.

Debate erupted in detention centers across the globe about how to get
detainees to talk. Were "stress techniques," such as isolation or sleep deprivation to decrease a detainee's resistance to questioning, acceptable? Before the
discussion concluded, however, the photos of prisoner abuse in Iraq's Abu Ghraib
prison appeared. Though they showed the sadism of a prison out of control, they
showed nothing about interrogation.

Nevertheless, Bush administration critics seized on the scandal as proof that
prisoner "torture" had become routine. A master narrative – call it the "torture
narrative" – sprang up: the government's 2002 decision to deny Geneva Convention status to al Qaeda fighters, it held, "led directly to the abuse of detainees
in Afghanistan and Iraq," to quote the *Washington Post*. In particular, torturous
interrogation methods, developed at Guantánamo Bay and in Afghanistan in illegal disregard of Geneva protections, migrated to Abu Ghraib and were manifest
in the abuse photos.

This story's success depends on the reader's remaining ignorant of the actual
interrogation techniques promulgated in the war on terror. Not only were they
light years from real torture and hedged around with bureaucratic safeguards,
but they had nothing to do with the Abu Ghraib anarchy. Moreover, the decision
on the Geneva Conventions was irrelevant to interrogation practices in Iraq.

No matter. The Pentagon's reaction to the scandal was swift and sweeping. It
stripped interrogators not just of stress options but of traditional techniques long
regarded as uncontroversial as well. Red tape now entangles the interrogation
process, and detainees know that their adversaries' hands are tied.

The need for rethinking interrogation doctrine in the war on terror will not go away, however. The Islamist enemy is unlike any the military has encountered in the past. If current wisdom on the rules of war prohibits making any distinction between a terrorist and a lawful combatant, then that orthodoxy needs to change.

The interrogation debate first broke out on the frigid plains of Afghanistan. Marines and other special forces would dump planeloads of al Qaeda and Taliban prisoners into a ramshackle detention facility outside the Kandahar airport; waiting interrogators were then supposed to extract information to be fed immediately back into the battlefield – whether a particular mountain pass was booby-trapped, say, or where an arms cache lay. That "tactical" debriefing accomplished, the Kandahar interrogation crew would determine which prisoners were significant enough to be shipped on to the Guantánamo naval base in Cuba for high-level interrogation.

Army doctrine gives interrogators sixteen "approaches" to induce prisoners of war to divulge critical information. Sporting names like "Pride and Ego Down" and "Fear Up Harsh," these approaches aim to exploit a detainee's self-love, allegiance to or resentment of comrades, or sense of futility. Applied in the right combination, they will work on nearly everyone, as the intelligence soldiers had learned in their training.

But the Kandahar prisoners were not playing by the army rule book. They divulged nothing. "Prisoners overcame the [traditional] model almost effortlessly," writes Chris Mackey in *The Interrogators*, his gripping account of his interrogation service in Afghanistan.[1] The prisoners confounded their captors "not with clever cover stories but with simple refusal to cooperate. They offered lame stories, pretended not to remember even the most basic of details, and then waited for consequences that never really came."

Some of the al Qaeda fighters had received resistance training, which taught that Americans were strictly limited in how they could question prisoners. Failure to cooperate, the al Qaeda manuals revealed, carried no penalties and certainly no risk of torture – a sign, gloated the manuals, of American weakness.

Even if a prisoner had not previously studied American detention policies before arriving at Kandahar, he soon figured them out. "It became very clear very early on to the detainees that the Americans were just going to have them sit there," recalls interrogator Joe Martin (a pseudonym). "They realized: 'The Americans will give us our Holy Book, they'll draw lines on the floor showing us where to pray, we'll get three meals a day with fresh fruit, do Jazzercise with the guards, . . . we can wait them out.'"

Even more challenging was that these detainees bore little resemblance to traditional prisoners of war. The army's interrogation manual presumed adversaries who were essentially the mirror image of their captors, motivated by emotions that all soldiers share. A senior intelligence official who debriefed prisoners in the 1989 U.S. operation in Panama contrasts the battlefield then and now: "There were no martyrs down there, believe me," he chuckles. "The Panamanian forces were more understandable people for us. Interrogation was pretty straightforward: 'Love of Family' [an army-manual approach, promising, say, contact with wife or children in exchange for cooperation] or, 'Here's how you get out of here as fast as you can.'"

"Love of family" often had little purchase among the terrorists, however – as did love of life. "The jihadists would tell you, 'I've divorced this life, I don't care about my family,'" recalls an interrogator at Guantánamo. "You couldn't shame them." The fierce hatred that the captives bore their captors heightened their resistance. The U.S. ambassador to Pakistan reported in January 2002 that prisoners in Kandahar would "shout epithets at their captors, including threats against the female relatives of the soldiers guarding them, knee Marines in the groin, and say that they will escape and kill 'more Americans and Jews.'" Such animosity continued in Guantánamo.

Battlefield commanders in Afghanistan and intelligence officials in Washington kept pressing for information, however. The frustrated interrogators constantly discussed how to get it. The best hope, they agreed, was to recreate the "shock of capture" – that vulnerable mental state when a prisoner is most frightened, most uncertain, and most likely to respond to questioning. Uncertainty is an interrogator's most powerful ally; exploited wisely, it can lead the detainee to believe that the interrogator is in total control and holds the key to his future. The Kandahar detainees, however, learned almost immediately what their future held, no matter how egregious their behavior: nothing untoward.

Many of the interrogators argued for a calibrated use of "stress techniques" – long interrogations that would cut into the detainees' sleep schedules, for example, or making a prisoner kneel or stand, or aggressive questioning that would put a detainee on edge.

Joe Martin – a crack interrogator who discovered that a top al Qaeda leader, whom Pakistan claimed to have in custody, was still at large and directing the Afghani resistance – explains the psychological effect of stress: "Let's say a detainee comes into the interrogation booth and he's had resistance training. He knows that I'm completely handcuffed and that I can't do anything to him. If I throw a temper tantrum, lift him onto his knees, and walk out, you can feel his uncertainty level rise dramatically. He's been told: 'They won't physically touch you,' and now you have. The point is not to beat him up but to introduce the reality into his mind that he doesn't know where your limit is." Grabbing someone by the top of the collar has had a more profound effect on the outcome of questioning than any actual torture could have, Martin maintains. "The guy knows: You just broke your own rules, and that's scary. He might demand to talk to my supervisor. I'll respond: 'There are no supervisors here,' and give him a maniacal smile."

The question was, was such treatment consistent with the Geneva Conventions?

President Bush had declared in February 2002 that al Qaeda members fell wholly outside the Geneva Conventions and that Taliban prisoners would not receive prisoner-of-war status, without which they, too, would not be covered by the Geneva rules. Bush ordered, however, that detainees be treated humanely and in accordance with Geneva principles, to the extent consistent with military necessity.[2] This second pronouncement sank in: all of the war on terror's detention facilities chose to operate under Geneva rules. Contrary to the fulminations of rights advocates and the press, writes Chris Mackey, "Every signal we interrogators got from above from the colonels at [the Combined Forces Land Component Command] in Kuwait to the officers at Central Command back in Tampa – had been . . . to observe the Conventions, respect prisoners' rights, and never cut corners."

What emerged was a hybrid and fluid set of detention practices. As interrogators tried to overcome the prisoners' resistance, their reference point remained Geneva and other humanitarian treaties. But the interrogators pushed into the outer limits of what they thought the law allowed, undoubtedly recognizing that the prisoners in their control violated everything the pacts stood for.

The Geneva Conventions embody the idea that even in as brutal an activity as war, civilized nations could obey humanitarian rules: no attacking civilians and no retaliation against enemy soldiers once they fall into your hands. Destruction would be limited as much as possible to professional soldiers on the battlefield. That rule required, unconditionally, that soldiers distinguish themselves from civilians by wearing uniforms and carrying arms openly.

Obedience to Geneva rules rests on another bedrock moral principle: reciprocity. Nations will treat an enemy's soldiers humanely because they want and expect their adversaries to do the same. Terrorists flout every civilized norm animating the conventions. Their whole purpose is to kill noncombatants, to blend into civilian populations, and to conceal their weapons. They pay no heed whatever to the golden rule; anyone who falls into their hands will most certainly not enjoy commissary privileges and wages, per the Geneva mandates. He – or she – may even lose his head.

Even so, terror interrogators tried to follow the spirit of the Geneva code for conventional, uniformed prisoners of war. That meant, as the code puts it, that the detainees could not be tortured or subjected to "any form of coercion" in order to secure information. They were to be "humanely" treated, protected against "unpleasant or disadvantageous treatment of any kind," and were entitled to "respect for their persons and their honour."

The Kandahar interrogators reached the following rule of thumb, reports Mackey: if a type of behavior toward a prisoner was no worse than the way the army treated its own members, it could not be considered torture or a violation of the conventions. Thus, questioning a detainee past his bedtime was lawful as long as his interrogator stayed up with him. If the interrogator was missing exactly the same amount of sleep as the detainee – and no tag-teaming of interrogators would be allowed, the soldiers decided – then sleep deprivation could not be deemed torture. In fact, interrogators were routinely sleep-deprived, catnapping maybe one or two hours a night, even as the detainees were getting long beauty sleeps. Likewise, if a boot camp drill sergeant can make a recruit kneel with his arms stretched out in front without violating the Convention Against Torture, an interrogator can use that tool against a recalcitrant terror suspect.

Did the stress techniques work? Yes. "The harsher methods we used ... the better information we got and the sooner we got it," writes Mackey, who emphasizes that the methods never contravened the Conventions or crossed over into torture.

Stress broke a young bomb maker, for instance. Six months into the war, Special Forces brought a young Afghan to the Kandahar facility, the likely accomplice of a Taliban explosives expert who had been blowing up aid workers. Joe Martin got the assignment.

"Who's your friend the Americans are looking for?" the interrogation began.
"I don't know."
"You think this is a joke? What do you think I'll do?"
"Torture me."
So now I understand his fear, Martin recollects.
The interrogation continued: "You'll stand here until you tell me your friend."
"No, sir, he's not my friend."
Martin picked up a book and started reading. Several hours later, the young Taliban was losing his balance and was clearly terrified. Moreover, he's got two "big hillbilly guards staring at him who want to kill him," the interrogator recalls.
"You think THIS is bad?!" the questioning starts up again.
"No, sir."
The prisoner starts to fall; the guards stand him back up. If he falls again, and can't get back up, Martin can do nothing further. "I have no rack," he says matter-of-factly. The interrogator's power is an illusion; if a detainee refuses to obey a stress order, an American interrogator has no recourse.
Martin risks a final display of his imaginary authority. "I get in his face, 'What do you think I will do next?'" he barks. In the captive's mind, days have passed, and he has no idea what awaits him. He discloses where he planted bombs on a road and where to find his associate. "The price?" Martin asks. "I made a man stand up. Is this unlawful coercion?"
Under a strict reading of the Geneva protections for prisoners of war, probably; the Army forbids interrogators from even touching lawful combatants. But there is a huge gray area between the gold standard of POW treatment reserved for honorable opponents and torture, which consists of the intentional infliction of severe physical and mental pain. None of the stress techniques that the military has used in the war on terror comes remotely close to torture, despite the hysterical charges of administration critics. (The CIA's behavior remains a

black box.) To declare nontorturous stress off-limits for an enemy who plays by no rules and accords no respect to Western prisoners is folly.

The soldiers used stress techniques to reinforce the traditional psychological approaches. Jeff (a pseudonym), an interrogator in Afghanistan, had been assigned a cocky English Muslim, who justified the 9/11 attacks because women had been working in the World Trade Center. The British citizen deflected all further questioning. Jeff questioned him for a day and a half, without letting him sleep and playing on his religious loyalties. "I broke him on his belief in Islam," Jeff recounts. "He realized he had messed up, because his Muslim brothers and sisters were also in the building." The Brit broke down and cried, then disclosed the mission that al Qaida had put him on before capture. But once the prisoner was allowed to sleep for six hours, he again "clammed up."

Halfway across the globe, an identical debate had broken out, among interrogators who were encountering the same obstacles as the Afghanistan intelligence team. The U.S. base at Guantánamo was supposed to be getting the Afghanistan war's worst of the worst: the al Qaeda Arabs and their high Taliban allies.

Usama bin Ladin's driver and bodyguard were there, along with explosives experts, al Qaeda financiers and recruiters, would-be suicide recruits, and the architects of numerous attacks on civilian targets. They knew about al Qaeda's leadership structure, its communication methods, and its plans to attack the United States And they weren't talking. "They'd laugh at you; 'You've asked me this before,' they'd say contemptuously," reports Major General Michael Dunlavey, a former Guantánamo commanding officer. "Their resistance was tenacious. They'd already had 90 days in Afghanistan to get their cover stories together and to plan with their compatriots."

Even more than Afghanistan, Guantánamo dissipated any uncertainty the detainees might have had about the consequences of noncooperation. Consistent with the president's call for humane treatment, prisoners received expert medical care, three culturally appropriate meals each day, and daily opportunities for prayer, showers, and exercise. They had mail privileges and reading materials. Their biggest annoyance was boredom, recalls one interrogator. Many prisoners disliked the move from Camp X-Ray, the first facility used at the base, to the more commodious Camp Delta, because it curtailed their opportunities for homosexual sex, says an intelligence analyst. The captives protested every perceived infringement of their rights but, as in Afghanistan, ignored any reciprocal obligation. They hurled excrement and urine at guards, used their blankets as garrotes, and created additional weapons out of anything they could get their hands on – including a sink wrenched off a wall. Guards who responded to the attacks – with pepper spray or a water hose, say – got punished and, in one case, court-martialed.

"Gitmo" personnel disagreed sharply over what tools interrogators could legally use. The FBI took the most conservative position. When a Bureau agent questioning Mohamedou Ould Slahi – a Mauritanian al Qaeda operative who had recruited two of the 9/11 pilots – was getting nothing of value, an army interrogator suggested, "Why don't you mention to him that conspiracy is a capital offense?" "That would be a violation of the Convention Against Torture," shot back the agent – on the theory that any covert threat inflicts "severe mental pain." Never mind that district attorneys and police detectives routinely invoke the possibility of harsh criminal penalties to get criminals to confess. Federal prosecutors in New York have even been known to remind suspects that they are more likely to keep their teeth and not end up as sex slaves by pleading to a federal offense, thus avoiding New York City's Rikers Island jail. Using such a method against an al Qaeda jihadist, by contrast, would be branded a serious humanitarian breach.

Top military commanders often matched the FBI's restraint, however. "It was ridiculous the things we couldn't do," recalls an army interrogator. "One guy said he would talk if he could see the ocean. It wasn't approved, because it would be a change of scenery" – a privilege that discriminated in favor of a cooperating detainee, as opposed to being available to all, regardless of their behavior.

Frustration with prisoner stonewalling reached a head with Mohamed al-Kahtani, a Saudi who had been fighting with Usama bin Ladin's bodyguards in Afghanistan in December 2001. By July 2002, analysts had figured out that Kahtani was the missing 20th hijacker. He had flown into Orlando International Airport from Dubai on August 4, 2001, but a sharp-eyed customs agent had denied him entry. Waiting for him at the other side of the gate was Mohamed Atta.

Kahtani's resistance strategies were flawless. Around the first anniversary of 9/11, urgency to get information on al Qaeda grew. Finally, army officials at Guantánamo prepared a legal analysis of their interrogation options and requested permission from Defense Secretary Donald Rumsfeld to use various stress techniques on Kahtani. Their memo, sent up the bureaucratic chain on October 11, 2002, triggered a fierce six-month struggle in Washington among military lawyers, administration officials, and Pentagon chiefs about interrogation in the war on terror.

To read the techniques requested is to understand how restrained the military has been in its approach to terror detainees – and how utterly false the torture narrative has been. Here's what the interrogators assumed they could not do without clearance from the secretary of defense: yell at detainees (though never in their ears), use deception (such as posing as Saudi intelligence agents), and put detainees on MREs (meals ready to eat – vacuum-sealed food pouches eaten by millions of soldiers, as well as vacationing backpackers) instead of hot rations. The interrogators promised that this dangerous dietary measure would be used only *in extremis*, pending local approval and special training.

The most controversial technique approved was "mild, non-injurious physical contact such as grabbing, poking in the chest with the finger, and light pushing," to be reserved only for a "very small percentage of the most unco-operative detainees" believed to possess critical intelligence. A detainee could be poked only after review by Gitmo's commanding general of intelligence and the commander of the U.S. Southern Command in Miami, and only pursuant to "careful coordination" and monitoring.

None of this remotely approaches torture or cruel or degrading treatment. Nevertheless, fanatically cautious Pentagon lawyers revolted, claiming that the methods approved for Kahtani violated international law. Uncharacteristically irresolute, Rumsfeld rescinded the Guantánamo techniques in January 2003.[3]

Kahtani's interrogation hung fire for three months, while a Washington committee, with representatives from the undersecretary of defense, the Defense Intelligence Agency, the Air Force, Army, Navy, and Marine Corps, and attorneys from every branch of the military, considered how to approach the twentieth hijacker.

The outcome of this massive deliberation was more restrictive than the Geneva Conventions themselves, even though they were to apply only to unlawful combatants, not conventional prisoners of war, and only to those held at Guantánamo Bay. It is worth scrutinizing the final twenty-four techniques Rumsfeld approved for terrorists at Gitmo in April 2003,[4] since these are the techniques that the media presents as the source of "torture" at Abu Ghraib. The torture narrative holds that illegal methods used at Guantánamo migrated to Iraq and resulted in the abuse of prisoners there.

So what were these cruel and degrading practices? For one, providing a detainee an incentive for cooperation – such as a cigarette or, especially favored in Cuba, a McDonald's Filet-O-Fish sandwich or a Twinkie unless specifically approved by the secretary of defense. In other words, if an interrogator had learned that Usama bin Ladin's accountant loved Cadbury chocolate, and intended to enter the interrogation booth armed with a Dairy Milk Wafer to extract the name of a Saudi financier, he needed to "specifically determine that military necessity requires" the use of the Dairy Milk Wafer and send an alert to Secretary Rumsfeld that chocolate was to be deployed against an al Qaeda operative.

Similar restrictions, such as a specific finding of military necessity and notice to Rumsfeld, applied to other tried-and-true army psychological techniques. These included "Pride and Ego Down," attacking a detainee's pride to goad him into revealing critical information, as well as "Mutt and Jeff," the classic good cop–bad cop routine of countless police shows. Isolating a detainee from other prisoners to prevent collaboration and to increase his need to talk required not just notice and a finding of military necessity but "detailed implementation instructions [and] medical and psychological review."

The only nonconventional "stress" techniques on the final Guantánamo list are such innocuous interventions as adjusting the temperature or introducing an unpleasant smell into the interrogation room, but only if the interrogator is present at all times; reversing a detainee's sleep cycles from night to day (call this the "Flying to Hong Kong" approach); and convincing a detainee that his interrogator is not from the United States.

Note that none of the treatments shown in the Abu Ghraib photos, such as nudity or the use of dogs, was included in the techniques certified for the unlawful combatants held in Cuba. And those mild techniques that were certified could only be used with extensive bureaucratic oversight and medical monitoring to ensure "humane," "safe," and "lawful" application.

After Rumsfeld cleared the twenty-four methods, interrogators approached Kahtani once again. They relied almost exclusively on isolation and lengthy interrogations. They also used some "psy-ops" (psychological operations). Ten or so interrogators would gather and sing the Rolling Stones' "Time Is on My Side" outside Kahtani's cell. Sometimes they would play a recording of "Enter Sandman" by the heavy-metal group Metallica, which brought Kahtani to tears, because he thought (not implausibly) he was hearing the sound of Satan.

Finally, at 4 am – after an 18-hour, occasionally loud, interrogation, during which Kahtani head-butted his interrogators – he started giving up information, convinced that he was being sold out by his buddies. The entire process had been conducted under the watchful eyes of a medic, a psychiatrist, and lawyers, to make sure that no harm was done. Kahtani provided detailed information on his meetings with Usama bin Ladin, on Jose Padilla and Richard Reid, and on Adnan El Shukrijumah, one of the FBI's most wanted terrorists, believed to be wandering between South and North America.

Since then, according to Pentagon officials, none of the nontraditional techniques approved for Kahtani has been used on anyone else at Guantánamo Bay.

The final strand in the "torture narrative" is the least grounded in actual practice, but it has had the most distorting effect on the public debate. In the summer of 2002, the CIA sought legal advice about permissible interrogation techniques for the recently apprehended Abu Zubaydah, Usama bin Ladin's chief recruiter in the 1990s. The Palestinian Zubaydah had already been sentenced to death in absentia in Jordan for an abortive plot to bomb hotels there during the millennium celebration; he had arranged to obliterate the Los Angeles airport on the same night. The CIA wanted to use techniques on Zubaydah that the military uses on marines and other elite fighters in Survive, Evade, Resist, Escape (SERE) school, which teaches how to withstand torture and other pressures to collaborate. The techniques are classified, but none allegedly involves physical contact. (Later, the CIA is said to have used "water-boarding" – temporarily submerging a detainee in water to induce the sensation of drowning – on Khalid Sheik Mohammad, the mastermind of the 9/11 attacks. Water-boarding is the most extreme method the CIA has applied, according to a former Justice Department attorney, and arguably it crosses the line into torture.)

In response to the CIA's request, Assistant Attorney General Jay S. Bybee produced a hair-raising memo that understandably caused widespread alarm.[5] Bybee argued that a U.S. law ratifying the 1984 Convention Against Torture – covering all persons, whether lawful combatants or not – forbade only physical pain equivalent to that "accompanying serious physical injury, such as organ failure, impairment of bodily function, or even death," or mental pain that resulted in "significant psychological harm of significant duration, e.g., lasting for months or even years." More troubling still, Bybee concluded that the torture statute and international humanitarian treaties did not bind the executive branch in wartime.[6]

This infamous August 2002 "torture memo" represents the high (or low) point of the Bush administration's theory of untrammeled presidential war-making power. But note: it had nothing to do with the interrogation debates and experiments unfolding among Pentagon interrogators in Afghanistan and Cuba. These soldiers struggling with al Qaeda resistance were perfectly ignorant about executive-branch deliberations on the outer boundaries of pain and executive power (which, in any case, were prepared for and seen only by the CIA). "We had no idea what went on in Washington," said Chris Mackey in an interview. A Guantánamo lawyer involved in the Kahtani interrogation echoes Mackey: "We were not aware of the [Justice Department and White House] debates." Interrogators in Iraq were equally unaware of the Bybee memo.

Nevertheless, when the Bybee analysis was released in June 2004, it became the capstone on the torture narrative, the most damning link between the president's decision that the Geneva Conventions didn't apply to terrorists and the sadistic behavior of the military guards at Abu Ghraib. Seymour Hersh, the left-wing journalist who broke the Abu Ghraib story, claims that the Bybee torture memo was the "most suggestive document, in terms of what was really going on inside military prisons and detention centers."

But not only is the Bybee memo irrelevant to what happened in Abu Ghraib; so, too, are the previous interrogation debates in Afghanistan and Cuba. The abuse at Abu Ghraib resulted from the Pentagon's failure to plan for any outcome of the Iraq invasion except the most rosy scenario, its failure to respond to the insurgency once it broke out, and its failure to keep military discipline from collapsing in the understaffed Abu Ghraib facility. Interrogation rules were beside the point.

As the avalanche of prisoners taken in the street fighting overwhelmed the inadequate contingent of guards and officers at Abu Ghraib, order within the ranks broke down as thoroughly as order in the operation of the prison itself. Soldiers talked back to their superiors, refused to wear uniforms, operated prostitution and bootlegging rings, engaged in rampant and public sexual misbehavior, covered the facilities with graffiti, and indulged in drinking binges while on duty. No one knew who was in command. The guards' sadistic and sexualized treatment of prisoners was just an extension of the chaos they were already wallowing in with no restraint from above. Meanwhile, prisoners regularly rioted; insurgents shelled the compound almost daily; the army sent only rotten, bug-infested rations; and the Iraqi guards sold favors to the highest bidders among the insurgents.

The idea that the abuse of the Iraqi detainees resulted from the president's decision on the applicability of the Geneva Conventions to al Qaeda and Taliban detainees is absurd on several grounds. Everyone in the military chain of command emphasized repeatedly that the Iraq conflict would be governed by the Conventions in their entirety. The interrogation rules that local officers developed for Iraq explicitly stated that they were promulgated under Geneva authority, and that the Conventions applied. Moreover, almost all the behavior shown in the photographs occurred in the dead of night among military police, wholly separate from interrogations. Most abuse victims were not even scheduled to be interrogated, because they were of no intelligence value. Finally, except for the presence of dogs, none of the behavior shown in the photos was included in the interrogation rules promulgated in Iraq. Mandated masturbation, dog leashes, assault, and stacking naked prisoners in pyramids – none of these depredations was an approved (or even contemplated) interrogation practice, and no interrogator ordered the military guards to engage in them.

It is the case that intelligence officers in Iraq and Afghanistan were making use of nudity and phobias about dogs at the time. Nudity was not officially sanctioned, and the official rule about dogs only allowed their "presence" in the interrogation booth, not their being "sicced" on naked detainees. The argument that such techniques contributed to a dehumanization of the detainees, which in turn led to their abuse, is not wholly implausible. Whether or not those two particular stressors are worth defending (and many interrogators say they are not), their abuse should not discredit the validity of other stress techniques that the military was cautiously experimenting with in the months before Abu Ghraib.

That experiment is over. Reeling under the public relations disaster of Abu Ghraib, the Pentagon shut down every stress technique but one – isolation – and that can be used only after extensive review. An interrogator who so much as requests permission to question a detainee into the night could be putting his career in jeopardy. Even the traditional army psychological approaches have fallen under a deep cloud of suspicion: deflating a detainee's ego, aggressive but nonphysical histrionics, and good cop–bad cop have been banished along with sleep deprivation.

Timidity among officers prevents the energetic application of those techniques that remain. Interrogation plans have to be triple-checked all the way up through the Pentagon by officers who have never conducted an interrogation in their lives.

In losing these techniques, interrogators have lost the ability to create the uncertainty vital to getting terrorist information. Since the Abu Ghraib scandal broke, the military has made public nearly every record of its internal interrogation debates, providing al Qaeda analysts with an encyclopedia of U.S. methods and constraints. Those constraints make perfectly clear that the interrogator is not in control. "In reassuring the world about our limits, we have destroyed our biggest asset: detainee doubt," a senior Pentagon intelligence official laments.

Soldiers on the ground are noticing the consequences. "The Iraqis already know the game. They know how to play us," a marine chief warrant officer told the *Wall Street Journal* in August. "Unless you catch the Iraqis in the act, it is very hard to pin anything on anyone.... We can't even use basic police interrogation tactics."

And now the human rights' advocates, energized by the Abu Ghraib debacle, are making one final push to halt interrogation altogether. In the *New York Times*'s words, the International Committee of the Red Cross (ICRC) is now condemning the thoroughly emasculated interrogation process at Guantánamo Bay as a "system devised to break the will of the prisoners [and] make them wholly dependent on their interrogators." In other words, the ICRC opposes traditional interrogation itself, since *all* interrogation is designed to "break the will of prisoners" and make them feel "dependent on their interrogators." But according to an ICRC report leaked to the *Times*, "the construction of such a system, whose stated purpose is the production of intelligence, cannot be considered other than an intentional system of cruel, unusual and degrading treatment and a form of torture."

But contrary to the fantasies of the international law and human rights lobbies, a world in which all interrogation is illegal and rights are indiscriminately doled out, is not a safer or more just world. Were the United States to announce that terrorists would be protected under the Geneva Conventions, it would destroy any incentive our ruthless enemies have to comply with the laws of war. The *Washington Post* and the *New York Times* understood that truth in 1987, when they supported President Ronald Reagan's rejection of an amendment to the Geneva Conventions that would have granted lawful-combatant status to terrorists. Today, however, those same opinion makers have done an about-face, though the most striking feature of their denunciations of the Bush administration's Geneva decisions is their failure to offer any explanation for how al Qaeda could possibly be covered under the plain meaning of the text.

The Pentagon is revising the rules for interrogation. If we hope to succeed in the war on terror, the final product *must* allow interrogators to use stress techniques against unlawful combatants. Chris Mackey testifies to how "ineffective schoolhouse methods were in getting prisoners to talk." He warns that his team "failed to break prisoners who I have no doubt knew of terrorist plots or at least terrorist cells that may one day do us harm. Perhaps they would have talked if faced with harsher methods."

The stress techniques that the military has used to date are not torture; the advocates can only be posturing in calling them such. On its website, Human Rights Watch lists the effects of real torture: "from pain and swelling to broken bones, irreparable neurological damage, and chronic painful musculoskeletal problems... [to] long-term depression, post-traumatic stress disorder, marked sleep disturbances and alterations in self-perceptions, not to mention feelings of powerlessness, of fear, guilt and shame." Though none of the techniques that Pentagon interrogators have employed against al Qaeda comes anywhere close to risking such effects, Human Rights Watch nevertheless follows up its list with an accusation of torture against the Bush administration.

The pressure on the Pentagon to outlaw stress techniques won't abate, as the American Civil Liberties Union continues to release formerly classified government documents obtained in a Freedom of Information Act lawsuit concerning detention and interrogation. As of late December 2004, the memos have merely confirmed that the FBI opposes stress methods, though the press breathlessly portrays them as confirming "torture."

Human Rights Watch, the ICRC, Amnesty International, and the other self-professed guardians of humanitarianism need to come back to earth, to the real world in which torture means what the Nazis and the Japanese did in their concentration and POW camps in World War II; the world in which evil regimes, like those we fought in Afghanistan and Iraq, don't follow the Miranda rules or the Convention Against Torture but instead gas children, bury people alive, set wild animals on soccer players who lose, and hang adulterous women by truckloads before stadiums full of spectators; the world in which barbarous death cults behead female aid workers, bomb crowded railway stations, and fly planes filled with hundreds of innocent passengers into buildings filled with thousands of innocent and unsuspecting civilians. By definition, our terrorist enemies and their state supporters have declared themselves enemies of the civilized order and its humanitarian rules. In fighting them, we must of course hold ourselves to our own high moral standards without, however, succumbing to the utopian illusion that we can prevail while immaculately observing every precept of the Sermon on the Mount. It is the necessity of this fallen world that we must oppose evil with force; and we must use all the lawful means necessary to ensure that good, rather than evil, triumphs.

NOTES

1. Chris Mackey and Greg Miller, *The Interrogators: Inside the Secret War Against Al Qaeda.* July, 2004.
2. Memorandum from President George W. Bush to the Vice President, the Secretary of State, the Secretary of Defense, the Attorney General, Chief of Staff to the President, Director of CIA, Assistant to the President for National Security Affairs, Chairman of the Joint Chiefs of Staff, February 7, 2002. ("Humane Treatment of al Qaeda and Taliban Detainess.") Memo #11 in *The Torture Papers*, Karen J. Greenberg and Joshua J. Dratel, eds., 2005, p. 134.
3. Memorandum from Secretary of Defence Donald Rumsfeld to Commander U.S. Southern Command, January 15, 2003. ("Counter-Resistance Techniques.") Memo #23 in *The Torture Papers*, 2005, p. 239.

4. Memorandum from Secretary of Defense Donald Rumsfeld to James T. Hill, Commander, U.S. Southern Command, April 16, 2003. ("Counter-Resistance Techniques in the War on Terrorism.") Memo #27 in *The Torture Papers*, 2005, p. 360.
5. Memorandum from Assistant Attorney General Jay S. Bybee to Alberto R. Gonzales, Counsel to the President, August 1, 2002. ("Standards of Conduct for Interrogation under 18 U.S.C. §§2340-2340A.") Memo #14 in *The Torture Papers*, 2005, p. 172.
6. *Id.*

3 Torture: Thinking about the Unthinkable

Andrew C. McCarthy

THE MORTIFICATION OF IRAQI PRISONERS BY AMERICAN MILITARY PERSON-
nel at the Abu Ghraib prison in Baghdad has been discomfiting far beyond the
impact of the now-infamous images. Coupled with other reports about harsh
post-9/11 tactics to garner information from captured terrorists, and with ongoing investigations into deaths alleged to have occurred in connection with interrogations, Abu Ghraib and the reaction to it have forced front and center a
profound national evasion: the propriety of torture.

As one would expect, the scandal has produced no small amount of righteous
indignation. The civil-libertarian lobby, operating in overdrive, has issued ringing declarations that torture is unacceptable under any circumstances, accused
the Bush administration of giving a green light to the humiliation of captives, and
demanded the jettisoning of established international norms in favor of protocols codifying new rights for mass murderers. The financier George Soros, who
has thrown millions of his billions behind various left-wing causes, recently proclaimed that Abu Ghraib was the functional equivalent of the 9/11 attack, only
committed this time by the United States.

On the other side, deep disapproval of the abuse has been joined to brave talk
about how we must make allowances for a "new kind of war," and to reminders
that Abu Ghraib under American malefactors was a day at the beach compared
with Abu Ghraib under Saddam and his ghouls and that our terrorist enemies:
instead of stripping their captives naked and leashing them like dogs, they tended
to behead them instead. This is all true, as far as it goes, but it has been largely
unaccompanied by any examination of the key question – namely, what are,
and what are not, appropriate methods of interrogation? Appropriate, that is,
according to American values and not the values of humanity's basest elements.

Finally, there are the centrists, who well understand that our enemies are
covert operatives bent on killing us in sneak attacks, and that the only way to
foil them is to get information about who they are and when and where they will

strike next. Unfortunately, zealots inspired by Islamic militancy and willing to immolate themselves in suicide assaults are not likely to share their secrets under the comparatively mild duress of humane captivity. Thus, the centrists figure, there is probably some necessary torture afoot, which they think wrong, or at the very least unsavory, but from which they would prefer to avert their gaze.

This is all, as I say, to be expected. If the spectacle of ruthless mass murder á la 9/11 evokes blind vengefulness in some, in others it triggers deepseated habits of denial or self-blame. In the meantime, the mere mention of torture is enough to engender disquieting thoughts of the dark brutality of which men (and women!) have historically shown themselves capable. Under the circumstances, rationality is not a good bet to rule the day. Nevertheless, it is where any discussion of the terrorist threat and how to deal with it must begin and end.

Terrorism in general is not a new phenomenon, but today's global and systematic menace is plainly not the threat that was contemplated when international humanitarian law, in the form of the Hague Convention, the Geneva Conventions, and the United Nations Convention Against Torture, took root. Those agreements were designed to institutionalize the laws of war, to promote the humane treatment of captured combatants, and to reduce civilian casualties in times of armed conflict. They were written for wars among readily identified forces – nation-states and, to some extent, intra-state liberation movements and organized insurgencies – in which conflict-appropriate tactics were well established and victory (or defeat) was easily visualized. They did not anticipate militant Islam: a subnational force of international scope, with access to weapons of unfathomed destructive power. They did not contemplate a core methodology, targeting civilians, randomly torturing and killing prisoners, that grossly and willfully violates the very premises of humanitarian law. They did not take account of a situation in which our highest priority would be to obtain not territory or treasure but intelligence, and in which victory would be exceedingly difficult to define.

Does this mean that the time has come to upend the entire structure of the law of armed conflict? Hardly. The impulse for making law is driven by a firm grasp of what kinds of conduct are condemnable. The fact that militant Islam has organized itself precisely within the parameters of the universally condemnable – that the terrorists, to adapt Daniel P. Moynihan's famous phrase, have defined deviancy right down to the bottom – is not a reason to reshape norms in order to license execrable behavior. Rather, it compels us to weigh the overriding imperative of our national security, without which our own civil liberties would be nonexistent, against the sanctity and dignity of human life, even when that life belongs to a captured terrorist. In the end, it compels us to ask rationally whether torture is ever permissible.

Before coming to that central issue, it would be helpful to clear away some underbrush surrounding the question of who may lawfully be held for questioning. This is necessary because humanitarian-law activists, many of whom seem more preoccupied with the treatment of terrorists than with the carnage wrought by terrorists, have been working feverishly to convince us that the government's denial of prisoner-of-war (POW) status to al Qaeda terrorists captured in Afghanistan and held in Guantanamo Bay, Cuba, somehow caused the abuse of actual POWs in Iraq.

As it happens, however, whether one is or is not a POW is a matter not of a moment's intuition but of long-settled principle of, one might even say, merit. "POW" is an honorable legal status. In order to earn that status and its protections, one is expected to conduct oneself honorably. Granting it to combatants who do not do so would only offer a further incentive to belligerents to act dishonorably. Granting it to terrorists, in particular, would gravely endanger the lives of countless civilians which, in the greater scheme of things, would lead to far worse evil than the deplorable treatment of a relative handful of prisoners.

It may well be that the failure adequately to regulate and monitor interrogation practices led to a culture that made Abu Ghraib more likely. That, however, has little to do with the legal status of those being interrogated. And it is incongruous, to say the least, to assail the Bush administration for the alleged consequence of a perfectly appropriate decision concerning the status of terrorists while ignoring the foreseeable (in truth, inevitable) consequence of abolishing the very distinctions on which that status rests. The whole rationale for having POW rules in the first place is to encourage civilized warfare and to protect civilians.

Where, then, do those distinctions come from? The relevant principles, developed over centuries, have been passed down to us primarily as codified in the Hague Convention IV of October 18, 1907 and the Geneva Conventions of August 12, 1949, particularly the Third, which addresses the "Treatment of Prisoners of War." It is crucial to remember that these are laws of war, and that the primary object in wartime is forcibly to defeat the enemy. In that sense, they constitute a practical effort to limit abuse and suffering while remaining ever cognizant of the martial context, which is to say of each side's drive to win. Moreover, these laws do not purport to prevent all discomfort to captives or all collateral damage to civilians and noncombatants. Rather, they seek to establish normative guidelines in which legitimate military objectives are pursued without causing disproportionate harm, fully understanding that harm is, to some extent, unavoidable.

The Hague Convention conveys the honorable notion of "lawful" or "privileged" combatant. During wartime, combatants are privileged to employ military force if they are members of a national army or of a militia that is part of such an army and that conducts itself accordingly, meaning that its members are subject to a formal chain of command; wear uniforms (i.e., "have a fixed distinctive emblem recognizable at a distance"); carry their weapons openly; and conduct their operations in accordance with "the laws and customs of war."

And what are those laws and customs? By the early 20th century, they comprised a well-founded balance of military necessity with humanitarian considerations based on the principles of "proportionality" and "distinction." The first called for factoring the likely damage to civilian infrastructure into the calculus for identifying proper military objectives; the second, for limiting acceptable targets to those objectives. The legal scholars David B. Rivkin, Jr. and Lee A. Casey have usefully summarized the resultant set of rules, which were long ago accepted "by all civilized states":

(1) only sovereign states have the right to make war;
(2) civilians cannot be deliberately attacked;
(3) combatants can be attacked either en masse or individually;
(4) quarter is to be granted when sought;
(5) lawful combatants, when taken prisoner or otherwise incapacitated by wounds, are to be accorded the respect and privileges due prisoners of war (POWs); and
(6) while all forms of force can be deployed in combat, certain weapons designed to cause unnecessary suffering are proscribed.[1]

Two other laws are likewise important for our purposes here, and are logically antecedent to rule (5) above: captured combatants may be held until the conclusion of hostilities, and they may be interrogated. Lately there has been much caterwauling over these points, particularly as they relate to captured members of al Qaeda. Leaving aside for the moment whether such persons may be classified as lawful combatants, their detention is routinely decried as unacceptable because it is "indefinite"-as if there has ever been a war in which captives could be assured that hostilities would end on a date certain.

In fact, the theory behind these laws is simple and irrefutable. Captives may be held "indefinitely" because if they are released they are likely to rejoin the battle, thus prolonging the war and its attendant suffering. By contrast, imposing a maximum and arbitrarily chosen period of detention (say, three years) would defeat the logical purpose of the detention. Similarly, captives may be questioned because they are likely to have information which, if learned by the captor state, will protect its forces, make it easier to pinpoint legitimate military targets of strategic importance, and secure victory more promptly, all of which saves lives.

The Geneva Conventions, promulgated in the middle of the last century, offered additional humanitarian protections. What impelled their drafting were the widespread atrocities visited upon captured prisoners of war during World War I and the savagery of World War II, in which civilians were broadly targeted, exterminated, and subjected to sundry lesser horrors. These 1949 accords are generally applicable only between and among national powers that have entered into them.

The Third Geneva Convention affords specific protections to prisoners of war: that is, lawful or privileged combatants who have been captured while taking part in hostilities. POW status is generally limited to two categories: members of the armed forces of nations that are parties to the conflict, and members of militias and organized resistance movements that belong to a nation that is a party to the conflict, provided they fulfill the conditions mentioned above (being part of a formal chain of command, wearing uniforms, etc.).

Those who satisfy these criteria are entitled "in all circumstances to respect for their persons and their honor." POWs, moreover, "must at all times be protected, particularly against acts of violence or intimidation and against insults and public curiosity." Similarly prohibited are "measures of reprisal against" them. The detaining power, in addition, is required to provide all POWs with health care and maintenance and to show no preference based "on race, nationality, religious belief, or political opinions, or any other distinction founded on similar criteria." Furthermore, while POWs may be questioned broadly, they are obligated to reveal in the time-honored formulation only their name, rank, and serial number. Finally, "prisoners of war who refuse to answer may not be threatened, insulted, or exposed to unpleasant or disadvantageous treatment of any kind."

Militant Islamic terrorists like those belonging to al Qaeda manifestly do not qualify for POW states because they are not lawful combatants: they are not part of a nation state, they are not signatories of the Geneva Conventions, they do not wear uniforms, they do not as a rule carry their weapons openly, they hide among (and thus gravely imperil) the civilian population and infrastructure, and they intentionally target civilians for indiscriminate mass homicide in order to extort concessions from governments they oppose. As a result, they do not enjoy the special privileges of POWs, such as entitlements during interrogation to limit their answers to "pedigree" information and to refuse to answer other questions.

But there is a complication. It is true that the 1949 protocols do not apply to al Qaeda. Nevertheless, even those who rightly maintain that the general protections of the Conventions are unavailable to terrorist organizations have found in them a highminded proscription against torture that extends to everyone, including terrorists. As best I can tell, this interpretation is rooted in a pertinent passage of Article 3 (common to all four Conventions):

> Persons taking no active part in the hostilities, including members of the armed forces who have laid down their arms and those placed hors de combat by . . . detention . . . shall in all circumstances be treated humanely [,] [and not subjected to] violence to life and person, in particular, murder of all kinds, mutilation, cruel treatment and torture [,] [nor to] outrages upon personal dignity, in particular humiliating and degrading treatment. [Emphasis added.]

This provision, it should be noted, does not literally compel the construction that has sometimes been placed on it. Indeed, it seems plausible that the phrase, "those placed hors de combat by . . . detention," was intended only to modify "members of the armed forces," i.e., lawful combatants belonging to the signatories' armies, some of whom may have been rendered hors de combat by detention. The fact that the provision is widely interpreted as extending anti-torture protection to nonsignatories almost certainly owes more to the general disrepute in which murder and torture are held by the civilized world than to any putative desire of the framers to create an entirely new category, otherwise left virtually unmentioned in the four Conventions.

But the bottom line is that, arguably, captured terrorists may not be lawfully subjected to torture. Is that the end of the matter?

To answer that question requires a look at more law: specifically, a convention developed more than a quarter-century after the 1949 Geneva Conventions took effect. This was a protocol to the Conventions, known as Protocol I Additional, dated June 8, 1977 and relating to the "Protection of Victims of International Armed Conflicts."

The late 1970s, one should recall, was the heyday of home-grown insurgencies and "national liberation" movements. These groups, in collusion with Western human-rights activists, pushed to extend Geneva protections to members of nonstate militias – often, guerrillas engaged in fighting colonial powers or other regimes backed by the West (especially the United States). Protocol I, as Rivkin and Casey have observed, was the fruit of that effort.

Not only does the accord grant POW status to such guerrillas, but it actually gives them a number of significant advantages over traditional nation-state armies. It allows them to maintain their privileged combatant status even if they have concealed their arms until very shortly before attacking, and it makes it unlawful to use force against them unless they are in the act of preparing an attack or attacking, thus permitting them to dictate the time and place of battle. Protocol I tips the scales even further by its rule of nonreciprocity, under which combatants in nonstate militias do not forfeit their privileged status even if they routinely violate international humanitarian law, which they are of course far more likely to do than are national armies.

It will come as no surprise that most of Europe, including England, signed on to Protocol I. The United States, however, did not, precisely because the protocol's loosening of traditional just war strictures would have the effect of protecting, and thus encouraging, irregular forces like terrorist organizations that pose a lethal threat to civilian populations. This disagreement between the United States and its key allies on so rudimentary a matter as what rules should apply to the treatment of nonstate combatants has caused no small number of problems in recent conflicts, including NATO's operations in the Balkans and coalition activities in Afghanistan and Iraq. The strains have induced Washington to fudge its opposition to Protocol I – formally opposing it but, for example, suggesting in such authoritative publications as the 2002 edition of the Army's Operational Law Handbook that much of its substance is "either legally binding as customary international law or acceptable practice though not legally binding."

Unfortunately, this purposeful ambiguity has not only fostered uncertainty about what the law requires but has created a platform for domestic activists whose interventions have redounded to the benefit of terrorists at the very time we are most threatened. Thus, Kenneth Roth, the executive director of Human Rights Watch, warned in a December 2002 letter to President Bush that our treatment of al Qaeda detainees held at Guantanamo Bay could place the United States in violation of Protocol I. Skirting the inconvenient fact that the United States is not a signatory to the protocol, Roth deftly observed that the document "is recognized as restating customary international law,"[2] which makes his position sound materially similar to the American army's.

Still, ambiguity aside, Protocol I has never been ratified and as such is not binding on the United States. I hasten to add that this is immaterial as far as the Iraqis held at Abu Ghraib are concerned. Iraq is a party to the Geneva Conventions; its military personnel, apprehended in wartime, were POWs. The United States conceded as much at the beginning of hostilities. Thus, even mild forms of abuse, much less the nightmarish indignities that occurred at Abu Ghraib, are violations of international law.

As for captured al Qaeda terrorists, however, none of this should be taken to suggest that it was, or is, improper to subject them to far more aggressive techniques of interrogation than can be applied to POWs. But torture? That is another matter.

Let me spell it out. It is illegal in the United States, under any circumstances, to torture anyone – even unlawful combatant terrorists who may have information about ongoing plots that, if revealed, could save thousands of lives. Period.[3]

There are two reasons for this, neither of them having to do with how one chooses to interpret the murky language of Article 3 of the 1949 Geneva Conventions (the one proscribing torture of some, or all, detainees). The first reason is that the United States is a signatory to an international treaty barring torture: this is the United Nations Convention Against Torture and Other Cruel, Inhuman, or Degrading Treatment or Punishment. The treaty is dated December 10, 1984 and was ratified in 1994, thus earning the force of binding law. The second reason is that federal law also categorically prohibits torture.

What constitutes torture under these laws? In Article 1 of the UN convention, torture is expressly and very broadly defined as any act, done at the direction or with the knowing acquiescence of a public official, by which

> severe pain or suffering, whether physical or mental, is intentionally inflicted on a person for such purposes as obtaining from him or a third person information or a confession, punishing him for an act he or a third person has committed or is suspected of having committed, or intimidating or coercing him or a third person, or for any reason based on discrimination of any kind.

What about exigent circumstances? What about a state of active combat in which causing severe "physical or mental" discomfort to a captive might elicit intelligence that will save the lives of troops? What about a war against a terrorist network in which nonlethal torture against a known mass murderer might induce him to reveal plans, say, to detonate a nuclear device in New York Harbor? The treaty turns a deaf ear. In Article 2, it states flatly: "No exceptional circumstances whatsoever, whether a state of war or a threat of war, internal political instability or any other public emergency, may be invoked as a justification of torture." Not content with that, the convention dictates (in Article 16) that each signatory state must "undertake to prevent in any territory under its jurisdiction other acts of cruel, inhuman, or degrading treatment or punishment" even if they are not so severe as to "amount to torture as defined in Article 1."

Pertinent questions arise here for Americans. What about the death penalty? What about when the police cause severe physical harm to a suspect during a disputed arrest? Well, such matters are indeed exempted from the treaty: its definition of torture excludes "pain or suffering arising only from, inherent in, or incidental to lawful sanctions." More importantly for our purposes, the U.S. Senate, in ratifying the treaty, registered some stringent caveats, insisting on the preservation of capital punishment and limiting our acceptance of the proscription of "cruel, inhuman, or degrading treatment or punishment" to the relevant understandings enshrined in the "Fifth, Eighth, and/or Fourteenth Amendments to the Constitution."

This was critical. As is well known, the Eighth Amendment bars "cruel and unusual punishments." But, as Alan M. Dershowitz reminds us in his 2002 book, *Why Terrorism Works*, American courts, including the Supreme Court, have held that its protection extends only to those already convicted of crimes; that is, the "punishments" it regulates are those meted out after guilty verdicts. Similarly with the government's mandate under the Fifth and Fourteenth Amendments to provide "due process of law": again, that term pertains almost exclusively to judicial proceedings and its substantive content is, to put it mildly, highly debatable.

Let us assume, for example, that the Abu Ghraib abuses were deemed to fall short of the "severe pain or suffering" needed to qualify as "torture." Could a humiliated prisoner find recourse in the "cruel, inhuman, or degrading treatment" provision of the UN treaty? No, according to Dershowitz: his plight has nothing to do with judicial proceedings – he is being held by the military in wartime. Indeed, Dershowitz contends that the Senate's caveats limit the applicability not only of the treaty's "cruel, inhuman, or degrading" clause but even of its proscription against torture itself.[4]

Whatever qualifications may attach to the treaty, however, it cannot credibly be argued that torture is permissible, that is, beyond the reach of U.S. law, as long as it occurs outside the parameters of a judicial proceeding. That is because, fulfilling an aspiration expressed in the torture convention, the United States in 1994 enacted stringent antitorture laws of its own.[5] In some ways, these laws define torture even more broadly than the UN convention. They proscribe any act (other than those incident to lawful sanctions like the death penalty) that is "specifically intended to inflict severe physical or mental pain or suffering." In other words, and contrary to the UN treaty's own slightly narrower definition, an act need not be motivated by a purpose to obtain information, to punish, or to intimidate for it to be considered torture in American law.

Nor is that all. Federal law also makes "severe mental pain or suffering" actionable with respect to a wide variety of menacing behavior. As long as mental harm is "prolonged," it is grounds for torture charges if the harm results from the intentional or threatened infliction of severe physical pain or suffering; from the administration or threatened administration of "mind-altering substances or other procedures calculated to disrupt profoundly the senses or the personality;" from a "threat of imminent death;" or from threats that another person will imminently be subjected to such abuses. Not only those who engage in such behavior but those who conspire to engage in it, even if they are unsuccessful, are subject to prosecution.

If such behavior results in death, it may itself be punished by the death penalty; in other cases, it may be punished with up to twenty years' imprisonment. Nor does it matter where in the world the offense takes place; an American citizen may be prosecuted, and so may a foreign torturer who happens to be found on U.S. soil.[6] As a matter of law, then, torture in this very expansive understanding is absolutely prohibited. The only question remaining is: should it be?

Just imagine, in this culture, having the temerity to say out loud: "I am in favor of torture." One might as well declare oneself in favor of child molestation (or tobacco). In point of fact, however, many people, probably most people, who claim to be opposed to torture are not against it in all cases or in every form. Many, indeed, are no doubt secretly relieved that it goes on regardless of what the laws and the regnant pieties may dictate.

Seventy percent of Americans, all of whom presumably oppose killing, favor the death penalty. A comparably sizable number who oppose abortion favor its availability in cases of rape, incest, or where the life of the mother is at risk. All sensible people oppose the slaughter of innocent civilians, but an overwhelming number favor war if the evil it seeks to defeat is worth fighting against, even if war will ineluctably lead to the slaughter of innocent civilians.

Torture is not meaningfully different. Considered in a vacuum, it is a palpable moral evil. Moral evils, however, do not exist in a vacuum; they exist in collision with other evils, and sometimes we are forced to choose. Ask the average person if he opposes torture and the answer will surely be yes. But present him with a real-world scenario and the answer may well change.

Let us posit a terrorist, credibly believed to have murdered thousands of people. Suppose this terrorist is aware that a radiological bomb will be detonated momentarily in the heart of a major metropolis, but is refusing to impart the details to interrogators. Now, suddenly, black and white becomes gray: perhaps there are worse evils than some forms of torture. That does not mean our average person "favors" torture, but he may well be amenable to keeping it on the table as an option, and henceforth not so disposed to declare confidently that he opposes it in any form under all circumstances.

The obverse goes for the proponent of torture. As Dershowitz notes, arguments for torture are often crudely cast in terms of raw numbers: for example, the torture of one guilty person would surely be justified to prevent the torture or death of a hundred innocent persons. But would it, without qualification? Are there lengths to which proponents might be unprepared to go? Of course there are. The vast majority of people who would favor torture in this case would oppose it if the form of abuse were inhumanly grisly; most would probably oppose a method that might lead to death (although that too might change if the situation were dire enough and especially if the person to be tortured were already facing execution). Moreover, most if not all people open to the rare application of torture in order to prevent terrorist acts would be immovably opposed if the torture involved abusing moral innocents – like harming a terrorist's children to induce him to talk – or in the absence of persuasive grounds for believing a terrorist attack was imminent.

All of which is to suggest that a significant gap exists between our wishes and reality. This is hardly unusual, either in life or in law. Take the canons of ethics that govern the behavior of attorneys. They are divided into two sections: ethical considerations and disciplinary rules. The former are the high principles that lawyers are enjoined to emulate; the latter are threshold commands of which they must not fall short on pain of sanction. So it is with torture. Even as we sincerely aspire never to resort to it, we are required to acknowledge that there are some instances in which it might be employed; therefore, it is incumbent upon us to regulate how and under what circumstances that could permissibly be done, and to prosecute aggressively those who step outside the parameters we undertake to define.

This conclusion, however reluctantly arrived at, is informed in part by the unpersuasiveness of the tactical and moral arguments parroted ubiquitously by the opponents of torture in the wake of Abu Ghraib. On the tactical level, it has been repeatedly asserted that torture simply does not work. The victim, it is said, has such a powerful incentive to tell the torturer what the torturer wants to hear that anything he says is by definition unreliable.

This claim might be made about countless other human endeavors in which inducements to act for ignoble reasons are similarly rampant, from politics to business to police work. It is thoroughly specious. A witness tempted to cooperate by the promise of a lenient sentence has a powerful motive to testify falsely to a version of events that he thinks might improve the prosecutor's case. A defendant who testifies in his own behalf has a different but no less strong incentive – namely, avoiding jail or perhaps death – to give a false exculpatory account. In neither situation is it necessarily the case that the witness will lie, or that if he does, the lie will escape notice. Information from witnesses beset by intense pressure is inherently suspect but far from intrinsically unreliable.

Torture is no different. The victim may have been given an incentive to say what he thinks his torturer wants to hear, but that does not mean his compelled words are untrue. Nor does the victim necessarily even know what his torturer wants to hear. Nor can he know that he will not be tortured further if he intentionally misleads his tormentor. In fact, it could just as plausibly be asserted that torture is an ironclad guarantee of honesty as of misinformation. Neither statement holds water as an absolute and, on the level of tactics, neither offers a sound reason either to permit or prohibit torture. As Dershowitz documents in detail, torture has been known to be a very effective method to get at truth; that it is not foolproof is hardly a reason to prohibit its selective use.

Then there is the moral argument: torture is an abomination so profound that permitting it, even if limited to rare and dire emergencies, constitutes an indelible blight on a society and its laws. So stated, the proposition has undeniable appeal. But "torture" is a loaded word. No one, it is fair to say, favors a policy of complete laissez-faire. What is envisioned instead is the administration of pressure that is capable of causing extreme pain – Dershowitz gives the example of sterile needles forced under the fingernails – but is nonlethal.

To be sure, even reading or thinking about such practices may make the teeth clench and the stomach churn. But consider: when sufficiently provoked, we already permit far worse. Capital punishment may be more humane than it used to be, thanks to lethal injection, but unlike torture it is forever. If we were to offer a choice, severe pain or execution, to convicts on death row, can there be any doubt which most of them would elect? Our weapons of war are "smarter" than they used to be, with precision targeting and the rest, but they still kill, mutilate, and maim with much less discrimination than we comfort ourselves to imagine. Is torture, with just cause and creating far less devastation, morally worse just because it is inflicted in a room looking the victim in the eye rather than from thousands of feet in the air where victims are unseen?

Equally significant from the moral point of view, one should think, are the consequences of the current system, in which we mouth our opposition to all torture while knowing full well that forms of it are occurring, with greater frequency than should be acceptable to anyone, inside many officially civilized countries that are signatories to the UN convention. It is here that Dershowitz is at his most trenchant: true civil libertarians are required to concern themselves with real-world outcomes rather than with proclaimed intentions, whether cynical or pure-hearted. By imposing an absolute ban on something we know is occurring, we promote disrespect for the rule of law in general and abdicate our duty to enact tailored and meaningful regulations. Both of these failings have the juggernaut effect of increasing the total amount of unjustifiable and otherwise preventable torture.

The task, then, is to create controlled, highly regulated, and responsibly accountable conditions. Toward this end, Dershowitz has proposed the notion of torture warrants. Under such a system, the government would have to apply to a federal court for permission to administer a predetermined form of nonlethal torture. The warrant would be issued only on a showing of reasonable grounds for believing that a catastrophe was impending, that the person to be subjected to torture had information about this event, that he had been given immunity (meaning, his statements could not be used against him in court and therefore he could not invoke the Fifth Amendment privilege against self-incrimination as a basis for refusing to answer), and that he had nevertheless remained silent.

Other conditions might be added. There could be limitations on who would be eligible for such treatment: for example, convicted terrorists or those who, even if not previously convicted, could be demonstrated to be terrorists according to some rigorous standard of proof. Application would have to be made with the approval of a high-ranking government official – the decision could not be entrusted to a twenty-three-year-old reservist assigned as custodian of a brig for mass murderers. Since torture would now be permitted, under stricture and with scrupulous judicial monitoring, no excuse would exist for engaging in torture outside the process, and those shown to have done so would be vigorously prosecuted.

In my estimation, this is a worthy proposal, far superior to the current hypocrisy that turns a blind eye to that which it purports to forbid. But my own approach, although based on the same underlying aims – minimizing the instances of actual torture and making its application more forthright, more transparent, and more accountable – is somewhat different. The struggle against militant Islamic terrorism, I believe, calls for an across-the-board rethinking of our current system as it relates not only to interrogations but also to the detention of unlawful combatants and to the trials of members of international terrorist networks, which our judicial system and its due-process standards are not designed to accommodate.

Elsewhere I have proposed the establishment of a national security court, structured along the lines of the current Foreign Intelligence Surveillance Court.[7] This would be a tribunal, drawn from the national pool of federal judges, that would have jurisdiction over, and develop an expertise in, matters of national security. It would monitor the detention of terrorist captives (deferring to the executive branch's decision to detain in the first place), and it would conduct trials of terrorists whom the government elected to charge under special rules that would apply only in national security cases. This would replace the current paradigm in which the enlightened procedures of our criminal justice system, designed to protect Americans accused of crimes and presumed innocent until proved otherwise, has been warped as we strain to apply them to terrorists in whose hands those same procedures imperil public safety.

Refining our consideration of torture would be of a piece with this proposed overhaul. With torture strictly limited to national security matters, and unavoidably involving highly classified information about terrorist networks, the new national security court would be the place to consider, and monitor the execution of, torture warrants. These could be sought, in turn, only by the attorney general or by a high-ranking Justice Department official designated for this purpose by the attorney general.

Centralizing this sensitive matter in a single court would ensure that the standards developed for warrants win rigorous adherence rather than (as in Dershowitz's proposal) being subject to tinkering by hundreds of federal judges in scores of districts throughout the country. It would also ensure speedy determinations – a critical point since torture would be permitted only under circumstances of imminent peril. Warrants would undoubtedly be rarely sought and rarely granted, but a judge who had previously dealt with even one would be in a far better position to decide quickly than a judge for whom this was uncharted territory. To bolster the new system's integrity and effectiveness, periodic reports would be made to the appropriate committees of Congress.

It goes without saying that amending our laws to permit limited, regulated torture would unleash torrents of obloquy throughout the world, not least in the Islamic countries and in Europe – two places, it must be observed, with shameful legacies of ruthless prisoner abuse. Nevertheless, our cause would be just: to demonstrate our seriousness about dealing with torture, to reduce its incidence, to make its practitioners accountable, and to ensure that in this new kind of war that is almost entirely about intelligence, we are not unduly deprived of information that may save thousands of lives.

Abu Ghraib presents an opportunity to deal with this wrenching issue in a practical, responsible, and honorable way. The wrong would lie in failing the summons.

NOTES

1. "Unleashing the Dogs of War," *The National Interest*, Fall 2003.
2. Roth's letter is available at <http://www.counterpunch.org/roth1227.html>.
3. The very clarity of the proscription is what prompted controversy earlier this month when reports emerged that government lawyers had struggled unconvincingly in 2003 to craft ways around these laws.
4. *Why Terrorism Works*, p. 136. I respectfully disagree: the Senate's caveats apply only to the "cruel, inhuman, or degrading" clause, not to torture. *See, e.g.,* Senate's Advice & Consent (www.umn.edu/humanrts/usdocs/tortres.html); and *see also* Douglass Cassel, "The United States and the Torture Convention: A Useful Dialogue," Center for Human Rights Commentaries (May 24, 2000).
5. Codified under Title 18, U.S. Code, Sections 2340, 2340A & 2340B.
6. The 1991 Torture Victim Protection Act, codified under Title 28, U.S. Code, Section 1350.
7. "Abu Ghraib and Enemy Combatants," National Review Online, May 11, 2004.

4 The Curious Debate

Joshua Dratel

THE DEBATE OVER THE UNITED STATES' POST-SEPTEMBER 11TH ENDORSE-ment of torture as a policy in aid of interrogation has been curious indeed. Official U.S. government memoranda defined torture so narrowly, in contravention of U.S. law and treaties, and interrogators and jailers engaged in abusive acts undoubtedly constituting torture under U.S. and international law, yet the United States has neither admitted that such policy existed, nor formally defended the mistreatment of detainees. However, former government officials and academics – often the same people – have presented what they consider justifications for torture, without conceding that the United States has adopted such measures. Do those reasons withstand scrutiny and analysis? And, if not, what is to be done with those who have constructed such a policy, and with the policy itself?

Certainly the intensity of the reaction to revelation of the government memoranda setting forth the policy, and the ensuing debate, has precipitated retrenchment already. Revising the policy formulated two-and-a-half years earlier in the wake of September 11, 2001, the U.S. Department of Justice agreed in December 2004 that torture is "abhorrent both to American law and values and to international norms."[1] That repudiation of the prior policy, however, does not end the controversy, since fundamental questions nonetheless remain: why the rush to condone torture and other coercive, abusive interrogation methods in the first place? Was there some finding or conclusion that traditional interrogation methods, consistent with established military or international standards, had failed, or would prove insufficient? Was there some empirical evidence that torture would constitute a more effective means of obtaining accurate or reliable information? Or was the haste to embrace torture and abuse merely a manifestation of panic, of helplessness, and of the desire to inflict pain upon an unconventional and difficult enemy?

The results of that initial policy which, in a curious paradox, the United States has claimed to reverse without acknowledging that it implemented the policy in the first place, also warrant examination and inquiry: has torture and abuse proved more effective in obtaining information? Has that information been valuable and/or reliable? Even if so, has the resort to torture and abuse been worth the price – the impairment of the reciprocal nature of treaties such as the Geneva Conventions as they pertain to the treatment of U.S. military and other personnel, the damage to international relations and the United States' reputation, the foreclosing of prosecution and punishment of potentially danger-ous terrorists, and the fostering of the degeneration of a national morality and standard of behavior that accompanies the abandonment of bedrock principles?

In embarking on its policy of authorizing torture and abuse, the United States did not provide any functional basis for jettisoning traditional interro-gation methods, not to mention the Geneva Conventions, the Uniform Code of Military Justice, and the Constitution. It did not rely on any historical parallel, cite statistics, quote any scholarly or field study, or refer to some body of anecdo-tal evidence that would justify the conclusion that torture would produce more, and more accurate, information more promptly than would ordinary methods of interrogation. Certainly, in late 2001, when the policy was first articulated, there had not been sufficient time to determine whether those time-honored methods were not working, and needed to be replaced. Just as surely, the United States did not produce any evidence of any such failure.

Instead, torture and abuse were justified colloquially in coordination with ominous catch-phrases: that torture would be necessary to discover the location of a "ticking time-bomb," that torture "saves lives," and that torture was part of a constellation of responses required to meet the "new paradigm" presented by al Qaeda and international terrorism.

Yet none of those rationalizations excuses torture and abuse – even assum-ing, for the time being, that torture constitutes an effective and swift means of obtaining the requisite information. For example, the "ticking time-bomb" ratio-nale ignores the fact that the torture approved in the current context occurred well after the detainees' apprehension, and continued for months, if not years, thereafter. Thus, any time-bomb would have ceased ticking, and detonated, long before any torture occurred. The same is true for the proposal that "torture war-rants," whereby judicial approval is obtained for such interrogation methods, are appropriate for the ticking time-bomb scenario. By the time judicial imprimatur were obtained, any ticking time-bomb would have already exploded – rendering the process entirely ineffective in addressing an emergency.

Also, the ticking time-bomb rationale slides inexorably down what law pro-fessors call the "slippery slope": at what point in the process of a terrorist, or even ordinary criminal, act is torture off-limits? What if there is indeed a time-bomb, but it is not yet ticking? What if it is not yet assembled? What if some, but not all, of the components have already been purchased? What if the time-bomb has been envisioned, but not yet constructed, with a time and target previously chosen?

Where does the rationale stop? Can it be stopped once it is accepted as valid? Who will be entrusted to stop it? In this context, the exception does indeed swallow the rule whole. The same is true, of course, with respect to the more general protestation that "torture saves lives," which has been trumpeted by some. That is simply a canard as, again, the intractable problem with the "saving lives" rationale is that it could apply to *any* situation. Torturing Japanese or German (or any enemy) soldiers – and certainly *officers* – would no doubt have "saved lives" during World War II. Yet we did not suspend the laws of war and treatment of prisoners to do so. Nor would the principle need be limited to war: torturing ordinary criminals, such as drug dealers or organized crime figures, would just as likely yield information that would "save lives." Again, though, we have not plumbed that depth.

Perhaps the most extreme, but illustrative, example of the fallacy of the "saving lives" hypothesis would not be attractive to those who argue that torture saves lives: the number of lives saved by torture of terrorists would pale, on an immeasurable scale, before the number of lives spared if cigarette and pharmaceutical manufacturers had been tortured to reveal their darkest industry secrets instead of being allowed to testify (or, more accurately, "testi-lie") before Congress in their crisp suits and smug defiance. Indeed, in the context of information about international terrorism, perhaps the most fruitful torture would have been of the personnel at various U.S. intelligence and regulatory agencies who, as documented in the 9/11 Commission Report, jealously husbanded notice of two of the hijackers' entry into the United States, and failed to share that intelligence with domestic law enforcement and immigration agencies.

Nor does any claim of a "new paradigm" provide any excuse, or even a viable explanation. The contention, set forth with great emphasis by various persons in and outside government, that al Qaeda, as a fanatic, violent, and intermittently capable international organization, represented some unprecedented enemy justifying abandonment of our principles is simply not borne out by historical comparison. The Nazi party's dominance of the Third Reich is not distinguishable in practical terms from al Qaeda's influence on the Taliban government.

Nor does al Qaeda present a military threat equal to Nazi Germany or the Japanese Empire in World War II, or the Soviet Union during the Cold War. Unlike Nazi Germany, al Qaeda does not control Europe; unlike the Japanese during that period, al Qaeda does not dominate Asia. Al Qaeda's status as an irregular organization, or as an ideology, does not distinguish it, either. There were almost undoubtedly more National Socialists and their sympathizers in the United States at the commencement of World War II than there are al Qaeda operatives and their associates present in the United States today. As for clandestine infiltration, the intellectual and political forbears of the architects of the United States' policy to permit torture and abuse believed with complete and unflinching conviction that communists had insinuated themselves into the highest levels of the U.S. government. As yet, there has not been any claim that al Qaeda has managed *any* incursion into government, much less one so ambitious or dramatic.

Al Qaeda's record of destruction, September 11th notwithstanding – and as a New Yorker who lived, and still lives, in the shadow of the twin towers, which cast a long shadow over lower Manhattan even in their absence, I am fully cognizant of the impact of that day – pales before the death machine assembled and operated by the Nazis. Yet we managed to eradicate Nazism as a significant threat without wholesale repudiation of the laws of war, or a categorical departure from international norms. Today, even while acknowledging the serious threat that al Qaeda constitutes, we can dispatch it to the same historical dust bin without, in the process, forsaking all of the precepts we hold dear, and upon which we distinguish ourselves from our enemies.

As Sir Thomas More said so eloquently in *A Man for All Seasons*, in response to his son-in-law's urging to "cut down all the laws in England" to get at the devil, that "if you cut them down, . . . do you really think you could stand upright in the winds that would follow then? Yes, I'd give the devil benefit of law for my own safety's sake." That lesson in law and politics, nearly five hundred years, old retains all of its vitality and value today.

The justifications for torture all presuppose the efficacy of torture as compared with traditional, nonabusive methods of interrogation – a conclusion reached without the slightest discussion or empirical proof. The abuse and torture of detainees at Guantánamo Bay provides an illuminating example on two levels: despite the abuse to which the detainees there were subjected, the consensus among intelligence, military, and criminal investigators is that the intelligence gathered from the Guantánamo Bay detainees has been minimal and of little value. That appraisal has been echoed by recently released FBI reports, which note that the FBI objected to coercive interrogation methods as ineffective and unreliable, and steadfastly adhered to its "rapport-based" system of interrogation, and its benefits with respect to accuracy and completeness.

Surely if there were some benefit from the torture practiced at Guantánamo Bay, the government would have announced it widely. Yet the government has not pointed to a single piece of information gleaned from the Guantánamo Bay detainees – and the response that such intelligence is classified is merely an excuse to hide behind, since the government has regularly leaked the information it has received from detainees in other locations (*i.e.*, from Khalid Sheikh Mohamed) – that has been useful in the war against terrorism.

In addition, the information the government obtained via torture at Guantánamo Bay has often proved *un*reliable. For example, the three British detainees (known colloquially as "the Tipton Three") released during the summer of 2004 had, while at Guantánamo Bay and in response to maltreatment by interrogators, "confessed" to appearing in a video with Usama bin Laden in Afghanistan. However, it was later indisputably established by British intelligence that all three were in fact in Great Britain at the time the video was recorded. So much for life-saving information. Also, as the 9/11 Commission Report confides, even coercive interrogation methods have not yielded complete information from detainees with respect to the identity of confederates and operations they have thus far declined to reveal.

In fact, the most useful information gleaned from al Qaeda captives has been through conventional intelligence and law enforcement methods. The first al Qaeda informant, whose version, encompassed within his testimony at the embassy bombings trial, serves as the foundation for much of the historical information in the 9/11 Commission Report, was a "walk-in" to a U.S. embassy in a foreign country. Another valuable source was lured by a classic intelligence sting (not conducted by the United States). Ironically, a third comprehensive confession was obtained because the suspect chose to speak to U.S. officials – without a lawyer – rather than submit to Kenyan authorities *with a lawyer*. Why? Because he knew that he would be beaten and abused by the Kenyans, and preferred to talk to the United States in order to *avoid* physical abuse. Of course, that confession might never have been obtained if that suspect had not possessed the confidence that the United States would not engage in torture. Thus, the departure from humane standards could very well impair intelligence-gathering and scare off potential informants.

Moreover, unacceptable and unsound methods of interrogation have caused the United States to forfeit criminal or other prosecution of persons it has deemed extremely dangerous. For example, the government acknowledged that the information it gleaned from Jose Padilla, declared an "enemy combatant" and subjected to uncounseled, incommunicado interrogation, would not be admissible in court proceedings, and that it could not prosecute Mr. Padilla as a result. Certainly statements obtained by physical torture would fare no better, and would similarly preclude prosecution and punishment of those who may very well merit both.

Nevertheless, those who constructed the United States' policy appear not to have considered these potential adverse consequences. By rejecting contributions from all elements of the government, and insisting on unilateralism instead, the government suffered the usual effects of such myopia and deliberately limited perspective: poor judgment, poor decision-making, and poor (even non-existent) contingency planning.

Despite these negative ramifications – and aside from the pure legal and moral wrongheadedness of the policy – none of those officials who participated in formulating and approving the government's policy on torture have suffered any sanction at all, in stark contrast to the discipline meted out to those who have had the misfortune of being responsible for the hands-on implementation of the policy and the culture it has bred. Instead, those who fashioned the policy have been appointed to the judiciary, elevated to other governmental positions, or found safe haven in academia.

Yet, some form of penalty is imperative if policy-makers are to be discouraged and dissuaded from future forays into such unsavory territory. Otherwise, it is a no-lose proposition for those who engage in contriving legal justifications for repugnant policies. Absent sanctions, they continue until they are discovered, all the while enjoying the fruits of their illegitimate conduct, whether it be in the form of coerced statements that have been used to justify the continued detention of hundreds of detainees at Guantánamo Bay, or the policy-makers' own career paths, which remain unimpeded by critical analysis from their peers or the public.

Indeed, any claim of good faith – that those who formulated the policies were merely misguided in their pursuit of security in the face of what is certainly a genuine terrorist threat – is belied by the policy makers' more than tacit acknowledgment of their unlawful purpose, which appears in writing in the December 28, 2001 memo analyzing whether the United States or any other court could exercise jurisdiction over the detainees if they were confined at Guantánamo Bay. Otherwise, why the need to find a location that is, Guantánamo Bay, purportedly outside the jurisdiction of the United States (or any other) court? Why the need to ensure those participating that they could proceed free of concern that they could face prosecution for war crimes as a result of their adherence to the policy? After all, if you intend to make a legitimate withdrawal from a bank, you do not need a getaway car at the ready. Rarely, if ever, has such a guilty governmental conscience been so starkly illuminated in advance.

That, of course, begs the question: what was it that these officials, lawyers, and lay persons feared from the federal courts? An independent judiciary? A legitimate, legislated, established system of justice designed to promote fairness and accuracy? The Uniform Code of Military Justice, which governs courts-martial and authorizes military commissions? The message that the government memoranda convey in response is unmistakable: these policy makers do not like our system of justice, with its checks and balances, and rights and limits, that they have been sworn to uphold. That antipathy for and distrust of our civilian and military justice systems is positively unAmerican.

Nonetheless, these architects of the torture policy, having retreated into academia, or ascended the rungs of the ladder of government, occupy important positions within American institutions that their policy so wantonly betrayed. In considering the appropriate outcome, perhaps it should start where the policymakers left off: they should be compelled to watch the application of "aggressive interrogation" techniques or "counter-resistance" measures on a human subject, or, better yet, perform such techniques themselves – or, even better still, be subjected to them.

Perhaps that would herald the arrival of a new government lawyer "Golden Rule": formulate policy unto others as you would have others *implement* unto you. Ultimately, though, whether torture is appropriate is not only a question of politics or law or professional disincentives, but also of morality and values. Long after Sir Thomas More articulated the concept in rich prose, an American statesman, George F. Kennan, a Cold War veteran who died March 17, 2005, at age 101, echoed the principle in a February 22, 1946, telegram regarding his evaluation of the Soviet and communist threat:

> Finally, we must have the courage and self-confidence to cling to our own methods and conceptions of human society. [T]he greatest danger that can befall us in coping with this problem of Soviet communism, is that we shall allow ourselves to become like those with whom we are coping.

Kennan's, and More's, analysis has proved not only cogent and durable, but prescient as well. As we contemplate and implement methods of meeting and conquering the threat posed by international terrorism, we must always be mindful of what differentiates us from the terrorists, and careful to safeguard those principles not only in word but in deed. Only fidelity to that doctrine will assure us that we are fighting for something worth preserving.

NOTE

1. Acting Assistant Attorney General Daniel Levin, December 30, 2004 Memorandum to Deputy Attorney General James B. Comey, in this volume, p. 361.

5 Is Defiance of Law a Proof of Success? Magical Thinking in the War on Terror

Stephen Holmes

"Are we litigating this war or fighting it?"
– interrogator with U.S. forces in Baghdad[1]

THE WAR ON TERROR HAS DISPLACED THE COLD WAR AS THE DEFINING framework of U.S. foreign and domestic policy. An ironic consequence is that the most infamous penal colony in a Communist country is now located at Guantánamo Bay Naval Base. We have come a long way since Solzhenitsyn. To Cuba, it turns out, the United States has spread not the blessings of liberty but the rule of manacles, stress positions, cages, and hoods. And Guantánamo Bay is merely one internment facility in a worldwide archipelago of U.S.-administered detention centers where terrorists, real and alleged, are incarcerated with little or no access to the outside world. Legal responsibility for what happens in these camps remains uncertain. But inside them detainees have been, and apparently continue to be, interrogated in a cruel, inhumane and degrading manner. We know that at least twenty or thirty prisoners have died in captivity, apparently from wounds inflicted by their American jailers. The sordid details have been widely publicized. Less evident are the reasons why the U.S. government has created such a system. The most paradoxical justification for what would otherwise be an odious violation of America's system of values is that such behavior alone makes it possible to protect America's system of values.

LAWYERS FOR TORTURE

To inflict what amounts to punishment on suspects before establishing their guilt through some sort of minimally fair judicial process seems contrary to the basic principles of the rule of law. But it is perfectly in tune with the general counter-terrorism policy of the current administration. Cruel interrogation techniques are certainly no more incompatible with ordinary principles of legality than the policy of extrajudicial executions. Today, U.S. officers, operating clandestinely around the world, are apparently licensed to kill suspected al Qaeda members (and others in the vicinity) on the basis of fragmentary evidence and uncorroborated hearsay. If U.S. agents, without criminal liability, can *kill* possibly innocent suspects, then it is not surprising that U.S. agents can also, shielded from judicial scrutiny, subject possibly innocent suspects to "extreme interrogation," verging on torture.

True, neither policy seems particularly compatible with "liberty and justice for all." To explain why such deviations from liberal practice are permitted, or even required, lawyers have been put to work. Their job has been to lend such policies a patina of respectability. Since ancient times, in fact, legal minds have proved willing to provide technically-refined justifications for the carefully dosed infliction of pain as a method for extracting information.[2] Whether or not lawyers have played a decisive role in introducing torture, they have historically helped deflect human compassion from victims of the practice. In late medieval and early modern Europe, doctors of law seem universally to have endorsed excruciating inquisitorial procedures as but one more versatile tool inherited from Roman Law.[3] Legal experts and scholars praised interlocutory torture, not only as an efficacious technique for compelling confession but also as a hard-to-resist way of coaxing suspects into betraying the identity of their accomplices. Evidence elicited by water torture, simulating the feeling of drowning up to the moment when the subject loses consciousness, was long said to be especially suitable for use in court to demonstrate guilt. But lawyers have not always been satisfied with their role as unprincipled servants of power, concocting ingenious justifications to lend an aroma of decorum to the schemes of the powerful. They have therefore occasionally added, with a flash of conscience, that torture, while legitimate in principle, should be applied only "as the due measure of well-regulated reason requires."[4]

What exactly does "reason" require in this domain of moans and screams? Attempting to establish when torture should and should not be used, legal thinkers have devoted themselves through the centuries to manufacturing subtle distinctions. According to Edward Gibbon, the selective embrace of the practice, in Rome, reflected an implicit disquiet:

> The deceitful and dangerous experiment of the criminal *quæstion*, as it is emphatically styled, was admitted rather than approved, in the jurisprudence of the Romans. They applied this sanguinary mode of examination only to servile bodies, whose sufferings were seldom weighed by those haughty republicans in the scale of justice or humanity; but they would never consent to violate the sacred person of a citizen till they possessed the clearest evidence of his guilt.[5]

The main point to take away from this passage is that, when it comes to rationalizing torture, lawyering has traditionally involved muffling unease by drawing distinctions to prevent terrifying policies from hitting too close to home. This tradition is very much alive.

Already in antiquity, the laws in force laid down boundaries between people who could be tortured, without any qualms, and others, the privileged, who were ordinarily exempt from judicially inflicted torments. Above all, aliens were treated more brutally than citizens. The worst cruelties were ordinarily reserved for "the other." In ancient Athens, for instance, inquiry by torture (*basanos*) was used under specified conditions, to extort evidence from slaves, but applied to citizens, if at all, only in cases of high treason. The Roman practice discussed by Gibbon was similar. From the outset, therefore, interlocutory torture was applied in a "republican" manner, with proper respect for the sensibilities and solidarities of citizens. It was also a rule-governed activity. The rules in question were many and evolved over time. A common maxim was that torturers should not to pose leading questions to those being tortured. Such guidelines were presumably set forth because spontaneous abuses, such as suggestive questioning, endangered the reliability of coerced confessions. But did apologists for torture really believe that truth could be extracted, like a rotten tooth, with a pair of pliers?

RELIABILITY ON TRIAL

Artfully crafted justifications or rationalizations of torture were met, from the very beginning, by tentative objections and counter-arguments. Although no rebel against Greek legal practice, Aristotle set forth very clearly what were to become the standard criticisms of a practice that was commonly condoned: "those under compulsion are as likely to give false evidence as true, some being ready to endure everything rather than tell the truth, while others are equally ready to make false charges against others, in the hope of being sooner released from torture."[6] The unreliability of testimony extracted under duress, even today, remains one of the most commonly invoked arguments against torture. Multiple allegations of false confession at Guantánamo, some of them now definitively confirmed, make it interesting to consider how Aristotle spelled out his hesitations: "It may also be said that evidence given under torture is not true; for many thick-witted and thick-skinned persons, and those who are stout-hearted heroically hold out under sufferings, while the cowardly and cautious, before they see the sufferings before them, are bold enough." Once they are actually facing torture, some subset of prisoners would lose their audacity and choose to confess to crimes they did not actually commit. "Wherefore," Aristotle concludes, "evidence from torture may be considered utterly untrustworthy."[7]

Torture's willing advocates, needless to say, took a much more "optimistic" line. They argued that extreme physical pain, artfully applied, will take away the examinee's freedom to keep secrets and withhold the truth. This "de-liberation" (or removal of free will) no doubt bore fruit some of the time. But the implicit theory that truth could be hauled out of an individual by physical violence was never without serious critics. One of them was Cicero, whose doubts about torture seem to build directly upon Aristotle's: "the course of examination under torture is steered by pain, is controlled by individual qualities of mind and body, is directed by the president of the court, is diverted by caprice, tainted by hope, invalidated by fear, and the result is that in all these straits there is no room left for the truth."[8] The turbulence and numbness injected into the interrogated individual's consciousness by intense bodily agony, combined with the inevitable partisan agendas of the all-too-human administrators of pain, may easily obscure rather than illuminate the facts of the case under examination.

As a servant of the law, he too accepted the admission at trial of evidence extracted by torture. But the Roman jurist Ulpian (d. 228) could not entirely ignore such compelling doubts: "It is stated in constitutions that reliance should not always be placed on torture...for it is a chancy and risky business and one which may be deceptive. For there are a number of people who, by their endurance and their toughness under torture, are so contemptuous of it that the truth can in no way be squeezed out of them. Others have so little endurance that they would rather tell any kind of lie than suffer torture; so it happens that they confess in various ways, incriminating not only themselves but others also."[9] So here again torture is presented as a trustworthy technique for probing endurance, but an unreliable method for establishing veracity.

Two centuries later, this time with a religious twist, Augustine recited these same doubts. He acknowledged that "the accused are often overcome by the pain of torture and so make false confessions and are punished, though innocent." In a vein that is distressingly pertinent to U.S. interrogation practice today, he went on to say: "although not condemned to death, they often die under torture or as a consequence of torture." True justice would be possible only if judges could peer directly into the minds of both accusers and accused to see who was lying and who was telling the truth. But judges are no more clairvoyant than other men. The truth of any criminal accusation, therefore, remains ultimately inscrutable even to the most discerning judge. Because human justice will always involve a fumbling in the dark, the city of man will never resemble the city of God.

Human law, nevertheless, instructs judges to try to ferret out the hidden truth by inflicting painful torments on witnesses as well as on the accused. But, Augustine laments, the rude means provided are wholly inadequate to the ideal end being pursued. Torture does *not* give the judge a privileged access to the innermost thoughts of those being tortured, for all of the reasons cited above, but especially because people will generally tell any untruth to make the torture stop. As a result, "the ignorance of the judge generally results in the calamity of the innocent." Christian judges must therefore pray to God to deliver them from the unbearable burdens of this miserable life, which obliges them to engage in torture, a calamitous practice that inevitably confounds the innocent with the guilty. Judicial torture is not technically a "sin," he concludes. But it is sickening enough to make any honorable judge feel morally unworthy and even to pray to escape from this vale of tears.[10]

By the sixteenth century these classical doubts about the reliability of testimony extracted via torture began to mature into a straightforward rejection of the practice. A fine example is Montaigne who repeated the ancient themes but this time from the point of view of someone expecting the practice to be abolished: "Torture is a dangerous innovation; it would appear that it is an assay not of truth but of a man's endurance. The man who can endure it hides the truth, so does he who cannot. For why should pain make me confess what is true rather than force me to say what is not true?"[11] In the seventeenth century, with even bitterer irony, La Bruyère reiterated that torture tests stamina not truthfulness: "The rack is a marvelous invention, and an unfailing method of ruining an innocent weakly man and saving one who is robust and guilty."[12] And, finally, in the eighteenth century, Blackstone expressed a growing scorn for interlocutory torture, accusing its advocates of "rating a man's virtue by the hardiness of his constitution, and his guilt by the sensibility of his nerves!"[13]

Most of the perennial dissatisfactions with interlocutory torture were transformed into a morally self-assured assault on the practice by Cesare Beccaria in his immensely influential treatise *On Crimes and Punishments* (1764). Beccaria's principal moral concern, which had been Augustine's and which remains alive today, is "the risk of torturing an innocent person."[14] Torture is randomly applied punishment, Beccaria argued. Such inflicting of penalties on mere suspects, before they are convicted of any crime, can be justified only by the corrosively antilegal principle that *might is right.*

It is absurd to make physical pain into "the crucible of truth," Beccaria explained.[15] The reason is simple: "the impression of pain may become so great that, filling the entire sensory capacity of the tortured person, it leaves him free only to choose what for the moment is the shortest way to escape from pain."[16] This is why, in all countries and in all ages, innocent people have confessed to crimes they did not commit. Beccaria's argument continues in a familiar vein. Far from being a reliable method for distinguishing the guilty from the innocent, he says, torture is better suited for helping the strong and hurting the weak. In practice, torture undermines the interrogator's capacity to distinguish between guilt and innocence, one proof being the plentiful (false) confessions to witchcraft extracted, in early modern Europe, by ingenious torments. The very same dynamic makes Beccaria doubt the veracity of testimony about accomplices extracted under torture: "As if a man who accuses himself would not more readily accuse others."[17]

Beccaria also mentions, more originally, the way in which interlocutory torture made tell-tale body language unintentionally illegible. Intelligent interrogators who are prohibited from inflicting physical agony during interrogation can sometimes read the body language of suspects to determine if they are lying or telling the truth. This is why physical torments ordinarily result in a loss of information. Subtle signals disappear when torture is employed to unearth truth: "if this truth is difficult to discover in the air, gesture, and countenance of a man at ease, much more difficult will its discovery be when the convulsions of pain have distorted all the signs by which truth reveals itself in spite of themselves in the countenances of the majority of men."[18]

Legal acceptance of torture, finally, creates a perverse incentive for interrogators. This is why a policy of torture tends to weaken the system of criminal justice in the long run, even if a single act of torture can turn up a useful piece of evidence. If they are *not* allowed to torture witnesses and suspects, interrogators have an incentive to search for evidence elsewhere or to develop alternative information-extracting skills. (In the case of U.S. interrogators at Guantánamo Bay and elsewhere, such useful skills might include, for example, mastery of relevant foreign languages.) If torture is allowed, by contrast, interrogators will have less motivation to develop more refined and conceivably more effective methods of seeking and establishing the truth.

Legalization effectively creates a self-justifying and self-perpetuating system of interlocutory torture. It discourages interrogators from seeking better evidence and honing their skills. It discourages supervisors from increasing the size and talent of their staff. Interrogators who have failed to acquire nonviolent skills can then "justify" their resort to torture by alleging, with superficial plausibility, that torture is the only method available to them for wringing information out of non-cooperating detainees. Although logically worthless, this justification is apparently both rhetorically effective and psychologically comforting.

ALTERNATIVES AND SIDE-EFFECTS

To know if torture is justified or not we must know more than whether or not "it works." Even if it were a totally reliable method for extracting information, contrary to classical case against the practice detailed by numerous writers including those cited above, torture might still be morally unjustifiable. In facing down Chechen terrorists, for instance, Moscow has sometimes adopted the posture that the best way to kill a few cockroaches is to burn down the apartment complex in which they were last seen scurrying about. This technique "works" in the sense that any terrorists trapped in collapsed and incinerated buildings are likely to be dead. But the achievement of such a desirable goal does not put a quietus to the question: Was the operation, conducted in this devastating way, with this massive amount of collateral damage, justified or not? Was the game worth the candle? What were the opportunity costs, and were they worth paying?

In the case of "successful" torture, in particular, we have to ask two further questions. First, could we have obtained the information we needed by other means, not involving physical torture of a defenseless detainee? Could we have learned virtually everything that the tortured prisoner confessed, simply by asking a U.S. official from a different agency who was sitting in an office elsewhere in the same facility? Could we have acquired the same information by less cruel methods, for example, by developing a rapport with the prisoner or offering him modest inducements? If it turns out that alternative techniques are just as effective as torture and just as easily available, then we cannot confidently say that the torture was justifiable even if, viewed in isolation, it "worked."

Montesquieu pressed this point in a famous passage in the *Spirit of the Laws* (1748). Proof that torture is not a necessary institution, he wrote, was provided by England, where criminal justice functioned perfectly well even though torture there was virtually unknown: "We have before us the example of a nation blessed with an excellent civil government, where without any inconvenience the practice of racking criminals is rejected. It is not, therefore, in its own nature necessary."[19] If judicial inquiry without torture works just as well as judicial inquiry with torture, then the observed utility of torture, to which its advocates point with pride, does not suffice to prove that it is legitimate or desirable.

Even if the practice of inquisitorial torture occasionally bears fruit, we must also examine its predictable side effects. Today, for example, we can ask: What will be the long-term effects on American political sensibilities, of normalizing torture as a means for increasing national security? What does it mean for America's attempt to "spread liberty" throughout the world if the United States is curtailing "liberty," at home and abroad, to increase security and defeat the enemy? Is the United States spreading liberty or curtailing it? How are the two projects related to each other? This mixed message is certainly confusing. Those concerned with American public diplomacy might want to know which part of it has been more forcefully conveyed.

Torture's effect on individuals is more concrete and less controversial. The searing psychic wounds and physical disabilities of individuals who have survived torture are difficult to heal. The scars of humiliation left by torture tend to endure for years, since it may be impossible to remember the experience of being tortured without vividly *reliving* the degradation. The moral-emotional effect on the individuals who do the torturing, of course, must also be taken into account. These breakers of men have triumphed over defenseless captives by inflicting intolerable pain. Their latent sadism was no doubt awakened by their freedom to abuse the helpless. They no doubt learn to compartmentalize. Their capacity for human sympathy and compassion for the weak must also have shriveled. Unlike soldiers on the battlefield, they did not expose themselves to any physical danger in order to confront their purported enemy. What is the likely result? Perhaps their sense of personal power became pathologically inflated. Perhaps they will return home depraved and disturbed? All this is uncertain, but it is interesting to note that America's interrogators in the war on terror were assured by their superiors that torture (that is, treating captives as less than human) was not only permissible but was noble and patriotic.

Finally, we need to consider the effect of the United States' embrace of cruel and inhuman interrogation techniques on the country's reputation abroad. We might recall, in this context, that one of the principal charges leveled against the Nazi war criminals at Nuremberg was the following: "Civilians were systematically subjected to tortures of all kinds, *with the object of obtaining information*" (my emphasis).[20] And the indictment continues: "Civilians of occupied countries were subjected systematically to 'protective arrests' whereby they were arrested and imprisoned without any trial and any of the ordinary protections of law."[21] One does not have to accept a wildly implausible comparison of Bush administration policy to the policy of the Nazis to realize that a public embrace of imprisonment without due process and coercive interrogation will further erode America's dying good name in the world. What are the concrete and practical consequences of this blemished reputation? How will it affect the number and quality of detainees that come into U.S. custody? How will it affect the inquisitorial practice of other nations? How will it affect the treatment of captured U.S. troops (including special forces who travel in combat zones without distinguishing military insignia)? It may well be that if we add up all of the negative side-effects of a policy of interlocutory torture, we will discover that, yes, torture occasionally "works," but that any short-term gain is nevertheless far outweighed by long-term losses.

It is remarkable that the handful of U.S. lawyers and law professors who, perhaps from partisan passion, have justified the practice of torture frequently linger over the claim that "it works," as if this consideration sufficed to put our critical faculties to sleep. Their failure to explore the available alternatives to torture and its likely side-effects is disturbing. Their assurance that inhumane and degrading interrogation will pacify potential enemies rather than radicalize them is presumptuous and wrong. So how can the untroubled consciences of torture's legal apologists be explained?

AN EMERGENCY POWER?

Classic arguments against resort to torture, even during national emergencies, are not iron-clad. But they are strong enough to warrant careful consideration. Some false confessions under torture are inevitable because "the sensitive innocent man will ... confess himself guilty when he believes that, by so doing, he can put an end to his torment."[22] Keeping open the torture option reduces the incentives for investigators to develop skills that might prove more effective in the long-run. A reputation for torture makes it less likely that investigators will get useful informants into their custody, and so forth. Many of these objections have been well-known for over two millennia. But they seem to have made little or no impression at all on the legal defenders of current U.S. policy about coercive interrogation. Why not?

Why is the United States continuing to send detainees to countries where they are certain to be tortured? Why are our military and intelligence officers presiding over grave-like "dungeons" across the globe where captives can disappear without a trace? Why is the United States itself engaged in interrogation practices designed to destroy the dignity and dismantle the personalities of possibly

innocent prisoners? Why have twenty or thirty individuals, of unknown culpabil-
ity, expired under U.S. interrogation? Are we really involved in such an unsavory
business because we *have* to be? Are such despicable practices truly necessary?
Would a refusal to do these things, which are repugnant and dishonorable, make
the country measurably less safe?

Lawyers have abetted these controversial policies in a number of ways. They
have identified loopholes in treaties and legislation, in an attempt to make highly
coercive and sexually humiliating interrogation seem less patently illegal than had
previously been believed. They have tried to develop defenses against criminal
and civil liability for supervisors and perpetrators involved in harsh and demean-
ing treatment of detainees. Above all, they have stressed the way national security, the unprecedented threat of terrorism and the Commander-in-Chief power
can be woven together into an all-purpose excuse for executive-branch activities, including inhumane interrogation, which would ordinarily be banned and
forbidden.

They have justified and rationalized brutally coercive questioning techniques,
including near suffocation. But the lawyers may not have played a decisive role
in initiating such policies. If the excuses were legal, the decisions were political.
The political motivation for the policy can in no way be inferred from the legal
justifications set forth. This is apparent from the famous torture memos themselves. The principal "legal" argument for highly coercive interrogation has been
that, in some settings, law simply does not apply. The lawyers who advanced this
claim, in other words, accepted the liberal view that torture is completely incompatible with the American system of criminal justice. From this they concluded
not that torture must be banned but rather that the American system of criminal
justice must be, for some purposes, set aside. In the current crisis, that is to say,
ordinary restrictions on executive-branch discretion must be temporarily lifted.
This is a very old story. Historically, even the most fastidious adherents of the
rule of law have excused, or at least understood, its breach in times of grave
crisis. In the late 16th century, for instance, England was faced with a serious
foreign threat from Spain. In this situation, even Blackstone acknowledged that
the "rack for torture," otherwise alien to English traditions, "was occasionally
used as an engine of state, not of law."[23]

This is a telling phrase. *Torture is an engine of state, not of law.* It is a "naked"
exercise of state power, whose victims, strangely enough, are often naked in a
nonmetaphorical sense. Harsh interrogation is an extra-legal tool, wielded by
political rulers, outside the ordinary system of legality, without the involvement
of judges and courts, to defend the political order from lethal enemies conspiring
to destroy it. Public safety trumps legalism and even constitutionality. This is
essentially the position taken by most of the legal professionals who continue
to defend the use of highly coercive interrogation in the war on terror. In this
conflict, they say, the executive branch cannot afford to fight with one hand
tied behind its back. It must therefore shed all ordinary restrictions, domestic

and international, upon the way it behaves, including especially the way it treats foreign prisoners held overseas. To gain the flexibility it needs to meet the lethal threat of transnational terrorism, the executive branch needs to suspend the rule of law, whenever it thinks that it is an obstacle, so long as the conflict endures.

This view is debatable, but it is not without some basis in reality. For instance, the legalistic requirement to ask permission of a judge is said to have prevented the FBI from examining Zaccarias Moussaui's computer. If they had examined the computer, FBI agents might conceivably have been able to foil the 9/11 conspiracy. Indirectly, therefore, judicial oversight of executive action increased the country's vulnerability to terrorism. Whatever the merits of this particular story, it exemplifies the way in which law and legalism can sometimes interfere with national security.

But do such incidents imply that the United States can successfully fight the war on terror only by abandoning due process? Critics of the administration vehemently disagree. To illustrate the way enemy prisoners can be given due process without compromising U.S. security, they sometimes mention the way the United States treated the Nazis at Nuremberg. As one reporter put it at the time: "in the courtroom at Nuremberg something more important is happening than the trial of a few captured prisoners. The inhuman is being confronted with the humane, ruthlessness with equity, lawlessness with patient justice, and barbarism with civilization."[24] This sounds noble enough. But, of course, those today who deny that the Bill of Rights and international covenants against torture are appropriate tools for confronting terrorism have a ready reply. The Nuremberg Trials occurred *after* World War II, they remind us, when the Nazi threat was already a thing of the past. We are not in that position today. The attack of 9/11 was only one episode in an ongoing war. We must therefore behave not like we did at Nuremberg, but rather as we did (around the same time) at Nagasaki. To respond to the savages who want to kill us, we must cast off our Christian-liberal meekness and embrace a "healthy savagery" of our own. We must confront ruthlessness with ruthlessness. We must pull out all the stops. After victory we will have plenty of time for civility, guilt feelings, and the rule of law.

THE SECRET OF THE TICKING BOMB

Academic commentaries on this controversy operate on a higher level of abstraction. They stress the way in which ordinary moral and legal prohibitions must sometimes be cast aside in order to meet a looming threat. The question of how to treat a prisoner who knows the whereabouts of a ticking time-bomb is commonly debated in this context. The stakes in the case are easily escalated by making the bomb into a nuclear devise. Although neither realistic nor representative, the hypothetical is nevertheless revealing. For one thing, the idea that the authorities might get a dangerous terrorist into their custody, after he has planned an attack but before he has executed it, is a utopian fantasy. The elusiveness of these criminal conspirators is intensely frustrating and naturally gives rise, among counter-terrorism officials, to daydreams of superman-style rescues. To set policies on the basis of such far-fetched scenarios would be folly.

The ticking bomb parable is also interesting for another reason. It makes the legitimacy of torture depend wholly on its future consequences, namely, on the prevention of grave harm. In this way, it tracks perfectly the thinking of administration lawyers and apologists. With its focus on the future, the hypothetical reveals the limited relevance of most historical debates about torture, which assumed that torture was justified or not depending on how useful it proved in uncovering reliable evidence of guilt for past crimes. The ground has now thoroughly shifted. Torture is morally justifiable, or will at least be publicly accepted, if it helps save a major urban center from Armageddon.

The ticking time-bomb fable also suggests the *quiet heroism* of those who, defying moral norms and legal conventions, choose torture. They sacrifice their scruples for the greater good. They follow the ethics of responsibility instead of the ethics of conscience. Those who torture (or approve the torture of) prisoners, according to the implicit storyline, are protecting their fellow Americans from mass death by nuclear incineration. No causal chain need be demonstrated in any particular case. Instead, the ticking time-bomb parable creates a presumption. What seemed illegitimate, because it yielded dubious confessions, now seems legitimate because it provides a ray of hope in a dark and dangerous world. And the once-scorned torturer now appears as a potential savior. This torturer/savior fusion does not seem all that remote from the self-image of those who support the current U.S. policies of harsh interrogation. This heroic self-image seems pervasive even though none of the prisoner abuse in Abu Ghraib, for example, could have contributed in any way to the safety of Americans back home.

So what is the most important implication of the ticking time-bomb parable? It is, quite simply, the insinuation, without evidence or argument, of an intimate connection between torture and terrorism. In the imaginary scenario, in fact, torture is the *only possible response* to terrorism. The suggestion is subliminal, to some extent. No *reasons* are given to explain why, faced with terrorism, the United States should resort to torture. But the correlation comes through loud and clear. So what should we make of such associational thinking?

To understand why torture might be thought to be an appropriate response to terrorism, it helps to look briefly at how the U.S. administration understands terrorism. The main points to stress are these: First, terrorism is an attack upon symbolic targets, aimed at displaying the attackers' power and the victims' impotence. Second, terrorism kills innocent civilians for the purpose of intimidation and to send a political message. And, third, terrorism is completely inexcusable.

Let us begin with this last point. Colin Powell is speaking for everyone when he says: "There can be no political justification [for terrorism]. There is no religious justification." And "the kind of evil and terror that we saw perpetrated against us three years ago on 9/11 ... must be fought. It must be resisted. There can be no compromise in this battle."[25] What is most interesting about the *absolutist* claim that terrorism admits of no justification is the way it is echoed, in international law, by the *absolutist* claim that torture admits of no justification. For instance: "No exceptional circumstances whatsoever, whether a state of war or a threat of war, internal instability or any other public emergency, may be invoked as a justification of torture."[26]

MIRROR-IMAGING

According to the consensus view of international law, neither terrorism nor torture can be justified, no matter how extreme the circumstances or how desperate the cause. The prohibition on both terrorism and torture is equally absolute, unambiguous, and final. The parallelism here may provide a clue to the unexplained choice of inhumane interrogation techniques by the American government and its approval after the fact by American voters. One of the greatest shocks to American liberals was that "The system of torture has, after all, survived its disclosure."[27] But why has the American public not been mortified or disillusioned by the revelations from Abu Ghraib? Historically, torture has sometimes turned a public violently against the policies of their government. For instance, "it was the very use of torture that in the end convinced most French people that the cause of Algérie-Française was not worth the enormous strain that it was placing on the societal fabric."[28] But this has not (or not yet) occurred in the United States. Why not? One possible answer is that the American public is prepared to accept any conceivable treatment of Arabs, including the torture of innocents unto death, so long such behavior is presented to them as a response to 9/11. We are facing a "new enemy" and must throw the old rules overboard.

Abuse of prisoners has proven politically acceptable in the United States, on this theory, not because, although shameful, it is especially useful in the war on terror. The absence of any metrics of success or failure in the war on terror is by now a commonplace. So the utility of torture cannot, whatever administration lawyers want us to believe, be invoked in its defense. Instead, harsh and humiliating interrogation may have been embraced by the public because it is widely perceived as an "appropriate" response. The 9/11 hijackers violated an absolute prohibition. What possible reaction could be adequate to what they did? A response that trespasses on equally sacred ground.

The absolute prohibition against torture, according to this line of argument, was not a legalistic obstacle to be swept aside to achieve important strategic aims (such as the extraction of timely information about future threats). On the contrary, the absolute prohibition provides an independent reason for resorting to torture. Because it violates an absolute prohibition, torture sends a message that there is nothing the United States is not willing to do. This is fairly close to the message sent by the 9/11 attack itself. To respond in kind the United States had to engage in behavior that was as universally condemned as terrorism against civilians. Overthrowing the Taliban was widely approved and therefore could not serve to convey America's audacity, ferocity, and readiness to throw away the rule book. Invading Iraq, a country that had nothing to do with 9/11, was a good start. But the inhumane and degrading treatment of randomly assembled prisoners was also very well suited to send this message.

Rules for the humane treatment of prisoners during wartime are based on expectations of reciprocity. One side treats its enemy captives humanely in the expectation that the enemy will treat its captive soldiers in the same way. This sort of reciprocity cannot be expected in the war on terror. Not only is al Qaeda not a "state party" to any of the international conventions concerning POWs. But al Qaeda is more of a network than an organization and is unlikely to have sufficient command-and-control powers to enforce any rules upon its far-flung and unruly operatives.

But if we cannot have this sort of civilized reciprocity with our new global enemy, what sort of reciprocity can we have? The answer is *uncivilized* reciprocity, and that means: a return to the original form of reciprocity, namely revenge. We can respond to their lawlessness with our own lawlessness. If they have renounced the laws of civilization, so will we. If they organized a sneak attack, then we will respond with a dirty war. If they terrorized us, we will terrorize them. If they symbolically humiliated us, we will symbolically humiliate them. If they desecrated our skyline, we will desecrate theirs. If they gloated about our dead, we will smile over their cadavers packed in ice. If they killed randomly assembled civilians, we will do the same in response. If they showed the world that their young warriors were willing to die for their cause, we will show the world that our young warriors are willing to do the same.

This attempt to explain America's anomalous torture policy is obviously speculative. The suggestion that torture has proved publicly acceptable because it is widely seen as a form of primitive reciprocity or "equivalent" response is no doubt difficult to prove. But it nevertheless seems a profitable line of research. A similar hypothesis about the motives behind administration policy is advanced by William Pfaff. He claims that "the Bush administration is not torturing prisoners because it is useful but because of symbolism,"[29] not because of the information that torture reveals, but because of the message that torture sends. Twenty years ago, Elaine Scarry provided slightly different, but perfectly compatible, view of the subject, arguing that "torture is a grotesque piece of compensatory drama,"[30] meaning that the brutal treatment of defenseless prisoners is common not because it provides vital clues but rather because it allows the torturing individuals or groups to see their own power mirrored in the torment of those they torture. It is the kind of behavior to be expected when people need to reassure themselves about their dominance after it has been called into question: "It is, of course, precisely because the reality of that power is so highly contestable, the regime is so unstable, that torture is being used."[31]

The claim that torture is meant to intimidate the victims' community and reassure the community of the perpetrators cannot be easily verified or falsified. But it certainly makes more sense of the observable facts than the principal alternative, namely that torture was employed and has proved acceptable because of its utility in extracting information necessary to prevent future calamities. The administration's defenders are unmoved by the numerous arguments against the *utility* of coercive interrogation because they are not really focused on the information extracted by these methods. (Compared to the French in Algeria or the Israelis in the West Bank and Gaza, the Americans at Abu Ghraib and Guantánamo Bay may have too little background knowledge to make much sense of the fragmentary information disgorged during harsh interrogations.) They may prize the cruel, inhumane, and degrading treatment of prisoners precisely *because* it violates international norms and the rules of war. Psychologically persuasive evidence that a medicine is effective is that it tastes unbearably foul. What this analogy suggests is that torture is more of a magical-emotional than a rational-strategic response to 9/11.

The debate between the opponents and defenders of U.S. torture policy, in fact, may be much more subtle, and psychologically twisted, than meets the eye. Those who oppose torture say that torture is illegal and does not work. Those who defend torture imply that torture is valuable, even if it does not work, *precisely because it defies the law.* Such magical thinking would help explain the otherwise inexplicable indifference of torture's apologists to the practice's less brutal alternatives and undesirable side-effects. As the violation of an absolute prohibition, torture sends a message about American determination, ruthless-ness, and willingness to act without asking permission or making excuses. By defying civilized conventions, the torturing authority shows its public, in an eye-catching way, that it is leaving no stone unturned. How else could it get this message across? But the underlying logic may even be less rational than this makes it seem. It is at least conceivable that the defenders of torture embrace the practice because they themselves have no other way to measure success in the war on terror. They may not know what works, but they know that torture shocks the conscience of mankind and may *therefore* infer that it is a fitting response to 9/11.

If this interpretation has any validity, then torture is not undertaken and accepted because it prevents specific harms. It is undertaken and accepted, rather, because it seems "adequate" to the harm that was done to us. An extreme injury requires an extreme remedy. George W. Bush may even have been re-elected, in part, because he was widely perceived as having fewer scruples than his oppo-nent and therefore as being more willing to give the terrorists a taste of their own medicine. With their brows furrowed over Vietnam, Democrats risk making Americans feel guilty about defending themselves ferociously in an increasingly dangerous world. Not so the Republicans. They are uninhibited and single-minded. They know how a sheriff must behave in the lawless frontier. They will not be hamstrung by legalisms or the opinion of other nations. Critics of the administration, of course, have ceaselessly asserted that torture is counterproductive as well as illegal. One reason why has this argument had so little political purchase may be that the supporters of prisoner abuse in Guantánamo Bay and Abu Ghraib are not thinking very clearly about consequences. They want to respond with appropriate ferocity to 9/11, interpret illegality as evidence of ferocity, and are seemingly untroubled by the thought that the vast majority of those being mistreated by the United States had nothing to do with the attack.

Torture is an emotionally satisfying (not useful) form of counterterrorism because it *mirrors* terrorism itself. For one thing, it is meant to terrorize. This primitive reciprocity has many disturbing implications. One is the way the United States, in the war on terror, mimics Osama bin Laden's "holy war." According to Judith Shklar, "no form of arrogance is more obnoxious than the claim that some of us are God's agents, his deputies on earth charged with punishing God's enemies."[32] In the war on terror, the United States has carbon-copied the obnoxious arrogance of the jihadists with an obnoxious arrogance of its own. To say that the United States, too, has a divine mission to punish God's enemies is to say that we are at war with "evil." It is to believe, with General William Boykin, Deputy Undersecretary of Defense for Intelligence, that the Christian God is "bigger" than the Muslim God.[33] Evil calls for wholesale exorcism not for a rational assessment of priorities. When faced with evil, moreover, we are allowed to use any possible means to help us prevail, including methods that would otherwise be forbidden.

On 9/11, al Qaeda gave Americans a burning inferno, a taste of hell. In the torture chambers of Guantánamo Bay and Abu Ghraib, the United States returned the favor. These sick facilities are not merely lawless zones, they are imitation hells. In one manual, written to prevent abuse of detainees, we read: "Placing a detainee on the ground or putting a foot on him implies that you are God. This is one of the worst things we can do."[34] That the jailers did this and worse is now a matter of public record.

Beccaria traces the roots of late medieval and early modern torture to Christian mythology. We torture a prisoner "to purge him of infamy in some metaphysical and incomprehensible way."[35] Torturers imitate the torments God inflicts upon sinners in Purgatory and Hell. Strangely enough, the photos of the Abu Ghraib prison abuse resemble nothing so much as Giotto's Last Judgment in the Scrovegni Chapel in Padova. Here too we see naked bodies piled up in painful mock promiscuity, naked limbs attacked by sharp-toothed beasts, naked men wearing hoods, manhandled, flagellated, in stress positions and pulled on leashes.

The hypothesis here is that torture is a blasphemous attempt to imitate God. That it is a perverted religious answer to a religiously inspired attack on America is strongly suggested by the following story. "One detainee, named in the report as Ameen Saeed al-Sheik, said he was asked by a soldier whether he believed in anything. 'I said to him, "I believe in Allah." So he said, "But I believe in torture and I will torture you."' He said one soldier struck his broken leg and ordered him to curse Islam. 'Because they started to hit my broken leg, I curse my religion,' the paper quoted him as saying. 'They ordered me to thank Jesus I'm alive.'"[36] Such random stories prove nothing, of course, but they do associate torture, plausibly, with self-divinization and an absurd belief that the laws of human fallibility do not apply to the U.S. side in the war on terror.

In explaining the greatest danger of anti-Communism, George Kennan wrote, in an often cited passage, that:

> something may occur in our own minds and souls which will make us no longer like the persons by whose efforts this republic was founded and held together, but rather like representatives of that very power we are trying to combat: intolerant, secretive, suspicious, cruel, and terrified of internal dissension because we have lost our own belief in ourselves and in the power of our ideals. The worst thing that our Communists could do to us, and the thing we have most to fear from their activities, is that we should become like them.[37]

Many commentators have stressed the continued relevance of this warning to the war on terror. We must beware of modeling ourselves on our mortal foes. What makes this danger loom so large today is well explained by the Israeli military historian and theorist, Martin van Creveld: "War being among the most imitative of all human activities, the very process of combating low-intensity conflict will cause both sides to become alike, unless it can be brought to a quick end."[38] Wartime's logic of imitation should perhaps make the United States rethink its hasty description of 9/11 as an act of war rather than a particularly atrocious crime in a serial crime spree.

By designing counter-terrorism in the image of terrorism, by answering terrorism with torture, the American government and electorate may experience a temporary feeling of adequacy to an obscure and unparalleled threat. But the ultimate effect on American political culture may resemble defeat more than victory. This is true even if the United States, by some miracle, prevails in a military sense. The story of the 9/11 hijackers reveals how a powerful psychological bond can be created among people who act together to commit an appalling crime. It would not be surprising if U.S. interrogators in Abu Ghraib and Guantánamo Bay felt linked by a similar emotional bond. The United States will certainly lose the moral dimension of its war on terror if it continues to build its sense of national solidarity around pride and pleasure at flouting the civilized norms that limit the way jailers treat defenseless prisoners of unknown guilt, who fall by chance into their hands.

NOTES

1. Patrick Radden Keefe, "Spy World," *Boston Globe* (February 13, 2005).
2. Danielle S. Allen, *The World of Prometheus: The Politics of Punishing in Democratic Athens* (Princeton University Press, 2000), p. 104.
3. Walter Ullmann, "Reflections on Medieval Torture," *Juridical Review* (vol. 56, 1944), p. 123.
4. *The Digest of Justinian*, trans. Alan Watson (Philadelphia: University of Pennsylvania Press, 1985), vol. IV, pp. 843; this extract comes from Aurellius Arcadius Charisius, a jurist from the age of Constantine.
5. Edward Gibbon, *Decline and Fall of the Roman Empire*, vol. I, p. 549.
6. Aristotle, *Rhetoric* 1376b 26-1377a 26, trans. by John Henry Freese (Cambridge, Mass.: Loeb Library, 1926), p. 163.
7. *Ibid.*
8. Cicero, *Pro Sulla*, 78, in *In Catilinam I-IV, Pro Murena, Pro Sulla, Pro Flacco*, trans. by C. MacDonald (Cambridge, Mass.: Loeb Library, 1977), p. 391.
9. *The Digest of Justinian*, trans. by Alan Watson (Philadelphia: University of Pennsylvania Press, 1985), vol. IV, pp. 841.
10. Augustine, *City of God*, XIX, 6, trans. by William Chase Greene (Cambridge, Mass.: Loeb Library, 1960), pp. 145–17.
11. Michel de Montaigne, *The Complete Essays*, trans. by M. A. Screech (London: Penguin, 1991), p. 414.
12. La Bruyère, *The Morals and Manners of the Seventeenth Century, being the Characters of La Bruyère* (Chicago: McClurg, 1890), p. 272.
13. William Blackstone, *Commentaries on the Laws of England* (Chicago: University of Chicago Press, 1979), vol. IV, p. 321.
14. Cesare Beccaria, *On Crimes and Punishments* (Indianapolis: Bobbs-Merrill, 1975), p. 31.
15. *Ibid.*
16. *Ibid.*, p. 32
17. *Ibid.*, p. 35.
18. *Ibid.*, p. 33.
19. Montesquieu, *Spirit of the Laws*, trans. by Thomas Nugent (New York: Hafner, 1949), vi.17, p. 91.
20. Indictment before the International Military Tribunal (October 6, 1945) in Michael Marrus (ed.), *The Nuremberg War Crimes Trial 1945–46* (Boston: St. Martin's, 1997), p. 65.
21. *Ibid.*
22. Beccaria, *On Crimes and Punishments*, p. 32.
23. William Blackstone, *Commentaries on the Laws of England* (Chicago: University of Chicago Press, 1979), vol. IV, p. 321.
24. Harold Nicolson, "Marginal Comment," *The Spectator* (May 10, 1946), p. 478.
25. Interview with Secretary of State Colin Powell by Barry Schweid and George Gedda, September 10, 2004.
26. The United Nations Convention Against Torture and Other Inhuman and Degrading Acts, Article 2.2.
27. Mark Danner, "We are All Torturers Now," *New York Times* (January 7, 2005).
28. George J. Andreopoulos, "The Age of National Liberation Movements," Michael Howard, George J. Andreopoulos, Mark R. Shulman (eds.), *The Laws of War: Constraints on Warfare in the Western World* (New Haven: Yale University Press, 1994), p. 205.

29. William Pfaff, "The Truth about Torture," *The American Conservative* (Feb. 14, 2005).

30. Elaine Scarry, *The Body in Pain* (Oxford University Press, 1985), p. 28.

31. *Ibid.*, p. 27.

32. Judith N. Shklar, *Ordinary Vices* (Cambridge, Mass.: Harvard University Press, 1984), p. 29.

33. David Rennie, "God put Bush in Charge, Says the General Hunting bin Laden," *Telegraph* (November 17, 2003).

34. Cited in Mark Danner, "Torture and Truth," in *Abu Ghraib: The Politics of Torture* (Berkeley: Terra Nova, 2004), p. 32.

35. Cesare Beccaria, *On Crimes and Punishments* (Indianapolis: Bobbs-Merrill, 1975), p. 30; *cf.* "An infallible dogma assures us that the stains contracted through our human frailty . . . must be purged by an incomprehensible fire" (*Ibid.*, p. 35).

36. "New Accounts of Prisoner Abuses," BBC News World Edition (May 21, 2004).

37. George F. Kennan, "Where Do You Stand on Communism?" *New York Times Magazine* (May 27, 1951).

38. Martin van Creveld, *The Transformation of War* (New York: Free Press, 1991), p. 225.

6 Through a Mirror, Darkly: Applying the Geneva Conventions to "A New Kind of Warfare"

Scott Horton

THE EIGHTEENTH CENTURY NEAPOLITAN PHILOSOPHER GIAMBATTISTA VICO wrote in his *New Science* (1725) about historical cycles (*ricorsi*) through which mankind progressed with eternal repetitions. Vico's cycles were not simple wheel spinning. Rather, he saw mankind engaged in a slow ascent: something like the march of the Ottoman Janissaries – two steps forward, and one to the side. Some generations would repeat the failings and mistakes of their forefathers; others would inch forward, and sometimes human progress would move in a lurch. Law in general, and the law of nations in particular, seems these days in a step to the side – if not backwards. This move has been driven by individuals who present themselves as scholars, but who are not. It has been driven by fear and by ignorance or willful disregard of our own history. The deterioration of policies governing the treatment of detainees in war time is a startling example.

In a recent statement issued in opposition to the nomination of Alberto Gonzales to serve as attorney general, a group of twelve retired generals and admirals questioned the nominee's legal judgment. In his decision to depart from traditional patterns of interpretation and application of the Geneva Conventions, the military leaders said, Gonzales had placed himself squarely on the "wrong side of history."[1] The comment was more than fair. In this brief essay, I aim to explore the historical precedents that Gonzales and his colleagues, most notably John Yoo, Jay Bybee, and Robert Delahunty have followed, whether consciously or not. As we will see, the Bush administration's position amounts not only to a complete reversal of America's historical posture on these issues;[2] it puts America behind positions the country once rightly condemned as road markers on a path to criminality.

The author expresses his thanks fo Fritz Stern, Detlev Vagts, Richard Bilder and Sanford Levinson for suggestions developed here; and to Gerhard Wegen and Angela Jung for assistance in procuring materials used in this study.

ANOTHER TIME, ANOTHER PLACE

The present study takes us back to a point still within the memory of some, to a nation renowned for its legal scholarship – a nation whose universities were considered at the forefront of the world and which drew scholars from around the world, including the United States. It was also a nation of great religious, philosophical, and artistic traditions.

Slowly, a radical political party came to power in this nation. This party first entered the government with a compromised and uncertain mandate. However, within a month a mysterious terrorist attack occurred on a building which was the very landmark of the nation's greatest city. This provided a pretext for the radicals to undermine the civil rights of the nation's citizens and construct a new government, first authoritarian, then totalitarian. The indispensable tool in this process was fear mongering – on a hitherto unknown scale. Government leaders spoke continuously of a "terrorist threat" to the nation. The threat was ideological, even fanatical, in nature and came from beyond the nation's borders. Still, suspicions were raised against certain elements of society linked to this threat. Building on the mass anxiety that they had induced, the radicals solidified their control over most aspects of society, including the government, the legislature, and the judiciary. They advanced the view that there was one supreme executive, one supreme legislator, one supreme judge. All resources of the state were subordinated to this leader with the goal of empowering him to vanquish the nation's mortal foes.

A system of detention facilities was constructed to house those viewed as threats to the nation. Persons held in these centers were beyond the reach of the law and the courts. Rumors of torture and abuse swirled around these centers, but the rumors were aggressively denied by the government.

This nation began aggressively to question the treatment of its nationals living within the borders of other states, claiming a role as guarantor of their rights. It did this in reliance on the work of politically loyal legal scholars who twisted the plain meaning of international agreements to suit the nation's political ends. These scholars were experts in asymmetrical application of the law; they ridiculed traditional scholarship and interpretation as the product of a cosmopolitan elite divorced from the needs and interests of the nation. Domestically, the nation's positions were justified by a messianic leader through a doctrine of national exceptionalism. In short order, however, this diplomacy receded, and the nation began wars against several of its neighbors.

Claiming dire threat to the nation and its people, the nation took preemptive action by invading and occupying a series of neighbors. In this manner, the government was forced to consider the requirements of the laws of armed conflict, particularly as reflected in the Hague Convention of 1907 and the Geneva Conventions of 1929, as applied to its military activities, and to fix rules for the treatment of detainees. Curiously, one institution in the nation contained isolated islands of resistance to the radical government, and that was the military, famed for its traditional conservative values.

The radical political leaders viewed international humanitarian law with ridicule and contempt. They argued that it was ill-suited to warfare targeting an unconventional adversary: an international ideological movement which itself disregarded the laws of war and that used terrorism as a principal tactic. Consequently, they denied application of the Geneva Conventions to combatants they labeled "terrorists." This viewpoint was sharply resisted by military lawyers, who argued that military morale and discipline depended on clear application of the rules of armed conflict. Moreover, the military felt that enlightened self-interest dictated such a stance, since a reputation for following these rules would protect the nation's soldiers generally and in future generations, even if there was no reason to expect reciprocity from the "terrorists."

The events described above occurred in Germany in 1933–44. They bear many unsettling similarities with events of more recent memory, though, to be clear, there are also many stark differences. But in the debate over application of international humanitarian law, the similarities dominate. Indeed, virtually all the arguments played out in the recent internal debate over detainee abuse were also raised and discussed in Germany in the opening phase of the Second World War. The position of military traditionalists, passionately supporting a faithful application of the law, was consistent; as were the dismissive comments of government leaders concerned about hard-nosed practicalities of warfare against a difficult opponent. In the balance of this essay, I will review some of the key decisions, and the arguments and rationalizations in each case.

1. Applying the Geneva and Hague Conventions on the Eastern Front

One scholar discussing Nazi Germany's engagement with the Hague and Geneva Conventions writes that while Germany adopted positions that were "at least within hailing distance" of traditional interpretations on the Western Front (with one notable exception we will discuss below),[3] its attitude towards the Eastern Front was strikingly different. This can only be understood in terms of the Nazi perception of an ideological menace emanating from Soviet Russia bolstered by anti-Slavic sentiments. Almost from the beginning of the Nazi movement, Soviet Russia had been a principal "bogeyman." The "international Bolshevik conspiracy" was a mainstay of the Nazi propaganda machine. The Reichstag fire was laid at the feet of this conspiracy, and domestic forces particularly German Communists, Social Democrats and Jews were often described as being in its thrall, or indeed, at its helm. This severe demonization tended to corrupt the application of the law of armed conflict on the Eastern Front. The leading Nazi scholar of international law, Carl Schmitt, provided a legal interpolation of this approach by arguing the fundamental proposition that while allies or friends had cognizable rights under international law, enemies did not.[4] It was but a short step from this principle to the blanket denial of humanitarian rights to enemy combatants fighting Germany on the Eastern Front.

Technical rules of construction also played an important rule. While imperial Russia had been a contracting state and had played an important role in both the Hague and Geneva processes, the Soviet Union stood consciously apart from the state systems of the old regime and declined to be viewed as a successor to Russia for purposes of the conventions. It had accepted the Geneva Convention on the treatment on the wounded and ill; but not the prisoner of war convention. Nazi leadership viewed Russian soldiers and their allies fighting on the Eastern Front as military formations in the service of a radical ideological movement rather than a traditional nation state. Clearly this viewpoint was not without a certain basis in fact: the Soviets themselves touted their "internationalism" and the ideological foundations of their cause. Building on these facts and the perception that the Soviets would not themselves abide by the laws of armed conflict but would apply "barbaric" practices the German political leadership concluded that the Geneva and Hague Conventions were technically inapplicable to the conflict with Soviet soldiers. The Nazis were also dismissive when, as a result of the intermediation of other nations (Sweden and Switzerland), the Soviets offered to apply the Geneva and Hague rules in the Second World War if Germany would agree to offer comparable assurances.

Military lawyers, led by the international law advisors attached to the *Abwehr* or Military Intelligence, led a valiant effort to challenge this viewpoint. Acknowledging that the Soviet Union was not a state-party, they argued that by virtue of their broad international acceptance, the rules in the Hague and Geneva Conventions had become international customary law, and were thus to be applied regardless of the status of the adversary. They also argued that this position was necessary to protect the interests of German soldiers captured on the front or, indeed, in future conflicts, as it established a German tradition of respecting the Conventions without technical quibbles. Finally, they asserted that such rules were essential to maintain order, discipline and morale within the German *Wehrmacht* itself.

The leader of this group of lawyers was Helmuth James von Moltke, the nephew of a former Army chief of staff, and the great-grand nephew of the celebrated general who led the Prussians to victory over France in 1870. Moltke was also half-English and the grandson of South Africa's famously liberal chief justice, James Rose Innes. He completed legal studies in Germany and England and was qualified as a lawyer in Germany and as a barrister in Britain. Moltke's special passion was international law, and he is said to have been much influenced by those scholars who saw in the medium of international law a path for the pacification of Europe. In 1939, Moltke became legal counsel to the German General Staff (*Oberkommando der Wehrmacht* or "OKW") with responsibility for international law and the law of war. Moltke was the principal author of a memorandum issued in the name of Admiral Wilhelm Canaris to the head of the OKW making the *Abwehr*'s case for application of the Geneva Conventions on the Eastern Front. It stated that

> The Geneva Convention on Prisoners of War is inapplicable between Germany and the USSR; consequently only the norms of international customary law apply to the treatment of prisoners of war. Since the 18th century, customary international law has clearly established that the state of prisoners of war is to be viewed neither as punitive nor retributory in character, but purely as a measure of security, whose sole purpose consists in denying the prisoner of war any further participation in the battle. This principle has developed in connection with the viewpoint dominant in all armies that it contradicts the military perspective to kill or wound those taken *hors de combat*. It corresponds simultaneously with the interest of those conducting war to protect their own soldiers from mistreatment in the event of their capture.
>
> The measures for the treatment of Soviet prisoners of war attached as App. 1, proceed, as is clear from the above sentences, from a thoroughly different approach. In accordance with these measures, military service for the Soviets is not viewed as the fulfillment of soldierly duty, but rather is characterized in its totality as criminal – this being justified on the basis of murderous deeds committed by the Soviet Russians. In this manner, the application of the norms of the law of war to the battle against Bolshevism is denied, and besides this manner other rules are put out of force which, in accordance with our experience to date, appear not only militarily useful, but also absolutely essential to the preservation of the morale and resolve of our own troops.[5]

The memorandum proceeded to review and critique in some detail the rules provided for treatment of Soviet prisoners of war, noting their inconsistency with international law and their blanket authorization of measures which could at best be justified only in severe cases. It pointed with concern to the practice of turning prisoners of war over to other government agencies well known for their disrespect for international humanitarian law, noting that the military might nevertheless be held accountable. It also noted the discovery of an order issued by the Soviets which appeared to provide for treatment consistent with the Geneva and Hague Conventions, and observed that the differing German position would present a propaganda shortcoming.

However, General-Field Marshal Wilhelm Keitel, chief of the OKW and *de facto* minister of war, would have none of this. He found no basis to give Russian soldiers on the Eastern Front the benefit of the conventions, deriding the Geneva Conventions in particular as obsolete.[6] He called them "the relic of a chivalrous notion of warfare!" words later quoted back to him by the American prosecutor in Nuremberg, in justification of a request for the death penalty.[7] Keitel stated that this was no ordinary war, but rather a struggle for the "destruction of an ideology." He thus echoed Hitler's propaganda line, under which the war on the Eastern Front was termed a "struggle to the death for the destruction of Bolshevist terrorism."[8] As a result, the lot of Russian soldiers on the Eastern Front who fell into German hands was horrific; the number of deaths was staggering. A formal policy of starvation was implemented in the area.

2. The "Kommissarbefehl"

A particularly striking example of the Eastern Front policies is found in the Commissar Order (*Kommissarbefehl*) issued on June 6, 1941 by Keitel. Under this order, political officers of the Communist Party were subject to summary execution upon detection. As is characteristic of totalitarian regimes, political officers were placed side-by-side with military officers in military units of the Soviet army. These political officers may have been uniformed and assigned service ranks. Their function was to provide a network of monitoring and oversight that cut through the formal military chain of command, and to insure fidelity to the party leadership by military units. In particular, the *Kommissarbefehl* provides

> In the struggle with Bolshevism the enemy cannot be expected to conduct itself in accordance with humanitarian principles or the rules of international law. In particular we can only expect that the political commissars of all sorts, as the actual leaders of the opposition, will treat our captured [soldiers] in a hateful, cruel and inhuman fashion.
>
> The armed forces must therefore be conscious of the following:
>
> 1. In this struggle, mercy and application of the rules of international law with respect to these individuals is a false approach. They are a threat to our very security and to the quick pacification of the conquered areas.
> 2. The political commissars employ barbaric Asiatic practices of warfare. We must therefore proceed against them with resolute strength.
>
> They are therefore, whenever captured in battle or in resistance, to be liquidated by force of arms.[9]

It is striking that the order relies upon (1) the Soviet Union's disrespect of international humanitarian law, (2) their use of "barbaric Asiatic practices" in the course of battle, and (3) an identification of the battle itself as an "ideological" struggle with terrorists rather than traditional warfare. Military lawyers in the *Abwehr* argued that the commissars should be treated in accordance with the Geneva and Hague rules. Those in uniformed military service should be held as prisoners of war subject to the rules of the Geneva Convention. Those who were purely political functionaries could be targeted as aspects of an enemy's command and control system, but once taken *hors de combat* they were entitled to basic humanitarian treatment, though not to the protections accorded prisoners of war.

However, for the Nazi leadership the commissars were leaders of an ideological terrorist movement that targeted Germany, and the fact that some wore uniforms was of no consequence. Following capture, the most brutal methods were employed against them in order to extract intelligence. Then they were to be quickly executed. Again, the ideological nature of the struggle and the fact that Soviet Russia was not formally a party to the Hague and Geneva rules was found to dispose of objections from the military lawyers.

3. The "Kommandobefehl"

The Nazi leadership issued an order providing that Allied commandos captured behind their lines were not to be taken prisoner but instead were subject to summary execution. The order relied upon allegations that the commandos themselves disrespected the laws of armed conflict and engaged in practices of summary execution. The order provided

> For some time our enemies have been using, in their warfare, methods which are outside the international Geneva agreements. Especially brutal and treacherous is the behavior of the so-called commandos, who, as is established, are partially recruited even from freed criminals in enemy countries. From captured orders it is divulged that they are directed not only to shackle prisoners, but also to kill defenseless prisoners on the spot at the moment in which they believe that the latter, as prisoners, represent a burden in the further pursuit of their purposes, or could otherwise be a hindrance. Finally, orders have been found in which the killing of prisoners has been demanded in principle.
>
> For this reason it was already announced, in an addendum to the *Wehrmacht* report of 7 October 1942, that, in the future, Germany in the face of these sabotage troops of the British and their accomplices, will resort to the same procedure, that is, that they will be ruthlessly mowed down by the German troops in combat, wherever they may appear.[10]

Military lawyers in the *Abwehr* argued that this order flagrantly contradicted the Hague Convention. The commandos were uniformed, were fully integrated into a military command and were led by responsible officers.[11] Accordingly they were subject to the same standards of treatment available to other uniformed soldiers. Moreover, unlike the *Kommissarbefehl*, this order applied to all Allied units – to British and later, American, units as well. The military lawyers noted that Germany also had commando units which were dropped behind enemy lines. They reasoned that the safety and protection of those units depended upon Germany's respect for the Hague Convention rules. Their reasoning was rejected by the OKW.[12]

4. The "Fliegerbefehl"

In 1944, the *Wehrmacht* leadership received a note to the effect that Allied airmen who were shot down should be executed without a court-martial if they had engaged in "acts of terror." The note evidently reflected a decision by Adolf

Hitler. Keitel responded to this document with a marginal notation to "arrange for an order to be drafted." Keitel noted that the following "acts of terror" would justify summary execution: strafing of civilians; shooting German aviators in parachutes; attacking civilian passenger planes; and attacks on Red Cross marked hospitals or trains. He reasoned that civilians and civilian targets were protected from attack under international humanitarian law, and that soldiers who disregarded these rules were "terrorists" and thus unprotected by the laws of armed conflict. The *Wehrmacht* thus sided with Nazi political leaders seeking to use ever harsher measures against advancing Allied forces.

Military and foreign office lawyers argued that the airmen were uniformed soldiers and were entitled to be treated as prisoners of war. They noted that if airmen engaged in conduct which violated the laws of war, such conduct might constitute war crimes. In this case, the airmen could be charged and tried before military tribunals that afforded them reasonable procedural protections. However, in no case could these procedural rights be short circuited. They also argued that any evidence of such a systematic violation of the Geneva Conventions would be damaging to Germany's war effort.[13]

It appears that the only deference given the objections of the military and foreign office lawyers was to further disguise the standards governing mistreatment of the airmen. In subsequently discovered documentation, German administrative authorities directed that "pilots shot down are in no case to be shielded against the anger of the people."[14] This language cloaked lynchings and beatings which were orchestrated by local police and other authorities.[15]

At Nuremberg, grave violations of the Hague and Geneva Conventions generally, and those associated with the *Fliegerbefehl* in particular, were classified as "criminal offenses of the first class," and were the first and most aggressively prosecuted charges.[16]

5. Armed Forces of Occupied Nations

With rapid successes on both fronts, German forces soon found themselves facing the remnant forces of governments-in-exile. The Germans quickly established their own administrations or created local puppet regimes. How, then, were military formations to be treated if they remained loyal to the government-in-exile or to local resistance leaders? Following the collapse of Poland, a significant number of Polish soldiers joined English units. Following the collapse of France and the creation of the Vichy regime, DeGaulle and Giraud continued to command the loyalty of French units. Yugoslav partisans fought under Tito and Mikhailovic. Military leaders in the field began to adopt the view that the units must be treated as renegades, unprotected by the Geneva and Hague rules.

This issue marked one of the few on which the *Abwehr* military lawyers achieved some success. They produced solid legal analysis for the application of the Geneva and Hague rules, but they also argued simple pragmatism. By treating the foreign military units with the dignity accorded by the laws of armed conflict, it was easier to bring them to surrender and thus bring hostilities to an end. This approach was followed with some success, from the German perspective, in French North Africa. However, it was not followed on the Eastern Front, and as the war effort began to collapse and Mussolini lost control over Italian forces, Germans were involved in many atrocities targeting their former Italian allies.

6. The "Nacht- und Nebelerlass"

Concerned about the level of resistance faced by German troops in the occupied territories, Hitler instructed Keitel to issue a special decree authorizing extraordinary measures pursuant to which political suspects would simply "disappear" to special detention facilities and might face summary court proceedings. The death penalty appears as the punishment most frequently contemplated.[17] The decree, issued on the same day the Japanese attacked Pearl Harbor (December 7, 1941) and as the German drive on Moscow stalled and the Soviet counteroffensive had begun, is known as the "Night and Fog Decree" (*Nacht- und Nebelerlaß*), a reference to the covert action it authorized. Contemporaneous documents make clear that it was motivated by the high level of casualties German soldiers were sustaining behind the front in occupied territory. Pacification of this territory was given a high priority.

A team of Justice Department lawyers worked with Keitel and his team at OKW on the drafting of the decree and further steps for its implementation. This included a series of highly particularized rules setting out how such detainees were to be treated by police, justice officials, and others. The rules specified how such individuals would be permitted to make wills, issue final letters of farewell, what would be done with children born to detainess, and how their deaths would be recorded in the registry. Other lawyers prepared parallel orders creating special secret courts and detention facilities for those interned under the *Nacht- und Nebelerlaß*. These courts were crafted under domestic German law and thus constituted a projection of German law into the occupied territories.

These arrangements flagrantly flouted the protections of the Hague Convention specifically the right of "family honor, lives of persons" and the right "to be judged under their own laws."[18] To the extent applied against uniformed service personnel, they also violated the Geneva Convention on Prisoners of War of 1929. However, the Justice Department lawyers advanced the view that the Haghe and Geneva Conventions were inapplicable.[19] This decree was applied brutally, and with particular force in France. A total of at least 7,000 persons were detained; a large number of them perished.

The Justice Department lawyers justified these acts as steps available to an occupying power in order to protect its troops against terrorist acts or insurgency. Further, the occupied territories could be divided, roughly, into three categories: (i) areas directly incorporated into the German State (for instance,

Austria, Alsace-Lorraine, the Eupen-Malmédy region of Belgium, Danzig, and portions of Poland); (ii) areas under German occupation and direct administration (such as Bohemia) and Moravia); and (iii) areas under puppet régimes (such as Hungary and Slovakia). As for the first, they asserted the right to treat persons found within those territories under German law. As to the second, they claimed the right as occupier to promulgate new rules and orders, and to derive them from Germany. As to the third, they relied on the acquiescence of régimes like Vichy France and Hungary. Their positions on these points were at least colorable from a legal perspective.

The Justice Department lawyers were indicated and charged with crimes against humanity and war crimes arising out of the issuance and implementation of the *Nacht- und Nebelerlaß*. The United States charged that as lawyers, "not farmers or factory workers," they must have recognized that their technical justifications for avoiding the application of the Hague and Geneva Conventions were unavailing, because these conventions were "recognized by all civilized nations, and were regarded as being declaratory of the laws and customs of war."[20] Further, the United States charged, this decree "would probably cause the death of human beings," grounding a charge of homicidal intent.[21]

After trial, the two principal Justice Department lawyers, one a deputy chief of the criminal division, were convicted and sentenced to ten years' imprisonment, less time served.[22] This judgment clearly established the concept of liability of the authors of bureaucratic policies that breach basic rules of the Hugue and Geneva Conventions for the consequences that predictably flow therefrom. Moreover, it establishes a particularly perilous standard of liability for government attorneys who adopt a dismissive attitude towards international humanitarian law.

SUMMARY: NAZI EVASIONS OF INTERNATIONAL HUMANITARIAN LAW

The Nazi evasions of the Geneva and Hague Conventions rested on a number of consistent concepts:

(1) Particularly on the Eastern Front, the conflict was a nonconventional sort of warfare being waged against a "barbaric" enemy which engaged in "terrorist" practices, and which itself did not observe the law of armed conflict.

(2) Individual combatants who engaged in "terrorist" practices, or who fought in military formations engaged in such practices, were not entitled to protections under international humanitarian law, and the adjudicatory provisions of the Geneva Conventions could therefore be avoided together with the substantive protections.

(3) The Geneva and Hague Conventions were "obsolete" and ill-suited to the sort of ideologically driven warfare in which the Nazis were engaged on the Eastern Front, though they might have limited application with respect to the Western Allies.

(4) Application of the Geneva Conventions was not in the enlightened self-interest of Germany because its enemies would not reciprocate such conduct by treating German prisoners in a humane fashion.

(5) Construction of international law should be driven in the first instance by a clear understanding of the national interest as determined by the executive branch. To this end, niggling, hypertechnical interpretations of the Conventions that disregarded the plain text, international practice, and even Germany's prior practice in order to justify their nonapplication were entirely appropriate.

(6) In any event, the rules of international law were subordinated to the military interests of the German state and to the law as determined and stated by the German *Führer*.

In a series of prosecutions at Nuremberg, Nazi political figures, generals, and lawyers were held to account for crimes against humanity. Violations of the Geneva and Hague Conventions frequently played focal roles in these prosecutions. Only very rarely did the Tribunal find any basis for acceptance of their technical parsing of the Conventions or their suggestions that the excuses offered above could justify crimes committed in violation of these Conventions.[23] The Allies solemnly undertook that this would not be "victor's justice," but rather the introduction of a new legal order for the post-war age. Has the conduct of a later American administration made a mockery of this pledge?

AN EXERCISE IN LEGAL ETHICS

The struggle over application of the Geneva and Hague Conventions at the outset of the Second World War presents a fascinating field for the study of legal ethics under the most stressful of conditions.[24] On one side stood a band of political lawyers, who with no compunction shredded the essence of international humanitarian law because they saw in it a hindrance to the effective prosecution of a war effort against an ideologically driven opponent. Speaking about these lawyers, the Nuremberg tribunal's judgment in the Justice Ministry case could well be quoted: they "prostitute[d] . . . a legal system for the accomplishment of criminal ends."[25]

On the other side stood a small group of dedicated and conscientious lawyers focused in the *Abwehr*. In advocating a faithful application of international humanitarian law, they showed supreme courage. It was not merely a "bad career move" to adopt these positions which openly challenged the views of their political ideologue masters – it was viewed as an act of betrayal, which put their lives at risk. By the end of the war, most in fact were victims of Hitler's Gestapo. Yet what moved these lawyers was not political opposition to an authoritarian regime but concern about the collapse of the rule of law at home, and faith in international humanitarian law as a vehicle to soften the ravages of war, as an affirmation of the most noble values of the uniformed services, as the necessary path to a better future for all mankind.

In these times, one can only look with amazement and respect at the unshakable resolve of men like Count Moltke, whose brilliant advocacy of the Geneva and Hague Conventions led inextricably to his execution in 1945. Disgusted by an atmosphere in which law was constantly subverted to political expedience, Moltke envisioned harsh prosecutions of politicians and lawyers who engaged in such antics as an essential purgative. In a draft dated June 14, 1943, Moltke envisioned a special international criminal tribunal to be convened at the conclusion of the Second World War for the purpose of bringing to justice all who had shamelessly violated the laws of war. In view of mounting evidence of a crime of genocide, and out of cencern that international customary law failed yet to provide a medium for its punishment, he advocated an expansive posture for prosecution. "Any person who violates the essential principles of divine or natural law, of international law, or of international customary law in such a fashion that makes clear that he contemptuously disregards the binding nature of such law shall be punished."[26] The Nuremberg model did not fully match Moltke's vision, but neither was it a bad approximation.

There is little doubt that under the professional responsibility regime binding on the German lawyers (not to mention their duties as military officers) at the time of these discussions, those who let themselves be guided by the political leadership were acting within the profession's rules. Conversely their adversaries who advocated a conscientious approach to the law may well have been acting at or beyond the limits of those rules.[27] Perhaps all of this serves to show how distant rules of "professional responsibility" can be from genuine ethics.

For those who invoke the image of a ticking bomb and Hobbes' *Leviathan*, the role of another man in this drama is particularly compelling. Justice Robert H. Jackson, a former Attorney General and one of the preëminent legal minds of his age, was a figure known for a pragmatic approach to law that gives full weight to the interests of state security. He is the author of the famous observation, of late often quoted by supporters of the Bush administration, that the Bill of Rights "is not a suicide pact."[28] However, Justice Jackson had no tolerance for those who evaded the "basic building blocks of civilization" found in the Geneva and Hague Conventions. His attitude on this point was hardly distinguishable from Moltke's. He spoke forcefully at the opening of the Nuremberg trials, stating that "[e]ven the most warlike of peoples have recognized in the name of humanity some limitations on the savagery of warfare. Rules to that end have been embodied in international conventions to which Germany became a party. This code had prescribed certain restraints as to the treatment of belligerents. The enemy was entitled to surrender and to receive quarter and good treatment as a prisoner of war."[29] Jackson saw no reason to show leniency to those who disrespected the laws of war; his demands for the death penalty, indeed, focused on those who demonstrated contempt for those rules and whose policies resulted in systematic violations.

Jackson stated:

> We must never forget that the record on which we judge these defendants today is the record on which history will judge us tomorrow. To pass these defendants a poisoned chalice is to put it to our lips as well.[30]

Jackson's words are prophetic and worthy of careful contemplation in these times. Those words and the entire legacy of Nuremberg – challenge those who argue that the perils of modern terrorism justify a retreat backward into the path of barbarity.

NOTES

1. The text of the letter may be found at <http://www.humanrightsfirst.org/us_law/etn/gonzales/statements/gonz_military_010405.pdf>.
2. *See, e.g.*, William H. Taft IV, Legal Adviser, U.S. Department of State, Draft Memorandum of January 11, 2002 concerning the Application of Treaties and Laws to Al Qaeda and Taliban Detainees at 2 (summarizing reasons why the Yoo/Delahunty memorandum of January 9, 2002 on application of treaties and laws to al Qaeda and Taliban detainees is incorrect and inconsistent with prior U.S. practice).
3. Vagts, *International Law in the Third Reich*, 84 Am. J. Int'l L. 661, 696 (1990).
4. *See, e.g.*, Schmitt, *Totaler Feind, totaler Krieg, totaler Staat*, 4 Völkerbund und Völkerrecht 139 (1937).
5. Memorandum from Admiral Wilhelm Canaris to the Chief, OKW, Sept. 15, 1941 *reproduced in* G. van Roon, Helmuth James Graf von Moltke: Völkerrecht im Dienste der Menschen, 258–59 (1986) (author's translation).
6. The notion that the main instruments of international humanitarian law were "obsolete" belonged to the Nazi mainstay and where invoked regularly. *See, e.g.*, T. Taylor, The Anatomy of the Nuremberg Trials, 443 (1992) (defense of obsolescence raised with respect to forced transport of civilian labor).
7. The full text of Keitel's pencil markings on the memorandum: "Die Bedenken entsprechen den soldatischen Auffassungen vom ritterlichen Krieg! Hier handelt es sich um die Vernichtung einer Weltanschauung. Deshalb billige ich die Maßnahmen und decke sie. K., 23.9." *Id.; see also* Vagts at 698.
8. C. Streit, Keine Kameraden: Die Wehrmacht und die sowjetischen Kriegsgefangenen, 1941–45 25–27, 182 (1978).
9. (Author's translation). "Im Kampf gegen den Bolschewismus ist mit einem Verhalten des Feindes nach den Grundsätzen der Menschlichkeit oder des Völkerrechts nicht zu rechnen. Insbesondere ist von den politischen Kommissaren aller Art als den eigentlichen Trägern des Widerstandes eine haßerfüllte, grausame und unmenschliche Behandlung unserer Gefangenen zu erwarten.
   Die Truppe muß sich bewußt sein:
   1. In diesem Kampf ist Schonung und völkerrechtliche Rücksichtnahme diesen Elementen gegenüber falsch. Sie sind eine Gefahr für die eigene Sicherheit und die schnelle Befriedung der eroberten Gebiete.
   2. Die Urheber barbarisch asiatischer Kampfmethoden sind die politischen Kommissare. Gegen diese muß daher sofort und ohne weiteres mit aller Schärfe vorgegangen werden.

Sie sind daher, wenn im Kampf oder Widerstand ergriffen, grundsätzlich sofort mit der Waffe zu erledigen."

Order of OKW, June 6, 1941, reproduced at <http://www.dhm.de/lemo/html/dokumente/kommissarbefehl/>.

10. (Author's translation). "Schon seit längerer Zeit bedienen sich unsere Gegner in ihrer Kriegführung Methoden, die außerhalb der internationalen Abmachungen von Genf stehen. Besonders brutal und hinterhältig benehmen sich die Angehörigen der sogenannten Kommandos, die sich selbst, wie feststeht, teilweise sogar aus Kreisen von in den Feindländern freigelassenen kriminellen Verbrechern rekrutieren. Aus erbeuteten Befehlen geht hervor, daß sie beauftragt sind, nicht nur Gefangene zu fesseln, sondern auch wehrlose Gefangene kurzerhand zu töten im Moment, in dem sie glauben, daß diese bei der weiteren Verfolgung ihrer Zwecke als Gefangene einen Ballast darstellen oder sonst ein Hindernis sein könnten. Es sind endlich Befehle gefunden worden, in denen grundsätzlich die Tötung der Gefangenen verlangt worden ist."

"Aus diesem Anlaß wurde in einem Zusatz zum Wehrmachtbericht vom 7. 10. 1942 bereits angekündigt, daß in Zukunft Deutschland gegenüber diesen Sabotagetrupps der Briten und ihren Helfershelfern zum gleichen Verfahren greifen wird, das heißt: daß sie durch die deutschen Truppen, wo immer sie auch auftreten, rücksichtslos im Kampf niedergemacht werden." OKW Order of Oct. 18, 1942, reproduced at <http://www.documentarchiv.de/ns/1942/-kommandobefehl.html.>

11. See Vagts at 698.

12. 15 Trial of the Major War Criminals Before the International Military Tribunal, 481–86 (1947).

13. 2 Nazi Conspiracy and Aggression, 528–65 (1946) (Trial of Defendant Wilhelm Keitel).

14. "Jabo-Piloten, die abgeschossen werden, sind grundsätzlich der Volksempörung nicht zu entziehen." Order issued by Albert Hoffmann, Gauleiter for Southern Westphalia, Feb. 25, 1945 (original in Public Records Office, London, WO 235/193).

15. Blank, *Gauleiter Albert Hoffmann und der 'Fliegerbefehl,'* 98 Märkisches Jahrbuch für Geschichte, 255 (1998).

16. Report to the President by Justice Robert H. Jackson, June 6, 1945, *reproduced at* <http://www.yale.edu/lawweb/avalon/imt/jackson/jack08.htm>.

17. Sec. I: "Within the occupied territories, the adequate punishment for offenses committed against the German State or the occupying power which endanger their security or a state of readiness is on principle the death penalty." 7 Nazi Conspiracy and Aggression (1946) (Doc. No. C-90).

18. Hague Convention of 1907, arts. 4–7, 23, 43, 45, 46 and 50.

19. 3 Nazi Conspiracy and Aggression at 64.

20. *Id.*

21. *Id.* at 69.

22. *United States v. Altstötter,* 3 Trials of War Criminals Before the Nürnberg Military Tribunals Under Control Council Law No. 10, 1086 (1949).

23. The most significant success achieved by Nuremberg defendants in this regard was the argument of German admirals led by Karl Dönitz that both sides had relaxed the rules concerning maritime economic war, and that it would be unjust to apply the old rules unilaterally to the Germans. *Final Judgment in the Admirals' Case,* 6 F.R.D. 69, 169 (1946) (concluding that the sentence against Dönitz did not rest on charges that he breached international law governing submarine warfare.) *See* Vagts at 699.

24. *See* Bilder & Vagts, *Speaking Law to Power: Lawyers and Torture,* 98 Am. J. Int'l L. 689 (2004).

25. *United States v. Altstötter,* 3 Trials of War Criminals at 1086.

26. Helmuth James von Moltke, Briefe an Freya 46 (1995) (author's translation).

27. It is noteworthy, for instance, that the *Volksgericht* decision condemning moltke dwells at some length with his professional duties as an attorney and the oath of loyalty sworn by attorneys in Nazi Germany to the *Führer*. Van Roon at 316.

28. *Terminiello v. City of Chicago*, 337 U.S. 1, 37 (1949) (dissenting opinion).

29. Opening Remarks of Justice Robert H. Jackson, 1 Nazi Conspiracy and Aggression, 172 (1946).

30. *Id.*

7 Speaking Law to Power: Lawyers and Torture

Richard B. Bilder and Detlev F. Vagts

THE DISCLOSURE OF GOVERNMENT LEGAL MEMORANDA SEEKING TO JUS-
tify coercive interrogation of U.S.-held detainees[1] raises important and recurrent
questions concerning the appropriate role and responsibilities of U.S. government
attorneys, particularly when they advise on questions of international and U.S.
foreign relations law.

As is now well known, these memoranda advised administration officials that,
among other things, the humanitarian Geneva Conventions[2] were inapplicable to
Taliban detainees or persons suspected of links with Al Qaeda or terrorism; that
the Torture Convention[3] and other treaties barring torture and cruel, inhuman,
or degrading treatment, as well as U.S. law implementing such treaties,[4] prohibit
only the most extreme methods of coercive interrogation; that the 1994 U.S.
statute criminalizing the commission of torture did not apply to interrogations
conducted at Guantánamo Bay, Cuba, because the U.S. naval station there was
within the definition of the special maritime and territorial jurisdiction of the U.S.
and thus outside the scope of the statute; and that, in any case, the president as
commander-in-chief has constitutional authority to disregard treaty or statutory
prohibitions on the use of torture or other coercive interrogation techniques in
conducting the "war on terror."[5] Indeed, White House counsel dismissed relevant
prohibitions of the Geneva Conventions as "obsolete."[6]

At least some State Department and military Judge Advocate General lawyers
protested those memoranda.[7] And many others – in the U.S. legal community
and beyond – have attacked them as legally and morally unsupportable, likely to
endanger our own military personnel, and damaging to our country's reputation
and national interest.[8] Critics argue, for example, that

- the provisions of the Geneva Conventions require that Taliban fighters be accorded prisoner-of-war status, or at least a fair hearing to determine that status;

Reproduced with permission from, 98 AJIL 689 (2004) © The American Society of International Law.

- the memoranda adopt an impermissibly narrow interpretation of the prohibitions on coercive interrogation mandated by the Torture Convention and other applicable treaties, ignoring the language and intent of these instruments, the injunction of the "Martens clause" in the humanitarian conventions requiring that they be liberally and protectively interpreted,[9] and recent decisions of the European Court of Human Rights raising the standard for permissible interrogations;[10]
- the memoranda's position that Guantánamo Bay is within the special admiralty and territorial jurisdiction of the U.S. and hence, that the 1994 Torture Statute is inapplicable, was contrary to the position taken by the administration in litigation involving Guantánamo Bay pending at the time;[11]
- the memoranda's contention that the president has constitutional discretion as commander-in-chief to disregard treaty and statutory prohibitions on the use of coercive interrogation techniques in conducting the "war on terror" is legally untenable in view of the Constitution's express grant to Congress of the power to establish rules relating to capture on land and sea, to make regulations for the governance of the land and naval forces, and to define crimes against the law of nations, and also in view of the Supreme Court's landmark decision in the *Steel Seizure* cases rejecting such broad presidential authority.[12]

Some critics charged that the memoranda focused less on a responsible analysis of the legal and policy issues involved than on proposing arguments to protect those involved in coercive interrogation from potential prosecution under U.S. law.[13] While it is not yet clear to what extent these legal memoranda may have contributed to the abuse of detainees at Abu Ghraib prison, Guantánamo Bay, and elsewhere, it has been suggested that they may at least have fostered a permissive climate in which such abuses were more likely.[14] Some critics propose that the government attorneys involved should be subject to professional sanctions.[15]

What, then, are the appropriate legal and ethical responsibilities of U.S. government attorneys in the "war on terror"? Are these responsibilities even greater when government lawyers deal with issues involving international or foreign relations law?[16]

Like all attorneys, lawyers working for the U.S. government or military are bound by U.S. law (constitutional and otherwise) and the ethical rules of the state in which they are licensed to practice, as well as by relevant rules of their own agencies or military branches of service.[17] The American Bar Association Model Rules of Professional Conduct,[18] adopted in most states, require a lawyer to provide competent representation to a client.[19] Importantly, these ethical rules prohibit a lawyer from knowingly counseling or assisting a client to violate the law.[20] Certainly, a lawyer may give an honest opinion about the consequences that are likely to result from a client's conduct, and may counsel or assist the client in a good faith effort to determine the validity, scope, meaning, or application of the law.[21] But the prospect that a client may not like the advice should not deter a lawyer from giving an honest assessment.[22] And, the American Bar Association Model Rules make clear that it is proper for a lawyer to refer to relevant moral and ethical considerations in giving such advice, since moral and ethical considerations impinge upon most legal questions and may decisively influence how the law should be applied.[23] Moreover, a lawyer employed or retained by an organization – including the government – represents the organization acting through its duly authorized constituents; indeed, such a lawyer is required to take certain steps if he or she knows that an officer or employee of the organization intends to act in violation of a legal obligation.[24]

But government attorneys also have responsibilities and obligations of loyalty that go beyond those of private attorneys.[25] Thus, the government lawyer's "client" is not simply his or her administrative superior but also the government agency or military service for which he or she works, the U.S. government as a whole, and indeed the American public and its collective interests and values. Moreover, government attorneys have a particular obligation to act responsibly in formulating advice or arguments regarding constitutional or international legal questions[26] because their opinions on such matters may often not be subject to definitive judicial or other impartial review. Even if government legal views are in theory subject to review, it is well known that federal courts, other government agencies, and the Congress have traditionally been especially deferential to such opinions. Consequently, in practice there may be no "safety net" other than these attorneys' own competence, care, integrity, and good faith; it is only these professional qualities that protect against legal advice or advocacy that might undermine the national interest in respect for law, or subvert or erode the international legal order.

Finally, foreign policy decisions are often highly political, and policymakers and others who influence policy are often skeptical concerning the relevance of international law.[27] Thus, there may be strong pressures on government lawyers to "bend" or ignore the law in order to support policy decisions,[28] pressures that responsible government attorneys have an obligation to resist.[29] For unless public officials are given competent, objective, and honest advice as to the legal consequences of their proposed actions and decisions, they cannot make informed and intelligent policy judgments or properly balance the national interests involved.

Controversy will continue as to whether the government attorneys preparing the memoranda met these responsibilities.[30] Absent the possibility of impartial judicial determination, it is difficult to agree on any clear criteria or tests for determining when a legal argument or position particularly one involving interpretations of treaties or international law is so clearly erroneous or politically slanted as to be simply "out of the ballpark" and beyond the range of permissible good-faith argument.[31] Thus, a final verdict on these matters is likely to emerge only out of the collective sentiment of the professional legal community.

Nevertheless, certain things may be said. First, these memoranda cannot in themselves insulate or immunize persons engaging or complicit in torture or war crimes from international or domestic criminal responsibility for their conduct. It is well settled that advice of counsel, the "My lawyer said it was OK" defense, cannot serve as an excuse for violating the law,[32] especially in cases where legal advice is deliberately sought and given for the very purpose of providing such an excuse.[33]

Second, an attorney who gives advice intended to assist or provide a "road map" for the client in violating or circumventing the law may be held complicit in the client's criminal conduct.[34] Nor should invocation of the supposedly overriding demands of the "war on terror" be presented as an excuse for violating the law. It is worth recalling that Ribbentrop was convicted at Nuremberg for having issued memoranda justifying the Nazi preemptive strikes against Norway, Denmark, and the Low Countries in 1940.[35] And the War Crimes Tribunal that convicted Schlegelberger, who headed the Reich Ministry of Justice, emphasized that he had "sold" his intellect and scholarship to Hitler and "prostitut[ed] . . . a judicial system for the accomplishment of criminal ends."[36]

Third, even if these memoranda somehow have the effect of protecting persons involved in torture or war crimes from prosecution under U.S. law, they may not provide protection from prosecution or liability in international tribunals or the courts of other countries. Under international and foreign law, such tribunals may be legally entitled to assert jurisdiction over these universally condemned crimes.[37]

Finally, it is questionable whether the policy that the memoranda sought to justify – avoiding U.S. obligations under international humanitarian treaties – has in fact furthered U.S. objectives in the "war on terror." A nation's reputation for decency and respect for law is a vital national asset that can strongly affect its influence and leadership. Unless U.S. foreign policy and actions in the "war on terror" are seen by its own citizens and other nations as legitimate and in compliance with broadly accepted legal and moral standards, they may fail to gain domestic and international support.[38] There is little doubt that disclosure of abuses at Abu Ghraib and elsewhere seriously damaged the United States' international standing. Greater respect for international law, as well as our traditional values, would have better served our national interest.

Ultimately, these memoranda raise even profounder issues regarding the government lawyers' commitment to principles of ordinary morality and common decency, as well as the rule of law, particularly in the context of an ongoing "war on terror." American lawyers still honor the courage, integrity, and fidelity to law of the government lawyers who were victims of the "Saturday Night massacre"- the top Department of Justice officials who, during the Watergate scandal, chose to resign rather than comply with President Nixon's order to fire the Special Prosecutor who had subpoenaed the Nixon White House tapes.[39] It should also be noted that the conduct of some other government lawyers during that same scandal met with such wide disapproval that renewed attention was focused on professional ethics.[40]

Across the years, one cannot help but admire the courage and integrity of German military lawyers who advised the German High Command that Hitler's infamous secret "Commando Order" (Kommandobefehl), which instructed the Wehrmacht to execute allied commandos as unlawful combatants, was illegal.[41] Those lawyers also advised that Russian prisoners should be handled humanely as a matter of customary international law even though the Soviet Union was not a party to the relevant conventions.[42] They did not hesitate to couple their legal analysis with practical and moral arguments. The German leadership scornfully rejected their advice; on the prisoner-of-war memorandum, General Keitel scrawled remarks about the obsolescence of the Geneva rules. But today the places where the Nazis executed those lawyers are national memorials.[43] In contrast, no one visits the graves of those who acted contrary to their legal advice and were later hanged at Nuremberg. Fortunately, American government lawyers can still remain faithful to the law and to their consciences with less dangerous consequences.

Perhaps Justice Brandeis said it best:

> In a government of laws, existence of the government will be imperilled if it fails to observe the law scrupulously. Our government is the potent, the omnipresent teacher. For good or for ill, it teaches the whole people by its example. . . . If the Government becomes a lawbreaker, it breeds contempt for law. . . . To declare that . . . the end justifies the means . . . would bring terrible retribution.[44]

NOTES

1. This essay focuses on three of these memoranda: (1) Memorandum from Assistant Attorney General Jay S. Bybee to White House Counsel Alberto R. Gonzales and Dept. of Defense General Counsel William J. Haynes, II (Jan. 22, 2002) ("Application of Treaties and Laws to al Qaeda and Taliban Detainees"), Memo 6 in *The Torture Papers* (Greenberg and Dratel, eds.), p. 81 [hereinafter Bybee Memo]; (2) Draft Memorandum from White House Counsel Alberto R. Gonzales to President George W. Bush (Jan. 25, 2002) ("Decision re Application of the Geneva Convention on Prisoners of War to the Conflict with al Qaeda and the Taliban"), Memo 7 in *The Torture Papers* (Greenberg and Dratel, eds.), p. 118 [hereinafter Gonzales Memo]; (3) Working Group Report on Detainee Interrogations in the Global War on Terrorism: Assessment of Legal, Historical, Policy, and Operational Considerations (Apr. 4, 2003), Memo 26 in *The Torture Papers* (Greenberg and Dratel, eds.), p. 286 [hereinafter Working Group Report – Detainee Interrogations].

   In June 2004, officials at the White House and the Justice Department distanced themselves from memoranda of the Office of Legal Counsel. *See* Press Briefing by White House Counsel Judge Alberto Gonzales, DOD General Counsel William Haynes, DOD Deputy General Counsel Daniel Dell'Orto, and Army Deputy Chief of Staff for Intelligence General Keith Alexander (June 22, 2004), at <http://www.whitehouse.gov/news/releases/2004/06/200406220-14.html> (statement by White House counsel that "[u]nnecessary, over-broad discussions in some of these memos that address abstract legal theories, or discussions subject to misinterpretation, but not relied upon by decision-makers are under review, and may be replaced, if appropriate, with more concrete guidance addressing only those issues necessary for the legal analysis of actual practices").

For some factual and legal background relating to the abuse of U.S.-held detainees, *see, e.g.*, Sean D. Murphy, Contemporary Practice of the United States, 98 AJIL 591 (2004). For the international legal issues, *see, e.g.*, Leila Nadya Sadat, International Legal Issues Surrounding the Mistreatment of Iraqi Detainees by American Forces, *ASIL Insights*, May 2004, and Frederic L. Kirgis, Distinctions Between International and U.S. Foreign Relations Law: Issues Regarding Treatment of Suspected Terrorists, *ASIL Insights*, June 2004 (both available at <http://www.asil.org/insights.htm>).

2. The Third Geneva Convention provides that prisoners of war "must at all times be humanely treated" and that "[n]o physical or mental torture, nor any other form of coercion, may be inflicted on prisoners of war to secure from them information of any kind whatever. Prisoners of war who refuse to answer may not be threatened, insulted, or exposed to unpleasant or disadvantageous treatment of any kind." Geneva Convention (No. III) Relative to the Treatment of Prisoners of War, Aug. 12, 1949, Arts. 13, 17, 6 UST 3316, 3328, 75 UNTS 135, 150. Similarly, the Fourth Geneva Convention provides that civilians detained by an occupying power are entitled, in all circumstances, to respect for their persons, their honour, their family rights, their religious convictions and practices, and their manners and customs. They shall at all times be humanely treated, and shall be protected especially against all acts of violence or threats thereof and against insults and public curiosity. Geneva Convention (No. IV) Relative to the Protection of Civilian Persons in Time of War, Art. 27, 6 UST 3516, 3536, 75 UNTS 287, 306; *see also id.*, Art. 31, 6 UST at 3538, 75 UNTS at 308 ("No physical or moral coercion shall be exercised against protected persons, in particular to obtain information from them or from third parties."). Further, torture and inhumane treatment of prisoners of war or protected civilians are considered war crimes under the 1949 Geneva Conventions.

3. The Convention Against Torture, to which the United States is a party, prohibits governments from engaging in acts of torture, which are defined as any act-when done by a person acting in an official capacity-by which "severe pain or suffering, whether physical or mental," is intentionally inflicted on a person for such purposes as obtaining information from him. The Convention also prohibits cruel, inhuman, and degrading treatment or punishment. Convention Against Torture and Other Cruel, Inhuman or Degrading Treatment or Punishment, Dec. 10, 1984, Arts. 1, 16, 1465 UNTS 85, 113–14, 116.

4. A U.S. statute criminalizes the commission of torture by a U.S. national outside the United States. 18 U.S.C. §2340A (2000). Further, it is a criminal offense for U.S. nationals to commit acts in violation of several provisions of treaties governing the law of war. 18 U.S.C. §2441 (2000).

5. The memoranda are summarized, with excerpts, in the summary of memoranda, *supra* note 1.

6. Gonzales Memo, *supra* note 1, at 2 in *The Torture Papers*, p. 119.

7. *See* Memorandum from Dep't of State Legal Adviser William H. Taft IV to White House Counsel Alberto R. Gonzales (Feb. 2, 2002) ("Comments on Your Paper on the Geneva Convention"), Memo 10 in *The Torture Papers* ("Greenberg and Dratel, eds.), p. 129; Draft Memorandum from Secretary of State Colin Powell to White House Counsel Alberto R. Gonzales (Jan. 26, 2002) ("The Applicability of the Geneva Convention to the Conflict in Afghanistan") (summarized in Summary of memoranda, *supra* note 1), Memo 8 in *The Torture Papers* (Greenberg and Dratel, eds.), p. 122; R. Jeffrey Smith, Lawyer for State Dept. Disputed Detainee Memo; Military Legal Advisers Also Questioned Tactics, WASH. POST, June 24, 2004, at A07 (reporting "strongly expressed

internal dissents at the State Department and the military services"); Final Report of the Independent Panel to Review DoD Detention Operations 33–34 (Aug. 24, 2004) in *The Torture Papers* (Greenberg and Dratel, eds.), p. 908. The promulgation of new guidelines for interrogation of Al Qaeda suspects in the war on terror led a group of military lawyers to organize a secret meeting with Scott Horton of the New York City Bar Association in the spring of 2003. They urged him to challenge the Bush administration about its standards for interrogation and detention, which they felt were a dangerous departure from the United States' historic approach to international law. See Anthony Dworkin, America's Interrogation Network: Rules on the Treatment of Prisoners in International Law, at <http://www.crimesofwar.org/onnews/news-prison2.html> (May 17, 2004) (Crimes of War Project).

8. *See, e.g.*, Lawyers' Statement on Bush Administration's Torture Memos (Aug. 4, 2004), at <http://www.allianceforjustice.org/spotlight/collection/spotlight_statement0804.html> (addressed to the president, vice president, secretary of defense, attorney general, and members of Congress; signed by some 130 prominent members of the American legal community, including former judges, elected officials, former attorneys general, American Bar Association presidents, and professors; posted on the Alliance for Justice Web site) [hereinafter Lawyers' Statement]; Letter Sent to the United States Congress Regarding Recent Human Rights Issues in Iraq (June 16, 2004), at <http://www.iraq-letter.com> (signed by over five hundred members of university faculties in law, international relations, diplomacy, and public policy).

9. The Martens clause, which requires that "civilians and combatants remain under the protection and authority of the principles of international law derived from established custom, from the principles of humanity and from the dictates of public conscience," appears in the Hague Conventions of 1899 and 1907, in the Geneva Conventions of 1949, and in Protocol I of 1977. See Helmut Strebel, Martens' Clause, 3 ENCYCLOPEDIA OF PUBLIC INTERNATIONAL LAW 326 (Rudolf Bernhardt ed., 1997).

10. The memoranda referred to *Ireland v. United Kingdom*, 25 Eur. Ct. H. R. (Ser. A) (1977). For more recent case law, however, see Human Rights Practice §§3.006-.013 (Jessica Simon et al. eds., 2001) (looseleaf).

11. *Rasul v. Bush*, 124 S.Ct. 2686 (2004).

12. *Youngstown Sheet & Tube Co. v. Sawyer*, 343 U.S. 579 (1952) (rejecting the argument that President Truman had inherent constitutional authority to seize private steel mills in order to prevent a strike during the Korean War); *United States v. Wappler*, 2 C.M.A. 393 (1953) (where president's Manual for Courts-Martial conflicts with the statutory Uniform Code of Military Justice, "the latter, of course, controls").

13. See, e.g., Lawyers' Statement, *supra* note 8 (asserting that the senior lawyers responsible for the memoranda "have counseled individuals to ignore the law and offered arguments to minimize their exposure to sanction or liability for doing so"); Neil A. Lewis, Justice Memos Explained How to Skip Prisoner Rights, N.Y. TIMES, May 21, 2004, at A10 (the memoranda "were crucial in building a legal framework for United States officials to avoid complying with international laws and treaties on handling prisoners, lawyers and former officials say" and "provided arguments to keep United States officials from being charged with war crimes for the way prisoners were detained and interrogated"); Jordan Paust, The Common Plan to Violate the Geneva Conventions (May 25, 2004), at <http://jurist.law.pitt.edu/forum/paust2.php> (Jurist forum).

14. *See, e.g.*, Bending the Rules? PBS ONLINE NEWSLETTER, May 13, 2004, at <http://pbs.org/newshour/bb/middle_east/jan-june04/interrogation_05-13.html> ("Recent images of Iraqi prisoner abuse have raised questions about, whether the Department of Defense created a climate for abuse by sidestepping international standards on the appropriate treatment for prisoners of war."); Michael Isikoff, Double Standards? A Justice Department

Memo Proposes That the United States Hold Others Accountable for International Laws on Detainees-but That Washington Did Not Have to Follow Them Itself (May 21, 2004), at <http://msnbc.msn.com/id/5032094/site/newsweek/>; The Roots of Abu Ghraib, N.Y. TIMES, June 9, 2004, at A24 (editorial) ("Each new revelation makes it more clear that the inhumanity at Abu Ghraib grew out of a morally dubious culture of legal expediency and a disregard for normal behavior fostered at the top of this administration."); John Barry, Michael Hirsh, & Michael Isikoff, The Roots of Torture, NEWSWEEK, May 24, 2004, at 28.

15. *See, e.g.*, Edward Alden, Attempt to Find Legal Justification for Torture Leaves Lawyers Aghast, FIN. TIMES, June 10, 2004, at 3 ("Scott Horton, past chairman of the international human rights committee of the New York City bar association says the government lawyers involved in preparing the documents could and should face professional sanctions. 'There are serious ethical shortcomings here,' he says."); Lawyers' Statement, *supra* note 8 ("The lawyers who approved and signed these memoranda have not met their high obligation to defend the Constitution."); Adam Liptak, Torture and Legal Ethics: How Far Can a Government Lawyer Go? N.Y. TIMES, June 21, 2004, §4 (Week in Review), at 3; Stephen Gillers, Tortured Reasoning, Am. Law., July 2004, at 65.

16. *See* The Role of the Legal Adviser of the Department of State. A Report of the Joint Committee Established by the American Society of International Law and the American Branch of the International Law Association (July 1990) (American Society of International Law, Oct. 1, 1990), reprinted in 85 AJIL 358 (1991) [hereinafter Report on the Role of the Legal Adviser]. For a discussion of the background, preparation, and issues raised by this report, see Richard B. Bilder, International Law and United States Foreign Policy: Some Reflections on the ASIL/ILA Report on the Role of the Legal Adviser, 1 TRANSNAT'L L. & CONTEMP. PROBS. 201 (1991) (includes report as appendix), and remarks by Richard B. Bilder in panel on "The Role of International Law in U.S. Foreign Policymaking," 86 ASIL PROC. 434, 436–40 (1992). On the role of the State Department legal adviser more generally, *see, e.g.*, Michael K. Young, Government Lawyering: The Role of the Attorney-Adviser in the U.S. Department of State: Institutional Arrangements and Structural Imperatives, 61 LAW & CONTEMP. PROBS. 133 (1998); Richard B. Bilder, The Office of the Legal Adviser: The State Department Lawyer and Foreign Affairs, 56 AJIL 633 (1962).

17. *See, e.g.*, Roger C. Cramton, The Lawyer as Whistleblower: Confidentiality and the Government Lawyer, 5 GEO. J. LEGAL ETHICS 291, 293–94 (1991).

18. CENTER FOR PROFESSIONAL RESPONSIBILITY, AMERICAN BAR ASSOCIATION, MODEL RULES OF PROFESSIONAL CONDUCT (2004).

19. Rule 1.1 ("Competence") provides: "A lawyer shall provide competent representation to a client. Competent representation requires the legal knowledge, skill, thoroughness and preparation reasonably necessary for the representation."

20. Rule 1.2 ("Scope of Representation"), paragraph (d), provides:

> A lawyer shall not counsel a client to engage, or assist a client, in conduct that the lawyer knows is criminal or fraudulent, but a lawyer may discuss the legal consequences of any proposed course of conduct with a client and may counsel or assist a client to make a good faith effort to determine the validity, scope, meaning or application of the law.

Comment [9] to that rule states:

> Paragraph (d) prohibits a lawyer from knowingly counseling or assisting a client to commit a crime or fraud. This prohibition, however, does not preclude the lawyer from giving an honest opinion about the actual consequences that appear likely to result from a client's conduct. Nor does the fact that a client uses advice in a course

of action that is criminal or fraudulent of itself make a lawyer a party to the course of action. There is a critical distinction between presenting an analysis of legal aspects of questionable conduct and recommending the means by which a crime or fraud might be committed with impunity.

21. See Rule 1.2(d), Comment [9] (quoted *supra* note 20).
22. Comment [1] to Rule 2.1 ("Advisor") states: "[1] A client is entitled to straightforward advice expressing the lawyer's honest assessment.... [A] lawyer should not be deterred from giving candid advice by the prospect that the advice will be unpalatable to the client."
23. Rule 2.1 provides: "In representing a client, a lawyer shall exercise independent professional judgment and render candid advice. In rendering advice, a lawyer may refer not only to law but to other considerations such as moral, economic, social and political factors, that may be relevant to the client's situation."
    Comment [2] to Rule 2.1 states:

    Advice couched in narrow legal terms may be of little value to a client, especially where practical considerations, such as cost or effects on other people, are predominant. Purely technical legal advice, therefore, can sometimes be inadequate. It is proper for a lawyer to refer to relevant moral and ethical considerations in giving advice. Although a lawyer is not a moral advisor as such, moral and ethical considerations impinge upon most legal questions and may decisively influence how the law will be applied.

24. Rule 1.13 ("Organization as Client") provides:
    (a) A lawyer employed or retained by an organization represents the organization acting through its duly authorized constituents.
    (b) If a lawyer for an organization knows that an officer, employee or other person associated with the organization is engaged in action, intends to act or refuses to act in a matter related to the representation that is a violation of a legal obligation to the organization, or a violation of law that reasonably might be imputed to the organization, and that is likely to result in substantial injury to the organization, then the lawyer shall proceed as is reasonably necessary in the best interest of the organization. Unless the lawyer reasonably believes that it is not necessary in the best interest of the organization to do so, the lawyer shall refer the matter to higher authority in the organization, including, if warranted by the circumstances, to the highest authority that can act on behalf of the organization as determined by applicable law.
        Furthermore, under 28 U.S.C. §535(b), government lawyers are bound to report to the attorney general "[a]ny information... received in a department or agency of the executive branch of the Government relating to violations of title 18 involving Government officers or employees."
25. *See, e.g.*, Report on the Role of the Legal Adviser, *supra* note 16; Roger C. Cramton, On the Steadfastness and Courage of Government Lawyers, 23 JOHN MARSHALL L. REV. 165 (1990).
26. For the role of State Department legal adviser in relation to international law, *see* Report on the Role of the Legal Adviser, *supra* note 16, at 360–62. *See also* Senate Committee on Foreign Relations, The ABM Treaty Interpretation Resolution, S. REP. No. 100–164, at 65 (1987), which comments as follows on the special responsibilities of the State Department legal adviser:

    The United States government needs such public servants-persons willing to place duty over ambition in defending the integrity of the law. Nowhere is this more true in the law of foreign relations. ...

The Legal Adviser stands alone among lawyers within our Federal Government. He is the first guardian, and often the last, of the United States government's commitment to the rule of law in two different legal systems-constitutional and international. . . .

The Legal Adviser is thus charged with American compliance with-and American efforts to enforce-the most momentous elements of the rule of law: rules of constitutional power, of international commitment, of war and peace. It is the Legal Adviser who, through his own integrity and the integrity of the legal analysis he oversees, must set the highest standards in honoring the law of the Constitution and the law of nations. It is the Legal Adviser who, when asked to "legalize" short-term policy ends over constitutional means, must be prepared to say no. It is the Legal Adviser who, regardless of political pressures, must revere law as the alternative to anarchy.

27. *See, e.g.*, John R. Bolton, Is There Really "Law" in International Affairs? 10 TRANSNATL. L. & CONTEMP. PROBS. 1 (2000); Charles Krauthammer, The Curse of Legalism: International Law? It's Purely Advisory, NEW REPUBLIC, Nov. 6, 1989, at 44; Jed Rubenfeld, The Two World Orders, WILSON Q., Autumn 2003, at 22.

28. *See, e.g.*, U.S. Is Said to Weigh Abducting Terrorists Abroad for Trials Here, NEW YORK TIMES, Jan. 19, 1986, at A1 (reporting that the State Department's legal adviser, in stating that he was prepared to support the "seizure" of terrorists in other countries, "acknowledged that such a move would violate international law, but said there were 'legitimate arguments in favor of'bending' the rules in extraordinary circumstances").

29. *See, e.g.*, Lawyers' Statement, *supra* note 8 ("Enforcement of all of our laws depends on lawyers telling clients not only what they can do but also what they can not [sic] do. This duty binds all lawyers and especially lawyers in government service.").

30. For views critical of the memoranda, see, for example, references cited *supra* note 15. For views defending the memoranda, see, for example, John C. Yoo, With 'All Necessary and Appropriate Force'; in Interrogations, U.S. Actions Align with Treaties and Congress" Wishes, LOS ANGELES TIMES, June 11, 2004, at B13.

31. *See* the discussion of this issue in Report on the Role of the Legal Adviser, *supra* note 16, at 363:

> [S]everal members noted the difficulty of determining impartially and authoritatively whether in a particular case the U.S. government was or was not complying with international law. An important reason for this difficulty in many cases is that legal conclusions depend on findings of fact and on judgments of reasonableness, necessity, proportionality or similar broad standards that are part of the law. In addition, in some cases, the content and interpretation of the applicable rules are in controversy.
>
> The Committee does not consider it useful to propose criteria or tests for determining when a legal argument or position is so slanted as to be beyond the range of responsible and good faith argument. Some members think that the international law community's good judgment and the public's common sense can generally be relied on to tell responsible arguments from those which are patently unfounded. Consequently, the most effective check on government advocacy of dubious or irresponsible legal positions will be the willingness of the Legal Adviser to publicly state, defend and be accountable for such arguments before other officials and Congress, the public and the community of international lawyers.

32. *See, e.g.*, WHARTON'S CRIMINAL LAW §79 ("Advice of Counsel") (Charles E. Torcia ed., 15th ed. 1993). But see News Hour report (Public Broadcasting System television broadcast, May 12, 2004) on Secretary of Defense Rumsfeld's appearance, along with General Richard Meyers, chairman of the Joint Chiefs of Staff, before a Senate hearing on

interrogation methods used in Iraq. In response to an assertion by Senator Richard Durbin of Illinois that such practices violate the Geneva Conventions, Secretary Rumsfeld stated: "General Myers, correct me if I'm wrong, but my recollection is that any instructions that have been issued or anything that's been authorized by the department was checked by the lawyers in your shop, in the office of the secretary of defense, and deemed to be consistent."

33. *See supra* note 13 and accompanying text.

34. *See id.*; Geoffrey C. Hazard, Jr., How Far May a Lawyer Go in Assisting a Client in Unlawful Conduct? 35 U. MIAMI L. REV. 669 (1981); CHARLES W. WOLFRAM, MODERN LEGAL ETHICS 692–98 (1986).

35. 1 TRIAL OF THE MAJOR WAR CRIMINALS BEFORE THE INTERNATIONAL MILITARY TRIBUNAL 286 (1947–49).

36. *United States v. Alstoetter*, 3 TRIALS OF WAR CRIMINALS BEFORE THE NUERN-BERG MILITARY TRIBUNALS UNDER CONTROL COUNCIL LAW No. 10, at 1086 (1949).

37. *See, e.g.*, LUC REYDAMS, UNIVERSAL JURISDICTION: INTERNATIONAL AND MUNICIPAL LEGAL PERSPECTIVES (2003); UNIVERSAL JURISDICTION: NATIONAL COURTS AND THE PROSECUTION OF SERIOUS CRIMES UNDER INTERNATIONAL LAW (Stephen Macedo ed., 2003); PRINCETON PROJECT ON UNIVERSAL JURISDICTION, THE PRINCETON PRINCIPLES ON UNIVERSAL JURISDICTION (2001), at <http://www.princeton.edu/~lapa/unive_jur.pdf>; but see Steven R. Ratner, Belgium's War Crimes Statute: A Postmortem, 97 AJIL 888 (2003); *Regina v. Barde, ex parte Pinochet*, [1999] 2 All E.R. 97, [1999] 2 W.L.R. 827 (H.L.).

38. *See* the latest 1992 revision of U.S. Army Field Manual 34–52, Intelligence Interrogation, which states: "Revelation of use of torture by U.S. personnel will bring discredit upon the U.S. and its armed forces while undermining domestic and international support for the war effort." *Id.* at 1–8. The field manual is available online at <http://atiam.train.army.mil/portal/atia/adlsc/view/public/302562–1/FM/34–52/FM34–52.HTM>.

39. KEN GORMLEY, ARCHIBALD COX: CONSCIENCE OF A NATION 338–58 (1997).

40. STEPHEN GILLERS, REGULATION OF LAWYERS: PROBLEMS OF LAW AND ETHICS 5 (6th ed. 2002).

41. 15 TRIAL OF THE MAJOR WAR CRIMINALS BEFORE THE INTERNATIONAL MILITARY TRIBUNAL 481–86 (1947–49).

42. 1 *id.* at 232.

43. Those involved in the preparation of the memoranda were also associated with the persons who sought to overthrow the Hitler regime on July 20, 1944. Although the memorandum on prisoners of war is signed by Admiral Canaris, not a lawyer, its drafting is attributed to Count von Moltke, a lawyer on his staff. See Detlev F. Vagts, International Law in the Third Reich, 84 AJIL 661, 698–99 (1990).

44. *Olmstead v. United States*, 277 U.S. 438, 485 (1928) (Brandeis, T., dissenting).

8 Torture: An Interreligious Debate

Joyce S. Dubensky and Rachel Lavery

IMAGES OF TORTURE ARE EVERYWHERE – ON TELEVISION, ON THE INTER-
net, in print. Today, the torturers and the tortured have faces, and physical abuse
is only one manifestation of the phenomenon. For too many, religious torment
seems to be the torturer's weapon of choice. It is what we see in the pictures
of smiling American soldiers from Abu Ghraib, taking pleasure in forcing their
prisoners into lewd acts that violate their cultural and religious beliefs. It is
also evident in the stories emerging from Guantanamo, including the explicit
allegations that a Muslim prisoner was forced to eat pork and ingest alcohol[1]
and that a female guard threw what appeared to be menstrual blood on Muslim
men, so that they would believe they were violating religious mandates.[2] The
straightforward pain of physical torture is impossible to fathom. And yet, torture
that is designed to strip a man or woman of his or her identity, religion, and core
beliefs seems somehow even more insidious.

Attacks on prisoners' religious identities are a time-honored tactic for dehumanizing the enemy, thereby making it easier to conduct military actions, to
pursue war and allow torture. Such use – and misuse – of religion needs to be
countered. Human rights activists are working to do so. But we also need to hear
from religious men and women. The voices of this too silent majority need to be
added to the national debate over ethics, the use of torture, and the proper limits
to be imposed on armies in power. At the Tanenbaum Center for Interreligious
Understanding, we believe that religiously identified individuals can and should
articulate common values across religious traditions to add a powerful rationale
to the legal and ethical proscriptions against the torture of men, women, and
children.

Such an articulation would be useful in the debate over torture. In general,
religious voices have not been prominent enough in the debate, even though the
conversation has large moral and ethical ramifications. In fact, Peter Steinfels, a
national observer and commentator on religion, noted a broad national failure
even to focus on moral issues with respect to Abu Ghraib, citing the "cursory $2\frac{1}{3}$
pages on ethical issues" that the Defense Department included in its extensive

report on the incidents.[3] In a related vein, the executive director of Amnesty International USA (an ordained Unitarian Universalist minister), observed that "[if] we could prove...that some universally recognized deity had imbued human beings with a set of rights that happened to coincide with the thirty articles of the Universal Declaration of Human Rights...my job [as an activist]...would suddenly become a lot easier."[4]

It is probably not surprising that religion has not been more dominant. Modern concepts of human rights are largely defined in terms of ethics and law.[5] As a creation of the international legal system, the mandates of the Universal Declaration of Human Rights (UDHR) are not grounded in an explicit philosophical or religious rationale.[6] In fact, none of the central international human rights conventions mentions God or a spiritual inspiration as a basis for protecting the welfare of all human beings.[7]

The history of these international conventions reveals the lack of a universally accepted, universal justification for human rights accepted by all societies – but we would suggest that one is critically needed. Shortly after the promulgation of the UDHR, the American Anthropological Association rejected the premise that all the rights specified in the Declaration were equally applicable to societies worldwide.[8] Similarly, in the Bangkok Declaration of 1993, a coalition of Asian governments asserted that human rights covenants must recognize "the significance of national and regional particularities and various historical, cultural, and religious backgrounds."[9] The 1993 Vienna Declaration on Human Rights then codified a very similar provision.[10]

These equivocations created a two-edged sword: they appealed to concepts of pluralism but simultaneously insulated governments from criticism for the failure to apply a universal definition of human rights.[11] This is why it is important to seek one or more universal bases to support human rights. We suggest that shared values in world religions are one place to start.

Religion is such a powerful societal force and personal experience that the voices of religion are needed to help protect human rights (and specifically, the right to be free from torture). In the words of one scholar: "to place complete confidence in a merely legal conception of human rights alone...seems to me to leave too much in the hands of the law."[12] While all religions worldwide do not identify the same theological basis for human rights, there are basic values across religious traditions that offer a powerful rationale for a shared condemnation of torture.

"Well of course the world's religions are against torture," you may be thinking. And for the most part, you would be accurate. But this is not the entire story. In nearly every religious tradition, you can also find justifications for war, violence, and even torture.

Given the diversity of the world's faiths and the variety of interpretations within each religious tradition at any point in time, this article will limit its focus to a small number of religious belief systems and some of the principles that define their views on torture as examples of the breadth of belief. We will provide an overview of how religion has been used in support of various forms of violence and torture, and then consider religious resources for identifying a universal religious commitment to human rights and the end of torture.* This analysis will reveal that religion is both a useful lens through which arguments on all sides of the torture debate can be viewed, and a rich resource for universally condemning it.

RELIGIOUS PERSPECTIVES: WHY HUMANS TORTURE

Religious traditions generally address how people come to mistreat others (including torture). But how they explain this varies. While it is beyond the scope of this paper to review many of these perspectives, it is instructive to consider an overview of a few of them.

Many Christians agree that, as a matter of faith, torture is intrinsically wrong, is a sin, and an insult to God.[13] However, different denominations offer different explanations for how and why torture occurs. Richard Mouw, a Calvinist, attributes acts of torture to original sin.[14] He sees the capacity of people to perform atrocities on other human beings as something that is within all of us: "[w]hen I recoil in horror, then, at the sight of American soldiers torturing Iraqi and Afghani prisoners, it is not because I am witnessing an evil that is unfathomable to me. . . . I see [this evil] lurking inside me, and once again I cry out to God for mercy and forgiveness."[15] However, Professor Mouw also believes that humans can resist original sin, provided they have God's help.[16]

Theologian William C. Placher echoes the view that all of us have the potential to torture, but he equates the potential of humans to sin as something akin to the psychological theory that all people are capable of evil.[17] These beliefs, for many Christians, mean that morality during war requires soldiers to restrain themselves, to follow Christian dictates, and seek help from God to treat others as God has mandated.[18]

Another Christian view is that the angel of darkness influences the torturer. For Miguel De La Torre, a professor and former pastor from the Southern Baptist tradition, it was the angel of darkness who seduced Abu Ghraib soldiers

---

* The United Nations Convention Against Torture and Other Cruel, Inhuman or Degrading Treatment or Punishment defines torture as:

> any act by which severe pain or suffering, whether physical or mental, is intentionally inflicted on a person for such purposes as obtaining from him or a third person information or a confession, punishing him for an act he or a third person has committed or is suspected of having committed, or intimidating or coercing him or a third person, or for any reason based on discrimination of any kind, when such pain or suffering is inflicted by or at the instigation of or with the consent or acquiescence of a public official or other person acting in an official capacity.

Opened for signature Dec. 10, 1984, art. 1 §1, S. Treaty Doc. No. 100-20 (1988), 1465 U.N.T.S. 113.

"into devouring and torturing those created in the image of God, all the while claiming that the blood we spill is the will of the Almighty and we are but God's instruments."[19] Again, this belief reflects the doctrine that all people are created in God's image with the infinite potential for good but also with the potential to be seduced from proper conduct.

Unlike many Christians, Muslims do not have a concept of original sin. Instead, Islam teaches that human beings' fundamental nature is one of moral innocence.[20] Each person innately knows moral right from wrong, but this knowledge dissipates as society corrupts people. As such, there will always be people who choose lives that violate their intrinsic innocence.[21] Professor Sohail H. Hashmi explains that this "uniquely human capacity for moral choice" not only means that people are destined not only to do good but also to mistreat their fellow human beings, often unjustifiably.[22]

Buddhists have a different explanation for torture. Though Buddhism has a core ethos of nonviolence, the Buddhist belief system views the human experience of the world as unsatisfactory and sees suffering as caused by desire for what is transitory and cannot be possessed. As such, some Buddhists explain conflict as coming from the same wellspring as all unwholesome acts, namely greed and desire, hatred, and delusion. When driven by these imperfections, people seek power to gain control over others and over transitory material things. This leads to an ever increasing desire for power and possessions, the loosening of ethical practices, and even to the persecution and torture of others.[23]

RELIGIOUS JUSTIFICATIONS FOR TORTURE

Throughout history, religion has had an intimate relationship with torture. And within a variety of religious traditions, one can find practices and beliefs that justify the use of torture in particular situations including self-torture to express spirituality, torture to save souls, and torture to preserve the greater good. The supporting religious beliefs range from assessments of the lesser of two evils to complex concepts of just war and the right of retribution.

Self-Torture
Inflicting pain on one's self as an act of spirituality has been recognized through-out history in different religious traditions. For example, one scholar explains that concepts of vicarious pain are at the center of Christian life.[24] Another asserts that Christianity is "about suffering, torture, the experience of Christ on the cross."[25] These foci embody the belief that God shares the suffering of torture victims,[26] and analogously, that individuals identify with Christ's sufferings.

In this vein, Christianity has a long history of asceticism, a practice that was widespread in the early centuries of the religion and throughout the Roman world. Held together by sharing the pain of Christ's suffering and sacrifice,[27] early Christian ascetics and martyrs often endured physical suffering because (stated simply) they believed that pain of the flesh was a validated pathway to enhance one's spiritual well-being and to remove the pain of the afterlife.[28] Self-torture is not merely historic; some Christians today still practice it as a religious exercise.[29]

Christianity is not alone in these kinds of practices.[30] *Mingzhen ke*, a Taoist text, contains liturgies that command practitioners to inflict pain and humiliation – torture – upon themselves to compensate for others' sins: "with your earnest heart and devoted mind, your sincerity is thorough and your suffering is sufficient; naturally [your supplications] will move [divine beings] pervasively."[31] Some Buddhists and Hindus perform acts of self-torture as *vrat*, vows, to keep themselves protected from illness and incarceration.[32] Some Shia Muslim men commemorate Ashura, a holiday marking the 680 C.E. martyrdom of Hussein, by flagellating themselves with chains or cutting their foreheads to emulate his suffering.[33] While the practice of self-torture, which many faiths encourage in limited situations, is distinguishable from the act of perpetrating torture on another, the acts are related in their violence on a person as a means to an end.

Saving Souls

In weighing proper conduct, many religious traditions throughout history have identified torture, in particular instances, as the lesser of two evils. The Inquisition is a clear, well-known example of how members of one religious community came to support the use of torture for what it believed were rightful ends. The Inquisition's tortures were intended as instruments of salvation targeting Muslims and Jews, and were used to identify heresy or other permutations of religious guilt, thereby saving the souls of sinners (and the souls of all people the heretic might influence) from eternal damnation.[34] Many of the torturers saw themselves as performing acts of Christian charity,[35] rooted in the Golden Rule's mandate to do good for others.[36]

The example of the Inquisition also shows how interpretations of religion and morality can evolve. In fact, the Roman Catholic Church has now moved 180 degrees from its position during the Inquisition. Ten years ago, Pope John Paul II condemned the use of physical and mental torture as one of the few actions that are evil "in themselves, independently of circumstances."[37]

For the Greater Good

Torture used with the objective of obtaining information in order to save lives – i.e., a lesser evil thesis – has also found religious justifications. In Jewish tradition, for example, some are inspired by the Talmud's emphasis on the innate and immeasurable worth in each human being: "One who saves but a single life is as if he has saved the entire world."[38] This exhortation emphasizes the value of each life in the Jewish tradition. But what if, by torturing just one individual, you could save thousands?

In the Jewish community today, a few thinkers postulate that torture might be acceptable if it meant that a great number would be saved from harm. In the perhaps far-fetched hypothetical where a prisoner knows the location of a nuclear bomb about to be detonated, an argument could be made that inflicting pain upon the prisoner may be justified to save the lives of countless others.

Rabbi Shraga Simmons, editor of a popular Jewish website, was posed this very question in his online column. Applying Maimonides' Laws of Murder 2:4–5,[39] which are based on the Talmud,[40] his opinion was that "reasonable physical pressure" would be justified in such a rare situation; indeed, he argued that there might be a *duty* to apply pressure to save other lives.[41] But Rabbi Simmons went on to emphasize that such drastic harm could only be justly inflicted on another person if the authorities had very accurate, specific evidence that the prisoner held the information necessary to save others from the horror of the nuclear bomb.[42]

Needless to say, even when articulating a justification for torture, the ultimate decision of whether to inflict such pressure is recognized as a difficult one. It is made more difficult by the Talmudic passage articulating Jewish law that, "One who destroys a single life is as if he has destroyed the entire world." In Judaism, each life has its intrinsic worth, and it is difficult to judge when one life may be subjected to pain for a *possibility* that the torture could save others.

Just Wars

Similarly, Christian traditions have developed concepts of just wars, which recognize limited circumstances in which force may be deemed justified. While most adherents of this theory oppose torture, its rejection under this theory is not absolute. For example, Saint Augustine, creator of the just war theory in Christianity, condoned the use of torture in order to learn necessary information from the person being tortured.[43]

The limitations on just wars vary among traditions but generally focus on whether the war is essential (e.g., have all alternatives been exhausted or must a nation defend itself from attack?) and how it is to be conducted (e.g., are operations proportional to the situation?).[44] Scholar John Finnis concludes that there is no place for the use of torture within this tradition. He maintains that one cannot weigh different moral constraints against each other (e.g., torture versus the need to save lives), and that every step in war must satisfy *all* moral requirements of the just war tradition.[45] While the military may carry out operations that may result in harm to noncombatants, this interpretation mandates that noncombatants may never be directly hurt or killed.[46] Military strategists may not intend harm to innocents either as an end or as a means (e.g., of breaking the other side's will or of gaining information).[47]

The just war theory, though generally associated with Christianity, has permutations in other faiths.[48] In Sikhism, for example, Guru Gobind Singh embraced the idea of a just war to protect oppressed people and preserve liberty: "When all efforts to restore peace prove useless and no words avail, Lawful is the flash of steel, it is right to draw the sword."[49]

Thich Nhat Hanh, a Buddhist, recognizes that an army may resort to violence and war but only in defense of itself or of an ally.[50] In a related line of thinking, some Buddhists have argued that violence can be condoned in the rare situation where it is the lesser of evils.[51] As Buddhism emphasizes intention and motive, defensive violence may be viewed as less wrong than other forms of violence.[52]

In a 1970s Thailand that was racked by violence and a struggle with communism, Buddhist monk Kittivuddho described the use of violence in self-defense (against the threat of invasion and communism) as less wrong than other forms of violence.[53] Indeed, he analyzed the national situation in terms of the lesser of two evils: it was legitimate to kill 5,000 people to protect the well-being of 42 million. He reasoned that "[i]f we want to preserve our nation, religion, and monarchy, we sometimes have to sacrifice *sila* (rules of morality) for the survival of these institutions."[54] Thus, Kittivuddho represents a strain of Buddhist thought that may accept violence, and possibly torture, when it is serving the greater good and therefore serving as a lesser evil even than killing. Kittivuddho's position is rare. Most Buddhists would be aghast at the thought of their religion justifying the use of violence – or torture – at all.

Retribution

History also tells how religious support for the use of cruel and inhuman treatment, potentially leading to acts that could constitute torture, has been used not just to save souls or gain information to save lives but, also, to punish. Retribution is built into the book of Exodus in the Hebrew Scriptures, when it says: "if there is serious injury, you are to take life for life, eye for eye, tooth for tooth, hand for hand, foot for foot, burn for burn, wound for wound, bruise for bruise."[55] Contrary to what a literal reading suggests, Rabbi David Freilich explains that these punishments were not meant to be meted out but were rather easily understood expressions of the seriousness of certain crimes and a means of deterrence.[56] Regardless, Jewish law has evolved to mandate monetary compensation and to prohibit physical retribution, thereby establishing a nonviolent concept of punishment. [57]

Islamic law, Sharia,[†] also supports the use of physical force for certain ends, namely the maintenance of law and order. In addition to regulating family law and interpersonal conduct, Sharia mandates a strict penal code that today is only followed in a handful of places, such as Pakistan and parts of Nigeria. For

---

[†] Sharia is the sacred law of the Islamic religion, which has also been enforced as law by religious courts in Muslim-controlled nations. The law is based primarily on four sources: the Qur'an, the practices of the Prophet Mohammed, the consensus of the Muslim community or scholars, and deductions from the previous sources. *See, e.g.,* Norman Anderson, *The Law of Islam, in* EERDMANS' HAND BOOK, *infra* note 113 at 326.

instance, the law requires that if someone is guilty of theft, his or her hands should be cut off to compensate for the crime, unless the criminal repents to God.[58] But before such retributive justice is meted out, strict conditions must be met. One must be tried in a Sharia court, and the punishment meted out by a judge. Likewise, if someone has been killed, the family of the deceased may choose to forgive the guilty person or demand blood money in lieu of physical punishment.[59]

A modern incarnation of retributive justice in the United States is the practice of capital punishment. While many would surely argue that capital punishment is not included within the definition of torture, it clearly must be understood as a form of cruel and inhuman treatment. In fact, capital punishment can viewed as on a continuum of conduct that begins with violence and war, allows for torture as a means to an end, and permits death at the hands of government as a proper form of societal punishment. As such, it is a relevant point of discussion because it involves governmentally-mandated pain and suffering.

There are a range of religious perspectives on the propriety of capital punishment and differences within the various traditions. The Southern Baptist Convention, for example, supports "the fair and equitable use of capital punishment . . . as a legitimate form of punishment" because human life is made in the image of God and those who take human lives must be properly punished.[60]

Conversely, the American Friends Service Committee founded the Religious Organizing Against the Death Penalty Project, which has distributed over 5,000 sample sermons against the use of capital punishment.[61] Pope John Paul II likewise spoke out against the practice, stating in a 1995 encyclical that the death penalty is only appropriate "in cases of absolute necessity, in other words, when it would not be possible otherwise to defend society."[62] To show how rarely capital punishment should be carried out, the late Pontiff pointed to a statement in the new *Catechism of the Catholic Church* that rings true in the torture context as well:

> If bloodless means are sufficient to defend human lives against an aggressor and to protect public order and the safety of persons, public authority must limit itself to such means, because they better correspond to the concrete conditions of the common good and are more in conformity to the dignity of the human person.[63]

In Japan, another industrialized democracy that permits capital punishment, the practice finds both religious supporters and detractors. For example, Megumu Sato, a former Buddhist priest, refused to sign execution orders during his term of office as Minister of Justice in the early 1990s. In contrast, Tomoko Sasaki, a former member of the Diet (Japanese Parliament) voiced religious support for the practice: "[a] basic teaching is retribution. . . . If someone evil does something bad, he has to atone with his own life."[64]

PRAGMATIC RELIGIOUS CONSIDERATIONS

While different religions articulate justifications for violence and torture, some religions (and religious leaders) also assess it from a pragmatic perspective. For example, Jewish law addresses the use of torture to coerce confessions. Though the Hebrew Bible actually mentions several confessions without disapprobation,[65] Jewish law now makes confessions by an accused inadmissible in criminal proceedings. The rationale is simple and based on an assessment of human nature. Because "no man calls himself a wrongdoer"[66] and because an offender is unlikely to be truthful about the wrongs he or she has committed,[67] self-incrimination is more likely to occur if the accused has been tortured or coerced. By making confessions of the accused inadmissible in a manner similar to the Fourth Amendment's exclusionary rule, therefore, Jewish law institutionalizes protections against torture.

Similarly, although St. Augustine condoned the use of torture to gain information, he also recognized an inherent weakness in the use of torture for this purpose:

> what is more intolerable . . . is that the judge, in the act of torturing the accused for the express purpose of avoiding the unwitting execution of an innocent man, through pitiable ignorance puts to death, both tortured and innocent, the very man whom he has tortured in order not to execute him if innocent.[68]

St. Augustine thus understood that torture often leads to unreliable results.

RELIGIOUS RESOURCES FOR CONDEMNING TORTURE

Beyond the pragmatic notion that torture yields results that cannot be trusted, there are also many interreligious beliefs that condemn the use of such violence and cruelty as intrinsically wrong.

Finding Divinity in the Tortured

The three Abrahamic faiths, Judaism, Christianity, and Islam, share more than a common ancestor, Abraham. They also share a fundamental belief that all humans are created in the image of the one God. The torture of another person, therefore, desecrates a being created in the divine image. And this is prohibited.

Judaism embraced this concept from its very beginnings. In fact, the first chapter of the first book of the Torah teaches that humans were created in God's image: ". . . God created humankind in his image, in the image of God he created them; male and female he created them."[69] In the words of Rabbi Arthur Waskow, "[t]orture shatters and defiles that Image."[70] Because the divine is within every person, Rabbi Waskow believes that every act of violence performed on a prisoner is the same as if it is performed upon God.[71] Rabbi Gerald Serotta of Rabbis for Human Rights refers to this concept as "the sacred dignity of the person."[72]

In a related context, Rabbi Marc H. Tanenbaum phrased it clearly:

> [E]ach human life is sacred and of infinite worth. In consequence, a human being cannot be treated as a chattel or an object to be disposed of for someone's program or project or ideology, but must be treated as a personality.[73]

Rabbi Tanenbaum's words serve as a powerful reminder that Judaism recognizes a transcendent nature in human beings that is trampled upon by acts of violence and disrespect, let alone torture.

Christianity retained the Jewish teaching that God is reflected in all humans and then built upon it through its theology. In fact, Christian clergy and commentators have invoked this divine image when speaking out against the abuses at Abu Ghraib and Guantanamo. When a group of over 200 religious (mostly – but not entirely – Christian) leaders sent an open letter to Attorney General Alberto Gonzales before his Senate confirmation, they beseeched him, as a man of religion, to stand against torture:

> As a self-professed evangelical Christian, you surely know that all people are created in the image of God. You see it as a moral imperative to treat each human being with reverence and dignity. We invite you to affirm with us that we are all made in the image of God – every human being. We invite you to acknowledge that no legal category created by mere mortals can revoke that status. You understand that torture – the deliberate effort to undermine human dignity – is a grave sin and affront to God.[74]

As in Judaism, this divine image inspires Christians around the world to respect the sanctity of all life.[75] Many Christians point to the Gospels to show the innate value in each individual: All people are so valuable that God sacrificed Jesus Christ for their salvation.[76] Jim Wallis, editor of the Christian *Sojourners* magazine, sees the belief that God's image is in every human as an "absolute barrier to the practice of torture" and as a foundation for international agreements such as the Geneva Convention.[77] While not all Christians would agree that the divine image is an absolute barrier to torture, Wallis' exhortation is potent.

Professor Jerry Irish, in seeking to articulate a Christian approach to human rights, states that the mandate to protect human rights for all people can be found in his faith's reverence for human dignity: "[t]hat respect is rooted for us in the love of God and in our participation in a common creation story...."[78] As such, Irish describes human rights as "not objects of faith but fruits of faith," and views the struggle for them as more than an ethical conviction. It is also a spiritual exercise.[79] For Irish and Christians who share his views, opposition to the U.S. government's use of torture is an act of faith.

Islam likewise teaches that humanity was created in God's image. According to many Muslims, God invested much of the "God-self" in each human being; Muslims are therefore expected to safeguard the well-being of all other human beings: "[t]o commit oneself to safeguarding and protecting the well-being of the individual is to take God's creation seriously."[80] Indeed, the Muslim holy book, the Qur'an, states that a person who kills another human unjustly is as if he or she has killed all of humankind.[81] And in this respect, the Qur'an makes no distinction between Muslims and non-Muslims, so that one cannot justify mistreatment of "the Other" simply on the basis of difference.[82] One scholar explains Islam as recognizing all humans as members of the same family; as such, one who tortures is actually harming his or her own brothers and sisters and should immediately perceive the wrong in so doing.[83]

The Abrahamic traditions influenced the Bahá'í faith, which likewise views humankind through a lens of divinity. The Bahá'ís see the divine image in each human, a belief which mandates that every life deserves protection: "I knew My love for thee, therefore I created thee, have engraved on thee Mine image and revealed to thee My beauty."[84] Bahá'í precepts firmly support human rights and are grounded in "the objective spiritual nature of the human."[85] Additionally, the Bahá'ís share the belief that all of humanity comprise one family, and that one should never want to cause harm to a family member in any way.[86] With this as a fundamental precept, it is difficult to find a position within the Bahá'í tradition that does anything other than oppose torture.

For Bahá'ís, protecting the rights of fellow human beings is a spiritual practice, an ethical one, and the fulfillment of one's responsibility for maintaining a stable society.[87] Recent in origin, the Bahá'í faith's revelations were first delivered in 1844, though it was several more decades before the faith was fully formed. Perhaps its genesis in the modern era explains why the religion included "modern" ethical as well as spiritual conceptions of human rights from the beginning.[88] Abdu'l-Bahá, leader of the Bahá'í faith from 1892 to 1921, asserted that humankind was then entering a new era of collective maturity in which people needed to continue their maturation and develop "new moral standards."[89]

Torture as Destroyer of Humanity

In every act of torture, there is the one who suffers the torture and the one(s) who perpetrate it. Many religious leaders have observed that torture occurs only when the torturer is unable to recognize the divinity in the other person. As such, many view both the individual being tortured and the one(s) who inflict the torture as victims. The person being tortured is assaulted, while the torturer's own humanity is lost with the inability to recognize the divine gift of humanity in each of us.[90] The all-encompassing inhumanity of an act of torture, therefore, makes it something to be decried.

Jim Wallis contemplated this phenomenon, noting that the dehumanization process is a prerequisite to torture: "[a]buse and torture are always more likely when the victims are objectified, made into an 'other' that is somehow different and less human than we are."[91] In this vein, the Reverend Barbara K. Lundblad, a Lutheran, characterized the treatment of "the other as less than human" as the greatest sin perpetrated at Abu Ghraib.[92] Validation for their conclusion was evident when a United States General proudly attributed his military success to the belief that "we're a Christian nation...and the enemy is a guy named Satan."[93]

The Vatican newspaper *L'Osservatore Romano* likewise condemned the acts at Abu Ghraib as sinful because they abused the human dignity of the detainees. Pointing to the now famous photo of a naked prisoner on a leash held by a U.S. soldier, the newspaper condemned the image as "the most 'tragically symbolic' because it [so graphically revealed the soldier's]...desire to treat the enemy almost as an animal."[94] This religiously-based concern regarding the impact of torture on the perpetrator again reflects Christian teachings that humans are created in God's image and that to violate a person's mental, physical, sexual, or religious integrity for any reason tears at the divine image within all of the parties involved – and deserves religious condemnation.[95]

The focus on the torturer is likewise evident in Islam. Taha Jabir Al- 'Alwani, an Islamic scholar, notes that a person's dignity is the "essence of his humanity."[96] When someone tortures another, his or her dignity is lost, and with it, that person's humanity. For many Muslims, when a human being tortures, it means that "animal qualities" have overwhelmed human ones.[97]

Buddhist monk Thich Nhat Hanh concluded that the acts of abuse at Abu Ghraib directly resulted from the soldiers' training, which caused them to lose their humanity: "preparing for war and fighting in a war means allowing our human nature to die and the animal nature in us to take over."[98] He believes that our human nature is protected when we adhere to our spiritual beliefs and refrain from mistreating others. Accordingly, he postulates that soldiers who go to war with a strong spiritual background are better able to retain their humanity during the preparation for and in the toils of combat. Nhat Hanh sees both torturers and their prisoners as victims. Each has lost his or her humanity, and each suffers as a result.[99] Indeed, some devout Buddhists may feel a sense of compassion even toward their torturers because they feel sorry for the abusers' "profound spiritual ignorance."[100] As Nhat Hahn phrased it: "When another person makes you suffer, it is because he suffers deeply within himself, and his suffering is spilling over. He doesn't need punishment – he needs help."[101]

This was the actual experience of a young Christian/Buddhist woman peacemaker, who started out as a radical activist and was then imprisoned and tortured. As Hyun Kyung explained at a working retreat of the Tanenbaum Center's *Peacemakers in Action* in 2004:

> I was in a radical student movement in Korea. When I was in Korea in my youth, I thought of bombing the U.S. embassy. During these days, I was arrested and tortured. I noticed something about my torturers.
>
> If I ever asked a torturer about his family, he couldn't torture me. This worked for three of the torturers. Then the fourth one, I could not make a connection with him. He was too broken. And he tortured me.
>
> At that time, I made the realization: Connection, no violence. No connection, violence. This is how I went from possible bomber to peacemaker.

These traditions – only a few examples of many – emphasize the value of each person. When identifying those beliefs that could provide a basis for a universal and interreligious condemnation of torture, the shared conviction that torture harms all involved, including those who perpetrate the torture, by destroying what makes us intrinsically human, is another place to begin.

Fair Treatment for Prisoners and Suspected Terrorists: A Religious Mandate

From the life, teachings, and death of Jesus Christ, many Christians derive a commandment to treat prisoners well.[102] Subjected to inhumane treatment as a prisoner and then crucified, Jesus' death graphically portrays the horror of torture.[103] The cross of Christ stands as a reminder to Christians not to be naïve because the cross represents what "humanity is capable of doing."[104] As one Baptist concluded, "[t]here's no doubt that Jesus stands with the victims of torture, not with the bystanders."[105] The Book of Hebrews therefore commands that Christians "[r]emember those who are in prison, as though you were in prison with them; those who are being tortured, as though you yourselves were being tortured."[106] And the Book of Matthew goes on to warn that nations will be judged by the way they treat prisoners.[107]

Islam also embraces concepts of fair treatment that directly impact their views on the use of torture in law enforcement or as a military device. Many Muslims take inspiration and guidance from the teachings of the Qur'an and from the sayings of the Prophet Mohammed and subsequent Islamic legal thinkers. Muslim jurists historically asserted that Mohammed prohibited the use of *muthla* (mutilations) in all situations and opposed the use of coerced confessions in political and legal matters. Over the years, Islamic legal scholars built on these prohibitions, concluding that Islam condemns torture in all situations.[108] But there are variations in Islamic thought. At least one scholar has observed that the jurists' understanding of what constituted torture, created in a different time, may differ from the more expansive understanding of torture that we have today, i.e., that sexual, psychological, and physical acts also can be torture.[109]

The Pacifist Impulse in Various Religions Traditions

Pacifism has roots in religions traditions that prohibit all forms of violence, including torture. Some of the 20th century's greatest heroes, including Gandhi and Martin Luther King, Jr. stand as icons of these beliefs. Hinduism, the religion of Gandhi, has a strong tradition of *Ahimsa*, or nonviolence. (*Himsa*, violence, is harm toward any living creature.) Therefore, to live by the virtue of Ahimsa, one must not cause pain to any being whatsoever.[110] While the Ahimsa tradition has not prevented all violence by Hindus[111] it serves as another basis for articulating a universal religious condemnation of torture.

Jainism[112] holds Ahimsa as its central tenet. The religion teaches that the only path to salvation of one's soul (i.e., *moksha*, freeing one's self from matter and from karma that weighs the soul down) is the protection of every other soul, both human and animal. Harm inflicted upon others is tantamount to hurting oneself because the act attracts karma and impedes the path toward liberation of the soul.[113] To this end, Jain scripture teaches that one must not "injure, abuse, oppress, enslave, insult, torment, *torture*, or kill any creature or living being."[114]

This principle of nonviolence is so strong that Jain monks can often be seen wearing cloths over their faces to prevent the accidental inhalation – and death – of insects, and carrying brooms to gently sweep the path so that they do not accidentally step on any creatures.[115] In such a tradition, a place for torture can hardly be contemplated. To violate the bodily, psychological, or sexual integrity of anyone goes directly against the core of Jainism, even with countervailing considerations such as public safety or a need for information.

Buddhism similarly exalts principles of nonviolence in its beliefs about right action. In the Buddhist worldview, suffering is recognized as the condition in which most people live. In this context, suffering is not directly analogous to the physical pain experienced in violence and torture. Rather, the concept is that life, as most people live it, is "unfulfilling and filled with insecurity." This reality influences all of human existence.[116] Buddha framed this in terms of Four Noble Truths, which, simplistically described, are:

1. There is suffering.
2. There is an origin of suffering, which comes from a failure to recognize the transitory nature of the world and therefore to desire to control it.
3. The end of suffering is possible.
4. There is a path [of proper conduct] to the end of suffering.[117]

The way to end suffering is known as the Eightfold Path, which articulates eight steps that constitute Right Action. When the eight steps are followed, one's suffering can end.[118] And Buddhism teaches that acting to stop others' suffering (such as the physical suffering of torture) is Right Action, a step in the path.[119]

The Quakers are among the best-known Christian representatives of nonviolence. Quakers believe that God is always present, and that God is in everyone. Drawing on this concept of the divine in each of us, therefore, the Quakers formed a fully pacifist religious tradition.[120] In 1661, in response to suppression and persecution, founder George Fox declared to King Charles II that: "All Bloody principles and practices, we as to our own particulars, do utterly deny, with all outward wards and strife and fighting with outward weapons, for any end or under any pretence whatsoever. And this is our testimony to the whole world."[121] While the pacifist tradition of the Quakers is the subject of many full-length books, it serves here merely to illustrate another religious movement that leaves absolutely no room for the practice of torture.

THE GOLDEN RULE

Each of the foregoing provides religious resources for a shared conviction that our common humanity precludes torture. But they do not stand alone. These beliefs are related to a nearly universal value, which can be found in almost every religion of the world: the Golden Rule. A classic formulation of the rule is that "you should do unto others as you would have them do unto you." Among the religious traditions that share this religious and – ethical – premise are:

Bahá'í: And if thine eyes be turned towards justice, choose thou for thy neighbor that which thou choosest for thyself.[122]

Buddhism: "Hurt not others in ways you yourself would find hurtful."[123]

Christianity: In everything do to others as you would have them do to you; for this is the law and the prophets.[124]

Confucianism: Do not unto others what you do not want them to do to you.[125]

Hinduism: This is the sum of duty: do naught unto others which would cause you pain if done to you.[126]

Islam: Not one of you is a believer until he loves for his brother what he loves for himself.[127]

Jainism: A man should wander about treating all creatures as he himself would be treated.[128]

Judaism: Love your neighbor as yourself.[129]

Native American: Respect for all life is the foundation.[130]

Sikhism: Treat others as thou wouldst be treated thyself.[131]

Taoism: Regard your neighbor's gain as your own gain and your neighbor's loss as your own loss.[132]

Zoroastrianism: That nature alone is good which refrains from doing unto another whatsoever is not good for itself.[133]

While the core value is the same, the rationale for the Golden Rule differs across the traditions. For example, one scholar bases the universality of the Golden Rule in the necessity to protect the person to person relationship.[134] This is the relationship all humans have with all other humans, simply on the basis of being human. In a similar vein, Christian (and, in many ways, Jewish and Muslim) ethics teach that the duty one owes to one's neighbor is also the duty one owes to God. When some Christians do good deeds for others, therefore, they may view their acts as helping Christ himself, and see acting immorally toward another as hurting Christ.[135]

Although each religion explains the principle a little differently, the universal mandate of the Golden Rule has a clear message: each person, friend or foe, neighbor or prisoner, is to be treated well and not to have pain inflicted upon him or her. Torture, here understood as the infliction of horrific pain regardless of the end for which it is done, is an anathema to the Golden Rule – a mandate that people across the world aspire to fulfill.

CONCLUSION

This cursory review of religious perspectives on torture is necessarily oversimplified and limited by the focus on only a few of the world's many religious traditions. And yet, even these few reveal a range of views on the use of torture. They also remind us that virtually universal resources exist within the religions of the world for unequivocally condemning torture.

Clearly, articulating an interreligious doctrine against torture is not an easy task. But it is necessary, because it can serve as a call to action to individuals motivated by religion. And action is needed. Abu Ghraib and Guantanamo leave us no choice.

Within every religious tradition, there are core values capable of providing the foundation for a shared perspective that all people must be treated with respect – as we would want for ourselves. When viewed as a fundamental doctrine within diverse religious traditions, the Golden Rule can serve as the basis for a shared belief in the sanctity of human life and a universal religious mandate condemning the horrors of torture and supporting human rights everywhere, worldwide.

This process was in play at the 2004 Parliament of the World's Religions, when it created a Universal Declaration of Human Rights, and included freedom from torture as one of the fundamental rights to be protected:

Article 5
1. No one shall be subjected to torture or to cruel, inhuman, or degrading treatment or punishment, inflicted either physically or mentally, whether on secular or religious grounds, inside the home or outside it.
2. No one shall subject anybody to such treatment.[136]

The statement is absolute and allows no room for torture. It sets the stage. Now, religious leaders and religious practitioners must turn these words into an activist movement in which diverse religious voices speak for human rights with one, clear message: *No More Torture*! If not now, when?

NOTES

1. *See* Andrew Sullivan, *Atrocities in Plain Sight*, NEW YORK TIMES, Jan. 23, 2005, at 7–1.
2. *See* Maureen Dowd, *Torture Chicks Gone Wild*, NEW YORK TIMES, Jan. 30, 2005, at A17.
3. Peter Steinfels, *The Ethical Questions Involving Torture of Prisoners are Lost in the Debate Over the War in Iraq*, NEW YORK TIMES, Dec. 4, 2004, at A16.
4. WILLIAM SCHULZ, TAINTED LEGACY 110 (2003).
5. *See* Arvind Sharma, *The Religious Perspective: Dignity as a Foundation for Human Rights Discourse, in* HUMAN RIGHTS AND RESPONSIBILITIES IN THE WORLD'S RELIGIONS 69 (Joseph Runzo, Nancy M. Martin, and Arvind Sharma eds., 2003) [hereinafter HUMAN RIGHTS AND RESPONSIBILITIES].
6. *See* Matthew Weinberg, *The Human Rights Discourse: A Bahai Perspective*, 1996–97 THE BAHÁ'Í WORLD 247, *at* <http://www.bahai.org/article-1-8-3-2.html> (last visited Jan. 31, 2005).
7. *See id.*

8. *See id*. However, this contention is now being subjected to serious revision. *See id*.

9. *See Report of the Regional Meeting for Asia of the World Conference on Human Rights*, World Conference on Human Rights, U.N. GAOR, at 293–95, U.N. Doc. A/Conf.157/ASRM/8 – A/CONF.157/PC/59, at 8 (1993).

10. *See* Vienna Declaration and Programme for Action, U.N. GAOR, World Conf. on Hum. Rts., 48th Sess., pt. II, para. 5, U.N. Doc. A/CONF. 157/124, available at <http://www.unhchr.ch/huridocda/huridoca.nsf/(Symbol)/A.CONF.157.23.En?OpenDocument> (last visited Feb. 7, 2005) ("While the significance of national and regional particularities and various historical, cultural and religious backgrounds must be borne in mind, it is the duty of States, regardless of their political, economic and cultural systems, to promote and protect all human rights and fundamental freedoms").

11. *See* Weinberg, *supra* note 6.

12. Sharma, *supra* note 5 at 70.

13. *See Religion & Ethics Newsweekly: Is Torture Ever Justified?* (PBS television broadcast, May 14, 2004), *transcript available at* <http://www.pbs.org/wnet/religionandethics/week737/p-perspectives.html> (last visited Jan. 14, 2005) [hereinafter *Is Torture Ever Justified?*].

14. The Apostle Paul brought the idea of original sin to Christianity – the thought that through the biblical Adam all of humankind has sinned and that Christ has saved humanity. In the orthodox interpretation, a belief grew that humankind had an original divine endowment of grace that mars the natural gift of free will. Protestant reformers saw it necessary to focus on a more sweeping doctrine of the absolute sinfulness of humankind. *See* WILLIAM L. REESE, DICTIONARY OF PHILOSOPHY AND RELIGION 706 (1996) (1980).

15. Richard Mouw, *Original Sin in Abu Ghraib, at* <http://www.beliefnet.com/story/145/story_14559.html> (last visited Jan. 7, 2005).

16. *See id*.

17. *Religion & Ethics Newsweekly: Abu Ghraib Prison Abuse Scandal* (PBS television broadcast, May 14, 2004), transcript available at <http://www.pbs.org/wnet/religionandethics/week737/commentary.html> (last visited Jan. 14, 2005) [hereinafter *Abu Ghraib Prison Abuse Scandal*].

18. *See Editorial: The Evil in Us*, CHRISTIANITY TODAY, June 10, 2004, available at <http://www.christianitytoday.com/ct/2004/007/2.22.html> (last visited Jan. 14, 2005).

19. Miguel De La Torre, *The Christian Ethics of Torture*, <http://www.beliefnet.com/story/158/story_15898.html> (last visited Jan. 7, 2005).

20. *See* Sohail H. Hashmi, *Interpreting the Islamic Ethics of War & Peace, in* ETHICS OF WAR & PEACE: RELIGIOUS AND SECULAR PERSPECTIVES 146, 149 (Terry Nardin ed 1996) [*hereinafter* ETHICS OF WAR & PEACE].

21. *See id*.

22. *Id*.

23. *See id*.

24. *See* ARIEL GLUCKLICH, SACRED PAIN 29 (2001).

25. Christopher Dickey & Rod Noland, *'Precious' Suffering*, NEWSWEEK, Feb. 28, 2005, at 24, 27.

26. A Lutheran columnist wrote of how he stared at drawings of torture victims hung in a Catholic Church and thought to himself: "God shared the sufferings of these people." John Hoffmeyer, *Would You Do It?: Some Question If Torture Is Always Wrong*, THE LUTHERAN, Jul. 2004, <http://www.thelutheran.org/0406/page12.html> (last visited Feb. 16, 2005).

27. *See id*.

28. *See* GLUCKLICH, *supra* note 24 at 21,17. See also H.J. THURSTON, I BUTLER'S LIVES OF THE SAINTS 27 (1990), *cited in* GLUCKLICH, *supra* note 24 at 17, for a description of a martyr's beliefs.

29. *See generally* Glucklich, *supra* note 24.
30. *See generally id.* for a thorough description and analysis of the relationship between religion and pain, and the ways that self-mutilation has been exercised as a religious experience.
31. *Mingzhen ke* 24b, *quoted in* Glucklich, *supra* note 24.
32. *See* Glucklich, *supra* note 24 at 18.
33. *See What is Ashura?* BBC News, <http://news.bbc.co.uk/1/hi/world/middle_east/4274749.stm> (last visited Mar. 4, 2005).
34. James Kellenberger, *Religious Moral Diversity and Relationships, in* Ethics in the World Religions 65, 81 (Joseph Runzo and Nancy M. Martin eds., 2001).
35. *See id.*
36. *See id. See also* section "The Golden Rule," *infra.*
37. Steinfels, *supra* note 3.
38. *Sanhedrin* 37a.
39. Maimonides' writings are generally considered authoritative interpretations of Jewish law, though he lived approximately 600 years after the compilation of the Talmud. Maimonides was the most influential scholar of medieval Jewish philosophy, and his works are widely cited as explanations of Jewish principles.
40. Sanhedrin 46a.
41. *Ask Rabbi Simmons: Torture, at* <http://judaism.about.com/library/3_askrabbi_o/bl_simmons_torture.htm> (last visited Jan. 18, 2005).
42. *See id.*
43. See Miguel De La Torre, Doing Christian Ethics from the Margins (2004), discussing Augustine, City of God 6:19:6
44. *See* John Finnis, *The Ethics of War and Peace in the Catholic Natural Law Tradition, in* Ethics of War & Peace, *supra* note 20 at 15, 25.
45. *See id.* at 26.
46. *See id.* at 27, 30.
47. *See id.* at 26.
48. *See generally* Religion, Law & The Role of Force (J. I. Coffey & Charles T. Mathewes eds., 2002); David R. Smock, Religious Perspectives on War (2002) (1992) (discussing just war in Christianity, Judaism, and Islam).
49. W. Owen Cole & Piara Singh Sambhi, The Sikhs: Their Religious Beliefs and Practices 140 (1978).
50. *See id.*
51. *See* Peter Harvey, An Introduction to Buddhist Ethics 255 (2000).
52. *See id.* at 254.
53. *See id.* at 254.
54. *Id.* at 261.
55. *Exodus* 21:23–25 (New International).
56. *See Ethos: Capital Punishment: A Brief History* (Australian Broadcasting Corporation Radio Broadcast, Nov. 2, 2003), *transcript available at* <http://www.abc.net.au/rn/relig/enc/stories/s970403.htm> (last visited Feb. 14, 2005) [hereinafter *A Brief History*].
57. *See id.* at 217–18.
58. *See* Philip Novak, The World's Wisdom 310 (1995).
59. *A Brief History, supra* note 56.
60. *See* Elizabeth Clarke, *In Religious Circles the Debate Rages: When Timothy McVeigh is Executed, Will God be Grieving?* Palm Beach Post, May 12, 2001, at 1D.
61. *See id.*
62. *Cited in The Death Penalty: Pro & Con: The Pope's Statement,* <http://www.pbs.org//pages/frontline/angel/procon/popestate.html> (last visited Feb. 16, 2005).

63. *Quoted in id.*
64. Charles Lane, *Why Japan Still Has the Death Penalty*, WASH. POST, Jan. 16, 2005, at B1.
65. COHN *supra* note XX at 213 (1984). *See Joshua* 7:19–20; *1 Samuel* 14:43; *2 Samuel* 1:16.
66. *B. Sanhedrin* 9b, *cited in* COHN, *supra* note XX at 213.
67. COHN, *supra* note XX at 213–14.
68. SAINT AUGUSTINE, CITY OF GOD 145 (W.C. Greene trans., 1960).
69. *Genesis* 1:27 (New Revised Standard).
70. *Statement by Rabbi Arthur Waskow, available at* <http://www.cfba.info/analyst/ Gonzales_press_conference.html> (last visited Feb. 14, 2005). *See also* Rabbis for Human Rights/North America, *Rabbinic Letter on Torture* (Jan. 27. 2005) *available at* <http://www.rhr-na.org/rabbinic-letter-Jan2005.html> (last visited Feb. 28, 2005).
71. *Id.*
72. Press Release, Rabbis for Human Rights/North America, *Rabbis for Human Rights Launches Campaign Against Torture* (Jan. 5, 2005), at <http://www.rhr-na.org/ torture-jan05.html> (last visited Feb. 2, 2005).
73. MARC H. TANENBAUM, RELIGIOUS VALUES IN AN AGE OF VIOLENCE 3–4 (1976).
74. *The Question of Torture: An Open Letter to Alberto Gonzales, available at* <http://www.informationclearinghouse.info/article7593.htm> (last visited Jan. 14, 2005).
75. *See* De La Torre, *supra* note 43.
76. *See John* 3:16.
77. Jim Wallis, *The Theology of Torture*, in SOJOURNERS, Aug. 2004, at 5, 6 (2004).
78. Jerry Irish, *A Christian Response to the Universal Declaration of Human Rights by the World's Religions, in* HUMAN RIGHTS AND RESPONSIBILITIES, *supra* note 5 at 159, 163.
79. *Id.*
80. Khaled Abou El Fadl, *The Human Rights Commitment in Modern Islam, in* HUMAN RIGHTS AND RESPONSIBILITIES, *supra* note 5 at 301, 338.
81. *Id.*
82. *Id.*
83. Taha Jabir Al- 'Alwani, *Of Torture and Abuse, at* <http://www.islamonline.net/english. introducingislam/politics/System/article07.shtml> (last visited Jan. 18, 2005).
84. Bahá'u'lláh, *The Hidden Words*, Arabic #3, 4.
85. Weinberg, *supra* note 6.
86. *See id.*
87. *See id.*
88. *See id.*
89. SHOGHI EFFENDI, THE WORLD ORDER OF BAHÁ'U'LLÁH: SELECTED LETTERS 165 (1991).
90. *See Religion & Ethics Newsweekly: The Ethics of Torture* (PBS television broadcast, Feb. 20, 2004), *transcript available at* <http://www.pbs.org/wnet/ religionandethics/week725/cover.html> (last visited Jan. 14, 2005).
91. *See* Wallis, *supra* note 77 at 6.
92. *Is Torture Ever Justified?*, *supra* note 13.
93. *See* Javed Akbar, *How Jesus' Message is Blatantly Subverted*, TORONTO STAR, Dec. 11, 2004, at M14; John Hendren, *General's Speeches Broke Pentagon Rules*, L.A. TIMES, Aug. 20, 2004, at A15.
94. John Thavis, *Vatican Newspaper Condemns "Inhuman Acts of Torture,"* CATHOLIC NEWS SERVICE, May 10, 2004), *available at* <http://www.catholicnews.com/data/stories/ cns/20040510a.htm> (last visited Jan. 14, 2005).
95. *See also* Hoffmeyer, *supra* note 26.
96. Al- 'Alwani, *supra* note 83.

97. *See id.*
98. Interview by Lisa Schneider with Thich Nhat Hanh, <http://www.beliefnet.com/story/146/story_14636_1.html> (last visited Feb. 28, 2005).
99. *See id.*
100. *Id.*
101. THICH NHAT HANH, THE HEART OF THE BUDDHA'S TEACHING 183 (1998).
102. Jack Miles, *Prisoners and Other Strangers, at* <http://www.beliefnet.com/story/146/story_14623.html> (last visited Jan. 7, 2005).
103. Crucifixion was a chosen mode of torturous death. Additionally, the Christian Bible tells of tortures inflicted upon Jesus before the crucifixion. *See, e.g., John* 19:1 ("Then Pilate took Jesus and had him flogged."); *Mark* 15:19 ("Again and again they struck him on the head with a staff and spit on him").
104. *Abu Ghraib Prison Abuse Scandal, supra* note 17.
105. Bob Allen, Religious Leaders Urge Attorney General to Denounce Torture, ETHICS DAILY, Jan. 6, 2005, available at <http://www.ethicsdaily.com/print_popup.cfm?AID=5195> (last visited Jan. 14, 2005).
106. *Hebrews* 13:3 (New Revised Standard).
107. *See Matthew* 25:31–46.
108. *See* Abou El Fadl, *supra* note 80 at 334.
109. *Id.* at 350 n.49.
110. *See* Klaus K. Klostermaier, *Himsa and Ahimsa Traditions in Hinduism, in* THE PACIFIST IMPULSE IN HISTORICAL PERSPECTIVE 227, 234 (Harvey L. Dyck ed., 1996).
111. Indeed, in the modern era, Hinduism has been aligned with militant political fundamentalism and violence, though at least one commentator blames the pressures of our time more than Hinduism itself. *See* Klaus K. Klostermaier, *Himsa and Ahimsa Traditions in Hinduism, in* THE PACIFIST IMPULSE IN HISTORICAL PERSPECTIVE 227, 235 (Harvey L. Dyck ed., 1996).
112. Jainism is an ancient Indian religion that emphasizes harmlessness and renunciation as the path towards bliss. Jains – like Hindus and Buddhists – believe in karma, that their actions, both good and bad, will be remembered in the next life. There are fewer than seven million Jains in the world. *See generally BBC Religion & Ethics: Jainism,* <http://www.bbc.co.uk/religion/religions/jainism/> (last visited Feb. 14, 2005).
113. *See Ahimsa – Non-Violence,* BBC RELIGION & ETHICS, *at* <http://www.bbc.co.uk/print/religion/religions/jainism/living/living2.shtml>.
114. *See id.* (emphasis added).
115. *See, e.g.,* Myrtle Langley, *Respect for All Life: Jainism, in* EERDMANS' HANDBOOK TO THE WORLD'S RELIGIONS 207, 215 (1994) [*hereinafter* EERDMANS' HANDBOOK].
116. HUSTON SMITH & PHILIP NOVAK, BUDDHISM 32–33 (2003).
117. THICH NHAT HANH, CREATING TRUE PEACE 87 (2004).
118. *See* SMITH & NOVAK, *supra* note 114 AT 31.
119. *Id.*
120. *See* ANTHONY BRADNEY & FIONA COWNIE, LIVING WITHOUT LAW 25 (2000).
121. *Cited in id.* at 27.
122. *Lawh'i 'Ibn'i 'Dhib, [Epistle to the Son of the Wolf]* 30.
123. *Udana-Varga* 5:18.
124. *Matthew* 7.12.
125. Confucius, *Analects* 15.13
126. *Mahabharata* 5:1517.
127. *Fortieth Hadith of an-Nawawi* 13.
128. *Sutrakritanga* 1.11.33.
129. *Leviticus* 19:18.

130. *The Great Law of Peace.*
131. *Adi Granth.*
132. *T'ai Shang Kan Ying P'ien.*
133. *Dadistan-I-Dinik* 94:5.
134. *See* Kellenberger, *supra* note 34 at 80–81.
135. *See* Miles, *supra* note 102.
136. Reprinted in HUMAN RIGHTS AND RESPONSIBILITIES, *supra* note 5 at 142.

9 Unwise Counsel: The War on Terrorism and the Criminal Mistreatment of Detainees in U.S. Custody

David W. Bowker

WITH GROUND ZERO STILL SMOLDERING, PRESIDENT BUSH BEGAN PREPAR-ing the nation for a new kind of war intended to destroy al Qaeda's terrorist network by any means necessary. In a memorable visit to the Pentagon on September 17, 2001, the President told the U.S. Armed Forces to be "ready to defend freedom at any cost" and reminded them of their duty to "respond to the call of the Commander-in-Chief and the Secretary of Defense." The President then used strong words to imply that the enemy in this new war may be sufficiently "barbaric" to justify "hunt[ing] them down" and taking no prisoners. Speaking directly to those under his command, he said:

> All I can tell you is that Osama bin Laden is a prime suspect, and the people who house him, encourage him, provide food, comfort or money are on notice.... [W]e're going to find those who – those evil-doers, those barbaric people who attacked our country and we're going to hold them accountable.... I know that an act of war was declared against America.... I know that this is a different type of enemy than we're used to. It's an enemy that likes to hide and burrow in, and their network is extensive. *There are no rules*. It's barbaric behavior. They slit throats of women in airplanes in order to achieve an objective that is beyond comprehension. And they like to hit, and then they like to hide out.
>
> *But we're going to smoke them out*. And we're adjusting our thinking to this new type of enemy.... It's going to require a new thought process. And I'm proud to report our military, led by the Secretary of Defense, understands that; understands *it's a new type of war*, it's going to take a long time to win this war ... *to get them running and find them and hunt them down*.
>
> *I want justice*. There's an old poster out west, as I recall, that said, "*Wanted: Dead or Alive.*" ... I remember that they used to put out there in the old west,

The views expressed in this article are strictly the author's and are not intended to reflect the views of the Office of the Legal Adviser, the Secretary of State, the U.S. Department of State, or the U.S. Government.

a wanted poster. It said: *"Wanted, Dead or Alive."* All I want and America wants [is for] him [to be] brought to justice. *That's what we want.*

Three days later, the President declared an all-out war on terrorism. Speaking to a special joint session of Congress on September 20, 2001, he explained that the nation's response to 9/11 would not be limited to traditional law enforcement means or to a few isolated missile strikes. Instead, he pledged to "direct every resource at [his] command – every means of diplomacy, every tool of intelligence, every instrument of law enforcement, every financial influence, and every necessary weapon of war – to the destruction and to the defeat of the global terror network." He avowed to destroy not only al Qaeda, but any group or nation that dared to protect, aid, or cooperate with al Qaeda: "Every nation in every region now has a decision to make – either you are with us or you are with the terrorists." The President's orders were clear: destroy al Qaeda and its supporters and use every possible means to do it.

The Secretary of Defense and the Vice President repeated those orders, again and again, both privately and publicly, and sometimes in even harsher terms. The Vice President, for example, delivered a speech in October 2001 in New York City, in which he declared that:

> We are dealing here with evil people, who dwell in the shadows, planning unimaginable violence and destruction. We have no alternative but to meet the enemy where he dwells.... *We must and we will use every means at our disposal* to ensure the freedom and security of the American people.... When you think of ... the merciless horror inflicted at the World Trade Center, *no punishment for the terrorist seems too harsh*.... [I]n dealing with the terrorists themselves, we will be relentless and they will come to understand the meaning of justice.... This is a struggle against evil. That is why people in every part of the world and of all faiths stand together against this foe. And that is why we will prevail.... The struggle can only end with their complete and permanent destruction ... and in victory for the United States and the cause of freedom.

The "tone at the top" had thus been set. The message was clear. "The gloves are off," according to an anonymous official quoted by the *Washington Post* on October 21, 2001. "The [P]resident has given the agency *the green light to do whatever is necessary.* Lethal operations that were *unthinkable* pre–September 11 are now under way." The President and Vice President had effectively elevated the mission of destroying the terrorists above all else.

AN EARLY (BUT FLEETING) CONSENSUS AMONG THE LAWYERS

Against this backdrop, the President turned to his legal advisor, Judge Alberto Gonzales, then-Counsel to the President ("WH Counsel"), for guidance regarding his legal authority to conduct the new war on terrorism. WH Counsel, in turn, convened a small cadre of ideologically-aligned, politically-appointed lawyers, including most notably David Addington, Counsel to the Vice President,

("VP Counsel"), William J. "Jim" Haynes II, General Counsel at the Department of Defense ("DoD/GC"), and John Yoo, a Deputy Assistant Attorney General in the Office of Legal Counsel at the Department of Justice ("OLC"). Together, WH Counsel and his team were the chief architects of U.S. legal policy in the war on terrorism. They provided legal opinions on countless questions of U.S. and international law, including, for example, the President's right to use military force against terrorists both inside and outside U.S. territory, the jurisdiction of federal courts over Guantanamo Bay, the status of enemy combatants under the Geneva Conventions, and the legality of interrogation methods under the Torture Convention.

The first fundamentally important legal question to arise – *i.e.*, whether the President has the authority to wage a "war" against a nonstate organization of terrorists – was (and is) the source of intense public debate, but generated surprisingly little controversy within the government. Most government lawyers involved readily agreed with the WH Counsel, VP Counsel, DoD/GC, and OLC's conclusion that the nature and intensity of al Qaeda's attacks cause them to be more akin to armed conflict than mere criminal acts and that, as a practical matter, the United States can no longer afford to deal with this enemy solely by traditional law enforcement means. In order to protect the country, the President had to have the legal authority to use all the assets of the U.S. government, including the armed forces, against this insidious and deadly enemy. For those who accepted that the President has the legal authority to wage war against al Qaeda and its supporters, it necessarily followed *a fortiori* that he has the legal authority to capture and detain enemy combatants for the duration of active hostilities. Similarly, most government lawyers readily accepted the notion of using military commissions to try enemy combatants in this new war.

None of these important threshold questions was particularly controversial among the experts – not at the National Security Council (NSC), not at DoD, not at Justice, and not even at State. Indeed, many government experts not only shared the conclusions, they actively assisted OLC with the research and analysis to support them. For many, however, their acceptance and support were based on the fundamentally important assumption that the President would adhere *as a matter of law* to domestic and international rules of war – as traditionally interpreted and understood – including in particular those rules that prohibit the mistreatment of detainees and require military courts to afford basic due process to the accused. We now know, however, that WH Counsel, VP Counsel, DoD/GC and OLC saw it differently. They were intent, it seems, on minimizing or avoiding the rule of law in this new war.

THE FACILITATORS: CIRCUMVENTING LEGAL CONSTRAINTS IN THE WAR ON TERRORISM

WH Counsel and his team repeatedly advised the President, the executive branch, and the U.S. Armed Forces that the traditional law of armed conflict does not apply in the war on terrorism. They told the President and his chain of command that the traditional rules of warfare do not constrain them in this "new kind of war." They warned the President that the traditional laws and customs of war could impede his ability to destroy the enemy and protect American citizens. OLC – and John Yoo in particular – played a critical role by working tirelessly to come up with novel arguments and narrow interpretations of the "old" rules, such that key provisions were either inapplicable or rendered meaningless in this new context. Yoo and others employed every argument imaginable to support a predetermined conclusion that the law affords no rights or protections to the enemy in this new war. Yoo and his team effectively reversed decades of U.S. legal policy and military doctrine by concluding that the United States has no binding legal obligation to treat enemy detainees humanely while in U.S. custody.

Relying on OLC's conclusions, White House Counsel advised the President that his power to fight, interrogate, and punish terrorists in this war is unlimited as a legal matter. To the extent any law may purport to limit the President's powers as the Commander-in-Chief, WH Counsel and his team concluded such law would be unconstitutional. Relying again on OLC, WH Counsel even went so far as to advise the President that he has the power – *as a matter of law* – to suspend or disregard treaties and laws that might impede his authority to effectively conduct the war on terrorism. These and countless other legal positions suggest that the President's lawyers may have been too focused on providing legal cover for whatever U.S. conduct might be operationally necessary, and not focused enough on providing independent legal judgment and reaching sound conclusions of law.

Evidence of this expedient approach to the law first surfaced when the President issued his first Military Order on November 13, 2001 (the "November 13 order" or the "order"). The order called for the establishment of military commissions for the trial of suspected terrorists and directed the Secretary of Defense to adopt rules consistent with the requirement that commission proceedings be "full and fair." Inexplicably, however, the order failed to ensure basic due process, completely ignored the Geneva Conventions, and failed to otherwise reflect universally-accepted judicial norms such as the presumption of innocence and the right to appeal. The order also sought to preclude judicial oversight by prohibiting any and all recourse to courts. Although the order closely resembled President Franklin Roosevelt's orders from World War II, it failed to take into account significant changes in the law since that time, including for example the ratification of the 1949 Geneva Conventions, the enactment of the Uniform Code of Military Justice, and the enactment of the War Crimes Act.

For these reasons, the order was met with fierce (and politically expensive) opposition at home and abroad. Although the order left open the possibility that the commission rules might ultimately afford more protections than the order required, it was nonetheless heavily criticized for omitting even the most basic procedural protections, violating modern military principles and regulations, disrespecting a co-equal branch of government, and failing to take important political and diplomatic considerations into account. Such defects might have been obvious to some experts in government, but most never even saw it because it was not formally vetted beyond the small team of lawyers working with WH Counsel and VP Counsel. To avoid dissent or disagreement, the team did not distribute drafts of the order to the Judge Advocates General for the U.S. Armed Forces, the legal staff for the Joint Chiefs of Staff, or the Legal Adviser to the Secretary of State, or otherwise initiate a standard interagency clearance process with the NSC staff. Nor was it vetted with any of our coalition partners, notwithstanding its potentially disastrous effects on their ability to cooperate in the war on terrorism (as several exasperated allies quickly pointed out when they first learned of the order in the newspapers).

Despite all the controversy and trouble, not a single military commission has been completed since the order was issued on November 13, 2001; not one verdict has been reached. The few military commissions that were convened were promptly halted last year when a federal district court in Washington D.C. held that the commissions had been established and administered in violation of the U.S. Constitution and the Geneva Conventions.

In an apparent attempt to mask these shortcomings, WH Counsel vigorously defended the November 13 order. In an OpEd published by *The New York Times* on November 30, 2001, WH Counsel reassured the American people that the order "preserves judicial review in civilian courts." In reality, however, the order attempted to do exactly the opposite. It purported to preclude judicial review for any purpose whatsoever; specifically, section 7(b) provides that detainees "shall not be privileged to seek any remedy or maintain any proceeding, directly or indirectly, or to have any such remedy or proceeding sought on [their] behalf, in (i) any court of the United States, or any State thereof, (ii) any court of any foreign nation, or (iii) any international tribunal." In the face of this clear prohibition, WH Counsel told the public not to worry because the order does not mean what it says. After all, he pointed out, "the language of the order is similar to the language of a military tribunal order issued by President Franklin Roosevelt" and that order was "construed by the Supreme Court to permit habeas corpus review." While it may be true that the November 13 order was modeled after a military order with a similar provision to which the Supreme Court chose not to defer, it is misleading to say that the November 13 order actually "*preserves* judicial review in civilian courts." In truth, the order does no such thing.

Even worse, we now know that WH Counsel and his team were working *at the time* to ensure that courts would be powerless to review U.S. conduct in the war on terrorism. According to official memoranda that have since been released to the public, it now appears that, at the time WH Counsel wrote his OpEd, he and OLC were crafting legal arguments to show that U.S. detention centers outside the United States are beyond the jurisdictional reach of any U.S. court. An OLC memorandum dated December 28, 2001, contains a painstakingly detailed analysis designed to show that a U.S. detention center at Guantanamo Bay would not fall within the jurisdiction of any federal court.[1] Thus, it was ideally suited for detaining, interrogating, and trying suspected terrorists without fear of judicial oversight. Within days, dozens of detainees were flown from Afghanistan to Guantanamo Bay, with hundreds more to follow over the course of 2002 and 2003, where they remain to this day. Tellingly, the U.S. government has vigorously opposed every effort to obtain habeas corpus review of these detentions, notwithstanding WH Counsel's public reassurance that the President's November 13 order "preserves judicial review in civilian courts."

This is not to say that enemy combatants detained in war are entitled to have access to lawyers and civilian courts – the law of war provides no such general right for enemy combatants – rather, it is to draw attention to the fact that WH Counsel publicly reassured the American people that military commissions would be subject to judicial oversight when neither he nor the President ever had any intention of allowing civilian courts to review any aspect of our conduct in the war on terrorism. These early efforts to avoid application of the rule of law to the war on terrorism were a sign of things to come.

Shortly before the detainees arrived at Guantanamo Bay in January 2002, OLC circulated a draft opinion in which Yoo provided an exhaustive legal blueprint explaining how the President could circumvent, suspend, or simply ignore the most fundamentally important laws of war, including the Geneva Conventions, the War Crimes Act, and customary international humanitarian law.[2] His analysis even explained how to avoid judicial oversight, referring back to the December 28 memorandum on Guantanamo Bay. Most of Yoo's arguments were neither frivolous nor unreasonable, but nearly all were novel, controversial, and contrary to the spirit of the Geneva Conventions, longstanding U.S. legal policy, standing military regulations, and a proud U.S. military tradition and ethos of respecting both the letter and spirit of the law of war.

To take just one example, Yoo concluded that the President can simply disregard the Geneva Conventions by "suspend[ing] our treaty obligations . . . during the period of the conflict." Yet, Article 131 of the third Geneva Convention on Prisoners of War (the "GPW") prohibits any party from "absolv[ing] itself of any liability" for grave breaches of the Conventions, e.g., for the commission of "torture or inhuman treatment." Moreover, Article 142 of the GPW states that any suspension or "denunciation" of the treaty "shall take effect one year after . . . notification," and, in the event a conflict is already ongoing, "shall not take effect until peace has been concluded" and all prisoners have been released. Inexplicably, however, neither OLC nor WH Counsel mentioned these articles in their written analysis for the President. Nor did they mention to the President that Yoo's suspension argument was inconsistent with both longstanding U.S. legal policy and standing military regulations in effect at the time.

Instead, the President was advised that he is free to suspend the Geneva Conventions at any time and for any reason including, for example, because

Afghanistan was a "failed state" and therefore no longer a legal entity for purposes of international law. Again, however, neither OLC nor WH Counsel told the President that the failed-state theory was novel, unprecedented in U.S. practice, and inconsistent with international law. Nor did they advise him that it had been rejected in the strongest terms by William H. Taft, IV, the Legal Adviser to the Secretary of State ("State/L"). Although WH Counsel acknowledged in his January 25, 2002 memorandum that State/L had expressed a different view, WH Counsel failed to describe the nature of the legal dispute or to mention that State/L had also taken issue with Yoo's version of the "facts," which were inconsistent with reports from regional and intelligence experts in the U.S. Government.[3] As it turns out, Yoo had cherry-picked his "facts" from a handful of public sources on the internet. Although the President ultimately chose not to invoke the failed-state theory – due in part to the Secretary of State's last-minute intervention – the President's February 7, 2002 decision memorandum says that he nonetheless accepted the OLC and WH Counsel's "legal conclusion" that he has the authority to suspend the Geneva Conventions at any time and for any reason.[4]

OLC's assault on the law of war did not stop at treaty law. To preclude a "back door" application of Geneva Convention rules and principles, OLC – and Yoo in particular – sought to do away with applicable customary international law. To that end, Yoo opined that customary international law does not bind the President as a matter of domestic law and that it "can have no legal effect on the government or on American citizens because it is not law." Even if it were law, he argued, the President would have "ample authority to override [it]" as a matter of constitutional law. In any event, Yoo warned, "relying on customary international law would undermine the President's control over foreign relations and his Commander-in-Chief authority."

Again, although not technically unreasonable or frivolous, Yoo's arguments read more like the zealous advocacy of an aggressive litigator than a rigorous and balanced analysis that has long been the hallmark of an OLC legal advisor. Contrary to traditional OLC practice, Yoo omitted or discounted information that undermined his conclusions. For example, notwithstanding that Yoo devoted nearly five pages of his January 2002 memorandum to showing that customary international law is irrelevant, he failed to say that the United States has long considered other countries bound by customary international law in armed conflict. Yoo also failed to mention that customary international law is binding as a matter of international law and that it affords minimum rights and protections to all war-time detainees. Although Yoo acknowledged that the U.S. Supreme Court has recognized that customary international law is binding in some circumstances, see, e.g., *The Paquete Habana*, 175 U.S. 677, 700 (1900), he dismissed the Court's conclusion as bad law. He added that customary international law is "subject to override by the action of the political branches," but then failed to note that any "override" of law in armed conflict would depart radically from longstanding U.S. legal policy and precedent. Tellingly, Yoo's analysis and advice are eerily silent on military considerations; nowhere does he disclose that a decision to follow his advice would be counter to U.S. military culture and tradition, U.S. military standing regulations, and the U.S. Uniform Code of Military Justice.

Yoo also did not hesitate to undercut "common Article 3," a bedrock provision of the Conventions that was meant to protect lawful and unlawful combatants alike by proscribing *in all circumstances* conduct that has been universally condemned as "grave breaches" of international humanitarian law including, for example, subjecting detainees to torture, medical experimentation and other "inhuman" treatment. Relying on the negotiating history and other nontextual arguments, Yoo concluded that common Article 3 applies only to "internal" wars and therefore does not cover "armed conflict between a nation-state and a transnational terrorist organization." Although his interpretation of common Article 3 is not unreasonable, Yoo failed to say that adopting such an interpretation would be contrary to longstanding U.S. legal policy and the legal policies of our allies in the war on terrorism. He also did not disclose that his interpretation had been soundly rejected by the U.S. Department of State, the U.S. Department of the Navy, the U.S. Department of the Army, the U.S. Department of the Air Force, the U.S. Joint Chiefs of Staff, and the highest-ranking Judge Advocates General in the U.S. military. Yoo did not mention that these departments and the Judge Advocates General viewed – and continue to view – common Article 3 as broadly applicable in all armed conflicts "not of an international character" and, in any event, binding as a matter of customary international law on *all parties* to such armed conflicts. He did not explain that accepting his advice *not* to apply the Geneva Conventions, common Article 3, or customary international law would effectively deprive the United States of any legal basis to prosecute war crimes and deprive U.S. soldiers of any claim to legal protections in the event they were to fall into enemy hands.

Relying on Yoo's analysis, WH Counsel, in turn, advised the President to disregard the Geneva Conventions in the war on terrorism. In a draft memorandum to the President dated January 25, 2002,[5] WH Counsel explained that "the war against terrorism is a new kind of war . . . [the nature of which] places a high premium on other factors, such as the ability to quickly obtain information from captured terrorists . . . in order to avoid further atrocities against American civilians. . . . [T]his new paradigm renders obsolete" various provisions of the Geneva Conventions, including "strict limitations on questioning of enemy prisoners." Avoiding the Geneva Conventions, WH Counsel reasoned, "preserves flexibility" and "[s]ubstantially reduces the threat of domestic criminal prosecution" for conduct that might otherwise be considered unlawful – in part because the War Crimes Act does not apply unless triggered by the underlying application of the Geneva Conventions. Thus, WH Counsel concluded, simply by deciding not to apply the Geneva Conventions, the President can "create a reasonable basis in law that [the War Crimes Act] does not apply, which would provide a solid defense to any future prosecution."

WH Counsel explained to the President that having such a defense is important because "it is difficult to predict with confidence" the types of actions that could be deemed "inhuman" or "cruel." Curiously, however, he failed to advise the President that these terms have a plain meaning and that, in any event, similar terms have been carefully defined by the U.S. Supreme Court in the context of the Eighth Amendment, by various international tribunals, by the International Committee of the Red Cross, by the U.N. Commission on Human Rights, and by U.S. military regulations. Rather than identifying and articulating these various interpretations of "cruel and inhuman" treatment or otherwise explaining to the President how he might adhere to the spirit of the rule, WH Counsel instead told the President that he should avoid the rules altogether by simply declaring the Geneva Conventions inapplicable. This, he said, would "avoid foreclosing options for the future" and minimize the risk of criminal liability.

WH Counsel's January 25 memorandum prompted a strong rebuke from Secretary of State Colin Powell. Secretary Powell advised WH Counsel and the NSC legal staff in writing that "[t]he President should know that a decision that the [Geneva] Conventions do apply is consistent with the plain language of the Conventions and the unvaried practice of the United States in introducing its forces into conflict for over fifty years."[6] Notwithstanding those concerns, the U.S. Attorney General, John Ashcroft (the "AG"), adopted OLC and WH Counsel's approach.

Parroting OLC and WH Counsel's result-oriented approach, the AG advised the President in a February 1, 2002 letter that "determin[ing] that the Geneva Convention does not apply" would be the surest way to minimize "various legal risks of liability, litigation and criminal prosecution."[7] The AG said that a presidential determination not to apply the Geneva Conventions would effectively provide the necessary "legal certainty" to avoid criminal liability "relating to [U.S.] field conduct, detention conduct or interrogation of detainees." Such a determination would likely preclude the courts from "entertain[ing] charges that American military officers, intelligence officials, or law enforcement officials violated Geneva Convention rules." With startling candor, the AG cautioned the President that a judicial review of his determination should be avoided at all costs because it *"could involve substantial criminal liability for involved U.S. officials."* Although the President referred to the Attorney General's letter as a "legal opinion," the AG's letter (tellingly) never discussed a single provision of the Geneva Convention.

Although the President ultimately decided to apply the Geneva Conventions to the war in Afghanistan, he decided that no combatants were entitled to prisoner-of-war status, that the Geneva Conventions would not apply to the global war on terrorism, that common Article 3 was inapplicable, and that neither treaty law nor customary international law could constrain his power as Commander-in-Chief. In short, WH Counsel and his team got their way.

The courts disagreed. Try as they might to prevent judicial intervention, the President's lawyers were unsuccessful in their efforts to avoid federal jurisdiction. Nor could they persuade the courts to accept their view that the President has unfettered authority to detain and interrogate enemy combatants as he sees fit. Although the courts have shown great deference to the President's authority as Commander-in-Chief, they have also firmly rejected the notion that the President's power is virtually unchecked in war. See, e.g., *Hamdi v. Rumsfeld*, 124 S. Ct. 2633 (2004); *Padilla v. Hanft*, Civ. No. 2:04-2221-26AJ,*_(U.S. Dist. S.C. Feb. 28, 2005).

In *Padilla*, the U.S. District Court for the District of South Carolina declined to adopt the U.S. government position that the President has unchecked power as the Commander-in-Chief to arrest U.S. citizens anywhere in the world (including in the United States), designate them "enemy combatants," and detain them *in communicado* in solitary confinement and without legal process for the indefinite duration of the war on terrorism. *See Padilla*, Civ. No. 2:04-2221-26AJ. Although the Supreme Court never reached the merits in *Padilla*, they firmly rejected similarly broad assertions in *Rasul v. Bush*, 124 S. Ct. 2686 (2004). There, the court found that the government's attempt to hold detainees indefinitely without affording them even the most perfunctory individual status determinations – e.g., under Article 5 of the Geneva Conventions – was an unconstitutional denial of due process. *Rasul*, 124 S. Ct. 2686.

Perhaps most troubling of all is the infamous "torture memorandum," dated August 1, 2002.[8] In that memorandum, OLC concluded that the laws against torture are "unconstitutional" to the extent they "interfere [ ] with the President's direction of . . . the detention and interrogation of enemy combatants. . . ." OLC stated that our domestic legislation implementing the Torture Convention does not apply to Guantanamo Bay and, even if it did, it would bar only the most severe acts "inflicting, and that are specifically intended to inflict, severe pain or suffering . . . equivalent in intensity to the pain accompanying serious physical injury, such as organ failure, impairment of bodily function, or even death." OLC further advised that even if U.S. officials committed torture at Guantanamo Bay, "certain justification defenses might be available that would potentially eliminate criminal liability." In short, OLC concluded that there is no criminal liability for individuals who commit acts tantamount to torture, so long as such acts are undertaken pursuant to the President's Commander-in-Chief authority.

The government has since disavowed the original torture memorandum and revised the underlying analysis in a new memorandum (the "new torture memorandum"), dated December 30, 2004. It did so, however, only after photographic evidence of the crimes at Abu Ghraib became public and only in the face of extraordinary public pressure, and the need to diffuse controversy immediately prior to Judge Gonzales' confirmation hearing for the position of the

U.S. Attorney General. Although we now know that evidence of these crimes was circulating within the government for months prior to the public exposure, neither WH Counsel nor his legal team did anything to amend their flawed legal analysis and advice until after the Abu Ghraib photographs were publicly available. Tellingly, the "new" OLC states in the amended torture memorandum that "[c]onsideration of the bounds of [the President's Commander-in-Chief] authority [to commit torture] would be inconsistent with the President's unequivocal directive that United States personnel not engage in torture" – a clear indication that the original torture memorandum is now seen as having been counterproductive and contrary to good policy.

In sum, these and other legal opinions and this advice together reveal a deeply troubling pattern of a sustained and conscious effort by the lawyers to eliminate, minimize, or circumvent basic legal constraints on U.S. conduct in the war on terrorism. Wherever the law of war could be interpreted to bestow legal rights on the enemy or to impose legal duties on the President, the lawyers sought to avoid or undermine it. This expedient approach to the law of war effectively reversed a proud, longstanding U.S. tradition of adhering to both the letter and the spirit of the law of war and applying that law broadly to afford basic legal protections to all detainees, even those suspected of war crimes. That had been every U.S. President's approach in the post–World War II era and – but for OLC's legal opinions and WH Counsel's advice – it could easily have been President Bush's approach in the war on terrorism. Instead, WH Counsel, OLC, and their team concluded that the President and, by delegation, U.S. soldiers and intelligence officers were essentially free *as a matter of law* to aggressively interrogate detainees – using cruel and inhuman treatment (or even torture, if deemed necessary by the President) – and to do so, at least until recently, without serious fear of criminal liability.

THE FORESEEABLE RESULT: CRIMINAL MISTREATMENT OF DETAINEES IN U.S. CUSTODY

This approach may have won favor with the President and certain members of his war cabinet, but it also led to a major breakdown in the rule of law and undermined the primary deterrent to war crimes.

By placing detainees beyond the protection of any law, the AG, WH Counsel, VP Counsel, OLC, and DoD/GC gave U.S. officials a false sense of impunity with regard to their conduct in the war on terrorism and, in particular, their treatment of detainees. It now appears that sense of impunity – and the interrogation policies and methods that developed as a result – led to a permissive atmosphere at U.S. detention centers, resulting in overly aggressive interrogations and, in some instances, criminal homicide, torture, and cruel and inhuman treatment.

Official military indicate that at least 75 detainees have died in U.S. custody since the beginning of 2002. Roughly 25 of those deaths are confirmed or suspected *homicides*, meaning that American soldiers or intelligence officials have murdered prisoners in U.S. custody. Many more have abused or tortured prisoners in U.S. custody. According to the official U.S. Army report on detention conditions in Iraq – the so-called "Taguba Report," named for the major general who oversaw the investigation – American soldiers and intelligence officials have engaged in a widespread pattern and practice of "sadistic, blatant, and wanton criminal abuse[]" toward enemy prisoners in our custody.[9] Acts of abuse have included punching, kicking, "beating . . . with a broom handle and a chair," "stomping," threatening with "deadly force," using blunt force to injure and intimidate, "slamming" against walls, "stomping" on body parts, "jumping on" detainees, "forcing groups of . . . detainees to masturbate . . . while being photographed and videotaped," "forcing detainees to remove their clothing and keeping them naked for several days at a time," "threatening male detainees with rape," "having sex with a female detainee," sexually assaulting detainees, "sodomizing [detainees] . . . with a chemical light and . . . a broom stick," threatening to electrocute detainees, "attaching wires to . . . fingers, toes, and penis to simulate electric torture," threatening with deadly force, using military attack dogs to intimidate and bite, "photograph[ing] dead Iraqi detainees," and other cruel, inhuman, and degrading treatment.

Reports from Guantanamo Bay – including recently-released FBI e-mails and various reports of internal investigations – provide startling evidence of other widespread abuses, such as the use of prolonged sensory deprivation, prolonged sleep deprivation, prolonged detention in solitary confinement, prolonged use of "stress positions" and shackling to produce severe pain, and excessively cruel treatment that is, in the words of the International Committee of the Red Cross, "tantamount to torture." Instances of homicide, rape, so-called "waterboarding," and various other means of torture have been corroborated and reported by various national media sources. These grave breaches, sadly, are war crimes of the highest order.

When the Abu Ghraib photographs were released, President Bush, Secretary Donald Rumsfeld, and others initially condemned the abusive acts they depicted as the work of "a few bad apples" – and many of us hoped that was the case – but we now know that the pattern and practice of abuse has been so widespread and pervasive (not only at Abu Ghraib, but elsewhere in Iraq, Afghanistan, and at Guantanamo Bay) as to strongly suggest a link to official policies and procedures. Indeed, the *Final Report of the Independent Panel to Review DoD Detention Operations* commissioned by Secretary Rumsfeld and chaired by former Secretary James Schlesinger (the "Schlesinger Report")[10] concludes:

> Abuses of varying severity occurred at different locations under different circumstances and contexts. They were widespread and, though inflicted on only a small percentage of those detained, they were serious both in number and in effect. . . . [T]he abuses were not just the failure of some individuals to

follow known standards, and they are more than the failure of a few leaders to enforce proper discipline. There is both institutional and personal responsibility at higher levels.

In short, this was more than the work of "a few bad apples." If, as the Schlesinger Report concludes, "[t]here is both institutional and personal responsibility at higher levels," the law of war imposes a duty to identify and punish those responsible.

RECOGNIZING THE CONNECTION BETWEEN
THE LEGAL ADVICE AND THE ABUSES

Countless other military memoranda, correspondence, and orders similarly demonstrate that our men and women in uniform relied on the lawyers' arguments to disregard standard protections for detainees. For example, a Joint Task Force 170 ("JTF 170") legal memorandum from a JAG lawyer at Guantanamo Bay ("GTMO") to the JTF 170 Commander at GTMO, dated October 11, 2002, states that "the Geneva Conventions limitations that ordinarily would govern captured enemy personnel interrogations *are not binding on U.S. personnel conducting detainee interrogations at GTMO.*"[11] Accordingly, the memorandum concludes that interrogation methods are generally lawful so long as "no severe physical pain is inflicted" and that "the use of scenarios designed to convince the detainee that death or several painful consequences are imminent is not illegal for the same aforementioned reasons that there is a compelling governmental interest and it is not done intentionally to cause prolonged harm." Given the wide range of misconduct that is permissible under the "no severe physical pain" standard, the lawyers' opinions and advice created the impression that it was legally permissible to subject detainees to cruel and inhuman treatment in the war on terrorism.

Indeed, that was the express *purpose* of the legal opinions and advice. As the written memoranda demonstrate, the legal opinions and advice were intended to minimize the risk of criminal prosecution for conduct that the lawyers knew to be legally questionable under the Geneva Conventions, the War Crimes Act, and the Torture Convention. This purpose is clear from documents such as the AG's February 1, 2002 legal "opinion,"[12] in which he warned of the possibility that a "court would subsequently entertain charges that American military officers, intelligence officials, or law enforcement officials violated Geneva Convention rules relating to field conduct, detention conduct or interrogation of detainees." WH Counsel apparently foresaw the same possibility when he advised the President in a memorandum dated January 25, 2002,[13] that avoiding the Geneva Conventions would "[s]ubstantially reduce [ ] the threat of criminal prosecution under the War Crimes Act." In a January 2002 memorandum regarding the Geneva Conventions,[14] Yoo similarly advised that OLC's opinions would effectively "preclude" prosecutions for war crimes.

In short, the AG, WH Counsel, VP Counsel, DoD/GC, and OLC were trying to provide legal cover – something akin to immunity – for U.S. soldiers and other officials who might subsequently be accused of criminal misconduct in the war on terrorism. Given this purpose, it seems unfair that lawyers like Yoo would publicly blame our men and women in uniform and other U.S. officials for misconduct that was entirely foreseeable and that Yoo and the other lawyers had tried to shield from future prosecution.

This is not to say that criminally abusive treatment was officially sanctioned or that the lawyers are solely or directly responsible for the crimes that have occurred. Rather, it is to say that such crimes were the foreseeable result of our official policies and that those policies were made legally possible by the legal opinions and advice of the AG, VP Counsel, WH Counsel, OLC, and DoD/GC.

We now know that the abusive treatment of detainees might not have become such a widespread practice had it not been for the legal opinions and advice of WH Counsel, OLC and others. For example, the Schlesinger Report states that, prior to the legal advice that the Geneva Conventions do not apply and the resulting conclusion in the President's memorandum that detainees in U.S. custody "are not legally entitled to [humane] treatment," the military had been faithfully adhering to standard Geneva Convention rules with respect to detainees. Will Taft, who recently left his position as the Legal Adviser to the Secretary of State, made a similar observation during a speech he delivered at the American University on March 24, 2005, stating:

> It has been a continuing source of amazement and, I may add, considerable disappointment to me that, notwithstanding the stated intention of the Pentagon's leadership to comply with the requirements of the Conventions without qualification, lawyers at the Department of Justice thought it was important to decide at that time that the Conventions did not apply to al Qaeda as a matter of law and to qualify the commitment to apply them as a matter of policy to situations where this was "appropriate' and "consistent with military necessity." This unsought conclusion unhinged those responsible for the treatment of the detainees in Guantanamo from the legal guidelines for interrogation of detainees reflected in the Conventions and embodied in the Army Field Manual for decades. Set adrift in uncharted waters and under pressure from their leaders to develop information on the plans and practices of al Qaeda, it was predictable that those managing the interrogation would eventually go too far, and news reports now indicate that from time to time this happened.[15]

In the face of mounting evidence, it now seems safe to say that OLC's legal opinions and advice, at a minimum, increased the likelihood that U.S. officials would engage in abusive interrogation practices. Because that result was entirely foreseeable, it can fairly be said that the lawyers knowingly facilitated such practices by emboldening U.S. officials to order, approve, supervise, or engage in conduct that would not otherwise have been an option. The lawyers knowingly facilitated such practices by causing U.S. officials to believe that they had the cover of law and thus, to feel a sense of impunity, when they mistreated detainees. To the extent that belief caused U.S. officials to engage in unlawful conduct, the lawyers must bear at least some of the blame.

DENYING RESPONSIBILITY, DEFLECTING BLAME ON TO OTHERS, AND MAKING EXCUSES

To date, WH Counsel, OLC, and the other lawyers involved have steadfastly denied responsibility for the abuses that have occurred, deflected the blame on to others – including the U.S. military – and offered a multitude of excuses.

First, the lawyers have denied having any responsibility whatsoever. In an OpEd dated January 2, 2005, Yoo claimed that the "abuses [at Abu Ghraib] had nothing to do with the memos defining torture."[16] Likewise, on June 22, 2004, shortly after the Abu Ghraib scandal became public, WH Counsel and DoD/GC told the public – incorrectly, it turns out – that the policies in Washington had nothing to do with the abuses that occurred in Iraq. WH Counsel erroneously asserted that "interrogation and detention policies in Iraq were issued by [Lieutenant] General [Ricardo] Sanchez in the field" and "are not related to legal opinions" issued by the AG, OLC or WH Counsel. WH Counsel stated emphatically – but again, incorrectly – that "the incidents at Abu Ghraib, they . . . have nothing to do with the policies contained in any of these memos" and that only the "misinformed have asked whether the President's February 7th determination contributed to the abuses at Abu Ghraib."[17]

But the abuses at Abu Ghraib were in fact linked to the President's February 7th determination and the underlying legal opinions of WH Counsel, the AG, and OLC. The official Schlesinger Report concludes that Lt. Gen. Sanchez, the commander of U.S. forces in Iraq, relied on the "President's Memorandum of February 7, 2002," which incorporated by reference OLC's January 22 opinion and the AG's February 1 opinion.[18] Thus, when the toughest measures of interrogation were approved in Iraq, including some of the abusive measures employed at Abu Ghraib, they were approved on the basis of the very opinions and advice that WH Counsel said had nothing to do with the policies in Iraq and the abuses at Abu Ghraib. The connection is clear. In the words of State/L former Legal Adviser Taft, OLC's "unsought [legal] conclusion[s] unhinged those responsible for the treatment of the detainees in Guantanamo from the legal guidelines for interrogation of detainees reflected in the Conventions and embodied in the Army Field Manual for decades . . . it was predictable that those managing the interrogation would eventually go too far." Likewise, Rr. Adm. Lohr, the former Judge Advocate General of the Navy, noted that there is an obvious connection between the legal policy decision to abandon the traditional law of war and the subsequent abuses that occurred in their absence.

Yoo nonetheless claims that neither he nor WH Counsel is to blame for the abuses that have occurred because, in his words, "the administration never ordered the torture of any prisoner...and these incidents did not result from any official orders." Yoo's denial misses the point. While it may be true that U.S. officials were not "ordered" to torture detainees, they were authorized to use cruel, inhuman and degrading treatment. Yoo even criticizes those who fail to recognize what he apparently thinks is an important distinction between "cruel" treatment and "torture" – the latter is criminally punishable but the former, he claims, is not. Yoo is mistaken on the law; in fact, cruel treatment is criminally punishable under U.S. law including, e.g., Article 55 of the Uniform Code of Military Justice ("UCMJ"). Even if one were to assume that there is no criminal punishment for cruelty toward another human, Yoo's argument does not take into account the fact that such treatment would nonetheless be *unlawful* under both U.S. and international law. Moreover, Yoo's argument is eerily silent on the ethical and moral implications of his legal advice. Although such considerations are not, strictly speaking, "*legal*," they obviously inform our understanding of the law and ought to inform our clients' consideration of the legal policy questions at issue.

The legal memoranda and opinions reinforced the pressure to explore the limits of what the law permits, concluding in many instances that U.S. officials could lawfully commit acts that went well beyond humane treatment. In the most egregious cases, OLC and others concluded that essentially any act could be justified if undertaken pursuant to the Commander-in-Chief authority. Thus, this policy was never intended to and in fact never did sufficiently constrain the actions of U.S. soldiers and agents charged with conducting this new war by any means necessary.

The result is that hundreds of detainees have suffered serious mistreatment and criminal abuse at the hands of U.S. interrogators and soldiers. Dozens more have been killed or been seriously injured by U.S. officials purportedly acting in accordance with U.S. legal policy. Thanks to that policy and the lawyers who created it, U.S. conduct in the war on terrorism has already done immeasurable harm to our reputation as a law-abiding nation, our credibility as a champion of human rights, our tradition of military discipline and respect for the rule of law, our sense of values, and our efforts to win the hearts and minds of those who oppose us in the war on terrorism.

SO WHAT WERE THE LAWYERS THINKING?

If we assume that the lawyers' legal opinions and advice have damaged U.S. interests, that such damage was foreseeable (and, in fact, foreseen), and that the lawyers did not intend to cause such damage, it is worth considering why they took the legal positions they did.

First, Their Desire to Help the President Win the War on Terrorism May Have Overshadowed Other Considerations. None of us will soon forget the President's speech on September 20th when he boldly declared that "our grief has turned to anger and anger to resolution. Whether we bring our enemies to justice or bring justice to our enemies, justice will be done." The atmosphere in government was intense. Understandably, some had a single-minded desire to help the President defend the country and win the war on terrorism. His advisors were expected to think "outside the box" about ways to thwart further acts of terrorism after 9/11, and the armed forces and the intelligence agencies were asked to be forward-leaning, aggressive, and willing to take risks. Although the President needed his lawyers to be equally focused and dedicated, lawyers have a different role from that of the armed forces and intelligence agencies. Legal advisors must maintain enough balance to provide candid, objective, and reasonable assessments of the law. Some lawyers may have been unable or unwilling to maintain the proper balance.

Second, They May Have Allowed Academic or Political Convictions to Displace Ethical and Moral Considerations, Historical Context, Common Sense, and the Proper Role of a Legal Advisor. It is neither unusual nor inappropriate that lawyers have strong preconceived academic and philosophical convictions that influence and guide their legal judgment. In this case, academic and political convictions may have caused some lawyers to assert and defend unnecessarily expansive views of presidential power. Ironically, some legal positions may have been so extreme as to provoke a backlash that ultimately may have undermined the President's power to conduct the war. Perhaps nowhere is this more apparent than in the context of the habeas corpus litigation, where the federal courts have shown a tendency to strike down controversial and extreme positions when fundamentally important national policies are at stake.

Third, They May Have Taken the View That the President Has the Discretion, Especially in War-Time, to Adopt Any Plausible View of the Law. The President has a constitutional duty to "take care that the laws be faithfully executed." The Constitution also requires the President to take an oath in which he swears to "faithfully execute the Office" and "protect, preserve, and defend the Constitution." According to the traditional view, the obligations to faithfully execute the law and defend the Constitution require the President to adopt the most reasonable view of the law and execute his duties on that basis. If this is the case, it is incumbent on the President to obtain accurate and objective assessments of the law. In that case, that duty would fall to the President's lawyers, most obviously, the Attorney General (and thus, by delegation, the Office of Legal Counsel) and the White House Counsel.

Here, the legal interpretations in question were generally plausible and, for the most part, technically defensible, but they were often not the most reasonable interpretations. In some cases, for example, the lawyers' interpretations were patently inconsistent with the commonly-accepted spirit and purpose of the law. Some interpretations appeared to be outcome-driven, e.g., to avoid potential liability, as opposed to good-faith attempts to determine the true meaning of the law. For example, as previously discussed, the AG, WH Counsel, OLC, and others advised the President to adopt a legal position on the Geneva Conventions, not because it was the most accurate or reasonable interpretation of the law, but because it was the surest way to minimize the risk of prosecution under the War Crimes Act. To the extent the President believed he was receiving the most reasonable and objective reading of the law, that advice may have prevented him from fulfilling his constitutional duty to faithfully execute the law.

Fourth, Their Preoccupation With Avoiding the Jurisdiction of the Courts May Have Caused Them to Take Extreme Positions That, Ironically, May Have Invited Judicial Review. Some lawyers evidently came into office with a strong bias against what they perceive to be an "activist" judicial branch. That bias likely caused some preoccupation with avoiding the jurisdiction of federal courts. That preoccupation, in turn, may have cause them to stake out and defend overly aggressive litigation positions. The problem is that the lawyers' preoccupation with avoiding federal jurisdiction may also have affected important *operational* issues, including the decision to detain prisoners at GTMO and to move certain prisoners away from GTMO.

This level of preoccupation suggests that the task of avoiding judicial review may have become an end in itself – outweighing other more practical considerations. While the fear of judicial review may or may not have been warranted under the circumstances, it was probably a mistake to allow that fear to drive operational decisions on the ground or litigation decisions in the courts. Ironically, it is possible that actions taken to avoid the courts ultimately caused the courts to play an even greater role than they otherwise would have played, had it not been for those actions.

Fifth, They Encouraged "Groupthink" by Discouraging Dissent and Rewarding Loyalty. Given the gravity of the issues and the specialized nature of the law of war issues facing us after 9/11, it was wise in the first days and weeks following the attacks to consult and include lawyers from different agencies and with subject matter expertise in the law of war. Unfortunately, however, some lawyers chose to discourage dissent by excluding from their inner circle those who disagreed with their approach or endorsed legal conclusions contrary to their own. The exclusivity of this inner circle may also have been a function of rewarding loyalty by increasing access for those who agreed with and endorsed the inner circle's conclusions. The resulting composition of their legal team, in turn, may have resulted in a "groupthink" problem, whereby those in the group tended toward uncritical acceptance and conformity with the prevailing point of view. Indeed, that might help explain why their legal opinions and advice became increasingly extreme over time, culminating in the *Padilla* arguments and the torture memorandum – both of which included truly extreme legal positions. Those legal positions may have seemed reasonable to insiders but came across as patently offensive to many outsiders, including not only academics and human rights advocates, but also federal judges, generals, members of Congress, and even Yoo's successors in OLC.

NOTES

1. Deputy Assistant Attorney General Patrick F. Philbin and Deputy Assistant Attorney General John Yoo, U.S. Department of Justice, December 28, 2001 Memorandum to General Counsel William J. Haynes, II, U.S. Department of Defense, in *The Torture Papers*, ed. Karen J. Greenberg and Joshua L. Dratel, Memo #3, p. 29 (New York: Cambridge University Press, 2005).
2. Deputy Assistant Attorney General John Yoo, U.S. Department of Justice, and Special Counsel Robert J. Delahunty, U.S. Department of Justice, January 9, 2002 Memorandum to General Counsel William J. Haynes, II, U.S. Department of Defense, in *The Torture Papers*, Memo #4, p. 38.
3. Counsel to the President Alberto R. Gonzales, January 25, 2002 Memorandum to President George W. Bush, in *The Torture Papers*, Memo #7, p. 118.
4. President George W. Bush, February 7, 2002 Memorandum to The Vice President, The Secretary of State, The Secretary of Defense, The Attorney General, Chief of Staff to the President, Director of CIA, Assistant to the President for National Security Affairs, Chairman of the Joint Chiefs of Staff in *The Torture Papers*, Memo #11, p. 134.
5. Memorandum from White House Counsel Alberto R. Gonzales to President Bush, *supra* note 4.
6. Memorandum from Secretary of State Colin L. Powell to White House Counsel ("Draft Decision Memorandum for the President on the Applicability of the Geneva Convention to the Conflict in Afghanistan") (January 26, 2002), in *The Torture Papers*, Memo #8, p. 122.
7. Memorandum from Attorney General John Ashcroft to President George W. Bush ("Justice Department's position on why the Geneva Convention did not apply to al Qaeda and Taliban detainees") (February 1, 2002), in *The Torture Papers*, Memo #9, p. 126.
8. Memorandum from Assistant Attorney General Jay S. Bybee, DoJ to White House Counsel Alberto R. Gonzales ("Standards of Conduct for Interrogation under 18 U.S.C. §§ 2340–2340A") (August 1, 2002), in *The Torture Papers*, Memo #14, p. 172.
9. Article 15-6 Investigation of the 800th Military Police Brigade (The Taguba Report) (March 2004), in *The Torture Papers*, p. 405.
10. Final Report of the Independent Panel to Review DoD Detention Operations (The Schlesinger Report) (August 2004), in *The Torture Papers*, p. 908.
11. Memo from Staff Judge Advocate Diane Beaver, DoD to General James T. Hill ("Legal Brief on Proposed Counter-Resistance Strategies") (October 11, 2002), in *The Torture Papers*, Memo #20, p. 229.

12. Memorandum from Attorney General John Ashcroft to President George W. Bush, *supra* note 8.
13. Memorandum from White House Counsel Alberto R. Gonzales to President Bush, *supra* note 4.
14. Memorandum from Deputy Assistant Attorney General John Yoo, DoJ Office of Legal Counsel, and Special Counsel Robert J. Delahunty, DoJ to General Counsel William J. Haynes, II, DoD, *supra* note 3.
15. "Former State Department Legal Adviser Blames Torture and Abuse on White House Decision to Deny Geneva Protections," *U.S. Law & Security Digest* 41, April 7, 2005.
16. John Yoo, "Behind the 'Torture Memos,'" January 2, 2005.
17. Press Briefing by White House Counsel Judge Alberto Gonzales, Dod General Counsel William Haynes, Dod Deputy General Counsel Daniel Dell'Orto and Army Deputy Chief of Staff for Intelligence General Keith Alexander, June 22, 2004, available at <http://www.whitehouse.gov/news/releases/2004/06/20040622-14.html>.
18. The Schlesinger Report, *supra* note 11.

10 Rethinking the Geneva Conventions

Lee A. Casey and David B. Rivkin, Jr.

They made him blow a bugle for his Uncle Sam
It really brought him down because he couldn't jam
The captain seemed to understand
Because the next day the cap' went out and drafted a band
And now the company jumps when he plays reveille
He's the boogie-woogie bugle boy of Company B.

– *Boogie-woogie Bugle Boy*, Don Raye & Hughie Prince
Popularized by The Andrews Sisters, 1941

IT'S HARD TO TALK SENSE ABOUT THE GENEVA CONVENTIONS. THEY ARE
Scripture for human rights activists – quite simply "the basis" of international
humanitarian law. Attorney General Alberto Gonzales was excoriated in the
media, and attacked during his January 2005, confirmation hearings, for merely
having suggested that some Geneva provisions were "quaint" when applied to
al Qaeda and the Taliban. Countless opponents of American policy in Iraq (and
of the war on terror generally) have shouted themselves hoarse claiming that the
Bush administration's refusal to grant Geneva prisoner of war (POW) status to
unlawful enemy combatants led to the criminal abuses at Abu Ghraib. Many
have suggested darkly that American POWs will one day pay for this failure.

In fact, it is high time that the American people had a long and informed talk
about the Geneva Conventions. To the extent that, in agreeing to the Geneva
treaties, the United States' goal was to obtain decent treatment for *Americans*,
particularly those held as POWs, the effort has failed. In nearly sixty years, three
generations of American forces have never been accorded the benefits to which

The authors are partners in the Washington, D.C., office of Baker & Hostetler LLP. They
served in the Justice Department during the Reagan and George H. W. Bush administrations,
and are currently members of the U.N. Subcommission on the Promotion and Protection of
Human Rights. The views expressed in this article are strictly the authors' own.

they are entitled under those instruments, at least not in any systematic way. The future looks equally bleak. In the current conflict with al Qaeda and its allies, America's enemies make no pretense of compliance with either the Geneva Conventions or the customary laws of war. In such circumstances, granting captured terrorists the manifold rights of POWs, to which they are not, in any case, legally entitled, would be foolhardy and irresponsible.[1]

One potential solution, both in terms of applying the Geneva Conventions in instances where the United States engages a noncompliant Geneva party and vis-à-vis al Qaeda, would be adoption of a reciprocity rule. This need not involve resort to tit-for-tat reprisals, but could be a flexible approach whereby the United States takes account of its opponent's compliance record in its own interpretation and application of the treaties. Human rights activists and the International Committee of the Red Cross (ICRC), which takes an absolutist position against reciprocity, considering it forbidden in all circumstances, certainly would decry this policy. However, such groups have failed to articulate any practical alternative capable of securing decent treatment for captured American service members or, in the context of the war on terror, preventing deliberate attacks on civilian targets in the United States and overseas. These too are humanitarian imperatives that must be vindicated.

THERE ARE, OF COURSE, FOUR GENEVA CONVENTIONS, ALL DATED AUGUST, 12, 1949. The first protects the wounded and sick on the battlefield; the second protects those shipwrecked at sea; the third deals with POWs; the fourth applies to civilians. The United States ratified these separate treaties in the 1950s, and there is no doubt that each represents an important aspect of the law of armed conflict, embodying fundamental humanitarian principles.[2] As always, however, the devil is in the details. When those are examined, Attorney General Gonzales's reference to quaint does not tell half the story. Although there were Geneva Conventions governing certain aspects of warfare and the treatment of POWs before World War II, the 1949 treaties were consciously drafted in response to the unique experience of that conflict, and they are replete with its artifacts.

This is especially true of the third, the POW convention (GPW). For example, in situations where that treaty applies, POWs must be housed "under conditions as favourable as those for the forces of the Detaining Power who are billeted in the same area."[3] They must be permitted to move about freely and socialize within their internment camp.[4] They are entitled to a camp "canteen," where they "may procure foodstuffs, soap and tobacco," at prevailing local prices.[5] Their representatives must be given a role in managing this establishment and the profits have to be used for their benefit.[6] POWs must be given the means of preparing food for themselves.[7] Their participation in sports, games, and other "recreational pursuits" must be encouraged, and the necessary equipment provided.[8] POWs are entitled to a monthly "advance of pay" in Swiss francs, and to wear their uniforms, badges of rank, and decorations.[9]

These rights and benefits – and this listing is by no means exhaustive – reflect a number of the fundamental assumptions on which the Geneva Conventions were based. First and foremost, it was taken for granted in 1949 that wars largely will be fought between the regular – and mostly conscripted – armed forces of sovereign states. Second, POWs are assumed to have a genuine interest in self-preservation and in maintaining a level of discipline among themselves more or less consistent with regular military service. Third, and perhaps most importantly, the treaties contemplate that belligerent countries will have both a moral and practical interest in ameliorating a conflict's effects on their citizens, in accordance with the conventions' requirements, and that violations of those requirements will be the exception rather than the rule. This, in fact, would be the only rational justification for the ICRC's view regarding reciprocity as applied to the Geneva Conventions.

Such a rule, of course, would have some very real problems in practical application. Like sending a gambler to the tables with an ironclad guarantee that he's "covered," eliminating any concept of reciprocity from the rules governing POW treatment also removes most of the ordinary incentives to moderation by a belligerent, not otherwise inclined to respect the treaties. Certainly, the highly speculative possibility of a later "war crimes" prosecution has rarely, if ever, deterred unscrupulous or brutal enemies from ignoring the Geneva Conventions, as well as customary international law, in their treatment of American POWs – even when the United States has concededly gone above and beyond its legal obligations under those instruments.[10]

THE FIRST TEST OF THE GPW WAS THE 1950–53 KOREAN WAR. ALTHOUGH neither the Peoples Republic of China nor its North Korean client had formally ratified the 1949 treaty during the war, they both committed to abide by its principles – at least some of which clearly represented the requirements of customary international law. (China, of course, had been a party to the 1929 Geneva POW convention.) In the event, however, that the Communist forces ever did comply with any Geneva requirements, it was by accident and not design. American POWs in the Korean War were treated with unparalleled savagery. As one expert noted, American prisoners "suffered from bitter cold and inadequate shelter, insufficient and filthy clothing, dangerously contaminated water, unsanitary conditions, lice and other pests, boredom and lethargy, debilitating diseases, uncertainty about their future, and, above all, acute hunger."[11]

The actual atrocities perpetrated by the Chinese and North Koreans on U.S. and allied forces, as well as South Korean soldiers and civilians alike, are too numerous to catalogue here. Suffice it to say that of the 7,245 Americans taken prisoner in the Korean War, more than one third, 2,847, died in enemy hands. In addition, nearly 400 were known to be alive at the war's end, but were not repatriated to the United States. By contrast, the United States and its allies pledged to treat captured Chinese and North Koreans in accordance with Geneva principles and, by and large, kept their word. Indeed, one of the greatest difficulties came at the end of the war, when thousands of such POWs begged to remain in allied hands, rather than be repatriated to China or North Korea.

The second major conflict in which American forces were engaged after the 1949 Geneva Conventions came into force was, of course, the 1965–73 Vietnam War. Unlike China or North Korea, Vietnam (North and South) was a party to the Geneva Conventions and bound by their provisions. Throughout the conflict, the United States acknowledged the application of the treaties, and worked with South Vietnam to ensure compliance. Although there were lapses, the majority of prisoners held by the United States and its allies were properly housed and fed, and received medical attention. The ICRC was permitted to visit and inspect POW camps in South Vietnam.

Moreover, the United States went far beyond the requirements of the treaties, and determined – in 1966 – to accord POW status to captured Viet Cong, regardless of whether they legally merited that treatment. In response to this decision, the ICRC delegate in South Vietnam waxed poetic, noting that for the first time "[a] government goes far beyond the requirements of the Geneva convention in an official instruction to its armed forces. The dreams of today are the realities of tomorrow."[12] Unfortunately, there was no reciprocity.

As in Korea, American POWs were treated savagely in Vietnam. Again, the ICRC was not permitted to visit American POWs nor to inspect North Vietnamese prison facilities. These were, and remain, notorious monuments to brutality and torture, the "Hanoi Hilton" first among them. The North Vietnamese government failed even to provide a proper list of the prisoners it held. As one authority noted, "[a]lthough both the Viet Cong and North Vietnamese consistently maintained that their prisoners received humane treatment, their efforts to comply with the provisions of the Geneva Prisoner of War Conventions were negligible."[13] Of 766 American taken prisoner in the Vietnam war, 114 (15 percent) died in captivity. More than 2,000 Americans remain missing and unaccounted for from the Vietnam era.

The situation was little better during the 1990–91 Gulf War, or today. Although Iraq was a party to the Geneva Conventions, Saddam Hussein ignored its requirements. American POWs were subjected to brutal treatment including "severe beatings, starvation, mock executions, dark and unsanitary living conditions."[14] They lived in "constant fear of death and torture."[15] Today, of course, American forces face an enemy that makes no pretense of compliance with the law of armed conflict – it has rejected that law outright as a foreign doctrine. Al Qaeda and its allies do not take prisoners, unless it is for the purpose of murder at a later time.

In short, the United States has never got the benefit of its bargain in ratifying the Geneva Conventions. After nearly six decades (fully a quarter of the nation's existence as an independent state), the American people are entitled to ask why they should continue to honor these instruments at all, let alone accept interpretations, such as those proffered by the ICRC regarding the grant of POW status to unprivileged or "unlawful" combatants, an interpretation that goes well beyond the obligations the United States originally accepted.

THE USUAL ANSWER TO THIS MOST FUNDAMENTAL QUESTION IS THAT THE United States must be true to its own principles, and cannot descend to the level of its adversaries. There are important truths here. A sovereign government, at least one which purports to value the rule of law, cannot behave like a group of "banditti." Moreover, even if the United States were to repudiate the Geneva Conventions entirely, it is unlikely that it would begin hacking the heads off of its al Qaeda or Taliban prisoners, or that the American people would ever support such tactics. At the same time, to paraphrase Justice Robert Jackson, the law is not a suicide pact. A commitment to the fundamental principles underlying the Geneva Conventions does not exclude a reassessment of their individual requirements, especially when new threats to national and global security emerge, nor does it necessarily require absolute rejection of a reciprocity rule. As suggested above, such a rule need not entail retaliatory acts of violence, but rather an overall recognition that the treatment of American prisoners will be taken into account both in the United States' interpretation of its Geneva obligations, as well as any decision to expand some or all of those protections to individuals not legally entitled to them.

Although the ICRC has claimed for decades that the Geneva Conventions, and particularly the POW treaty, are not subject to reciprocity, this is a considerable overstatement of the case. This view is based on the language of Common Article 1, which states that "[t]he High Contracting Parties undertake to respect and to ensure respect for the present Convention in all circumstances."[16] The above language suggests to the ICRC that:

> By undertaking this obligation at the very outset, the Contracting Parties drew attention to the fact it is not merely an engagement concluded on a basis of reciprocity, binding each party to the contract only in so far as the other party observes its obligations. It is rather a series of unilateral engagements solemnly contracted before the world as represented by the other Contracting Parties. [17]

However, like all of the Convention's requirements, Common Article 1 remains subject to the general rules governing the interpretation and application of treaties.

Those norms have traditionally permitted a state to suspend its performance in the face of a material breach by another party.[18] As noted in the Restatement Third of the Foreign Relations Law of the United States: "A material breach of a multilateral agreement by one of the parties generally entitles... (b) a party specifically affected by the breach to invoke it as a ground for suspending the operation of the agreement in whole or in part in the relations between itself and the defaulting state."[19] Moreover, the GPW's actual text and structure do not support an absolutist position with regard to reciprocity.

First, the text of Common Article 1 does not directly address the question of reciprocity, but only requires the parties to "respect and to ensure respect for" the treaty "in all circumstances." Both respecting the treaty and ensuring respect by other parties are obligations equal in dignity, and how these requirements can be met is left to the parties. Second, Common Article 2, governing the Convention's application, itself clearly contemplates that reciprocity will be the rule in certain critical circumstances. In this respect, it provides that a nonparty state may obtain Geneva benefits, but only if "the latter accepts *and applies* the provisions thereof."[20] If merely accepting Geneva's obligations is insufficient to guarantee its benefits to a nonparty, there is little reason to interpret the treaty to afford those guarantees, in the face of a widespread or systematic failure of compliance, to a party.

Thus, despite the contrary claims by the ICRC and others, the Geneva Conventions need not be interpreted to eliminate the concept of reciprocity. Moreover, applying the general rule, which permits a state to suspend its performance only in the face of another's material breach, would avoid a simple rule of reprisal approach to the treatment of POWs, which has indeed resulted over time in terrible injustices to otherwise innocent individuals. It was for this very reason, for example, that the Lincoln Administration opted not to retaliate after Confederate officials refused to treat African-American soldiers as POWs, and effectively countenanced their massacre on several occasions.[21] As Lincoln himself explained to Frederic Douglass, "'if once begun, there is no telling where [retaliation] would end.'"[22]

At the same time, there have been circumstances in which actual application of a reciprocity rule obtained real and immediate results. Taking another example from the American Civil War, when Confederate commanders in Virginia and South Carolina forced black prisoners to build fortifications under Union fire, local Federal commanders deployed a similar number of Confederate prisoners under enemy fire. This promptly ended the practice, which now is clearly accepted as a war crime.[23] In other words, as in so many other areas, a balance must be struck. In those instances where the GPW actually does apply, i.e., an armed conflict between Geneva parties, there is no reason not to make plain that the United States, in interpreting its own obligations under the treaty, will take account of its adversary's interpretations. More importantly, in the far more likely situation where the United States finds itself fighting a non-Geneva party, the treaty itself establishes a rule of reciprocity.

THIS IS ESPECIALLY TRUE WITH RESPECT TO THE WAR ON TERROR AND THE tactics of "asymmetric" warfare it represents. Indeed, as armed conflicts between states, and especially between the Great Powers, become increasingly rare, the relevance of the 1949 conventions will continue to diminish. As suggested above, those instruments were not drafted with the purpose of establishing rules for a war waged on one side by guerilla fighters or irregular forces, let alone by suicidal jihadists. Indeed, it was the ICRC's express purpose, in sponsoring Protocol I Additional in the 1970s, to bring irregular forces within the "system." Evidently the ICRC hoped that granting legal status to guerillas would prompt them into general compliance with international humanitarian norms.[24] Time has proven these hopes to have been, at best, quixotic. More to the point, the United States flatly rejected Protocol I on this very ground. As President Reagan explained in 1987:

> Protocol I is fundamentally and irreconcilably flawed. It contains provisions that would undermine humanitarian law and endanger civilians in war. . . . It would give special status to "wars of national liberation," an ill-defined concept expressed in vague, subjective, politicized terminology. Another provision would grant combatant status to irregular forces even if they do not satisfy the traditional requirements to distinguish themselves from the civilian population and otherwise comply with the laws of war. This would endanger civilians among whom terrorists and other irregulars attempt to conceal themselves.[25]

Indeed, if the Geneva Conventions were to be applied in the context of a terrorist war – and the actual practice of states suggests that they never have been – they would lead to absurd results. In particular, as interpreted by the ICRC and other critics of American policy, the Geneva Conventions would require that captured al Qaeda members be treated as POWs or processed as civilian criminal defendants. Neither option is legally required and neither is realistic. Not only does granting captured terrorists the rights of honorable POWs reward their own rejection of the laws of war – especially their preference for targeting civilians – but permitting them to govern their own affairs in captivity would undercut basic security needs. The disciplinary provisions incorporated into the GPW are designed to address individual misbehavior among the prisoners, not a mass refusal to accept the authority of the detaining power.

In addition, granting detainees POW status would eliminate any realistic hope of obtaining information from them regarding the capabilities and future plans of their compatriots. Intelligence collection, of course, is crucial in a war where the enemy's primary tactic is launching deliberate attacks on the civilian population. Indeed, the civilian population has an affirmative and unqualified right, inherent in Article 6 of the International Covenant on Civil and Political Rights, to be protected against such attacks, and states have an unqualified obligation to vindicate that right. However, under Article 17 of the Third Geneva Convention, a detaining power's ability to interrogate POWs is very severely restricted. POWs cannot be subject to any form of "coercion," and any who refuse to answer questions cannot be "threatened, insulted, or exposed to any unpleasant or disadvantageous treatment of any kind."[26] A strict reading of this provision would, in fact, eliminate even interrogation methods routinely utilized by domestic police forces, such as "good cop, bad cop." The reason is simple. POWs have a right to keep their country's military secrets. Terrorists, on the other hand, have no "right" to keep their secrets.

Treating captured al Qaeda or Taliban members as "civilians" is also no answer. First, the Geneva Civilian Convention severely restricts interrogations, requiring that "[n]o physical or moral coercion" be used.[27] Second, if al Qaeda and the Taliban are treated as civilians, rather than enemy combatants, then they are not subject to military attack. The members of these organizations would have to be handled as criminal suspects. Of course, this is exactly the position taken by many critics of American policy in the war on terror, and was the ICRC's constant refrain in defending Protocol I's efforts to privilege guerillas.[28] Unfortunately, these critics rarely, if ever, grapple with the consequences that would inevitably flow from adopting the criminal justice model in these circumstances. The rules governing an armed conflict are fundamentally different from those applicable to civilian criminal systems, and they do not mix and match.

For example, if the United States had pursued a criminal justice path in the aftermath of September 11, it could not have dispatched its armed forces to eliminate al Qaeda's operational centers and activities in Afghanistan. Rather, an investigation would have been commenced, and a grand jury convened. Once individual indictments were secured, extradition requests would have to have been directed to the Afghani government. Of course, the United States – like most of the rest of the world – did not recognize the Taliban as that government, and the Northern Alliance was in no position to execute such requests. The net result would have been no meaningful action at all. Al Qaeda would have remained free to launch additional attacks against the United States from its Afghan fortress.

In fact, the criminal justice system is manifestly inadequate to deal with the existential threat posed by radical Islam in general, or al Qaeda in particular. Law enforcement must, of course, constitute an element of the nation's strategy, but reliance on prosecutors and police would result in what would rightly be considered an unacceptable number of civilian casualties – as it did in the years leading up to September 11. The criminal justice system is reactive. Although it generally assumes that, by punishing the offender, others will be deterred, it nevertheless depends on a basically law-abiding population that accepts the legitimacy and authority of the government. It is assumed that the government has a legal and, more or less, actual monopoly of deadly force. In such circumstances, it makes perfect sense to constrain the use of that force. These assumptions rapidly dissolve when the "criminal," who hopes to escape detection and punishment, is not a part and parcel of the surrounding society but is a foreign "power" determined to challenge the state's authority by doing as much damage as possible to the citizenry.

Of course, even the most vociferous critics of American policy post – September 11 rarely go so far as to demand that there be no role for the armed forces. Rather, they appear to support a hybrid system, where the military will act as especially well-armed constables, collaring "suspected" terrorists and shipping them to civilian courts for trial. Leaving aside legal impediments, such as the Posse Comitatus Act,[29] this too is wildly unrealistic. First, as noted above, if al Qaeda and Taliban members are not "enemy combatants" then they are not legally subject to military attack. That rule would have to change, creating a class of "civilians" who could be directly attacked. Second, battlefields make poor crime scenes. Courts must have evidence, and evidence must be collected and preserved so that its origins and authenticity can later be proven. This often is difficult in the ordinary, domestic criminal case in which the police have absolute control over the area – it would be nearly impossible in the context of ongoing hostilities. Third, even assuming that sufficient evidence could be collected to convict more than a handful of individuals, it would have to be presented in open court, revealing and endangering any intelligence sources or methods used in military courts to obtain it. This list could be expanded.[30]

Overall, criminal prosecution is certainly appropriate for al Qaeda and Taliban members, as they have violated the laws of war. However, it is unlikely that any but the most senior actors will ever face trial. They must surely know this. They have chosen the tactics of terror because this gives them an inestimable advantage in making war on a government that cares for the lives of its citizens. Granting such individuals the rights and privileges of lawful combatants increases this advantage, along with the real and present danger to their civilian targets. In short, those who insist that the United States must conduct the war on terror as if it is fighting another sovereign state pursuant to the Geneva Conventions, or behave as if it is faced by a particularly virulent crime wave, have missed at least one half of the humanitarian equation – and the better half at that.

NOTES

1. The Attorney General's conclusion that neither al Qaeda nor Taliban detainees legally qualify for Geneva POW status is correct. *See* Lee A. Casey, David B. Rivkin, Jr., & Darin R. Bartram, *Detention and Treatment of Combatants in the War on Terrorism* (The Federalist Society for Law and Public Policy Policy Studies 2002).
2. In addition, there are two "protocols," Protocol Additional to the Geneva Conventions of 12 August 1949, and Relating to the Protection of Victims of International Armed Conflicts (Protocol I), of 8 June 1977, and Protocol Additional to the Geneva Conventions of 12 August 1949, and Relating to the Protection of Victims of Non-International Armed Conflicts (Protocol II), of 8 June 1977. The United States has affirmatively rejected Protocol I, because it would grant unlawful combatants legal status under the laws of war, and has not ratified Protocol II.
3. *See* Geneva Conventions of 12 August 1949, Geneva Convention III Relative to the Treatment of Prisoners of War, art. 25, 6 U.S.T. 3316 [hereinafter GPW].
4. *Id.*, art. 21.
5. *Id.*, art. 28.

6. *Id.*
7. *Id.*, art. 26.
8. *Id.*, art. 38.
9. *Id.*, arts. 40, 60.
10. In fact, in the post–World War II era, there appear to have been no prosecutions of foreign belligerents for the abuse of American POWs.
11. Lewis H. Carlson, *Remembered Prisoners of a Forgotten War: An Oral History of Korean War POWs* 121 (2002).
12. Major General George S. Prugh, *Law at War Vietnam 1964–1973* 66 (1975), available at <http://www.army.mil/cmh-pg/books/Vietnam/Law-War/law-fm.htm>.
13. *Id.* at 72.
14. *Acree v. Iraq*, 370 F.3d 41 (2004).
15. *Id.*
16. *See* ICRC, *Commentary on the Geneva Conventions of 12 August 1949, Geneva Convention III Relative to the Treatment of Prisoners of War* 18 (1960) [hereinafter ICRC Commentaries]. In fact, the ICRC itself acknowledged – a few paragraphs on – that this view was not universally held at the time the treaties were negotiated, noting that "[t]he Geneva Conventions are *coming to be regarded less and less* as contracts concluded on the basis of reciprocity in the national interests of the parties, and more and more as a solemn affirmation of principles respected for their own sake, a series of unconditional engagements on the part of each of the Contracting Parties vis-à-vis the others." *Id.* at 20 (emphasis added).
17. *Id.*
18. *See, e.g.,* William Edward Hall, *A Treatise on International Law* 352 (1890). ("There can be no question that the breach of a stipulation which is material to the main object . . . liberates the party other than that committing the breach from the obligations of the contract.")
19. *See, e.g., Restatement Third of the Foreign Relations Law of the United States* §335 (2)(b) (1986). Article 60 of the Vienna Convention on the Law of Treaties, to which the United States is not a party, adopted this rule but with an important gloss: it would not apply "to provisions relating to the protection of the human person contained in treaties of a humanitarian character, in particular to the provisions prohibiting any form of reprisals against persons protected by such treaties." Vienna Convention on the Law of Treaties, art. 60(5), 8 I.L.M. 679. Whether Article 60(5) can, based on the actual practice of states, meet the exacting test of customary international law is highly debatable.
20. GPW, *supra* note 3, Art. 2. (emphasis added). Indeed, the ICRC's own commentaries recognize that the obligations of Article 1 are fully subordinate to the restrictions of Article 2. ICRC Commentaries, *supra* note 16, at 18.
21. *See* James M. McPherson, *Battle Cry of Freedom: The Civil War Era* 793–796 (1988).
22. *Id.* at 794.
23. *Id.* at 795.
24. In its commentaries on Protocol I, the ICRC claims that its aim was to "increas[e] the legal protection of guerilla fighters as far as possible, and thereby encourage them to comply with the applicable rules of armed conflict, without at the same time reducing the protection of the civilian population in an unacceptable manner." ICRC, *Commentary on the Protocol Additional to the Geneva Conventions of 12 August 1949 and Relating to the Protection of Victims of International Armed Conflicts* 522 (1987) [hereinafter Commentaries (Protocol I)].
25. Message to the Senate Transmitting Protocol II Additional to the Geneva Conventions of 12 August 1949, 23 Weekly Comp. Pres. Doc. 91 (Jan. 29, 1987). That instrument's provisions benefiting irregular combatants also are not customary law. Even the ICRC

has admitted that they were innovations, and the United States has – in any case – openly and persistently objected to those peculiar norms.

26. GPW, *supra* note 3, art. 17.
27. Geneva Conventions of 12 August 1949, Geneva Convention IV Relative to the Protection of Civilian Persons in Time of War, art 31, 6 U.S.T. 3516 [hereinafter GC].
28. *See, e.g.*, Commentaries (Protocol I), *supra* note 24, at 385.
29. 18 U.S.C. §1385. ("Whoever, except in cases and under circumstances expressly authorized by the Constitution or Act of Congress, willfully uses any part of the Army or the Air Force as a *posse comitatus* or otherwise to execute the laws shall be fined under this title or imprisoned not more than two years, or both.")
30. The successful prosecution of the first World Trade Center "bombers" is often cited as proof that the criminal law system can work in these circumstances. Suffice it to say that the incarceration of those men did not prevent the far more successful September 11 attacks, any more than it prevented al Qaeda's other attacks on American targets, including the Kobar Towers, U.S. Embassies in Kenya and Tanzania, or the U.S.S. Cole.

David D. Caron

INTRODUCTION

Amidst the focus on the way in which Bush administration legal advisors defined the crime of torture,[1] a fundamentally radical "doctrine" of law has slipped through almost unnoticed. This essay points to a startling and exceptionally dangerous concoction – the "failed state doctrine" – invoked in Bush Administration legal memoranda.[2]

To be blunt, the failed state doctrine is a fabrication. There is no historical precedent. As much as I am troubled by the definition of torture in the memoranda, the failed state doctrine in my view is more troubling in that it provided the basis for concluding the international humanitarian law of the four 1949 Geneva Conventions did not apply *at all* to Afghanistan.

International humanitarian law is concerned with the humane treatment of soldiers and civilians during armed conflict. As treaties, the four 1949 Geneva Conventions both codified and progressively developed international humanitarian law and are the core, although by no means all, of international humanitarian law today. The United States was one of the primary drafters of the four 1949 Geneva Conventions. The Geneva Conventions are open for ratification by all nations. States that join the treaties are called "High Contracting Parties."

On January 9, 2002, the Office of the Solicitor General in the Department of Justice sent a Memorandum, stamped "Draft," to William Haynes, the General Counsel for the Department of Defense.[3] The memorandum opens, "[y]ou have asked for our Office's view concerning the effect of international treaties and federal laws on the treatment of individuals detained by U.S. Armed Forces during the conflict in Afghanistan." Expressed more directly, Haynes was asking for an opinion as to the applicability of the four 1949 Geneva Conventions to the conflict in Afghanistan.

Both the United States and Afghanistan are High Contracting Parties to the Geneva Conventions. Given that both states accepted the obligations of the Geneva Conventions, an international legal analysis would begin with the position that the four 1949 Geneva Conventions applied to the armed conflict between the United States and Afghanistan, and then proceed to consider whether some extraordinary circumstance denied such applicability. The January 9, 2002 memorandum concludes that the Conventions do not apply. This conclusion, thus, is extraordinary. This essay focuses on the reasons and analysis the memorandum provides in support of its conclusion that the Geneva Conventions do not apply to the State of Afghanistan.

It should be noted that the memorandum separates the question asked into two: 1) Do the Geneva Conventions apply to the State of Afghanistan? and 2) Do they apply to al Qaeda, an international terrorist organization operating from the territory of Afghanistan? I leave the question of al Qaeda to the side, however, because this essay focuses only on the first question, namely the applicability of the Geneva Conventions to Afghanistan. This focus should not be taken as an endorsement of any other specific portion of the memorandum. Errors, poor legal reasoning, and an inferior grasp of the substantive law pervade the memorandum.[4] I focus on the analysis of the applicability of the Geneva Conventions to Afghanistan because it is in that context that the memorandum concocts and then invokes the failed state doctrine.

I. THE OPINION

The authors of the January 9, 2002 memorandum opine that the four 1949 Geneva Conventions do not apply to Afghanistan because Afghanistan is not a High Contracting Party.[5] The memorandum's opening paragraph states, "Afghanistan's status as a failed state is ground alone to find that members of the Taliban militia are not entitled to enemy POW status under the Geneva Conventions."[6]

The four 1949 Geneva Conventions do not apply – the memorandum answers – because Afghanistan is not a party to the treaties. Thus Afghanistan is not entitled to the rights of a state party.

Well, that was an easy opinion to provide.

Do we take this reply to mean that Afghanistan never ratified the treaties? No, it did so in September of 1956. Do we take this reply to mean that Afghanistan has withdrawn from the treaties? No, it did not. The answer is that Afghanistan is not a party because it is no longer a "state." In other words, Afghanistan had ceased to exist as a state some time prior to the U.S. invasion and had as of the date of the memorandum – several months after U.S. military operations – not yet come back into being.

II. THREE SLEIGHTS OF HAND

To reach the conclusion that Afghanistan is no longer a state, the memorandum invokes the "failed state doctrine." A definition of a failed state is provided. Evidence relevant to that definition is reviewed. The opinion concludes that Afghanistan meets this definition. Afghanistan is therefore a failed state. Afghanistan therefore no longer exists. The Geneva Conventions therefore do not apply because they cannot apply.

Three sleights of hand (false assertions or omissions) are required to pull this rabbit out of a hat. First, the memorandum must invoke, while not acknowledging that it is manufacturing, the failed state doctrine which provides the theoretical leap for the conclusion that a failed state is no longer a state. Second, the memorandum must conclude that Afghanistan is a failed state. Third, the memorandum must ignore the fact that no state, including the United States of America, ever suggested that Afghanistan had gone out of existence, and no international organization, including the United Nations, ever questioned Afghanistan's existence or its continued membership. To the contrary, all had acted as if Afghanistan had continuously possessed statehood.

A. The Manufacture of the "Failed State Doctrine"

In international law, the primary holder of rights and obligations is the state. States are the primary subject, and quite often the object of international law. Because of this central role, intellectual effort has been devoted to the legal definition of what constitutes a state. A widely accepted definition, containing four elements, is to be found in the 1933 Montevideo Convention on Rights and Duties of States. Article 1 provides: The State as a person of international law should possess the following qualifications: (a) a permanent population; (b) a defined territory; (c) government; and (d) capacity to enter into relations with other States. It is appropriately difficult for a state to come into being. Once a state has come into existence, it is likewise difficult for it to die. Importantly, a state does not automatically cease to exist when it is "temporarily deprived of an effective government as a result of civil war or similar upheavals."[7]

The difficulty with the idea of a state simply disappearing is reflected in the presumption toward the continuity of the state. The Soviet Union, for example, following the revolution establishing it, argued that its transformation was so foundational that it was a new state and not merely a successor to the obligations and rights of Czarist Russia. This argument, and many others like it since then, however, was rejected by the United States and other states as contrary to the presumption in favor of the continuity of the state.

If one examines the older theoretical discussions of the basis of the state, there are isolated speculations that a state which experienced a protracted absence of government could lose its status as a state.[8] But no examples of such a self-annihilating state are ever offered. To my knowledge, there is no example.

If there is little *legal* distinction between the 180 states of the world, states vary tremendously along every conceivable dimension of *political* significance: population, wealth, size, and power, to name only a few. Political scientists categorize states with reference to such qualities. For example, they refer to "developed

countries" and to "super powers." Two political science characterizations of
states relevant to the present discussion are that of the "rogue state" and the
"failed state." The rogue state is a state that behaves outside of the expectations
of even the most tolerant members of the international community and in ways
that threaten that community or members of it. The failed state may also be
lawless, but not because it has chosen to be so but rather because lawlessness
increases as the governance structures of the state fail. In determining whether
a state has failed, a variety of factors can be involved. It is a political description, not an exact science. State failure is defined by political scientists as having
occurred when there is widespread presence of violence and when the appara-
tus of government is so dysfunctional that it no longer delivers positive political
goods.[9]

It is critical to note that political scientists undertook the task of studying
failed states in order to, as Rothberg describes it, "design methods to prevent
failure and, in cases of states that nevertheless fail . . . , to revive them and assist in
the rebuilding process."[10] Political scientists did not assume that the conclusion
that a state had failed for the purpose of policy analysis meant that the state also
no longer existed in the legal sense.

The sleight of hand in the memorandum is that the authors take the social science description of "failed states" (without acknowledging its roots in political
science) and conflate that political science description with the legal possibility of
a state that ceases to exist.[11] It is as though one conflated a social science description of homeless people as spiritually dead with the legal conclusion that such
persons are dead. The theoretical leap made by the authors of the memorandum
is without support in international law and without precedent.

B. Afghanistan as "Failed State"

Defining state failure as "the collapse or near-collapse of State authority,"[12] the
memorandum provides a description of the situation in Afghanistan prior to the
United States' invasion in 2001 and argues that the regime was unable to control
effectively or provide basic services to the population.[13] The authors of the memorandum state that when the Taliban were in control of Afghanistan there was
no "functioning central government" capable of providing basic services to the
people, "suppressing endemic internal violence," or "maintaining normal relations with other governments."[14] The memorandum concludes that Afghanistan
under the Taliban in 2001 was a "failed state."

First, it is important to emphasize that the definition of failed state was constructed for political science analysis. If it had been developed in a context where
the consequence of meeting the definition would be that the state no longer
existed, one can be sure that the definition would be far more demanding and
precise.

Second, given the looseness of the political science definition, there are likely
several scholars and analysts who would have regarded Afghanistan under the

Taliban as dysfunctional or, in some sense, "failed." These scholars and analysts likely would have a substantial list of other states that are dysfunctional or "failed." I very much doubt that any of these scholars or analysts would have stated that those states because of their "failed" status no longer existed as states in a legal sense.

Third, the weight of opinion would have been that Afghanistan under the Taliban was an oppressive and violent state, but not a "failed state" as that term is defined in political science. The Taliban constituted the *de facto* government of Afghanistan since their capture of Kabul, the capital, in September 1996.[15] In its ascension to power during the fighting of 1999–2000, the Taliban took control of most of the country.[16] By early 2001, the Taliban controlled 90–97 percent "of national territory, although in many areas this control amounted to little more than a small armed presence in the major towns."[17] Many Afghans initially supported the Taliban for bringing security to their lawless country (particularly since control over the country had been essentially divided amongst seven warlords).[18] Later the Taliban would enforce oppressive edicts in these same areas.

It is important to note that the Taliban was not recognized as the government of the State of Afghanistan by the vast majority of states.[19] Moreover, the Taliban government was unable to secure Afghanistan's seat in the United Nations General Assembly.[20] Thus, states such as the United States, France, the United Kingdom, and Australia chose to leave in place as diplomatic representatives the agents of the previous Afghan government, the Rabanni government.[21] Likewise, from 1996 to 2001, the Credential Committee of the UN General Assembly left the Rabbani government representatives in control of Afghanistan's UN seat.[22] The memorandum stresses this lack of recognition of the Taliban government. It overlooks, however, that a necessary implication of the continued recognition of the Rabbani government as the government of Afghanistan is that the State of Afghanistan continued to exist.

C. Afghanistan as State

Finally, the January 9, 2002 memorandum is careful to avoid mentioning that its conclusion that Afghanistan did not exist as a state in 2001 was contrary to the official position of the United States, the United Nations, and any other state that considered the question. Indeed, both the United States and many others nations of the world acting through the United Nations General Assembly and the Security Council had called upon the *State* of Afghanistan to fulfill its obligations under numerous treaties and international customary law.

ENTERTAINING A FAILED STATE DOCTRINE

The conclusion that there is no precedent for the failed state doctrine does not mean that there should not be one. Indeed, a theme in the effort to justify a number of the legal positions taken in the Bush administration's war on terror has been that the old rules do not fit this new type of conflict. Thus, we should ask whether a doctrine such as the failed state doctrine – even if not presently a doctrine – should be created and encouraged.

It does make sense that states that are failing or have failed present a range of problems for other states, not to mention the residents of those failed states. Indeed, it is this fact that leads political scientists and international lawyers to consider the challenges presented by failed states and to offer policy prescriptions. Importantly, none of these analysts to my knowledge suggest the removal of statehood as a helpful policy approach. The reason for this is quite obvious: the removal of statehood is a very blunt policy tool, possibly accomplishing some beneficial ends, but overall resulting in numerous unproductive and unintended consequences. For example, the January 9, 2002 memorandum apparently did not consider that along with the removal of the protections of the Geneva Conventions, all of the state debt of Afghanistan to lending institutions and private businesses around the world also would have been extinguished with the death of the State of Afghanistan. (Indeed, one can imagine that one of the groups that would be most interested in promoting a failed state doctrine would be the poorest states of the world. For them, the failed state doctrine is the closest thing to an international bankruptcy regime yet imagined.) Thus, the failed state doctrine not only removes the rights of the failed state (such as protections under the Geneva Conventions), it removes all of the obligations of the failed state which in all likelihood will lead in many cases to de facto exercise of some authority over an area.

Ironically, despite the effort to have a more structured removal of some rights or obligations for a failed state as a policy response to its failure, the four 1949 Geneva Conventions and international humanitarian law would not be among the list considered. Thus, to the extent that the creation of such a doctrine might be entertained, its implications are far reaching yet simultaneously unlikely to accomplish the specific goals for which President Bush's advisors conceived it.

CONCLUSION

There are legal opinions that are debatable. There are legal opinions that are wrong. The purpose of this essay is to emphasize that the January 9, 2002 memorandum's invocation and application of a "failed state doctrine" is about as wrong as opinion gets. If it were only an opinion, stamped "draft," from a Deputy Assistant Attorney General, then one might think it neither the position of the United States nor the final corrected version.

Indeed, the U. S. Department of State immediately saw the sleights of hand just described. The January 9, 2002 draft memorandum was forwarded to the Department of State for comment; it was given two days to do so. The Legal Advisor for the Department of State, William H. Taft, wrote a two page letter to John C. Yoo in the Department of Justice on January 11th. Attached to his letter was a forty page analytical critique of the January 9th memorandum. Taft sent a copy of this packet to both Secretary of State Colin Powell and the White House Counsel, Judge Alberto Gonzales. On the first page of his letter, Taft states plainly the fundamental problem with the January 9th memorandum:

> [The memorandum's] conclusion that 'failed states' cease to be parties to treaties they have joined is without support. Its arguments that Afghanistan became a "failed state" and thus was no longer bound by treaties to which it had been a party is contrary to the official position of the United States, the United Nations and all other states that have considered the issue.[23]

The Department of Justice, however, did not change its opinion, allowing the draft opinion to stand. Moreover, the White House Counsel Alberto Gonzales, aware of the views of both the Departments of Justice and of State, advised President Bush on January 18th of the Department of Justice's opinion that "there are reasonable grounds for you to conclude that the [Geneva Conventions] do not apply to the conflict with the Taliban."[24] The President accepted the recommendation that the Conventions do not apply and Secretary of State Colin Powell requested the President to reconsider his decision.[25] Alberto Gonzales on January 25th, in a "draft" memorandum advising the President on Secretary's Powell's request, repeated the advice that the President has the authority to determine that the Geneva Conventions do not apply because "Afghanistan was a failed state."[26] Secretary Powell wrote to Alberto Gonzales on January 26th with comments on his draft memorandum noting, among other things, that "any determination that Afghanistan is a failed state would be contrary to the official U.S. government position."[27] President Bush shortly thereafter reversed his earlier decision stating that the Geneva Conventions would apply to the Taliban "because Afghanistan is a party to the Convention."[28] Whether the President's reversal should be seen as a repudiation of the failed state doctrine or a reversal of the conclusion that Afghanistan was a failed state is unclear. Thus, the failed state doctrine, unfortunately, can not be seen as merely an opinion stamped "draft."

At best, the failed state doctrine, which finds its origins in the quasi-judicial advisory function of the Office of Legal Counsel, can be seen as an overzealous piece of judicial activism during a difficult time for the nation. It also was both dead wrong and deeply unwise. The purpose of this essay has been to make clear how unsupported and unwise this doctrine was, and remains.

NOTES

1. *See* Memorandum from U.S. Department of Justice, Office of Legal Counsel, Office of the Assistant Attorney General, to Counsel to the President (Aug. 1, 2002) (on file with author) (asserting that "Where the pain is physical, it must be of an intensity akin to that which accompanies serious physical injury such as death or organ failure ... Because the acts inflicting torture are extreme, there is a significant range of acts that though they

might constitute cruel, inhuman, or degrading treatment or punishment fail to rise to the level or torture.")

2. The initiation of this line of advocacy is to be found in a Draft Memorandum from the U.S. Department of Justice, Office of Legal Counsel, Office of the Deputy Assistant Attorney General, to General Counsel, Department of Defense (Jan. 9, 2002) (on file with author) (hereinafter "Jan. 9, 2002 DOJ Memo").

3. Its title is "Application of Treaties and Laws to al Qaeda and Taliban Detainees." The authors of memorandum are John C. Yoo and Robert Delahunty.

4. There is, for example, a repeated fundamental confusion of doctrines concerning the recognition of a government and the recognition of a state.

5. Jan. 9, 2002 DOJ Memo, *supra* note 2, at 14 (concluding that "Afghanistan was without the attributes of statehood necessary to continue as a party to the Geneva Conventions, and the Taliban militia ... is therefore not entitled to the protections of the Geneva Conventions.")

6. Jan. 9, 2002 DOJ Memo, *supra* note 2, at 2.

7. Malanczuk, *infra* note 8, at 77. ("The long period of *de facto* partition of Lebanon did not hinder its continued legal appearance as a state ... nor did the case of Somalia, which was described as a 'unique case' in the resolution of the Security Council authorizing the UN humanitarian intervention, abolish the international legal personality of the country as such.")

8. As to late 19th and early 20th century writers who express the view that prolonged anarchy may terminate the existence of the state, *see* A. RIVIER, DROIT DES GENS i, 66 (1896); R. LE NORMAND, LA RECONNAISSANCE INTERNATIONALE ET SES DIVERSES APPLICATIONS 207 (1899); F. DESPAGNET, COURS DE DROIT INTERNATIONAL PUBLIC 111–12 (1910); H. BONFILS, MANUEL DE DROIT INTERNATIONAL PUBLIC 140–1 (1914); W. E. HALL, A TREATISE ON INTERNATIONAL LAW 21 (1917); and E. VON WALDKIRCH, DAS VOLKERRECHT IN SEINEN GRUNDZUGEN DARGESTEELT 115 (1926). One scholar writing recently who perhaps supports this possibility is Peter Malanczuk: "a state cannot exist for long ..., unless it has a government." PETER MALANCZUK, AKEHURST'S MODERN INTRODUCTION TO INTERNATIONAL LAW 81 (7th revised ed. 1997). The more common recent trend, however, is to favor the continuation of the state. James Brierly in his THE LAW OF NATIONS (1955) at 137 writes: "the identity of a state is not affected ... by a temporary anarchy."

9. *See, e.g.*, Robert I. Rothberg, *Failed States, Collapsed States, Weak States: Causes and Indicators* in STATE FAILURE AND WEAKNESS IN A TIME OF TERROR 1 (Robert Rothberg, ed., 2003). Political goods refer to the services a state is normally expected to provide to its citizens. These include security, education, and health services. *See, e.g.*, S. Rice, *The New National Security: Focus on Failed States*, Policy Brief #116, The Brookings Institution (Feb. 2003).

Seeking to be rigorous in their analysis, political scientists outlined characteristics of state failure. *See* R. Rothberg, *The New Nature of Nation-State Failure*, THE WASHINGTON QUARTERLY 85–96 (2003). State failure is not the absence of a government's intention to protect its population, it is more accurately the point at which the government is unable to achieve any goal, no matter what the intentions of the leaders may be. T. Magner, *Does a Failed State Country of Origin Result in a Failure of International Protection? A Review of Policies Toward Asylum-Seekers in Leading Asylum Nations*, 15 GEO. IMMIGR. L.J. 703 (2001). Failure can occur gradually. C. Crocker, *Bridges, Bombs, or Bluster*, FOREIGN AFFAIRS 32 (Sept.–Oct. 2003). Failure will be evident in the absence of all governmental structures. G. Kreijen, *The Transformation of Sovereignty and African Independence: No Shortcuts to Statehood* in STATE, SOVEREIGNTY, AND INTERNATIONAL GOVERNANCE 45–46 (G. Kreijen, M. Brus, J. Duursma, E. de Vos, and J. Dugard eds.,

2002). The failed state finally becomes the collapsed state. As one author describes the collapsed state of Somalia, "The mob had replaced tyranny and it could be said, not that Somalis had returned to the anarchical order of the clan, but that factional warlords had unraveled the last shreds of the Somali social fabric." J. Chopra, *'Achilles' Heel in Somalia: Learning from Conceptual Failure*, 31 TEX. INT'L L.J. 495, 507 (1996).

10. Rothberg, *Failed States, supra* note 9, at 2.
11. For example, the memorandum states:

> International law recognizes many situations in which there may be a territory that has no "State." A variety of situations can answer to this description. Of chief relevance here is the category of the "failed state."

Jan. 9, 2002 DOJ Memo, *supra* note 2, at 16–17 (footnotes omitted). Note the structure of these sentences incorrectly suggests that "failed states" is a category of international law and a category previously considered in international law as a situation in which a territory has no state.

12. Jan. 9, 2002 DOJ Memo, *supra* note 2, at 17.
13. *Id.*
14. *Id.*
15. Larry Goodson, AFGHANISTAN'S ENDLESS WARS: STATE FAILURE, REGIONAL POLITICS, AND THE RISE OF THE TALIBAN 80 (2001).
16. *Id.* at 85.
17. Larry Goodson, *Afghanistan*, 1, 3 JANE'S SENTINEL SECURITY ASSESSMENT, SOUTH ASIA (1999).
18. *See* Rifaat Hussein et al., THE ANATOMY OF A CONFLICT: AFGHANISTAN AND 9/11 (2002); AHMED RASHID, TALIBAN: MILITANT ISLAM, OIL AND FUNDAMENTALISM IN CENTRAL ASIA (2000).
19. The Taliban was recognized as the government of the State of Afghanistan by the United Arab Emirates (UAE), Pakistan, and Saudi Arabia.
20. WILLIAM MALEY, THE AFGHANISTAN WARS 243 (2002).
21. *Id.*
22. *Id.*
23. Memorandum from William H. Taft, IV, Legal Adviser of the Department of State to John C. Yoo, Deputy Assistant Attorney General, Department of Justice, dated January 11, 2002, at 1 (on file with author).
24. Memorandum from Alberto Gonzales, White House Legal Counsel, to President George W. Bush, dated January 25, 2002, at 1 (on file with author).
25. *Id.*
26. *Id.*
27. Memorandum from Colin Powell, Secretary of State to Alberto Gonzales, White House Counsel, dated January 26, 2002, at 5 (on file with author).
28. Statement by White House Press Secretary Ari Fleischer February 7, 2002, available at <http://us-mission.ch/press2002/0802fleischerdetainees.htm> (last visited May 9, 2005).

12 War Not Crime

William H. Taft, IV

TO BEGIN WITH, I WOULD LIKE TO THANK AMERICAN UNIVERSITY'S WASHING-
ton College of Law and the International Law Review for putting on this conference. The subject – the Geneva Convention and the Rules of War in the post–9/11
world and in Iraq – could not be more timely and potentially useful. We are at a
point now where we have enough experience in the war the terrorists are fighting against us to know how it is being fought by them and needs to be defended
against by us. Specifically, we now have a fair idea of how this conflict varies
from both traditional wars and normal law enforcement operations – the two
familiar structures through which uses of force against civil societies have been
customarily dealt with. We need to take the knowledge our experience has given
us to establish a new system whose rules are well understood and take account
of both the need to protect our citizens and assure that we accurately identify,
effectively deter, and appropriately punish those who pose threats to our society
or have committed criminal acts.

During the course of the day, I have no doubt the various panels will be
exploring the issues implicit in the assignment I have described in detail. In this
short keynote address, I will try just to make a few general points that I hope
will assist in that work.

At the outset, let me declare my own preference for using the law of war rather
than traditional criminal law as at least the starting point for any new system of
rules for dealing with the terrorist challenge we currently confront. In saying this,
I do not exclude that a better day may come when nations may be able to protect
their citizens effectively through traditional law enforcement methods, but at the
moment it does not seem to me that such an approach will succeed or properly
takes account of the nature and extent of the threat. Al Qaeda is not simply

These remarks were presented at the Washington College of Law on March 24, 2005, at
the American University International Law Review's annual conference, entitled "The Geneva
Conventions and the Rules of War in the post–9/11 and Iraq World." An edited version of the
remarks will appear in 21 Am. U. Int'l L. Rev. (forthcoming Fall 2005).

a criminal enterprise that uses violence to achieve particular, limited, material objectives. Its objectives, insofar as they can be determined from its actions and the statements of its leaders, are essentially political and amount to nothing less than the overthrow of recognized governments and the destruction of as much of civil society as it can manage in certain states, including the United States. Moreover, it pursues its political objectives in ways that are the ways of war, not the ways of crime. Al Qaeda, of course, is not a state, but nor is it simply the Red Brigades or even the IRA or the Basque movement, with their specific goals to change the policy of a single national state. Al Qaeda's program addresses itself directly to the conduct of national governments around the world. Its methods, moreover, are the methods of war, and the scale and international character of its activity are similarly familiar to us only in war. Finally, on our side it is clear that the deployment of our own armed forces and the conduct of military operations are essential to deal with al Qaeda and its affiliate terrorist groups. In short, as was clearly recognized by our allies and the unanimous vote of the United Nations Security Council immediately after the attacks on September 11, 2001, we are engaged in an armed conflict. While it is undoubtedly true that this armed conflict with al Qaeda has its unconventional aspects, the law of armed conflict modified to adapt to those unconventional aspects appears to me to be the best place to start.

I mentioned just now what I believe should be the purposes of the set of rules we apply in dealing with al Qaeda – the effective protection of our citizens and the need to assure that we accurately identify, effectively deter, and appropriately punish the terrorists who are fighting us. With regard to each of these purposes, the law of armed conflict provides several distinct advantages over traditional law enforcement approaches.

First, the law of armed conflict authorizes the detention and interrogation of persons who may have critically important information about terrorists' plans and capabilities. While detained persons are not, of course, required to provide information and certainly may not be coerced into doing so, experience suggests that many of them will do so voluntarily or, perhaps as often, inadvertently, and this can save many lives. Because under the law of war it is not necessary to provide detained persons with lawyers, advise them of their rights to remain silent or charge them with any crime – they may not, after all, have committed one – they are more likely to provide vital intelligence information than would be the case in a law enforcement setting. The law of war, which traditionally has immunized lawful combatants for acts that in other contexts would be criminal, recognizes that a belligerent's interest in gaining intelligence may outweigh his interest in prosecuting individual members of the opposing force for criminal acts – apart, of course, for war crimes, which present a special case. The same balance of interests would seem to apply in the war with terrorists.

A second area where the traditional law of war seems to correspond well with the balance of interests in the conflict with al Qaeda concerns the right to detain persons who, if they are released, will re-engage in the fight. Again, the law of war recognizes that it is not necessary to charge a detained person with a crime to keep him off the battlefield while hostilities continue. Preventing his further participation in the conflict will, presumably, hasten its end and could significantly reduce the risk of additional casualties to our population. Such preventive detention obviously has no place in our concept of criminal law enforcement, but it has long been accepted in the law of war and, again, seems sensibly to apply to the conflict with al Qaeda.

A third advantage of applying the law of war to the conflict with al Qaeda is that it embodies an established set of rules for the conduct of our own troops. It immunizes them for various acts involving the use of force that in a law enforcement context would not be permitted, at the same time as it prohibits acts that unnecessarily endanger noncombatants; it assures detained combatants of humane treatment; it provides a basis for charging terrorists for war crimes and holding them accountable for how they treat our servicemen who fall into their hands. Our troops, moreover, are trained to comply with the law of war in conducting operations. Inasmuch as the terrorists can only be defeated by our armed forces, discarding familiar rules of conduct and improvising new ones as we go along creates a situation full of temptations to cut corners and adopt practices that seem desirable at the moment but are not well thought through and are bad precedents for other situations that we fail to anticipate.

On the whole, then, it seems to me that, for these and other reasons, the law of armed conflict provides the best foundation for a system governing the war the terrorists have declared and are pursuing against us. However, in applying it to this new type of war with nonstate actors operating in a loose, erratically disciplined structure, we need to recognize that this war varies in important respects from the state-against-state wars for which the law of war was designed, and we should be prepared to make appropriate modifications to accommodate the differences. Two points, in particular, stand out in this regard, both of them having to do with detention of enemy combatants.

First, we need to exercise great care in taking persons into custody in the first place to assure that they are indeed enemy combatants. In the traditional state-against-state war this is generally not difficult. The enemy wears his country's uniform, has a rank and serial number he is obliged and typically pleased to specify, and is assigned to a regular military unit. Most often he is captured in the course of actual combat, leaving no doubt as to his status. In the war the terrorists are fighting, the situation is much less clear. Persons are handed over to our forces by third parties whose reports about the circumstances of capture are not always reliable; they do not wear uniforms or other identifying insignia; and they are often arrested on the basis of information that they are plotting terrorist events while they sit in their apartments far from the battlefield rather than in a national Ministry of Defense. In short, in all these circumstances it is a lot more difficult to be sure that persons we suspect are terrorists actually are enemy combatants who may be detained. It appears now, in fact, that not many but at least a few of the persons detained in Guantanamo for more than two years were not properly classified as combatants and should have been sent there at all. Errors occur in war, of course, and often with tragic consequences, but it is hard not to think that providing an individualized determination of each individual's status at the time of capture rather than waiting until the Supreme Court required this years later would have avoided some mistakes and, perhaps incidentally, would have increased public support both at home and abroad for detaining enemy combatants while the war with al Qaeda continues.

Second, there is the issue of how long an individual detainee may be held while the conflict with al Qaeda continues. In view of the fact that the conflict may extend indefinitely, there has been concern that persons who have not been charged with any crime may nonetheless be effectively imprisoned for life because a war in which they were perhaps only briefly involved when they were young has not ended. People expressing this concern in this way – and there are many of them – evidently do not accept that the law of war, permitting detention of combatants while hostilities continue, is the applicable body of law for the conflict with al Qaeda. Nonetheless, even assuming as I do that it is, the situation, in my judgment, calls for another adjustment to the practice of holding captured enemy combatants until the end of hostilities under the traditional law of war to reflect the special circumstances of the war with al Qaeda.

The traditional rule assumed that the belligerent state had the ability both to initiate the war and require its citizens to participate in it and, subsequently, to end hostilities by ordering its forces to surrender. Military discipline would enforce each decision in its turn. In this situation the consequences of repatriating captured combatants whether during hostilities or after were clear: persons repatriated while hostilities continued would rejoin their country's forces, and those repatriated later would have no war to fight in and thus present no danger. The key consideration here, of course, is simply whether the released detainee will rejoin the fight. Rather than seeking the answer to this question in the formal position of a belligerent state, however, in the war with the terrorists it would seem that a periodic individual assessment of a detainee's intentions is appropriate. This is the approach reflected in the annual review board process recently established for Guantanamo detainees.

There remains the important question of what rules should govern the treatment of enemy combatants captured in this new type of war. It seems clear that strictly speaking the Geneva Conventions do not apply to a conflict with al Qaeda, a nonstate and a nonparty to the Conventions. While it is less clear, it is likely that in most cases even if the Conventions did apply, the terrorist combatants in this conflict do not qualify for treatment as prisoners of war because of their failure to comply with the laws of war. None of this is to say, however, that the Conventions' general requirement that detained persons not be subjected to cruel, inhumane, or humiliating treatment is not a sound guideline. If we are to use the law of war as the point of departure for the system to be used in this new type of war, there ought in any event to be some particular justification – or at least some practical benefit – for departing from this guideline. It is significant that, seeing no such justification or benefit when they were considering this issue initially in January of 2002, neither the military nor the civilian leadership of the Department of Defense proposed to deviate from the requirements of the Geneva Conventions in their treatment of the detainees in Guantanamo. The original rules of engagement issued to the forces fighting in Afghanistan had rather directed that the Geneva Conventions be complied with in the treatment of persons taken into custody, regardless of whether they were strictly speaking entitled to this. In this respect they followed the American practice in Vietnam, where the Viet Cong were treated in accordance with the Conventions even though it was understood that this was not required. It has been a continuing source of amazement and, I may add, considerable disappointment to me that, notwithstanding the stated intention of the Pentagon's leadership to comply with the requirements of the Conventions without qualification, lawyers at the Department of Justice thought it was important to decide at that time that the Conventions did not apply to al Qaeda as a matter of law and to qualify the commitment to apply them as a matter of policy to situations where this was "appropriate" and "consistent with military necessity." This unsought conclusion unhinged those responsible for the treatment of the detainees in Guantanamo from the legal guidelines for interrogation of detainees reflected in the Conventions and embodied in the Army Field Manual for decades. Set adrift in uncharted waters and under pressure from their leaders to develop information on the plans and practices of al Qaeda, it was predictable that those managing the interrogation would eventually go too far, and news reports now indicate that from time to time this happened. I do not exclude that some important information – perhaps very important, life-saving information – may have resulted from the application of methods of interrogation that are prohibited by the Conventions and the Manual. I would note, however, that in adopting any new system authorizing such methods, some justification more than that unlawful combatants have no rights or that the laws of war prohibiting the use of such methods do not apply to our conflict with al Qaeda would be highly desirable. This would seem to be a job for Congress, but perhaps this conference can make a start.

Before ending, I should mention one more area where there is some work to be done.

The International Committee of the Red Cross ("ICRC") and several human rights advocacy groups have on a number of occasions publicly raised concerns about other alleged deviations from the customary law of war as it relates to the treatment of detainees in our conflict with al Qaeda. Specifically, the ICRC has alleged that the U.S. is holding persons whose identities have not been declared to the ICRC, that it is operating undisclosed detention facilities, and arranging unlawful transfers of detainees to third countries. There is no basis in the law of war, criminal law, or human rights law for such practices. Nor is it tenable after the Supreme Court's rulings last summer to assert that detainees have no legal rights of any kind, that they may not contest with the assistance of competent counsel of their own choosing the legal basis of their detention, that the government has complete discretion to determine the conditions of their detention, or that whether they are treated humanely or not is a question only of policy. How our government treats people should never, at bottom, be a matter merely of policy, but a matter of law.

13 Legal Ethics and Other Perspectives

Jeffrey K. Shapiro

I SERVED IN THE JUSTICE DEPARTMENT'S OFFICE OF LEGAL COUNSEL, OR OLC, from 1991 to 1994. I read with interest, therefore, OLC's draft memorandum of January 9, 2002, on whether the protections of the Geneva Convention apply to al Qaeda and Taliban detainees.[1] It was brought to my attention by Stephen Gillers' opinion column last year in *The American Lawyer*, criticizing the legal ethics of the OLC lawyers who prepared the memorandum.[2] His essay in this volume reiterates and amplifies the criticism. I believe that Professor Gillers' position is demonstrably ill-informed and without merit. In the discussion below, I will present the factual background necessary to fairly judge OLC's work on Geneva. Then, I will explain where I think Professor Gillers errs.

THE PRESIDENT'S DETERMINATION

It is the President's determination with regard to Geneva that is at issue. On February 7, 2002, the President issued a memorandum of determination addressed to the Vice President, Secretary of State, Secretary of Defense, Attorney General, Chief of Staff to the President, Director of Central Intelligence, Assistant to the President for National Security Affairs, and the Chairman of the Joint Chiefs of Staff.[3]

His memorandum begins: "Our recent extensive discussions regarding the status of al Qaeda and Taliban detainees confirm that the application of the Geneva Conventions . . . to the conflict with the al Qaeda and the Taliban involves complex legal questions."[4] Chief among these, says the President, is that Geneva

applies to conflicts involving "High Contracting Parties," which can only be states. Moreover, it assumes the existence of "regular" armed forces fighting on behalf of states. However, the war against terrorism ushers in a new paradigm, one in which groups with broad, international reach commit horrific acts against innocent civilians, sometimes with the direct support of states. Our Nation recognizes that this new paradigm – ushered in not by us, but by terrorists – requires new thinking that should nevertheless be consistent with the principles of Geneva."[5]

The President then notes that he is "relying on the opinion of the Department of Justice dated January 22, 2002, and on the legal opinion rendered by the Attorney General in his letter of February 1, 2002."[6] His determination is as follows:

- "I accept the legal conclusion of the Department of Justice and determine that none of the provisions of Geneva apply to our conflict with al Qaeda in Afghanistan or elsewhere throughout the world because . . . al Qaeda is not a High Contracting Party to Geneva."
- "I accept the legal conclusion of the Attorney General and the Department of Justice that I have authority . . . to suspend Geneva as between the United States and Afghanistan, but I decline to exercise that authority at this time. Accordingly, I determine that . . . Geneva will apply to our present conflict with the Taliban."
- "I also accept the legal conclusion of the Department of Justice and determine that common Article 3 of Geneva does not apply to either al Qaeda or Taliban detainees, because . . . the relevant conflicts are international in scope and common Article 3 applies only to 'armed conflict not of an international character.'"
- "Based on the facts supplied by the Department of Defense and the recommendation of the Department of Justice, I determine that the Taliban detainees are unlawful combatants and, therefore, do not qualify as prisoners of war under Article 4 of Geneva. I note that, because Geneva does not apply to our conflict with al Qaeda, al Qaeda detainees also do not qualify as prisoners of war."

Finally, the President announced, as the policy of the United States, that the armed forces, "shall continue to treat detainees humanely and, to the extent appropriate and consistent with military necessity, in a manner consistent with the principles of Geneva." He also expressly reaffirmed the Secretary of Defense's previous order to that effect.[7]

OLC'S JANUARY 22 MEMO

As the President's memorandum noted, his determination was made in light of extensive discussions among the Departments of Justice, State, and Defense, the CIA, and their various legal and policy advisors. One of the participants in the discussions was the Office of Legal Counsel (OLC), which is an important office with a long history in the Justice Department. OLC assists the Attorney General in his function as legal advisor to the President and all the Executive Branch agencies. OLC drafts legal opinions of the Attorney General and also provides its own written opinions and oral advice in response to requests from the Counsel to the President and the various agencies of the Executive Branch.

As the name implies, the "Office of *Legal* Counsel" exists to provide legal counsel. OLC does not provide significant policy, political, or public relations advice. OLC's narrow but important function is to read the law and provide reasonably objective legal analysis for the Executive Branch, especially on matters important to the Attorney General and the President. OLC's pronouncements on the law are treated as authoritative within the Executive Branch.

As part of the interagency deliberation, OLC circulated a draft memorandum dated January 9, 2002, on the applicability of the Geneva Conventions to al Qaeda and Taliban detainees.[8] This memorandum was finalized with essentially the same reasoning and conclusions on January 22, 2002.[9] In the memoranda, OLC expressed its view that Geneva did not apply to the al Qaeda detainees, because al Qaeda is not a contracting party, and the conflict is of an international character, thus precluding application of common Article 3, which applies to traditional wars between state parties or noninternational civil wars. As to the Taliban, OLC opined that the President could find that Geneva does not apply. To do so, the President would need to find that, in the relevant time period, Afghanistan had become a failed state (or, alternatively, that the Taliban had become so intertwined with al Qaeda that they were more akin to a terrorist organization than a government). As an alternative, the President could conclude that Geneva was in force in Afghanistan but that members of the Taliban militia as a class were ineligible for prisoner of war, or POW, status for failing to comply with Geneva's requirements (command by responsible individuals, wearing insignia, carrying arms openly, and obeying the laws of war).

Finally, OLC explained at length that, even if the President chose to suspend specific provisions of Geneva as a legal matter, he would be free legally to apply the same requirements as a matter of policy. OLC discussed historical examples in which this approach was followed, including Korea (which began before the parties had ratified Geneva), Vietnam (regarding the Viet Cong), and recent interventions in Panama, Somalia, Haiti, and Bosnia.

THE ATTORNEY GENERAL'S FEBRUARY 1 LETTER

The State Department did not want the President to suspend Geneva in Afghanistan, primarily on policy grounds. As noted above, OLC concluded that the President possessed the legal authority to do so. On February 1, 2002, the Attorney General sent a short letter to the President on this subject.[10] The Attorney General told the President there were two potential theories supporting the conclusion that the Taliban are not legally entitled to the protections of Geneva. One theory would require the President to find that Afghanistan was a failed state and not a party to Geneva, which would deny the Taliban the benefits of Geneva. Under existing case law, said the Attorney General, this option would virtually foreclose judicial review and thereby minimize the Administration's risk of liability, litigation, and criminal prosecution.

Alternatively, wrote the Attorney General, the President could uphold the applicability of Geneva in Afghanistan, but interpret the treaty to deny the Taliban protection for failure to comply. This option, said the Attorney General, would expose the Administration to judicial review that "could involve substantial criminal liability for involved U.S. officials"[11] and "judicially-imposed conditions of detainment – including mandated release of a detainee."[12] Despite this warning, the President nonetheless chose the latter option with greater legal risk.

PROFESSOR GILLERS' CRITICISM

Professor Gillers begins by figuratively slapping his forehead: "*I should have realized there would be legal memos.* We cannot issue stock or mount a hostile takeover in the United States without lawyers. Neither can we wage war without lawyers." (Italics added.) After sharing this epiphany, Gillers then gravely reports on the great undertaking to unravel the role of these lawyers in providing legal cover for the would-be torturers in the Bush administration. An air of mystery wafts through his narrative: "I then tried to dig a little deeper," "so far as we can tell based on what has come to light," "the press revealed," "I think what happened here was not an accident," "We do not know, and may never know, all of the conversations," "the entire sequence suggests an orchestrated plan." And, finally, the future seen darkly through the looking glass: "I suspect we are going to see more memoranda leaked. We are going to get more information about what the lawyers did and did not do. And I fear, in the end, that the news is going to be even worse than it now appears."[13]

This little detective story is very entertaining. But the President's February 7 Geneva determination is quite transparent. In the determination, the President concisely summarizes the legal issues, the Justice Department's legal conclusions, and his final determination. He even notes the "extensive discussions" within the Executive Branch that preceded his determination.[14] It is odd that Gillers is focused so exclusively on these discussions. Why does he not criticize the lawfulness of the President's determination itself? Is that not relevant to evaluating the legal advice behind it? In particular, if Gillers were of the view that the President's determination misconstrues or misapplies Geneva, then it might be fair for him to ask if the OLC lawyers upon whom the President relied had led him astray. But Gillers does not challenge the lawfulness of the President's determination.

Odder still, Gillers never contends that the OLC lawyers themselves misconstrued or misapplied Geneva. His failure to do so seems to be a silent admission that their advice was analytically sound. Indeed, I would challenge Gillers to argue that it was not. I predict he will not do so, because deep down he knows that the OLC lawyers correctly construed and applied the treaty.

If OLC's legal advice was sound, and the President's determination in reliance upon the advice was lawful, what is there to criticize from a legal ethics perspective? Can a lawyer provide sound legal advice that is nonetheless incompetent and unethical? Does Gillers really believe that is possible? He does not face up to this interesting conundrum. Instead, he conveniently mischaracterizes the advice that OLC was asked to provide. He states that the subject of OLC's January 9 memorandum is "the legal protection, if any, for Taliban and al Qaeda members taken prisoner in Afghanistan."[15] That is a fictional description of the OLC memorandum. Relying on this fictional description, he then argues that the authors of the memorandum left such prisoners in a "lawless world" by omitting discussion of humanitarian laws such as the Convention Against Torture that would protect them. He argues, in other words, that the OLC advice was incomplete on a basic point.

The question put to OLC, however, was not whether al Qaeda and Taliban detainees enjoy "any" legal protection. Had that question been asked, the answer doubtless would have included the Torture Convention. OLC was asked to opine only as to the applicability of Geneva to these detainees. As proof, consider the second sentence of the January 9 memorandum: "[Y]ou have asked whether the laws of armed conflict apply to the conditions of detention and procedures for trial of members of al Qaeda and the Taliban militia."[16] Or, even more specifically, consider the revised second sentence in the final January 22 memorandum: "[Y]ou have asked whether certain treaties forming part of the laws of armed conflict apply to the conditions of detention and the procedures for trial of members of al Qaeda and the Taliban militia."[17] It is well established that the "laws of armed conflict" do not include the Torture Convention and other general humanitarian laws that apply at all times and not just during armed conflict. Gillers thus falsely describes OLC's assignment in order to criticize the absence of the Torture Convention from their discussion.

Gillers also faults the OLC lawyers for a "tone" that is overly "confident . . . about the accuracy of [their] advice" and the absence of "significant qualifying language" that "even the most aggressive corporate lawyer" would include "as a matter of self-protection and self-respect." He speculates that OLC lawyers omitted contrary arguments at the request of the White House and because they "may have felt confident" about their immunity from criminal, civil, or disciplinary liability, "unlike corporate lawyers, whose opinions would not have been so one-sided."[18]

It is a bit tendentious of Gillers to fault the OLC lawyers for having too much confidence in their advice when he fails to challenge its accuracy. More important, Gillers never explains why a "corporate lawyer" model applies. He never discusses the role OLC plays within the Executive Branch, the nature of its work, its typical work product, or any other context that might bear on a fair evaluation of OLC's work. He simply assumes without discussion that OLC's work product in this case should have resembled what one would expect from a good corporate lawyer. I have raised this issue with Professor Gillers previously in writing and on a panel; since he has never responded, it would appear that he does not have a good answer.

In truth, OLC has never adhered to a "corporate lawyer" model in its legal practice. OLC's standard practice is to answer legal questions as posed, neither more nor less. Asked about Geneva and other, related laws of war, OLC will address those legal instruments and not others. Moreover, while a good corporate lawyer is expected to provide practical judgment on the risks and consequences of a legal position, with all the hedging and qualifications that implies, OLC is not. An OLC opinion essentially announces the legal position of the Executive Branch on specific legal questions. In this respect, the more appropriate analogue is an appellate court decision, not an advice memo from a corporate lawyer. If Gillers would trouble himself to look at even a sampling of the hundreds of opinion memoranda posted on OLC's home page going back to 1992 <http://www.usdoj.gov/olc>, he would see that they have a similar tone. There is nothing at all special or distinctive about the Geneva memoranda in this regard.

Gillers also fails to explain why a White House intent on obtaining legal cover to commit torture chose to do so on a legal theory that maximized exposure to criminal and civil liability, while overtly rejecting a valid alternative legal theory that would have virtually foreclosed judicial review, as was explained to the President in the Attorney General's February 1 letter. This fact alone tends to puncture Gillers' speculation that the White House sought OLC's legal cover for planned depredations against detainees.

I have dwelled at some length on the specifics of the President's determination, OLC's advice, and OLC's general charter, because all of this necessary context is either absent or glossed over in Professor Giller's legal ethics analysis. It is disturbing that he would impugn the legal work of OLC lawyers by name based upon a specious description of their assignment, while concurrently omitting the relevant context in which to fairly evaluate their work product. In the future, I would hope that Professor Gillers will support his criticisms of OLC with an honest description of the relevant facts, and the application of a legal ethics construct that is appropriate to the work in question.

NOTES

1. Deputy Assistant Attorney General John Yoo, U.S. Department of Justice, and Special Counsel Robert J. Delahunty, U.S. Department of Justice, January 9, 2002 Memorandum to General Counsel William J. Haynes, II, U.S. Department of Defense, in *The Torture Papers*, ed. Karen J. Greenberg and Joshua L. Dratel, Memo #4, p. 38 (New York: Cambridge University Press, 2005).
2. Gillers, Stephen. "Tortured Reasoning." *The American Lawyer*, September 2004.
3. President George W. Bush, February 7, 2002 Memorandum to The Vice President, The Secretary of State, The Secretary of Defense, The Attorney General, Chief of Staff to the President, Director of CIA, Assistant to the President for National Security Affairs, Chairman of the Joint Chiefs of Staff, in *The Torture Papers*, Memo #11, p. 134.

4. *Id.*, p. 134.
5. *Id.*, p. 134.
6. *Id.*
7. *Id.*, pp. 134–5.
8. *See* note 1.
9. Assistant Attorney General Jay S. Bybee, U.S. Department of Justice, January 22, 2002 Memorandum to Alberto R. Gonzales, Counsel to the President, and General Counsel William J. Haynes, U.S. Department of Defense, in *The Torture Papers*, Memo #6, p. 81.
10. Attorney General John Ashcroft, February 1, 2002 Memorandum to President George W. Bush, in *The Torture Papers*, Memo #9, p. 126.
11. *Id.*, p. 126.
12. *Id.*, p. 127.
13. Stephen Gillers, "Legal Ethics: A Debate," p. 236.
14. *See* note 3.
15. *See* note 13.
16. *See* note 1.
17. *See* note 9.
18. *See* note 13.

14 Legal Ethics: A Debate

Stephen Gillers

READERS OF THIS BOOK AND OF THE DOCUMENTS PRINTED IN THE EARLIER volume have abundant information with which to evaluate my contribution and Jeffrey K. Shapiro's response. This audience does not need to be led through the texts. But Mr. Shapiro says several things that deserve reply, the better to facilitate independent judgment. I will limit my comments to those matters.

Mr. Shapiro claims that the Office of Legal Counsel (OLC) memoranda of January 9 and 22 answered the question the client posed. They did their job. He argues that the question posed did not ask the authors to address the Torture Convention or Statute. He quotes as proof the "second sentence" of the memoranda. The first sentence of each memo is also relevant: "You have asked our Office's views concerning the effect of international treaties and federal law on the treatment of individuals detained by the U.S. Armed Forces during the conflict in Afghanistan." Mr. Shapiro's point seems to be that the second sentence, beginning "In particular," limits the scope of the inquiry to the Geneva Conventions and the OLC had no responsibility to go beyond them or to explain the perceived limitation.

Of course, both sentences were written by the authors of the memoranda. We do not (yet) have the text of the client's original request. But taking these sentences as the full scope of the request, I reject Mr. Shapiro's effort to defend the omission of the Torture Convention and the Torture Statute in the way he does.

First, the initial sentence does refer to "international treaties and federal laws," which encompass the documents not mentioned or discussed. At the very least, then, the authors should have made it clear that they were ignoring the broader language in the first sentence so the client was put on notice.

Second, a client's interest in a legal document "in particular" does not limit the lawyer's responsibility to respond fully to the client's broader, stated request. It means only that within the broader request, the client has a "particular" interest. Certainly, the authors should have entertained that possibility. Instead, the authors narrowly interpreted what is at best an ambiguity – was the "In particular" sentence meant to be restrictive or only to identify one concern "in particular?" – without telling the client how they had decided to resolve the purported ambiguity.

Third, even if the client had specifically limited its request to the Geneva Conventions by name, it would still have been irresponsible to fail to address the Torture Convention and Statute, or at least to identify their existence and say that they were not addressed. It is the duty of the lawyer to recognize relevant sources of law, not the client. If a client asked whether a particular issue of stock "violated the Securities and Exchange Act of 1934," surely we would expect the lawyer, in answering that question, either to address the legality of the issue under the 1933 Securities Act if relevant, or at the very least to make it clear that he or she was not doing so. Lawyers have been successfully sued for such mundane omissions as the failure to tell a client who identifies his need as "workers compensation" that he also has a tort claim arising from the same incident.

Here, the duty to reference other sources of relevant law was particularly high because the two memoranda concluded that detainees did not enjoy any protection from torture under Geneva. A reasonable – and I suggest an inevitable – reading of the January memoranda was that the detainees existed outside of all legal protection. But as the Justice Department later acknowledged on August 1, after more than six months had elapsed, other sources of law did protect them, if barely. (More than two years later, the Justice Department disowned the August 1 memo as insufficiently protective of detainees.)

Next, Mr. Shapiro "would challenge [me] to argue that" the advice on Geneva was not sound. I accept the challenge. Focusing solely on Geneva, then, here is my response.

First, although the advice was that Taliban and al Qaeda enjoyed no protection from Geneva, OLC counsel nowhere addressed the risk of misidentification and the legal risks to the client in that event. Mr. Shapiro, if I read him correctly, seems to say that that was not OLC's job. It was asked a pure question of law and it answered the pure question of law. If it had been asked another question it would have answered that one, too, but it wasn't. (See below on Mr. Shapiro's view of the role of OLC lawyers.)

In fact, however, Mr. Bybee did later attempt to explain how the government might avoid the individualized determinations by a "competent tribunal," which Geneva Three required should there be "any doubt" of a person's identity. Mr. Bybee told the government that it could avoid this process through presidential fiat, a position so far rejected by two district courts. Whether or not Mr. Bybee's advice eventually proves correct, the failure to deal with risks to the client from misidentification of prisoners as al Qaeda or Taliban when they are not – or even to describe the issue in a paragraph – is not competent.

Second, as many have pointed out, neither of the two memoranda nor the later Bybee and Yoo memoranda of August 1, 2002, on the Torture Convention and Statute, discuss or even cite the Supreme Court's leading decision in *Youngstown*

Sheet & Tube, Co. v. Sawyer, 343 U.S. 579 (1952), which emphatically limits the scope of presidential power even in time of war. This is a remarkable omission given the authors' strong reliance on the President's constitutional power as the basis for some of their more aggressive opinions. Addressing the August 1 memorandum on the Torture Convention and Statute, Yale Law Dean Harold Koh called the failure to "mentio[n] the landmark Supreme Court decision" in *Youngstown* "a stunning failure of lawyerly craft." Others have made the same point.

Third, the memoranda failed to acknowledge powerful contrary arguments. In finding no problem here, Mr. Shapiro posits a disturbingly crabbed view of the responsibilities of government counsel. "OLC's standard practice," he writes, "is to answer legal questions as posed, neither more nor less."

Legal issues are not litmus paper. As any practicing lawyer knows, the tough issues are loaded with ambiguities and uncertainties. They invite debate and disagreement. Is Mr. Shapiro saying that it is not the job of the lawyer as advisor to ensure that the client appreciates these uncertainties if that lawyer happens to work for the government? I hope not. The government would be terribly ill-served if so. Mr. Shapiro rejects the analogy to corporate lawyers and claims I haven't addressed his criticism of it. I am unaware that I haven't addressed it but let me do so now. I think the analogy is compelling. I do not claim *identity* between the relationship of a private lawyer for his or her private client, corporate or not, and the relationship of government lawyers to their client. But for one important professional responsibility – which is the reason I drew the analogy in the first place – Mr. Shapiro is dangerously wrong and the analogy quite correct.

When a lawyer, public or private, is asked to predict what the law is so the client may take action, perhaps very consequential action, based on the lawyer's advice, the lawyer is not in the traditional role of the courtroom advocate. He or she is professionally obligated to explore and explain well-founded conclusions contrary to those the lawyer has reached and to identify the risks to the client if, contrary to the lawyer's belief, a different view prevails. Only then can the client make an informed choice.

I would hope that any Attorney General would tell the head of his or her OLC:

> I know you won't simply tell me what you think I want to hear. I wouldn't have hired you if I thought you would. I expect you to tell me your best judgment on the question. But many of the questions I ask you will not have a clearly correct answer. When you answer these, I need you also to tell me why your judgment may be wrong and to do so in a way that respects the best arguments for other points of view. This is particularly important when the action the government will take based on your advice can have profound effect for the nation and individuals. Only if you do this, can I do my job of evaluating your advice and assessing how to proceed.

Although you'd never know it from the Yoo and Bybee memos (and it must be said that the Bybee memo *is* the Yoo memo reorganized), there is a rather substantial body of opinion from scholars and lawyers in the field that categorically rejects their conclusions. One such criticism, from more than 100 lawyers from all areas of practice and both political parties, states that the argument in the January memoranda "ignores that the treaty, by its own terms, governs all conflicts 'at any time and in any place whatsoever,' and protects even unlawful combatants who do not qualify as prisoners of war from 'humiliating and degrading treatment' and 'mutilation, cruel treatment and torture'" (quoting the treaty).

In various interviews or talks that Yoo has lately given he does not appear to defend the reasoning of the memoranda, but rather asserts that presidential power cannot be constrained by treaty in any event (to Jane Mayer of *The New Yorker* in the issue of February 14, 2005), or that terrorism means that "[w]e ought to establish a new set of rules" (in a recent speech at William & Mary School of Law), or (said both places) that the Bush victory means the debate is over. This last comment is quite a remarkable statement for a law professor. As for the need for a new set of rules, if we do need them, proper ways are available to adopt them.

It is important, finally, to recognize that the issue is not whether the memoranda got Geneva right. The answer to that question may come in litigation by persons claiming to be treated in violation of Geneva. But we don't have to wait for a judicial answer. The quality of the OLC work should be judged as of the time the memoranda issued. A badly done legal analysis is not saved by the fact that a court happens to accept its conclusion, no more than a poorly done brief turns into a good one because its author wins the case. The converse is also true. Competent advice does not lose that status because the courts ultimately reject it. OLC advised the government that United States courts would not have jurisdiction over Guantanamo. The memorandum offering that advice recognized the opposing view and was appropriately qualified. As it happens, the advice proved wrong. But it is not thereby incompetent.

Professor Yoo said (at William & Mary) that the soldiers who abused detainees were "people going off the reservations." But the effort to distance himself and OLC from the subsequent abuse may not prove so easy. More information will come out and we will be able to determine the extent to which abuse can be traced to OLC's advice in 2002. We do know, of course, that the OLC advice was accepted. The President, "relying on the opinion of the Department of Justice," did so in his memorandum of February 7, 2002, and even earlier. Secretary Rumsfeld cited OLC's specific conclusions on January 19, 2002, in a memorandum to the Joint Chiefs of Staff. While both men wrote that the Armed Forces (at least) would treat detainees "humanely" and "to the extent appropriate...in a manner consistent with the principles of Geneva," that of course is not the same as legal protection. We should not have been surprised, then, to learn that on December 2, 2002, Mr. Rumsfeld approved sixteen inter-rogation techniques for Guantanamo including "exploiting individual phobias, e.g., dogs," "stress positions," "hooding," and "20-hour interrogations." Most of these were rescinded on January 15, 2003 following expression of concern from the Navy General Counsel.

We await the leak or release of more information in the months and years ahead. But Mr. Shapiro's effort to exonerate his former office from any criticism on the ground that its members were just lawyers, just doing their jobs, saying what the law is in response to specific questions as posed by the client, and "neither more nor less," must be rejected as unacceptable for the profession and the nation.

15 The Lawyers Know Sin: Complicity in Torture

Christopher Kutz

"THE PHYSICISTS HAVE KNOWN SIN, AND THIS IS A KNOWLEDGE WHICH they cannot lose," reflected Robert Oppenheimer on the dropping of the atomic bombs in Japan.[1] Oppenheimer was referring both to the particular physicists involved in the Manhattan Project, including himself, and to physicists in general. A discipline whose traditional aim was the production of knowledge had become, in the pressures of war, a discipline producing fear and death.

When the Justice Department torture memos were initially leaked to the press, Oppenheimer's line floated through my mind. The lawyers too now know sin. The government lawyers who produced, reviewed, and apparently endorsed these memoranda, including lawyers at both the Department of Justice and the Department of Defense, spent their creative energies shaping a policy whose aim and effect was to legitimate previously illegitimate forms of interrogation and captive treatment – forms ranging from the cruelty and degradation of forced nudity, sexual humiliation, sensory deprivation, and prolonged use of stress positions – to the clearly torturous, most notably including the practice of "waterboarding," wherein interrogees are submerged in cold water so as to create the impression of imminent suffocation.[2]

As a result of these memoranda, law itself also now knows sin, or at least has become profoundly reacquainted with it. One of the signal, if incomplete, victories for the Enlightened rule of law – a campaign fought by Voltaire and Beccaria – has been the erasure of torture from the menu of governmental policy choices. Where there is law there can be no torture. The constellation of law, dignity, and governmental legitimacy has come to have iconic significance for legal thought in recent centuries, as Jeremy Waldron has recently observed.[3] With the torture memoranda, law's role was precisely to strip away the regulation of state violence.

I acknowledge the melodrama in the analogy to Oppenheimer's regrets, not least because law's relation to violence has always been close and complex, as have particular lawyers' relations to illegality. And I think we must recognize that the torture memoranda were written by civil servants whose sincere aim was the collective national security of the United States, as furthered through the selective use of torture and other extreme forms of interrogation. Second, and importantly, the policy decision to use (or not use) torture was taken by political officials, not these lawyers. They were not consulted about the wisdom or utility of torture, but only its legality; and they discharged their duty not by recommending torture directly, but by opening the field of policy choices as widely as possible. More generally, we expect our government to keep us safe, and to free us from the responsibility of knowing how this was done. The torture memos, it might be thought, were simply a case in which hard political choices saw the light of day.

The caveats are warranted. I will not here argue for what I believe: that the categorical prohibition of torture is the only legitimate governmental policy, and that the road to the violation of that norm is paved with expedient but cruel and degrading practices. If you reject that claim, then the issue of the lawyers' moral responsibility for the cruel and torturous acts they address is unproblematic: if they are responsible at all, they are to be praised, not blamed, for their roles. I too regard the lawyers' moral responsibility as unproblematic: they are morally complicit in the CIA and military intelligence interrogations they ratified in retrospect, those they warranted in prospect, and even in the unauthorized abuses their memos arguably occasioned, however unintentionally, in Abu Ghraib and elsewhere. But this I will not argue either.

What I do want to argue (or, given the brevity, really to suggest) is that there is a case for the *criminal* responsibility of these lawyers for the acts of torture they explicitly contemplated, if not under the default principles limiting attorneys' liability for their legal advice, then under a defensible, and more fine-grained, alternative to that scheme. Such liability exists most persuasively for the interrogations that took place after the memoranda's composition. It is a political fact that prosecution is extraordinarily unlikely in the United States, but the increasingly aggressive assertions of universal jurisdiction by other countries mean that it remains a live possibility.

To focus this discussion, let me simplify issues slightly. By the "torture memoranda," I mean to focus especially on the Office of Legal Counsel memoranda of January 2002, which argued that the Geneva Conventions, and hence the War Crimes Act, did not apply to treatment of Taliban and al Qaeda detainees, and the famous memorandum of August 2002, which argued that 18 U.S.C. sections 2340-2340a (the criminal statute implementing the Convention against Torture) fails to apply to evidently cruel and degrading forms of interrogation, and arguably fails to apply even to evident torture under current wartime conditions, and especially to interrogations ordered by the President as Commander-in-Chief. The legal effect of the memoranda was to give a green light to inhuman and degrading forms of interrogation, as well as to procedures and conditions of internment that were potentially in grave breach of the Geneva Conventions, and a yellow light to actual torture, by way of the proposed defenses of necessity and Presidential authority.[4]

The memoranda chiefly bear on three different sets of events: the harsh interrogations conducted by the CIA or the military in Afghanistan, Guantánomo, and elsewhere, whose questionable legality gave rise to the request for the memorandum of August; the interrogations conducted after the memoranda's issuance, including (apparently) the waterboarding of Khalid Sheikh Mohammed; and the prison abuse scandal at Abu Ghraib, which was certainly not contemplated by these memoranda. I will assume that, because of the legal effect of the President's determination that the Geneva Conventions do not apply to Taliban and al Qaeda detainees, War Crimes Act liability is off the table.[5] The relevant events for criminal liability, then, are those forms of interrogation that meet the standard of section 2340, namely acts specifically intended to "inflict severe physical or mental pain or suffering," including "the threat of imminent death," or "other procedures calculated to disrupt profoundly the senses or personality."[6] Waterboarding clearly fits the statutory definition of torture, as possibly do techniques of profound humiliation, fear inducement, and physical stress, notwithstanding the memoranda's cramped argument that the latter techniques would be merely cruel.

The actual causal relations between the memoranda and the acts of torture are unclear. The following is not overly contentious: the memoranda obviously had no effect on any prior acts of torture; they may have encouraged the subsequent acts (by way of independent decisions by political authorities); and they may have made likelier the unauthorized abuses of Abu Ghraib by helping to establish a climate of deep uncertainty regarding the limits of interrogation techniques. The central question for criminal liability is whether the text of the memos, coupled with their possible policy effects, suffices for accessorial liability for the subsequently authorized acts of torture.[7]

Accessorial liability lies most naturally when one person has aided or encouraged another to commit a criminal act, with the intent that the second person commit the act. Let the act here be torture in the course of interrogation, conducted after the issuance of the memoranda. Could there be liability for the lawyers whose opinion encouraged policymakers to green light such interrogations? Putting aside the crucial complication that what is at issue is legal advice, at first cut, the answer would seem to be yes, or at least enough of a yes to get to a jury.

As an analogy, consider a company considering making an illegal discharge of waste into a stream. The plant manager asks a nonlawyer vice-president whether he ought to discharge the waste; the vice-president responds with a long memo discussing the costly nature of compliance with environmental regulations, considers the pros and cons of the illegal discharge, concludes that the risk of detection and prosecution for the discharge is quite low, and indicates her office's anticipated acquiescence in the discharge, but does not actually recommend it. If the plant manager engages in the discharge, the vice-president is arguably an accomplice in the crime: given the question at stake, her clearing of the option could be interpreted to manifest an intent that the manager engage in the discharge; and it encouraged (or "abetted") the manager's decision to perform that act, by suggesting to him that the expected cost of engaging in the act was relatively low. As a matter of law, the vice-president could be convicted as an accomplice in the discharge (as could the company itself). Moreover, this seems true even if the vice-president's memorandum went through a number of other decisionmakers who themselves dictated whether the plant manager would engage in the discharge. Her motives are also irrelevant: she might genuinely believe that the regulations are socially inefficient, the harm *de minimis*, and the benefits substantial. Yet so long as the vice-president's intent was to encourage the discharge, and it had an effect on whoever made the decision to engage in the discharge, there could be accomplice liability.

Now assume that the vice-president is also general counsel, and her memorandum discusses not the likelihood of detection, but the actual legality of the discharge. She argues in her memo that some of the substances discharged by the plant might differ in chemical form from the list of designated legal pollutants that a court might not regard them as included in the regulations; and that even for those substances clearly prohibited, there is a good argument that the regulations were issued by the EPA pursuant to an unconstitutional delegation of Congressional authority, a claim that a sympathetic court might recognize. Her memorandum further insinuates that pushing the legal envelope in this direction would be a good policy choice. Alas, her legal analysis is flawed; the manager engages in the discharge after considering her counsel, is prosecuted and convicted. Though he might try to claim a defense of mistake of law, reliance on private counsel's mistake (however reasonable) would not be a defense.

One might think that the vice-president would be on the hook as well: the memo provides grounds for ascribing intent, and her authority as a lawyer makes her advice all the more persuasive, thus increasing the weight of her causal contribution to the discharge. But, of course, her being a lawyer counts profoundly against her accomplice liability. For it is a general legal rule that a lawyer will not be criminally liable for her clients' acts unless she either directly encourages them to act contrary to a known legal duty (for example by facilitating fraudulent transactions or destroying documents so as to minimize detection) or by representing a course of conduct as legal without being able to offer a good-faith, nonfrivolous legal argument for that position.[8] If she can offer a nonfrivolous argument for her client's position, she is not as a general matter exposed to criminal liability (or civil liability) even if a court later determines that her client committed a crime. Assuming the lawyer's arguments for the unconstitutionality of the regulations are not frivolous – even in the Pickwickian sense that they have been published in academic journals – she likely cannot be prosecuted as an accomplice. The reasons for this comparatively generous treatment of lawyers are familiar, and parallel the general argument for the attorney-client privilege: a rule imposing greater liability might make lawyers excessively risk-averse, rather than candid, in the advice they give; and lawyers' traditional role in civil disobedience and test-case litigation would be undermined, to the detriment of social experimentation and change. As a result, lawyers get a mistake of law defense denied to their own clients.

The case for the government lawyers would seem to be similar. Even if we grant that their counsel on the question of torture had the effect of encouraging acts of torture, and we can interpret their memoranda as offering an argument for considering torture as a viable legal option, not merely addressing its legality under the circumstances, the grounds for that argument have formed a distinctive, if highly contentious, body of academic work in recent years. Their arguments may have been silly, or wrong, or morally misguided, but they do not seem to be frivolous.[9] As a result, they would not be liable even if the actual interrogators could be.

Criminal liability for the government lawyers would thus seem to be foreclosed. But it is worth noting that the presumptive legal rule, limiting their liability to occasions of frivolous counsel or direct aid, has uncertain legal status in this application. The general rule, as I mentioned, is supported by very general policy considerations that aim to increase clients' range of activity and to protect possibilities of social change across the whole spectrum of law. At stake here is a very specific issue: when, and with what responsibility, may lawyers counsel acts of violence, in clear apparent conflict with statutory intent, and supported principally by extremely controversial legal arguments? There are no obvious precedents for this particular issue, and it is easy to see why: the domain of potential cases will typically involve government counsel to police or military (executive) functions, and prosecutions are virtually unthinkable. But a more refined rule for attorney accountability should be thinkable. Whatever the merits of protecting lawyers' advice in civil rights test cases (or even highly aggressive tax planning cases), counseling the violation of a statute regulating gross violence is a prime occasion for risk-aversion on the part of both counsel and clients.

There is thus a plausible case to be made that government counsel should bear the same risks as their clients: counseling the permissibility of what turns out to be a war crime puts both operative and attorney on the hook. Distinguishing the scope of a lawyer's complicity-free autonomy by reference to the content of their advice is at odds with the formalism of legal ethics, but it makes sense on policy grounds. To the extent international norms of legal conduct are more restrictive than American norms, the government lawyers may already be exposed to prosecutorial risk. One of the prime lessons of the torture memos has been how quickly the use of torture or other extraordinary interrogatory practices spreads from the limited instance of the "high-value" detainee to general practice and then general chaos. It is law's nature to be generalizable, and when the generalizability moves in the direction of greater use of force, extra caution is needed. Safe harbors for governmental lawyers could be designed as well: counsel might make clear the limited nature of their analyses, and include full accounts of contrary arguments when evaluating aggressive legal positions. Alternatively, special provision for the nature of attorney complicity might be recognized: they might be sentenced not as principals, but as providers of limited assistance, and so subject to substantial discounts in sentencing. There is surely room for a duty of government lawyers' own fidelity to law. Perhaps the punishment for sin should be left to other agencies, but the flouting of the U.S. and international law against torture could get an earthly hearing.

NOTES

1. J. Robert Oppenheimer, Arthur D. Little Memorial Lecture at MIT, 1947, quoted in Barton J. Bernstein, "The Oppenheimer Loyalty-Security Case Reconsidered," 42 Stanford L. Rev. 1383, 1400 (1990).
2. Douglas Jehl and David Johnston, "CIA Expands Its Inquiry into Interrogation Tactics," *New York Times* (August 29, 2004); Mark Danner, "Abu Ghraib: The Hiden Story," *New York Review of Books* (October 7, 2004).
3. Jeremy Waldron, "Torture and Positive Law: Jurisprudence for the White House," <http://repositories.cdlib.org/berkeley_gala/fall2004/1/> (forthcoming in the *Columbia Law Review*).
4. The light is actually yellowish-green: the August memorandum says that prosecution "may be barred" but that "Any effort by Congress to regulate the interrogation of battle-field combatants *would violate* the Constitution's sole vesting of the Commander-in-Chief authority in the President." *The Torture Papers*, p. 173, 207.
5. *See* Memorandum from John Ashcroft of February 1, 2002, *The Torture Papers*, p. 126.
6. 18 U.S.C. §2340, 2340(2).
7. There are also possibilities of conspiratorial liability or – especially under foreign or international law – accessorial liability on the basis of recklessness; but these cases would be substantially harder to make out.
8. Restatement (Third) of the Law of Lawyering, §§8, 94. For additional discussion, *see* Geoffrey Hazard, "How Far May A Lawyer Go In Assisting A Client In Legally Wrongful Conduct?" 35 U. Miami L. Rev. 669 (1981).
9. Moreover, it is possible that here (in contrast to the pollution case) the actual torturers could avail themselves of a defense of mistake of law grounded in an official (mis)statement by a government office charged with the interpretation or enforcement of the statute. *See, e.g.,* Model Penal Code §2.04. On the other hand, the August memo did not present itself as a clear statement that torture would be legal under the circumstances, but was couched in weak qualifiers.

16 Renouncing Torture

Michael C. Dorf

AS 2004 DREW TO A CLOSE, THE OFFICE OF LEGAL COUNSEL OF THE UNITED
States Department of Justice took an important step towards restoring its own
integrity: It released a memorandum[1] essentially repudiating its earlier analysis
of the circumstances under which someone could be found criminally liable for
engaging in torture. That earlier memorandum of August 2002[2] had turned
intellectual somersaults to find loopholes and excuses for the commission of
what a lay observer would surely consider torture.

The new memo, in contrast, is fair-minded and reasonable. Accordingly, its
author, Acting Assistant Attorney General Daniel Levin, deserves considerable
praise. As I explain below, the memo definitively repudiates two of the most
outrageous positions set forth in the August 2002 memo: the almost impossibly
high threshold for finding an act of torture, and the contention that a torturer
can escape criminal liability if he engages in torture with a noble goal in mind,
such as to extract vital information from the torture victim.

In one particular, however, the new memo could have gone further. The
August 2002 memo had set forth a third outrageous proposition: that Congress
lacks the power to prohibit torture undertaken at the behest of the President, acting in his capacity as Commander-in-Chief. Although the new memo laudably
declines to endorse this view, it does not formally repudiate the position either.
That is unfortunate, because the August 2002 memo's contentions regarding
the wartime powers of the President are truly frightening. They deserve to be
repudiated expressly and unequivocally.

THE POLITICAL BACKGROUND OF THE TORTURE MEMOS

The Office of Legal Counsel (OLC) provides legal advice to the Executive Branch
of the federal government on important matters of public policy. Its August 2002
memo was signed by Jay Bybee, then the head of OLC and now a federal appeals
court judge. Judge Bybee, who was confirmed by the Senate before the memo
came to light, has refused to comment on it.

Much of the political heat produced by the Bybee memo has accordingly been directed elsewhere – at the Bush administration in general and at White House Counsel Alberto Gonzales, to whom the memo is addressed, in particular. Gonzales will shortly face his own Senate confirmation hearings on his nomination to become Attorney General.[3] When he does, he will likely be asked why he sought legal advice about the "standards of conduct" under the international treaty and the federal statute barring torture.

The August 2002 memo recites OLC's understanding that the torture issue arose "in the context of the conduct of interrogations outside of the United States."[4] One can reasonably infer, therefore, that the Bush administration, with the approval of Gonzales, was interested in pushing the envelope in its treatment of suspected al Qaeda terrorists and others detained in Afghanistan, at Guantanamo Bay, and elsewhere. That inference receives further support from reports of the treatment of prisoners in Iraq. Together, the evidence suggests that U.S. military and civilian interrogators were given the green light to engage in practices that the International Committee of the Red Cross has described as "tantamount to torture."[5]

The Senate is thus entitled to inquire whether Gonzales knew or should have known that his request for legal advice regarding potential criminal liability for torture was part of a scheme to authorize – or at least turn a blind eye toward – torture. In the wake of last week's release of the new memo, some commentators have suggested that the administration is hoping to defuse the potentially explosive issue of the role Gonzales played with respect to the August 2002 memo. If that is the administration's hope, however, it seems a vain one; the fact that OLC has now repudiated the views it expressed earlier sheds little light on Gonzales' fitness to serve as the nation's chief law enforcement officer.

If one were to conclude that Gonzales showed poor judgment and disrespect for the rule of law by asking for the August 2002 memo, then it is hard to see how OLC's more recent change of heart would alter this conclusion. A confession of error by Gonzales himself might be relevant, but why should an about-face by OLC be relevant?

THE LEGAL SIGNIFICANCE OF THE OLC MEMOS

These political considerations will be addressed when Gonzales goes before the Senate. For now, let us focus on the law. What is the legal significance of the August 2002 memo and the December 2004 memo repudiating it?

OLC memos do not have the force of law in quite the way that opinions of the Supreme Court do, but neither are they mere opinion pieces in the way that, say, a scholarly article or a law professor's column on FindLaw's Writ is. OLC is often asked to address constitutional issues that will never to make it to court – what lawyers call nonjusticiable political questions. In these circumstances, the formal advice of OLC may be the only sort of "precedent" that exists.

Moreover, although the head of OLC and the top deputies are political appointees, the office as a whole has long had a culture of independence. The dedicated and talented lawyers who work at OLC typically see themselves not as mere servants of the administration that happens to seek their advice, but also as keepers of an inter-generational trust. Thus, one commonly sees OLC memos taking seriously the views expressed in prior OLC memos prepared for Presidents of either political party. The OLC under Republican administrations approvingly cites the memos of its predecessors in Democratic administrations, and vice-versa.

Against this background, the August 2002 memo can only be described as a serious departure from longstanding OLC practice. In content and tone, the memo reads much like a document that an overzealous young associate in a law firm would prepare in response to a partner's request for whatever arguments can be concocted to enable the firm's client to avoid criminal liability.

The December 2004 memo, however, is markedly different. Although its analysis is no less lawyerly than that contained in the August 2002 memo, it shows a sensitivity to the important role that OLC plays in shaping national policy – a sensitivity that was sorely lacking in the earlier memo.

HOW SEVERE IS THE PAIN OR SUFFERING THAT TORTURE MUST CAUSE?

As its title suggests, the United Nations Convention Against Torture and Other Cruel, Inhuman, or Degrading Acts, prohibits not only torture but also less serious forms of cruelty, inhumanity, and degradation. The United States ratified the Convention and subsequently enacted federal legislation that defines torture and establishes criminal liability for Americans and others found in the United States who commit torture abroad.

Significantly, however, the federal statute does not impose criminal liability for cruel, inhuman, or degrading acts. Under a reservation adopted by the Senate when it ratified the U.N. Convention, such lesser acts are equated with treatment that would be considered unconstitutional under the Fifth, Eighth, and Fourteenth Amendments.

The August 2002 memo seizes on the distinction between, on the one hand, torture as defined in both the U.N. Convention and the U.S. implementing legislation as the infliction of "severe pain or suffering," and, on the other hand, "mere" cruel, inhuman or degrading acts. The basic strategy of the August 2002 memo on this point is to treat all but the most horrific acts as insufficiently severe to constitute torture. Thus, the August 2002 memo sets the torture threshold at "excruciating and agonizing" pain or pain "equivalent in intensity to the pain accompanying serious physical injury, such as organ failure, impairment of bodily function, or even death."[6]

Although the December 2004 memo recognizes that the plain text of the Convention and federal law do distinguish between torture and lesser degradations, it disavows the extremely high threshold advocated in the August 2002 memo. To be sure, the new memo is not especially helpful in establishing exactly how much pain or suffering is necessary to count as "severe." For the most part, the memo simply describes cases in which the courts have and have not found torture to have occurred. But this is probably the prudent course. Cruel, inhuman, and degrading forms of treatment are, after all, no more lawful than torture, even if they do not give rise to criminal liability in the U.S. courts. To draw sharp distinctions between torture and these "lesser" horrors, as the August 2002 memo attempted to do, could only serve to signal to potential torturers how they can avoid imprisonment while still inflicting great pain and suffering. OLC apparently now realizes that it is inappropriate to send such signals.

WHEN, IF EVER, IS TORTURE JUSTIFIED?

Perhaps the most jarring aspect of the August 2002 memo was its argument that a defendant could escape criminal liability for committing torture by presenting a defense of necessity or self-defense.[7] Under either defense, the torturer could argue that he tortured his victim in order to prevent some terrible harm. To use the classic example, one could claim that he had in custody a suspect believed to have planted a time-bomb that, if not defused, would kill many innocents. If the defendant reasonably believed that by torturing the suspect, he would learn the location of the bomb and thus save the innocents, the argument goes, he cannot be punished for having done so.

The notion that torture is sometimes morally justified has real appeal. If one stipulates sufficiently great certainty of a catastrophe, all but the most punctilious Kantians will be tempted to say that it is better to torture the terrorist than to allow the catastrophe to occur. The difficulty, though, is that the real world provides probabilities rather than certainties. Categorical prohibitions against torture like the one contained in the U.N. Convention and federal law are based on the sensible assumption that if torture is condoned in the extreme case of the known terrorist who has certainly planted the ticking time-bomb, security officers will come to believe that they hear bombs ticking everywhere, and will use torture against people merely suspected of posing a security threat. Only by prohibiting torture under all circumstances, such laws assume, can we prevent an extremely limited authorization, for torture in extreme circumstances, from becoming a license for routine torture.

It is possible that this logic is wrong. Perhaps, as Alan Dershowitz and others have argued recently, careful regulation can prevent us from slipping down the slope from rare to common torture. But if so, that is an argument for a dramatic change in the law, rather than an argument for reading nonexistent exceptions into the existing international and U.S. categorical bans on torture. The August 2002 memo, in proposing such exceptions, would have gutted the laws it purported to interpret.

Accordingly, the December 2004 memo states unequivocally that "there is no exception under the statute permitting torture to be used for a 'good reason.'"[8]

CAN CONGRESS LIMIT THE PRESIDENT'S ABILITY TO ORDER TORTURE?

The principal disappointment in the December 2004 memo is its failure to condemn the view of Presidential power expressed in the August 2002 memo. That earlier memo asserted that "the President enjoys complete discretion in the exercise of his Commander-in-Chief authority and in conducting operations against hostile forces."[9] It argued that Congress lacks the constitutional power to limit the President's decisions about how to treat captives.

The August 2002 memo had attempted to justify these sweeping propositions largely by presenting selective, out-of-context citations of broad language in a few Supreme Court opinions, and citing OLC's own recent post–9/11 memos.

The December 2004 memo should have unequivocally repudiated the unlimited view of Presidential power espoused in August 2002. Article I, Section 8 of the Constitution commits to Congress the authority "to make Rules concerning Captures on Land and Water." From this language, Congress's authority to limit the President's treatment of captives is clear.

If the August 2002 memo's view of Presidential power were accepted, the President could unilaterally order discipline of U.S. service members even if that discipline clearly contradicted the Uniform Code of Military Justice, enacted by Congress. He could even order that all enemy captives be shot, notwithstanding clear treaty obligations to the contrary. These extreme examples show the absurdity of any claim that the President has an entirely free hand in the treatment of captives or the conduct of war more generally.

The December 2004 memo, by its terms, "supersedes the August 2002 Memorandum in its entirety." For that reason, the August 2002 assertion of the President's virtually unlimited power as Commander-in-Chief can no longer be said to constitute official OLC policy. However, the December 2004 memo does not specifically disavow the August 2002 view of Presidential authority. Deeming analysis of such power "unnecessary," the December 2004 memo simply declines to address the subject.

Why did the memo's author feel it was unnecessary to address this key point? The memo itself claims that "[c]onsideration of the bounds of any ..." Presidential authority to authorize torture in violation of Acts of Congress "would be inconsistent with the President's unequivocal directive that United States personnel not engage in torture." But this explanation for the new memo's reticence as to the scope of Presidential authority does not quite wash, for none of the OLC analysis is, strictly speaking, necessary; if the new memo had been limited to necessary analysis, there would have been no memo at all.

Given that U.S. personnel are not supposed to engage in torture or cruel, inhuman, or degrading treatment of prisoners, there is no necessity to clarify the line between the two categories of forbidden conduct; yet the December 2004 memo does just that. Similarly, with respect to the question of whether there is a good-reason exception to the torture prohibition, and a number of other issues, the December 2004 memo does not simply wash away the conclusions of the August 2002 memo; it affirmatively draws contrary conclusions. Accordingly, one is left to worry that OLC declined to assert limits on Presidential authority because OLC may continue to entertain a dangerously broad view of that authority.

Nonetheless, putting aside the legitimate worry about what the December 2004 memo does not say about Presidential power, the memo is, on the whole, a most welcome development. Whatever the actual motives of the Justice Department officials who released it when they did, the memo itself should have the salutary effect of communicating to personnel overseas that the United States neither encourages nor tolerates torture.

NOTES

1. This volume, on FindLaw.com. *See* "Relevant Documents," p. 281.
2. *See* Karen J. Greenberg and Joshua L. Dratel, eds. *The Torture Papers: The Road to Abu Ghraib* (New York: Cambridge University Press, 2005), p. 172.
3. Editor's note: Alberto Gonzales was confirmed as U.S. Attorney General on February 3, 2005.
4. *Id.*
5. *See* Greenberg and Dratel, eds., *The Torture Papers*, p. 383.
6. *See* Greenberg and Dratel, eds., *The Torture Papers*, pp. 172–183, 194–196.
7. *See* Greenberg and Dratel, eds., *The Torture Papers*, pp. 207–213.
8. *See* Levin–Comey December 30, 2004 Memo Re: Legal Standards Applicable Under 18 U.S.C. Sec. 2340–2340A p. 361.
9. *See* Greenberg and Dratel, eds., *The Torture Papers*, pp. 202, 204–207.

17 Reconciling Torture with Democracy

Deborah Pearlstein

THE DEBATE IN THIS COUNTRY SINCE SEPTEMBER 11 ABOUT THE USE OF torture or other forms of coercive interrogation has proceeded along two, oddly irreconcilable tracks. On the one hand is the national reaction following the publication of actual photos of torture and humiliation committed by U.S. troops at Abu Ghraib – a reaction that was swift, uniform, and bipartisan in its revulsion. The Secretary of Defense called the conduct "unacceptable" and "un-American." John McCain, Republican Senator and former prisoner of war, emphasized that "history shows – and I know a little bit about this – that mistreatment of prisoners and torture is not productive.... You don't get information that's usable from people under torture, because they just tell you what you want to hear." And John Warner, Republican Chair of the Senate Armed Services Committee, said the abuses, if true, were "an appalling and totally unacceptable breach of military conduct that could undermine much of the courageous work and sacrifice by our forces in the war on terror."

There remains, on the other hand, a vigorous abstract debate in academic and policy circles about the need to abandon some existing laws governing detention and interrogation, and to adopt new rules permitting the use of physical or mental coercion to extract intelligence information, our best weapon, it is argued, against a new and potentially devastating terrorist threat. Human rights scholar Michael Ignatieff has insisted that "defeating terror requires violence," and that "to defeat evil, we may have to traffic in evils," including indefinite detention and coercive interrogation. Harvard lawyer Alan Dershowitz is more specific, proposing the use of physical coercion in exceptional cases if a judge authorizes its use in advance. And Judge Richard Posner goes further still, writing that "only the most doctrinaire civil libertarians (not that there aren't plenty of them) deny [that] if the stakes are high enough, torture is permissible. No one who doubts that this is the case should be in a position of responsibility."

The apparent disconnect between our attraction to coercive interrogation in theory, and our repulsion from it in practice is mediated by a few (like Mark Bowden) who have argued that coercive interrogation "should be banned but also

253

quietly practiced." We need to do it in the interest of national security, but we need
to not know about it to preserve the appearance of public morality. Whatever the
merits of such a view – and there is substantial question where the rule of law fits
in to such a calculus – our ability to pursue it is soon to be overtaken by events.
The 109th Congress, sworn in on January 4, 2005, will almost certainly be asked
to consider authorizing new powers for detaining and interrogating terrorist
suspects. There will be a range of proposed circumstances – only in a state of
emergency, only if there is a ticking bomb, only for suspected "terrorists" –
along with a range of proposed procedural safeguards – right to counsel, to
judicial supervision, to limited duration – and a range of proposed techniques,
from prolonged solitary confinement and sleep deprivation to moderate physical
force.

The good news, as it were, for Congress is that the past four years have produced substantial empirical data to guide its deliberations about how the theory
of coercive interrogation plays out in the real world. As official investigations,
press reports, and NGO studies beyond the photos at Abu Ghraib have now
made clear, U.S. authorities have practiced various forms of torture and coercive
interrogation from Iraq to Afghanistan to Guantánamo Bay. Since Fall 2001,
the Pentagon has reported more than 300 allegations of abuse by U.S. officials
(66 substantiated as of mid-August); there are some 30 pending investigations
into detainee deaths in U.S. custody by torture or abuse; and there are currently underway about two dozen criminal prosecutions of military and civilian
personnel. While public information about the effects of this practice remains
incomplete, it is worth identifying some of what our experience has shown.

Take, for example, the argument that the use of coercive techniques could
be limited to only the most exceptional circumstances – only where there was
a real "ticking bomb" to be diffused – and real "torture" would not be authorized, but only lesser techniques like sleep deprivation, sensory deprivation, or
uncomfortable "stress" positions – only "torture lite." The past few years have
demonstrated our failure to limit the use of coercion by circumstances or technique. A U.S. Army interrogator deployed to Afghanistan in 2001 wrote of one
example, explaining that the stress positions that had been prohibited early in
the war in Afghanistan were soon adopted by soldiers there as a means of prison
discipline. By the time of the Iraq war (where, unlike in Afghanistan, the administration had announced its intention to apply the Geneva Conventions), the use of
stress positions, practiced in Afghanistan, had become an accepted interrogation
technique. While the specific behavior at Abu Ghraib may not have been part
of the rules of engagement, the former interrogator argues, they "represented
the gravitational laws that govern human behavior when one group of people is
given complete control over another in a prison. Every impulse tugs downward."

What of the argument that the use of coercive interrogation in some form
may be the only way to secure intelligence critical to saving lives? The past few
years have seen mixed reports about the value of intelligence gleaned as a result

of coercive practices. Some insist that Guantánamo, for instance, has produced valuable information, while other military and intelligence officials contend that those held there have yielded little or no intelligence value. But Senator McCain's view that abusive tactics have long been understood as counterproductive has been echoed by many, including a group of retired admirals and generals, who wrote in a letter to the President that information gathered through coercion is "notoriously unreliable," and has "a demoralizing, dehumanizing effect not only on those subject to violations, but also on our own troops." The Army Field Manual itself reinforces this view, instructing that coercive techniques are not to be practiced not only because they are against the law, but because they are ineffective. Meanwhile, the negative consequences of such tactics for U.S. security interests are apparent. Polling in Iraq suggests that evidence of coercive practices by the United States helped galvanize public opinion in Iraq against U.S. efforts there. And the Pakistani Sunni extremist group Lashkar-e-Tayba has used the internet to call for sending holy warriors to Iraq to take revenge for the torture at Abu Ghraib.

The opportunity to evaluate these and other lessons of the past few years in a semipublic forum in Congress is, to be sure, far closer to how a democracy should operate than the unilateral, unreviewable use of such techniques behind closed doors. But getting to the right result in the coming debate is tricky. And it depends critically on our willingness to hold our theory of coercion up against the reality of what makes us secure.

18 Great Nations and Torture

M. Cherif Bassiouni

THE GENESIS OF THE UNITED NATIONS CONVENTION AGAINST TORTURE AND Other Cruel, Inhuman, or Degrading Treatment or Punishment (Torture Convention), which was adopted by the General Assembly in 1984, is in a resolution adopted by the Fifth United Nations Congress on Crime Prevention and Criminal Justice held in Geneva in 1975. On that occasion, a special resolution condemning torture and other forms of cruel, inhuman, or degrading treatment or punishment was adopted. The resolution was based on the prohibition of cruel, inhuman, or degrading treatment or punishment contained in the Universal Declaration of Human Rights and the International Covenant on Civil and Political Rights.

The 1975 resolution by the Fifth Congress on Crime Prevention and Criminal Justice was then adopted by the General Assembly that same year, with a proviso that the Secretary General implement said resolution. The Secretary General then sent the resolution to the Sub-Commission on the Prevention of Discrimination and Protection of Minorities, which, pursuant to a submission jointly made by the International Association of Penal Law and the International Commission of Jurists in accordance with the Commission on Human Rights Resolution 1503, proposed to organize a committee of experts chaired by the respective secretary generals of the two co-sponsoring organizations to prepare a draft convention for the prohibition of torture and other forms of cruel, inhuman, and degrading treatment or punishment. The co-chairs, namely, M. Cherif Bassiouni and Neil MacDermott (of late), then convened an international committee of experts consisting of 20 distinguished jurists from different countries acting in their personal capacities. In 1977, the experts met at the International Institute of Higher Studies in Criminal Sciences (Siracusa, Italy) to review the draft convention prepared by this writer. The text of the draft convention, as well as a commentary, was then published in the *Revue Internationale de Droit Pénal*. Three thousand copies of the *Revue* were distributed to permanent missions to the United Nations in New York and Geneva, and the official text contained in UN Doc. E/CN.4/NGO/213 (1 Feb. 1978) was submitted by the undersigned on behalf of the International

Association of Penal Law and the International Commission of Jurists to the Sub-Commission.

Shortly thereafter, the government of Sweden, which was represented in the committee of experts mentioned above by its Attorney General, submitted a substantially similar official text to the Commission on Human Rights. The Commission then established a working group, which completed its work in 1984.

During this period, there was no doubt that any form of physical or psychological abuse intended to be coercive in order to obtain any statements by a person held in official custody was prohibited. The definition of torture contained in the Convention makes that quite explicit. There is no exception or derogation, and there can be no interpretation of the Torture Convention that justifies the infliction of pain and suffering of any degree. The consensus of the international community, as reflected by the overwhelming majority of United Nations' member states as well as by international civil society, was clear and unequivocal.

In the years following the entry into effect of the Torture Convention, the conduct of states engaging in torture as a systematic practice was significantly reduced, though individual occurrences continued to take place in a number of countries, many of which were recidivists in this regard. The Committee on Torture (CAT) established by the Convention monitored these activities and issued annual reports, which named and shamed those governments that engaged in this practice. As a result, such governments became more circumspect, and the practice became more limited.

The United Nations Commission on Human Rights also established a special mandate to monitor the implementation of the Torture Convention. Over the years, the reports of the special rapporteur on torture gained more prominence and attention within the United Nations and the international community. International civil society and, more particularly, human rights organizations, such as Amnesty International, Human Rights Watch, the International Commission of Jurists, Redress, and others became more active and more effective in their monitoring, prevention, and denunciation of torture practices. National legislation in many countries implemented the Torture Convention, and civil remedies were used in many countries to ensure that the perpetrators of torture would incur civil liability even though they may have benefitted from the protection of their governments while they were public officials.

In short, the international community and international civil society's combined efforts produced notable effects in the reduction of the practices of torture, and the deterrent effect of private causes of action also contributed to that end.

During the course of this evolution, which started with the Universal Declaration of Human Rights, regional organizations also followed the same path as that of the United Nations. The European Convention on the Protection of Fundamental Freedoms and the American Convention on Human Rights also contain prohibitions on torture and cruel, inhuman, or degrading treatment or punishment. Within the context of these conventions, remedies were available through, at first, the European Commission of Human Rights and then the European Court of Human Rights, and the Inter-American Commission on Human Rights and the Inter-American Court of Human Rights. The two commissions and courts issued several landmark decisions condemning the practices of certain states and providing remedies to those aggrieved. In Europe, the practice was nearly eliminated except for individual abusive cases that do not reflect the policies of governments. In the Americas, the progress was slower, but it has now reached a much higher standard of compliance. In both the European and Inter-American regions, there is no doubt that the prohibition against torture is viewed as a violation of fundamental human rights, not only because it is so proscribed in the applicable regional conventions and national legislation, but also because it represents a fundamental moral and ethical violation.

The African Charter on Human Rights has also followed the same path, though with less effective means of implementation and with more reported practices among its member states. Still, the recognition that torture constitutes a legal, moral, and ethical violation is well established.

The world community had reached a point believed to be one of no return with respect to allowing governments to practice torture, either as a matter of policy or by the agents of governments as a matter of practice. But that point of no return was breached by the United States in the post-9/11 era with the advent of officially authorized practices of torture, which were sanctioned by the National Security Council of the White House, the Department of Defense, and the Department of Justice. The application of torture under the guise of physical and psychological coercive practices was, and, it seems, still is, conducted at the Guantanamo Bay military facilities, as well as at U.S. military bases in Afghanistan and Iraq. Although the blatant practices of torture resulting in deaths in Abu Ghraib and in Afghanistan became publicly known, other practices in these and other U.S. military facilities were not. The defense department conducted several investigations, most of which remain classified, and some military prosecutions and disciplinary actions were taken against lower-ranking military personnel, never reaching those in the chain of command in accordance with the theory of command responsibility established in the Uniform Code of Military Justice. In addition, no national review of the policies of torture described in different ways by government memoranda and authorizations has ever been undertaken.

In addition, the United States engaged in the practice of extraordinary rendition, which under the Torture Convention, as well as other sources of international law, is unlawful. These practices consist in the kidnaping of individuals by the CIA or other U.S. officials, and their illegal transfer to countries where they are subjected to torture. Published reports indicate that a number of such persons have been kidnaped in Sweden, Italy, Canada, the United States, and Afghanistan, and transferred to countries such as Syria, Egypt, Jordan, and Pakistan, where they reportedly have been tortured. To date, only Italy has issued an indictment against 13 CIA officers accused of kidnaping an Egyptian religious leader in Milano, a resident of Italy, and effecting his forceful transfer to Egypt where he is reported to have been tortured and kept in detention for nearly two years. The removal of two persons from Sweden by the same forceful tactic was reported to the CAT in its spring 2005 session, which committee condemned the action. In the United States, an action was filed pursuant to the Alien Tort Claims Act by a Canadian citizen of Syrian origin kidnaped by the CIA and transferred to Syria, where he was tortured and then released.

The position of the United States is that torture called by another name is permissible and that torture which does not cause the risk of death is considered only coercive – ignoring the obvious conclusion that a rose by any other name is still a rose. In this case, torture by any other name is still torture.

The practices of the United States described above have re-opened a question that the world community thought had been answered conclusively by the 1984 Convention. Arguments of exigencies have also proven to be spurious in that none of these cases of torture has ever produced any evidence leading to the elimination of an imminent danger against the United States. Some of the proponents of these euphemistically referred-to coercive practices argue the *in extremis* case of a hypothetical situation where torture is resorted to as a way of avoiding a rather certain and imminent danger to a large group of innocent victims. The usual argument refers to scenarios about an explosion likely to kill thousands of people where the person subjected to these coercive practices is known to have the information necessary to prevent the greater harm. But assuming arguendo that this rationalization can be accepted, there has never been a known case involving persons tortured in Iraq, Afghanistan, Guantanamo or elsewhere under the infamous practice of extraordinary rendition that falls into that category – thus the false analogy and the spurious nature of the argument.

Torture, or torture by any other name, is legally, morally, and ethically reprehensible. Civilized nations do not engage in that practice as a reflection of their human values and also as a reflection of their adherence to the rule of law and respect for human rights. The practice of torture and other coercive measures similar thereto and in violation of the 1984 Convention are those engaged in by dictatorial regimes as evidenced by history. They go to the very core of those values that are the foundations of democratic societies based on the rule of law and respect for human rights.

Even when *in extremis* situations may occur, one would expect that, in those cases, governments would not seek to rationalize these actions or justify them, but, in following Henry David Thoreau, acknowledge such abhorrent individual practices when done to avoid a greater imminent and certain harm, and submit those who engage in them to the legal consequences for their violations. For a government like that of the United States, which has historically championed human rights at the international level and which is based on the rule of law as reflected in its constitution and laws, blatantly to violate its international and national legal obligations by an established governmental policy exceeds any possible description. Regrettably, the United States administration that has developed and carried out these policies and practices, while admittedly carrying out these practices to a lesser extent as a result of international and domestic pressures, is nonetheless in violation of international and national law. What is more, it is in breach of a national trust in accordance with the Constitution of the United States.

The difference between a great nation and a mighty nation is not measured by its military wherewithal or its ability to exercise force, but by its adherence to higher values and principles of law. This is what the United States is based on, and this is what has made it a great nation.

19 Litigating Against Torture: The German Criminal Prosecution

Michael Ratner and Peter Weiss

ON NOVEMBER 30, 2004 THE CENTER FOR CONSTITUTIONAL RIGHTS (CCR)[1], a U.S. based human rights legal organization, filed a criminal complaint in Germany seeking an investigation of and prosecution against ten high level U.S. officials allegedly involved in the torture and inhumane treatment of detainees in Iraq.[2] Complainants were CCR as well as four Iraqis who had been brutally tortured. The 160-page complaint was filed with the prosecutor in Karlsruhe, Germany. It charged Secretary of Defense Donald Rumsfeld, former CIA Director George Tenet, Lt. General Ricardo Sanchez, the former Commander of U.S. forces in Iraq, and seven other high-ranking officials[3] and officers with war crimes under the German Code of Crimes under International Law (CCIL).[4] CCR later added an eleventh defendant, U.S. Attorney General Alberto Gonzales, subsequent to his admission at his confirmation hearing that he had been involved with drafting and approving legal memoranda authorizing torture and inhumane treatment of detainees.

CCR decided to bring this case in a national court of a foreign state because there was no U.S. or international forum where the criminal responsibility of high U.S. officials for war crimes could be investigated and prosecuted. Although it would have been preferable to prosecute war crimes domestically or in an international court, that was not possible. In the United States there is no legal procedure under which victims can file criminal complaints; only prosecutors, who have complete discretion whether or not to do so, can file such cases. While a victim can bring a crime to the attention of a prosecutor, the prosecutor can ignore any suggestion and there is no court remedy for the victim. The situation is different in many European countries; victims can initiate criminal proceedings and appeal to a court if the prosecutor refuses to go forward. Although the Bush administration has brought some prosecutions for the torture that has occurred in Iraq, these have all been against lower-level soldiers; no proceedings have been brought against those in the extended chain of command. We at CCR believe high officials were and are responsible for the crimes.

None of the many U.S. government investigations of the torture and abuse that occurred in Iraq have undertaken any serious investigation of the chain of command. In fact, the investigations were run by the Department of Defense, CIA, and other agencies deeply involved in the war crimes, and while they have documented so many incidents of torture that investigators have called the use of torture "almost routine," nowhere has responsibility been laid on top officials. This is despite clear evidence in the public record that Secretary of Defense Rumsfeld, General Sanchez, and others authorized many of the illegal techniques used against detainees, and failed in their duty to prevent numerous war crimes, which they knew or should have known were occurring.[5]

In thinking about bringing suit outside of the United States CCR also looked at international courts. However, the United States has refused to ratify the treaty creating the International Criminal Court and there is no other international court with jurisdiction over these alleged war crimes. For these reasons, CCR was compelled to turn to the courts of other states with universal jurisdiction over war crimes.

In exploring the courts of other states, we soon recognized that Germany, under its 2002 Code of Crimes Against International Law (CCIL), had an extremely good war crimes law. The German CCIL more or less parallels the definition of crimes set forth in the statute of the International Criminal Court. The CCIL makes criminal grave breaches of the Geneva Conventions as well as violations of the customary laws of war. Under German law, torture and inhumane treatment of detainees constitute war crimes. In addition, the German code covers both war crimes committed directly, and those committed by the superior who orders the crime. The German code makes liable superiors, whether military or civilian, who knew or had reason to know that a subordinate was about to commit a crime and failed to prevent it; it also imposes liability if the superior, knowing about a war crime, failed to punish it.

A concrete example will help explain the law. If a U.S. soldier tortures or abuses a detainee as happened at Abu Ghraib – for example, threatening detainees with unmuzzled dogs that – soldier has committed a war crime under both U.S. law and the German code. If a soldier was ordered to commit that crime or authorized to use the dog by a superior, that superior would also be guilty of war crimes under both U.S. and German law. In fact, we know that authorization to use dogs against detainees was given for Guantánamo by Secretary of Defense Rumsfeld, and we know Lt. General Sanchez also authorized the use of dogs for interrogations in Iraq. Under the German code, if it were proven that the superiors directly ordered the use of dogs against detainees, both Rumsfeld and Sanchez would have direct responsibility for war crimes, and could be punished as perpetrators by a term of imprisonment in Germany.

Superiors such as Rumsfeld and Sanchez would also be guilty of war crimes if it could be proved they were aware of torture and abuse like that at Abu Ghraib and either failed to prevent the crimes or failed to bring the guilty to justice. Again, in fact, we know that the Red Cross complained often to high-level U.S. officials about the abuse and torture of detainees, yet nothing was done by these officials to stop the crimes or punish the perpetrators. In these circumstances, the officials would also be guilty of what the German code calls "indirect responsibility" for war crimes.

This definition of war crimes in the German Code is a traditional one in the law and would certainly encompass the conduct carried out by U.S. soldiers and their superiors in detention facilities in Afghanistan, Guantanamo, and Iraq as well as in secret CIA detention facilities around the world. But it was not just the definition of the crimes which made the German code interesting to the lawyers at CCR. It was another part of the code called the universal jurisdiction provision. Under that section the German courts are given what lawyers call universal jurisdiction over war crimes, meaning that a prosecutor and the courts of Germany can investigate, charge, and convict persons of war crimes no matter where in the world the crimes are committed, no matter by whom they are committed. The crime, the perpetrator, and the victim need have no connection to Germany.

A recent example of the exercise of universal jurisdiction was the Pinochet case in Spain. Pinochet was responsible for acts of torture in Chile against Chileans. Despite this, a Spanish court indicted him under Spanish law that gave Spain universal jurisdiction over acts of torture and genocide no matter where in the world such acts were committed. Although Chile had refused to extradite him to Spain, when he traveled to England he was arrested. If not for the finding that Pinochet was incompetent to stand trial, he would have been sent to Spain and tried there for the crime of torture.

Universal jurisdiction for certain heinous crimes is not something new in law. It began with piracy; a pirate could be tried in any country of the world. In the nineteenth century the concept was extended to cover the crimes of slave traders, in the twentieth century to cover acts of genocide, war crimes, and torture. The Geneva Conventions require every country that is a party to the Conventions to seek out and punish alleged war criminals without any geographical limitation. The underlying theory is that certain very serious crimes are a concern of the entire world; the perpetrators of such crimes are considered to be "enemies of all mankind" and can be brought to justice wherever found. However, the United States, as its power has grown, has become less willing to support universal jurisdiction in any forum or court where it could not determine against whom criminal prosecutions could be initiated. U.S. officials wanted to ensure that no U.S. soldiers or officials, no matter what crimes they may have committed, would wind up in the dock of a foreign country. The hostility of the United States to universal jurisdiction, whether exercised by the International Criminal court or national courts of states, has grown in recent years and is now practically a principle of U.S. political discourse.

Nonetheless, CCR decided to bring suit in Germany, and found support in a provision of the German law mandating investigations of war crimes if a case has links to Germany. The U.S. military has major bases in Germany. The 205th intelligence brigade, the very brigade involved in the torture and abuse at Abu Ghraib, is stationed at Wiesbaden. The head of that military brigade, U.S. Army Col. Pappas, who was allegedly involved in the war crimes, is stationed there as well. Lt. General Ricardo Sanchez and his deputy Maj. Gen. Walter Wojdakowski, the leadership of the Army's V Corps, the occupying force in Iraq during what was apparently the worst of the Abu Ghraib scandal, are all stationed in Heidelberg. This means not only that a German prosecutor could do a genuine investigation of the war crimes, but also investigate some of the main alleged perpetrators who were living in Germany. Under the German code it is obligatory to investigate and prosecute alleged war criminals living on German soil.

Germany, thus, was ideal for our case, and CCR named as defendants Sanchez, Wojdakowski and Pappas, among others. We also gave the German prosecutor sufficient uncontested evidence in the 160-page complaint to ensure that the criminality of the defendants could be demonstrated with little further investigation. Many of the facts indicating guilt are part of the public record.

We were, however, aware that for a prosecutor in Germany to exercise his authority to investigate a universal jurisdiction case, he must find that the state having "primary jurisdiction" is "unwilling" to do its own investigation. As U.S. officials committed the alleged crimes, it was the United States that had this "primary" jurisdiction and would be looked to first to prosecute the crimes. Therefore, it was critical for us to demonstrate that the U.S. was "unwilling" to investigate and prosecute the high-level officials we wanted brought to justice.

It seemed obvious to us, in relation to allegations of torture and war crimes, that the main strategy of the Bush administration had been to blame lower-level soldiers, call them "bad apples," and focus attention on their trials. In press briefings and statements, the administration claimed that those up the chain of command and civilians in the Pentagon such as Secretary of Defense Rumsfeld were not involved in the torture and abuses.

The issue of "unwillingness" to investigate on the part of the state holding primary jurisdiction became the central issue in the case. We used the declaration of a prominent U.S. lawyer and international law expert, Scott Horton, to bolster our case.[6] Horton, Chair of the Committee of International Law of the Association of the Bar of the City of New York, had been visited in May 2003, a year before the photographs of Abu Ghraib were revealed, by a delegation of senior military lawyers who advised him that policy decisions taken in Rumsfeld's office would lead to the abuse of detainees. Horton's declaration in our case demonstrated conclusively that no investigation of the officials named in our lawsuit would occur in the United States and that, in fact, there was a cover-up of high level involvement in war crimes. As Horton said to the German prosecutor:

> I have formed the opinion that no such criminal investigation or prosecution would occur in the near future in the United States for the reason that the criminal investigative and prosecutorial functions are currently controlled by individuals who are involved in the conspiracy to commit war crimes.

Horton's powerful declaration detailed the basis for his conclusion that high-level Bush administration officials are involved in a conspiracy to commit war crimes and cover them up. First, Horton pointed out that the Department of Defense was under the control of defendant Secretary of Defense Rumsfeld who therefore had "effective immunity." Second, he found that the criminal investigations pursuant to army regulations look only down the chain of command and not up, and thus eliminate any "meaningful inquiry into the criminal misconduct of the defendants." Third, he found that the criminal investigations were influenced from above with the "intention of producing a 'whitewash' exculpating those up the chain of command." Fourth, he found that the responsibility of the legislative branch to investigate had been abdicated, since Senator John Warner, chairman of the Senate Armed Services Committee, "was threatened [by other Republicans] with sharp political retaliation if he carried through on his plans to conduct real hearings." Fifth, he found that the Attorney General controls war crimes prosecutions under the U.S. War Crimes Act and that since former Attorney General Ashcroft was "complicit in a scheme for the commission of war crimes" he had not undertaken a criminal investigation. Alberto Gonzales, the current Attorney General, Horton said, was the "principal author of a scheme to undertake war crimes" and was motivated in writing his January 25, 2002 memo by a fear of prosecution for war crimes, which he sought to evade in that memo.

In filing the case in Germany we were not unaware of the power of the Bush administration to bludgeon countries into dropping such prosecutions. When a case regarding the Iraq war was filed in Belgium against U.S. General Tommy Franks, the United States threatened to pull NATO headquarters out of Brussels unless Belgian law were changed to exclude such prosecutions. Belgium complied. Our hopes were that the Bush administration could not use similar tactics on the more powerful Germany and that the case was incredibly strong – much of Europe understood that high officials in the U.S. had authorized torture.

We do not know what occurred behind the scenes. We do know that Rumsfeld showed his displeasure with the lawsuit and attempted to bully Germany. He and the Pentagon announced that Rumsfeld would not attend the important annual Munich Security conference as long as the lawsuit was pending. This and probably other threats had the desired effect. Despite the strength of the case, a day prior to the Munich conference, the prosecutor dismissed the case and Rumsfeld went to Munich.

In dismissing the case the prosecutor did not dispute that the criminal complaint had set forth allegations of war crimes by high-level officials. The key issue he focused on was whether or not the Bush administration was "unwilling" to investigate and prosecute the violations in the complaint. He concluded that "there are no indications that the authorities and courts of the United States of America are refraining from, or would refrain, from penal measures as regards violations in the complaint." In support he mentioned proceeding against low-level soldiers in the United States.

The prosecutor's conclusion defies logic and the evidence presented. We are taking all legal avenues against this decision. First, we have asked the prosecutor to reconsider his decision. Considering that it was more than likely a politically motivated result, though, it is unlikely we will get him to modify his conclusion. We are at the same time appealing to the court on the basis that the prosecutor's decision that the Bush administration is willing to investigate and prosecute high-level officials is completely contrary to all the evidence. We believe we will eventually prevail.

As the months and possibly years pass, what we have demonstrated in this case will become even more obvious: U.S. officials have committed war crimes and there is conspiracy within the Bush administration to ensure that none of the high-level perpetrators will be brought to justice. Whether it takes only a few years or the thirty it has taken to initiate proceedings against Pinochet, those officials accused of war crimes will be brought to justice.

NOTES

1. The Center for Constitutional Rights is a nonprofit litigation organization in the United States that is involved in lawsuits to protect U.S. constitutional and human rights. Our most recent major victory was the Supreme Court ruling in the Guantánamo cases, which won the right to hearings for those detained. We are currently the legal organization mounting most major challenges to the violations of civil and human rights in the Bush administration's "war on terror." In addition to continuing to represent the Guantánamo detainees, we have challenged the thousands of noncitizen detentions in the Untied States, the practice of rendition (sending of persons to countries or places where they are tortured), and brought various lawsuits against private interrogators and U.S. officials for torture in Guantánamo and Iraq.
2. The complaint and other materials regarding the German prosecution are available at the CCR website: <www.ccr-ny.org>.
3. The seven other defendants named in the initial criminal complaint were: Maj. Gen. Walter Wojdakowski, Brigadier Gen. Janis Karpinski, Lt. Col. Jerry L. Phillabaum, Lt. Col. Stephen L. Jordan, Maj. Gen. Geoffrey Miller, Col. Thomas M. Pappas, Stephen Cambone, Undersecretary of Defense.
4. The German CCIL can be found in English at <http://www.iuscrim.mpg.de/forsch/legaltext/vstgbleng.pdf>.
5. "Lawsuit Against Rumsfeld Threatens U.S.-German Relations," <http://www.dw-world.de/dw/article/0,1564,142700.html>.
6. The Horton declaration is available at <www.ccr-ny.org>.

20 Ugly Americans

Noah Feldman

THE CANAANITE KING ADONI-BEZEK HAS JUST A SINGLE LINE OF DIALOGUE
in the Bible, but it is one not easily forgotten. Defeated by the combined forces of
the tribes of Judah and Simeon, he is subjected to the ordeal of having his index
fingers and great toes cut off. Adoni-bezek's philosophical response is that in his
day he himself lopped off the fingers and toes of seventy kings: "As I have done,
so God hath requited me." With these last words, the captive king is brought to
Jerusalem, where he dies.

Today prisoners of war are protected by the Geneva Conventions – but the
principle of reciprocity articulated in the king's reflection on the customs of
victors still pervades the laws of war. The assumption that all sides might torture
or kill prisoners has given way, at least in theory, to the principle that all sides are
reciprocally obligated to treat prisoners of war and civilians under occupation
humanely. It is fair to say that this norm of international law grew as much
from the mutual interests of belligerents in having their own prisoners of war
treated humanely as from any deeply held commitment to the dignity of the
person. Otherwise it would be almost impossible to explain the anomaly that,
according to the rules of war, the enemy may be killed even while he is fleeing,
but if captured must be sheltered, fed, and returned to his home when the war
is over. The motivation to frame and to follow the rule is surely the reciprocal
concern about what might happen to troops captured by the other side, which
lends the fuel of self-interest to the fire of moral principle.

I.

In the wake of September 11, 2001, the principle of reciprocity in the laws of
war was dealt a substantial blow. In a series of secret memoranda – some of
which have since been leaked or declassified, and collected by Mark Danner and
more comprehensively by Karen J. Greenberg and Joshua L. Dratel – government

Reprinted with permission from *The New Republic*.

attorneys in the Office of Legal Counsel of the Department of Justice, working closely with the White House, developed a theory of why the Geneva Conventions did not apply to members of al Qaeda and the Taliban forces whom the United States was already in the process of defeating in Afghanistan. The lawyers advanced a number of creative and often doubtful hypotheses in support of their views, including the suggestion that, since Afghanistan was a failed state, the president could suspend the conventions in a war there. But the core of their theory followed from the accurate observation that the al Qaeda terrorists (and the Taliban, who harbored them) were not playing by the rules of war, and never would. Al Qaeda was a terrorist organization, rather than a state actor covered by the conventions. Worse, the enemy had broken the model of reciprocal respect for the laws of war. "Al Qaeda members," argued the lawyers, ". . . hijacked civilian airliners, took hostages, and killed them; and they themselves do not obey the laws of war concerning the protection of the lives of civilians or the means of legitimate combat."[1] It therefore made no sense to follow those laws in fighting the terrorists.

Once it could be argued that the Geneva Conventions did not apply to al Qaeda and the Taliban, there naturally arose the question of what limits, if any, did apply to American conduct in what the lawyers assumed must be characterized as a war. The United States is a signatory to an international treaty prohibiting torture. In fulfillment of that treaty, Congress passed a statute that defines torture as any act "specifically intended to inflict severe physical or mental pain or suffering," and criminalizes such torture abroad anywhere, anytime. The treaty and those federal laws applied to all citizens and personnel of the United States; so whatever counted as "torture" would ordinarily be subject to prosecution. Fear of such prosecution might restrain intelligence officers or others from engaging in aggressive interrogation techniques that some in the government thought would be valuable in seeking information from captured terrorists.

The government lawyers set out to solve the problem of prior American participation in this humane and prudential arrangement. In order to expand the range of coercive tactics that could lawfully be used against suspected terrorists, they pared down the legal definition of torture to the barest minimum. "Physical pain amounting to torture must be equivalent in intensity to the pain accompanying serious physical injury, such as organ failure, impairment of bodily function, or even death," they wrote. "For purely mental pain or suffering to amount to torture . . . it must result in significant psychological harm of significant duration, e.g., lasting for months or even years." Cruel, inhuman, or degrading punishment or treatment that fell short of this definition would not be prohibited by the torture treaty or the U.S. torture statute. According to the official interpretation of the American government, then, the gloves were off, so long as the very circumscribed category now delineated as "torture" was avoided.

Not content with this newly expansive approach, the government lawyers also suggested two further justifications for American personnel who might cross the line into prohibited torture. They might be able to argue that their actions were dictated by necessity, and so defend themselves against prosecution by arguing that the law excused their actions in the same way that it would excuse a starving hiker who broke into an abandoned cabin looking for food. (In 1999, the Israeli Supreme Court rejected the view that the necessity defense provides a source of authority to torture, although it preserved the possibility that such a defense might be available at trial to an officer charged with human rights abuses.) Alternatively, it could be argued that neither the torture treaty nor American laws could bind the president when he was exercising his constitutional powers as commander-in-chief leading the United States in war. Never mind that it was Congress that both authorized the president to use force against al Qaeda and also prohibited torture: once war was under way, went the argument, the Constitution put the president above Congress in conducting it.

These arguments were astonishing. Absent from them was any serious concern about either the morality of the actions being contemplated or their desirability as a matter of policy. Some of the silence may be blamed on lawyerly obtuseness, derived from the mistaken view that moral and practical questions are beyond the province of law and are best left to the client, in this case the President of the United States. But this explanation misses the moral and practical premises that were smuggled into the arguments of the so-called torture memos just described. In fact, both the realities of the immediate post–September 11 environment and the moral theories being developed at the time are necessary to explain the thought world of these memoranda.

The moral grounding for the position of the government's lawyers was the paramount value of protecting the United States without being constrained by rules that the enemy had flouted. Practically speaking, had the United States been worried that its citizens might be subjected to torture by other signatories to the torture treaty, it would have been extremely unlikely to reduce the definition of torture so drastically. But no such reciprocal fear existed. Americans captured by al Qaeda or the Taliban had no hope of avoiding mistreatment because of the treaty's protection: they would likely have had their heads cut off, or worse. And to the extent that other countries might choose to adopt a similarly restrictive definition of torture, the government's lawyers simply presumed that the overwhelming military might of the United States and the threat of retaliation would scare them out of it.

Ironically, then, the circumstances after September 11 made reciprocity seem irrelevant along two opposite dimensions. On the one hand, the United States was newly understood to be vulnerable to asymmetrical threats from terrorists who ignored the laws of war and engaged in "a new type of warfare – one not contemplated in 1949 when the [Geneva Convention] was framed."[2] On the other, in a unipolar world, there was no nation-state with the strength and the willingness to defy the United States by torturing our citizens, even if the United States were to adopt an asymmetrically minimalist definition of torture. In the judgment of then–White House counsel (now attorney general) Alberto Gonzales, "this new paradigm renders obsolete Geneva's strict limitations on questioning of enemy prisoners."[3] Waiving the Geneva Conventions and loosening the ban on torture did not merely seem justifiable. The lawyers also believed that they, and we, could get away with it.

II.

How did the memoranda translate into practice? This question figures centrally in evaluating the treatment, the interrogation, and sometimes the death of prisoners in Afghanistan, Guantanamo, and elsewhere in the world. But it has assumed even greater significance in light of the revelations of the gross violations of the Geneva Conventions, and in some cases of the ban on torture, that were committed by Americans against Iraqis in the Abu Ghraib prison on the outskirts of Baghdad.

No event since My Lai has so publicly shown American soldiers violating the human dignity of citizens of a foreign country. The humiliation of the Iraqi civilians, not to mention the physical injuries they suffered, including death, are and always will be a national shame for the United States. In the minds of many people, not just in the Arab world, the claims of the United States to moral justification for its invasion and occupation of Iraq were permanently vitiated by what happened in what had been one of Saddam Hussein's worst prisons. The Iraqis, some said, had traded one oppressor for another.

In a democracy, one of the consequences of such a horror being revealed is a debate over responsibility. With the government memoranda leaking around the same time as the pictures from Abu Ghraib, it was natural, and it was necessary, to explore the relationship between the government lawyers' theories and the actions of the military police units in Iraq. That there must be some relationship between the human atrocity in Iraq and the legal atrocity in Washington seemed self-evident to many. Danner, in *Torture and Truth: America, Abu Ghraib, and the War on Terror*, suggests a direct causal connection between the memoranda and the horror. He introduces his collection with several articles that he wrote for *The New York Review of Books* while the torture story was breaking. Emphasizing military links between Guantanamo and Abu Ghraib, he argues that "there simply was no clear dividing line" between what was legally authorized at Guantanamo but banned in Iraq. Greenberg and Dratel's volume, *The Torture Papers*, which at twice the length contains many more primary documents, makes a similar point by implication in its subtitle, "*The Road to Abu Ghraib*," even though this book, less political than Danner's, generally – and wisely – lets the documents speak for themselves. The idea of a link has in particular seemed especially convincing to lawyers, who always want to believe that their quiddities matter beyond the courtroom.

Although most of those who argue for a direct link are harsh critics of the Bush administration, at whose feet they wish to lay the responsibility, there is also something reassuring in blaming lawyers for what went wrong. If the problem is with the law, after all, then fixing it can prevent another Abu Ghraib. If it lies elsewhere, in policy or politics or philosophy, we may have to work harder to identify both the causes and the potential long-term solutions.

Neither the Bush administration nor the military has been prepared to acquiesce fully in the claim of a direct connection between the Army's torturers and the government's lawyers. The unclassified executive summary of a recent report issued by a commission led by Naval Inspector General Admiral Albert T. Church III (to be included in a forthcoming volume by Greenberg and Dratel) stakes out the position neatly. First, it maintains that several of the most extreme legal arguments in the memoranda were never adopted by the administration as policy. Although Secretary of Defense Donald Rumsfeld did issue an order to the troops stating that al Qaeda and Taliban detainees were not to be considered prisoners of war under the Geneva Conventions, the President soon supplemented that order with one specifying that they were nonetheless as a matter of policy to be treated in accordance with the Geneva guidelines, "to the extent appropriate and consistent with military necessity." The Church report assumes that the Geneva Conventions obviously applied in Iraq (in fact the administration has intimated that they would not apply to al Qaeda in Iraq); accordingly, the Church report implies, the entire legal edifice of the torture memos was legally irrelevant to Abu Ghraib.

Moreover, the Church report continues, the actual abusive treatment of prisoners in Abu Ghraib fell outside the guidelines for interrogation developed in the memoranda and in a subsequent Defense Department working-group report. (Rumsfeld declined to authorize several of the more extreme measures that the working group proposed, except on an individual basis with his personal permission. How often this occurred is classified and unknown.) In particular, sexual humiliation, dog attacks (as opposed to the use of dogs to inspire fright), and all forms of physical violence were prohibited. Finally, argues the Church report, the U.S. soldiers in Iraq were bound by the provisions of the Uniform Code of Military Justice, which certainly prohibited cruel and inhumane treatment falling short of torture. Yet the published memoranda essentially ignored the Code, and so cannot have been understood to authorize the military police in Abu Ghraib to act as they did.

When it came to assigning blame, the bowdlerized version of the Church report followed earlier military reports, such as the report of March 2004, commissioned by the Army and prepared by Major General Antonio Taguba, which first reviewed the evidence, in blaming the abuses at Abu Ghraib on the combination of an inadequate command structure and the personal initiative of several reservist military police with prior job experience as guards in domestic American prisons. The subtext of this position is to blame the Bush administration, and Rumsfeld in particular, for sending an inadequate military force to Iraq. Understaffed and undertrained, the military acted in an improvisatory fashion that highlighted the greatest structural weakness of any system based on following commands. Where clear regulations and orders are in place, the U.S. military, including the Reserves, does very well in carrying them out. Where there is little or no guidance, individual soldiers may end up drawing on their civilian experiences.

Pointing the finger at former civilian prison guards, as all the military reports have done, also has the effect of shifting the responsibility for Abu Ghraib onto America's own shadowy prison-industrial complex, where abuses occur with a regularity that is rarely discussed or acknowledged. Seen one way, this assignment of responsibility impugns American practices and values. In the aftermath of the revelations, politicians were quick to assert that what happened in Abu Ghraib was not "the American way," though a closer examination of the role of our prison system might produce the opposite conclusion. Seen from the military's perspective, however, the suggestion is faintly exculpatory. It suggests that the source of the problem lies not in the military, but in the introduction of civilian methods of incarceration under crisis conditions in Iraq.

To the Church report's denial of a connection between the memoranda and Abu Ghraib, two types of answers may be made. One approach accepts the difficulty of finding a smoking gun, but is satisfied with a general association of the memoranda's thought-world and the abuses that took place. The torture memos signaled the Bush administration's belief that every possible step, including evading or bending the law, should be taken in order to discover information about terrorist attacks. The administration's famous conflation of the war in Iraq with what its insiders call the GWOT, or global war on terror, makes it likely that in dealing with suspected insurgents in Iraq, military personnel, not to mention the civilian contract interrogators, followed the lead that had been set by the president and secretary of defense and was captured, in snapshot form, in the memoranda. The general who supervised interrogations at Guantanamo visited Iraq in the fall of 2003 and, shocked by the disorganization of Abu Ghraib, proposed that it be "Gitmoized" through the introduction of specific regulations that in fact drew closely on the framework produced by the Defense Department working group. (It is unclear precisely when the Abu Ghraib photographs were taken, but they may well have pre-dated this visit.) On this view, the treatment at Abu Ghraib, intended to "soften up" prisoners so that they would give information, is of a piece with the techniques authorized by the working-group documents, even if it does not fit neatly within their legal categories. Both involved stress positions. Both involved dogs. Sexual humiliation was never explicitly prohibited. The general pattern suffices to prove the point.

Another answer points to an agency almost entirely unmentioned in the Church report: the CIA, which in military parlance falls under the catchall heading of "OGA," or "other governmental agencies." In a careful piece of reasoning that first appeared on the blog "Balkinization," which is frequented by constitutional advocates and law professors, Martin Lederman, an eight-year veteran of the Office of Legal Counsel who was not privy to the memos when they were written, has argued that the initial memoranda were drafted not with the military in mind, but with the goal of immunizing CIA agents against prosecution for the use of techniques that would otherwise have amounted to torture. The key to Lederman's argument is that while the government lawyers certainly knew that military personnel would be bound by the Uniform Code of Military Justice, those laws do not restrict the CIA, and the statements of policy that order the military to act as though the Geneva Conventions applied and to treat the detainees humanely do not expressly include the CIA in their ambit. It would follow that the CIA, unlike the military, would be authorized to do anything except violate the U.S. anti-terror statute – which is precisely the statute whose reach the memoranda sought to diminish.

Further support for Lederman's position may be gleaned from a stray bullet point that appears at the end of an unsigned document in Greenberg and Dratel's collection. Recording a conversation among lawyers for various government agencies, it notes that lawyers for the CIA specifically sought clarification from the president for the fact that the policy of applying the Geneva Conventions did not apply to its agents. Ominously, it notes also that lawyers from the Justice and State departments "made no comment."[4] In his written responses to the Senate during his recent confirmation hearings for the post of attorney general, Gonzales acknowledged that the presidential order directing that prisoners be treated in compliance with the Geneva Conventions did not apply to the CIA or other non-military agencies. This belated acknowledgment provides the best evidence yet that Lederman's analysis was correct.

So if the memoranda were aimed at the CIA, then Abu Ghraib may be understood either as a space in which the CIA approach went awry (there were, by all accounts, "OGA" personnel in the prison, though they, too, ought to have been governed by the Geneva Conventions while in Iraq), or as a sideshow that accidentally cast light on the whole question of torture. The really upsetting American actions to be considered would include, on this view, the Guantanamo detentions without hearing, which were subsequently modified by the Supreme Court's decision to require due process. But, more prominently, they would include also renditions to other nations where intelligence services routinely torture, and the CIA's use of techniques as extreme as "waterboarding," in which a prisoner is strapped upside down to a board and immersed in water to simulate drowning. This technique or something like it appears to have been used to interrogate Khalid Shaikh Mohammed, to some effect.

The problem with this CIA-focused line of analysis, of course, is that so far it rests mostly on informed conjecture. It would be a grave mistake to think that the memoranda contained in these volumes, even supplemented by further documents that may come to light, represent the totality of the relevant government evidence on these questions. Plenty of material certainly remains classified, and it will remain so for the foreseeable future, as perhaps some of it should in light of the continuing terrorist threat. We cannot at present answer responsibly the question of the exact consequences of the memoranda by the administration's lawyers. The Office of Legal Counsel has issued a new memorandum with a less restrictive and more legally responsible definition of torture. But that memorandum contains a footnote stating that OLC does not believe that the conclusions of the office's earlier memoranda addressing the treatment of detainees "would be different under the standards set forth in this memorandum." One possible implication is that at least some government officials have already acted on the basis of those early memos, and OLC does not want to leave their actions legally unprotected. In this sense, at least, the damage to the definition of torture may already have been done.

III.

The impossibility of knowing all the consequences of the government memoranda makes it all the more urgent to ask the deeper question of what exactly is wrong with their argument from reciprocity – or, more precisely, from the breakdown of the argument from reciprocity that these documents attempt to enact. Law provides one sort of answer to this question, and the ideology of human rights another. Each, in different ways, challenges the idea that the principle of reciprocity lies behind the duty to comply with the laws of war.

The response of the American legal community to the memos has in the first instance been that they are bad law, poorly framed by the standards of the craft. Sifting assiduously through the memoranda, refuting one argument after another, lawyers and legal academics have done much to show the flimsiness of the reasoning. Often the targets are easily hit. The law students in my seminar had no trouble spotting inconsistencies in the memos. One federal court decision cited there, for example, found torture to have occurred when a woman was removed from a ship, interrogated, held incommunicado for months, and threatened with death if she tried to escape – yet the same memos were defining torture to permit treatment virtually indistinguishable from this, and indeed far worse. Another sure loser is the casuistic argument that failure to comply with U.N. Security Council resolutions renders a state "failed" and therefore removes it from the protection of the Geneva Conventions. The most frequent justification for war under international law is that a state, like Iraq, has ignored the Security Council's command. It can hardly be the case that the Geneva Conventions do not apply in an archetypally lawful war.

More broadly, the core of the legal response to the official memoranda is that the United States is not excused from its legal obligations just because the other side has decided not to play by the rules. Even where the Geneva Conventions do not apply – as, for example, to combatants out of uniform – other legal standards must be considered. These include not only the ban on torture or the constitutional prohibition of treatment that shocks the conscience, but also relevant legal procedures for determining who actually is a terrorist and under what conditions such persons may be detained. In this vein, the Supreme Court has required hearings for the Guantanamo detainees, many of whom have already been released. To much of the legal community, the greatest flaw in the torture memos is that they sought to evade the law by finding categories and spaces where no law applied. In so doing, they resisted and ultimately subverted the rule of law itself.

Vindication of the rule of law deserves the support of anyone committed to the possibility of legal justice and a constitutional order of limited government. Going outside the law – or above it – ensures a disrespect for institutions and individuals alike, and it comes as no surprise that torture can be a result. But such a criticism of the memoranda is too formalistic, or too general, insofar as it concerns the rule of law as such; and it runs the risk of missing the essentially moral claim on which the memoranda drew, namely that the reason for obeying law is the reciprocal agreement of all sides to be bound, and so the old rules could not apply in a war against the new terrorists. Troubling as this claim might be, it cannot be dismissed out of hand merely by asserting that moral claims cannot justify distortions of legal craft or deviations from the rules.

Imagine that the scenario was the enforcement of the fugitive slave laws of the antebellum United States. Careful lawyers would be able to argue – many did – that the purported immorality of slavery made no difference to the deployment of legal principles. Meanwhile, morally inspired lawyers would go to great lengths to pressure, to massage, and even to distort accepted legal doctrine to try to avoid returning slaves to their Southern masters. Who would be right as a matter of law? The answer turns on the role that morality plays in the American legal system. That role is immense. Even if one believed that there might exist, somewhere in the world, legal systems that strictly separate law from morals, it is hard to look at the great sweep of American law and conclude that ours is one of them. Our constitutional law, certainly, incorporates principles of moral force.

So moral considerations must indeed be a part of the legal debate. And once morality is in the conversation, we cannot simply reject the government memoranda for their attack on the rule of law. We need to acknowledge that the imperative of self-preservation is itself a moral value to which the law is sensitive; and we must ask whether we are convinced by the implicit moral theory of the government's lawyers, which was that the circumstances of the war on terror justified deviation from the bounds of ordinary legal interpretation and practice. To do so we must turn to the human rights arguments deployed against the memoranda, because these arguments rest directly on moral grounds.

The human rights community offers a powerful moral objection to the claim that the enemy's nonreciprocity dissolves our duty to obey the law. The claim is that the Geneva Conventions, or U.S. statutes, or the Constitution, are to be respected not because they are conventional legal agreements between parties, but because they embody the universally true and indefeasible value of human dignity. No matter how the enemy may treat you, he is still a human being, and so are you. From those two inexorable facts, from the fact of his human dignity and the fact of your human dignity, flows a duty of biblical – or, if you prefer, Kantian – weight. It is that he, the enemy, must be treated humanely no matter what the consequences. His lack of reciprocity is, quite simply, morally irrelevant. The principle of nonreciprocity invoked by the government's lawyers represents, say the human rights advocates, a moral mistake, which led to similar moral mistakes at Abu Ghraib.

The argument from human dignity has not been asserted with sufficient clarity in the public debate about the torture memos and Abu Ghraib. There should be nothing disconcerting to Americans about the claim that all humans are created equal and endowed by their Creator with certain inalienable rights. Surely dignity is to be found within the rubric of life, liberty, and the pursuit of happiness. Some may be uncomfortable with the avowedly religious basis of this American belief, preferring the Kantian substitute; but whichever argument would be more powerful with the American public or the Bush administration itself, the fundamental human right to dignity cannot be gainsaid, except by introducing cost–benefit analysis into the discussion.

Yet the human dignity argument does not, alas, settle the matter. Its drawback lies in a different quarter, far away from philosophy. The problem is that such an ideal cannot, as a general rule, be expected to do all the work in the real world of war and national interest, especially when lined up against the powerful human impulse to revenge. That is why the laws of war have historically had to depend on reciprocity, rather than the unilateral adoption of wise moral restraints. Moralists, if they are actually to improve the human world, must also be realists; and moral reflection on war must regard war as it really is, in all its brutality and its appeal to the darker impulses. When the French at Agincourt kill the boys, Shakespeare's Henry V retaliates in kind by killing the French prisoners he has taken, Fluellen's protestations that both actions are expressly against the laws of war notwithstanding. Henry does not act without compunction, but he does avenge his subjects' deaths. Vengeance, too, is a form of reciprocity. Against it, a commitment to acting morally no matter what the other side may do is difficult, almost impossible, to sustain.

IV.

The limitations of the legal and the human rights arguments against the torture memoranda suggest a third possibility: that the principle of reciprocity does, in fact, have something to teach us about what was wrong with the worldview of the administration, or of its lawyers. Perhaps the memos did not err in raising the question of whether the terrorists' tactics broke the principle of reciprocity that underlay traditional law-of-war norms. The problem may have been, rather, that the memos gave the wrong answer to this question, mistakenly judging that al Qaeda's deviation from the laws of war made it prudent for the United States to circumvent them as well.

The first error that the memoranda made was in assuming that only the terrorists and the United States were relevant parties in determining whether reciprocity still gave a reason for rule-following. In fact, reciprocity is almost always more than bilateral. It need not narrowly mean that I follow the agreement that we have reached on the expectation and hope that you will do the same. Reciprocity extends also to my desire to convince other parties, third parties, that agreements are worth keeping, even when such parties might be able to get away with violating them. Just as important, reciprocity includes the proposition that I have an interest to signal that I am the kind of person or entity who keeps agreements in spirit as well as in letter.

The rule of law, understood from this perspective of reciprocal interest in keeping to the rules, is not only a good in itself. It is also a tool for promoting a habit of rule-following that serves the interests of stability. No wonder a proper-tied bourgeoisie always prefers the rule of law, while autocrats and revolutionaries favor the possibility of bending or breaking the rules when it is expedient. If enough people follow the rules, the custom of doing so may harden into a social norm. But if everyone is potentially what Oliver Wendell Holmes Jr. called a "bad man," constantly weighing the risks of breaking the law against what he can gain from breaking it, the rule of law is unlikely to find much traction, and the costs of enforcing compliance will rise drastically. To make any legal system work, most people most of the time need to follow the law without giving it much thought. Moreover, the most salient actor in the system – the state, typically – will always be the most effective promoter of it. If it breaks the law, then it signals that anything goes. If it follows the law, the habit of obedience is encouraged.

It was precisely this richer conception of reciprocity that led the United States during the Cold War to champion international treaties and the rule of international law. The United States perceived it to be in our interest to encourage obedience to treaties that we helped to draft; and it was equally in our interest to condemn our enemies for their deviations. The Geneva Conventions themselves reflected American influence and pressure, and of course the United Nations was also conceived as a creature of Roosevelt's vision of how the United States might lead through a combination of soft influence and hard power. It helped that, during the Cold War, the Soviet bloc existed to provide the threat of someone else capturing our soldiers or torturing our civilians; but the foreign policy realists of the era understood perfectly well that behind the Iron Curtain, legal agreements alone would not necessarily protect our prisoners.

The disappearance of the Soviet threat helped to set the conditions in which the United States could begin to imagine that it could get away with deviating from international law reciprocity with no significant added cost. But this was a profoundly shortsighted view, fundamentally at odds with the Bush administration's own stated objective of holding nations accountable for their actions or those of terrorists whom they might be harboring. In a hastily drafted response to the OLC memorandum on applying the Geneva Conventions in Afghanistan, State Department lawyers pointed out that it could be harmful to American soldiers in future wars to declare the Geneva Conventions irrelevant; but even this formulation fell far short of what needed to be said. The central and crucial point should have been that if the United States aimed to demand accountability with international norms, it had better begin by actively and visibly upholding those norms itself. Whatever the merits of unilateralism in foreign policy, unilateralism in law and morals is incoherent and dangerous.

There is another consideration. In the frenzied days after September 11, when the memoranda were being written, the Bush administration had not yet settled on a policy of combating terror by promoting democracy in the Muslim world. But it should rapidly have become clear that this objective, too, requires special vigilance to the promotion of international legal norms. After all, the purported advantage of democracy from the perspective of the United States lies in the assumption that democracies follow the norms of international good behavior better than monarchies or proletarian dictatorships. Democratization would do the United States no good if new democracies in the Muslim world were to adopt policies of exporting terror against us. The other great appeal of democracy lies in its dependence on the proposition of human equality and universal rights – and that idea, too, can be promoted efficaciously only by a country that respects fundamental rights, including very prominently a right against torture.

It emerges that in these memoranda, as in a broad range of subsequent detention decisions, the Bush administration erred disastrously by its failure to consider the costs of the world's perception that it was acting without concern for the reciprocity inherent in a legal order. Had the administration decided to treat the Guantanamo detainees as prisoners of war, al Qaeda members could still have been tried for war crimes; but the world would not now see Guantanamo as a symbol of American flouting of international humanitarian law. There would also have been no strong legal objection to repatriating them at will, as there is today.

It is of course possible – though at present unknowable – that under the sort of harsh CIA interrogation that would have been barred by the Geneva Conventions, one or a few al Qaeda detainees might have disclosed information that saved lives. But a more careful evaluation of who had been brought to Guantanamo, the case-by-case investigations that the Geneva Conventions in fact require for persons whose prisoner-of-war status is unclear, would have spared much, if not all, of the international condemnation that the United States has incurred. What is more, by opening detention facilities to reporters, the

United States could have gained enormous leverage in the international press, including in the Arab world.

The important point is that the United States was not invulnerable to the costs of noncompliance by virtue of the collapse of the Soviet bloc. Quite the contrary. The costs of failing to comply were great in light of the objectives that the United States has sought to pursue since September 11. When it came to international law, detention, and interrogation, the Bush administration failed to understand why reciprocity is valuable, even when the immediate enemy is never going to comply. This was not only moral obtuseness. It was also something worse for the consequentialist (and all strategists are consequentialists): a profound and damaging error of judgment.

NOTES

1. Assistant Attorney General Jay S. Bybee, U.S. Department of Justice, January 22, 2002 Memorandum to Counsel to the President Alberto R. Gonzales and General Counsel William J. Haynes, II, Department of Defense, in *The Torture Papers*, ed. Karen J. Greenberg and Joshua L. Dratel, Memo #6, p. 90 (New York: Cambridge University Press, 2005).
2. Counsel to the President Alberto R. Gonzales, January 25, 2002 Memorandum to President George W. Bush, in *The Torture Papers*, Memo #7, p. 120.
3. Counsel to the President Alberto R. Gonzales, January 25, 2002 Memorandum to President George W. Bush, in *The Torture Papers*, Memo #7, p. 119 (New York: Cambridge University Press, 2005).
4. President George W. Bush, February 7, 2002 Memorandum to the Vice President, the Secretary of State, the Secretary of Defense, the Attorney General, Chief of Staff to the President, Director of CIA, Assistant to the President for National Security Affairs, Chairman of the Joint Chiefs of Staff in *The Torture Papers*, Memo #11, p. 133.

RELEVANT DOCUMENTS

THE LEGAL ADVISOR

DEPARTMENT OF STATE

WASHINGTON

March 22, 2002

NOTE FOR JIM HAYNES

Attached is a memorandum concerning the President's recent decisions about the applicability of the Geneva Conventions to the conflicts with al Qaeda and the Taliban and the treatment of persons detained by the U.S. in those conflicts. The memorandum concludes that the President's decisions are consistent with our treaty obligations and customary international law. I hope the memorandum will be useful to you and others in responding to questions on this subject.

William H. Taft, IV

Attachment:
    As stated.

1949 GENEVA CONVENTIONS
THE PRESIDENT'S DECISIONS UNDER INTERNATIONAL LAW

SUMMARY

- The President's decisions. President Bush has concluded that the *Geneva Convention Relative to the Treatment of Prisoners of War of August 12, 1949* (GPW) does not apply to the conflict with al Qaeda and does apply to the conflict in Afghanistan with the Taliban. He also has decided that neither the al Qaeda terrorists nor the Taliban qualify for prisoner of war (POW) status under the GPW. Finally, the President has decided to treat all Taliban and al Qaeda detainees humanely, consistent with the general principles of the GPW. Statement by the President's Press Secretary, in White House press briefing (Feb. 7, 2002).
- These decisions are consistent with international law. This paper addresses the Geneva Conventions as well as customary international law and is divided according to legal conclusions into nine sections as follows:

  I.   The detainees are receiving humane treatment in accordance with customary international law [*see* pp. 4–7];

  II. The GPW is not applicable to the conflict with al Qaeda because al Qaeda is not a High Contracting Party under Article 2 [*see* pp. 8–15];

  III. Even if al Qaeda were covered by the GPW, al Qaeda does not meet the Article 4 criteria for groups entitled to POW status [*see* pp. 16–38];

  IV. The GPW is applicable to the conflict with the Taliban in Afghanistan because Afghanistan and the United States are High Contracting Parties under Article 2 [*see* pp. 38–41];

  V.   Although the conflict with the Taliban is covered by the GPW, the Taliban does not meet the Article 4 criteria for groups entitled to POW status [*see* pp. 41–62];

  VI. The President has made proper group determinations regarding POW status, consistent with GPW Articles 4 and 5, and the detainees are receiving protections consistent with Article 5 [*see* pp. 62–74];

  VII. Common Article 3 of the GPW does not apply by its terms to either the armed conflict with al Qaeda or the armed conflict with the Taliban because these conflicts are not internal conflicts; standards equivalent to those in common Article 3 do apply to the conflicts under customary international law [*see* pp. 74–75];

  VIII. The detainees are receiving protections consistent with the *Geneva Convention Relative to the Protection of Civilian Persons in Time of War of August 12, 1949* (GCC) even though the President has determined that they are unlawful combatants. The detainees do not fall precisely within the definitions of the Geneva Conventions. Those individuals currently in detention are not "protected persons" under the definitions of the GCC, but will continue to receive humane treatment consistent with the GCC and in accordance with customary international law [*see* pp. 76–89];

  IX. Under customary international law and the GPW, the President may use military commissions or other courts to try detainees suspected of violating international law, including the laws and customs of war [*see* 89–94].

- Before proceeding with the section by section analysis, it is important to note that the determination of GPW coverage is essentially a three-step process. The first step is to determine whether the GPW applies to a particular conflict. Under Article 2, the only conflicts that are covered are armed conflicts that arise between any two High Contracting Parties, i.e., states which are a party to the GPW. The second step is to determine whether groups of combatants participating in that conflict are entitled to coverage. According to Article 4, groups of combatants are not covered unless they meet certain criteria and are the armed forces of a party, or militias and volunteer corps belonging to a party. The third step is to determine the status of individuals by assessing whether they belong to a group that is entitled to coverage. The point of highlighting this three-step process is to demonstrate the possibility that the GPW may cover a given conflict, but that certain groups or individuals may nonetheless not be entitled to POW status.

I.   THE DETAINEES ARE RECEIVING HUMANE TREATMENT IN ACCORDANCE WITH THE REQUIREMENTS OF CUSTOMARY INTERNATIONAL LAW.

- The President remains deeply committed to the Geneva Conventions and is fulfilling the United States obligations under customary international law. The President's Press Secretary said:

> Today President Bush affirms our enduring commitment to the important principles of the Geneva Convention. Consistent with American values and the principles of the Geneva Convention, the United States has treated and will continue to treat all Taliban and al Qaeda detainees in Guantanamo Bay humanely and consistent with the principles of the Geneva Convention. They will continue to receive three appropriate meals a day, medical care, clothing, shelter, showers, and the opportunity to worship. The International Committee of the Red Cross can visit each detainee privately. . . . The Convention remains as important today as it was the day it was signed, and the United States is proud of its 50-year history in compliance with the Convention.

> Statement by the President's Press Secretary, White House press briefing (Feb. 7, 2002)

- Customary international law incorporates standards of basic humane treatment as reflected in common Article 3 of the four Geneva Conventions of 1949, Articles 27–34 of the GCC, Article 75 of 1977 *Protocol Additional to the Geneva Conventions of 12 August 1949, and Relating to the Protection of Victims of International Armed Conflicts* (Protocol I), and Articles 4 and 6 of 1977 *Protocol Additional to the Geneva Conventions of 12 August 1949, and Relating to the Protection of Victims of Non-International Armed Conflicts* (Protocol II). Murder, torture, corporal punishment, mutilation, unlawful medical experiments, pillage, terrorism, and other despicable acts are expressly prohibited.
- It is widely recognized internationally, for example, by the United Nations, the International Court of Justice, the International Criminal Tribunal for the Former Yugoslavia, and the International Criminal Tribunal for Rwanda, that common Article 3 reflects minimum customary international law standards for both internal and international armed conflicts.
- As indicated by the practice of states, the negotiating record of the 1949 Geneva Conventions, the opinions of scholars, and the authoritative commentary of the International Committee of the Red Cross (ICRC), the standards equivalent to those found in

common Article 3 at a minimum are applicable in any armed conflict, whether internal or international. *See, e.g.,* JEAN S, PICTET, COMMENTARY III GENEVA CONVENTION 35 (1960) (noting that common Article 3 simply demands respect for rules "recognized as essential in all civilized countries, and embodied in the municipal law" of States); *see also,* Howard S. Levie, *Maltreatment of Prisoners of War in Vietnam* in 2 THE VIETNAM WAR AND INTERNATIONAL LAW 361, 374–75 (1969).

- Although not a party to Protocol I (for reasons unrelated to Article 75), the United States has stated that "certain provisions of Protocol I reflect customary international law. . . ." SECRETARY OF STATE GEORGE SHULTZ, LETTER OF SUBMITTAL, *accompanying* MESSAGE FROM THE PRESIDENT OF THE UNITED STATES TRANSMITTING PROTOCOL II TO THE U.S. SENATE, *reprinted in* S. TREATY DOC. NO. 100-2 at X (1st Sess., Dec. 13, 1986).
- Shortly thereafter, the United States expressed its support for the fundamental guarantees contained in Article 75. *See Remarks of the U.S. Department of State Deputy Legal Adviser,* Michael J. Matheson, *Session One: The United States Position on the Relation of Customary International Law to the 1977 Protocols Additional to the 1949 Geneva Conventions,* 2 AM. U.J. INT'L L. & POLICY 419, 427 (Fall 1987).
- The fundamental guarantees in Article 75 of Protocol I are similar to those contained in Articles 4 and 6 of Protocol II. Although the United States is not a party to Protocol II (for reasons unrelated to Articles 4 and 6), President Reagan did transmit Protocol II to the Senate requesting advice and consent to ratification. As Secretary of State Shultz indicated in his accompanying report, these obligations "are no more than a restatement of the rules of conduct with which U.S. military forces would almost certainly comply as a matter of national policy, constitutional and legal protections, and common decency." *See* S. TREATY DOC. NO. 100-2 at VIII.
- Based upon the President's decision, the detainees will continue to receive the basic humanitarian protections required under the customary international law of war as reflected in common Article 3 of the 1949 Geneva Conventions, Articles 27–34 of the GCC, Article 75 of Protocol I, and Articles 4 and 6 of Protocol II.
- The President's decision to provide these humanitarian protections is consistent with long-standing policies of the United States Armed Forces, including those contained in U.S. Department of Defense Directive 5100.77 on the Law of War, which provides that the Heads of Department of Defense components shall "ensure that the members of their components comply with the law of war during all armed conflicts, however such conflicts are characterized, and with the principles and spirit of the law during all other operations." U.S. DOD Directive 5100.77 at para. 5.3.1 (1998 ed.).

II.   THE GPW IS NOT APPLICABLE TO THE CONFLICT WITH
      AL QAEDA BECAUSE AL QAEDA IS NOT A HIGH CONTRACTING
      PARTY UNDER ARTICLE 2.

- GPW Article 2 states that "the present Convention shall apply to all cases of declared war or of *any other armed conflict which may arise between two or more of the High Contracting Parties. . . .*" (emphasis added). Thus, for non-internal conflicts, two threshold requirements exist for application of the GPW or any of the other three Geneva Conventions of 1949: (1) there must be an armed conflict; and (2) it must exist between High Contracting Parties.

- Whether an armed conflict exists in a particular case presents a question that is appropriately reserved to the political branches of government. *See. e.g.*, The Three Friends, 166 U.S. 1, 63 (1887) ("(I)t belongs to the political branches to determine when belligerency shall be recognized, and its action must be accepted according to its terms and intention expressed."); Ludecke v. Watkins, 335 U.S. 160, 168–69 (1948) (Whether a war had ended was a question "...too fraught with gravity to be formulated when not compelled" and is left to "political agencies").

- It has long been the policy of the United States to adopt a liberal construction of the term "armed conflict" for purposes of GPW application. According to the U.S. Department of State, an armed conflict "includes any situation in which there is hostile action between the armed forces of two parties, regardless of the duration, intensity or scope of the fighting and irrespective of whether a state of war exists between the two parties." Legal Regulation of Use of Force: The Laws of War, 1981–88 DIGEST OF U.S. PRACTICE IN INTERNATIONAL LAW III, §2 at 3457 (citing U.S. Dept. of State to American Embassy at Damascus, telegram 348126, Dec. 8, 1983, and ARTICLE 1, PROTOCOL II, 16 I.L.M. 1443 ("treaty applicable if armed forces of a state are involved in the fighting")).

- A similarly broad view was taken by the International Criminal Tribunal for the Former Yugoslavia. *Prosecutor v. Dusko Tadic*, Case No. IT-94-1-AR at 37 (Appeals Chamber, Oct. 2, 1995) ("...an armed conflict exists whenever there is a resort to armed force between States or protracted armed violence between governmental authorities and organized armed groups or between such groups within a State."); *see also* PICTET at 36; Arthur Rovine, *Notes from the President*, ASIL NEWSLETTER (Amer. Soc. Int'l L., Washington, D.C.), Sept.–Oct. 2001, at 1 ("If the United States replies using armed force...then there is clearly an armed conflict.").

- In this case, al Qaeda is engaged in a protracted war of terrorism against the United States and its allies. Established in the late-1980s by Osama bin Laden, al Qaeda has been attacking United States personnel and citizens at least since 1998 and perhaps as far back as 1993. *See, e.g.*, U.S. Dep't of State, PATTERNS OF GLOBAL TERRORISM 2000 at 68–69 (April, 2001).

- Al Qaeda "claims to have shot down US helicopters and killed US servicemen in Somalia in 1993 and to have conducted three bombings that targeted US troops in Aden, Yemen, in December 1992." *Id.* at 69. According to the U.S. Department of State Coordinator for Counter-terrorism, al Qaeda is linked to multiple unsuccessful conspiracies, including to assassinate Pope John Paul II during his visit to Manila in late 1994, to carry out simultaneous bombings of the United States and Israeli Embassies in Manila in late 1994, to kill President Clinton during a visit to the Philippines in early 1995, and to bomb a dozen U.S. trans-Pacific flights in 1995. *Id.*

- As early as 1998, al Qaeda's leader, Osama bin Laden, called upon Muslims everywhere, including his al Qaeda organization, "to kill U.S. citizens – civilian or military – and their allies everywhere." *Id.* at 68; *see also* Interview with Osama bin Laden, in UK Arabic weekly news publication, *Al-Quds Al-Arabi* (1998). Shortly thereafter, al Qaeda killed at least 301 individuals and injured more than 5,000 others in August 1998 when it bombed the United States Embassies in Nairobi, Kenya, and Dar es Salaam, Tanzania. *Id.* at 68–69.

- It is believed that al Qaeda unsuccessfully conspired to set off a bomb in 1999 at Los Angeles International Airport and to carry out terrorist operations against United States and Israeli tourists visiting Jordan for millennial celebrations. U.S. Dep't of State, PATTERNS OF GLOBAL TERRORISM 2001 at 143 (draft, Feb. 20, 2002)

("Jordanian authorities thwarted the planned attacks and put 28 suspects on trial."). Intelligence sources indicate that al Qaeda directed an attack in October 2000 on the U.S.S. Cole in the port of Aden, Yemen, killing 17 U.S. Navy members, and injuring another 39, *Id*. at 142.

- Most recently, on September 11, 2001, 19 al Qaeda suicide attackers hijacked and crashed four U.S. commercial jets, two into the World Trade Center towers in New York City, one into the Pentagon near Washington, D.C., and a fourth into a field in Shanksville, Pennsylvania, leaving about 3,000 individuals dead or missing. *Id*. at 142.

- These latest attacks were of sufficient magnitude to persuade most of the world, including NATO and the United Nations, that the United States was warranted in invoking its right to use force in self-defense under Article 51 of the United Nations Charter. *See* U.N. Sec. Council Res., U.N. Doc. No. S/RES/1368 (Sept. 12, 2001) (condemning acts as a "threat to international peace and security"); Statement by NATO Secretary General, Lord Robertson, (Oct. 2, 2001) (announcing NATO determination that September 11 attack "shall [ ] be regarded as an action covered by Article 5 of the Washington Treaty, which states that an armed attack on one or more of the Allies of Europe or North America shall be considered an attack against them all").

- As the President stated in his Military Order of November 13, 2001, "[i]nternational terrorists, including members of al Qaeda, have carried out attacks on United States diplomatic and military personnel and facilities abroad and on citizens and property within the United States on a scale that has created a state of armed conflict that requires the use of the United States Armed Forces."

- The United States and al Qaeda are engaged in a worldwide armed conflict, but the GPW provisions on prisoners of war apply only to international armed conflicts "which may arise between two or more of the High Contracting Parties...." *See* GPW ARTICLE 2.

- Only states can become High Contracting Parties. GPW Article 136 provides that it is open to signature by the "Powers represented at the Conference" or by the "Powers...which are parties to the Convention of July 27, 1929". All such Powers are states. *See also* DIGEST OF U.S. PRACTICE at 3443 (citing GPW Article 136 for the proposition that only states can become parties). The fact that only states can become High Contracting Parties to the Geneva Conventions was reemphasized during the 1974–77 negotiations of Protocol I. PROTOCOL I COMMENTARY on preamble (The term "'High Contracting Parties' must be understood in the Conventions and the Protocol in the sense given by the Vienna Convention to the ward 'Party' namely a 'State which has consented to be bound by the treaty, and for which the treaty is in force.'" (citation omitted)).

- It is widely recognized that "there is no room for an insurgent faction to become a High Contracting Party" under this treaty. DIGEST OF U.S. PRACTICE at 3443 (citing U.S. Dep't of State Office of the Legal Adviser memorandum filed with U.S. Dep't of Justice affidavit in the case of *U.S. v. Shakur*, 690 F. Supp. 1291 (S.D.N.Y. 1988) (citing Richard Baxter, *Ius in Bello Interno: The Present and Future Law*, LAW AND CIVIL WAR IN THE MODERN WORLD 518, 527 (J. N. Moore ed: 1974))).

- Al Qaeda is not a state and therefore, not a High Contracting Party. Instead, al Qaeda is a private terrorist organization comprised of a network of individuals from numerous foreign countries. Thus, the threshold Article 2 requirement that the conflict in question arise between High Contracting Parties is not met with respect to the global conflict between the United States and al Qaeda.

- Even if al Qaeda were a state, the United States still would not be bound to apply the GPW in its relations with al Qaeda. GPW Article 2 states in pertinent part:

   Although one of the Powers in conflict may not be a party to the present Convention, the Powers who are parties thereto shall remain bound by it in their mutual relations. They shall furthermore be bound by the Convention in relation to said Power, *if the latter accepts and applies the provisions thereof.* (emphasis added).

- In order for a non-Party state to be deemed to have "accepted and applied" the GPW, it must: (1) declare its acceptance; and (2) avoid "manifestly disregarding the main [GPW] provisions". ALLAN ROSAS, THE LEGAL STATUS OF PRISONERS OF WAR 112–13 (1976). The GPW therefore applies to a non-party state only if it "both (1) agrees to apply the agreement and (2) actually does so in practice." U.S. BACKGROUND PAPERS AND ANALYSIS at Tab A, at 2–3 (1995) (citing 2B Final Record, Dipl. Conf. Of Geneva 128). "If the [non-party] fails to abide by the Convention, the [party] is not bound by it and is released from it obligations to apply its provisions." *Id.*

- In this case, al Qaeda is not a state, and even if it were, it has neither declared its acceptance of the GPW nor applied its provisions. As discussed more completely at Section III, *infra*, al Qaeda systematically attacks civilians by perfidious means, does not wear uniforms or otherwise distinguish itself from the civilian population, does not carry its arms openly, and is not subject to adequate command authority. The United States owes no GPW obligations to *non-state, non-Party* terrorist organizations. This is especially true in this case, where al Qaeda has neither accepted nor applied the GPW.

III.   EVEN IF AL QAEDA WERE COVERED BY THE GPW, AL QAEDA DOES NOT MEET THE ARTICLE 4 CRITERIA FOR GROUPS ENTITLED TO POW STATUS.

- The status of being a POW is important from a legal standpoint because POWs are entitled to immunity from prosecution for their legitimate acts of war. *See, e.g.,* ROSAS at 305; *see also* Waldemar A. Solf and Edward R. Cummings, *A Survey of Penal Sanctions Under Protocol 1 to the Geneva Convention of August 12, 1949,* 9 CASE W. J. OF INT'L L. 205, 212–16 (1977). They are combatants who "have a right to participate directly in hostilities." PROTOCOL I, ART. 43(2); *see also* ROSAS at 222–23; *cf.* Ex parte Quirin, 317 U.S. 1, 31 (1942).

- In the words of a prominent law of war scholar and commentator, "[u]nder the Conventions and customary international law governing international armed conflicts, prisoner of war status flows directly from the combatant's privilege.... This privilege immunizes members of the armed forces from criminal prosecution by their captors for their violent acts that do not transgress the laws of war, but that might otherwise be crimes under domestic law." Robert K. Goldman, *International Humanitarian Law and the Armed Conflicts in El Salvador and Nicaragua,* 2 AM. U.J. INT'L L. & POLICY 539, 545 (Fall 1967) (citing W. Solf, *The American Red Cross – Washington College of Law Conference; International Humanitarian Law,* 31 AM. U.L. REV. 927, 928 (1982)).

- On the other hand, those who participate in hostilities and who are not entitled to POW status historically have been deemed to be unlawful or unprivileged combatants who may be prosecuted for acts which make their belligerency unlawful. ROSAS at

419; *see also* Ex parte Quirin, 317 U.S. at 31 (citing GREAT BRITAIN, WAR OFFICE, MANUAL OF MILITARY, ch. xiv, §§ 445–451; REGOLAMENTO DI SERVIZIO IN GUERRA, § 133, 3 LEGGI E DECRETI DEL REGNO D'ITALIA (1896) 3184; 7 MOORE, DIGEST OF INTERNATIONAL LAW, § 1109; 2 HYDE, INTERNATIONAL LAW, §§ 654, 652; 2 HALLECK, INTERNATIONAL LAW (4th Ed. 1908) § 4; 2 OPPENHEIM, INTERNATIONAL LAW, § 254; HALL, INTERNATIONAL LAW, §§ 127, 135; BATY & MORGAN, WAR, ITS CONDUCT AND LEGAL RESULTS (1915) 172; BLUNTSCHI, DROIT INTERNATIONAL, §§ 570 bis.). As stated by a professor of international law in Sweden, "Unlawful combatants...though they are a legitimate target for any belligerent action, are not, if captured, entitled to any prisoner of war status." INGRID DETTER, THE LAW OF WAR 148 (2000) (adding that "[t]hey are also personally responsible for any action they have taken and may thus be prosecuted and convicted for murder if they have killed an enemy soldier. They are often summarily tried and enjoy no protection under international law.").

- The GPW does not apply to the international conflict with al Qaeda, but even if it did, al Qaeda would not be entitled to POW status. This is because al Qaeda fails to meet the Article 4 criteria for lawful combatants.
- GPW Article 4(A), in pertinent part, sets forth the basic categories of lawful forces whose members are entitled to POW protections. They are:
  (1) armed forces of a Party and militias and volunteer corps forming part of such armed forces;
  (2) members of other militia and volunteer corps who meet the four basic requirements of being commanded within a hierarchy, wearing a uniform or distinctive sign, carrying arms openly, and observing the laws and customs of war; and
  (3) members of regular armed forces who profess allegiance to an authority not recognized.
- Although the GPW does not define "armed force of a Party", the phrase is understood to refer only to organized military units of a Party, subject to the Party's command authority and a disciplinary system which enforces the laws and customs of war. PICTET at 52, 63. This interpretation is consistent with subsequent international efforts to define "armed force". *See, e.g.*, PROTOCOL I, ARTICLE 43 ("The armed forces of a Party to a conflict consist of all organized armed forces, groups and units which are under a command responsible to that Party for the conduct of its subordinates.... Such armed forces shall be subject to an internal disciplinary system which, *inter alia*, shall enforce compliance with the rules of international law applicable in armed conflict.").
- In this case, al Qaeda does not qualify under Article 4(A)(1), which covers "armed forces of a Party and militias and volunteer corps forming part of such armed forces".
- Al Qaeda is not the "armed force" of Afghanistan or any other High Contracting Party. Al Qaeda, as a group, was not under a military command responsible to Afghanistan or any other High Contracting Party. Rather, al Qaeda is an independent terrorist organization, which does not fight under the military command authority of any single nation.
- Al Qaeda is fighting a private terrorist war for reasons it claims are related to, *inter alia*, its religious beliefs and ideology. In the words of al Qaeda's leader, Osama bin Laden (a former national of Saudi Arabia), al Qaeda is fighting a holy war or "Jihad" in the name of Islam. Videotape: Osama bin Laden monologue (as reported in THE NEW YORK TIMES, Sept. 9, 2001) (stating that the Taliban, the Islamic militant movement

that has sheltered him since 1996, has built an ideal, purified Islamic state that provides the perfect base for a "worldwide holy war" against "infidels").

- Al Qaeda is comprised of individual terrorists from many different countries. It exists in numerous regions of the world and its members do not belong to any national armed force or government. Al Qaeda previously operated its camps in the Sudan, perhaps in Southeast Asia and elsewhere.

- Most recently, al Qaeda appears to have been based in Afghanistan, not because of any allegiance to that nation or its people, but rather for the terrorist "safehaven" the Taliban regime was able to provide. See, e.g., U.N. Sec. Council Res. 1267, U.N. Doc. No. S/RES/1267 (1999) ("Deploring the fact that the Taliban continues to provide safehaven to Usama bin Laden and to allow him and others associated with him to operate a network of terrorist training camps from Taliban-controlled territory and to use Afghanistan as a base from which to sponsor international terrorist operations. . . .");U.N. Sec. Council Res. 1333, U.N. Doc. S/RES/1333 (2000) (repeating language from Res. 1267).

- Al Qaeda has used the safehaven in Afghanistan to construct and operate terrorist training camps and to plan, prepare for, and conduct global terrorist operations. In light of its purpose and method, al Qaeda cannot be said to form part of the "armed force" of Afghanistan or any other High Contracting Party for purposes of Article 4(A) (1).

- Even if al Qaeda were part of Afghanistan's "armed force," it would not qualify for POW status under Article 4(A) (1) because it fails to meet the fundamental GPW criteria for lawful forces: (a) that of being commanded by a person responsible for his subordinates; (b) that of having a fixed distinctive sign recognizable at a distance; (c) that of carrying arms openly; and (d) that of conducting their operations in accordance with the laws and customs of war. Rosas at 328 (noting that regular armed forces are presumed to fulfill these conditions which originally were set forth at the Brussels Conference of 1874, and the Hague Conferences of 1899 and 1907).

- Although Article 4(A) (1) omits mention of these four criteria, which are explicitly set forth in Article 4(A) (2) (by its terms applicable only to militia and volunteer corps), it is widely understood that even regular armed forces must meet the fundamental criteria for lawful belligerency. See id,; see also PICTET at 52, 63; Ex Parte Quirin, 317 U.S. at 36 n. 12; In Re Yamashita, 327 U.S. 1, 15–16 (1945); Asman Bin Haji Mohamed Ali v. Public Prosecutor (decided by the Judicial Committee of the Privy Council in 1968), [1969] A.C. 430, 453–54 (P.C. Malaysia 1968) (quoting the British Government, Manual of Military Law, stating "[s]hould regular combatants fail to comply with these four conditions, they may in certain cases become unprivileged belligerents. This would mean that they would not be entitled to the status of prisoners of war upon their capture." (emphasis in orginal)); THE WAR OFFICE, THE LAW OF WAR ON LAND BEING PART III OF THE MANUAL OF MILITARY WAR at 34, para. 96 (1958); Richard Baxter, So-Called "Unprivileged Belligerency": Spies, Guerillas, and Saboteurs, 28 BRIT. Y.B. OF INT'L L. 332 (1951).

- The authoritative commentary on Article 4 states that

> The drafters of the 1949 Convention, like those of the Hague Convention, considered that it was unnecessary to specify the sign which members of the armed forces should have for purposes of recognition. It is the duty of each State to take steps so that members of its armed forces can be immediately recognized as such and to see to

it that they are easily distinguishable from members of the enemy armed forces or from civilians ... the Convention ... merely assumes ... that there can be no room for doubt.

PICTET at 52.

- Thus, the commentary continues, the "delegates to the 1949 Diplomatic Conference were ... fully justified in considering that there was no need to specify for such armed forces the requirements stated in sub-paragraph (2) (a), (b), (c) and (d)." *Id.* at 63; *see also* MICHAEL BOTHE, KARL JOSEF PARTSCH, AND WALDEMAR SOLF, NEW RULES FOR VICTIMS OF ARMED CONFLICTS at 234 (1982) ("It is generally assumed that these conditions were deemed, by the 1874 Brussels Conference and the 1899 and 1907 Hague Peace Conferences, to be inherent in the regular armed forces of States. Accordingly, it was considered to be unnecessary and redundant to spell them out."); cf. ROSAS at 328 n.496, 370 (citing *The Military Prosecutor v. Omar Mahmud Kassem and Others* (Israeli Mil. Ct., 1969); article 34 of the regulations of France; and *Verri*, 11 RDPMDG 1972, p. 94); *cf.* Howard S. Levie, *Prisoners of War in International Armed Conflict*, 59 INT'L L. STUD. 1, 37 n.142 (1977) (citing Pictet for the principle that Article 4(A) (1) requires only a fixed distinctive sign on the grounds that the other three elements can be assumed to follow from the mere fact of membership in the regular armed forces).
- The United States has long held the view that regular armed forces, militias, and volunteer corps must meet the four criteria in order to qualify for protections as POWs. *See, e.g.*, S. EXEC. REP. No. 84-9, at 5 (1st Sess., 1955) (stating that militias and volunteer corps and partisans "must conform to article I of the [1907] Hague regulations, which requires such persons to act under orders of a responsible commander, to wear a fixed emblem recognizable at a distance, to carry arms openly, and to obey the laws and customs of war.").
- President Reagan based his decision not to submit Protocol I to the Senate for advice and consent in part on the fact that it would have provided protections where the GPW had not, i.e., to fighters not in uniform who fail to obey the laws and customs of war. MESSAGE FROM THE PRESIDENT OF THE UNITED STATES TRANSMITTING PROTOCOL II TO THE U.S. SENATE, *reprinted in* S. TREATY DOC. No. 100-2, at X (1st *Sess.*, 1987) (explaining his decision not to submit Protocol I on the ground that it "would grant combatant status to irregular forces even if they do not satisfy the traditional requirements to distinguish themselves from the civilian population and otherwise comply with the laws of war").
- In this case, al Qaeda systematically violates the four fundamental criteria applicable to lawful forces. There can be no question that al Qaeda, whose members disguise themselves as civilians and willfully and wantonly attack civilians in contravention of the most basic rules of war, does not meet these threshold requirements.
- First, al Qaeda is not commanded by any authority that properly disciplines its members or otherwise enforces the laws and customs of war. The purpose of the command requirement is to ensure that all lawful combatants are subject to an organizational hierarchy which enforces the laws and customs of war. *See, e.g.*, PICTET at 59.
- Second, its members do not wear distinctive signs or otherwise distinguish themselves from civilians. In carrying out the attacks of September 11, al Qaeda used so-called "sleepers" who were specially trained by the organization to blend in with the civilian population, and succeeded in doing so for months while planning and then conducting

their attacks. Nor did al Qaeda wear uniforms or other insignia during the fighting in Afghanistan, where they continued to wear clothes that closely resembled civilian dress.

- Third, al Qaeda routinely and by tactical design does not carry its arms openly. As previously discussed, its members disguise themselves as civilians in planning and carrying out attacks. They used such tactics for example in the bombings of September 11, the U.S.S. Cole, and the U.S. Embassies in East Africa.
- Fourth, al Qaeda does not adhere to the laws and customs of war. In the words of Osama bin Laden, "[w]e do not differentiate between those dressed in military uniforms and civilians; they are all targets in this fatwa." John Miller, *Greetings, America, My Name [sic] Osama bin Laden*, ESQUIRE, Feb. 1, 1999 ("A reporter describes his journey to interview alleged terrorist."); *see also*, Videotape: Osama bin Laden monologue (*as reported in* THE WASHINGTON POST, Nov. 13, 2001): "Yes, we kill their innocents.... We will not stop killing them and whoever supports them." Thus, al Qaeda has declared its intent to violate the most fundamental provisions of the laws and customs of war and in practice has done precisely that.
- Its resolve to attack civilians flagrantly violates the "letter and spirit of the law of armed conflict, which seeks as one of its primary purposes to protect those persons." LT. COL. RICHARD J. ERICKSON, LEGITIMATE USE OF MILITARY FORCE AGAINST STATE-SPONSORED INTERNATIONAL TERRORISM 79 (1989) (explaining why terrorists are not entitled to law of war protections).
- In addition to attacking civilians, al Qaeda carries out its attacks by unlawful and perfidious means which include exploding truck bombs in civilian areas, directing fully-loaded civilian aircraft into civilian buildings, and using suicide bombers feigning civilian status. The law of war expressly forbids the use of such means. *See, e.g.,* PROTOCOL I, ARTICLE 37.
- Nor is al Qaeda a "militia or volunteer corps forming part of" a Party's armed force under Article 4(A) (1). Volunteer corps and militia under Article 4(A) (1) must be integrated formally into an armed force. PICTET at 51–2.
- The common understanding of the drafters evidently was that any part of an "armed force," including militias and volunteer corps, had to fulfill basic traditional requirements of "military organization." PICTET at 58. While the extent to which these requirements include traditional uniforms or insignia is unclear, they include at a minimum "discipline, hierarchy, responsibility, and honour." *Id.* It is "the duty of each State to take steps so that members of its armed forces can be immediately recognized as such and to see that they are easily distinguishable from members of the enemy armed forces or from civilians." *Id.* at 51–52.
- As discussed, al Qaeda does not use insignia or otherwise distinguish itself from civilians. Nor does it belong to any state with the responsibility and disciplinary authority to require it to distinguish itself. In this connection, al Qaeda is not "part of" any national armed force in the sense that it is not "effectively subordinated to the High Command and to the military penal legislation of the party concerned." ROSAS at 330.
- Even if the Taliban did at some point exercise some kind of *de facto* command authority over limited numbers of al Qaeda fighters on the battlefield (this is not at all clear), the Taliban did not control al Qaeda as an organized military unit and subject it to any sort of effective military discipline. The Taliban took no steps to ensure that al Qaeda distinguishes itself from the civilian population and adheres to the laws and customs of war.

- Instead, the Taliban "allowed" Osama bin Laden and others associated with him "to operate a network of terrorist training camps from Taliban-controlled territory and to use Afghanistan as a base from which to sponsor international terrorist operations." U.N. Sec. Council Res. 1267, U.N. Doc. S/RES/1267 (1999); U.N. Sec. Council Res. 1333, U.N. Doc. S/RES/1333 (2000).
- Nor does al Qaeda qualify for coverage under Article 4(A) (2). Article 4(A) (2) refers to "[m] embers of other militias and members of other volunteer corps, including those of organized resistance movements, belonging to a Party to the conflict ... provided that such militias or volunteer corps ... fulfill the following [four] conditions: (a) that of being commanded by a person responsible for his subordinates; (b) that of having a fixed distinctive sign recognizable at a distance; (c) that of carrying arms openly; and (d) that of conducting their operations in accordance with the laws and customs of war."
- Al Qaeda does not qualify under Article 4(A) (2) in the first instance because, as described above, it is not a militia or volunteer corps that *belongs* to Afghanistan or some other High Contracting Party. *See, e.g.*, Bothe, Partsch & Solf, New Rules for Victims of Armed Conflict at 237 (1982) (noting that "belonging to" means not acting on own behalf). Al Qaeda is not part of any organized resistance movement fighting to regain occupied territory as in the case of the Free French during World War II. *See, e.g.*, Pictet at 62; *see also* W. Thomas Mallison and Sally V. Mallison, *The Juridical Status of Irregular Combatants under the International Humanitarian Law of Armed Conflict*, 9 Case W. Res. J. Int'l L. 39, 42 (1977) ("If the partisans are organized and are engaged in what international law regards as legitimate warfare for the defense of their own country, they are entitled to be protected as combatants." (quoting *The Einsatzgruppen Case*, 4 U.S. Trials of War Crim. 1 (1949)). Al Qaeda's terrorist agenda is an independent one, not linked to Afghanistan. Al Qaeda's terrorist war extends geographically far beyond Afghanistan to a global battlefield that includes nearly every continent. Al Qaeda and its independent network of terrorists have attacked or taken steps to attack the United States and its allies in Africa, Asia, North America, Europe, and the Middle East. *See, e.g.*, U.S. Dep't of State, Global Terrorism 2000 at 68–9 (April 2001).
- More importantly, even if al Qaeda were sufficiently linked to Afghanistan or the Taliban, it still would not be covered by Article 4(A) (2) because it fails to meet the four criteria as discussed in detail above and summarized briefly below.
- Al Qaeda is not commanded by any authority that adequately disciplines its members, and its members do not wear distinctive signs or otherwise distinguish themselves from civilians. In many cases, they do not carry arms openly. Al Qaeda clearly does not adhere to the laws and customs of war.
- Nor are al Qaeda fighters covered as "members of a regular armed forces" under. Article 4(A) (3). Article 4(A) (3) refers to "[m] embers of regular armed forces who profess allegiance to an authority not recognized by the Detaining Power." As discussed, al Qaeda fighters are not regular armed forces and have not professed allegiance to Afghanistan or the Taliban.
- According to authoritative commentary, regular armed forces for purposes of Article 4(A) (3) must fulfill the same conditions as those pertaining to armed forces under Article 4(A) (1); the only difference is that armed forces under 4(A) (3) fight for a party that is not recognized by the opposing party. *See* Pictet at 61 et seq. Regular armed forces under Article 4(A) (3) therefore "have all the material characteristics

and all the attributes of armed forces in the sense of sub-paragraph(1) : they wear uniform, they have an organized hierarchy and they know and respect the laws and customs of war. The delegates to the 1949 Diplomatic Conference were therefore fully justified in considering that there was no need to specify for such armed forces the requirements stated in sub-paragraph (2) (a), (b), (c), and (d)." *See id.* at 63.

- As discussed, al Qaeda terrorists do not meet these criteria. It is beyond debate that al Qaeda does not comprise the "regular armed force" of any High Contracting Party.

- To interpret the GPW as requiring the United States to extend POW coverage to al Qaeda would lead to results clearly not intended by the framers of the GPW.

- In setting out the types of organizations that would be covered by the GPW, the framers sought to eliminate the possibility of "abusive interpretations" resulting in coverage for every group that happened to be fighting in conjunction with a High Contracting Party. *See, e.g.*, PICTET at 62. It was widely recognized at that time, as it is today, that abusive interpretations would only serve to blur the distinction between lawful and unlawful combatants. Blurring this distinction ultimately puts civilians, the same civilians the drafters intended to protect, at greater risk during armed conflict. *See, e.g.*, ERICKSON at 77 (explaining why terrorists are not entitled to law of war protections). One expert states that "[i]nevitably, regular forces would treat civilians more harshly and with less restraint if they believed that their opponents were free to pose as civilians while retaining their right to act as combatants and their POW status if captured." Abraham D. Sofaer, *Agora: The U.S. Decision Not to Ratify Protocol I to the Geneva Conventions on the Protection of War Victims (Cont'd)*, 82 AM. J. INT'L L. 784, 786 (1988).

- Events subsequent to the 1949 negotiations also make clear that the GPW was not intended to provide POW status to terrorists such as al Qaeda. There was widespread recognition that the provisions of the GPW were in certain respects unrealistic with regard to modern guerilla warfare or so-called wars of national liberation. The lack of GPW coverage for non-traditional forces ultimately led states parties and international humanitarian organizations such as the International Committee of the Red Cross (ICRC) to propose a new set of rules which later became the 1977 Protocols I and II.

- It should be emphasized that even Article 43 of Protocol I, which expanded the class of persons receiving POW status, refers to armed forces "of a Party to the conflict." Leading scholars on the Protocols have pointed out the relation of this phrase to the traditional "belonging to a Party to the conflict" in Article 4 of the GPW. They indicate that the purpose of the Article 43 language was not to "require more formality in the link than was inherent under Article 4(A) (2) of the Third Convention. The rationale of this condition is to provide recognition and protection only to those organizations and individuals who act on behalf of a State or an entity which is a subject of international law, and to exclude private wars whether conducted by individuals or groups. Thus gangs of terrorists acting on their own behalf and not linked to a subject of international law are excluded." BOTHE, PARTSCH & SOLF, NEW RULES FOR VICTIMS OF ARMED CONFLICT 237 (1982). Similarly, it has long been recognized that "individuals who undertake to wage a war in their private capacity are not entitled to the treatment of prisoners of war." HERBERT C. FOOKS, PRISONERS OF WAR 40 (1924): *see also* Mallison and Mallison, *supra*, at 42 ("The requirements that all privileged combatants act for a public purpose and that violence for private gain (the acts of marauders on land or pirates at sea) is prohibited are as fundamental today as they have been historically" (citations omitted).)

- The United States is not prepared to give such a right, let alone POW status, to terrorists such as al Qaeda. Although the United States participated actively in the negotiations of Protocol I, President Reagan declined to recommend it for ratification in part to ensure that terrorist organizations such as al Qaeda could not legitimately claim POW status. *See* MESSAGE FROM THE PRESIDENT OF THE UNITED STATES TRANSMITTING PROTOCOL II TO THE U.S. SENATE, *reprinted in* S. TREATY DOC. 100-2, at IV (1st Sess., 1987) ("It is unfortunate that Protocol I must be rejected.... But we cannot allow other nations of the world, however numerous, to impose upon us and our allies and friends an unacceptable and thoroughly distasteful price for joining a convention drawn to advance the laws of war. *In fact we must not, and need not, give recognition and protection to terrorist groups as a price for progress in humanitarian law.*" (emphasis added).); *see also id.* at IX, *accompanying* LETTER FROM U.S. SECRETARY OF STATE GEORGE SHULTZ (Dec. 13, 1986) ("As the essence of terrorist criminality is the obliteration of the distinction between combatants and non-combatants, it would be hard to square ratification of [Protocol I] with the United States' announced policy of combatting terrorism.")
- Even if the more relaxed Protocol I standards did apply, al Qaeda still would not qualify for POW status. Protocol I sets forth the requirements for combatant and POW status at Section II, Articles 43 and 44. As a general matter, combatants must belong to an armed force as defined in Article 43 ("armed forces, groups, and units which are under a command responsible to [a Party] ... subject to an internal disciplinary system ... which, *inter alia*, shall enforce compliance with the rules of international law applicable in armed conflict"), and as discussed in detail above, al Qaeda fighters clearly do not.
- Even if al Qaeda met the Article 43 threshold requirements, it still would not qualify under Protocol I. Article 44 of Protocol I provides, in pertinent part, that combatants must at a minimum distinguish themselves by carrying their arm openly "during each military engagement" and "during such time as he is visible to the adversary while he is engaged in a military deployment preceding the launching of an attack in which he is to participate." Al Qaeda does not meet this standard because, *inter alia*, it conducts its war by feigning civilian status, blending in with civilian populations, and crashing civilian aircraft into civilian targets. Such perfidious means and methods of warfare constitute violations of Protocol I (Article 37) as well as grave breaches under the GPW and the laws and customs of war. Those who use them do not qualify for the status granted to legitimate combatants under Protocol I.
- The United States' political branches and the federal courts long have recognized that the GPW, which is intended to protect lawful combatants and innocent non-combatants, is not available for the protection of "terrorists" such as al Qaeda. *See* 1981–88 DIGEST, U.S. PRACTICE AT 3450 (citing U.S. brief filed in *U.S. v. Shakur*, 690 F. Supp. 1291 (S.D.N.Y. 1988) (citing PICTET, BAXTER, GREENSPAN, and FEITH)).
- Customary international law does not require the United States to depart from the terms of the GPW or otherwise afford al Qaeda the same legal rights it affords the Taliban. This is true with respect to belligerent states as well. The GPW by its terms entitles states parties to its protections in their mutual relations, even if in the same conflict there are non-party states that would not be so entitled. Article 2 states that "[a]lthough one of the Parties in conflict may not be a party to the present Convention, the Powers who are parties thereto shall remain bound by it in their mutual relations."
- It is expected that states will differentiate between legally distinct categories of combatants as well. The United States and others have long distinguished between lawful

and unlawful combatants, as was done in Vietnam and World War II. *Contemporary Practice of the United States*, 62 Am. J. Int'l L. 766–68 (1968) (citing MACV, Annex A of Directive Number 381-46 of December 27, 1967).

IV. THE GPW IS APPLICABLE TO THE CONFLICT WITH THE TALIBAN IN AFGHANISTAN BECAUSE AFGHANISTAN AND THE UNITED STATES ARE HIGH CONTRACTING PARTIES UNDER ARTICLE 2.

- Article 2 of the GPW provides that the Convention "shall apply" to armed conflict which "may arise between two or more of the High Contracting Parties." In this case, both states are High Contracting Parties; the United States and Afghanistan ratified the GPW in 1955 and 1956, respectively.
- Some have argued that Afghanistan was a "failed state" or in a condition of state-lessness when the conflict began and that therefore, the United States had no GPW obligations to the Taliban or any other authorities in Afghanistan.
- However, the weight of authority recognizes that there is a presumption in international law against the extinction of a State, even after a lengthy period of internal anarchy. *See generally*, JAMES CRAWFORD, THE CREATION OF STATES IN INTERNATIONAL LAW 405–12, 417–20 (1979). The international community generally has not taken the position that long-established States such as Afghanistan cease to exist as legal entities on the grounds of internal conflict and the absence of a single effective or recognized government.
- Even in extreme cases of complete civil war or enemy occupation in wartime, disrupted States have continued to exist for purposes of international law (e.g., occupied Germany and Japan after World War II; civil wars in Somalia, the United States, Spain, etc.). *See generally* Clark v. Allen, 331 U.S. 503, 514 (1947) (rejecting the argument that a treaty "failed to survive the [Second World War], since Germany, as a result of its defeat and the occupation by the Allies, has ceased to exist as an independent national or international community"); *see also* JENNINGS AND WATTS, OPPENHEIM'S INTERNATIONAL LAW, §§ 34, 120, 122 (1992) (stating that once a state is established, "temporary interruption of the effectiveness of its government, as in civil war or as a result of belligerent occupation, is not inconsistent with the continued existence of a state").
- While only a handful of nations officially recognized the Taliban as the legitimate government of Afghanistan, the United Nations, the United States, and many other governments and organizations nonetheless treated the Taliban as the *de facto* governing authority in Afghanistan. *See, e.g.*, Letter from the U.S. Permanent Representative, to the President of the U.N. Security Council, U.N. Doc. No. S/2001/946 (Oct. 7, 2001) (referring to the "Taliban regime"); *see also* U.N. Sec. Council Res. 1333, U.N. Doc. S/RES/1333 (2000) (making demands on the basis of the Taliban's *de facto* control over Afghan territory); U.N. Sec. Council Res. 1193, U.N. Doc. S/RES/1193 (1998) (reaffirming that Taliban and others "are bound to comply with their obligations under international humanitarian law and in particular the Geneva Conventions of 12 August 1949...").
- The Taliban exercised *de facto* governmental control over parts of Afghanistan, and clearly did not consent to the U.S. use of force with respect to the parts of Afghanistan under its control. In the absence of such consent, the President is justified in concluding that an armed conflict exists between two High Contracting Parties to the GPW. *See, e.g.*, W. Michael Reisman and James Silk, *Which Law Applies to the Afghan*

Conflict?, 82 Am. J. Int'l L. 459, 483 (1988) (concluding that the Soviet invasion of Afghanistan constituted an "international armed conflict" for purposes of GPW Article 2, notwithstanding an alleged "invitation" from the Afghan government).

V.   ALTHOUGH THE CONFLICT WITH THE TALIBAN IS COVERED BY
     THE GPW, THE TALIBAN DOES NOT MEET THE ARTICLE 4
     CRITERIA FOR GROUPS ENTITLED TO POW STATUS.

- GPW Article 4(A), as discussed in the context of al Qaeda, sets forth in pertinent part the basic categories of individuals entitled to POW protections. They are:
  (1) armed forces of a Party and militias and volunteer corps forming part of such armed forces;
  (2) members of other militia and volunteer corps who meet the four basic requirements; and
  (3) members of regular armed forces who profess allegiance to an authority not recognized.
- The Taliban does not qualify for coverage under Article 4(A) (1) as they were not "the armed forces of a Party" or the "militias and volunteer corps forming part of such armed forces". In this case, the High Contracting Party is the state of Afghanistan. The regular armed forces and the militias or volunteer corps which may at one time have been a part of such forces were disbanded and ceased to exist well before the current conflict. The recognized leadership of Afghanistan, as represented at the United Nations by exiled King Zahir Shah, had no standing army or armed forces of any kind during the period in question.
- The armed forces of Afghanistan, and all its constituent parts, ceased to exist as organized entity well before the current conflict. Former Afghan leader Mohammad Najibullah's armed forces ceased to exist sometime in the mid-1990s as "officers in the government's frightened forces ... delivered entire garrisons into *mujahedin* hands. ..." Michael Griffin, Reaping the Whirlwind: The Taliban Movement in Afghanistan 12 (2001). The armed forces disintegrated and became part of the existing "patchwork of rival warlords, each with his ramshackle facsimile of the Soviet war machine." *Id.* The Taliban was part of this patchwork, and although it became more powerful than other opposition forces, it was never the regular armed force of Afghanistan.
- Nor is the Taliban a militia or volunteer corps entitled to coverage under Article 4(A) (1) or 4(A) (2). As discussed, the Taliban was never part of the armed forces of the state of Afghanistan. In addition, it does not fulfill the basic requirements applicable to any armed force, militia or volunteer corps under GPW Article 4(A).
- As discussed previously, although Article 4(A) (1) omits mention of the four criteria, it is widely understood that even regular armed forces and militias and volunteer corps forming part of such armed forces must fulfill the four fundamental conditions for lawful belligerency. *See detailed discussion, supra* at Section III; *see also* Mallison and Mallison, *supra,* at 44, 48 ("These four fundamental criteria [from the Brussels Declaration of 1874], which are equally applicable to regulars, have been repeated in Hague Convention II of 1899 as well as in Hague Convention IV of 1907 and the Geneva Prisoner of War Convention of 1949. ... [T]he matter of applicability to regulars was so well established in customary law that a treaty provision would have been superfluous.").

- In this case, the Taliban fail to meet the requirements necessary to qualify for coverage under Article 4(A) (1) because they do not generally wear uniforms, are not subject to command that enforces the laws and customs of war, and do not sufficiently adhere to the laws and customs of war.

- First, the Taliban's members do not wear proper uniforms or fixed distinctive signs. *See, e.g.*, U.S. Dep't of Defense, OGC Draft, *Status of Taliban Forces*, Nov. 21, 2001 (citing Agence France Press, June 28, 2001) (reporting that Taliban forces wore uniforms for the first time in June 2001, when a mere 50 soldiers were outfitted for purposes of patrolling Kabul). The U.S. Department of Defense has noted that the Taliban's failure to wear uniforms complicated the U.S. bombing campaign since the Taliban were indistinguishable from civilians. *See id.* (citing THE NEW YORK TIMES, Oct. 26, 2001 at A3(1)).

- Although some sources indicate that the Taliban wore black turbans, the authoritative commentary on the GPW indicates that a cap or hat "way frequently be taken off and does not seem fully adequate" as a distinctive sign. PICTET at 60. Even if turbans were generally adequate, it is not clear that the Taliban turbans were recognizable at a distance or, in any event, distinguishable from turbans worn by civilians.

- A London journalist who was taken by the Taliban to interview Osama bin Laden in 1996 states that the Taliban made him dress in "an Afghan costume consisting of baggy trousers, a long shirt and a turban.... [in] the same style as everyone else.... [so that he would] pass for a Pashtun tribal leader...." Abdul Bari Atwan (editor of UK weekly, *Al-Quds Al-Arabi), Inside Osama's Mountain Lair*, reprinted in THE GUARDIAN, Nov. 12, 2001. The implication is that the Taliban wore garments that were indistinguishable from those worn by non-combatants as well as enemy forces.

- This is consistent with another independent journalist's account in which he describes the dress of civilian men, and then notes that the military wore the same things:

  > Men had to wear the traditional perahan and tumban, a pyjama suit of long loose shirt and incredibly baggy trousers. Over this you had to wear a waistcoat, and it had to be striped. Turbans, or lungi, were compulsory, and had to be worn with a long loose end called the alaga hanging below the shoulder. Decrees were posted in public, signed by the Taliban's supreme leader himself, Mullah Mohammed Omar, saying that the those who did not wear their turbans crooked would go to jail. *Taliban soldiers wore the same clothes; they had no uniform except that their turbans were either black or white*

  > Justin Hugler, *Campaign against terrorism: Stallholders selling out of Afghanistan's new must-have hat.* THE INDEPENDENT – LONDON, Nov. 26, 2001 (emphasis added)

- Assuming that the Taliban military generally wore turbans that were either black or white, it still is not clear that this feature alone was sufficient to distinguish them from non-military Taliban, other civilians, or even enemy combatants. In one experts' book, there are detailed photographs showing Taliban soldiers wearing turbans of different colors (not merely black or white) and styles, many of which appear to closely resemble the turbans worn by non-military Taliban and other civilians. KANAL MATINUDDIN, THE TALIBAN PHENOMENON: AFGHANISTAN 1994–97 at 70–71. Another report as recent as January 27, 2002, states that "since the October action [with Karzai's Popalazi troops], the Taliban and [al Qaeda] have had no presence near Tarin Kot, the provincial capital. Mullah Mohammed Omar, the Taliban's fugitive leader, was born in the province, and the black or white turbans favored by the Taliban *are the*

*traditional headgear of the province. Gunmen there yesterday were indistinguishable
from Taliban fighters ... it is not uncommon to spot bands of armed men who look
like Taliban fighters, but whose allegiance is unclear."* See, e.g.; Craig Smith, *Victims
were no al-Qaeda or Taliban members,* The San Diego Union-Tribune, Jan. 27, 2002,
(citing THE NEW YORK TIMES NEWS SERVICE) (emphasis added).

- The White House and the U.S. Department of Defense have stated publicly that the
Taliban members did not "effectively distinguish themselves from the civilian population." Statement by the President's Press Secretary, White House press briefing, Feb. 7,
2002. Independent news agencies, including The New York Times, have made similar
observations, indicating that the Taliban members were able to switch allegiances, in
part because they looked like their adversaries in the Northern Alliance. *See, e.g.,* THE
NEW YORK TIMES NEWS SERVICE, Jan. 27, 2002. As the United States made progress
in the war, thousands of Taliban apparently blended in with the civilian population
to some extent, making it possible for many of them to avoid capture.

- The problem therefore with the Taliban turbans is two-fold: (1) they were not worn
by all the members of the Taliban and those who did wear them evidently did not wear
a uniform style or color; and (2) they were similar to the headgear worn by civilians
in many areas. *See, e.g.,* Mallison and Mallison, *supra,* at 57 ("The sign should be the
same for all members of a particular resistance organization.... [And must] remain
distinguishable from noncombatants").

- Second, the Taliban was not subject to adequate command authority. GPW Article 4
requires that forces be "commanded by a person responsible for his subordinates."
This military command requirement is intended to ensure widespread compliance with
the laws and customs of war. *See generally* PICTET at 59 ("Respect for [the command
requirement] is moreover in itself a guarantee of the discipline which must prevail
in volunteer corps and should therefore provide reasonable assurance that the other
[three conditions] will be observed."). During the 1949 Diplomatic Conference, the
requirements "... of organization and responsible command were generally regarded
as essential so as to ensure a certain degree of responsible behaviour [sic], including respect for international humanitarian law...." ROSAS at 340. According to two
experts on the subject, "[t]he main purpose for having a 'responsible commander' is
to provide for reasonable assurance of adherence by irregulars to the fundamental
requirement of compliance with the laws of war." Mallison and Mallison, *supra,* at
55. The requirement of military command indicates "a special emphasis on the principle that irregulars or partisans should be organized in belligerent groups which better
facilitate their compliance with the other conditions of the Article." *Id.* at 42.

- In this case, the Taliban failed to satisfy the command requirement for purposes
of the GPW. According to the U.S. Department of Defense, the Taliban "are not
commanded by any person responsible for his subordinates". *See* U.S. Department of
Defense memorandum, *Why Taliban are unlawful combatants* at 1 (Oct. 19, 2001).
"The command structure is loose and subject to change." *Id.*

- Independent experts have come to the same conclusions. One Taliban expert states
that "there is no clear military structure with a hierarchy of officers and commanders,
while unit commanders are constantly being shifted around." AHMED RASHID, THE
TALIBAN 99 (2000). "There is constant coming and going as family members change
places at the front, allowing soldiers to go home for long spells.... [the Taliban's]
haphazard style of enlistment, which contrasted sharply with Masud's 12,000 to
15,000 regular troops, *does not allow for a regular or disciplined army to be created."*
Id. at 100 [emphasis added]. Another expert states that "[t]he Taliban are *not to*

be compared to an organized army. Their commanders do not carry out a military appreciation." MATINUDDIN at 59 (emphasis added).

- The Taliban's military command evidently was informal and disorganized and (assuming it even tried) did not effectively ensure widespread compliance with the laws and customs of war. There necessarily is a "close relationship between this [command] condition and the condition of respect for the law of armed conflicts." ROSAS at 341. The Taliban failed on both conditions.

- Third, the Taliban did not comply *as a group* with the laws and customs of war. Rather, the Taliban had the systematic and widespread practice of violating the laws and customs of war. The United States' view is that if an armed force as a whole has the policy and practice of complying with the laws and customs of war, individuals within the group (even those who may have violated the laws and customs of war) are presumptively entitled to POW status providing the other requirements are met. *See, e.g.,* THE UNITED STATES ARMY FIELD MANUAL ON THE LAW OF LAND WARFARE at para. 64 (1956). It follows that where most of the members of the group do not wear distinctive uniforms and observe the laws and customs of war, the group as a whole cannot meet the requirements of Article 4(A) (2) (d).

- In this case, the Taliban as a whole dose not generally adhere to the laws and customs of war. According to the laws and customs of war, parties must take precautions to protect civilians, for example by verifying the military nature of targets, respecting the principles of proportionality and necessity, and minimizing incidental loss of civilian life. *See generally GCC; see also* PROTOCOL I PART IV – CIVILIAN POPULATION (setting forth fundamental protections for civilian populations). The "basic rule" relating to the protection of civilians, as reflected in Protocol I, is that "the Parties to the conflict shall at all times distinguish between the civilian population and combatants and between civilian objects and military objectives and accordingly shall direct their operations only against military objectives." PROTOCOL I, ARTICLE 48.

- In this case, the Taliban has violated these norms by failing to distinguish between civilians and military objectives, and even worse, intentionally targeting civilians and civilian objects. In this connection, one independent expert has stated:

> These non-Afghan fighters, along with the Taliban army, have not only broken the traditional norms of Afghan civil societies, they have also committed massive crimes against humanity by beheading and killing prisoners of war (POWs) and massacring thousands of civilians in different parts of the country. In 1998 to 1999, the International Red Cross reported that the Taliban and their non-Afghan army killed thousands of civilians in Bamyan and set fire to 8,000 houses and shops.
>
> NEAMATOLLAH NOJUMI, THE RISE OF THE TALIBAN IN AFGHANISTAN at 229 (2002); *see also* Lee A. Casey, David B. Rivkin Jr. and Darin R. Bartram, *By the Laws of War, They Aren't POWs*, WASHINGTON POST, March, 3, 2002, at B03 (quoting Nojumi)

- In another example, the Taliban unlawfully targeted and killed civilians, as such:

> The Taliban forces also retaliated while they retreated from Mazar-e-Sharif [in 1997] by firing on hundreds of civilians.... [A year later,] a revengeful [Taliban] operation for their losses in Mazar was launched against the civilian population.... Taliban fighters did a door-to-door search and shot the males of the families or slit their throats. According to eyewitnesses, hundreds of women were kidnapped and became concubines for the Taliban fighters.
>
> NOJUMI at 161, 168.

- Another author and expert on the Taliban writes that "[o]n 9 and 10 September [1997], Taliban troops lined up and shot 100 Shia civilians in the villages of Qazelbad and Qul Mohammad...." GRIFFIN at 177–8 (2001). He and others have described in great detail the widespread atrocities committed by the Taliban during their offensive across the Shomali Plain is 1998. *Id.* at 227 (stating that "[s]ix thousand Taliban and their Pakistani allies were allotted the task of clearing the district of Massoud sympathizers, 'killing wantonly, emptying entire towns, machine-gunning livestock, sawing down fruit trees, blasting apart irrigation canals'") (citing THE NEW YORK TIMES, Oct. 19, 1999).

- In an independent account of incidents involving the targeted killings of civilians, another expert wrote that "[a]s the Taliban retreated they massacred at least 70 Shia Hazaras in Qazil Abad...and perhaps hundreds more". RASHID at 62–63. "Fighting continued through the winter months [of 1997–98] in the western province of Faryab, where the Taliban carried out another massacre in January – this time of some 600 Uzbek villagers." *Id.* at 70.

- Journalists and news agencies reported quite recently that the Taliban have continued to engage in the unlawful killing of civilians in plain violation of the laws of war. The Taliban "may have systematically killed more than 500 civilians following their recapture of an area in central Afghanistan last month, travelers from the area said." *Taliban Killed Hundreds of Afghans*, REUTERS, Feb. 19, 2001. "[W]itnesses and international aid workers in the region have provided detailed accounts of the mass killings, in which Taliban troops were repeatedly described as rounding up unarmed men and boys from their homes and work sites and shooting them in the head." Pamela Constable, *Rights Groups Say Taliban Forces Killed Civilians*, THE WASHINGTON POST, Feb. 19, 2001, at A25.

- Similar incidents are reflected in U.S. Government publications on the Taliban. The Department of State has reported that the Taliban "massacred hundreds of Afghan civilians, including women and children, in Yakaoloang, Mazar-I-Sharif, Bamiyan, Qezelbad, and other towns." *Fact Sheet: Taliban Actions Imperil Afghan Civilians* (Nov. 2, 2001) (visited March 6, 2002) <http://www.usinfo.state.gov/topical/pol/terror/01110203.htm> (describing each massacre, with citations to independent non-governmental sources, including Human Rights watch and Amnesty International). For example, "[t]here were reports that as many as 5,000 persons, mostly ethnic Hazara civilians, were massacred by the Taliban after the takeover of Mazar-i-Sharif." *U.S. Department of State Country Reports on Human Rights Practices – Afghanistan 2000* at sec. 1(g) (Feb. 2001).

- The Taliban routinely failed in its attacks to discriminate between, military objectives and civilians, as required under the law of armed conflict. *See, e.g.,* PROTOCOL I, ARTICLE 51(4) ("Indiscriminate attacks are prohibited."). According to the State Department, the Taliban was a party to fighting characterized by "sporadic and indiscriminate shelling and bombing." *U.S. Dep't of State Human Rights Report at* sec. 1 (Feb. 2001). "Taliban forces were responsible for indiscriminate bombardment of civilian areas." *Id.* "The Taliban's aerial bombing of civilian areas has resulting [sic] in the deaths of civilians, property damage, and the displacement of residents." *Id.* at 1(g).

- The State Department also reported that in response to the U.S. and coalition bombing in the present conflict, "[t]he Taliban have put the Afghan civilian population in grave danger by deliberately hiding their soldiers and equipment in civilian areas, including mosques." *See Fact Sheet: Taliban Actions Imperil Afghan Civilians.*

- The State Department also publicized reports by *The Washington Post* that the Taliban was using entire villages as human shields to protect their stockpiles of ammunition and weapons, that they were relocating the police ministry in Kandahar to mosques, that they had taken over humanitarian relief organization buildings, and that they were discovered transporting tanks and mortar shells in the guise of humanitarian relief. *Fact Sheet: The Taliban's Betrayal of the Afghan People* (Nov. 6, 2001) (visited Mar. 6, 2002) <http://www.usinfo.state.gov/topical/pol/terror/01110608>. Such conduct violates the laws and customs of war, as reflected, for example, in Article 51(7) of Protocol I, which states that "[t]he presence or movements of the civilian population or individual civilians shall not be used to render certain points or areas immune from military operations, in particular attempts to shield military objectives from attacks or to shield, favour [sic] or impede military operations...." *See also, e.g.,* PROTOCOL I, ARTICLE 53 (prohibiting use of cultural objects in support of military); PROTOCOL I, ARTICLE 57 (requiring combatants to take care to "spare" the civilian population, civilians, and civilian objects").
- The Taliban militia also violated the laws and customs of war by torturing and summarily executing prisoners in plain violation of the most basic principles of civilized nations. Summary justice and torture of detained persons in wartime is impermissible. *See, e.g.,* GPW common ARTICLE 3 (prohibiting torture and "at any time and in any place whatsoever... the passing of sentences and the carrying out of executions without previous judgment pronounced by a regularly constituted court affording all the judicial guarantees which are recognized as indispensable by civilized peoples").
- In this case, there have been reports. (denied by the Taliban) "of summary executions of prisoners by the Taliban forces in conflict areas." *U.S. Dep't of State Human Rights Report* at sec. 1(a). The Taliban "carried out summary justice in the areas they controlled" and "Taliban militiamen often judged accused offenders and meted out punishments, such as beatings, on the spot." *Id.* at intro. "In 1998 the Taliban reportedly executed as many as 189 prisoners it captured during fighting near Mazar-I-Sharif in order to avoid exchanging them with the Northern Alliance." *Id.* at 1(a) (acknowledging that the Taliban denied these and other allegations, and noting that the Taliban has not conducted any investigations). "The Taliban is believed to have used torture against opponents and POWs." *Id.* at 1(c).
- In one instance, it is alleged that foreign Taliban soldiers "gunned down more than 400 Afghan Taliban soldiers trying to defect to the Northern Alliance", rather than detain and punish such defectors in accordance with the laws and customs of war, i.e., by proper court-martial. *See* Dexter Filkins, *Foes Claim Taliban Are Killing Soldiers Who Seek to Defect,* THE NEW YORK TIMES, Nov, 19, 2001.
- These accounts are consistent with the independent reporting of prominent human rights groups. For example, Amnesty International publicly condemned the Taliban's reported summary execution of Abdul Haq and others on October 26, 2001. Public Statement, Amnesty International, AI Index ASA 11/025/2001 (Oct. 30, 2001) (stating that the 1949 Geneva Conventions prohibits murder and that prisoners "must be treated humanely and should not be executed") (visited Mar. 6, 2002) <http://web.amnesty.org/ai.nsf/Index/ASA110252001?OpenDocument&of=COUNTRIES/AFGHANISTAN>. In an earlier incident at Yakaolong, Amnesty International reported that "[f]or several days [Taliban] forces massacred [or summarily executed] over 300 unarmed men and a number of civilian women and children." *Id.* at AI Index ASA 11/008/2001 (Jan. 3, 2001). According to Human Rights Watch, "Taliban forces subjected local civilians to a ruthless and systematic policy of collective punishment,

Summary executions, the deliberate destruction of homes, and confiscation of farmland were recurrent practices...." 2001 Afghanistan Report (visited Mar. 6, 2002) <http://hrw.org/wr2k2/asial.html>.

- The United Nations has made similar observations. The U.N. Security Council has expressed "its deep concern over the continuing violations of international humanitarian law [i.e., laws and customs of war]...." *See* U.N. Sec. Council Res. 1333, U.N. Doc. S/RES/1333 (2000); U.N. Sec. Council Res. 1267, U.N. Doc. S/RES/1267 (1999) ("Reiterating its deep concern over the continuing violations of international humanitarian law and of human rights, ... and stressing that the capture by the Taliban of the Consulate-General of the Islamic Republic of Iran and the murder of Iranian diplomats and a journalist in Mazar-i-Sharif constituted flagrant violations of established international law, ...").
- In 1999, the President of the U.N. Security Council stated:

> The Security Council deplores the worsening human rights situation in Afghanistan. It expresses particular alarm at the continuing disregard by the Taliban of the concerns expressed by the international community. The Council underlines the unacceptability of the forced displacement of the civilian population, in particular that conducted by the Taliban during their recent offensive, summary executions, the deliberate abuse and arbitrary detentions of civilians, violence and continuing discrimination against women and girls, the separation of men from their families, the use of child soldiers, the widespread burning of crops and destruction of homes, the indiscriminate bombing and other violations of human rights [sic] international humanitarian law in Afghanistan.
>
> *Statement by the President of the Security Council*, U.N. Doc. No. S/PRST/1999/29 (Oct. 22, 1999)

- The United Nations has accused the Taliban of waging a "scorched earth war" and systematically violating international humanitarian law. GRIFFIN at 227–28 (citing INTERNATIONAL HERALD TRIBUNE, Aug. 16, 1998).
- The U.N. Secretary General stated:

> This pattern of warfare – international abuse of civilians coupled with the destruction of their property – has characterized the latest bout of fighting in the Shomali plains north of Kabul.... The separation of men from families, arbitrary detention, violence against women, the use of child soldiers, indiscriminate bombing and use of landmines continue to add to the dismal human rights record of Afghanistan.
>
> Report of the Secretary General, *The Situation in Afghanistan and its Implications for International peace and Security*, U.N. Doc. No. S/1999/994 (Sept. 21, 1999)

- In a similar report from a year earlier, the Secretary General condemned the Taliban for its alleged role in the killing of two U.N. aid workers, and in a separate incident, the killing of eleven Iranian diplomats. Report of the Secretary General, *The Situation in Afghanistan and its Implications for International Peace and Security*, U.N. Doc. No. S/1998/913 (Oct. 2, 1998). The Secretary General also expressed concerns regarding unconfirmed reports that Taliban forces were responsible for massacring as many as 2,000 people following the battle at Mazar-e-Sharif. *Id.*
- These independent sources provide strong support for the president's conclusion that the Taliban flagrantly violated the laws and customs of war, failed to wear insignia or otherwise distinguish itself from civilians, and had inadequate military command.

Under these circumstances, the Taliban does not meet the Article 4 criteria for groups entitled to POW status.

- As discussed at greater length in the next section, the failure of the group as a whole or collectively to meet the four conditions makes it difficult for any of its individual members to qualify independently for POW status. *See, e.g.,* LEVIE at 52–53 (citations omitted). Thus, only by complying generally with the preconditions may the group as a whole bring its members presumptively within the provisions of Article 4.

- Although the United States may choose to extend POW protections even to those forces that fail to meet the Article 4 criteria, the President has sound policy reasons for not doing so in this case. To extend POW status to the Taliban in this case would have the unacceptable effect of removing a strong disincentive to those who would choose to flout the laws and customs of war and support terrorist organizations such as al Qaeda.

- In this case, the Taliban harbored and supported al Qaeda's unlawful terrorist objectives. *See, e.g., Statement by* Taliban ambassador to Pakistan, M. Zaeef, Oct. 1, 2001 (admitting that "Osama bin Laden is under our control," but refusing to reveal his whereabouts); *Statement by* Taliban senior leader, M. Omar, Oct. 18, 2001 (indicating support for al Qaeda objectives). To make matters worse, the Taliban ignored the repeated demands of the U.N. Security Council that they stop harboring known terrorists and turn over Osama bin Laden "to appropriate authorities without further delay". *See* U.N. Sec. Council Res. 1373, U.N. Doc. S/RES/1373 (2001); U.N. Sec. Council Res. 1333, U.N. Doc. S/RES/1333 (2000); U.N. Sec. Council Res. 1267, U.N. Doc. S/RES/1267 (1999).

- The war on terrorism necessarily involves bringing to justice those who, like the Taliban, violate the laws and customs of war and support and harbor terrorists, thereby allowing them to commit horrific acts such as those on September 11. *See generally* President Bush remarks to the press, Nov. 21, 2001 ("America has a message for the nations of the world. If you harbor terrorists, you are terrorists. If you train or arm a terrorist, you are a terrorist. If you feed a terrorist or fund a terrorist, you're a terrorist, and you will be held accountable by the United States and our friends."); *see also* President Bush's Military Order, Nov. 13, 2001 (permitting the President to designate for trial by military commission those individuals who harbor and support terrorists).

VI. THE PRESIDENT HAS MADE PROPER GROUP DETERMINATIONS REGARDING POW STATUS, CONSISTENT WITH GPW ARTICLES 4 AND 5, AND THE DETAINEES ARE RECEIVING PROTECTIONS CONSISTENT WITH ARTICLE 5.

- Article 5 of the GPW provides:

  "Should any doubt arise as to whether persons, having committed a belligerent act and having fallen into the hands of the enemy, belong to any of the categories enumerated in Article 4, such persons shall enjoy the *protection* of the present Convention *until* such time as their status has been determined by a competent tribunal" [emphasis added].

- The negotiating record and subsequent commentaries suggest that the drafters of the 1949 Geneva Conventions intended, by operation of Article 5, "to avoid arbitrary decisions by a local commander, who may be of a very low rank. He may be a corporal and we do not want a corporal deciding on the life or death of any human being." Statement by the Representative of the Netherlands, FINAL RECORD OF THE DIPLOMATIC CONFERENCE OF GENEVA OF 1949, Vol. II., Sec. B, 13th Plenary meeting at 270 (1949). "This rule, which has been applied e.g. by the United States in Vietnam and by Israel in the Middle East, removes the risk of arbitrary decision on the part of individual commanders and creates at least the possibility of a duly considered decision." FRITZ KALSHOVEN AND LIESBETH ZEGVELD, CONSTRAINTS ON THE WAGING OF WAR 53 (2001) ("An Introduction to International Humanitarian Law," written for use in legal training by the ICRC).

- In this case, the decision on status was not based upon the arbitrary opinion of an individual commander. The decision in this case was neither arbitrary nor low-level. Rather, the President himself made the decision based upon a careful analysis involving his most senior advisers. The deliberative process in this case occurred at the highest levels of the Executive Branch of the United States Government. This was a process consistent with the drafters' intent to avoid arbitrary and low-level decision-making on questions of status.

- Article 5 was designed to deal with the problems experienced in World War II, and it significantly improved the 1929 Geneva Convention on POWs. The original text for Article 5 proposed at the 1949 Diplomatic Conference would have accorded the "benefit" rather than "protection" of the Convention in cases of doubt. However, the final text of Article 5 focuses on the humanitarian *protections* of the GPW, as opposed to its *benefits or privileges* (as might have been the case if the text originally proposed had been adopted in 1949).

- The GPW *protections* are contained in Part II of the GPW, entitled "General Protection of Prisoners of War." They include respect for the persons and honor of POWs, and protection against intimidation and against insults and public curiosity and reprisals. These protections are distinct from the privileges and benefits accorded under the GPW, such as respect for rank, pay, and traditional courtesies by members of the military to others in the profession of arms, including soldiers of a defeated enemy. *See, e.g., Comments of the Denmark Delegation*, Volume IIA, Committee II, Special Committee, 7th Mtg. at 433 (noting in a related context "that it was not a question of granting the persons referred to in the paragraph the same rights and privileges as those of prisoners of war, but simply affording them 'a minimum of protection.'").

- The United States is providing protections consistent with Article 5. It is providing the protections of the GPW (i.e., those enumerated in Part II) to all those in detention. *See id.* (quoting the representative of Denmark, who noted that providing a minimum of protections, as opposed to the rights and privileges of POWs, is a matter of "simply preventing such persons from being subjected to inhuman treatment or summarily shot").

- As previously discussed, the United States is providing humane treatment in accordance with customary international law and consistent with common Article 3, GCC Articles 27–34, Protocol I Article 75, and Protocol II Articles 4 and 6. Such protections satisfy Article 5.

- Article 5 by its terms does not require the convening of a tribunal to make a factual determination on whether or not all captured individuals are entitled to prisoner of war protection, treatment, or status. Rather, it provides that the protections are to be provided in cases of doubt, until a contrary decision is made by a competent tribunal.

- In this case, the detainees currently are enjoying the GPW protections. The United states is protecting them from insults, public curiosity, and reprisals. The United States is affording them humane treatment consistent with the general principles of the GPW. They are being provided three culturally sensitive meals a day, shelter, clothing and shoes, showers, sleeping pads and blankets, and excellent medical care.

- They also are receiving additional privileges, including the use of toiletries, laundered towels and washcloths, the ability to send and receive mail (including packages of food and clothing, subject to security measures), the opportunity to visit individually and privately with the ICRC, and the chance to worship freely with the assistance of a Muslim chaplain provided by the U.S. Navy.

- The detainees will continue to enjoy these protections and privileges, consistent with Article 5 and the general principles of the GPW. Article 5 requires nothing more.

- Critics of the U.S. approach have argued that the President was wrong not to convene an Article 5 tribunal in each individual case. Under U.S. Army procedures, such a tribunal normally would be comprised of three army officers. *See* U.S. ARMY FIELD MANUAL 27-10 at para, 71(c). In this case, the President convened the U.S. National Security Council and consulted the expertise of his most senior advisors before making a decision on status. This level and degree of attention exceeds the type of attention envisaged by the drafters of Article 5 in 1949.

- Moreover, the President's decision to deal initially with groups, versus individuals, is consistent with the GPW, state practice and the negotiators' intent.

- In World War II, the United States, its allies, and enemy nations all made group status determinations as a routine matter. LEVIE at 61. Likewise, the U.S. and its allies made collective decisions on POWs in Korea and Vietnam, although Article 5 tribunals were established in Vietnam to deal with individual cases of doubt. *See, e.g.*, Adam Roberts, *Counter-terrorism, Armed Force and the Laws of War*, 44 SURVIVAL no. 1, 23–24 (Spring 2002) (discussing the U.S. cases involving the Viet Cong "irregulars"; noting that they would not be entitled to POW status if engaged in terrorism, sabotage, or spying). In the Gulf War, the U.S. also convened tribunals to deal with every individual detainee.

- Group determinations, however, are not uncommon and consistent with past practice by other states as well. The French in Algeria in the 1960s and the United Kingdom in Northern Ireland with respect to the IRA both have made sweeping legal decisions that affected the legal status of detainees as a group, without regard to any given individual's circumstances. In these cases, proper decisions were made that the conflict was internal and not international and therefore, that POW status, which exists as a matter of law only in international armed conflicts, was not available to any group under the GPW, regardless of the analysis under Article 4 criteria.

- Articles 2 and 4 in fact compel Detaining Powers to make certain determinations that necessarily affect groups as a whole. For example, a Detaining Power must decide whether a given group *as a whole ("collectively")* is a High Contracting Party under Article 2. Such a decision necessarily affects whether an individual belonging to the group is entitled to status, regardless of his or her individual situation. Additionally, individual status determinations under Article 4 may turn initially on whether groups have adequate command structure and follow the laws and customs of war. In the words of a prominent Swiss scholar on the law of war:

> These conditions concern the movement as a whole and individual violations of these rules [do] not deprive its members of their protection. Those who violate these principles are responsible for this violence. On the contrary, if the movement itself does not respect those conditions, any member of this movement, even if he personally

respects the rules, does not receive the benefits of privileged treatment...the fundamental principles of the law of war exclude the terrorist activities. This prohibition is based on the lack of distinction between legitimate and illegitimate attacks.

DR. JIRI TOMAN, former deputy director of the Henri Dunant Institute, *quoted in* ERICKSON at 79–80 (1989)

- "According to the accepted view, if the group does not meet the first three criteria (organization, association with a party to the conflict, and military command), the individual member cannot qualify for privileged status as a POW." Mallison and Mallison, *supra*, at 62 (citing Draper, *The Status of Combatants and the Question of Guerilla Warfare*, 45 Brit. Y.B. Int' I L. 172, 196 (1973)). "The last three criteria (distinctive sign, open arms, and adhering the laws and customs) must be met by both the group as a whole and the individual member to entitle the latter to POW status." *Id.* (citing Draper).
- Thus, if the group as a whole has the policy and practice of complying with the laws and customs of war, individuals within the group, even those who may have violated the laws and customs of war, are presumptively entitled to POW status providing the other requirements are met. *See, e.g.*, THE UNITED STATES ARMY FIELD MANUAL at para. 64 (stating that Article 4A(2) (d) is presumptively fulfilled "if most of the members of the body observe the laws and customs of war, notwithstanding the fact that the individual member concerned may have committed a war crime").
- It follows that where most of the members of the group do not wear distinctive uniforms or observe the laws and customs of war, the group as a whole does not meet the requirement of Article 4A(2) (d). The failure of the group as a whole or collectively to meet the four conditions makes it difficult for any of its individual members to qualify independently for POW status. LEVIE at 52–53 (citations omitted); *see also* TOMAN in ERICKSON at 79–80. Thus, only by complying generally with the preconditions may the group as a whole bring its members presumptively within the scope of Article 4.
- In this case, al Qaeda and the Taliban fail as groups to meet the Article 4 requirements and therefore, there is a presumption against POW status for members of these groups. Although other countries may contend that captured individuals in an international armed conflict generally have a presumption of POW status under Article 45 of Protocol I, the United States is not a party to this treaty. In this connection, Article 45 clearly was new law in 1977 and did not purport to reflect customary international law. However, even if Protocol I were applicable, the facts in this case demonstrate overwhelmingly that these detainees have not met the Article 43 and 44 criteria.
- The United States is, of course, bound by Article 5 in situations where the GPW applies, and notwithstanding the appropriateness of a group determination in particular situations, the longstanding view of the U.S. armed forces has been that the Detaining Power should establish competent tribunals in all cases of doubt involving specific individuals. The President's decision in this case is consistent with that view.
- Here, there is no genuine doubt regarding the proper status of any detainee in Guantanamo. The President has made carefully reasoned and proper group determinations for the Taliban and al Qaeda, consistent with Article 4. *See supra*, Sections III and V.
- Although not an Article 5 process as such, the U.S. has a careful process in place to screen the detainees taken to Guantanamo. The detainees were screened individually at least twice before they were transferred. They were screened by U.S. armed forces before they were taken to Qandahar, and they were interviewed a second time in

Qandahar. Although U.S. screening under Article 5 historically has been done by a tribunal comprised of three army officers (e.g., as in the cases of Vietnam and the Gulf War, under para. 71(c) of U.S. Army Field Manual 27-10), the double screening here appears to be equally, if not more, rigorous than the single field-screening process used by the U.S. during the 1983 Rescue Operation in Grenada. *See* DIGEST, U.S. PRACTICE at 3455 ("Determination of precise status is accomplished through screening by the capturing or detaining unit commander; in this case, the U.S. Army ground force commander.")

- That said, the United States will also revisit its Article 4 determinations should any genuine doubt about status arise in individual cases. Statement by U.S. Dept. of State Spokesperson Richard Boucher, U.S. Department of State press briefing (Feb. 8, 2002). This is consistent with past U.S. practice, as well as Article 5.
- This could be accomplished using various types of tribunals. Ultimately, the issue of status could be addressed in an administrative hearing or a criminal proceeding convened for other purposes, such as a war crimes prosecution. *See, e.g.,* Roberts, 44 SURVIVAL at 23 ("The possibilities that the proceedings could take place *after* a trial for an offence [sic], and also *in camera* in the interest of state security, are not excluded." (emphasis in original)). As the ICRC has indicated, an Article 5 tribunal can be administrative in nature or a military commission. *See* COMMENTARY ON THE PROTOCOLS at 551–52.
- Historically, courts also have made POW determinations because individual defendants charged with common crimes have made motions claiming such status and courts have had to decide on such motions. Article 5 was proposed largely because decisions on status could have the greatest of consequences due to the fact that "persons taking part in the fight without the right to do so are liable to be prosecuted for murder or attempted murder, and might even be sentenced to capital punishment." PICTET at 77.
- In the United States, individuals on criminal trial in federal courts have claimed rights to POW status and ultimately had their claims addressed and decided in U.S: District Court. *See, e.g., U.S. v. Morales,* 464 F. Supp. 325 (1979) (denying POW status to individuals allegedly fighting for Puerto Rican independence); *U.S. v. Shakur,* 690 F. Supp. 1291 (S.D.N.Y. 1988) (denying POW status to bank robbers allegedly fighting for political independence); *U.S. v. Noriega,* 808 F. Supp. 791 (S.D. Fla. 1992) (granting POW status to member of Panamanian military).
- In any case and regardless of how an individual's status ultimately is determined, the fact remains that the United States is complying with Article 5 by providing the GPW protections to those in detention and will revisit individual cases should any doubt arise.

VII.   COMMON ARTICLE 3 OF THE GPW DOES NOT APPLY BY ITS TERMS
       TO EITHER THE ARMED CONFLICT INVOLVING THE UNITED STATES
       BECAUSE THE CONFLICTS ARE NOT INTERNAL CONFLICTS;
       STANDARDS EQUIVALENT TO THOSE IN COMMON ARTICLE 3
       DO APPLY AT A MINIMIM TO THE CONFLICTS UNDER
       CUSTOMARY INTERNATIONAL LAW.

- Common Article 3, by its express terms, applies only "[i]n the case of armed conflict *not of an international character* occurring in the territory of one of the High Contracting Parties..." [emphasis added]. This generally refers to civil wars.

- However, it is widely recognized internationally for example by the United Nations, the International Court of Justice, the International Criminal Tribunal for the Former Yugoslavia, and the International Criminal Tribunal for Rwanda, that common Article 3 reflects customary international law standards for both internal and international armed conflicts. As indicated at Section I, *supra*, the United States is adhering to the customary international law standards which reflect common Article 3 protections.
- That said, the United States has interpreted the plain language of the GPW as limiting common Article 3 application to "internal" conflicts. U.S. BACKGROUND PAPERS & ANALYSIS at 3–4 (citing the Committee report and stating that GPW Article 3 is intended to deal "[e]ssentially with civil wars").
- In this case, the conflicts with al Qaeda and the Taliban are not covered under common Article 3 because, as recognized by the United Nations and NATO, these conflicts are not internal. With respect to the Taliban, the United States is engaged in an international armed conflict.
- In the case of al Qaeda, the conflict is unquestionably global in nature. Al Qaeda has committed terrorist atrocities of a shocking magnitude against U.S. personnel and citizens and the citizens of its allies in multiple countries, including for example Kenya, Tanzania, Yemen, and America. Thus, as non-internal conflicts, they are not covered by the express terms of Common Article 3.

VIII. THE DETAINEES ARE RECEIVING PROTECTIONS CONSISTENT WITH THE *GENEVA CONVENTION RELATIVE TO THE PROTECTION OF CIVILIAN PERSONS IN TIME OF WAR OF AUGUST 12, 1949* (GCC) EVEN THOUGH THE PRESIDENT HAS DETERMINED THAT THEY ARE UNLAWFUL COMBATANTS. THE DETAINEES DO NOT FALL PRECISELY WITHIN THE DEFINITIONS OF THE GENEVA CONVENTIONS. THOSE INDIVIDUALS CURRENTLY IN DETENTION ARE NOT "PROTECTED PERSONS" UNDER THE DEFINITIONS OF THE GCC, BUT WILL CONTINUE TO RECEIVE HUMANE TREATMENT CONSISTENT WITH THE GCC AND IN ACCORDANCE WITH CUSTOMARY INTERNATIONAL LAW.

- The European Parliament recently adopted a resolution recognizing that the United States finds itself in what the European Parliament deemed to be an "uncharted legal limbo." Specifically, the European Parliament "agrees that the prisoners . . . do not fall precisely within the definitions of the Geneva Convention. . . ." *See Euro. Parliament Res.*, B5-0066/2002 (Feb. 7, 2002); *see also*, H. Lauterpacht, *The Problem of the Revision of the Law of War* 1952 BRIT. Y.B. INT'L L. 360, 380 ("For the Conventions, beneficent as they are, abound in gaps, compromises, obscurities, and somewhat nominal provisions resulting from the inability of the parties to achieve an agreed effective solution. . . ."); Roberts, 44 SURVIVAL at 27 ("Events in Afghanistan have confirmed that there are particular difficulties in applying the laws of war to anti-terrorist operations. [This war] . . . involves many awkward issues for which the existing laws of war are not a perfect fit.").
- Notwithstanding the legal ambiguities, the President has decided to apply traditional Geneva Convention principles to the new and difficult set of circumstances in the war on terrorism. The war against terrorism is a new kind of war. It is neither large-scale conflict between two nation-states nor a civil or internal war between a nation-state and an insurgent or rebel group. In this war, global terrorists transcend

national boundaries, owe no loyalties to any country and intentionally target innocent civilians by perfidious means.

- Rather than dismiss the Conventions as inapplicable or out of date, the President has invoked them as a guide in this difficult time. He is applying their general principles in a way that affords all the detainees, regardless of status, basic protections consistent with customary international law.

- As indicated by the President's Press Secretary Ari Fleischer on February 8, 2002, the President "believes in the principles and the law of the Geneva Convention; he believes in its importance; he believes that [it] plays a role even in today's modern world where the applicability gets somewhat more complicated as a result of an international terrorist organization that doesn't wear uniforms or insignias."

- The President's approach is consistent with the Geneva Conventions, the customary international law, and the ICRC view that "the rules for armed conflict are not static; on the contrary, they must be adapted to a constantly changing world by means of appropriate modifications." COMMENTARY ON THE ADDITIONAL PROTOCOLS at 521; *see also* Euro. Parliament Res., B5-0066/2002 (agreeing that "the standards set out in [the Geneva Conventions] must be revised to respond to the new situations created by the development of international terrorism"). In this case, the President has adapted the U.S. approach to fit new and difficult circumstances, while continuing to provide humane treatment, consistent with the general principles of the Geneva Conventions.

- The question has been raised as to whether the Geneva Convention on the Protection of Civilian Persons (GCC) applies to the conflict in Afghanistan and whether those in detention fall within its definition of "protected persons."

- This question is largely academic because the President is applying the principles and protections of the GPW (i.e., the Convention on POWs as opposed to the one on civilians). Its provisions are essentially the same as those contained in Parts II and III of the Fourth Convention (e.g., humane treatment, and freedom from insults, coercion, murder, etc). To conclude that GCC does or does not apply would in effect make no difference in terms of the protections provided to those individuals currently in custody.

- It bears noting, however, that the legal standard for the applicability of the GCC is contained in common Article 2 of that Convention, and it is thus identical to the standard for applying the GPW. The practical effect of common Article 2 is that whenever one of the four Geneva Conventions applies, so do the others. In this case, since the President has stated that the GPW applies to the conflict with the Taliban, the logical implication is that the same is true with respect to the GCC.

- Unlike the other three 1949 Geneva Conventions which had existed as 1929 Geneva Conventions, the GCC was completely new in 1949. The GCC was designed to fill a specific gap in the law of war that became evident during World War II, i.e., that civilians who did not participate in hostilities or who occasionally committed hostile acts against an occupying Power had virtually no legal protections.

- It is clear from the negotiating record that the GCC was never intended to provide protections to armies or organized military forces, including unlawful combatants, that engaged in sustained or systematic combat activities.

- For example, the representative of the ICRC stated during the negotiations that the 1949 Diplomatic Conference was engaged in the framing of one Convention to protect members of the armed forces and similar categories of persons, and another Convention to protect civilians. The ICRC representative pointed out that "although the two conventions might appear to cover all the categories concerned, irregular belligerents were not actually protected." Vol. IIA Final Record of the Diplomatic Conference of Geneva of 1949 at 622. Indeed, he pointed out that "it was an open question whether it was desirable to give protections to persons who did not conform to the laws and customs of war...." *Id.*

- Similar views were stated by several prominent delegations. For example, the representative of the United Kingdom stated that "the whole conception of the Civilians Convention was the protection of civilian victims of war and not the protection of illegitimate bearers of arms." *Id.* at 621. The representative of Switzerland pointed out that "in regard to those who violated the laws of war, the [Civilians] Convention could not of course cover criminals or saboteurs." *Id.* The representative of the Netherlands took a similar view. He pointed out that to conclude that individuals who are not prisoner of war under Article 4 of the GPW "are automatically protected by other Conventions is certainly untrue. The Civilians Convention, for instance, deals only with civilians under certain circumstances; such as civilians in an occupied country or civilians who are living in a belligerent country, *but it certainly does not protect civilians who are in the battlefield, the adverse party.*" *Id.*, Vol. IIB, at 271 (emphasis added).

- The United States long ago took the position that the GCC was intended to address the circumstances of peaceful civilians, as opposed to unlawful combatants. U.S. BACKGROUND PAPERS AND ANALYSIS at Tab A, p. 2 ("The terrible suffering undergone by the peaceful population during World War II pointed to the need for a treaty which would spell out with particularity the rights and privileges of the populations of occupied areas, civilians who had been interned (who previously had been assimilated in a rather rough and ready way to prisoners of war), and to the peaceful population generally, wherever they might be."); *see also S.* EXEC. REP. NO. 84-9 at 5 (1st Sess. 1995) (noting that the Geneva Conventions were not intended to protect any partisan civilian "who performs the role of farmer by day, guerilla by night").

- The negotiating history and subsequent U.S. Government analysis of the GCC indicate that it was never intended to afford rights or privileges to unprivileged combatants engaged in "unlawful belligerency". Enemy combatants who organize and take up arms to wage war have no claim to the protections of the GCC. Rather, combatants of whatever category, lawful or unlawful, are governed by the principles of the GPW.

- This was the United States' position in 1949, as reflected in the negotiating history of the GCC:

> Certain delegations wished to extend the application of the [GCC] to cover still other categories of persons. They had particularly in mind civilians who had taken up arms to defend their life, their health, their livelihood, under an attack which violated the laws and conditions of war.... Numerous possible solutions of this problem were carefully considered but in the end a majority of the Committee came to the conclusion that it would be difficult to take the course proposed without the risk of indirectly weakening the protection afforded to persons coming under the various categories of Article 3. One delegation pointed out, in particular, that the acceptance of the proposed extension would be tantamount to rejecting the principles generally accepted at the Hague, and recognized in the Prisoner of War Convention. *It was, according to the views of this delegation, essential that war, even illegal war, should be governed by those [GPW] principles....*
>
> *See U.S.* BACKGROUND PAPERS AND ANALYSIS at 4–7 (referring to the understanding of the U.S. delegation) (emphasis added).

- On the other hand, there has been substantial support for the view that any captured persons who are not covered by the GPW are protected persons under the GCC. There are thus two schools of thought on the meaning of the terms of the conventions.
- For example, the ICRC stated in 1958, that "every person in enemy hands must have some status under international law; he is either a prisoner of war and, as such covered by the [GPW], a civilian covered by the [GCC], or again, a member of the medical personnel of the armed forces who is covered by the First Convention. There is no intermediate status." *See* PICTET COMMENTARY IV 51 (1958).
- The authoritative U.S. Army Field Manual 27-10 on the Law of Land Warfare appears to take the same position. *See* paras. 73, 247b. As indicated above, however, the negotiating record of the Convention strongly suggests otherwise. The negotiating record is supported by the work of many scholars who also have acknowledged the existence of gaps in the Geneva Conventions.
- Scholars have recognized that international humanitarian law "... defines categories of individuals to whom it grants specific rights and protection ... [and as a result] certain individuals may not receive adequate protection if the actors in a conflict do not recognize them as belonging to one of the categories of protected persons." FRANÇOISE BOUCHET-SAULNIER, THE PRACTICAL GUIDE TO HUMANITARIAN LAW 302 (2002). In order to protect the individuals who do not fall neatly into any of the categories, the drafters established "certain fundamental guarantees that are applicable to all individuals in times of conflict." *Id.*
- Some of the most prominent European scholars have noted that "the [GCC] is more narrow than it would appear at first glance." ROSAS at 412; *see also* KALSHOVEN and ZEGVELD at 52 ("In spite of its sweeping title, it is neither intended to protect civilians from the dangers of warfare ... to which they may be exposed in their own territory nor does it offer them protection against the acts of their own State of nationality."). The reason is that there are separate provisions on the treatment of (1) aliens in the territory of a party to the conflict and (2) on protected persons in occupied territory, and (3) "provisions *common to these two categories*." ROSAS at 412. "These provisions seem to be based on the assumption that protected persons are *either* foreign civilians who are *in the territory of a party to the conflict* when hostilities break out *or* civilians who are in occupied territory. . . . This has lead some experts to the conclusion that the status of combatants who do not fulfill the conditions of article 4 of the Third Convention in the zone of operations was not taken into account in the drafting of the Fourth Convention." *See id.* (emphasis in original); *cf.* F. Kalshoven, *The Position of Guerrilla Fighters under the Law of War*, 11 MIL. L. & L. OF WAR REV. 55, 70–71 (1972) (adopting the same narrow view).
- The Senate Foreign Relations Committee apparently also took this narrow view of the GCC during the 1955 ratification process on the Geneva Conventions. *See* S. EXEC. REP. No. 84-9 at 2 ("... a new Convention [the GCC] was drawn up at the Geneva Convention in 1949, which spells out to a degree never before attempted the obligations of the parties to furnish humanitarian treatment to two broad categories of civilians: enemy aliens present within the home territory of a belligerent, and civilian persons found in territory which it occupies in the course of military operations").
- It thus appears difficult to reconcile the inclusive position taken in the U.S. Army Field Manual in 1956 and the view of the U.S. Senate and of the negotiators and scholars cited above. However, it also appears that the position taken by the U.S. Army in its 1956 Field Manual was made on the basis of the desire and operational need to

provide clear guidance to troops in the field to eliminate gaps in practice, rather than on the basis that such a result was legally compelled.

- In any event, the situation in 1956 was very different from the situation that exists today. At the time the Field Manual was written, it was probably not contemplated that armed civilian terrorists would be able to pose a global threat of the kind that now exists. *See, e.g.*, Roberts, 44 SURVIVAL at 7 ("...in anti-terrorist military operations, certain phases and situations may well be different from what was envisaged in the main treaties on the laws of war.") Groups such as al Qaeda, a well-organized, international, and extensive network of well-trained terrorists committed to systematic attacks against the civilian population did not exist, nor is it likely that such forces were then foreseen. In 1956, soon after ratification of the four Geneva Conventions of 1949, it may have made good military sense to treat unlawful belligerents as civilians rather than as combatants for purposes of guidance to soldiers in the field. This is not the case today.

- One reason for this conclusion is that even if the United States were to choose to treat the detainees as civilians for purposes of the GCC, it still is not clear that they would be entitled to "protected person" status. Article 4 of the GCC defines "protected persons" (with some exceptions) as "those who, at any given moment and in any manner whatsoever, find themselves, in case of a conflict or occupation, in the hands of a party to the conflict or Occupying Power of which they are not nationals." Article 4 excludes from the definition of "protected persons" those who are nationals of neutral states or nationals of co-belligerent states, if normal diplomatic relations exist between their own states and the detaining state.

- Almost all of the detainees in Guantanamo are nationals of countries with which the United States has normal diplomatic relations. As such, they do not fall within the definition of "protected persons" under the GCC. Indeed, they were captured in a foreign combat zone and not in occupied territory. They were not captured in the United States. As indicated above, it is widely recognized that only individuals who fall into enemy hands in occupied territory or the enemy's territory are protected persons for purposes of the GCC.

- As indicated at the outset of this section, the issue of whether the GCC applies is largely academic because all of the detainees are being provided the basic protections of the GPW and the GCC. It bears noting, however, that Article 5 of the GCC expressly recognizes that protected persons who are definitely suspected of or engaged in activities hostile to the security of the state are not entitled to claim rights and privileges that might be prejudicial to the security of the state.

- All of the limitations in the text of the GCC and perceived gaps in the Geneva Conventions system led many to believe that the Geneva Conventions system should be revised. *See, e.g.*, Solf and Esgain, *The 1949 Geneva Convention Relative to the Treatment of Prisoners of War: Its Principles, Innovations, and Deficiencies*, 41 N.C. L. REV. 537, 595 (1963) (recognizing positive aspects and deficiencies in the 1949 Geneva Conventions). This view led to the negotiation and adoption of the 1977 Protocols to the Geneva Conventions. As stated previously, Protocol I left unaddressed many important issues, including some that are present in the current war on terrorism.

- For example, experts have noted that ambiguities in the 1949 Geneva Conventions "led the ICRC to study the question of the status and treatment of combatants not fulfilling the conditions of article 4 of the Third Convention." ROSAS at 412. The

ICRC appears to have taken the view in a 1971 report that "all combatants not fulfilling the conditions of article 4 of the [GPW] should, as a minimum, be granted the guarantees of article 3 common to the Geneva Conventions." *Id.*

- As indicated in Section I, the United States has taken this view and is providing the fundamental guarantees of common Article 3, as well as other protections and benefits, to the detainees in Gauntanamo.

IX. UNDER CUSTOMARY INTERNATIONAL LAW AND THE GPW, THE PRESIDENT MAY USE MILITARY COMMISSIONS OR OTHER COURTS TO TRY DETAINESS SUSPECTED OF VIOLATING INTERNATIONAL LAW, INCLUDING THE LAWS AND CUSTOMS OF WAR.

- The longstanding position of the United States is that "there is nothing in international law to prevent the trial and punishment of violators of international rules in time of war." U.S. BACKGROUND PAPERS AND ANALYSIS, Tab C at 5.
- Al Qaeda and Taliban detainees at Guantanamo Bay are unlawful combatants for reasons previously discussed (i.e., al Qaeda has inadequate command structure, fails to wear uniforms, chooses in some cases not to carry arms openly, and systematically flouts the laws and customs of war; and the Taliban has inadequate command structure, fails to wear adequate uniforms, and violates the laws and customs of war).
- Unlawful combatants are not entitled to the protections of the GPW and may be prosecuted for the acts that make their belligerency unlawful. ROSAS at 419 ("Still more important is that persons who are not entitled to prisoner-of-war status are as a rule regarded as unlawful combatants, and can thus be prosecuted for the mere fact of having participated in hostilities."); R. C. HINGORANI, PRISONERS OF WAR 18 (1982) ("The rest of the combatants [i.e., hostile persons who are denied POW status] are considered to be violators of international law or national prescriptions which thus make them liable to arrest and punishment according to the law of the land of the captor State.").
- The U.S. Supreme Court, citing numerous authoritative international sources, shares the view that unlawful combatants "are subject to capture and detention, [as well as] trial and punishment by military tribunals for acts which render their belligerency unlawful." *See* Ex parte Quirin, 317 U.S. at 31 (citing GREAT BRITAIN, WAR OFFICE, MANUAL OF MILITARY, ch. xiv, §§ 445–451; REGOLAMENTO DI SERVIZIO IN GUERRA, § 133, 3 LEGGI E DECRETI DEL REGENO D'ITALIA (1896) 3184; 7 MOORE, DIGEST OF INTERNATIONAL LAW, § 1109; 2 HYDE, INTERNATIONAL LAW, §§ 654, 652; 2 HALLECK, INTERNATIONAL LAW (4th Ed. 1908) § 4; 2 OPPENHEIM, INTERNATIONAL LAW, § 254; HALL, INTERNATIONAL LAW, §§ 127, 135; BATY & MORGAN, WAR, ITS CONDUCT AND LEGAL RESULTS (1915) 172; BLUNTSCHI, DROIT INTERNATIONAL, §§ 570 bis.).
- Trial and punishment of enemy individuals for violations of the laws of war historically has been accomplished by means of military commission, but may also be accomplished by domestic courts, foreign courts, and international tribunals. *See, e.g.,* U.S. BACKGROUND PAPERS AND ANALYSIS, Tab C at 7; *see also* Ex parte Quirin, 317 U.S. at 31 (holding that unlawful combatants who take up arms and commit hostilities can be punished in military commissions as war criminals); *see generally* Application of Yamashita, 327 U.S. 1 (1946) (holding that military commissions may administer a system of military justice during wartime for the trial and punishment of enemy combatants who have violated the laws of war); Eisentrager v. Johnson,

339 U.S. 763 (1950) (holding that military commissions have a well-established juris-diction to try and punish individuals, including members of the armed forces, those directly connected with such forces, or enemy belligerents, prisoners of war, or others charged with violating the laws of war).

- Trying and punishing individuals for war crimes is an internationally accepted and effective method for enforcing the provisions of international law. *See, e.g., The International Military Commission for the Trial of War Criminals at Nuremberg* and the *International Criminal Tribunals in The Hague (for Yugoslavia and Rwanda); see also* U.S. BACKGROUND PAPERS AND ANALYSIS, Tab C at 9. The nationality of victims is not dispositive for purposes of jurisdiction nor is the fact that the prosecuting nation was not at war when the offense occurred. *Id.*

- Military commissions may try and punish individuals for any war crimes, especially grave breaches (of the Geneva Conventions) which include, for example, engaging in willful killing, torture or inhuman treatment including biological experiments, the willful causing of suffering or serious injury, extensive destruction of property not justified by military necessity, compelling prisoners of war to serve in the forces of a hostile power, deprivation of prisoner of war rights, and deprivation of rights of civilians.

- The laws of war in addition forbid such acts as mistreatment of the dead, firing on undefended localities without military significance, use of civilian clothing by troops during battle, the bombardment of hospitals, pillage, etc. *See* U.S. BACKGROUND PAPERS AND ANALYSIS, Tab C at 9.

- The mere act of engaging in hostilities as an unlawful combatant is, without more, a violation of the laws and customs of war. ROSAS at 419 (noting "that persons who are not entitled to prisoner of war status are as a rule regarded as unlawful combatants, and thus can be prosecuted for the mere act of having participated in hostilities"); *see also* COMMENTARY ON THE PROTOCOLS at 383–84 (1987) (noting the traditional legal view that "anyone who violate[s] the four conditions of 1907 [e.g., fixed insignia, uniforms, carrying arms openly, command, respecting the laws and customs of war] [is] a non-privileged combatant, i.e., [ ] a civilian with no right to carry arms").

U.S. Department of Justice
Office of Legal Counsel

Office of the Assistant Attorney General   *Washington, D.C. 20530*

August 1, 2002

MEMORANDUM FOR ALBERTO R. GONZALES COUNSEL TO THE PRESIDENT

RE: Standards of Conduct for Interrogation Under 18 U.S.C. §§ 2340–2340A

You have asked for our Office's views regarding the standards of conduct under the Convention Against Torture and Other Cruel, Inhuman and Degrading Treatment or Punishment as implemented by Sections 2340–2340A of title 18 of the United States Code. As we understand it, this question has arisen in the context of the conduct of interrogations outside of the United States. We conclude below that Section 2340A proscribes acts inflicting, and that are specifically intended to inflict, severe pain or suffering, whether mental or physical. Those acts must be of an extreme nature to rise to the level of torture within the meaning of Section 2340A and the Convention. We further conclude that certain acts may be cruel, inhuman, or degrading, but still not produce pain and suffering of the requisite intensity to fall within Section 2340A's proscription against torture. We conclude by examining possible defenses that would negate any claim that certain interrogation methods violate the statute.

In Part I, we examine the criminal statute's text and history. We conclude that for an act to constitute torture as defined in Section 2340, it must inflict pain that is difficult to endure. Physical pain amounting to torture must be equivalent in intensity to the pain accompanying serious physical injury, such as organ failure, impairment of bodily function, or even death. For purely mental pain or suffering to amount to torture under Section 2340, it must result in significant psychological harm of significant duration, e.g., lasting for months or even years. We conclude that the mental harm also must result from one of the predicate acts listed in the statute, namely: threats of imminent death; threats of infliction of the kind of pain that would amount to physical torture; infliction of such physical pain as a means of psychological torture; use of drugs or other procedures designed to deeply disrupt the senses, or fundamentally alter an individual's personality; or threatening to do any of these things to a third party. The legislative history simply reveals that Congress intended for the statute's definition to track the Convention's definition of torture and the reservations, understandings, and declarations that the United States submitted with its ratification. We conclude that the statute, taken as a whole, makes plain that it prohibits only extreme acts.

In Part II, we examine the text, ratification history, and negotiating history of the Torture Convention. We conclude that the treaty's text prohibits only the most extreme acts by reserving criminal penalties solely for torture and declining to require such penalties for "cruel, inhuman, or degrading treatment or punishment." This confirms our view that the criminal statute penalizes only the most egregious conduct. Executive branch interpretations and representations to the Senate at the time of ratification further confirm that the treaty was intended to reach only the most extreme conduct.

In Part III, we analyze the jurisprudence of the Torture Victims Protection Act, 28 U.S.C. § 1350 note (2000), which provides civil remedies for torture victims, to predict the standards that courts might follow in determining what actions reach the threshold of torture in the criminal context. We conclude from these cases that courts are likely to take a totality-of-the-circumstances approach, and will look to an entire course of conduct, to determine whether certain acts will violate Section 2340A. Moreover, these cases demonstrate that most often torture involves cruel and extreme physical pain. In Part IV, we examine international decisions regarding the use of sensory deprivation techniques. These cases make clear that while many of these techniques may amount to cruel, inhuman or degrading treatment, they do not produce pain or suffering of the necessary intensity to meet the definition of torture. From these decisions, we conclude that there is a wide range of such techniques that will not rise to the level of torture.

In Part V, we discuss whether Section 2340A may be unconstitutional if applied to interrogations undertaken of enemy combatants pursuant to the President's Commander-in-Chief powers. We find that in the circumstances of the current war against al Qaeda and its allies, prosecution under Section 2340A may be barred because enforcement of the statute would represent an unconstitutional infringement of the President's authority to conduct war. In Part VI, we discuss defenses to an allegation that an interrogation method might violate the statute. We conclude that, under the current circumstances, necessity or self-defense may justify interrogation methods that might violate Section 2340A.

I. 18 U.S.C. §§ 2340–2340A

Section 2340A makes it a criminal offense for any person "outside the United States [to] commit or attempt to commit torture."[1] Section 2340 defines the act of torture as an:

> act committed by a person acting under the color of law specifically intended to inflict severe physical or mental pain or suffering (other than pain or suffering incidental to lawful sanctions) upon another person within his custody or physical control.

[1] If convicted of torture, a defendant faces a fine or up to twenty years' imprisonment or both. If, however, the act resulted in the victim's death, a defendant may be sentenced to life imprisonment or to death. *See* 18 U.S.C.A. § 2340A(a). Whether death results from the act also affects the applicable statute of limitations. Where death does not result, the statute of limitations is eight years; if death results, there is no statute of limitations. *See* 18 U.S.C.A. § 3286(b) (West Supp. 2002); *id.* § 2332b(g)(5)(B) (West Supp. 2002). Section 2340A as originally enacted did not provide for the death penalty as a punishment. *See* Omnibus Crime Bill, Pub. L. No. 103–322, Title VI, Section 60020, 108 Stat. 1979 (1994) (amending section 2340A to provide for the death penalty); H. R. Conf. Rep. No. 103–711, at 388 (1994) (noting that the act added the death penalty as a penalty for torture).

Most recently, the USA Patriot Act, Pub. L. No. 107–56, 115 Stat. 272 (2001), amended section 2340A to expressly codify the offense of conspiracy to commit torture. Congress enacted this amendment as part of a broader effort to ensure that individuals engaged in the planning of terrorist activities could be prosecuted irrespective of where the activities took place. *See* H. R. Rep. No. 107–236, at 70 (2001) (discussing the addition of "conspiracy" as a separate offense for a variety of "Federal terrorism offense[s]").

18 U.S.C.A. § 2340(1); *see id.* § 2340A. Thus, to convict a defendant of torture, the prosecution must establish that: (1) the torture occurred outside the United States; (2) the defendant acted under the color of law; (3) the victim was within the defendant's custody or physical control; (4) the defendant specifically intended to cause severe physical or mental pain or suffering; and (5) that the act inflicted severe physical or mental pain or suffering. *See also* S. Exec. Rep. No. 101–30, at 6 (1990) ("For an act to be 'torture,' it must...cause severe pain and suffering, and be intended to cause severe pain and suffering."). You have asked us to address only the elements of specific intent and the infliction of severe pain or suffering. As such, we have not addressed the elements of "outside the United States," "color of law," and "custody or control."[2] At your request, we would be happy to address these elements in a separate memorandum.

A. "Specifically Intended"

To violate Section 2340A, the statute requires that severe pain and suffering must be inflicted with specific intent. *See* 18 U.S.C. § 2340(1). In order for a defendant to have acted with specific intent, he must expressly intend to achieve the forbidden act. *See United States v. Carter*, 530 U.S. 255, 269 (2000); Black's Law Dictionary at 814 (7th ed. 1999) (defining specific intent as "[t]he intent to accomplish the precise criminal act that one is later charged with"). For example, in *Ratzlaf v. United States*, 510 U.S. 135, 141 (1994), the statute at issue was construed to require that the defendant act with the "specific intent to commit the crime." (Internal quotation marks and citation omitted). As a result, the defendant had to act with the express "purpose to disobey the law" in order for the *mens rea* element to be satisfied. *Ibid.* (internal quotation marks and citation omitted)

Here, because Section 2340 requires that a defendant act with the specific intent to inflict severe pain, the infliction of such pain must be the defendant's precise objective. If the statute had required only general intent, it would be sufficient to establish guilt by showing that the defendant "possessed knowledge with respect to the *actus reus* of the crime." *Carter*, 530 U.S. at 268. If the defendant acted knowing that severe pain or suffering was reasonably likely to result from his actions, but no more, he would have acted only with general intent. *See id.* at 269; Black's Law Dictionary 813 (7th ed. 1999) (explaining that general intent "usu[ally] takes the form of recklessness (involving actual awareness of a risk and the culpable taking of that risk) or negligence (involving blameworthy inadvertence)"). The Supreme Court has used the following example to illustrate the difference between these two mental states:

> [A] person entered a bank and took money from a teller at gunpoint, but deliberately failed to make a quick getaway from the bank in the hope of being arrested so that he would be returned to prison and treated for alcoholism. Though this defendant knowingly engaged in the acts of using force and taking money (satisfying "general intent"), he did not intend permanently to deprive the bank of its possession of the money (failing to satisfy "specific intent").

---

[2] We note, however, that 18 U.S.C. § 2340(3) supplies a definition of the term "United States." It defines it as "all areas under the jurisdiction of the United States including any of the places described in" 18 U.S.C. §§ 5 and 7, and in 49 U.S.C. § 46501(2). Section 5 provides that United States "includes all places and waters, continental or insular, subject to the jurisdiction of the United States." By including the definition set out in Section 7, the term "United States" as used in Section 2340(3) includes the "special maritime and territorial jurisdiction of the United States." Moreover, the incorporation by reference to Section 46501(2) extends the definition of the "United States" to "special aircraft jurisdiction of the United States."

Carter, 530 U.S. at 268 (citing 1 W. LaFave & A. Scott, Substantive Criminal Law §§ 3.5, at 315 (1986)).

As a theoretical matter, therefore, knowledge alone that a particular result is certain to occur does not constitute specific intent. As the Supreme Court explained in the context of murder, "the . . . common law of homicide distinguishes . . . between a person who knows that another person will be killed as a result of his conduct and a person who acts with the specific purpose of taking another's life[.]" *United States v. Bailey*, 444 U.S. 394, 405 (1980). "Put differently, the law distinguishes actions taken 'because of' a given end from actions taken in spite of their unintended but foreseen consequences." *Vacco v. Quill*, 521 U.S. 793, 802–03 (1997). Thus, even if the defendant knows that severe pain will result from his actions, if causing such harm is not his objective, he lacks the requisite specific intent even though the defendant did not act in good faith. Instead, a defendant is guilty of torture only if he acts with the express purpose of inflicting severe pain or suffering on a person within his custody or physical control. While as a theoretical matter such knowledge does not constitute specific intent, juries are permitted to infer from the factual circumstances that such intent is present. *See, e.g., United States v. Godwin*, 272 F.3d 659, 666 (4th Cir. 2001); *United States v. Karro*, 257 F.3d 112, 118 (2d Cir. 2001); *United States v. Wood*, 207 F.3d 1222, 1232 (10th Cir. 2000); *Henderson v. United States*, 202 F.2d 400, 403 (6th Cir. 1953). Therefore, when a defendant knows that his actions will produce the prohibited result, a jury will in all likelihood conclude that the defendant acted with specific intent.

Further, a showing that an individual acted with a good faith belief that his conduct would not produce the result that the law prohibits negates specific intent. *See, e.g., South Atl. Lmtd. Ptrshp. of Tenn. v. Reise*, 218 F.3d 518, 531 (4th Cir. 2002). Where a defendant acts in good faith, he acts with an honest belief that he has not engaged in the proscribed conduct. *See Cheek v. United States*, 498 U.S. 192, 202 (1991); *United States v. Mancuso*, 42 F.3d 836, 837 (4th Cir. 1994). For example, in the context of mail fraud, if an individual honestly believes that the material transmitted is truthful, he has not acted with the required intent to deceive or mislead. *See, e.g., United States v. Sayakhom*, 186 F.3d 928, 939–40 (9th Cir. 1999). A good faith belief need not be a reasonable one. *See Cheek*, 498 U.S. at 202.

Although a defendant theoretically could hold an unreasonable belief that his acts would not constitute the actions prohibited by the statute, even though they would as a certainty produce the prohibited effects, as a matter of practice in the federal criminal justice system it is highly unlikely that a jury would acquit in such a situation. Where a defendant holds an unreasonable belief, he will confront the problem of proving to the jury that he actually held that belief. As the Supreme Court noted in *Cheek*, "the more unreasonable the asserted beliefs or misunderstandings are, the more likely the jury . . . will find that the Government has carried its burden of proving" intent. *Id.* at 203–04. As we explained above, a jury will be permitted to infer that the defendant held the requisite specific intent. As a matter of proof, therefore, a good faith defense will prove more compelling when a reasonable basis exists for the defendant's belief.

B. *"Severe Pain or Suffering"*

The key statutory phrase in the definition of torture is the statement that acts amount to torture if they cause "severe physical or mental pain or suffering." In examining the meaning of a statute, its text must be the starting point. *See INS v. Phinpathya*, 464

U.S. 183, 189 (1984) ("This Court has noted on numerous occasions that in all cases involving statutory construction, our starting point must be the language employed by Congress,... and we assume that the legislative purpose is expressed by the ordinary meaning of the words used.") (internal quotations and citations omitted). Section 2340 makes plain that the infliction of pain or suffering per se, whether it is physical or mental, is insufficient to amount to torture. Instead, the text provides that pain or suffering must be "severe." The statute does not, however, define the term "severe." "In the absence of such a definition, we construe a statutory term in accordance with its ordinary or natural meaning." *FDIC v. Meyer*, 510 U.S. 471, 476 (1994). The dictionary defines "severe" as "[u]nsparing in exaction, punishment, or censure" or "[I]nflicting discomfort or pain hard to endure; sharp; afflictive; distressing; violent; extreme; as *severe* pain, anguish, torture." Webster's New International Dictionary 2295 (2d ed. 1935); *see* American Heritage Dictionary of the English Language 1653 (3d ed. 1992) ("extremely violent or grievous: *severe* pain") (emphasis in original); IX The Oxford English Dictionary 572 (1978) ("Of pain, suffering, loss, or the like: Grievous, extreme" and "of circumstances...: hard to sustain or endure"). Thus, the adjective "severe" conveys that the pain or suffering must be of such a high level of intensity that the pain is difficult for the subject to endure.

Congress' use of the phrase "severe pain" elsewhere in the United States Code can shed more light on its meaning. *See, e.g., West Va. Univ. Hosps., Inc. v. Casey*, 499 U.S. 83, 100 (1991) ("[W]e construe [a statutory term] to contain that permissible meaning which fits most logically and comfortably into the body of both previously and subsequently enacted law."). Significantly, the phrase "severe pain" appears in statutes defining an emergency medical condition for the purpose of providing health benefits. *See, e.g.*, 8 U.S.C. § 1369 (2000); 42 U.S.C § 1395w-22 (2000); *id.* § 1395x (2000); *id.* § 1395dd (2000); *id.* § 1396b (2000); *id.* § 1396u-2 (2000). These statutes define an emergency condition as one "manifesting itself by acute symptoms of sufficient severity (including *severe pain*) such that a prudent lay person, who possesses an average knowledge of health and medicine, could reasonably expect the absence of immediate medical attention to result in – placing the health of the individual... (i) in serious jeopardy, (ii) serious impairment to bodily functions, or (iii) serious dysfunction of any bodily organ or part." *Id.* § 1395w-22(d)(3)(B) (emphasis added). Although these statutes address a substantially different subject from Section 2340, they are nonetheless helpful for understanding what constitutes severe physical pain. They treat severe pain as an indicator of ailments that are likely to result in permanent and serious physical damage in the absence of immediate medical treatment. Such damage must rise to the level of death, organ failure, or the permanent impairment of a significant body function. These statutes suggest that "severe pain," as used in Section 2340, must rise to a similarly high level – the level that would ordinarily be associated with a sufficiently serious physical condition or injury such as death, organ failure, or serious impairment of body functions – in order to constitute torture.[3]

[3] One might argue that because the statute uses "or" rather than "and" in the phrase "pain or suffering" that "severe physical suffering" is a concept distinct from "severe physical pain." We believe the better view of the statutory text is, however, that they are not distinct concepts. The statute does not define "severe mental pain" and "severe mental suffering" separately. Instead, it gives the phrase "severe mental pain or suffering" a single definition. Because "pain or suffering" is single concept for the purposes of "severe mental pain or suffering," it should likewise be read as a single concept for the purposes of severe physical pain or suffering. Moreover, dictionaries define the words "pain" and "suffering" in terms of each other. *Compare, e.g.*, Webster's Third New International Dictionary 2284 (1993) (defining suffering as "the endurance of... pain" or "a pain

C. "Severe Mental Pain or Suffering"

Section 2340 gives further guidance as to the meaning of "severe mental pain or suffering," as distinguished from severe physical pain and suffering. The statute defines "severe mental pain or suffering" as:

the prolonged mental harm caused by or resulting from –

(A) the intentional infliction or threatened infliction of severe physical pain or suffering;

(B) the administration or application, or threatened administration or application, of mind-altering substances or other procedures calculated to disrupt profoundly the senses or the personality;

(C) the threat of imminent death; or

(D) the threat that another person will imminently be subjected to death, severe physical pain or suffering, or the administration or application of mind-altering substances or other procedures calculated to disrupt profoundly the senses or personality.

18 U.S.C. § 2340(2). In order to prove "severe mental pain or suffering," the statute requires proof of "prolonged mental harm" that was caused by or resulted from one of four enumerated acts. We consider each of these elements.

1. "Prolonged Mental Harm." As an initial matter, Section 2340(2) requires that the severe mental pain must be evidenced by "prolonged mental harm." To prolong is to "lengthen in time" or to "extend the duration of, to draw out." Webster's Third New International Dictionary 1815 (1988); Webster's New International Dictionary 1980 (2d ed. 1935). Accordingly, "prolong" adds a temporal dimension to the harm to the individual, namely, that the harm must be one that is endured over some period of time. Put another way, the acts giving rise to the harm must cause some lasting, though not necessarily permanent, damage. For example, the mental strain experienced by an individual during a lengthy and intense interrogation – such as one that state or local police might conduct upon a criminal suspect – would not violate Section 2340(2). On the other hand, the development of a mental disorder such as post-traumatic stress disorder, which can last months or even years, or even chronic depression, which also can last for a considerable period of time if untreated, might satisfy the prolonged harm requirement. *See* American Psychiatric Association, *Diagnostic and Statistical Manual of Mental Disorders* 426, 439–45 (4th ed. 1994) ("DSM-IV"). *See also* Craig Haney & Mona Lynch, *Regulating Prisons of the Future: A Psychological Analysis of Supermax and Solitary Confinement*, 23 N.Y.U. Rev. L. & Soc. Change 477, 509 (1997) (noting that post-traumatic stress disorder is frequently found in torture victims); *cf.* Sana Loue, *Immigration Law and Health* § 10:46 (2001) (recommending evaluating for post-traumatic stress disorder

---

endured"); Webster's Third New International Dictionary 2284 (1986) (same); XVII The Oxford English Dictionary 125 (2d ed. 1989) (defining suffering as "the bearing or undergoing of pain"); *with, e.g.,* Random House Webster's Unabridged Dictionary 1394 (2d ed. 1999) (defining "pain" as "physical suffering"); The American Heritage Dictionary of the English Language 942 (College ed. 1976) (defining pain as "suffering or distress"). Further, even if we were to read the infliction of severe physical suffering as distinct from severe physical pain, it is difficult to conceive of such suffering that would not involve severe physical pain. Accordingly, we conclude that "pain or suffering" is a single concept within the definition of Section 2340.

immigrant-client who has experienced torture).[4] By contrast to "severe pain," the phrase "prolonged mental harm" appears nowhere else in the U.S. Code nor does it appear in relevant medical literature or international human rights reports.

Not only must the mental harm be prolonged to amount to severe mental pain and suffering, but also it must be caused by or result from one of the acts listed in the statute. In the absence of a catch-all provision, the most natural reading of the predicate acts listed in Section 2340(2)(A)–(D) is that Congress intended it to be exhaustive. In other words, other acts not included within Section 2340(2)'s enumeration are not within the statutory prohibition. *See Leatherman v. Tarrant Country Narcotics Intelligence & Coordination Unit*, 507 U.S. 163, 168 (1993) (*"Expressio unius est exclusio alterius."*); Norman Singer, 2A Sutherland on Statutory Construction § 47.23 (6th ed. 2000) ("[W]here a form of conduct, the manner of its performance and operation, and the persons and things to which it refers are designated, there is an inference that all omissions should be understood as exclusions.") (footnotes omitted). We conclude that torture within the meaning of the statute requires the specific intent to cause prolonged mental harm by one of the acts listed in Section 2340(2).

A defendant must specifically intend to cause prolonged mental harm for the defendant to have committed torture. It could be argued that a defendant needs to have specific intent only to commit the predicate acts that give rise to prolonged mental harm. Under that view, so long as the defendant specifically intended to, for example, threaten a victim with imminent death, he would have had sufficient *mens rea* for a conviction. According to this view, it would be further necessary for a conviction to show only that the victim factually suffered prolonged mental harm, rather than that the defendant intended to cause it. We believe that this approach is contrary to the text of the statute. The statute requires that the defendant specifically intend to inflict severe mental pain or suffering. Because the statute requires this mental state with respect to the infliction of severe mental pain, and because it expressly defines severe mental pain in terms of prolonged mental harm, that mental state must be present with respect to prolonged mental harm. To read the statute otherwise would read the phrase "the prolonged mental harm caused by or resulting from" out of the definition of "severe mental pain or suffering."

A defendant could negate a showing of specific intent to cause severe mental pain or suffering by showing that he had acted in good faith that his conduct would not amount to the acts prohibited by the statute. Thus, if a defendant has a good faith belief that his actions will not result in prolonged mental harm, he lacks the mental state necessary for his actions to constitute torture. A defendant could show that he acted in good faith by taking such steps as surveying professional literature, consulting with experts, or reviewing

---

[4] The DSM-IV explains that post-traumatic disorder ("PTSD") is brought on by exposure to traumatic events, such as serious physical injury or witnessing the deaths of others and during those events the individual felt "intense fear" or "horror." *Id.* at 424. Those suffering from this disorder reexperience the trauma through, *inter alia*, "recurrent and intrusive distressing recollections of the event," "recurrent distressing dreams of the event," or "intense psychological distress at exposure to internal or external cues that symbolize or resemble an aspect of the traumatic event." *Id.* at 428. Additionally, a person with PTSD "[p]ersistent[ly]" avoids stimuli associated with the trauma, including avoiding conversations about the trauma, places that stimulate recollections about the trauma; and they experience a numbing of general responsiveness, such as a "restricted range of affect (e.g., unable to have loving feelings)," and "the feeling of detachment or estrangement from others." *Ibid.* Finally, an individual with PTSD has "[p]ersistent symptoms of increased arousal," as evidenced by "irritability or outbursts of anger," "hypervigilance," "exaggerated startle response," and difficulty sleeping or concentrating. *Ibid.*

evidence gained from past experience. *See, e.g., Ratlzlaf*, 510 U.S. at 142 n.10 (noting that where the statute required that the defendant act with the specific intent to violate the law, the specific intent element "might be negated by, e.g., proof that defendant relied in good faith on advice of counsel" (citations omitted)). All of these steps would show that he has drawn on the relevant body of knowledge concerning the result proscribed that the statute, namely prolonged mental harm. Because the presence of good faith would negate the specific intent element of torture, it is a complete defense to such a charge. *See, e.g., United States v. Wall*, 130 F.3d 739, 746 (6th Cir. 1997); *United States v. Casperson*, 773 F.2d 216, 222–23 (8th Cir. 1985).

2. Harm Caused By Or Resulting From Predicate Acts. Section 2340(2) sets forth four basic categories of predicate acts. First in the list is the "intentional infliction or threatened infliction of severe physical pain or suffering." This might at first appear superfluous because the statute already provides that the infliction of severe physical pain or suffering can amount to torture. This provision, however, actually captures the infliction of physical pain or suffering when the defendant inflicts physical pain or suffering with general intent rather than the specific intent that is required where severe physical pain or suffering alone is the basis for the charge. Hence, this subsection reaches the infliction of severe physical pain or suffering when it is but the means of causing prolonged mental harm. Or put another way, a defendant has committed torture when he intentionally inflicts severe physical pain or suffering with the specific intent of causing prolonged mental harm. As for the acts themselves, acts that cause "severe physical pain or suffering" can satisfy this provision.

Additionally, the threat of inflicting such pain is a predicate act under the statute. A threat may be implicit or explicit. *See, e.g., United States v. Sachdev*, 279 F.3d 25, 29 (1st Cir. 2002). In criminal law, courts generally determine whether an individual's words or actions constitute a threat by examining whether a reasonable person in the same circumstances would conclude that a threat had been made. *See, e.g., Watts v. United States*, 394 U.S. 705, 708 (1969) (holding that whether a statement constituted a threat against the President's life had to be determined in light of all the surrounding circumstances); *Sachdev*, 279 F.3d at 29 ("a reasonable person in defendant's position would perceive there to be a threat, explicit, or implicit, of physical injury"); *United States v. Khorrami*, 895 F.2d 1186, 1190 (7th Cir. 1990) (to establish that a threat was made, the statement must be made "in a context or under such circumstances wherein a reasonable person would foresee that the statement would be interpreted by those to whom the maker communicates a statement as a serious expression of an intention to inflict bodily harm upon [another individual]") (citation and internal quotation marks omitted); *United States v. Peterson*, 483 F.2d 1222, 1230 (D.C. Cir. 1973) (perception of threat of imminent harm necessary to establish self-defense had to be "objectively reasonable in light of the surrounding circumstances"). Based on this common approach, we believe that the existence of a threat of severe pain or suffering should be assessed from the standpoint of a reasonable person in the same circumstances.

Second, Section 2340(2)(B) provides that prolonged mental harm, constituting torture, can be caused by "the administration or application or threatened administration or application, of mind-altering substances or other procedures calculated to disrupt profoundly the senses or the personality." The statute provides no further definition of what constitutes a mind-altering substance. The phrase "mind-altering substances" is found nowhere else in the U.S. Code nor is it found in dictionaries. It is, however, a commonly used synonym for drugs. *See, e.g., United States v. Kingsley*, 241 F.3d 828, 834 (6th Cir.) (referring to controlled substances as "mind-altering substance[s]") *cert. denied*, 122 S. Ct. 137 (2001); *Hogue v. Johnson*, 131 F.3d 466, 501 (5th Cir. 1997) (referring to drugs and alcohol as "mind-altering substance[s]"), *cert. denied*, 523 U.S. 1014 (1998). In addition, the phrase appears in a number of state statutes, and the context in which it appears confirms this understanding of the phrase. *See, e.g.,* Cal. Penal Code § 3500(c) (West Supp. 2000) ("Psychotropic drugs also include mind-altering...drugs...."); Minn. Stat. Ann. § 260B.201(b) (West Supp. 2002) ("'chemical dependency treatment'" define as programs designed to "reduc[e] the risk of the use of alcohol, drugs, or other mind-altering substances").

This subparagraph, however, does not preclude any and all use of drugs. Instead, it prohibits the use of drugs that "disrupt profoundly the senses or the personality." To be sure, one could argue that this phrase applies only to "other procedures," not the application of mind-altering substances. We reject this interpretation because the terms of Section 2340(2) expressly indicate that the qualifying phrase applies to both "other procedures" *and* the "application of mind-altering substances." The word "other" modifies "procedures calculated to disrupt profoundly the senses." As an adjective, "other" indicates that the term or phrase it modifies is the remainder of several things. *See* Webster's Third New International Dictionary 1598 (1986) (defining "other" as "the one that remains of two or more") Webster's Ninth New Collegiate Dictionary 835 (1985) (defining "other" as "being the one (as of two or more) remaining or not included"). Or put another way, "other" signals that the words to which it attaches are of the same kind, type, or class as the more specific item previously listed. Moreover, where statutes couple words or phrases together, it "denotes an intention that they should be understood in the same general sense." Norman Singer, 2A Sutherland on Statutory Construction § 47:16 (6th ed. 2000); *see also Beecham v. United States*, 511 U.S. 368, 371 (1994) ("That several items in a list share an attribute counsels in favor of interpreting the other items as possessing that attribute as well."). Thus, the pairing of mind-altering substances with procedures calculated to disrupt profoundly the senses or personality and the use of "other" to modify "procedures" shows that the use of such substances must also cause a profound disruption of the senses or personality.

For drugs or procedures to rise to the level of "disrupt[ing] profoundly the senses or personality," they must produce an extreme effect. And by requiring that they be "calculated" to produce such an effect, the statute requires for liability the defendant has consciously designed the acts to produce such an effect.28 U.S.C. § 2340(2)(B). The word "disrupt" is defined as "to break asunder; to part forcibly; rend," imbuing the verb with a connotation of violence. Webster's New International Dictionary 753 (2d ed. 1935); *see* Webster's Third New International Dictionary 656 (1986) (defining disrupt as "to break apart: Rupture" or "destroy the unity or wholeness of"); IV The Oxford English Dictionary 832 (1989) (defining disrupt as "[t]o break or burst asunder; to break in pieces; to separate forcibly"). Moreover, disruption of the senses or personality alone is insufficient to fall within the scope of this subsection; instead, that disruption must be profound. The word "profound" has a number of meanings, all of which convey a significant depth. Webster's New International Dictionary 1977 (2d ed. 1935) defines profound as: "Of very great depth; extending far below the surface or top; unfathomable[;]...[c]oming from, reaching to, or situated at a depth or more than ordinary depth; not superficial; deep-seated; chiefly with reference to the body; as a *profound* sigh, wound, or pain[;]...[c]haracterized by intensity, as of feeling or quality; deeply felt or realized; as, *profound* respect, fear, or melancholy; hence, encompassing; thorough-going; complete; as, *profound* sleep, silence, or ignorance." *See* Webster's Third New International Dictionary 1812 (1986) ("having very great depth: extending far below the surface...not superficial"). Random House Webster's Unabridged Dictionary 1545 (2d ed. 1999) also defines profound as "originating in or penetrating to the depths of one's being" or "pervasive or intense; thorough; complete" or "extending, situated, or originating far down, or far beneath the surface." By requiring that the procedures and the drugs create a *profound* disruption, the statute requires more than that the acts "forcibly separate" or "rend" the senses or personality. Those acts must penetrate to the core of an individual's ability to perceive the world around him, substantially interfering with his cognitive abilities, or fundamentally alter his personality.

The phrase "disrupt profoundly the senses or personality" is not used in mental health literature nor is it derived from elsewhere in U.S. law. Nonetheless, we think the following examples would constitute a profound disruption of the senses or personality. Such an effect might be seen in a drug-induced dementia. In such a state, the individual suffers from significant memory impairment, such as the inability to retain any new information or recall information about things previously of interest to the individual. *See* DSM-IV at 134.[5] This impairment is accompanied by one or more of the following: deterioration of language function, e.g., repeating sounds or words over and over again; impaired ability to execute simple motor activities, e.g., inability to dress or wave goodbye; "[in]ability to recognize [and identify] objects such as chairs or pencils" despite normal visual functioning; or "[d]isturbances in executive level functioning," i.e., serious impairment of abstract thinking. *Id.* at 134–35. Similarly, we think that the onset of "brief psychotic disorder" would satisfy this standard. *See id.* at 302–03. In this disorder, the individual suffers psychotic symptoms, including among other things, delusions, hallucinations, or even a catatonic state. This can last for one day or even one month. *See id.* We likewise think that the onset of obsessive-compulsive disorder behaviors would rise to this level. Obsessions are intrusive thoughts unrelated to reality. They are not simple worries, but are repeated doubts or even "aggressive or horrific impulses." *See id.* at 418. The DSM-IV further explains that compulsions include "repetitive behaviors (e.g., hand washing, ordering, checking)" and that "[b]y definition, [they] are either clearly excessive or are not connected in a realistic way with what they are designed to neutralize or prevent." *See id.* Such compulsions or obsessions must be "time-consuming." *See id.* at 419. Moreover, we think that pushing someone to the brink of suicide, particularly where the person comes from a culture with strong taboos against suicide, and it is evidenced by acts of self-mutilation, would be a sufficient disruption of the personality to constitute a "profound disruption." These examples, of course, are in no way intended to be exhaustive list. Instead, they are merely intended to illustrate the sort of mental health effects that we believe would accompany an action severe enough to amount to one that "disrupt[s] profoundly the senses or the personality."

---

[5] Published by the American Psychiatric Association, and written as a collaboration of over a thousand psychiatrists, the DSM-IV is commonly used in U.S. courts as a source of information regarding mental health issues and is likely to be used in trial should charges be brought that allege this predicate act. *See, e.g., Atkins v. Virginia,* 122 S. Ct. 2242, 2245 n.3 (2002); *Kansas v. Crane,* 122 S. Ct. 867, 871 (2002); *Kansas v. Hendricks,* 521 U.S. 346, 359–60 (1997); *McClean v. Merrifield,* No. 00-CV-0120E(SC), 2002 WL 1477607 at *2 n.7 (W.D.N.Y. June 28, 2002); *Peeples v. Coastal Office Prods.,* 203 F. Supp. 2d. 432, 439 (D. Md. 2002); *Lassiegne v. Taco Bell Corp.,* 202 F. Supp. 2d 512, 519 (E.D. La. 2002).

The third predicate act listed in Section 2340(2) is threatening a prisoner with "imminent death." 18 U.S.C. § 2340(2)(C). The plain text makes clear that a threat of death alone is insufficient; the threat must indicate that death is "imminent." The "threat of imminent death" is found in the common law as an element of the defense of duress. *See Bailey*, 444 U.S. at 409. "[W]here Congress borrows terms of art in which are accumulated the legal tradition and meaning of centuries of practice, it presumably knows and adopts the cluster of ideas that were attached to each borrowed word in the body of learning from which it was taken and the meaning its use will convey to the judicial mind unless otherwise instructed. In such case, absence of contrary direction may be taken as satisfaction with widely accepted definitions, not as a departure from them." *Morissette v. United States*, 342 U.S. 246, 263 (1952). Common law cases and legislation generally define imminence as requiring that the threat be almost immediately forthcoming. 1 Wayne R. LaFave & Austin W. Scott, Jr., Substantive Criminal Law § 5.7, at 655 (1986). By contrast, threats referring vaguely to things that might happen in the future do not satisfy this immediacy requirement. *See United States v. Fiore*, 178 F.3d 917, 923 (7th Cir. 1999). Such a threat fails to satisfy this requirement not because it is too remote in time but because there is a lack of certainty that it will occur. Indeed, timing is an indicator of certainty that the harm *will* befall the defendant. Thus, a vague threat that someday the prisoner *might* be killed would not suffice. Instead, subjecting a prisoner to mock executions or playing Russian roulette with him would have sufficient immediacy to constitute a threat of imminent death. Additionally, as discussed earlier, we believe that the existence of a threat must be assessed from the perspective of a reasonable person in the same circumstances.

Fourth, if the official threatens to do anything previously described to a third party, or commits such an act against a third party, that threat or action can serve as the necessary predicate for prolonged mental harm. *See* 18 U.S.C. § 2340(2)(D). The statute does not require any relationship between the prisoner and the third party.

3. Legislative History. The legislative history of Sections 2340–2340A is scant. Neither the definition of torture nor these sections as a whole sparked any debate. Congress criminalized this conduct to fulfill U.S. obligations under the U.N. Convention Against Torture and Other Cruel, Inhuman or Degrading Treatment or Punishment ("CAT"), adopted Dec. 10, 1984, S. Treaty Doc. No. 100-20 (1988), 1465 U.N.T.S. 85 (entered into force June 26, 1987), which requires signatories to "ensure that all acts of torture are offenses under its criminal law." CAT Article 4. These sections appeared only in the Senate version of the Foreign Affairs Authorization Act, and the conference bill adopted them without amendment. *See* H. R. Conf. Rep. No. 103-482, at 229 (1994). The only light that the legislative history sheds reinforces what is already obvious from the texts of Section 2340 and CAT: Congress intended Section 2340's definition of torture to track the definition set forth in CAT, as elucidated by the United States' reservations, understandings, and declarations submitted as part of its ratification. *See* S. Rep. No. 103-107, at 58 (1993) ("The definition of torture emanates directly from Article 1 of the Convention."); *id.* at 58–59 ("The definition for 'severe mental pain and suffering' incorporates the understanding made by the Senate concerning this term.").

4. Summary. Section 2340's definition of torture must be read as a sum of these component parts. *See Argentine Rep. v. Amerada Hess Shipping Corp.*, 488 U.S. 428, 434–35 (1989) (reading two provisions together to determine statute's meaning); *Bethesda Hosp.*

Ass'n v. Bowen, 485 U.S. 399, 405 (1988) (looking to "the language and design of the statute as a whole" to ascertain a statute's meaning). Each component of the definition emphasizes that torture is not the mere infliction of pain or suffering on another, but is instead a step well removed. The victim must experience intense pain or suffering of the kind that is equivalent to the pain that would be associated with serious physical injury so severe that death, organ failure, or permanent damage resulting in a loss of significant body function will likely result. If that pain or suffering is psychological, that suffering must result from one of the acts set forth in the statute. In addition, these acts must cause long-term mental harm. Indeed, this view of the criminal act of torture is consistent with the term's common meaning. Torture is generally understood to involve "intense pain" or "excruciating pain," or put another way, "extreme anguish of body or mind." Black's Law Dictionary at 1498 (7th Ed. 1999); Random House Webster's Unabridged Dictionary 1999 (1999); Webster's New International Dictionary 2674 (2d ed. 1935). In short, reading the definition of torture as a whole, it is plain that the term encompasses only extreme acts.[6]

---

[6] Torture is a term also found in state law. Some states expressly proscribe "murder by torture." *See*, e.g., Idaho Code § 18-4001 (Michie 1997); N.C. Gen. Stat. Ann. § 14-17 (1999); *see also* Me. Rev. Stat. Ann. tit. 17-A, § 152-A (West Supp. 2001) (aggravated attempted murder is "[t]he attempted murder . . . accompanied by torture, sexual assault or other extreme cruelty inflicted upon the victim"). Other states have made torture an aggravating factor suppositing imposition of the death penalty. *See*, e.g., Ark. Code Ann. § 5-4-604(8)(B); Del. Code Ann. tit. 11, § 4209(e)(1)(*l*) (1995); Ga. Code Ann. § 17-10-30(b)(7) (1997); 720 Ill. Comp. Stat. Ann. 5/9-1(b)(14) (West Supp. 2002); Mass. Ann. Laws ch. 279, § 69(a) (Law. Co-op. 1992); Mo. Ann. Stat. § 565.032(2)(7) (West 1999); Nev. Rev. Stat. Ann. 200-033(8) (Michie 2001); N.J. Stat. Ann. § 2C:11-3 (West Supp. 2002) (same); Tenn. Code Ann. § 39-13-204(i)(5) (Supp. 2001); *see also* Alaska Stat. § 12.55.125(a)(3) (2000) (term of 99 years' imprisonment mandatory where defendant subjected victim to "substantial physical torture"). *All of these laws support the conclusion that torture is generally an extreme act far beyond the infliction of pain or suffering alone.*
    California law is illustrative on this point. The California Penal Code not only makes torture itself an offense, see Cal. Penal Code § 206 (West Supp. 2002), it also prohibits murder by torture, see Cal. Penal Code § 189 (West Supp. 2002), and provides that torture is an aggravating circumstance supporting the imposition of the death penalty, see Cal. Penal Code § 190.2 (West Supp. 2002). California's definitions of torture demonstrate that the term is reserved for especially cruel acts inflicting serious injury. Designed to "fill a gap in existing law dealing with extremely violent and callous criminal conduct[,]" *People v. Hale*, 88 Cal. Rptr. 2d 904, 913 (1999) (internal quotation marks and citation omitted), Section 206 defines the offense of torture as:

> [e]very person who, with the intent to cause *cruel* or *extreme* pain and suffering for the purpose of revenge, extortion, persuasion, or for any sadistic purpose, inflicts great bodily injury . . . upon the person of another, is guilty of torture. The crime of torture does not require any proof that the victim suffered pain.

(Emphasis added). With respect to sections 190.2 and 189, neither of which are statutorily defined, California courts have recognized that torture generally means an "[a]ct or process of inflicting severe pain, esp[ecially] as a punishment to extort confession, or in revenge. . . . Implicit in that definition is the requirement of an intent to cause pain and suffering in addition to death." *People v. Barrera*, 18 Cal. Rptr. 2d 395, 399 (Ct. App. 1993) (quotation marks and citation omitted). Further, " 'murder by torture was and is considered among the most reprehensible types of murder because of the calculated nature of the acts causing death." *Id.* at 403 (quoting *People v. Wiley*, 133 Cal. Rptr. 135, 138 (1976) (in bank)). The definition of murder by torture special circumstance, proscribed under Cal. Penal Code § 190.2, likewise shows an attempt to reach the most heinous acts imposing pain beyond that which a victim suffers through death alone. To establish murder by torture special circumstance, the "intent to kill, intent to torture, and infliction of an extremely painful act upon a living victim" must be present. *People v. Bemore*, 94 Cal. Rptr. 2d 840, 861 (2000). The intent

II. U.N. Convention Against Torture and Other Cruel Inhuman or Degrading Treatment or Punishment

Because Congress enacted the criminal prohibition against torture to implement CAT, we also examine the treaty's text and history to develop a fuller understanding of the context of Sections 2340–2340A. As with the statute, we begin our analysis with the treaty's text. *See Eastern Airlines Inc. v. Floyd*, 499 U.S. 530, 534–35 (1991) ("When interpreting a treaty, we begin with the text of the treaty and the context in which the written words are used.) (quotation marks and citations omitted). CAT defines torture as:

> any act by which *severe* pain or suffering, whether physical or mental, is intentionally inflicted on a person for such purposes as obtaining from him or a third person information or a confession, punishing him for an act he or a third person has committed or is suspected of having committed, or intimidating or coercing him or a third person, or for any reason based on discrimination of any kind, when such pain or suffering is inflicted by or at the instigation of or with the consent or acquiescence of a public official or other person acting in an official capacity.

Article 1(1) (emphasis added). Unlike Section 2340, this definition includes a list of purposes for which such pain and suffering is inflicted. The prefatory phrase "such purposes as" makes clear that this list is, however, illustrative rather than exhaustive. Accordingly, severe pain or suffering need not be inflicted for those specific purposes to constitute torture; instead, the perpetrator must simply have a purpose of the same kind. More importantly, like Section 2340, the pain and suffering must be severe to reach the threshold of torture. Thus, the text of CAT reinforces our reading of Section 2340 that torture must be an extreme act.[7]

CAT also distinguishes between torture and other acts of cruel, inhuman, or degrading treatment or punishment.[8] Article 16 of CAT requires state parties to "undertake to

---

to torture is characterized by a "'sadistic intent to cause the victim to suffer pain in addition to the pain of death.'" *Id.* at 862 (quoting *People v. Davenport*, 221 Cal. Rptr. 794, 875 (1985)). Like the Torture Victims Protection Act and the Convention Against Torture, discussed *infra* at Parts II and III, each of these California prohibitions against torture require an evil intent – such as cruelty, revenge or even sadism. Section 2340 does not require this additional intent, but as discussed *supra* pp. 2–3, requires that the individual specifically intended to cause severe pain or suffering. Furthermore, unlike Section 2340, neither section 189 nor section 206 appear to require proof of actual pain to establish torture.

[7] To be sure, the text of the treaty requires that an individual act "intentionally." This language might be read to require only general intent for violations of the Torture Convention. We believe, however, that the better interpretation is that the use of the phrase "intentionally" also created a specific intent-type standard. In that event, the Bush administration's understanding represents only an explanation of how the United States intended to implement the vague language of the Torture Convention. If, however, the Convention established a general intent standard, then the Bush understanding represents a modification of the obligation undertaken by the United States.

[8] Common Article 3 of Geneva Convention on prisoners of war, Convention Relative to the Treatment of Prisoners of War, 6 U.S.T. 3517 ("Geneva Convention III") contains somewhat similar language. Article 3(1)(a) prohibits "violence to life and person, in particular murder of all kinds, mutilation, *cruel treatment and torture*." (Emphasis added). Article 3(1)(c) additionally prohibits "outrages upon personal dignity, in particular, humiliating and degrading treatment." Subsection (c) must forbid more conduct than that already covered in subsection (a) otherwise subsection (c) would be superfluous. Common Article 3 does not, however, define either of the phrases "outrages upon personal dignity" or "humiliating and degrading treatment." International criminal tribunals, such as those respecting Rwanda and former Yugoslavia have used common Article 3 to try individuals for committing inhuman acts lacking any military necessity whatsoever. Based on our review of the

prevent... other acts of cruel, inhuman or degrading treatment or punishment *which do not amount to torture* as defined in Article 1." (Emphasis added). CAT thus establishes a category of acts that are not to be committed and that states must endeavor to prevent, but that states need not criminalize, leaving those acts without the stigma of criminal penalties. CAT reserves criminal penalties and the stigma attached to those penalties for torture alone. In so doing, CAT makes clear that torture is at the farthest end of impermissible actions, and that it is distinct and separate from the lower level of "cruel, inhuman, or degrading treatment or punishment." This approach is in keeping with CAT's predecessor, the U.N. Declaration on the Protection from Torture. That declaration defines torture as "an aggravated and deliberate form of cruel, inhuman or degrading treatment or punishment." Declaration on Protection from Torture, UN Res. 3452, Art. 1(2) (Dec. 9, 1975).

A. Ratification History

Executive branch interpretation of CAT further supports our conclusion that the treaty, and thus Section 2340A, prohibits only the most extreme forms of physical or mental harm. As we have previously noted, the "division of treaty-making responsibility between the Senate and the President is essentially the reverse of the division of lawmaking authority, with the President being the draftsman of the treaty and the Senate holding the authority to grant or deny approval." *Relevance of Senate Ratification History to Treaty Interpretation*, 11 Op. O.L.C. 28, 31 (Apr. 9, 1987) ("Sofaer Memorandum"). Treaties are negotiated by the President in his capacity as the "sole organ of the federal government in the field of international relations." *United States v. Curtiss-Wright Export Corp.*, 299 U.S. 304, 320 (1936). Moreover, the President is responsible for the day-to-day interpretation of a treaty and retains the power to unilaterally terminate a treaty. *See Goldwater v. Carter*, 617 F.2d 697, 707–08 (D.C. Cir.) (en banc) *vacated and remanded with instructions to dismiss on other grounds*, 444 U.S. 996 (1979). The Executive's interpretation is to be accorded the greatest weight in ascertaining a treaty's intent and meaning. *See, e.g., United States v. Stuart*, 489 U.S. 353, 369 (1989) (" 'the meaning attributed to treaty provisions by the Government agencies charged with their negotiation and enforcement is entitled to great weight' ") (quoting *Sumitomo Shoji America, Inc. v. Avagliano*, 457 U.S. 176, 184–85 (1982)); *Kolovrat v. Oregon*, 366 U.S. 187, 194 (1961) ("While courts interpret treaties for themselves, the meaning given them by the department of government particularly charged with their negotiation and enforcement is given great weight."); *Charlton v. Kelly*, 229 U.S. 447, 468 (1913) ("A construction of a treaty by the political departments of the government, while not conclusive upon a court..., is nevertheless of much weight.").

case law, however, these tribunals have not yet articulated the full scope of conduct prohibited by common Article 3. Memorandum for John C. Yoo, Deputy Assistant Attorney General, Office of Legal Counsel, from James C. Ho, Attorney-Advisor, Office of Legal Counsel, *Re: Possible Interpretations of Common Article 3 of the 1949 Geneva Convention Relative to the Treatment of Prisoners of War* (Feb. 1, 2002).

We note that Section 2340A and CAT protect any individual from torture. By contrast, the standards of conduct established by common Article 3 of Convention III, do not apply to "an armed conflict between a nation-state and a transnational terrorist organization." Memorandum for Alberto R. Gonzales, Counsel to the President and William J. Haynes, II, General Counsel, Department of Defense, from Jay S. Bybee, Assistant Attorney General, Office of Legal Counsel, *Re: Application of Treaties and Laws to al Qaeda and Taliban Detainees* at 8 (Jan. 22, 2002).

A review of the Executive branch's interpretation and understanding of CAT reveals that Congress codified the view that torture included only the most extreme forms of physical or mental harm. When it submitted the Convention to the Senate, the Reagan administration took the position that CAT reached only the most heinous acts. The Reagan administration included the following understanding:

> The United States understands that, in order to constitute torture, an act must be a deliberate and calculated act of an extremely cruel and inhuman nature, specifically intended to inflict excruciating and agonizing physical or mental pain or suffering.

S. Treaty Doc. No. 100–20, at 4–5. Focusing on the treaty's requirement of "severity," the Reagan administration concluded, "The extreme nature of torture is further emphasized in [this] requirement." S. Treaty Doc. No. 100–20, at 3 (1988); S. Exec. Rep. 101–30, at 13 (1990). The Reagan administration also determined that CAT's definition of torture fell in line with "United States and international usage, [where it] is usually reserved for extreme deliberate and unusually cruel practices, for example, sustained systematic beatings, application of electric currents to sensitive parts of the body and tying up or hanging in positions that cause extreme pain." S. Exec. Rep. No. 101–30, at 14 (1990). In interpreting CAT's definition of torture as reaching only such extreme acts, the Reagan administration underscored the distinction between torture and other cruel, inhuman, or degrading treatment or punishment. In particular, the administration declared that Article 1's definition of torture ought to be construed in light of Article 16. See S. Treaty Doc. No. 100–20, at 3. Based on this distinction, the administration concluded that: " 'Torture' is thus to be distinguished from lesser forms of cruel, inhuman, or degrading treatment or punishment, which are to be deplored and prevented, but are not so universally and categorically condemned as to warrant the severe legal consequences that the Convention provides in case of torture." S. Treaty Doc. 100–20, at 3. Moreover, this distinction was "adopted in order to emphasize that torture is at the extreme end of cruel, inhuman and degrading treatment or punishment." S. Treaty Doc. No. 100–20, at 3. Given the extreme nature of torture, the administration concluded that "rough treatment as generally falls into the category of 'police brutality,' while deplorable, does not amount to 'torture.' " S. Treaty Doc. No. 100–20, at 4.

Although the Reagan administration relied on CAT's distinction between torture and "cruel, inhuman, or degrading treatment or punishment," it viewed the phrase "cruel, inhuman, or degrading treatment or punishment" as vague and lacking in a universally accepted meaning. Of even greater concern to the Reagan administration was that because of its vagueness this phrase could be construed to bar acts not prohibited by the U.S. Constitution. The administration pointed to *Case of X v. Federal Republic of Germany* as the basis for this concern. In that case, the European Court of Human Rights determined that the prison officials' refusal to recognize a prisoner's sex change might constitute degrading treatment. See S. Treaty Doc. No. 100–20, at 15 (citing European Commission on Human Rights, *Dec. on Adm.*, Dec. 15, 1977, *Case of X v. Federal Republic of Germany* (No. 6694/74), 11 Dec. & Rep. 16)). As a result of this concern, the Administration added the following understanding:

> The United States understands the term, 'cruel, inhuman or degrading treatment or punishment,' as used in Article 16 of the Convention, to mean the cruel, unusual, and inhumane treatment or punishment prohibited by the Fifth, Eighth and/or Fourteenth Amendments to the Constitution of the United States."

S. Treaty Doc. No. 100–20, at 15–16. Treatment or punishment must therefore rise to the level of action that U.S. courts have found to be in violation of the U.S. Constitution in order to constitute cruel, inhuman, or degrading treatment or punishment. That which fails to rise to this level must fail, *a fortiori*, to constitute torture under Section 2340.[9]

The Senate did not give its advice and consent to the Convention until the first Bush administration. Although using less vigorous rhetoric, the Bush administration joined the Reagan administration in interpreting torture as only reaching extreme acts. To ensure that the Convention's reach remained limited, the Bush administration submitted the following understanding:

> The United States understands that, in order to constitute torture, an act must be specifically intended to inflict severe physical or mental pain or suffering and that mental pain or suffering refers to prolonged mental pain caused by or resulting from (1) the intentional infliction or threatened infliction of severe physical pain or suffering; (2) administration or application, or threatened administration or application, of mind altering substances or other procedures calculated to disrupt profoundly the senses or the personality; (3) the threat of imminent death; or (4) the threat that another person will imminently be subjected to death, severe physical pain or suffering, or the administration or application of mind-altering substances or other procedures calculated to disrupt profoundly the senses or personality.

S. Exec. Rep. No. 101–30, at 36. This understanding accomplished two things. First, it ensured that the term "intentionally" would be understood as requiring specific intent. Second, it added form and substance to the otherwise amorphous concept of *mental* pain or suffering. In so doing, this understanding ensured that mental torture would rise to a severity seen in the context of physical torture. The Senate ratified CAT with this understanding, and as is obvious from the text, Congress codified this understanding almost verbatim in the criminal statute.

To be sure, it might be thought significant that the Bush administration's language differs from the Reagan administration understanding. The Bush administration said that it had altered the CAT understanding in response to criticism that the Reagan administration's original formulation had raised the bar for the level of pain necessary for the act or acts to constitute torture. *See* Convention Against Torture: Hearing Before the Senate Comm. On Foreign Relations, 101st Cong. 9–10 (1990) ("1990 Hearing") (prepared statement of Hon. Abraham D. Sofaer, Legal Adviser, Department of State). While

---

[9] The vagueness of "cruel, inhuman and degrading treatment" enables the term to have a far-ranging reach. Article 3 of the European Convention on Human Rights similarly prohibits such treatment. The European Court of Human Rights has construed this phrase broadly, even assessing whether such treatment has occurred from the subjective standpoint of the victim. *See* Memorandum from James C. Ho, Attorney-Advisor to John C. Yoo, Deputy Assistant Attorney General, *Re: Possible Interpretations of Common Article 3 of the 1949 Geneva Convention Relative to the Treatment of Prisoners of War* (Feb. 1, 2002) (finding that European Court of Human Right's construction of inhuman or degrading treatment "is broad enough to arguably forbid even standard U.S. law enforcement interrogation techniques, which endeavor to breakdown a detainee's 'moral resistance' to answering questions.").

Moreover, despite the Reagan and Bush administrations' efforts to limit the reach of the cruel, inhuman and degrading treatment language, it appears to still have a rather limitless reach. *See id.* (describing how the Eighth Amendment ban on "cruel and unusual punishment" has been used by courts to, *inter alia*, "engage in detailed regulation of prison conductions, including the exact size cells, exercise, and recreational activities, quality of food, access to cable television, Internet, and law libraries.")

it is true that there are rhetorical differences between the understandings, both administrations consistently emphasize the extraordinary or extreme acts required to constitute torture. As we have seen, the Bush understanding as codified in Section 2340 reaches only extreme acts. The Reagan understanding, like the Bush understanding, ensured that "intentionally" would be understood as a specific intent requirement. Though the Reagan administration required that the "act be deliberate and calculated" *and* that it be inflicted with specific intent, in operation there is little difference between requiring specific intent alone and requiring that the act be deliberate and calculated. The Reagan understanding's also made express what is obvious from the plain text of CAT: torture is an extreme form of cruel and inhuman treatment. The Reagan administration's understanding that the pain be "excruciating and agonizing" is in substance not different from the Bush administration's proposal that the pain must be severe.

The Bush understanding simply took a rather abstract concept – excruciating and agonizing mental pain – and gave it a more concrete form. Executive branch representations made to the Senate support our view that there was little difference between these two understandings and that the further definition of mental pain or suffering merely sought to remove the vagueness created by concept of "agonizing and excruciating" mental pain. *See* 1990 Hearing, at 10 (prepared statement of Hon. Abraham D. Sofaer, Legal Adviser, Department of State) ("no higher standard was intended" by the Reagan administration understanding than was present in the Convention or the Bush understanding); *id.* at 13–14 (statement of Mark Richard, Deputy Assistant Attorney General, Criminal Division, Department of Justice) ("In an effort to overcome this unacceptable element of vagueness [in the term "mental pain"], we have proposed an understanding which defines severe mental pain constituting torture with sufficient specificity . . . to protect innocent persons and meet constitutional due process requirements.") Accordingly, we believe that the two definitions submitted by the Reagan and Bush administrations had the same purpose in terms of articulating a legal standard, namely, ensuring that the prohibition against torture reaches only the most extreme acts. Ultimately, whether the Reagan standard would have been even higher is a purely academic question because the Bush understanding clearly established a very high standard.

Executive branch representations made to the Senate confirm that the Bush administration maintained the view that torture encompassed only the most extreme acts. Although the ratification record, i.e., testimony, hearings, and the like, is generally not accorded great weight in interpreting treaties, authoritative statements made by representatives of the Executive Branch are accorded the most interpretive value. *See* Sofaer Memorandum, at 35–36. Hence, the testimony of the executive branch witnesses defining torture, in addition to the reservations, understandings and declarations that were submitted to the Senate by the Executive branch, should carry the highest interpretive value of any of the statements in the ratification record. At the Senate hearing on CAT, Mark Richard, Deputy Assistant Attorney General, Criminal Division, Department of Justice, offered extensive testimony as to the meaning of torture. Echoing the analysis submitted by the Reagan administration, he testified that "[t]orture is understood to be that barbaric cruelty which lies at the top of the pyramid of human rights misconduct." 1990 Hearing, at 16 (prepared statement of Mark Richard). He further explained, "As applied to physical torture, there appears to be some degree of consensus that the concept involves conduct, the mere mention of which sends chills down one's spine[.]" *Id.* Richard gave the following examples of conduct satisfying this standard: "the needle under the fingernail, the application of electrical shock to the genital area, the piercing of eyeballs, etc."

Id. In short, repeating virtually verbatim the terms used in the Reagan understanding, Richard explained that under the Bush administration's submissions with the treaty "the essence of torture" is treatment that inflicts "excruciating and agonizing physical pain." *Id.* (emphasis added).

As to mental torture, Richard testified that "no international consensus had emerged [as to] what degree of mental suffering is required to constitute torture[,]" but that it was nonetheless clear that severe mental pain or suffering "does not encompass the normal legal compulsions which are properly a part of the criminal justice system[:] interrogation, incarceration, prosecution, compelled testimony against a friend, etc, – notwithstanding the fact that they may have the incidental effect of producing mental strain." *Id.* at 17. According to Richard, CAT was intended to "condemn as torture intentional acts such as those designed to damage and destroy the human personality." *Id.* at 14. This description of mental suffering emphasizes the requirement that any mental harm be of significant duration and lends further support for our conclusion that mind-altering substances must have a profoundly disruptive effect to serve as a predicate act.

Apart from statements from Executive branch officials, the rest of a ratification record is of little weight in interpreting a treaty. *See generally* Sofaer Memorandum. Nonetheless, the Senate understanding of the definition of torture largely echoes the administrations' views. The Senate Foreign Relations Committee Report on CAT opined: "[f]or an act to be 'torture' it must be an *extreme* form of cruel and inhuman treatment, cause *severe* pain and suffering and be *intended to cause severe* pain and suffering." S. Exec. Rep. No. 101–30, at 6 (emphasis added). Moreover, like both the Reagan and Bush administrations, the Senate drew upon the distinction between torture and cruel, inhuman or degrading treatment or punishment in reaching its view that torture was extreme.[10] Finally, the Senate concurred with the administrations' concern that "cruel, inhuman, or degrading treatment or punishment" could be construed to establish a new standard above and beyond that which the Constitution mandates and supported the inclusion of the reservation establishing the Constitution as the baseline for determining whether conduct amounted to cruel, inhuman, degrading treatment or punishment. *See* 136 Cong. Rec. 36,192 (1990); S. Exec. Rep. 101–30, at 39.

B. Negotiating History

CAT's negotiating history also indicates that its definition of torture supports our reading of Section 2340. The state parties endeavored to craft a definition of torture that reflected the term's gravity. During the negotiations, state parties offered various formulations of the definition of torture to the working group, which then proposed a definition based on those formulations. Almost all of these suggested definitions illustrate the consensus that torture is an extreme act designed to cause agonizing pain. For example, the United States proposed that torture be defined as "includ[ing] any act by which extremely severe pain or suffering ... is deliberately and maliciously inflicted on a person." J. Herman

---

[10] Hearing testimony, though the least weighty evidence of meaning of all of the ratification record, is not to the contrary. Other examples of torture mentioned in testimony similarly reflect acts resulting in intense pain: the "gouging out of childrens' [sic] eyes, the torture death by molten rubber, the use of electric shocks," cigarette burns, hanging by hands or feet. 1990 Hearing at 45 (Statement of Winston Nagan, Chairman, Board of Directors, Amnesty International USA); *id.* at 79 (Statement of David Weissbrodt, Professor of Law, University of Minnesota, on behalf of the Center for Victims of Torture, the Minnesota Lawyers International Human Rights Committee).

Burgers & Hans Danelius, *The United Nations Convention Against Torture: A Handbook on the Convention Against Torture and Other Cruel Inhuman and Degrading Treatment or Punishment* 41 (1988) ("CAT Handbook"). The United Kingdom suggested an even more restrictive definition, i.e., that torture be defined as the "*systematic and intentional* infliction of *extreme* pain or suffering rather than *intentional* infliction of *severe* pain or suffering." *Id.* at 45 (emphasis in original). Ultimately, in choosing the phrase "severe pain," the parties concluded that this phrase "sufficient[ly] ... convey[ed] the idea that only acts of a certain gravity shall ... constitute torture." *Id.* at 117.

In crafting such a definition, the state parties also were acutely aware of the distinction they drew between torture and cruel, inhuman, or degrading treatment or punishment. The state parties considered and rejected a proposal that would have defined torture merely as cruel, inhuman or degrading treatment or punishment. *See id.* at 42. Mirroring the Declaration on Protection From Torture, which expressly defined torture as an "aggravated and deliberate form of cruel, inhuman or degrading treatment or punishment," some state parties proposed that in addition to the definition of torture set out in paragraph 2 of Article 1, a paragraph defining torture as "an aggravated and deliberate form of cruel, inhuman or degrading treatment or punishment" should be included. *See id.* at 41; *see also* S. Treaty Doc. No. 100–20, at 2 (the U.N. Declaration on Protection from Torture (1975) served as "a point of departure for the drafting of [CAT]"). In the end, the parties concluded that the addition of such a paragraph was superfluous because Article 16 "impl[ies] that torture is the gravest form of such treatment or punishment." *CAT Handbook* at 80; *see* S. Exec. Rep. No. 101–30, at 13 ("The negotiating history indicates that [the phrase 'which do not amount to torture'] was adopted in order to emphasize that torture is at the extreme end of cruel, inhuman and degrading treatment or punishment and that Article 1 should be construed with this in mind.").

Additionally, the parties could not reach a consensus about the meaning of "cruel, inhuman, or degrading treatment or punishment." *See CAT Handbook* at 47. Without a consensus, the parties viewed the term as simply " 'too vague to be included in a convention which was to form the basis for criminal legislation in the Contracting States.' " *Id.* This view evinced by the parties reaffirms the interpretation of CAT as purposely reserving criminal penalties for torture alone.

CAT's negotiating history offers more than just support for the view that pain or suffering must be extreme to amount to torture. First, the negotiating history suggests that the harm sustained from the acts of torture need not be permanent. In fact, "the United States considered that it might be useful to develop the negotiating history which indicates that although conduct resulting in permanent impairment of physical or mental faculties is indicative of torture, it is not an essential element of the offence." *Id.* at 44. Second, the state parties to CAT rejected a proposal to include in CAT's definition of torture the use of truth drugs, where no physical harm or mental suffering was apparent. This rejection at least suggests that such drugs were not viewed as amounting to torture per se. *See id.* at 42.

C. Summary

The text of CAT confirms our conclusion that Section 2340A was intended to proscribe only the most egregious conduct. CAT not only defines torture as involving severe pain and suffering, but also it makes clear that such pain and suffering is at the extreme end of the spectrum of acts by reserving criminal penalties solely for torture. Executive interpretations confirm our view that the treaty (and hence the statute) prohibits only the worst forms of cruel, inhuman, or degrading treatment or punishment. The ratification history further substantiates this interpretation. Even the negotiating history displays a recognition that torture is a step far-removed from other cruel, inhuman or degrading treatment or punishment. In sum, CAT's text, ratification history and negotiating history all confirm that Section 2340A reaches only the most heinous acts.

III. U.S. Judicial Interpretation

There are no reported cases of prosecutions under Section 2340A. *See* Beth Stephens, *Corporate Liability: Enforcing Human Rights Through Domestic Litigation*, 24 Hastings Int'l & Comp. L. Rev. 401, 408 & n.29 (2001); Beth Van Schaack, *In Defense of Civil Redress: The Domestic Enforcement of Human Rights Norms in the Context of the Proposed Hague Judgments Convention*, 42 Harv. Int'l L. J. 141, 148–49 (2001); Curtis A. Bradley, *Universal Jurisdiction and U.S. Law*, 2001 U. Chi. Legal F. 323, 327–28. Nonetheless, we are not without guidance as to how United States courts would approach the question of what conduct constitutes torture. Civil suits filed under the Torture Victims Protection Act ("TVPA"), 28 U.S.C. § 1350 note (2000), which supplies a tort remedy for victims of torture, provide insight into what acts U.S. courts would conclude constitute torture under the criminal statute.

The TVPA contains a definition similar in some key respects to the one set forth in Section 2340. Moreover, as with Section 2340, Congress intended for the TVPA's definition of torture to follow closely the definition found in CAT. *See Xuncax v. Gramajo*, 886 F. Supp. 162, 176 n.12 (D. Mass 1995) (noting that the definition of torture in the TVPA tracks the definitions in Section 2340 and CAT).[11] The TVPA defines torture as:

(1)... any act, directed against an individual in the offender's custody or physical control, by which severe pain or suffering (other than pain or suffering arising only from or inherent in, or incidental to, lawful sanctions), whether physical or mental, is intentionally inflicted on that individual for such purposes as obtaining from that individual or a third person information or a confession, punishing that individual for an act that individual or a third person has committed or is suspected of having committed, intimidating or coercing that individual or a third person, or for any reason based on discrimination of any kind; and

(2) mental pain or suffering refers to prolonged mental harm caused by or resulting from –

(A) the intentional infliction or threatened infliction of severe physical pain or suffering;

(B) the administration or application, or threatened administration or application, of mind altering substances or other procedures calculated to disrupt profoundly the senses or the personality;

(C) the threat of imminent death; or

---

[11] *See also* 137 Cong. Rec. 34,785 (statement of Rep. Mazzoli) ("Torture is defined in accordance with the definition contained in [CAT]"); *see also* Torture Victims Portection Act: Hearing and Markup on H.R. 1417 Before the Subcomm. On Human Rights and International Organizations of the House Comm. on Foreign Affairs, 100th Cong. 38 (1988) (Prepared Statement of the Association of the Bar of the City of New York, Committee on International Human Rights) ("This language essentially tracks the definition of 'torture' adopted in the Torture Convention.").

(D) the threat that another individual will imminently be subjected to death, severe physical pain or suffering, or the administration or application of mind altering substances or other procedures calculated to disrupt profoundly the senses or personality

28 U.S.C. § 1350 note § 3(b). This definition differs from Section 2340's definition in two respects. First, the TVPA definition contains an illustrative list of purposes for which such pain may have been inflicted. *See id.* Second, the TVPA includes the phrase "arising only from or inherent in, or incidental to lawful sanctions"; by contrast, Section 2340 refers only to pain or suffering "incidental to lawful sanctions." *Id.* Because the purpose of our analysis here is to ascertain acts that would cross the threshold of producing "severe physical or mental pain or suffering," the list of illustrative purposes for which it is inflicted, generally would not affect this analysis.[12] Similarly, to the extent that the absence of the phrase "arising only from or inherent in" from Section 2340 might affect the question of whether pain or suffering was part of lawful sanctions and thus not torture, the circumstances with which we are concerned here are solely that of interrogations, not the imposition of punishment subsequent to judgment. These differences between the TVPA and Section 2340 are therefore not sufficiently significant to undermine the usefulness of TVPA cases here.[13]

In suits brought under the TVPA, courts have not engaged in any lengthy analysis of what acts constitute torture. In part, this is due to the nature of the acts alleged. Almost all of the cases involve physical torture, some of which is of an especially cruel and even sadistic nature. Nonetheless, courts appear to look at the entire course of conduct rather than any one act, making it somewhat akin to a totality-of-the-circumstances analysis. Because of this approach, it is difficult to take a specific act out of context and conclude that the act in isolation would constitute torture. Certain acts do, however, consistently reappear in these cases or are of such a barbaric nature, that it is likely a court would find that allegations of such treatment would constitute torture: (1) severe beatings using instruments such as iron barks, truncheons, and clubs; (2) threats of imminent death, such as mock executions; (3) threats of removing extremities; (4) burning, especially burning with cigarettes; (5) electric shocks to genitalia or threats to do so; (6) rape or sexual assault, or injury to an individual's sexual organs, or threatening to do any of these sorts of acts; and (7) forcing the prisoner to watch the torture of others. Given the highly contextual nature of whether a set of acts constitutes torture, we have set forth in the attached appendix the circumstances in which courts have determined that the plaintiff has suffered torture, which include the cases from which these seven acts are drawn. While we cannot say with certainty that acts falling short of these seven would *not* constitute torture under Section 2340, we believe that interrogation techniques would have to be similar to these in their extreme nature and in the type of harm caused to violate the law.

---

[12] This list of purposes is illustrative only. Nevertheless, demonstrating that a defendant harbored any of these purposes "may prove valuable in assisting in the establishment of intent at trial." Matthew Lippman, *The Development and Drafting of the United Nations Convention Against Torture and Other Cruel Inhuman or Degrading Treatment or Punishment*, 17 B.C. Int'l & Comp. L. Rev. 275, 314 (1994).

[13] The TVPA also requires that an individual act "intentionally." As we noted with respect to the text of CAT, see *supra* n. 7, this language might be construed as requiring general intent. It is not clear that this is so. We need not resolve that question, however, because we review the TVPA cases solely to address the acts that would satisfy the threshold of inflicting "severe physical or mental pain or suffering."

Despite the limited analysis engaged in by courts, a recent district court opinion provides some assistance in predicting how future courts might address this issue. In *Mehinovic v. Vuckovic*, 198 F. Supp. 2d 1322, (N.D. Ga. 2002), the plaintiffs, Bosnian Muslims, sued a Bosnian Serb, Nikola Vuckovic, for, among other things, torture and cruel and inhumane treatment. The court described in vivid detail the treatment the plaintiffs endured. Specifically, the plaintiffs experienced the following:

Vuckovic repeatedly beat Kemal Mehinovic with a variety of blunt objects and boots, intentionally delivering blows to areas he knew to already be badly injured, including Mehinovic's genitals. *Id.* at 1333–34. On some occasions he was tied up and hung against windows during beatings. *Id.* Mehinovic, was subjected to the game of "Russian roulette" *See id.* Vuckovic, along with other guards, also forced Mehinovic to run in a circle while the guards swung wooden planks at him. *Id.*

Like Mehinovic, Muhamed Bicic was beaten repeatedly with blunt objects, to the point of loss of consciousness. *See Id* at 1335. He witnessed the severe beatings of other prisoners, including his own brother. "On one occasion, Vuckovic ordered Bicic to get on all fours while another soldier stood or rode on his back and beat him with a baton – a game the soldiers called 'horse.'" *Id.* Bicic, like Mehinovic, was subjected to the game of Russian roulette. Additionally, Vuckovic and the other guards forcibly extracted a number of Bicic's teeth. *Id.* at 1336.

Safet Hadzialijagic was subjected to daily beatings with "metal pipes, bats, sticks, and weapons." *Id.* at 1337. He was also subjected to Russian roulette *See id.* at 1336–37.

Hadzialijagic also frequently saw other prisoners being beaten or heard their screams as they were beaten. Like Bicic, he was subjected to the teeth extraction incident. On one occasion, Vuckovic rode Hadzialijagic like a horse, simultaneously hitting him in the head and body with a knife handle. During this time, other soldiers kicked and hit him. He fell down during this episode and was forced to get up and continue carrying Vuckovic. *See id.* "Vuckovic and the other soldiers [then] tied Hadzialijagic with a rope, hung him upside down, and beat him. When they noticed that Hadzialijagic was losing consciousness, they dunked his head in a bowl used as a toilet." *Id.* Vuckovic then forced Hadzialijagic to lick the blood off of Vuckovic's boots and kicked Hadzialijagic as he tried to do so. Vuckovic then used his knife to carve a semi-circle in Hadzialijagic's forehead. Hadzialijagic went into cardiac arrest just after this incident and was saved by one of the other plaintiffs. *See id.*

Hasan Subasic was brutally beaten and witnessed the beatings of other prisoners, including the beating and death of one of his fellow prisoners and the beating of Hadzialijagic in which he was tied upside down and beaten. *See id.* at 1338–39. *Id.* at 1338. Subasic also was subjected to the teeth pulling incident. Vuckovic personally beat Subasic two times, punching him and kicking him with his military boots. In one of these beatings, "Subasic had been forced into a kneeling position when Vuckovic kicked him in the stomach." *Id.*

The district court concluded that the plaintiffs suffered both physical and mental torture at the hands of Vuckovic.[14] With respect to physical torture, the court broadly

---

[14] The court also found that a number of acts perpetrated against the plaintiffs constituted cruel, inhuman, or degrading treatment but not torture. In its analysis, the court appeared to fold into cruel, inhuman, or degrading treatment two distinct categories. First, cruel, inhuman, or degrading treatment includes acts that "do not rise to the level of 'torture.'" *Id.* at 1348. Second, cruel, inhuman, or degrading treatment includes acts that "do not have the same purposes as 'torture.'" *Id.* By including this latter set of treatment as cruel, inhuman or degrading, the court appeared to take

outlined with respect to each plaintiff the acts in which Vuckovic had been at least complicit and that it found rose to the level of torture. Regarding Mehinovic, the court determined that Vuckovic's beatings of Mehinovic in which he kicked and delivered other blows to Mehinovic's face, genitals, and others body parts, constituted torture. The court noted that these beatings left Mehinovic disfigured, may have broken ribs, almost caused Mehinovic to lose consciousness, and rendered him unable to eat for a period of time. As to Bicic, the court found that Bicic had suffered severe physical pain and suffering as a result of Vuckovic's repeated beatings of him in which Vuckovic used various instruments to inflict blows, the "horse" game, and the teeth pulling incident. *See id.* at 1346. In finding that Vuckovic inflicted severe physical pain on Hadzialijagic, the court unsurprisingly focused on the beating in which Vuckovic tied Hadzialijagic upside down and beat him. *See id.* The court pointed out that in this incident, Vuckovic almost killed Hadzialijagic. *See id.* The court further concluded that Subasic experienced severe physical pain and thus was tortured based on the beating in which Vuckovic kicked Subasic in the stomach. *See id.*

The court also found that the plaintiffs had suffered severe mental pain. In reaching this conclusion, the court relied on the plaintiffs' testimony that they feared they would be killed during beatings by Vuckovic or during the "game" of Russian roulette. Although the court did not specify the predicate acts that caused the prolonged mental harm, it is plain that both the threat of severe physical pain and the threat of imminent death were present and persistent. The court also found that the plaintiffs established the existence of prolonged mental harm as each plaintiff "*continues* to suffer long-term psychological harm as a result of [their] ordeals." *Id.* (emphasis added). In concluding that the plaintiffs had demonstrated the necessary "prolonged mental harm," the court's description of that harm as ongoing and "long-term" confirms that, to satisfy the prolonged mental harm requirement, the harm must be of a substantial duration.

The court did not, however, delve into the nature of psychological harm in reaching its conclusion. Nonetheless, the symptoms that the plaintiffs suffered and continue to suffer are worth noting as illustrative of what might in future cases be held to constitute mental harm. Mehinovic had "anxiety, flashbacks, and nightmares and has difficulty sleeping." *Id.* at 1334. Similarly, Bicic, "suffers from anxiety, sleeps very little, and has frequent nightmares" and experiences frustration at not being able to work due to the physical and mental pain he suffers. *Id.* at 1336. Hadzialijagic experienced nightmares, at times required medication to help him sleep, suffered from depression, and had become reclusive as a result of his ordeal. *See id.* at 1337–38. Subasic, like the others, had nightmares and flashbacks, but also suffered from nervousness, irritability, and experienced difficulty trusting people. The combined effect of these symptoms impaired Subasic's ability to work. *See id.* at 1340. Each of these plaintiffs suffered from mental harm that destroyed his ability to function normally, on a daily basis, and would continue to do so into the future.

In general, several guiding principles can be drawn from this case. First, this case illustrates that a single incident can constitute torture. The above recitation of the case's facts shows that Subasic was clearly subjected to torture in a number of instances, e.g., the teeth pulling incident, which the court finds to constitute torture in discussing Bicic. The

the view that acts that would otherwise constitute torture fall outside that definition because of the absence of the particular purposes listed in the TVPA and the treaty. Regardless of the relevance of this concept to the TVPA or CAT, the purposes listed in the TVPA are not an element of torture for purposes of sections 2340–2340A.

court nevertheless found that the beating in which Vuckovic delivered a blow to Subasic's stomach while he was on his knees sufficed to establish that Subasic had been tortured. Indeed, the court stated that this incident "caus[ed] Subasic to suffer severe pain." *Id.* at 1346. The court's focus on this incident, despite the obvious context of a course of torturous conduct, suggests that a course of conduct is unnecessary to establish that an individual engaged in torture. It bears noting, however, that there are no decisions that have found an example of torture on facts that show the action was isolated, rather than part of a systematic course of conduct. Moreover, we believe that had this been an isolated instance, the court's conclusion that this act constituted torture would have been in error, because this single blow does not reach the requisite level of severity.

Second, the case demonstrates that courts may be willing to find that a wide range of physical pain can rise to the necessary level of "severe pain or suffering." At one end of the spectrum is what the court calls the "nightmarish beating" in which Vuckovic hung Hadzialijagic upside down and beat him, culminating in Hadzialijagic going into cardiac arrest and narrowly escaping death. *Id.* It takes little analysis or insight to conclude that this incident constitutes torture. At the other end of the spectrum, is the court's determination that a beating in which "Vuckovic hit plaintiff Subasic and kicked him in the stomach with his military boots while Subasic was forced into a kneeling position [ ]" constituted torture. *Id.* To be sure, this beating caused Subasic substantial pain. But that pain pales in comparison to the other acts described in this case. Again, to the extent the opinion can be read to endorse the view that this single act and the attendant pain, considered in isolation, rose to the level of "severe pain or suffering," we would disagree with such a view based on our interpretation of the criminal statute.

The district court did not attempt to delineate the meaning of torture. It engaged in no statutory analysis. Instead, the court merely recited the definition and described the acts that it concluded constituted torture. This approach is representative of the approach most often taken in TVPA cases. The adoption of such an approach suggests that torture generally is of such an extreme nature – namely, the nature of acts are so shocking and obviously incredibly painful – that courts will more likely examine the totality of the circumstances, rather than engage in a careful parsing of the statute. A broad view of this case, and of the TVPA cases more generally, shows that only acts of an extreme nature have been redressed under the TVPA's civil remedy for torture. We note, however, that *Mehinovic* presents, with the exception of the single blow to Subasic, facts that are well over the line of what constitutes torture. While there are cases that fall far short of torture, see *infra* app., there are no cases that analyze what the lowest boundary of what constitutes torture. Nonetheless, while this case and the other TVPA cases generally do not approach that boundary, they are in keeping with the general notion that the term "torture" is reserved for acts of the most extreme nature.

IV. International Decisions

International decisions can prove of some value in assessing what conduct might rise to the level of severe mental pain or suffering. Although decisions by foreign or international bodies are in no way binding authority upon the United States, they provide guidance about how other nations will likely react to our interpretation of the CAT and Section 2340. As this Part will discuss, other Western nations have generally used a high standard in determining whether interrogation techniques violate the international prohibition on torture. In fact, these decisions have found various aggressive interrogation methods to, at worst, constitute cruel, inhuman, and degrading treatment, but not torture. These decisions only reinforce our view that there is a clear distinction between the two standards and that only extreme conduct, resulting in pain that is of an intensity often accompanying serious physical injury, will violate the latter.

A. European Court of Human Rights

An analogue to CAT's provisions can be found in the European Convention on Human Rights and Fundamental Freedoms (the "European Convention"). This convention prohibits torture, though it offers no definition of it. It also prohibits cruel, inhuman, or degrading treatment or punishment. By barring both types of acts, the European Convention implicitly distinguishes between them and further suggests that torture is a grave act beyond cruel, inhuman, or degrading treatment or punishment. Thus, while neither the European Convention nor the European Court of Human Rights decisions interpreting that convention would be authority for the interpretation of Sections 2340–2340A, the European Convention decisions concerning torture nonetheless provide a useful barometer of the international view of what actions amount to torture.

The leading European Court of Human Rights case explicating the differences between torture and cruel, inhuman, or degrading treatment or punishment is *Ireland v. the United Kingdom* (1978).[15] In that case, the European Court of Human Rights examined interrogation techniques somewhat more sophisticated than the rather rudimentary and frequently obviously cruel acts described in the TVPA cases. Careful attention to this case is worthwhile not just because it examines methods not used in the TVPA cases, but also because the Reagan administration relied on this case in reaching the conclusion that the term torture is reserved in international usage for "extreme, deliberate, and unusually cruel practices." S. Treaty Doc. 100–20, at 4.

The methods at issue in *Ireland* were:

(1) Wall Standing. The prisoner stands spreadeagle against the wall, with fingers high above his head, and feet back so that he is standing on his toes such that his all of his weight falls on his fingers.

(2) Hooding. A black or navy hood is placed over the prisoner's head and kept there except during the interrogation.

---

[15] According to one commentator, the Inter-American Court of Human Rights has also followed this decision. *See* Julie Lantrip, *Torture and Cruel, Inhuman and Degrading Treatment in the Jurisprudence of the Inter-American Court of Human Rights*, 5 ILSA J. Int'l & Comp. L. 551, 560–61 (1999). The Inter-American Convention to Prevent and Punish Torture, however, defines torture much differently than it is defined in CAT or U.S. law. *See* Inter-American Convention to Prevent and Punish Torture, opened for signature Dec. 9, 1985, art. 2, OAS T.S. No. 67 (entered into force Feb. 28, 1987 but the United States has never signed or ratified it). It defines torture as "any act intentionally performed whereby physical or mental pain or suffering is inflicted on a person for purposes of criminal investigation, as a means of intimidation, as personal punishment, as a preventive measure, as a penalty or for any other purpose. Torture shall also be understood to be the use of methods upon a person intended to obliterate the personality of the victim or to diminish his physical or mental capacities, even if they do not cause physical pain or mental anguish." Article 2. While the Inter-American Convention to Prevent and Punish Torture does not require signatories to criminalize cruel, inhuman, or degrading treatment or punishment, the textual differences in the definition of torture are so great that it would be difficult to draw from that jurisprudence anything more than the general trend of its agreement with the *Ireland* decision.

(3) Subjection to Noise. Pending interrogation, the prisoner is kept in a room with a loud and continuous hissing noise.

(4) Sleep Deprivation. Prisoners are deprived of sleep pending interrogation.

(5) Deprivation of Food and Drink. Prisoners receive a reduced diet during detention and pending interrogation.

The European Court of Human Rights concluded that these techniques used in combination, and applied for hours at a time, were inhuman and degrading but did not amount to torture. In analyzing whether these methods constituted torture, the court treated them as part of a single program. *See Ireland.* ¶ 104. The court found that this program caused "if not actual bodily injury, at least intense physical and mental suffering to the person subjected thereto and also led to acute psychiatric disturbances during the interrogation." *Id.* ¶ 167. Thus, this program "fell into the category of inhuman treatment[.]" *Id.* The court further found that "[t]he techniques were also degrading since they were such as to arouse in their victims feeling of fear, anguish and inferiority capable of humiliating and debasing them and possible [sic] breaking their physical or moral resistance." *Id.* Yet, the court ultimately concluded:

> Although the five techniques, as applied in combination, undoubtedly amounted to inhuman and degrading treatment, although their object was the extraction of confession, the naming of others and/or information and although they were used systematically, they did not occasion suffering of the particular *intensity* and *cruelty* implied by the word torture...

Id. (emphasis added). Thus, even though the court had concluded that the techniques produce "intense physical and mental suffering" and "acute psychiatric disturbances," they were not sufficient intensity or cruelty to amount to torture.

The court reached this conclusion based on the distinction the European Convention drew between torture and cruel, inhuman, or degrading treatment or punishment. The court reasoned that by expressly distinguishing between these two categories of treatment, the European Convention sought to "attach a special stigma to deliberate inhuman treatment causing very serious and cruel suffering." *Id.* ¶ 167. According to the court, "this distinction derives principally from a difference in the intensity of the suffering inflicted." *Id.* The court further noted that this distinction paralleled the one drawn in the U.N. Declaration on the Protection From Torture, which specifically defines torture as " 'an aggravated and deliberate form of cruel, inhuman or degrading treatment or punishment.' " *Id.* (quoting U.N. Declaration on the Protection From Torture).

The court relied on this same "intensity/cruelty" distinction to conclude that some physical maltreatment fails to amount to torture. For example, four detainees were severely beaten and forced to stand spreadeagle up against a wall. *See id.* ¶ 110. Other detainees were forced to stand spreadeagle while an interrogator kicked them "continuously on the inside of the legs." *Id.* ¶ 111. Those detainees were beaten, some receiving injuries that were "substantial" and, others received "massive" injuries. *See id.* Another detainee was "subjected to...'comparatively trivial' beatings" that resulted in a perforation of the detainee's eardrum and some "minor bruising." *Id.* ¶ 115. The court concluded that none of these situations "attain[ed] the particular level [of severity] inherent in the notion of torture." *Id.* ¶ 174.

B. Israeli Supreme Court

The European Court of Human Rights is not the only other court to consider whether such a program of interrogation techniques was permissible. In *Public Committee Against Torture in Israel v. Israel*, 38 I.L.M. 1471 (1999), the Supreme Court of Israel reviewed a challenge brought against the General Security Service ("GSS") for its use of five techniques. At issue in *Public Committee Against Torture In Israel* were: (1) shaking, (2) the Shabach, (3) the Frog Crouch, (4) excessive tightening of handcuffs, and (5) sleep deprivation. "Shaking" is "the forceful shaking of the suspect's upper torso, back and forth, repeatedly, in a manner which causes the neck and head to dangle and vacillate rapidly." *Id.* ¶ 9. The "Shabach" is actually a combination of methods wherein the detainee

> is seated on a small and low chair, whose seat is tilted forward, towards the ground. One hand is tied behind the suspect, and placed inside the gap between the chair's seat and back support. His second hand is tied behind the chair, against its back support. The suspect's head is covered by an opaque sack, falling down to his shoulders. Powerfully loud music is played in the room.

Id. ¶ 10.

The "frog crouch" consists of "consecutive, periodical crouches on the tips of one's toes, each lasting for five minute intervals." *Id.* ¶ 11. The excessive tightening of handcuffs simply referred to the use handcuffs that were too small for the suspects' wrists. *See id.* ¶ 12. Sleep deprivation occurred when the Shabach was used during "intense non-stop interrogations."[16] *Id.* ¶ 13.

While the Israeli Supreme Court concluded that these acts amounted to cruel, and inhuman treatment, the court did not expressly find that they amounted to torture. To be sure, such a conclusion was unnecessary because even if the acts amounted only to cruel and inhuman treatment the GSS lacked authority to use the five methods. Nonetheless, the decision is still best read as indicating that the acts at issue did not constitute torture. The court's descriptions of and conclusions about each method indicate that the court viewed them as merely cruel, inhuman or degrading but not of the sufficient severity to reach the threshold of torture. While its descriptions discuss necessity, dignity, degradation, and pain, the court carefully avoided describing any of these acts as having the severity of pain or suffering indicative of torture. *See id.* at ¶ ¶ 24–29. Indeed, in assessing the *Shabach* as a whole, the court even relied upon the European Court of Human Right's *Ireland* decision for support and it did not evince disagreement with that decision's conclusion that the acts considered therein did not constitute torture. *See id.* ¶ 30.

Moreover, the Israeli Supreme Court concluded that in certain circumstances GSS officers could assert a necessity defense.[17] CAT, however, expressly provides that "[n]o

---

[16] The court did, however, distinguish between this sleep deprivation and that which occurred as part of routine interrogation, noting that some degree of interference with the suspect's regular sleep habits was to be expected. *Public Committee Against Torture in Israel* ¶ 23.

[17] In permitting a necessity defense, the court drew upon the ticking time bomb hypothesis proffered by the GSS as a basis for asserting a necessity defense. In that hypothesis, the GSS has arrested a suspect, who holds information about the location of a bomb and the time at which it is set to explode. The suspect is the only source of this information, and without that information the bomb will surely explode, killing many people. Under those circumstances, the court agreed that the necessity defense's requirement of imminence, which the court construed as the "imminent nature of the act rather than that of danger," would be satisfied. *Id.* ¶ 34. It further agreed "that in appropriate circumstances" this defense would be available to GSS investigators. *Id.* ¶ 35.

exceptional circumstance whatsoever, whether a state of war or a threat of war, internal political instability or any other public emergency may be invoked as a justification of torture." Article 2(2). Had the court been of the view that the GSS methods constituted torture, the Court could not permit this affirmative defense under CAT. Accordingly, the court's decision is best read as concluding that these methods amounted to cruel and inhuman treatment, but not torture.

In sum, both the European Court on Human Rights and the Israeli Supreme Court have recognized a wide array of acts that constitute cruel, inhuman, or degrading treatment or punishment, but do not amount to torture. Thus, they appear to permit, under international law, an aggressive interpretation as to what amounts to torture, leaving that label to be applied only where extreme circumstances exist.

V. The President's Commander-in-Chief Power

Even if an interrogation method arguably were to violate Section 2340A, the statute would be unconstitutional if it impermissibly encroached on the President's constitutional power to conduct a military campaign. As Commander-in-Chief, the President has the constitutional authority to order interrogations of enemy combatants to gain intelligence information concerning the military plans of the enemy. The demands of the Commander-in-Chief power are especially pronounced in the middle of a war in which the nation has already suffered a direct attack. In such a case, the information gained from interrogations may prevent future attacks by foreign enemies. Any effort to apply Section 2340A in a manner that interferes with the President's direction of such core war matters as the detention and interrogation of enemy combatants thus would be unconstitutional.

A. The War with Al Qaeda

At the outset, we should make clear the nature of the threat presently posed to the nation. While your request for legal advice is not specifically limited to the current circumstances, we think it is useful to discuss this question in the context of the current war against the al Qaeda terrorist network. The situation in which these issues arise is unprecedented in recent American history. Four coordinated terrorist attacks, using hijacked commercial airliners as guided missiles, took place in rapid succession on the morning of September 11, 2001. These attacks were aimed at critical government buildings in the Nation's capital and landmark buildings in its financial center. These events reach a different scale of destructiveness than earlier terrorist episodes, such as the destruction of the Murrah Building in Oklahoma City in 1994. They caused thousands of deaths. Air traffic and communications within the United States were disrupted; national stock exchanges were shut for several days; and damage from the attack has been estimated to run into the tens of billions of dollars. Moreover, these attacks are part of a violent campaign against the United States that is believed to include an unsuccessful attempt to destroy an airliner in December 2001; a suicide bombing attack in Yemen on the *U.S.S. Cole* in 2000; the bombings of the United States Embassies in Kenya and in Tanzania in 1998; a truck bomb attack on a U.S. military housing complex in Saudi Arabia in 1996; an unsuccessful attempt to destroy the World Trade Center in 1993; and the ambush of U.S. servicemen in Somalia in 1993. The United States and its overseas personnel and installations have been attacked as a result of Osama Bin Laden's call for a "jihad against the U.S. government, because the U.S. government is unjust, criminal and tyrannical."[18]

In response, the Government has engaged in a broad effort at home and abroad to counter terrorism. Pursuant to his authorities as Commander-in-Chief, the President in October, 2001, ordered the Armed Forces to attack al Qaeda personnel and assets in Afghanistan, and the Taliban militia that harbored them. That military campaign appears to be nearing its close with the retreat of al Qaeda and Taliban forces from their strongholds and the installation of a friendly provisional government in Afghanistan. Congress has provided its support for the use of forces against those linked to the September 11 attacks, and has recognized the President's constitutional power to use force to prevent and deter future attacks both within and outside the United States. S. J. Res. 23, Pub. L. No. 107–40, 115 Stat. 224 (2001). We have reviewed the President's constitutional power to use force abroad in response to the September 11 attacks in a separate memorandum. *See* Memorandum for Timothy E. Flanigan, Deputy Counsel to the President, from John C. Yoo, Deputy Assistant Attorney General, Office of Legal Counsel, *Re: The President's Constitutional Authority to Conduct Military Operations Against Terrorists and Nations Supporting Them* (Sept. 25, 2001) ("September 11 War Powers Memorandum"). We have also discussed the President's constitutional authority to deploy the armed forces domestically to protect against foreign terrorist attack in a separate memorandum. *See* Memorandum for Alberto R. Gonzales, Counsel to the President and William J. Haynes, II, General Counsel, Department of Defense, from John C. Yoo, Deputy Assistant Attorney General and Robert J. Delahunty, Special Counsel, Office of Legal Counsel, *Re: Authority for Use of Military Force to Combat Terrorist Activities Within the United States* at 2–3 (Oct. 17, 2001). The Justice Department and the FBI have launched a sweeping investigation in response to the September 11 attacks, and last fall Congress enacted legislation to expand the Justice Department's powers of surveillance against terrorists. *See* The USA Patriot Act, Pub. L. No. 107–56, 115 Stat. 272 (Oct. 26, 2001). This spring, the President proposed the creation of a new cabinet department for homeland security to implement a coordinated domestic program against terrorism.

Despite these efforts, numerous upper echelon leaders of al Qaeda and the Taliban, with access to active terrorist cells and other resources, remain at large. It has been reported that the al Qaeda fighters are already drawing on a fresh flow of cash to rebuild their forces. *See* Paul Haven, *U.S.: al-Qaida Trying to Regroup*, Associated Press, Mar. 20, 2002. As the Director of the Central Intelligence Agency has recently testified before Congress, "al Qaeda and other terrorist groups will continue to plan to attack this country and its interests abroad. Their modus operandi is to have multiple attack plans in the works simultaneously, and to have al Qaeda cells in place to conduct them." Testimony of George J. Tenet, Director of Central Intelligence, Before the Senate Armed Services Committee at 2 (Mar. 19, 2002). Nor is the threat contained to Afghanistan. "Operations against US targets could be launched by al Qaeda cells already in place in major cities in Europe and the Middle East. al Qaeda can also exploit its presence or connections to other groups in such countries as Somalia, Yemen, Indonesia, and the Philippines." *Id.* at 3. It appears that al Qaeda continues to enjoy information and resources that allow it to organize and direct active hostile forces against this country, both domestically and abroad.

---

[18] *See Osama Bin Laden v. The U.S.: Edicts and Statements*, CNN Interview with Osama bin Laden, March 1997, *available at* http://www.pbs.org/wgbh/pages/frontline/shows/binladen/who/edicts.html.

Al Qaeda continues to plan further attacks, such as destroying American civilian air-liners and killing American troops, which have fortunately been prevented. It is clear that bin Laden and his organization have conducted several violent attacks on the United States and its nationals, and that they seek to continue to do so. Thus, the capture and interrogation of such individuals is clearly imperative to our national security and defense. Interrogation of captured al Qaeda operatives may provide information concerning the nature of al Qaeda plans and the identities of its personnel, which may prove invaluable in preventing further direct attacks on the United States and its citizens. Given the massive destruction and loss of life caused by the September 11 attacks, it is reasonable to believe that information gained from al Qaeda personnel could prevent attacks of a similar (if not greater) magnitude from occurring in the United States. The case of Jose Padilla, a.k.a. Abdullah Al Mujahir, illustrates the importance of such information. Padilla allegedly had journeyed to Afghanistan and Pakistan, met with senior al Qaeda leaders, and hatched a plot to construct and detonate a radioactive dispersal device in the United States. After allegedly receiving training in wiring explosives and with a substantial amount of currency in his position, Padilla attempted in May, 2002, to enter the United States to further his scheme. Interrogation of captured al Qaeda operatives allegedly allowed U.S. intelligence and law enforcement agencies to track Padilla and to detain him upon his entry into the United States.

B. Interpretation to Avoid Constitutional Problems

As the Supreme Court has recognized, and as we will explain further below, the President enjoys complete discretion in the exercise of his Commander-in-Chief authority and in conducting operations against hostile forces. Because both "[t]he executive power and the command of the military and naval forces is vested in the President," the Supreme Court has unanimously stated that it is "*the President alone* who is constitutionally invested with the *entire charge of hostile operations.*" *Hamilton v. Dillin*, 88 U.S. (21 Wall.) 73, 87 (1874) (emphasis added). That authority is at its height in the middle of a war.

In light of the President's complete authority over the conduct of war, without a clear statement otherwise, we will not read a criminal statute as infringing on the President's ultimate authority in these areas. We have long recognized, and the Supreme Court has established a canon of statutory construction that statutes are to be construed in a manner that avoids constitutional difficulties so long as a reasonable alternative construction is available. *See, e.g., Edward J. DeBartolo Corp. v. Florida Gulf Coast Bldg. & Constr. Trades Council*, 485 U.S. 568, 575 (1988) (citing *NLRB v. Catholic Bishop of Chicago*, 440 U.S. 490, 499–501, 504 (1979)) ("[W]here an otherwise acceptable construction of a statute would raise serious constitutional problems, [courts] will construe [a] statute to avoid such problems unless such construction is plainly contrary to the intent of Congress."). This canon of construction applies especially where an act of Congress could be read to encroach upon powers constitutionally committed to a coordinate branch of government. *See, e.g., Franklin v. Massachusetts*, 505 U.S. 788, 800–1 (1992) (citation omitted) ("Out of respect for the separation of powers and the unique constitutional position of the President, we find that textual silence is not enough to subject the President to the provisions of the [Administrative Procedure Act]. We would require an express statement by Congress before assuming it intended the President's performance of his statutory duties to be reviewed for abuse of discretion."); *Public Citizen v. United States Dep't of Justice*, 491 U.S. 440, 465–67 (1989) (construing Federal Advisory Committee Act not to apply to advice given by American Bar Association to the President on judicial nominations, to avoid potential constitutional question regarding encroachment on Presidential power to appoint judges).

In the area of foreign affairs, and war powers in particular, the avoidance canon has special force. *See, e.g., Dep't of Navy v. Egan*, 484 U.S. 518, 530 (1988) ("unless Congress specifically has provided otherwise, courts traditionally have been reluctant to intrude upon the authority of the Executive in military and national security affairs."); *Japan Whaling Ass'n v. American Cetacean Soc'y*, 478 U.S. 221, 232–33 (1986) (construing federal statutes to avoid curtailment of traditional presidential prerogatives in foreign affairs). We do not lightly assume that Congress has acted to interfere with the President's constitutionally superior position as Chief Executive and Commander-in-Chief in the area of military operations. *See Egan*, 484 U.S. at 529 (quoting *Haig v. Agee*, 453 U.S. 280, 293–94 (1981)). *See also Agee*, 453 U.S. at 291 (deference to Executive Branch is "especially" appropriate "in the area ... of ... national security").

In order to respect the President's inherent constitutional authority to manage a military campaign against al Qaeda and its allies, Section 2340A must be construed as not applying to interrogations undertaken pursuant to his Commander-in-Chief authority. As our Office has consistently held during this Administration and previous Administrations, Congress lacks authority under Article I to set the terms and conditions under which the President may exercise his authority as Commander-in-Chief to control the conduct of operations during a war. *See, e.g.*, Memorandum for Daniel J. Bryant, Assistant Attorney General, Office of Legislative Affairs, from Patrick F. Philbin, Deputy Assistant Attorney General, Office of Legal Counsel, *Re: Swift Justice Authorization Act* (Apr. 8, 2002); Memorandum for Timothy E. Flanigan, Deputy Counsel to the President, from John C. Yoo, Deputy Assistant Attorney General, Office of Legal Counsel, *Re: The President's Constitutional Authority to Conduct Military Operations Against Terrorists and Nations Supporting Them* (Sep. 25, 2001) ("Flanigan Memorandum"); Memorandum for Andrew Fois, Assistant Attorney General, Office of Legislative Affairs, from Richard L. Shiffrin, Deputy Assistant Attorney General, Office of Legal Counsel, *Re: Defense Authorization Act* (Sep. 15, 1995). As we discuss below, the President's power to detain and interrogate enemy combatants arises out of his constitutional authority as Commander-in-Chief. A construction of Section 2340A that applied the provision to regulate the President's authority as Commander-in-Chief to determine the interrogation and treatment of enemy combatants would raise serious constitutional questions. Congress may no more regulate the President's ability to detain and interrogate enemy combatants than it may regulate his ability to direct troop movements on the battlefield. Accordingly, we would construe Section 2340A to avoid this constitutional difficulty, and conclude that it does not apply to the President's detention and interrogation of enemy combatants pursuant to his Commander-in-Chief authority.

This approach is consistent with previous decisions of our Office involving the application of federal criminal law. For example, we have previously construed the congressional contempt statute not to apply to executive branch officials who refuse to comply with congressional subpoenas because of an assertion of executive privilege. In a published 1984 opinion, we concluded that

> if executive officials were subject to prosecution for criminal contempt whenever they carried out the President's claim of executive privilege, it would significantly burden and immeasurably impair the President's ability to fulfill his constitutional duties. Therefore, the separation of powers principles that underlie the doctrine of executive privilege also would preclude an application of the contempt of Congress statute to punish officials for aiding the President in asserting his constitutional privilege.

Prosecution for Contempt of Congress of an Executive Branch Official Who Has Asserted A Claim of Executive Privilege, 8 Op. O.L.C. 101, 134 (May 30, 1984). Likewise, we believe that, if executive officials were subject to prosecution for conducting interrogations when they were carrying out the President's Commander-in-Chief powers, "it would significantly burden and immeasurably impair the President's ability to fulfill his constitutional duties." These constitutional principles preclude an application of Section 2340A to punish officials for aiding the President in exercising his exclusive constitutional authorities. *Id.*

C. The Commander-in-Chief Power

It could be argued that Congress enacted 18 U.S.C. § 2340A with full knowledge and consideration of the President's Commander-in-Chief power, and that Congress intended to restrict his discretion in the interrogation of enemy combatants. Even were we to accept this argument, however, we conclude that the Department of Justice could not enforce Section 2340A against federal officials acting pursuant to the President's constitutional authority to wage a military campaign.

Indeed, in a different context, we have concluded that both courts and prosecutors should reject prosecutions that apply federal criminal laws to activity that is authorized pursuant to one of the President's constitutional powers. This Office, for example, has previously concluded that Congress could not constitutionally extend the congressional contempt statute to executive branch officials who refuse to comply with congressional subpoenas because of an assertion of executive privilege. We opined that "courts . . . would surely conclude that a criminal prosecution for the exercise of a presumptively valid, constitutionally based privilege is not consistent with the Constitution." 8 Op. O.L.C. at 141. Further, we concluded that the Department of Justice could not bring a criminal prosecution against a defendant who had acted pursuant to an exercise of the President's constitutional power. "The President, through a United States Attorney, need not, indeed may not, prosecute criminally a subordinate for asserting on his behalf a claim of executive privilege. Nor could the Legislative Branch or the courts require or implement the prosecution of such an individual." *Id.* Although Congress may define federal crimes that the President, through the Take Care Clause, should prosecute, Congress cannot compel the President to prosecute outcomes taken pursuant to the President's own constitutional authority. If Congress could do so, it could control the President's authority through the manipulation of federal criminal law.

We have even greater concerns with respect to prosecutions arising out of the exercise of the President's express authority as Commander-in-Chief than we do with prosecutions arising out of the assertion of executive privilege. In a series of opinions examining various legal questions arising after September 11, we have explained the scope of the President's Commander-in-Chief power.[19] We briefly summarize the findings of those opinions here. The President's constitutional power to protect the security of the United States and the lives and safety of its people must be understood in light of the Founders' intention to create a federal government "clothed with all the powers requisite to the complete execution of its trust." *The Federalist* No. 23, at 147 (Alexander Hamilton) (Jacob E. Cooke ed. 1961). Foremost among the objectives committed to that trust by the Constitution is the

---

[19] *See, e.g.,* September 11 War Powers Memorandum; Memorandum for Alberto R. Gonzales, Counsel to the President, from Patrick F. Philbin, Deputy Assistant Attorney General, Office of Legal Counsel, *Re: Legality of the Use of Military Commissions to Try Terrorists* (Nov. 6, 2001).

security of the nation. As Hamilton explained in arguing for the Constitution's adoption, because "the circumstances which may affect the public safety" are not "reducible within certain determinate limits,"

> it must be admitted, as a necessary consequence, that there can be no limitation of that authority, which is to provide for the defence and protection of the community, in any matter essential to its efficacy.

Id. at 147–48. Within the limits that the Constitution itself imposes, the scope and distribution of the powers to protect national security must be construed to authorize the most efficacious defense of the nation and its interests in accordance "with the realistic purposes of the entire instrument." *Lichter v. United States*, 334 U.S. 742, 782 (1948).

The text, structure and history of the Constitution establish that the Founders entrusted the President with the primary responsibility, and therefore the power, to ensure the security of the United States in situations of grave and unforeseen emergencies. The decision to deploy military force in the defense of United States interests is expressly placed under Presidential authority by the Vesting Clause, U.S. Const. Art. I, § 1, cl. 1, and by the Commander-in-Chief Clause, *id.*, § 2, cl. 1.[20] This Office has long understood the Commander-in-Chief Clause in particular as an affirmative grant of authority to the President. *See, e.g.*, Memorandum for Charles W. Colson, Special Counsel to the President, from William H. Rehnquist, Assistant Attorney General, Office of Legal Counsel, *Re: The President and the War Power: South Vietnam and the Cambodian Sanctuaries* (May 22, 1970) ("Rehnquist Memorandum"). The Framers understood the Clause as investing the President with the fullest range of power understood at the time of the ratification of the Constitution as belonging to the military commander. In addition, the structure of the Constitution demonstrates that any power traditionally understood as pertaining to the executive – which includes the conduct of warfare and the defense of the nation – unless expressly assigned in the Constitution to Congress, is vested in the President. Article II, Section 1 makes this clear by stating that the "executive Power shall be vested in a President of the United States of America." That sweeping grant vests in the President an unenumerated "executive power" and contrasts with the specific enumeration of the powers – those "herein" – granted to Congress in Article I. The implications of constitutional text and structure are confirmed by the practical consideration that national security decisions require the unity in purpose and energy in action that characterize the Presidency rather than Congress.[21]

---

[20] *See Johnson v. Eisentrager*, 339 U.S. 763, 789 (1950) (President has authority to deploy United States armed forces "abroad or to any particular region"); *Fleming v. Page*, 50 U.S. (9 How.) 603, 614–15 (1850) ("As Commander-in-Chief, [the President] is authorized to direct the movements of the naval and military forces placed by law at his command, and to employ them in the manner he may deem most effectual") *Loving v. United States*, 517 U.S. 748, 776 (1996) (Scalia, J., concurring in part and concurring in judgment) (The "inherent powers" of the Commander-in-Chief "are clearly extensive."); *Maul v. United States*, 274 U.S. 501, 515–16 (1927) (Brandeis & Holmes, JJ., concurring) (President "may direct any revenue cutter to cruise in any waters in order to perform any duty of the service"); *Commonwealth of Massachusetts v. Laird*, 451 F.2d 26, 32 (1st Cir. 1971) (the President has "power as Commander-in-Chief to station forces abroad"); *Ex parte Vallandigham*, 28 F.Cas. 874, 922 (C.C.S.D. Ohio 1863) (No. 16,816) (in acting "under this power where there is no express legislative declaration, the president is guided solely by his own judgment and discretion"); *Authority to Use United States Military Forces in Somalia*, 16 Op. O.L.C. 6, 6 (Dec. 4, 1992) (Barr, Attorney General).

[21] Judicial decisions since the beginning of the Republic confirm the President's constitutional power and duty to repel military action against the United States and to take measures to prevent the

As the Supreme Court has recognized, the Commander-in-Chief power and the President's obligation to protect the nation imply the ancillary powers necessary to their successful exercise. "The first of the enumerated powers of the President is that he shall be Commander-in-Chief of the Army and Navy of the United States. And, of course, the grant of war power includes all that is necessary and proper for carrying those powers into execution." *Johnson v. Eisentrager*, 339 U.S. 763, 788 (1950). In wartime, it is for the President alone to decide what methods to use to best prevail against the enemy. *See, e.g.*, Rehnquist Memorandum; Flanigan Memorandum at 3. The President's complete discretion in exercising the Commander-in-Chief power has been recognized by the courts. In the *Prize Cases*, 67 U.S. (2 Black) 635, 670 (1862), for example, the Court explained that whether the President "in fulfilling his duties as Commander-in-Chief" had appropriately responded to the rebellion of the southern states was a question "to be *decided by him*" and which the Court could not question, but must leave to "the political department of the Government to which this power was entrusted."

One of the core functions of the Commander-in-Chief is that of capturing, detaining, and interrogating members of the enemy. *See, e.g.*, Memorandum for William J. Haynes, II, General Counsel, Department of Defense, from Jay S. Bybee, Assistant Attorney General, Office of Legal Counsel, *Re: The President's Power as Commander in Chief to Transfer Captured Terrorists to the Control and Custody of Foreign Nations* at 3 (March 13, 2002) ("the Commander-in-Chief Clause constitutes an independent grant of substantive authority to engage in the detention and transfer of prisoners captured in armed conflicts"). It is well settled that the President may seize and detain enemy combatants, at least for the duration of the conflict, and the laws of war make clear that prisoners may be interrogated for information concerning the enemy, its strength, and its plans.[22] Numerous Presidents have ordered the capture, detention, and questioning of enemy combatants during virtually every major conflict in the Nation's history, including recent conflicts such as the Gulf, Vietnam, and Korean wars. Recognizing this authority, Congress has never attempted to restrict or interfere with the President's authority on this score. *Id.*

---

recurrence of an attack. As Justice Joseph Story said long ago, "[i]t may be fit and proper for the government, in the exercise of the high discretion confided to the executive, for great public purposes, to act on a sudden emergency, or to prevent an irreparable mischief, by summary measures, which are not found in the text of the laws." *The Apollon*, 22 U.S. (9 Wheat.) 362, 366–67 (1824). If the President is confronted with an unforeseen attack on the territory and people of the United States, or other immediate, dangerous threat to American interests and security, it is his constitutional responsibility to respond to that threat with whatever means are necessary. *See, e.g., The Prize Cases*, 67 U.S. (2 Black) 635, 668 (1862) ("If a war be made by invasion of a foreign nation, the President is not only authorized but bound to resist force by force ... without waiting for any special legislative authority."); *United States v. Smith*, 27 F. Cas. 1192, 1229–30 (C.C.D.N.Y. 1806) (No. 16,342) (Paterson, Circuit Justice) (regardless of statutory authorization, it is "the duty ... of the executive magistrate ... to repel an invading foe"); *see also* 3 Story, *Commentaries* § 1485 ("[t]he command and application of the public force ... to maintain peace, and to resist foreign invasion" are executive powers).

[22] The practice of capturing and detaining enemy combatants is as old as war itself. *See* Allan Rosas, The Legal Status of Prisoners of War 44–45 (1976). In modern conflicts, the practice of detaining enemy combatants and hostile civilians generally has been designed to balance the humanitarian purpose of sparing lives with the military necessity of defeating the enemy on the battlefield. *Id.* at 59–80. While Article 17 of the Geneva Convention Relative to the Treatment of Prisoners of War, Aug. 12, 1949, 6 U.S.T. 3517, places restrictions on interrogation of enemy combatants, members of al Qaeda and the Taliban militia are not legally entitled to the status of prisoners of war as defined in the Convention. *See* Memorandum for Alberto R. Gonzales, Counsel to the President and William J. Haynes, II, General Counsel, Department of Defense, from Jay S. Bybee, Assistant Attorney General, Office of Legal Counsel, *Re: Application of Treaties and Laws to al Qaeda and Taliban Detainees* (Jan. 22, 2002).

Any effort by Congress to regulate the interrogation of battlefield combatants would violate the Constitution's sole vesting of the Commander-in-Chief authority in the President. There can be little doubt that intelligence operations, such as the detention and interrogation of enemy combatants and leaders, are both necessary and proper for the effective conduct of a military campaign. Indeed, such operations may be of more importance in a war with an international terrorist organization than one with the conventional armed forces of a nation-state, due to the former's emphasis on secret operations and surprise attacks against civilians. It may be the case that only successful interrogations can provide the information necessary to prevent the success of covert terrorist attacks upon the United States and its citizens. Congress can no more interfere with the President's conduct of the interrogation of enemy combatants than it can dictate strategic or tactical decisions on the battlefield. Just as statutes that order the President to conduct warfare in a certain manner or for specific goals would be unconstitutional, so too are laws that seek to prevent the President from gaining the intelligence he believes necessary to prevent attacks upon the United States.

VI. Defenses

In the foregoing parts of this memorandum, we have demonstrated that the ban on torture in Section 2340A is limited to only the most extreme forms of physical and mental harm. We have also demonstrated that Section 2340A, as applied to interrogations of enemy combatants ordered by the President pursuant to his Commander-in-Chief power would be unconstitutional. Even if an interrogation method, however, might arguably cross the line drawn in Section 2340, and application of the statute was not held to be an unconstitutional infringement of the President's Commander-in-Chief authority, we believe that under the current circumstances certain justification defenses might be available that would potentially eliminate criminal liability. Standard criminal law defenses of necessity and self-defense could justify interrogation methods needed to elicit information to prevent a direct and imminent threat to the United States and its citizens.

A. Necessity

We believe that a defense of necessity could be raised, under the current circumstances, to an allegation of a Section 2340A violation. Often referred to as the "choice of evils" defense, necessity has been defined as follows:

> Conduct that the actor believes to be necessary to avoid a harm or evil to himself or to another is justifiable, provided that:
>
>   (a) the harm or evil sought to be avoided by such conduct is greater than that sought to be prevented by the law defining the offense charged; and
>   (b) neither the Code nor other law defining the offense provides exceptions or defenses dealing with the specific situation involved; and
>   (c) a legislative purpose to exclude the justification claimed does not otherwise plainly appear.

Model Penal Code § 3.02. *See also* Wayne R. LaFave & Austin W. Scott, 1 Substantive Criminal Law § 5.4 at 627 (1986 & 2002 supp.) ("LaFave & Scott"). Although there is no federal statute that generally establishes necessity or other justifications as defenses to federal criminal laws, the Supreme Court has recognized the defense. *See United States v.*

Bailey, 444 U.S. 394, 410 (1980) (relying on LaFave & Scott and Model Penal Code definitions of necessity defense).

The necessity defense may prove especially relevant in the current circumstances. As it has been described in the case law and literature, the purpose behind necessity is one of public policy. According to LaFave and Scott, "[t]he law ought to promote the achievement of higher values at the expense of lesser values, and sometimes the greater good for society will be accomplished by violating the literal language of the criminal law." LaFave & Scott, at 629. In particular, the necessity defense can justify the intentional killing of one person to save two others because "it is better that two lives be saved and one lost than that two be lost and one saved." *Id.* Or, put in the language of a choice of evils, "the evil involved in violating the terms of the criminal law (. . . even taking another's life) may be less than that which would result from literal compliance with the law (. . . two lives lost)." *Id.*

Additional elements of the necessity defense are worth noting here. First, the defense is not limited to certain types of harms. Therefore, the harm inflicted by necessity may include intentional homicide, so long as the harm avoided is greater (i.e., preventing more deaths). *Id.* at 634. Second, it must actually be the defendant's intention to avoid the greater harm; intending to commit murder and then learning only later that the death had the fortuitous result of saving other lives will not support a necessity defense. *Id.* at 635. Third, if the defendant reasonably believed that the lesser harm was necessary, even if, unknown to him, it was not, he may still avail himself of the defense. As LaFave and Scott explain, "if A kills B reasonably believing it to be necessary to save C and D, he is not guilty of murder even though, unknown to A, C and D could have been rescued without the necessity of killing B." *Id.* Fourth, it is for the court, and not the defendant to judge whether the harm avoided outweighed the harm done. *Id.* at 636. Fifth, the defendant cannot rely upon the necessity defense if a third alternative is open and known to him that will cause less harm.

It appears to us that under the current circumstances the necessity defense could be successfully maintained in response to an allegation of a Section 2340A violation. On September 11, 2001, al Qaeda launched a surprise covert attack on civilian targets in the United States that led to the deaths of thousands and losses in billions of dollars. According to public and governmental reports, al Qaeda has other sleeper cells within the United States that may be planning similar attacks. Indeed, al Qaeda plans apparently include efforts to develop and deploy chemical, biological and nuclear weapons of mass destruction. Under these circumstances, a detainee may possess information that could enable the United States to prevent attacks that potentially could equal or surpass the September 11 attacks in their magnitude. Clearly, any harm that might occur during an interrogation would pale to insignificance compared to the harm avoided by preventing such an attack, which could take hundreds or thousands of lives.

Under this calculus, two factors will help indicate when the necessity defense could appropriately be invoked. First, the more certain that government officials are that a particular individual has information needed to prevent an attack, the more necessary interrogation will be. Second, the more likely it appears to be that a terrorist attack is likely to occur, and the greater the amount of damage expected from such an attack, the more that an interrogation to get information would become necessary. Of course, the strength of the necessity defense depends on the circumstances that prevail, and the knowledge of the government actors involved, when the interrogation is conducted. While every interrogation that might violate Section 2340A does not trigger a necessity defense, we can say that certain circumstances could support such a defense.

Legal authorities identify an important exception to the necessity defense. The defense is available "only in situations wherein the legislature has not itself, in its criminal statute, made a determination of values." *Id.* at 629. Thus, if Congress explicitly has made clear that violation of a statute cannot be outweighed by the harm avoided, courts cannot recognize the necessity defense. LaFave and Israel provide as an example an abortion statute that made clear that abortions even to save the life of the mother would still be a crime; in such cases the necessity defense would be unavailable. *Id.* at 630. Here, however, Congress has not explicitly made a determination of values vis-à-vis torture. In fact, Congress explicitly removed efforts to remove torture from the weighing of values permitted by the necessity defense.[23]

B. Self-Defense

Even if a court were to find that a violation of Section 2340A was not justified by necessity, a defendant could still appropriately raise a claim of self-defense. The right to self-defense, even when it involves deadly force, is deeply embedded in our law, both as to individuals and as to the nation as a whole. As the Court of Appeals for the D.C. Circuit has explained:

> More than two centuries ago, Blackstone, best known of the expositors of the English common law, taught that "all homicide is malicious, and of course amounts to murder, unless ... excused on the account of accident or self-preservation ..." Self-defense, as a doctrine legally exonerating the taking of human life, is as viable now as it was in Blackstone's time.

United States v. Peterson, 483 F.2d 1222, 1228–29 (D.C. Cir. 1973). Self-defense is a common-law defense to federal criminal law offenses, and nothing in the text, structure or history of Section 2340A precludes its application to a charge of torture. In the absence of any textual provision to the contrary, we assume self-defense can be an appropriate defense to an allegation of torture.

The doctrine of self-defense permits the use of force to prevent harm to another person. As LaFave and Scott explain, "one is justified in using reasonable force in defense of another person, even a stranger, when he reasonably believes that the other is in immediate danger of unlawful bodily harm from his adversary and that the use of such force is necessary to avoid this danger." *Id.* at 663–64. Ultimately, even deadly force is permissible, but "only when the attack of the adversary upon the other person reasonably appears to

---

[23] In the CAT, torture is defined as the intentional infliction of severe pain or suffering "for such purpose as obtaining from him or a third person information or a confession." CAT Article 1.1. One could argue that such a definition represented an attempt to to indicate that the good of of obtaining information – no matter what the circumstances – could not justify an act of torture. In other words, necessity would not be a defense. In enacting Section 2340, however, Congress removed the purpose element in the definition of torture, evidencing an intention to remove any fixing of values by statute. By leaving Section 2340 silent as to the harm done by torture in comparison to other harms, Congress allowed the necessity defense to apply when appropriate.

Further, the CAT contains an additional provision that "no exceptional circumstances whatsoever, whether a state of war or a threat of war, internal political instability or any other public emergency, may be invoked as a justification of torture." CAT Article 2.2. Aware of this provision of the treaty, and of the definition of the necessity defense that allows the legislature to provide for an exception to the defense, see Model Penal Code § 3.02(b), Congress did not incorporate CAT Article 2.2 into Section 2340. Given that Congress omitted CAT's effort to bar a necessity or wartime defense, we read Section 2340 as permitting the defense.

the defender to be a deadly attack." *Id.* at 664. As with our discussion of necessity, we will review the significant elements of this defense.[24] According to LaFave and Scott, the elements of the defense of others are the same as those that apply to individual self-defense.

First, self-defense requires that the use of force be *necessary* to avoid the danger of unlawful bodily harm. *Id.* at 649. A defender may justifiably use deadly force if he reasonably believes that the other person is about to inflict unlawful death or serious bodily harm upon another, and that it is necessary to use such force to prevent it. *Id.* at 652. Looked at from the opposite perspective, the defender may not use force when the force would be as equally effective at a later time and the defender suffers no harm or risk by waiting. *See* Paul H. Robinson, 2 Criminal Law Defenses § 131(c) at 77 (1984). If, however, other options permit the defender to retreat safely from a confrontation without having to resort to deadly force, the use of force may not be necessary in the first place. La Fave and Scott at 659–60.

Second, self-defense requires that the defendant's belief in the necessity of using force be reasonable. If a defendant honestly but unreasonably believed force was necessary, he will not be able to make out a successful claim of self-defense. *Id.* at 654. Conversely, if a defendant reasonably believed an attack was to occur, but the facts subsequently showed no attack was threatened, he may still raise self-defense. As LaFave and Scott explain, "one may be justified in shooting to death an adversary who, having threatened to kill him, reaches for his pocket as if for a gun, though it later appears that he had no gun and that he was only reaching for his handkerchief." *Id.* Some authorities, such as the Model Penal Code, even eliminate the reasonability element, and require only that the defender honestly believed – regardless of its unreasonableness – that the use of force was necessary.

Third, many legal authorities include the requirement that a defender must reasonably believe that the unlawful violence is "imminent" before he can use force in his defense. It would be a mistake, however, to equate imminence necessarily with timing – that an attack is immediately about to occur. Rather, as the Model Penal Code explains, what is essential is that, the defensive *response* must be "immediately necessary." Model Penal Code § 3.04(1). Indeed, imminence may be merely another way of expressing the requirement of necessity. Robinson at 78. LaFave and Scott, for example, believe that the imminence requirement makes sense as part of a necessity defense because if an attack is not immediately upon the defender, the defender has other options available to avoid the attack that do not involve the use of force. LaFave and Scott at 656. If, however, the fact of the attack becomes certain and no other options remain, the use of force may be justified. To use a well-known hypothetical, if A were to kidnap and confine B, and then tell B he would kill B one week later, B would be justified in using force in self-defense, even if the opportunity arose before the week had passed. *Id.* at 656; *see also* Robinson at § 131(c)(1) at 78. In this hypothetical situation, while the attack itself is not imminent, B's use of force becomes immediately necessary whenever he has an opportunity to save himself from A.

Fourth, the amount of force should be proportional to the threat. As LaFave and Scott explain, "the amount of force which [the defender] may justifiably use must be reasonably related to the threatened harm which he seeks to avoid." LaFave and Scott at 651. Thus, one may not use deadly force in response to a threat that does not rise to death or serious

---

[24] Early cases had suggested that in order to be eligible for defense of another, one should have some personal relationship with the one in need of protection. That view has been discarded. LaFave & Scott at 664.

bodily harm. If such harm may result, however, deadly force is appropriate. As the Model Penal Code § 3.04(2)(b) states, "[the] use of deadly force is not justifiable ... unless the actor believes that such force is necessary to protect himself against death, serious bodily injury, kidnapping or sexual intercourse compelled by force or threat."

Under the current circumstances, we believe that a defendant accused of violating Section 2340A could have, in certain circumstances, grounds to properly claim the defense of another. The threat of an impending terrorist attack threatens the lives of hundreds if not thousands of American citizens. Whether such a defense will be upheld depends on the specific context within which the interrogation decision is made. If an attack appears increasingly likely, but our intelligence services and armed forces cannot prevent it without the information from the interrogation of a specific individual, then the more likely it will appear that the conduct in question will be seen as necessary. If intelligence and other information support the conclusion that an attack is increasingly certain, then the necessity for the interrogation will be reasonable. The increasing certainty of an attack will also satisfy the imminence requirement. Finally, the fact that previous al Qaeda attacks have had as their aim the deaths of American citizens, and that evidence of other plots have had a similar goal in mind, would justify proportionality of interrogation methods designed to elicit information to prevent such deaths.

To be sure, this situation is different from the usual self-defense justification, and, indeed, it overlaps with elements of the necessity defense. Self-defense as usually discussed involves using force against an individual who is about to conduct the attack. In the current circumstances, however, an enemy combatant in detention does not himself present a threat of harm. He is not actually carrying out the attack; rather, he has participated in the planning and preparation for the attack, or merely has knowledge of the attack through his membership in the terrorist organization. Nonetheless, leading scholarly commentators believe that interrogation of such individuals using methods that might violate Section 2340A would be justified under the doctrine of self-defense, because the combatant by aiding and promoting the terrorist plot "has culpably caused the situation where someone might get hurt. If hurting him is the only means to prevent the death or injury of others put at risk by his actions, such torture should be permissible, and on the same basis that self-defense is permissible." Michael S. Moore, *Torture and the Balance of Evils*, 23 Israel L. Rev. 280, 323 (1989) (symposium on Israel's Landau Commission Report).[25] Thus, some commentators believe that by helping to create the threat of loss of life, terrorists become culpable for the threat even though they do not actually carry out the attack itself. They may be hurt in an interrogation because they are part of the mechanism that has set the attack in motion, *id.* at 323, just as is someone who feeds ammunition or targeting information to an attacker. Under the present circumstances, therefore, even though a detained enemy combatant may not be the exact attacker – he is not planting the bomb, or piloting a hijacked plane to kill civilians – he still may be harmed in self-defense if he has knowledge of future attacks because he has assisted in their planning and execution.

Further, we believe that a claim by an individual of the defense of another would be further supported by the fact that, in this case, the nation itself is under attack and has the

---

[25] Moore distinguishes that case from one in which a person has information that could stop a terrorist attack, but who does not take a hand in the terrorist activity itself, such as an innocent person who learns of the attack from her spouse. Moore, 23 Israel L. Rev. at 324. Such individuals, Moore finds, would not be subject to the use of force in self-defense, although they might be under the doctrine of necessity.

right to self-defense. This fact can bolster and support an individual claim of self-defense in a prosecution, according to the teaching of the Supreme Court in *In re Neagle*, 135 U.S. 1 (1890). In that case, the State of California arrested and held deputy U.S. Marshal Neagle for shooting and killing the assailant of Supreme Court Justice Field. In granting the writ of habeas corpus for Neagle's release, the Supreme Court did not rely alone upon the marshal's right to defend another or his right to self-defense. Rather, the Court found that Neagle, as an agent of the United States and of the executive branch, was justified in the killing because, in protecting Justice Field, he was acting pursuant to the executive branch's inherent constitutional authority to protect the United States government. *Id.* at 67 ("We cannot doubt the power of the president to take measures for the protection of a judge of one of the courts of the United States who, while in the discharge of the duties of his office, is threatened with a personal attack which may probably result in his death."). That authority derives, according to the Court, from the President's power under Article II to take care that the laws are faithfully executed. In other words, Neagle as a federal officer not only could raise self-defense or defense of another, but also could defend his actions on the ground that he was implementing the Executive Branch's authority to protect the United States government.

If the right to defend the national government can be raised as a defense in an individual prosecution, as *Neagle* suggests, then a government defendant, acting in his official capacity, should be able to argue that any conduct that arguably violated Section 2340A was undertaken pursuant to more than just individual self-defense or defense of another. In addition, the defendant could claim that he was fulfilling the Executive Branch's authority to protect the federal government, and the nation, from attack. The September 11 attacks have already triggered that authority, as recognized both under domestic and international law. Following the example of *In re Neagle*, we conclude that a government defendant may also argue that his conduct of an interrogation, if properly authorized, is justified on the basis of protecting the nation from attack.

There can be little doubt that the nation's right to self-defense has been triggered under our law. The Constitution announces that one of its purposes is "to provide for the common defense." U.S. Const., Preamble. Article I, § 8 declares that Congress is to exercise its powers to "provide for the common Defence." *See also* 2 Pub. Papers of Ronald Reagan 920, 921 (1988–89) (right of self-defense recognized by Article 51 of the U.N. Charter). The President has a particular responsibility and power to take steps to defend the nation and its people. *In re Neagle*, 135 U.S. at 64. *See also* U.S. Const., Article IV. § 4 ("The United States shall . . . protect [each of the States] against Invasion"). As Commander-in-Chief and Chief Executive, he may use the armed forces to protect the nation and its people. *See, e.g., United States v. Verdugo-Urquidez*, 494 U.S. 259, 273 (1990). And he may employ secret agents to aid in his work as Commander-in-Chief. *Totten v. United States*, 92 U.S. 105, 106 (1876). As the Supreme Court observed in *The Prize Cases*, 67 U.S. (2 Black) 635 (1862), in response to an armed attack on the United States "the President is not only authorized but bound to resist force by force . . . without waiting for any special legislative authority." *Id.* at 668. The September 11 events were a direct attack on the United States, and as we have explained above, the President has authorized the use of military force with the support of Congress.[26]

---

[26] While the President's constitutional determination alone is sufficient to justify the nation's resort to self-defense, it also bears noting that the right to self-defense is further recognized under international law. Article 51 of the U.N. Charter declares that "[n]othing in the present Charter shall impair the inherent right of individual or collective self-defense if an armed attack occurs

As we have made clear in other opinions involving the war against al Qaeda, the nation's right to self-defense has been triggered by the events of September 11. If a government defendant were to harm an enemy combatant during an interrogation in a manner that might arguably violate Section 2340A, he would be doing so in order to prevent further attacks on the United States by the al Qaeda terrorist network. In that case, we believe that he could argue that his actions were justified by the executive branch's constitutional authority to protect the nation from attack. This national and international version of the right to self-defense could supplement and bolster the government defendant's individual right.

Conclusion

For the foregoing reasons, we conclude that torture as defined in and proscribed by Sections 2340–2340A, covers only extreme acts. Severe pain is generally of the kind difficult for the victim to endure. Where the pain is physical, it must be of an intensity akin to that which accompanies serious physical injury such as death or organ failure. Severe mental pain requires suffering not just at the moment of infliction but it also requires lasting psychological harm, such as seen in mental disorders like post-traumatic stress disorder. Additionally, such severe mental pain can arise only from the predicate acts listed in Section 2340. Because the acts inflicting torture are extreme, there is significant range of acts that though they might constitute cruel, inhuman, or degrading treatment or punishment fail to rise to the level of torture.

Further, we conclude that under the circumstances of the current war against al Qaeda and its allies, application of Section 2340A to interrogations undertaken pursuant to the President's Commander-in-Chief powers may be unconstitutional. Finally, even if an interrogation method might violate Section 2340A, necessity or self-defense could provide justifications that would eliminate any criminal liability.

Please let us know if we can be of further assistance.

Jay S. Bybee
Assistant Attorney General

against a Member of the United Nations until the Security Council has taken the measures necessary to maintain international peace and security." The attacks of September 11, 2001 clearly constitute an armed attack against the United States, and indeed were the latest in a long history of al Qaeda sponsored attacks against the United States. This conclusion was acknowledged by the United Nations Security Council on September 28, 2001, when it unanimously adopted Resolution 1373 explicitly "reaffirming the inherent right of individual and collective self-defence as recognized by the charter of the United Nations." This right of self-defense is a right to effective self-defense. In other words, the victim state has the right to use force against the aggressor who has initiated an "armed attack" until the threat has abated. The United States, through its military and intelligence personnel, has a right recognized by Article 51 to continue using force until such time as the threat posed by al Qaeda and other terrorist groups connected to the September 11th attacks is completely ended" Other treaties reaffirm the right of the United States to use force in its self-defense. *See, e.g.,* Inter-American Treaty of Reciprocal Assistance, art. 3, Sept. 2, 1947, T.I.A.S. No. 1838, 21 U.N.T.S. 77 (Rio Treaty); North Atlantic Treaty, art. 5, Apr. 4, 1949, 63 Stat 2241, 34 U.N.T.S. 243.

APPENDIX

Cases in which U.S. courts have concluded the defendant tortured the plaintiff:

- Plaintiff was beaten and shot by government troops while protesting the destruction of her property. *See Wiwa v. Royal Dutch Petroleum*, 2002 WL 319887 at *7 (S.D.N.Y. Feb. 28, 2002).

- Plaintiff was removed from ship, interrogated, and held incommunicado for months. Representatives of the defendant threatened her with death if she attempted to move from quarters where she was held. She was forcibly separated from her husband and unable to learn of his welfare or whereabouts. *See Simpson v. Socialist People's Libyan Arab Jamahiriya*, 180 F. Supp. 2d 78, 88 (D.D.C. 2001) (Rule 12(b)(6) motion).

- Plaintiff was held captive for five days in a small cell that had no lights, no window, no water, and no toilet. During the remainder of his captivity, he was frequently denied food and water and given only limited access to the toilet. He was held at gunpoint, with his captors threatening to kill him if he did not confess to espionage. His captors threatened to cut off his fingers, pull out his fingernails, and shock his testicles. *See Daliberti v. Republic of Iraq*, 146 F. Supp. 2d 19, 22–23, 25 (D.D.C. 2001) (default judgment).

- Plaintiff was imprisoned for 205 days. He was confined in a car park that had been converted into a prison. His cell had no water or toilet and had only a steel cot for a bed. He was convicted of illegal entry into Iraq and transferred to another facility, where he was placed in a cell infested with vermin. He shared a single toilet with 200 other prisoners. While imprisoned he had a heart attack but was denied adequate medical attention and medication. *See Daliberti v. Republic of Iraq*, 146 F. Supp. 2d 19, 22–23 (D.D.C. 2001) (default judgment).

- Plaintiff was imprisoned for 126 days. At one point, a guard attempted to execute him, but another guard intervened. A truck transporting the plaintiff ran over a pedestrian at full speed without stopping. He heard other prisoners being beaten and he feared being beaten. He had serious medical conditions that were not promptly or adequately treated. He was not given sufficient food or water. *See Daliberti v. Republic of Iraq*, 146 F. Supp. 2d 19, 22–23 (D.D.C. 2001) (default judgment).

- Allegations that guards beat, clubbed, and kicked the plaintiff and that the plaintiff was interrogated and subjected to physical and verbal abuse sufficiently stated a claim for torture so as to survive Rule 12(b)(6) motion. *See Price v. Socialist People's Libyan Arab Jamahiriya*, 110 F. Supp. 2d 10 (D.D.C. 2000).

- Plaintiffs alleged that they were blindfolded, interrogated and subjected to physical, mental, and verbal abuse while they were held captive. Furthermore, one plaintiff was held eleven days without food, water, or bed. Another plaintiff was held for four days without food, water, or a bed, and was also stripped naked, blindfolded, and threatened with electrocution of his testicles. The other two remaining plaintiffs alleged that they were not provided adequate or proper medical care for conditions that were life threatening. The court concluded that these allegations sufficiently stated a claim for torture and denied defendants Rule 12(b)(6) motion. *See Daliberti v. Republic v. Iraq*, 97 F. Supp. 2d 38, 45 (D.D.C. 2000) (finding that these allegations were "more than enough to meet the definition of torture in the [TVPA]").

- Plaintiff's kidnappers pistol-whipped him until he lost consciousness. They then stripped him and gave him only a robe to wear and left him bleeding, dizzy, and in severe pain. He was then imprisoned for 1,908 days. During his imprisonment, his captors sought to force a confession from him by playing Russian roulette with him and threatening him with castration. He was randomly beaten and forced to watch the beatings of others. Additionally, he was confined in a rodent and scorpion infested cell. He was bound in chains almost the entire time of his confinement. One night during the winter, his captors chained him to an upper floor balcony, leaving him exposed to the elements. Consequently, he developed frostbite on his hands and feet. He was also subjected to a surgical procedure for an unidentified abdominal problem. *See Cicippio v. Islamic Republic of Iran*, 18 F. Supp. 2d 62 (D.D.C. 1998).

- Plaintiff was kidnapped at gunpoint. He was beaten for several days after his kidnapping. He was subjected to daily torture and threats of death. He was kept in solitary confinement for two years. During that time, he was blindfolded and chained to the wall in a six-foot by six-foot room infested with rodents. He was shackled in a stooped position for 44 months and he developed eye infections as a result of the blindfolds. Additionally, his captors did the following: forced him to kneel on spikes, administered electric shocks to his hands; battered his feet with iron bars and struck him in the kidneys with a rifle; struck him on the side of his head with a hand grenade, breaking his nose and jaw; placed boiling tea kettles on his shoulders; and they laced his food with arsenic. *See Cicippio v. Islamic Republic of Iran*, 18 F. Supp. 2d 62 (D.D.C. 1998).

- Plaintiff was pistol-whipped, bound and gagged, held captive in darkness or blindfold for 18 months. He was kept chained at either his ankles or wrists, wearing nothing but his undershorts and a t-shirt. As for his meals, his captors gave him pita bread and dry cheese for breakfast, rice with dehydrated soup for lunch, and a piece of bread for dinner. Sometimes the guards would spit into his food. He was regularly beaten and incessantly interrogated; he overheard the deaths and beatings of other prisoners. *See Cicippio v. Islamic Republic of Iran*, 18 F. Supp. 2d 62, (D.D.C. 1998).

- Plaintiff spent eight years in solitary or near solitary confinement. He was threatened with death, blindfolded and beaten while handcuffed and fettered. He was denied sleep and repeatedly threatened him with death. At one point, while he was shackled to a cot, the guards placed a towel over his nose and mouth and then poured water down his nostrils. They did this for six hours. During this incident, the guards threatened him with death and electric shock. Afterwards, they left him shackled to his cot for six days. For the next seven months, he was imprisoned in a hot, unlit cell that measured 2.5 square meters. During this seven-month period, he was shackled to his cot – at first by all his limbs and later by one hand or one foot. He remained shackled in this manner except for the briefest moments, such as when his captors permitted him to use the bathroom. The handcuffs cut into his flesh. *See Hilao v. Estate of Marcos*, 103 F.3d 789, 790 (9th Cir. 1996). The court did not, however, appear to consider the solitary confinement per se to constitute torture. *See id.* at 795 (stating that to the extent that [the plaintiff's] years in solitary confinement do not constitute torture, they clearly meet the definition of prolonged arbitrary detention.").

- High-ranking military officers interrogated the plaintiff and subjected him to mock executions. He was also threatened with death. *See Hilao v. Estate of Marcos*, 103 F.3d 789, 795 (9th Cir. 1996).

- Plaintiff, a nun, received anonymous threats warning her to leave Guatemala. Later, two men with a gun kidnapped her. They blindfolded her and locked her in an unlit room for hours. The guards interrogated her and regardless of the answers she gave to their questions, they burned her with cigarettes. The guards then showed her surveillance photographs of herself. They blindfolded her again, stripped her, and raped her repeatedly. *See Xuncax v. Gramajo*, 886 F. Supp. 162, 176 (1995).

- Plaintiffs were beaten with truncheons, boots, and guns and threatened with death. Nightsticks were used to beat their backs, kidneys, and the soles of their feet. The soldiers pulled and squeezed their testicles. When they fainted from the pain, the soldiers revived them by singeing their nose hair with a cigarette lighter. They were interrogated as they were beaten with iron barks, rifle butts, helmets, and fists. One plaintiff was placed in the "djak" position, i.e., with hands and feet bound and suspended from a pole. Medical treatment was withheld for one week and then was sporadic and inadequate. *See Paul v. Avril*, 901 F. Supp. 330, 332 (S.D. Fla. 1994).
- Alien subjected to sustained beatings for the month following his first arrest. After his second arrest, suffered severe beatings and was burned with cigarettes over the course of an eight-day period. *Al-Saher v. INS*, 268 F.3d 1143, 1147 (9th Cir. 2001) (deportation case).
- Decedent was attacked with knifes and sticks, and repeatedly hit in the head with the butt of a gun as he remained trapped in his truck by his attackers. The attackers then doused the vehicle with gasoline. Although he managed to get out of the truck, he nonetheless burned to death. *Tachiona v. Mugabe*, No. 00 Civ. 6666VMJCF, 2002 WL 1424598 at *1 (S.D.N.Y. July 1, 2002).
- Decedent was attacked by spear, stick, and stone wielding supporters of defendant. He was carried off by the attackers and "was found dead the next day, naked and lying in the middle of the road[.]" From the physical injuries, it was determined that he had been severely beaten. According to his death certificate, he died from "massive brain injury from trauma; assault; and laceration of the right lung." *Tachiona v. Mugabe*, No. 00 Civ. 6666VMJCF, 2002 WL 1424598 at *2 (S.D.N.Y. July 1, 2002).
- Decedent was abducted, along with five others. He and the others were severely beaten and he was forced to drink diesel oil. He was then summarily executed. *Tachiona v. Mugabe*, No. 00 Civ. 6666VMJCF, 2002 WL 1424598 at *4(S.D.N.Y. July 1, 2002).
- Forced sterilization constitutes torture. *Bi Zhu Lin v. Ashcroft*, 183 F. Supp. 2d 551 (D. Conn. 2002) (noting determination by immigration judge that such conduct constitutes torture).

There are two cases in which U.S. courts have rejected torture claims on the ground that the alleged conduct did not rise to the level of torture. In *Faulder v. Johnson*, 99 F. Supp. 2d 774 (S.D. Tex. 1999), the district court rejected a death row inmate's claim that psychological trauma resulting from repeated stays of his execution and his 22-year-wait for that execution was torture under CAT. The court rejected this contention because of the United States' express death penalty reservation to CAT. *See id.* In *Eastman Kodak v. Kavlin*, 978 F. Supp. 1078, 1093 (S.D. Fla. 1997), the plaintiff was held for eight days in a filthy cell with drug dealers and an AIDS patient. He received no food, no blanket and no protection from other inmates. Prisoners murdered one another in front of the plaintiff. *Id.* The court flatly rejected the plaintiff's claim that this constituted torture.

U.S. Department of Justice

Office of Legal Counsel

Office of the Assistant Attorney General   *Washington, D.C. 20530*

December 30, 2004

MEMORANDUM FOR JAMES B. COMEY
DEPUTY ATTORNEY GENERAL

RE: Legal Standards Applicable Under 18 U.S.C. §§ 2340–2340A

Torture is abhorrent both to American law and values and to international norms. This universal repudiation of torture is reflected in our criminal law, for example, 18 U.S.C. §§ 2340–2340A; international agreements, exemplified by the United Nations Convention Against Torture (the "CAT")[1]; customary international law[2]; centuries of Anglo-American law[3]; and the longstanding policy of the United States, repeatedly and recently reaffirmed by the President.[4]

This Office interpreted the federal criminal prohibition against torture – codified at 18 U.S.C. §§ 2340–2340A – in *Standards of Conduct for Interrogation under 18 U.S.C. §§ 2340–2340A* (Aug. 1, 2002) ("August 2002 Memorandum"). The August 2002 Memorandum also addressed a number of issues beyond interpretation of those

---

[1] Convention Against Torture and Other Cruel, Inhuman or Degrading Treatment or Punishment, Dec. 10, 1984, S. Treaty Doc. No. 100–20, 1465 U.N.T.S. 85. *See also, e.g.,* International Covenant on Civil and Political Rights, Dec. 16, 1966, 999 U.N.T.S. 171.

[2] It has been suggested that the prohibition against torture has achieved the status of *jus cogens* (*i.e.*, a peremptory norm) under international law. *See, e.g., Siderman de Blake v. Republic of Argentina*, 965 F.2d 699, 714 (9th Cir. 1992); *Regina v. Bow Street Metro. Stipendiary Magistrate Ex Parte Pinochet Ugarte (No. 3)*, [2000] 1 AC 147, 198; *see also* Restatement (Third) of Foreign Relations Law of the United States § 702 reporters' note 5.

[3] *See generally* John H. Langbein, *Torture and the Law of Proof: Europe and England in the Ancien Régime* (1977).

[4] *See, e.g.,* Statement on United Nations International Day in Support of Victims of Torture, 40 Weekly Comp. Pres. Doc. 1167 (July 5, 2004) ("Freedom from torture is an inalienable human right...."); Statement on United Nations International Day in Support of Victims of Torture, 39 Weekly Comp. Pres. Doc. 824 (June 30, 2003) ("Torture anywhere is an affront to human dignity everywhere."); *see also Letter of Transmittal from President Ronald Reagan to the Senate* (May 20, 1988), *in Message from the President of the United States Transmitting the Convention Against Torture and Other Cruel, Inhuman or Degrading Treatment or Punishment,* S. Treaty Doc. No. 100–20, at iii (1988) ("Ratification of the Convention by the United States will clearly express United States opposition to torture, an abhorrent practice unfortunately still prevalent in the world today").

statutory provisions, including the President's Commander-in-Chief power, and various defenses that might be asserted to avoid potential liability under sections 2340–2340A. *See id.* at 31–46.

Questions have since been raised, both by this Office and by others, about the appropriateness and relevance of the non-statutory discussion in the August 2002 Memorandum, and also about various aspects of the statutory analysis, in particular the statement that "severe" pain under the statute was limited to pain "equivalent in intensity to the pain accompanying serious physical injury, such as organ failure, impairment of bodily function, or even death." *Id.* at 1.[5] We decided to withdraw the August 2002 Memorandum, a decision you announced in June 2004. At that time, you directed this Office to prepare a replacement memorandum. Because of the importance of – and public interest in – these issues, you asked that this memorandum be prepared in a form that could be released to the public so that interested parties could understand our analysis of the statute.

This memorandum supersedes the August 2002 Memorandum in its entirety.[6] Because the discussion in that memorandum concerning the President's Commander-in-Chief power and the potential defenses to liability was – and remains – unnecessary, it has been eliminated from the analysis that follows. Consideration of the bounds of any such authority would be inconsistent with the President's unequivocal directive that United States personnel not engage in torture.[7]

We have also modified in some important respects our analysis of the legal standards applicable under 18 U.S.C. §§ 2340–2340A. For example, we disagree with statements in the August 2002 Memorandum limiting "severe" pain under the statute to "excruciating and agonizing" pain, *id.* at 19, or to pain "equivalent in intensity to the pain accompanying serious physical injury, such as organ failure, impairment of bodily function, or even death," *id.* at 1. There are additional areas where we disagree with or modify the analysis in the August 2002 Memorandum, as identified in the discussion below.[8]

---

[5] *See, e.g.*, Anthony Lewis, *Making Torture Legal*, N.Y. Rev. of Books, July 15, 2004; R. Jeffrey Smith, *Slim Legal Grounds for Torture Memos*, Wash. Post, July 4, 2004, at A12; Kathleen Clark & Julie Mertus, *Torturing the Law; the Justice Department's Legal Contortions on Interrogation*, Wash. Post, June 20, 2004, at B3; Derek Jinks & David Sloss, *Is the President Bound by the Geneva Conventions?*, 90 Cornell L. Rev, 97 (2004).

[6] This memorandum necessarily discusses the prohibition against torture in sections 2340–2340A in somewhat abstract and general terms. In applying this criminal prohibition to particular circumstances, great care must be taken to avoid approving as lawful any conduct that might constitute torture. In addition, this memorandum does not address the many other sources of law that may apply, depending on the circumstances, to the detention or interrogation of detainees (for example, the Geneva Conventions; the Uniform Code of Military Justice, 10 U.S.C. § 801 et seq.; the Military Extraterritorial Jurisdiction Act, 18 U.S.C. §§ 3261–3267; and the War Crimes Act, 18 U.S.C. § 2441, among others). Any analysis of particular facts must, of course, ensure that the United States complies with all applicable legal obligations.

[7] *See, e.g.*, Statement on United Nations International Day in Support of Victims of Torture, 40 Weekly Comp. Pres. Doc. 1167–68 (July 5, 2004) ("America stands against and will not tolerate torture. We will investigate and prosecute all acts of torture ... in all territory under our jurisdiction.... Torture is wrong no matter where it occurs, and the United States will continue to lead the fight to eliminate it everywhere").

[8] While we have identified various disagreements with the August 2002 Memorandum, we have reviewed this Office's prior opinions addressing issues involving treatment of detainees and do not believe that any of their conclusions would be different under the standards set forth in this memorandum.

The Criminal Division of the Department of Justice has reviewed this memorandum and concurs in the analysis set forth below.

I.

Section 2340A provides that "[w]hoever outside the United States commits or attempts to commit torture shall be fined under this title or imprisoned not more than 20 years, or both, and if death results to any person from conduct prohibited by this subsection, shall be punished by death or imprisoned for any term of years or for life."[9] Section 2340(1) defines "torture" as "an act committed by a person acting under the color of law specifically intended to inflict severe physical or mental pain or suffering (other than pain or suffering incidental to lawful sanctions) upon another person within his custody or physical control."[10]

In interpreting these provisions, we note that Congress may have adopted a statutory definition of "torture" that differs from certain colloquial uses of the term. *Cf. Cadet v. Bulger*, 377 F.3d 1173, 1194 (11th Cir. 2004) ("[I]n other contexts and under other definitions [the conditions] might be described as torturous. The fact remains, however, that the only relevant definition of 'torture' is the definition contained in [the] CAT. . . ."). We must, of course, give effect to the statute as enacted by Congress.[11]

---

[9] Section 2340A provides in full:

(a) Offense. – Whoever outside the United States commits or attempts to commit torture shall be fined under this title or imprisoned not more than 20 years, or both, and if death results to any person from conduct prohibited by this subsection, shall be punished by death or imprisoned for any term of years or for life.

(b) Jurisdiction. – There is jurisdiction over the activity prohibited in subsection (a) if –

(1) the alleged offender is a national of the United States; or

(2) the alleged offender is present in the United States, irrespective of the nationality of the victim or alleged offender.

(c) Conspiracy. – A person who conspires to commit an offense under this section shall be subject to the same penalties (other than the penalty of death) as the penalties prescribed for the offense, the commission of which was the object of the conspiracy.

18 U.S.C. § 2340A (2000).

[10] Section 2340 provides in full:

As used in this chapter –

(1) "torture" means an act committed by a person acting under color of law specifically intended to inflict severe physical or mental pain or suffering (other than pain or suffering incidental to lawful sanctions) upon another person within his custody or physical control;

(2) "severe mental pain or suffering" means the prolonged mental harm caused by or resulting from –

(A) the intentional infliction or threatened infliction of severe physical pain or suffering;

(B) the administration or application, or threatened administration or application, of mind-altering substances or other procedures calculated to disrupt profoundly the senses or the personality;

(C) the threat of imminent death; or

(D) the threat that another person will imminently be subjected to death, severe physical pain or suffering, or the administration or application of mind-altering substances or other procedures calculated to disrupt profoundly the senses or personality; and

(3) "United States" means the several States of the United States, the District of Columbia, and the commonwealths, territories, and possessions of the United States.

18 U.S.C. § 2340 (as amended by Pub. L. No. 108–375, 118 Stat. 1811 (2004)).

[11] Our task is only to offer guidance on the meaning of the statute, not to comment on policy. It is of course open to policymakers to determine that conduct that might not be prohibited by the statute is nevertheless contrary to the interests or policy of the United States.

Congress enacted sections 2340–2340A to carry out the United States' obligations under the CAT. *See* H.R. Conf. Rep. No. 103–482, at 229 (1994). The CAT, among other things, obligates state parties to take effective measures to prevent acts of torture in any territory under their jurisdiction, and requires the United States, as a state party, to ensure that acts of torture, along with attempts and complicity to commit such acts, are crimes under U.S. law. *See* CAT arts. 2, 4–5. Sections 2340–2340A satisfy that requirement with respect to acts committed outside the United States.[12] Conduct constituting "torture" occurring within the United States was – and remains – prohibited by various other federal and state criminal statutes that we do not discuss here.

The CAT defines "torture" so as to require the intentional infliction of "severe pain or suffering, whether physical or mental." Article 1(1) of the CAT provides:

> For the purposes of this Convention, the term "torture" means any act by which severe pain or suffering, whether physical or mental, is intentionally inflicted on a person for such purposes as obtaining from him or a third person information or a confession, punishing him for an act he or a third person has committed or is suspected of having committed, or intimidating or coercing him or a third person, or for any reason based on discrimination of any kind, when such pain or suffering is inflicted by or at the instigation of or with the consent or acquiescence of a public official or other person acting in an official capacity. It does not include pain or suffering arising only from, inherent in or incidental to lawful sanctions.

The Senate attached the following understanding to its resolution of advice and consent to ratification of the CAT:

> The United States understands that, in order to constitute torture, an act must be specifically intended to inflict severe physical or mental pain or suffering and that mental pain or suffering refers to prolonged mental harm caused by or resulting from (1) the intentional infliction or threatened infliction of severe physical pain or suffering; (2) the administration or application, or threatened administration or application, of mind altering substances or other procedures calculated to disrupt profoundly the senses or the personality; (3) the threat of imminent death; or (4) the threat that another person will imminently be subjected to death, severe physical pain or suffering, or the administration or application of mind altering substances or other procedures calculated to disrupt profoundly the senses or personality.

S. Exec. Rep. No. 101–30, at 36 (1990). This understanding was deposited with the U.S. instrument of ratification, *see* 1830 U.N.T.S. 320 (Oct. 21, 1994), and thus defines the scope of the United States' obligations under the treaty. *See Relevance of Senate Ratification History to Treaty Interpretation*, 11 Op. O.L.C. 28, 32–33 (1987). The criminal prohibition against torture that Congress codified in 18 U.S.C. §§ 2340–2340A generally tracks the prohibition in the CAT, subject to the U.S. understanding.

---

[12] Congress limited the territorial reach of the federal torture statute, providing that the prohibition applies only to conduct occurring "outside the United States," 18 U.S.C. § 2340A(a), which is currently defined in the statute to mean outside "the several States of the United States, the District of Columbia, and the commonwealths, territories, and possessions of the United States." *Id.* § 2340(3).

II.

Under the language adopted by Congress in sections 2340–2340A, to constitute "torture," the conduct in question must have been "specifically intended to inflict severe physical or mental pain or suffering." In the discussion that follows, we will separately consider each of the principal components of this key phrase: (1) the meaning of "severe"; (2) the meaning of "severe physical pain or suffering"; (3) the meaning of "severe mental pain or suffering"; and (4) the meaning of "specifically intended."

(1) The Meaning of "Severe."

Because the statute does not define "severe," "we construe [the] term in accordance with its ordinary or natural meaning." *FDIC v. Meyer*, 510 U.S. 471, 476 (1994). The common understanding of the term "torture" and the context in which the statute was enacted also inform our analysis.

Dictionaries define "severe" (often conjoined with "pain") to mean "extremely violent or intense: *severe pain.*" *American Heritage Dictionary of the English Language* 1653 (3d ed. 1992); *see also* XV *Oxford English Dictionary* 101 (2d ed. 1989) ("Of pain, suffering, loss, or the like: Grievous, extreme" and "Of circumstances . . . : Hard to sustain or endure").[13]

The statute, moreover, was intended to implement the United States' obligations under the CAT, which, as quoted above, defines as "torture" acts that inflict "severe pain or suffering" on a person. CAT art. 1(1). As the Senate Foreign Relations Committee explained in its report recommending that the Senate consent to ratification of the CAT:

> The [CAT] seeks to define "torture" in a relatively limited fashion, corresponding to the common understanding of torture as an extreme practice which is universally condemned. . . .
>
> . . . .
>
> . . . The term "torture," in United States and international usage, is usually reserved for extreme, deliberate and unusually cruel practices, for example, sustained systematic beating, application of electric currents to sensitive parts of the body, and tying up or hanging in positions that cause extreme pain.

S. Exec. Rep. No. 101-30 at 13-14. *See also* David P. Stewart, *The Torture Convention and the Reception of International Criminal Law Within the United States*, 15 Nova L. Rev. 449, 455 (1991) ("By stressing the extreme nature of torture, . . . [the] definition [of

---

[13] Common dictionary definitions of "torture" further support the statutory concept that the pain or suffering must be severe. *See Black's Law Dictionary* 1528 (8th ed. 2004) (defining "torture" as "[t]he infliction of *intense pain* to the body or mind to punish, to extract a confession or information, or to obtain sadistic pleasure") (emphasis added); *Webster's Third New International Dictionary of the English Language Unabridged* 2414 (2002) (defining "torture" as "the infliction of *intense pain* (as from burning, crushing, wounding) to punish or coerce someone") (emphasis added); *Oxford American Dictionary and Language Guide* 1064 (1999) (defining "torture" as "the infliction of *severe bodily pain*, esp. as a punishment or a means of persuasion") (emphasis added).

This interpretation is also consistent with the history of torture. *See generally* the descriptions in Lord Hope's lecture, *Torture*, University of Essex/Clifford Chance Lecture 7-8 (Jan. 28, 2004), and in Professor Langbein's book, *Torture and the Law of Proof: Europe and England in the Ancien Régime.* We emphatically are not saying that only such historical techniques – or similar ones – can constitute "torture" under sections 2340–2340A. But the historical understanding of "torture" is relevant to interpreting Congress's intent. *Cf. Morissette v. United States*, 342 U.S. 246, 263 (1952).

torture in the CAT] describes a relatively limited set of circumstances likely to be illegal under most, if not all, domestic legal systems.").

Further, the CAT distinguishes between torture and "other acts of cruel, inhuman or degrading treatment or punishment which do not amount to torture as defined in article 1." CAT art. 16. The CAT thus treats torture as an "extreme form" of cruel, inhuman, or degrading treatment. *See* S. Exec. Rep. No. 101-30 at 6, 13; *see also* J. Herman Burgers & Hans Danelius, *The United Nations Convention Against Torture: A Handbook on the Convention Against Torture and Other Cruel, Inhuman or Degrading Treatment or Punishment* 80 (1988) ("*CAT Handbook*") (noting that Article 16 implies "that torture is the *gravest form* of [cruel, inhuman, or degrading] treatment [or] punishment") (emphasis added); Malcolm D. Evans, *Getting to Grips with Torture*, 51 Int'l & Comp. L.Q. 365, 369 (2002) (The CAT "formalises a distinction between torture on the one hand and inhuman and degrading treatment on the other by attributing different legal consequences to them.").[14] The Senate Foreign Relations Committee emphasized this point in its report recommending that the Senate consent to ratification of the CAT. *See* S. Exec. Rep. No. 101-30 at ("'Torture' is thus to be distinguished from lesser forms of cruel, inhuman, or degrading treatment or punishment, which are to be deplored and prevented, but are not so universally and categorically condemned as to warrant the severe legal consequences that the Convention provides in the case of torture. . . . The requirement that torture be an extreme form of cruel and inhuman treatment is expressed in Article 16, which refers to

---

[14] This approach – distinguishing torture from lesser forms of cruel, inhuman, or degrading treatment – is consistent with other international law sources. The CAT's predecessor, the U.N. Torture Declaration, defined torture as "an *aggravated* and deliberate form of cruel, inhuman or degrading treatment or punishment." Declaration on the Protection of All Persons from Being Subjected to Torture and Other Cruel, Inhuman or Degrading Treatment or Punishment, U.N. Res. 3452, art. 1(2) (Dec. 9, 1975) (emphasis added); *see also* S. Treaty Doc. No. 100–20 at 2 (The U.N. Torture Declaration was "a point of departure for the drafting of the [CAT]."). Other treaties also distinguish torture from lesser forms of cruel, inhuman, or degrading treatment. *See, e.g.*, European Convention for the Protection of Human Rights and Fundamental Freedoms, art. 3, 213 U.N.T.S. 221 (Nov. 4, 1950) ("European Convention") ("No one shall be subjected to torture or to inhuman or degrading treatment or punishment."); Evans, *Getting to Grips with Torture*, 51 Int'l & Comp. L.Q. at 370 ("[T]he ECHR organs have adopted . . . a 'vertical' approach . . . , which is seen as comprising three separate elements, each representing a progression of seriousness, in which one moves progressively from forms of ill-treatment which are 'degrading' to those which are 'inhuman' and then to 'torture.' The distinctions between them is [*sic*] based on the severity of suffering involved, with 'torture' at the apex."); Debra Long, Association for the Prevention of Torture, *Guide to Jurisprudence on Torture and Ill-treatment: Article 3 of the European Convention for the Protection of Human Rights* 13 (2002) (The approach of distinguishing between "torture," "inhuman" acts, and "degrading" acts has "remained the standard approach taken by the European judicial bodies. Within this approach torture has been singled out as carrying a special stigma, which distinguishes it from other forms of ill-treatment."). *See also CAT Handbook* at 115–17 (discussing the European Court of Human Rights ("ECHR") decision in *Ireland v. United Kingdom*, 25 Eur. Ct. H.R. (ser. A) (1978) (concluding that the combined use of wall-standing, hooding, subjection to noise, deprivation of sleep, and deprivation of food and drink constituted inhuman or degrading treatment but not torture under the European Convention)). Cases decided by the ECHR subsequent to *Ireland* have continued to view torture as an aggravated form of inhuman treatment. *See, e.g., Aktas v. Turkey*, No. 24351/94 ¶ 313 (E.C.H.R. 2003); *Akkoc v. Turkey*, Nos. 22947/93 22948/93 ¶ 115 (E.C.H.R. 2000); *Kaya v. Turkey*, No. 22535/93 ¶ 117 (E.C.H.R. 2000).

The International Criminal Tribunal for the Former Yugoslavia ("ICTY") likewise considers "torture" as a category of conduct more severe than "inhuman treatment." *See, e.g., Prosecutor v. Delalic*, IT-96-21, Trial Chamber Judgment ¶ 542 (ICTY Nov. 16, 1998) ("[I]nhuman treatment is treatment which deliberately causes serious mental and physical suffering that falls short of the severe mental and physical suffering required for the offence of torture.").

'other acts of cruel, inhuman or degrading treatment or punishment *which do not amount to torture....*'"). *See also Cadet*, 377 F.3d at 1194 ("The definition in CAT draws a critical distinction between 'torture' and 'other acts of cruel, inhuman, or degrading punishment or treatment.'").

Representations made to the Senate by Executive Branch officials when the Senate was considering the CAT are also relevant in interpreting the CAT's torture prohibition – which sections 2340–2340A implement. Mark Richard, a Deputy Assistant Attorney General in the Criminal Division, testified that "[t]orture is understood to be that barbaric cruelty which lies at the top of the pyramid of human rights misconduct." *Convention Against Torture: Hearing Before the Senate Comm. on Foreign Relations*, 101st Cong. 16 (1990) ("*CAT Hearing*") (prepared statement). The Senate Foreign Relations Committee also understood torture to be limited in just this way. *See* S. Exec. Rep. No. 101-30 at 6 (noting that "[f]or an act to be 'torture,' it must be an extreme form of cruel and inhuman treatment, causing severe pain and suffering, and be intended to cause severe pain and suffering"). Both the Executive Branch and the Senate acknowledged the efforts of the United States during the negotiating process to strengthen the effectiveness of the treaty and to gain wide adherence thereto by focusing the Convention "on torture rather than on other relatively less abhorrent practices." *Letter of Submittal from George P. Shultz, Secretary of State, to President Ronald Reagan* (May 10, 1988), *in* S. Treaty Doc. No. 100-20 at v; *see also* S. Exec. Rep. No. 101-30 at 2-3 ("The United States" helped to focus the Convention "on torture rather than other less abhorrent practices"). Such statements are probative of a treaty's meaning. *See* 11 Op. O.L.C. at 35–36.

Although Congress defined "torture" under sections 2340–2340A to require conduct specifically intended to cause "severe" pain or suffering, we do not believe Congress intended to reach only conduct involving "excruciating and agonizing" pain or suffering. Although there is some support for this formulation in the ratification history of the CAT,[15] a proposed express understanding to that effect[16] was "criticized for setting too high a threshold of pain," S. Exec. Rep. No. 101-30 at 9, and was not adopted. We are not aware of any evidence suggesting that the standard was raised in the statute and we do not believe that it was.[17]

---

[15] Deputy Assistant Attorney General Mark Richard testified: "[T]he essence of torture" is treatment that inflicts "excruciating and agonizing physical pain." *CAT Hearing* at 16 (prepared statement).

[16] *See* S. Treaty Doc. No. 100–20 at 4–5 ("The United States understands that, in order to constitute torture, an act must be a deliberate and calculated act of an extremely cruel and inhuman nature, specifically intended to inflict excruciating and agonizing physical or mental pain or suffering.").

[17] Thus, we do not agree with the statement in the August 2002 Memorandum that "[t]he Reagan administration's understanding that the pain be 'excruciating and agonizing' is in substance not different from the Bush administration's proposal that the pain must be severe." August 2002 Memorandum at 19. Although the terms are concededly imprecise, and whatever the intent of the Reagan Administration's understanding, we believe that in common usage "excruciating and agonizing" pain is understood to be more intense than "severe" pain.

The August 2002 Memorandum also looked to the use of "severe pain" in certain other statutes, and concluded that to satisfy the definition in section 2340, pain "must be equivalent in intensity to the pain accompanying serious physical injury, such as organ failure, impairment of bodily function, or even death." *Id.* at 1; *see also id.* at 5–6, 13, 46. We do not agree with those statements. Those other statutes define an "emergency medical condition," for purposes of providing health benefits, as "a condition manifesting itself by acute symptoms of sufficient severity (including severe pain)" such that one could reasonably expect that the absence of immediate medical care might result in death, organ failure or impairment of bodily function. *See, e.g.*, 8 U.S.C. § 1369 (2000); 42 U.S.C.

Drawing distinctions among gradations of pain (for example, severe, mild, moderate, substantial, extreme, intense, excruciating, or agonizing) is obviously not an easy task, especially given the lack of any precise, objective scientific criteria for measuring pain.[18] We are, however, aided in this task by judicial interpretations of the Torture Victims Protection Act ("TVPA"), 28 U.S.C. § 1350 note (2000). The TVPA, also enacted to implement the CAT, provides a civil remedy to victims of torture. The TVPA defines "torture" to include:

> any act, directed against an individual in the offender's custody or physical control, by which *severe pain or suffering* (other than pain or suffering arising only from or inherent in, or incidental to, lawful sanctions), *whether physical or mental*, is intentionally inflicted on that individual for such purposes as obtaining from that individual or a third person information or a confession, punishing that individual for an act that individual or a third person has committed or is suspected of having committed, intimidating or coercing that individual or a third person, or for any reason based on discrimination of any kind....

28 U.S.C. § 1350 note, § 3(b)(1) (emphases added). The emphasized language is similar to section 2340's "severe physical or mental pain or suffering."[19] As the Court of Appeals for the District of Columbia Circuit has explained:

> The severity requirement is crucial to ensuring that the conduct proscribed by the [CAT] and the TVPA is sufficiently extreme and outrageous to warrant the universal condemnation that the term "torture" both connotes and invokes. The drafters of the [CAT], as well as the Reagan Administration that signed it, the Bush Administration that submitted it to Congress, and the Senate that ultimately ratified it, therefore all sought to ensure that "only acts of a certain gravity shall be considered to constitute torture."

§ 1395w-22(d)(3)(B) (2000); *id.* § 1395dd(e) (2000). They do not define "severe pain" even in that very different context (rather, they use it as an indication of an "emergency medical condition"), and they do not state that death, organ failure, or impairment of bodily function cause "severe pain," but rather that "severe pain" may indicate a condition that, if untreated, could cause one of those results. We do not believe that they provide a proper guide for interpreting "severe pain" in the very different context of the prohibition against torture in sections 2340–2340A. *Cf. United States v. Cleveland Indians Baseball Co.*, 532 U.S. 200, 213 (2001) (phrase "wages paid" has different meaning in different parts of Title 26); *Robinson v. Shell Oil Co.*, 519 U.S. 337, 343–44 (1997) (term "employee" has different meanings in different parts of Title VII).

[18] Despite extensive efforts to develop objective criteria for measuring pain, there is no clear, objective, consistent measurement. As one publication explains:

> Pain is a complex, subjective, perceptual phenomenon with a number of dimensions – intensity, quality, time course, impact, and personal meaning – that are uniquely experienced by each individual and, thus, can only be assessed indirectly. *Pain is a subjective experience and there is no way to objectively quantify it.* Consequently, assessment of a patient's pain depends on the patient's overt communications, both verbal and behavioral. Given pain's complexity, one must assess not only its somatic (sensory) component but also patients' moods, attitudes, coping efforts, resources, responses of family members, and the impact of pain on their lives.

Dennis C. Turk, *Assess the Person, Not Just the Pain*, Pain: Clinical Updates, Sept. 1993 (emphasis added). This lack of clarity further complicates the effort to define "severe" pain or suffering.

[19] Section 3(b)(2) of the TVPA defines "mental pain or suffering" similarly to the way that section 2340(2) defines "severe mental pain or suffering."

The critical issue is the degree of pain and suffering that the alleged torturer intended to, and actually did, inflict upon the victim. The more intense, lasting, or heinous the agony, the more likely it is to be torture.

Price v. Socialist People's Libyan Arab Jamahiriya, 294 F.3d 82, 92–93 (D.C. Cir. 2002) (citations omitted). That court concluded that a complaint that alleged beatings at the hands of police but that did not provide details concerning "the severity of plaintiffs' alleged beatings, including their frequency, duration, the parts of the body at which they were aimed, and the weapons used to carry them out," did not suffice "to ensure that [it] satisf[ied] the TVPA's rigorous definition of torture." *Id.* at 93.

In *Simpson v. Socialist People's Libyan Arab Jamahiriya*, 326 F.3d 230 (D.C. Cir, 2003), the D.C. Circuit again considered the types of acts that constitute torture under the TVPA definition. The plaintiff alleged, among other things, that Libyan authorities had held her incommunicado and threatened to kill her if she tried to leave. *See id.* at 232, 234. The court acknowledged that "these alleged acts certainly reflect a bent toward cruelty on the part of their perpetrators," but, reversing the district court, went on to hold that "they are not in themselves so unusually cruel or sufficiently extreme and outrageous as to constitute torture within the meaning of the [TVPA]." *Id.* at 234. Cases in which courts have found torture suggest the nature of the extreme conduct that falls within the statutory definition. *See, e.g., Hilao v. Estate of Marcos*, 103 F.3d 789, 790–91, 795 (9th Cir. 1996) (concluding that a course of conduct that included, among other things, severe beatings of plaintiff, repeated threats of death and electric shock, sleep deprivation, extended shackling to a cot (at times with a towel over his nose and mouth and water poured down his nostrils), seven months of confinement in a "suffocatingly hot" and cramped cell, and eight years of solitary or near-solitary confinement, constituted torture); *Mehinovic v. Vuckovic*, 198 F. Supp. 2d 1322, 1332–40, 1345–46 (N.D. Ga. 2002) (concluding that a course of conduct that included, among other things, severe beatings to the genitals, head, and other parts of the body with metal pipes, brass knuckles, batons, a baseball bat, and various other items; removal of teeth with pliers; kicking in the face and ribs; breaking of bones and ribs and dislocation of fingers; cutting a figure into the victim's forehead; hanging the victim and beating him; extreme limitations of food and water; and subjection to games of "Russian roulette," constituted torture); *Daliberti v. Republic of Iraq*, 146 F. Supp. 2d 19, 22–23 (D.D.C. 2001) (entering default judgment against Iraq where plaintiffs alleged, among other things, threats of "physical torture, such as cutting off . . . fingers, pulling out . . . fingernails," and electric shocks to the testicles); *Cicippio v. Islamic Republic of Iran*, 18 F. Supp. 2d 62, 64–66 (D.D.C. 1998) (concluding that a course of conduct that included frequent beatings, pistol whipping, threats of imminent death, electric shocks, and attempts to force confessions by playing Russian roulette and pulling the trigger at each denial, constituted torture).

(2) The Meaning of "Severe Physical Pain or Suffering."

The statute provides a specific definition of "severe mental pain or suffering," *see* 18 U.S.C. § 2340(2), but does not define the term "severe physical pain or suffering." Although we think the meaning of "severe physical pain" is relatively straightforward, the question remains whether Congress intended to prohibit a category of "severe physical suffering" distinct from "severe physical pain." We conclude that under some circumstances "severe physical suffering" may constitute torture even if it does not involve "severe physical pain." Accordingly, to the extent that the August 2002 Memorandum suggested that "severe physical suffering" under the statute could in no circumstances be distinct from "severe physical pain," *id.* at 6 n.3, we do not agree.

We begin with the statutory language. The inclusion of the words "or suffering" in the phrase "severe physical pain or suffering" suggests that the statutory category of physical torture is not limited to "severe physical pain." This is especially so in light of the general principle against interpreting a statute in such a manner as to render words surplusage. *See, e.g., Duncan v. Walker*, 533 U.S. 167, 174 (2001).

Exactly what is included in the concept of "severe physical suffering," however, is difficult to ascertain. We interpret the phrase in a statutory context where Congress expressly distinguished "physical pain or suffering" from "mental pain or suffering." Consequently, a separate category of "physical suffering" must include something other than any type of "mental pain or suffering."[20] Moreover, given that Congress precisely defined "mental pain or suffering" in the statute, it is unlikely to have intended to undermine that careful definition by including a broad range of mental sensations in a "physical suffering" component of "physical pain or suffering."[21] Consequently, "physical suffering" must be limited to adverse "physical" rather than adverse "mental" sensations.

The text of the statute and the CAT, and their history, provide little concrete guidance as to what Congress intended separately to include as "severe physical suffering." Indeed, the record consistently refers to "severe physical pain or suffering" (or, more often in the ratification record, "severe physical pain *and* suffering"), apparently without ever disaggregating the concepts of "severe physical pain" and "severe physical suffering" or discussing them as separate categories with separate content. Although there is virtually no legislative history for the statute, throughout the ratification of the CAT – which also uses the disjunctive "pain or suffering" and which the statutory prohibition implements – the references were generally to "pain *and* suffering," with no indication of any difference in meaning. The *Summary and Analysis of the Convention Against Torture and Other Cruel, Inhuman or Degrading Treatment or Punishment*, which appears in S. Treaty Doc. No. 100–20 at 3, for example, repeatedly refers to "pain *and* suffering." *See also* S. Exec. Rep. No. 101–30 at 6 (three uses of "pain and suffering"); *id.* at 13 (eight uses of "pain

---

[20] Common dictionary definitions of "physical" confirm that "physical suffering" does not include mental sensations, *See, e.g., American Heritage Dictionary of the English Language* at 1366 ("Of or relating to the body as distinguished from the mind or spirit"); *Oxford American Dictionary and Language Guide* at 748 ("of or concerning the body (*physical exercise; physical education*)").

[21] This is particularly so given that, as Administration witnesses explained, the limiting understanding defining mental pain or suffering was considered necessary to avoid problems of vagueness. *See, e.g., CAT Hearing* at 8, 10 (prepared statement of Abraham Sofaer, Legal Adviser, Department of State: "The Convention's wording...is not in all respects as precise as we believe necessary.... [B]ecause [the Convention] requires establishment of criminal penalties under our domestic law, we must pay particular attention to the meaning and interpretation of its provisions, especially concerning the standards by which the Convention will be applied as a matter of U.S. law.... [W]e prepared a codified proposal which...clarifies the definition of mental pain and suffering."); *id.* at 15–16 (prepared statement of Mark Richard: "The basic problem with the Torture Convention – one that permeates all our concerns – is its imprecise definition of torture, especially as that term is applied to actions which result solely in mental anguish. This·definitional vagueness makes it very doubtful that the United States can, consistent with Constitutional due process constraints, fulfill its obligation under the Convention to adequately engraft the definition of torture into the domestic criminal law of the United States."); *id.* at 17 (prepared statement of Mark Richard: "Accordingly, the Torture Convention's vague definition concerning the mental suffering aspect of torture cannot be resolved by reference to established principles of international law. In an effort to overcome this unacceptable element of vagueness in Article I of the Convention, we have proposed an understanding which defines severe mental pain constituting torture with sufficient specificity to...meet Constitutional due process requirements").

and suffering"); *id.* at 14 (two uses of "pain and suffering"); *id.* at 35 (one use of "pain and suffering"). Conversely, the phrase "pain or suffering" is used less frequently in the Senate report in discussing (as opposed to quoting) the CAT and the understandings under consideration, *e.g., id.* at 5–6 (one use of "pain or suffering"), *id.* at 14 (two uses of "pain or suffering"); *id.* at 16 (two uses of "pain or suffering"), and, when used, it is with no suggestion that it has any different meaning.

Although we conclude that inclusion of the words "or suffering" in "severe physical pain or suffering" establishes that physical torture is not limited to "severe physical pain," we also conclude that Congress did not intend "severe physical pain or suffering" to include a category of "physical suffering" that would be so broad as to negate the limitations on the other categories of torture in the statute. Moreover, the "physical suffering" covered by the statute must be "severe" to be within the statutory prohibition. We conclude that under some circumstances "physical suffering" may be of sufficient intensity and duration to meet the statutory definition of torture even if it does not involve "severe physical pain." To constitute such torture, "*severe* physical suffering" would have to be a condition of some extended duration or persistence as well as intensity. The need to define a category of "severe physical suffering" that is different from "severe physical pain," and that also does not undermine the limited definition Congress provided for torture, along with the requirement that any such physical suffering be "severe," calls for an interpretation under which "severe physical suffering" is reserved for physical distress that is "severe" considering its intensity and duration or persistence, rather than merely mild or transitory.[22] Otherwise, the inclusion of such a category would lead to the kind of uncertainty in interpreting the statute that Congress sought to reduce both through its understanding to the CAT and in sections 2340–2340A.

(3) The Meaning of "Severe Mental Pain or Suffering."

Section 2340 defines "severe mental pain or suffering" to mean:

the prolonged mental harm caused by or resulting from –

(A) the intentional infliction or threatened infliction of severe physical pain or suffering;

(B) the administration or application, or threatened administration or application, of mind-altering substances or other procedures calculated to disrupt profoundly the senses or the personality;

(C) the threat of imminent death; or

(D) the threat that another person will imminently be subjected to death, severe physical pain or suffering, or the administration or application of mind-altering substances or other procedures calculated to disrupt profoundly the senses or personality[.]

18 U.S.C. § 2340(2). Torture is defined under the statute to include an act specifically intended to inflict severe mental pain or suffering. *Id.* § 2340(1).

---

[22] Support for concluding that there is an extended temporal element, or at least an element of persistence, in "severe physical suffering" as a category distinct from "severe physical pain" may also be found in the prevalence of concepts of "endurance" of suffering and of suffering as a "state" or "condition" in standard dictionary definitions. *See, e.g., Webster's Third New International Dictionary* at 2284 (defining "suffering" as "the endurance of or submission to affliction, pain, loss"; "a pain endured"); *Random House Dictionary of the English Language* 1901 (2d ed. 1987) ("the state of a person or thing that suffers"); *Funk & Wagnalls New Standard Dictionary of the English Language* 2416 (1946) ("A state of anguish or pain"); *American Heritage Dictionary of the English Language* at 1795 ("The condition of one who suffers").

An important preliminary question with respect to this definition is whether the statutory list of the four "predicate acts" in section 2340(2)(A)-(D) is exclusive. We conclude that Congress intended the list of predicate acts to be exclusive – that is, to constitute the proscribed "severe mental pain or suffering" under the statute, the prolonged mental harm must be caused by acts falling within one of the four statutory categories of predicate acts. We reach this conclusion based on the clear language of the statute, which provides a detailed definition that includes four categories of predicate acts joined by the disjunctive and does not contain a catchall provision or any other language suggesting that additional acts might qualify (for example, language such as "including" or "such acts as").[23] Congress plainly considered very specific predicate acts, and this definition tracks the Senate's understanding concerning mental pain or suffering when giving its advice and consent to ratification of the CAT. The conclusion that the list of predicate acts is exclusive is consistent with both the text of the Senate's understanding, and with the fact that it was adopted out of concern that the CAT's definition of torture did not otherwise meet the requirement for clarity in defining crimes. *See supra* note 21. Adopting an interpretation of the statute that expands the list of predicate acts for "severe mental pain or suffering" would constitute an impermissible rewriting of the statute and would introduce the very imprecision that prompted the Senate to adopt its understanding when giving its advice and consent to ratification of the CAT.

Another question is whether the requirement of "prolonged mental harm" caused by or resulting from one of the enumerated predicate acts is a separate requirement, or whether such "prolonged mental harm" is to be presumed any time one of the predicate acts occurs. Although it is possible to read the statute's reference to "*the* prolonged mental harm caused by or resulting from" the predicate acts as creating a statutory presumption that each of the predicate acts always causes prolonged mental harm, we do not believe that was Congress's intent. As noted, this language closely tracks the understanding that the Senate adopted when it gave its advice and consent to ratification of the CAT:

> in order to constitute torture, an act must be specifically intended to inflict severe physical or mental pain or suffering and that mental pain or suffering refers to prolonged mental harm caused by or resulting from (1) the intentional infliction or threatened infliction of severe physical pain or suffering; (2) the administration or application, or threatened administration or application, of mind altering substances or other procedures calculated to disrupt profoundly the senses or the personality; (3) the threat of imminent death; or (4) the threat that another person will imminently be subjected to death, severe physical pain or suffering, or the administration or application of mind altering substances or other procedures calculated to disrupt profoundly the senses or personality.

S. Exec. Rep. No. 101–30 at 36. We do not believe that simply by adding the word "the" before "prolonged harm," Congress intended a material change in the definition of mental pain or suffering as articulated in the Senate's understanding to the CAT. The legislative history, moreover, confirms that sections 2340–2340A were intended to fulfill – but

---

[23] These four categories of predicate acts "are members of an 'associated group or series,' justifying the inference that items not mentioned were excluded by deliberate choice, not inadvertence." *Barnhart v. Peabody Coal Co.*, 537 U.S. 149, 168 (2003) (quoting *United States v. Vonn*, 535 U.S. 55, 65 (2002). *See also, e.g., Leatherman v. Tarrant County Narcotics Intelligence & Coordination Unit*, 507 U.S. 163, 168 (1993); 2A Norman J. Singer, *Statutes and Statutory Construction* § 47.23 (6th ed. 2000). Nor do we see any "contrary indications" that would rebut this inference. *Vonn*, 535 U.S. at 65.

not go beyond – the United States' obligations under the CAT: 'This section provides the necessary legislation to implement the [CAT]. . . . The definition of torture emanates directly from article I of the [CAT]. The definition for 'severe mental pain and suffering' incorporates the [above mentioned] understanding." S. Rep. No. 103–107, at 58–59 (1993). This understanding, embodied in the statute, was meant to define the obligation undertaken by the United States. Given this understanding, the legislative history, and the fact that section 2340(2) defines "severe mental pain and suffering" carefully in language very similar to the understanding, we do not believe that Congress intended the definition to create a presumption that any time one of the predicate acts occurs, prolonged mental harm is deemed to result.

Turning to the question of what constitutes "prolonged mental harm caused by or resulting from" a predicate act, we believe that Congress intended this phrase to require mental "harm" that is caused by or that results from a predicate act, and that has some lasting duration. There is little guidance to draw upon in interpreting this phrase.[24] Nevertheless, our interpretation is consistent with the ordinary meaning of the statutory terms. First, the use of the word "harm" – as opposed to simply repeating "pain or suffering" – suggests some mental damage or injury. Ordinary dictionary definitions of "harm," such as "physical or mental *damage: injury*," *Webster's Third New International Dictionary* at 1034 (emphasis added), or "[p]hysical or psychological *injury or damage*," *American Heritage Dictionary of the English Language* at 825 (emphasis added), support this interpretation. Second, to "prolong" means to "lengthen in time" or to "extend in duration," or to "draw out," *Webster's Third New International Dictionary* at 1815, further suggesting that to be "prolonged," the mental damage must extend for some period of time. This damage need not be permanent, but it must continue for a "prolonged" period of time.[25] Finally, under section 2340(2), the "prolonged mental harm" must be "caused by" or "resulting from" one of the enumerated predicate acts.[26]

---

[24] The phrase "prolonged mental harm" does not appear in the relevant medical literature or elsewhere in the United States Code. The August 2002 Memorandum concluded that to constitute "prolonged mental harm," there must be "significant psychological harm of significant duration, e.g., lasting for months or even years." *Id.* at I; *see also id.* at 7. Although we believe that the mental harm must be of some lasting duration to be "prolonged," to the extent that formulation was intended to suggest that the mental harm would have to last for at least "months or even years," we do not agree.

[25] For example, although we do not suggest that the statute is limited to such cases, development of a mental disorder – such as post-traumatic stress disorder or perhaps chronic depression – could constitute "prolonged mental harm." *See* American Psychiatric Association, *Diagnostic and Statistical Manual of Mental Disorders* 369–76, 463–68 (4th ed. 2000) ("DSM-IV-TR"). *See also, e.g., Report of the Special Rapporteur on Torture and Other Cruel, Inhuman or Degrading Treatment or Punishment*, U.N. Doc. A/59/324, at 14 (2004) ("The most common diagnosis of psychiatric symptoms among torture survivors is said to be post-traumatic stress disorder."); *see also* Metin Basoglu et al., *Tortured and Mental Health: A Research Overview*, in Ellen Gerrity et al. eds., *The Mental Health Consequences of Torture* 48–49 (2001) (referring to findings of higher rates of post-traumatic stress disorder in studies involving torture survivors); Murat Parker et al., *Psychological Effects of Torture: An Empirical Study of Tortured and Non-Tortured Non-Political Prisoners, in* Metin Basoglu ed., *Torture and Its Consequences: Current Treatment Approaches* 77 (1992) (referring to findings of post-traumatic stress disorder in torture survivors).

[26] This is not meant to suggest that, if the predicate act or acts continue for an extended period, "prolonged mental harm" cannot occur until after they are completed. Early occurrences of the predicate act could cause mental harm that could continue – and become prolonged – during the extended period the predicate acts continued to occur. For example, in *Sackie v. Ashcroft*, 270 F. Supp. 2d 596, 601–02 (E.D. Pa. 2003), the predicate acts continued over a three-to-four-year period, and the court concluded that "prolonged mental harm" had occurred during that time.

Although there are few judicial opinions discussing the question of "prolonged mental harm," those cases that have addressed the issue are consistent with our view. For example, in the TVPA case of *Mehinovic*, the court explained that:

> [The defendant] also caused or participated in the plaintiffs' mental torture. Mental torture consists of "prolonged mental harm caused by or resulting from: the intentional infliction or threatened infliction of severe physical pain or suffering; . . . the threat of imminent death. . . ." As set out above, plaintiffs noted in their testimony that they feared that they would be killed by [the defendant] during the beatings he inflicted or during games of "Russian roulette." *Each plaintiff continues to suffer long-term psychological harm as a result of the ordeals they suffered at the hands of defendant and others.*

198 F. Supp. 2d at 1346 (emphasis added; first ellipsis in original). In reaching its conclusion, the court noted that the plaintiffs were continuing to suffer serious mental harm even ten years after the events in question: One plaintiff "suffers from anxiety, flashbacks, and nightmares and has difficulty sleeping. [He] continues to suffer thinking about what happened to him during this ordeal and has been unable to work as a result of the continuing effects of the torture he endured." *Id.* at 1334. Another plaintiff "suffers from anxiety, sleeps very little, and has frequent nightmares. . . . [He] has found it impossible to return to work." *Id.* at 1336. A third plaintiff "has frequent nightmares. He has had to use medication to help him sleep. His experience has made him feel depressed and reclusive, and he has not been able to work since he escaped from this ordeal." *Id.* at 1337–38. And the fourth plaintiff "has flashbacks and nightmares, suffers from nervousness, angers easily, and has difficulty trusting people. These effects directly impact and interfere with his ability to work." *Id.* at 1340. In each case, these mental effects were continuing years after the infliction of the predicate acts.

And in *Sackie v. Ashcroft*, 270 F. Supp. 2d 596 (E. D. Pa. 2003), the individual had been kidnapped and "forcibly recruited" as a child soldier at the age of 14, and over the next three to four years had been forced to take narcotics and threatened with imminent death. *Id.* at 597–98, 601–02. The court concluded that the resulting mental harm, which continued over this three-to-four year period, qualified as "prolonged mental harm." *Id.* at 602.

Conversely, in *Villeda Aldana v. Fresh Del Monte Produce, Inc.*, 305 F. Supp. 2d 1285 (S. D. Fla. 2003), the court rejected a claim under the TVPA brought by individuals who had been held at gunpoint overnight and repeatedly threatened with death. While recognizing that the plaintiffs had experienced an "ordeal," the court concluded that they had failed to show that their experience caused lasting damage, noting that "there is simply no allegation that Plaintiffs have suffered any prolonged mental harm or physical injury as a result of their alleged intimidation." *Id.* at 1294–95.

(4) The Meaning of "Specifically Intended."

It is well recognized that the term "specific intent" is ambiguous and that the courts do not use it consistently. *See* 1 Wayne R. LaFave, *Substantive Criminal Law* § 5.2(e), at 355 & n.79 (2d ed. 2003). "Specific intent" is most commonly understood, however, "to designate a special mental element which is required above and beyond any mental state required with respect to the *actus reus* of the crime." *Id.* at 354; *see also Carter v. United States*, 530 U.S. 255, 268 (2000) (explaining that general intent, as opposed to specific intent, requires "that the defendant possessed knowledge [only] with respect to the *actus reus* of the crime"). As one respected treatise explains:

> With crimes which require that the defendant intentionally cause a specific result, what is meant by an "intention" to cause that result? Although the theorists have not always been in agreement . . . , the traditional view is that a person who acts . . . intends a result of his act . . . under two quite different circumstances: (1) when he consciously desires that result, whatever the likelihood of that result happening from his conduct; and (2) when he knows that that result is practically certain to follow from his conduct, whatever his desire may be as to that result.

1 LaFave, *Substantive Criminal Law*, § 5.2(a), at 341 (footnote omitted).

As noted, the cases are inconsistent. Some suggest that only a conscious desire to produce the proscribed result constitutes specific intent; others suggest that even reasonable foreseeability suffices. In *United States v. Bailey*, 444 U.S. 394 (1980), for example, the Court suggested that, at least "[i]n a general sense," *id.* at 405, "specific intent" requires that one consciously desire the result. *Id.* at 403–05. The Court compared the common law's *mens rea* concepts of specific intent and general intent to the Model Penal Code's *mens rea* concepts of acting purposefully and acting knowingly. *Id.* at 404–05. "[A] person who causes a particular result is said to act purposefully," wrote the Court, "if 'he consciously desires that result, whatever the likelihood of that result happening from his conduct.'" *Id.* at 404 (internal quotation marks omitted). A person "is said to act knowingly," in contrast, "if he is aware 'that result is practically certain to follow from his conduct, whatever his desire may be as to that result.'" *Id.* (internal quotation marks omitted). The Court then stated: "In a general sense, 'purpose' corresponds loosely with the common-law concept of specific intent, while 'knowledge' corresponds loosely with the concept of general intent." *Id.* at 405.

In contrast, cases such as *United States v. Neiswender*, 590 F.2d 1269 (4th Cir. 1979), suggest that to prove specific intent it is enough that the defendant simply have "knowledge or notice" that his act "would have likely resulted in" the proscribed outcome. *Id.* at 1273. "Notice," the court held, "is provided by the reasonable foreseeability of the natural and probable consequences of one's acts." *Id.*

We do not believe it is useful to try to define the precise meaning of "specific intent" in section 2340.[27] In light of the President's directive that the United States not engage in torture, it would not be appropriate to rely on parsing the specific intent element of the statute to approve as lawful conduct that might otherwise amount to torture. Some observations, however, are appropriate. It is clear that the specific intent element of section 2340 would be met if a defendant performed an act and "consciously desire[d]" that act to inflict severe physical or mental pain or suffering. 1 LaFave, *Substantive Criminal Law* § 5.2(a), at 341. Conversely, if an individual acted in good faith, and only after reasonable investigation establishing that his conduct would not inflict severe physical or mental pain or suffering, it appears unlikely that he would have the specific intent necessary to violate sections 2340–2340A. Such an individual could be said neither consciously to desire the proscribed result, *see, e.g., Bailey*, 444 U.S. at 405, nor to have "knowledge or notice"

---

[27] In the August 2002 Memorandum, this Office concluded that the specific intent element of the statute required that infliction of severe pain or suffering be the defendant's "precise objective" and that it was not enough that the defendant act with knowledge that such pain "was reasonably likely to result from his actions" (or even that that result "is certain to occur"). *Id.* at 3–4. We do not reiterate that test here.

that his act "would likely have resulted in" the proscribed outcome, *Neiswender*, 590 F.2d at 1273.

Two final points on the issue of specific intent: First, specific intent: must be distinguished from motive. There is no exception under the statute permitting torture to be used for a "good reason." Thus, a defendant's motive (to protect national security, for example) is not relevant to the question whether he has acted with the requisite specific intent under the statute. *See Cheek v. United States*, 498 U.S. 192, 200–01 (1991). Second, specific intent to take a given action can be found even if the defendant will take the action only conditionally. *Cf., e.g., Holloway v. United States*, 526 U.S. 1, 11 (1999) ("[A] defendant may not negate a proscribed intent by requiring the victim to comply with a condition the defendant has no right to impose."). *See also id.* at 10–11 & nn. 9–12; Model Penal Code § 2.02(6). Thus, for example, the fact that a victim might have avoided being tortured by cooperating with the perpetrator would not make permissible actions otherwise constituting torture under the statute. Presumably that has frequently been the case with torture, but that fact does not make the practice of torture any less abhorrent or unlawful.[28]

Please let us know if we can be of further assistance.

Daniel Levin
Acting Assistant Attorney
General

---

[28] In the August 2002 Memorandum, this Office indicated that an element of the offense of torture was that the act in question actually result in the infliction of severe physical or mental pain or suffering. *See id.* at 3. That conclusion rested on a comparison of the statute with the CAT, which has a different definition of "torture" that requires the actual infliction of pain or suffering, and we do not believe that the statute requires that the defendant actually inflict (as opposed to act with the specific intent to inflict) severe physical or mental pain or suffering. *Compare* CAT art. 1(1) ("the term 'torture' means any act by which severe pain or suffering, whether physical or mental, *is intentionally inflicted*") (emphasis added) *with* 18 U.S.C. § 2340 ("'torture' means an act ... *specifically intended to inflict* severe physical or mental pain or suffering") (emphasis added). It is unlikely that any such requirement would make any practical difference, however, since the statute also criminalizes attempts to commit torture. *Id.* § 2340A(a).

UNCLASSIFIED

DEPARTMENT OF THE AIR FORCE

OFFICE OF THE JUDGE ADVOCATE GENERAL

5 February 2003

MEMORANDUM FOR SAF/GC

FROM: AF/JA

SUBJECT: Final Report and Recommendations of the Working Group to Assess the Legal, Policy and Operational Issues Relating to Interrogation of Detainees Held by the U.S. Armed Forces in the War on Terrorism (U)

1. (U) In drafting the subject report and recommendations, the legal opinions of the Department of Justice, Office of Legal Counsel (DoJ/OLC), were relied on almost exclusively. Although the opinions of DoJ/OLC are to be given a great deal of weight within the Executive Branch, their positions on several of the Working Group's issues are contentious. As our discussion demonstrate, others within and outside the Executive Branch are likely to disagree. The report and recommendations caveat that it only applies to "strategic interrogations" of "unlawful combatants" at locations outside the United States. Although worded to permit maximum flexibility and legal interpretation, I believe other factors need to be provided to the DoD/GC before he makes a final recommendation to the Secretary of Defense.

2. (SNF) Several of the more extreme interrogation techniques, on their face, amount to violations of domestic criminal law and the UCMJ (e.g., assault). Applying the more extreme techniques during the interrogation of detainees places the interrogators and the chain of command at risk of criminal accusations domestically. Although a wide range of defenses to these accusations theoretically apply, it is impossible to be certain that any defense will be successful at trial; our domestic courts may well disagree with DoJ/OLC's interpretation of the law. Further, while the current administration is not likely to pursue prosecution, it is impossible to predict how future administrations will view the use of such techniques.

3. (SNF) Additionally, other nations are unlikely to agree with DoJ/OLC's interpretation of the law in some instances. Other nations may disagree with the President's status determination regarding the Operation ENDURING FREEDOM (OEF) detainees; they may conclude that the detainees are POWs entitled to all of the protections of the Geneva Conventions. Treating OEF detainees inconsistently with the Conventions arguably "lowers the bar" for the treatment of U.S. POWs in future conflicts. Even where nations agree with the President's status determination, many would view the more extreme interrogation techniques as violative of other international law (other treaties or customary international law) and perhaps violative of their own domestic law. This puts the interrogators and the chain of command at risk of criminal accusations abroad, either in foreign domestic courts or in international fora, to include the ICC.

~~SECRET//NOFORN~~
UNCLASSIFIED

4. (SNF) Should any information regarding the use of the more extreme interrogation techniques become public, it is likely to be exaggerated/distorted in both the U.S. and international media. This could have a negative impact on international, and perhaps even domestic, support for the war on terrorism. Moreover, it could have a negative impact on public perception of the U.S. military in general.

5. (SNF) Finally, the use of the more extreme interrogation techniques simply is not how the U.S. armed forces have operated in recent history. We have taken the legal and moral "high-road" in the conduct of our military operations regardless of how others may operate. Our forces are trained in this legal and moral mindset beginning the day they enter active duty. It should be noted that law of armed conflict and code of conduct training have been mandated by Congress and emphasized since the Viet Nam conflict when our POWs were subjected to torture by their captors. We need to consider the overall impact of approving extreme interrogation techniques as giving official approval and legal sanction to the application of interrogation techniques that U.S. forces have consistently been trained are unlawful.

V/R

JACK L. RIVES
Major General, USAF
Deputy Judge Advocate General

Derived from: SAF/GC Memo
Declassify on: ~~4 February 2013~~
Date of Source: 4 February 2003
Declassified by ExecSec. Decl of
WG Final Report; Exec Decl of JTF
170 Memo dtd 11 Oct 02; Faye Report
p. 63; OGC E-Mail 15 Apr 05

~~Declassify Under the Authority of Executive Order 12958~~
~~By Executive Secretary, Office of the Secretary of Defense~~
~~William P. Marriott, CAPT, USN~~
~~June 21, 2005~~

~~SECRET//NOFORN~~
UNCLASSIFIED

UNCLASSIFIED
DEPARTMENT OF THE AIR FORCE
OFFICE OF THE JUDGE ADVOCATE GENERAL

6 February 2003

MEMORANDUM FOR SAF/GC

FROM: AF/JA

SUBJECT: Comments on Draft Report and Recommendations of the Working Group to Assess the Legal, Policy and Operational Issues Relating to Interrogation of Detainees Held by the U.S. Armed Forces in the War on Terrorism (U)

1. (U) Please note that while I accept that the Department of Justice, Office of Legal Counsel (DoJ/OLC), speaks for the Executive Branch and that its legal opinions in this matter are to be followed, I continue to maintain that DoJ/OLC's opinions on several of the Working Group's issues are contentious. Others may disagree with various portions of the DoJ/OLC analysis. I believe we should recognize this fact and therefore urge that certain factors should be prominently provided to the DoD/GC before he makes a final recommendation to the Secretary of Defense. I recommend the following specific modifications to the draft report dated 4 February 2003:

    a. Page 2, add the following sentence to the end of paragraph 2:

        It should be noted that several of the legal opinions expressed herein are likely to be viewed as contentious outside the Executive Branch, both domestically and internationally.

    b. Page 54, change fourth full paragraph to read as follows

        (U) Choice of interrogation techniques involves a risk benefit analysis in each case, bounded by the limits of DOD policy and law. When assessing whether to use exceptional interrogation techniques, consideration should be given to the possible adverse effects on U.S. Armed Forces culture and self-image, which suffered during the Vietnam conflict and at other times due to perceived law of armed conflict violations. DoD policy, indoctrinated in the DoD Law of War Program in 1979 and subsequent service regulations, greatly restored the culture and self-image of U.S. Armed Forces by establishing high benchmarks of compliance with the principles and spirit of the law of war, and humane treatment of all persons in U.S. Armed Forces custody. U.S. Armed Forces are continuously trained to take the legal and moral "high-road" in the conduct of our military operations regardless of how others may operate. While the detainees' status as unlawful belligerents may not entitle them to protections of the Geneva Conventions, that is a legal distinction that may be lost on the members of the armed forces. Approving exceptional interrogation techniques

~~SECRET/NOFORN~~
UNCLASSIFIED

may be seen as giving official approval and legal sanction to the application of
interrogation techniques that U.S. Armed Forces have heretofore been trained are
unlawful. In addition, consideration should be given to whether implementation of
such techniques is likely to result in adverse impacts for DOD personnel who become
POWs, including possible perceptions by other nations that the United States is ·
lowering standards related to the treatment of prisoners, generally.

Alternatively, change the last paragraph on page 68, to read as follows:

~~(U)~~ The cultural and self-image of the U.S. Armed Forces suffered during the
Vietnam conflict and at other times due to perceived law of armed conflict violations.
DoD policy, indoctrinated in the DoD Law of War Program in 1979 and subsequent
service regulations, greatly restored the culture and self-image of U.S. Armed Forces.
U.S. Armed Forces are continuously trained to take the legal and moral "high-road" in
the conduct of our military operations regardless of how others may operate. While
the detainees' status as unlawful belligerents may not entitle them to protections of the
Geneva Conventions, that is a legal distinction that may be lost on the members of the
armed forces. Approving exceptional interrogation techniques may be seen as giving
official approval and legal sanction to the application of interrogation techniques that
U.S. Armed Forces have heretofore been trained are unlawful. General use of
exceptional techniques (generally, having substantially greater risk than those
currently, routinely used by U.S. Armed Forces interrogators), even though lawful,
may create uncertainty among interrogators regarding the appropriate limits of
interrogations, and may adversely affect the cultural self-image of the U.S. armed
forces.

c. Page 68, add the following new paragraphs after the sixth full paragraph:

~~(U)~~ Several of the exceptional techniques, on their face, amount to violations of
domestic criminal law and the UCMJ (e.g., assault). Applying exceptional techniques
places interrogators and the chain of command at risk of criminal accusations
domestically. Although one or more of the aforementioned defenses to these
accusations may apply, it is impossible to be certain that any of these defenses will be
successful as the judiciary may interpret the applicable law differently from the
interpretation provided herein.

~~(U)~~ Other nations are likely to view the exceptional interrogation techniques as
violative of international law and perhaps violative of their own domestic law. This
places interrogators and the chain of command at risk of criminal accusations abroad,
either in foreign domestic courts or in international fora, to include the ICC.

d. Page 68, add the following new paragraphs after the eighth full paragraph:

~~(U)~~ Employment of exceptional interrogation techniques may have a negative
effect on the treatment of U.S. POWs. Other nations may disagree with the President's
status determination regarding Operation ENDURING FREEDOM (OEF) detainees,
concluding that the detainees are POWs entitled to all of the protections of the Geneva

~~SECRET/NOFORN~~
UNCLASSIFIED

Conventions. Treating OEF detainees inconsistently with the Conventions arguably "lowers the bar" for the treatment of U.S. POWs in future conflicts. Even where nations agree with the President's status determination, many may view the exceptional techniques as violative of other law.

2. (U) ~~(S/NF)~~ Should any information concerning the exceptional techniques become public, it is likely to be exaggerated/distorted in both the U.S. and international media. This could have a negative impact on international, and perhaps even domestic, support for the war on terrorism. It could likewise have a negative impact on public perception of the U.S. military in general.

/s/

JACK L. RIVES
Major General, USAF
Deputy Judge Advocate General

Derived from: SAF/GC Memo
Declassify on: ~~4 February 2013~~
Date of Source: 4 February 2003
Declassified by ExecSec. Decl of WG
Final Report; Exec Decl of JTF 170
Memo dtd 11 Oct 02; Faye Report,
p. 63; OGC E-Mail 15 Apr 05

~~Declassify Under the Authority of Executive Order 12958
By Executive Secretary, Office of the Secretary of Defense
William P. Marriott, CAPT, USN June 21, 2004~~

~~SECRET/NOFORN~~
UNCLASSIFIED

WASHINGTON NAVY YARD DC 20374-5066

IN REPLY REFER TO

·6 Feb 03

⁻SECRET - NOFORN

Memorandum for General Counsel of the Air Force

Subj: WORKING GROUP RECOMMENDATIONS RELATING TO INTERROGATION OF
       DETAINEES

1. Earlier today, I provided to you a number of suggested changes, additions, and deletions to the subject
    document.

2. . I would like to further recommend that the document make very clear to decision-makers that its legal
    conclusions are limited to the arguably unique circumstances of this group of detainees, i.e., unlawful
    combatants held "outside" the United States. Because of these unique circumstances, the U.S.
    Torture Statute, the Constitution, the Geneva Conventions and customary international law do not
    apply, thereby affording policy latitude that likely does not exist in almost any other circumstance.
    (The UCMJ, however, does apply to U.S. personnel conducting the interrogations.)

3. Given this unique set of circumstances, I believe policy considerations continue to loom very large.
    Should service personnel be conducting the interrogations? How will this affect their treatment when
    incarcerated abroad and our ability to call others to account for their treatment? More broadly, while
    we may have found a unique situation in GTMO where the protections of the Geneva Conventions,
    U.S. statutes, and even the Constitution do not apply, will the American people find we have missed
    the forest for the trees by condoning practices that, while technically legal, are inconsistent with our
    most fundamental values? How would such perceptions affect our ability to prosecute the Global
    War on Terrorism?

4. I accept the premise that this group of detainees is different, and that lawyers should identify legal
    distinctions where they exist. It must be conceded, however, that we are preparing to treat these
    detainees very differently than we treat any other group, and differently than we permit our own
    people to be treated either at home or abroad. At a minimum, I recommend that decision-makers be
    made fully aware of the very narrow set of circumstances – factually and legally – upon which the
    policy rests. Moreover, I recommend that we consider asking decision-makers directly: is this the
    "right thing" for U.S. military personnel?

                                              MICHAEL F. LOHR
                                              Rear Admiral, JAGC, U.S. Navy
                                              Judge Advocate General

·Cc:
DoD GC
Navy GC
Classified by: Navy JAG, Feb 03
Reason: 1.5c
DECLAS ON: X1

~~SECRET/NOFORN~~ DECLASSIFIED

DEPARTMENT OF THE NAVY
HEADQUARTERS UNITED STATES MARINE CORPS
2 NAVY ANNEX
WASHINGTON, DC 20380-1775

IN REPLY REFER TO:

5800
JAO
27 Feb 03

Memorandum for General Counsel of the Air Force

Subj: WORKING GROUP RECOMMENDATIONS ON DETAINEE INTERROGATIONS

1. In addition to comments we submitted 5 February, we concur with the recommendations submitted by the Navy (TJAG RADM Lohr), the Air Force (TJAG MGen Rives), and the Joint Staff Legal Counsel's Office. Their recommendations dealt with policy considerations, contention with the OLC opinion, and foreign interpretations of GC IV (Civilians) and customary international law, respectively.

2. The common thread among our recommendations is concern for servicemembers. OLC does not represent the services; thus, understandably, concern for servicemembers is not reflected in their opinion. Notably, their opinion is silent on the UCMJ and foreign views of international law.

3. We nonetheless recommend that the Working Group product accurately portray the services' concerns that the authorization of aggressive counter-resistance techniques by servicemembers will adversely impact the following:

    a. Treatment of U.S. Servicemembers by Captors and Compliance with International Law.

    b. Criminal and Civil Liability of DOD Military and Civilian Personnel in Domestic, Foreign, and International Forums.

    c. U.S. and International Public Support and Respect of U.S. Armed Forces.

    d. Pride, Discipline, and Self-Respect within the U.S. Armed Forces.

    e. Human Intelligence Exploitation and Surrender of Foreign Enemy Forces, and Cooperation and Support of Friendly Nations.

KEVIN M. SANDKUHLER
Brigadier General, USMC
Staff Judge Advocate to CMC

DECLASSIFIED BY EXECSEC
DECLASSIFICATION OF WG FINAL
REPORT; EXECSEC DECLASSIFICATION
OF JTF-170 MEMO DATED 11 OCT 02;
FAYE REPORT, P.63; OGC e-mail
15 APR 05

~~SECRET/NOFORN~~ DECLASSIFIED

SECRET/NOFORN DECLASSIFIED

Comments on Draft Working Group Report on Detainee Interrogations

1. Change p. 54, fifth paragraph, to read as follows (new language highlighted):

(S/NF U) Choice of interrogation techniques involves a risk benefit analysis in each case, bounded by the limits of DOD policy and law. When assessing whether to use exceptional interrogation techniques, consideration should be given to the possible adverse effects on U.S. Armed Forces culture and self-image In addition, consideration should be given to whether implementation of such techniques is likely to result in adverse impacts for DOD personnel who are captured or detained become POWs, including possible perceptions by other nations that the United States is lowering standards related to the treatment of prisoners and other detainees, generally.

2. Add to p. 68, a paragraph after the seventh paragraph that reads:

See DODD 5100.77 DoD Law of War Program, para 5.3.1 (9 Dec 98, canceling DODD 5100.77 of 10 Jul 79); DODD 2310.1 DoD Program for EPOW and Other Detainees, para 3.1 (18 Aug 94); CJCSI 5819.01B Implementation of the DoD LOW Program, para 4a (25 Mar 02); AR 190-8/OPNAVINST 3461.6/AFJI31-304/MCO 3461.1 EPWs, Retained Personnel, Civilian Internees and Other Detainees, para 1-5a; SECNAVINST 3461.3 Program for POWs and Other Detainees, para 3a (30 Apr 73); SECNAVINST 3300.1A LOAC Program to Insure Compliance by the Naval Establishment, para 4a (23 Mar 88); OPNAVINST 3300.52 LOAC Program to Ensure Compliance by USN and USNR, para 2 (18 Mar 83); MCO 3300.3 Marine Corps LOW Program, para 4 (2 Aug 84 cancelled pending revision).

[2] Even Article 98 agreements under the Rome Statute of the ICC are limited. In Article 98 agreements, a nation agrees not to turn over U.S. personnel without U.S. consent. Such agreements do not bind other nations.

[3] The Restatement 3d of the Foreign Relations Law of the U.S., § 702 Customary International Law of Human Rights, states, "A state violates international law if, as a matter of state policy, it practices, encourages, or condones...torture or other cruel, inhuman, or degrading treatment or punishment, [or] prolonged arbitrary detention..."

SECRET/NOFORN DECLASSIFIED

INSERT:

which suffered during the Vietnam conflict and at other times due to perceived law of war violations. DOD policy indoctrinated in the DOD Law of War Program in 1979 and subsequent service regulations, greatly restored the culture and self-image of U.S. Armed Forces by establishing high benchmarks of compliance with the principles and spirit of the law of war and humane treatment of all persons in U.S. Armed Forces custody. In addition, consideration should be given to whether implementation of such techniques is likely to result in adverse impacts for DOD personnel who are captured or detained <become POWs,> including possible perceptions by other nations that the United States is lowering standards related to the treatment of prisoners and other detainees, generally.

2. Add to p. 68, a paragraph after the seventh paragraph that reads:
(U) Comprehensive protection is lacking for DOD personnel who may be tried by other nations and/or international bodies for violations of international law, such as violations of the Geneva or Hague Conventions, the Additional Protocols, the Torture Convention, the Rome Statute of the ICC, or the Customary International Law of Human Rights. This risk has the potential to impact future operations and overseas travel of such personnel, both on and off duty.

DEPARTMENT OF THE ARMY
OFFICE OF THE JUDGE ADVOCATE GENERAL
2200 ARMY PENTAGON
WASHINGTON, DC 20310-2200

REPLY TO
ATTENTION OF

DAJA-ZA   3 March 2003

MEMORANDUM FOR GENERAL COUNSEL OF THE DEPARTMENT OF THE AIR
FORCE

SUBJECT: Draft Report and Recommendations of the Working Group to Access the
Legal, Policy and Operational Issues Related to Interrogation of Detainees Held by the
U.S. Armed Forces in the War on Terrorism (U)

1. (U) The purpose of this memorandum is to advise the Department of Defense (DOD)
General Counsel of a number of serious concerns regarding the draft Report and
Recommendations of the Working Group to Access the Legal, Policy and Operational
Issues Related to Interrogation of Detainees Held by the U.S. Armed Forces in the War
on Terrorism (Final Report). These concerns center around the potential Department of
Defense (DOD) sanctioning of detainee interrogation techniques that may appear to
violate international law, domestic law, or both.

(U)
2. (S/NF) The Office of Legal Counsel (OLC), Department of Justice (DOJ), provided
DOD with its analysis of international and domestic law as it relates to the interrogation
of detainees held by the United States Government. This analysis was incorporated
into the subject draft Report and forms, almost exclusively, the legal framework for the
Report's Conclusions, Recommendations, and PowerPoint spreadsheet analysis of the
interrogation techniques in issue. I am concerned with several pivotal aspects of the
OLC opinion.

(U)
3. (S/NF) While the OLC analysis speaks to a number of defenses that could be raised
on behalf of those who engage in interrogation techniques later perceived to be illegal,
the "bottom line" defense proffered by OLC is an exceptionally broad concept of
"necessity." This defense is based upon the premise that any existing federal statutory
provision or international obligation is unconstitutional per se, where it otherwise
prohibits conduct viewed by the President, acting in his capacity as Commander-in-
Chief, as essential to his capacity to wage war. I question whether this theory would
ultimately prevail in either the U.S. courts or in any International forum. If such a
defense is not available, soldiers ordered to use otherwise illegal techniques run a
substantial risk of criminal prosecution or personal liability arising from a civil lawsuit.

(U)
4. (S/NF) The OLC opinion states further that customary international law cannot bind
the U.S. Executive Branch as it is not part of the federal law. As such, any presidential

DAJA-ZA
SUBJECT: Draft Report and Recommendations of the Working Group to Access the Legal, Policy and Operational Issues Related to Interrogation of Detainees Held by the U.S. Armed Forces in the War on Terrorism (U)

decision made in the context of the ongoing war on terrorism constitutes a "controlling" Executive act; one that immediately and automatically displaces any contrary provision of customary international law. This view runs contrary to the historic position taken by the United States Government concerning such laws and, in our opinion, could adversely impact DOD interests worldwide. On the one hand, such a policy will open us to international criticism that the "U.S. is a law unto itself." On the other, implementation of questionable techniques will very likely establish a new baseline for acceptable practice in this area, putting our service personnel at far greater risk and vitiating many of the POW/detainee safeguards the U.S. has worked hard to establish over the past five decades.

(U)

5. (S/NF) I recommend that the aggressive counter-resistance interrogation techniques under consideration be vetted with the Army intelligence community before a final decision on their use is made. Some of these techniques do not comport with Army doctrine as set forth in Field Manual (FM) 34-52, Intelligence Interrogation, and may be of questionable practical value in obtaining reliable information from those being interrogated.

THOMAS J. ROMIG
Major General, US Army
The Judge Advocate General

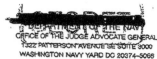

DEPARTMENT OF THE NAVY
OFFICE OF THE JUDGE ADVOCATE GENERAL
1322 PATTERSON AVENUE SE SUITE 3000
WASHINGTON NAVY YARD DC 20374-5066

IN REPLY REFER TO

13 Mar 02

MEMORANDUM FOR THE AIR FORCE GENERAL COUNSEL

Subj: COMMENTS ON THE 6 MARCH 2003 DETAINEE INTERROGATION
       WORKING GROUP REPORT

1. My comments on subject report are provided below. These
comments incorporate and augment those submitted by my action
officer earlier this week. New comments are highlighted within
the previously submitted text.

    1.(U) Page 2, second paragraph: Add new penultimate
    sentence to read, "In addition this paper incorporates
    significant portions of work product provided by the Office
    of Legal Counsel, United States Department of Justice." In
    the last sentence change "by a Department..." to "by the
    Department..." Finally, add new footnote to reference the
    OLC opinion to read "Memorandum dated March xx, 2003, Re:
    xxxxxxxxxx.
            -- Rationale: this WG paper contains large segments
    of DOJ work product, rather than being "informed" by DOJ.
    We believe the OLC opinion should be incorporated by
    reference into the WG report.

    2. (U) Page 24, second paragraph, last sentence: delete.
         -- Rationale: this sentence is not true. There are
    domestic limits on the President's power to interrogate
    prisoners. One of them is Congress's advice and consent to
    the US ratification to the Geneva Conventions that limit
    the interrogation of POWs. The willingness of the
    Executive, and of the Legislative Branch, to enforce those
    restrictions is a different matter.

    3. (U) Page 24, footnote 20: delete or rewrite to read,
    "This is the stated view of the Department of Justice."
         -- Rationale: Mr. Yoo clearly stated that he believes
    the viability of these defenses is greatly enhanced by
    advance Presidential direction in the matter. He
    specifically recommended obtaining such direction in
    writing.

    4.(U) Page 26, first full paragraph, first sentence:
    delete.

Derived from: AF/GC Interrogations WG draft report of 6 Mar 03
Reason: 1.5(e)
Declassify on: 10 years

Subj: COMMENTS ON THE 6 MARCH 2003 DETAINEE INTERROGATION
       WORKING GROUP REPORT

    -- Rationale: this statement is too broad. The similar
language used at the end of the following paragraph is more
accurate.

5. (U) (S) Page 29, second paragraph, fifth sentence: Rewrite
sentence to read, "A leading scholarly commentator..." and
later in the sentence change "...section 2340 would be
justified under ..." to "...section 2340 should be
justified under..."

    -- Rationale: There is only one article written by one
person cited. Also the quoted language from the commentator
indicates his view that torture should be permissible, not
a statement that international law allows such.

6. (U) (S) Page 29, second paragraph, last sentence: delete.
    -- Rationale: this conclusion is far too broad but the
general principle can be inferred from the discussion.

7. (U) Page 31, para d, third sentence and penultimate
sentences: delete
    -- Rationale: This analogy is inapt. There is nothing
in law enforcement that would authorize the use of torture
or excessive force against persons for intelligence
gathering.

8. (U) (S) Page 41, second paragraph, penultimate sentence:
delete.
    -- Rationale: it is not clear what the meaning of the
sentence is.

9. (U) (S) Page 59, second paragraph: it is unclear if SECDEF
must approve exceptional techniques on a case-by-case
basis, or just approve their use generally.

10. (U) Page 63, footnote 86. The text of this footnote
does not correspond to its citation in the paper. It
appears that the current text of footnote 86 belongs as
part of the discussion of API in the paragraph above, or
as part of the text of footnotes 83 or 84. Footnote 86
should detail the rationale for the Justice Department
determination that GCIV does not apply.

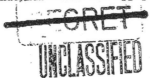

Subj: COMMENTS ON THE 6 MARCH 2003 DETAINEE INTERROGATION
      WORKING GROUP REPORT

11. (S) Page 67, technique 26: Add last sentence to read,
"Members of the armed forces will not threaten the detainee
with the possible results of the transfer, but will instead
limit the threat to the fact of transfer to allow the
detainee to form their own conclusions about such a move."
       -- Rationale: threatening the detainee with death or
injury (by the transfer) may be considered torture under
international law.

12. (S) Page 72, second paragraph: in the last sentence
replace "protections of the Geneva Conventions" with
"protections of the third Geneva Convention."
       -- Rationale: clarity

13. (S) Page 72, second paragraph: add new last sentence to
read: "Under international law, the protections of the
fourth Geneva Convention may apply to the detainees."
       -- Rationale: this view is shared by Chairman's Legal
and all the services.

14. (U) Page 72, third paragraph: at the beginning add, "In
those cases where the President has made a controlling
executive decision or action..."
       -- Rationale: this is the standard by which the
President may "override" CIL.

15. (S) Page 73, sixth paragraph: Add new last sentence to
read, "Presidential written directive to engage in these
techniques will enhance the successful assertion of the
potential defenses discussed in this paper."
       -- Rationale: much of the analysis in this paper is
premised on the authority of the President as
delegated/directed, in writing, to SECDEF and beyond. This
point needs to be made prominently.

16. (S) Matrix Annex, Technique 33: delete.
       -- Rationale: It is not clear what the intent of
this technique is. If it loses its effectiveness after the
first or second use, it appears to be little more than a
gratuitous assault. Other methods are equally useful in
getting/maintaining the attention of the detainee. It also
has the potential to be applied differently by different
individuals.

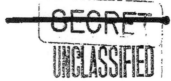

Subj: COMMENTS ON THE 6 MARCH 2003 DETAINEE INTERROGATION
WORKING GROUP REPORT

17. (U) Page 75, first paragraph, in the discussion re
technique 36: Rewrite 3rd to last and penultimate sentences
to read, "The working group believes use of technique 36
would constitute torture under international and U.S. law
and, accordingly, should not be utilized. In the event
SECDEF decides to authorize this technique, the working
group believes armed forces personnel should not
participate as interrogators as they are subject to UCMJ
jurisdiction at all times."

-- This is a correct statement of the positions of the
services party to the working group, who all believe this
technique constitutes torture under both domestic and
international law.

18. Thank you for the opportunity to comment. My action
officer in this matter is CDR Steve Gallotta, 614-4385.

MICHAEL F. LOHR
Rear Admiral, JAGC, U.S. Navy
Judge Advocate General

AFTERTHOUGHT

TO THE AMERICAN PEOPLE

REPORT

UPON THE

ILLEGAL PRACTICES

OF THE

UNITED STATES DEPARTMENT OF JUSTICE

Prepared, May, 1920

R. G. Brown,
    Memphis, Tenn.

Zechariah Chafee, Jr.,
    Cambridge, Mass.

Felix Frankfurter,
    Cambridge, Mass.

Ernst Freund,
    Chicago, Ill.

Swinburne Hale,
    New York City.

Francis Fisher Kane,
    Philadelphia, Pa.

Alfred S. Niles,
    Baltimore, Md.

Roscoe Pound,
    • Cambridge, Mass.

Jackson H. Ralston,
    Washington, D. C.

David Wallerstein,
    Philadelphia, Pa.

Frank P. Walsh,
    New York City.

Tyrrell Williams,
    St. Louis, Mo.

REPRINTED FOR

WORKERS' DEFENSE UNION

7 EAST 15TH STREET

NEW YORK CITY

NOVEMBER, 1920

Price, 25 Cents

The N. Y. Call Printing Co., 112 Fourth Ave., N. Y.

TO THE AMERICAN PEOPLE:

For more than six months we, the undersigned lawyers, whose sworn duty it is to uphold the Constitution and Laws of the United States, have seen with growing apprehension the continued violation of that Constitution and breaking of those Laws by the Department of Justice of the United States government.

Under the guise of a campaign for the suppression of radical activities, the office of the Attorney General, acting by its local agents throughout the country, and giving express instructions from Washington, has committed continual illegal acts. Wholesale arrests both of aliens and citizens have been made without warrant or any process of law; men and women have been jailed and held *incomunicado* without access of friends or counsel; homes have been entered without search-warrant and property seized and removed; other property has been wantonly destroyed; workingmen and working-women suspected of radical views have been shamefully abused and maltreated. Agents of the Department of Justice have been introduced into radical organizations. for the purpose of informing upon their members or inciting them to activities; these agents have even been instructed from Washington to arrange meetings upon certain dates for the express object of facilitating wholesale raids and arrests. In support of these illegal acts, and to create sentiment in its favor, the Department of Justice has also constituted itself a propaganda bureau, and has sent to newspapers and magazines of this country quantities of material designed to excite public opinion against radicals, all at the expense of the government and outside the scope of the Attorney General's duties.

We make no argument in favor of any radical doctrine as such, whether Socialist, Communist or Anarchist. No one of us belongs to any of these schools of thought. Nor do we now raise any question as to the Constitutional protection of free speech and a free press. We are concerned solely with bringing to the attention of the American people the utterly illegal acts which have been committed by those charged with the highest duty of enforcing the laws—acts which have caused widespread suffering and unrest, have struck at the foundation of American free institutions, and have brought the name of our country into disrepute.

These acts may be grouped under the following heads:

(1) Cruel and Unusual Punishments:

The Eighth Amendment to the United States Constitution provides:

> "Excessive bail shall not be required nor excessive fines imposed, nor cruel and unusual punishments inflicted."

Punishments of the utmost cruelty, and heretofore unthinkable in America, have become usual. Great numbers of persons arrested, both aliens and citizens, have been threatened, beaten with blackjacks, struck with fists, jailed under abominable conditions, or actually tortured. Annexed hereto as Exhibits 1-1c, 2-2f, 5a, 5b, and 9 are affidavits and evidence of these practices.

(2) Arrests without Warrant:

The Fourth Amendment to the Constitution provides:

> "The right of the people to be secure in their persons, houses, papers, and effects, against unreasonable searches and seizures, shall not be violated, and no Warrants shall issue, but upon probable cause, supported by Oath or affirmation, and particularly describing the place to be searched, and the persons or things to be seized."

Many hundreds of citizens and aliens alike have been arrested in wholesale raids, without warrants or pretense of warrants. They have then either been released, or have been detained in police stations or jails for indefinite lengths of time while warrants were being applied for. This practice of making mass raids and mass arrests without warrant has resulted directly from the instructions, both written and oral, issued by the Department of Justice at Washington. The cases are far too numerous to catalogue, but typical instances may be found in Exhibits 1-1b, 2-2f, 5 and 13. The secret instructions of the Department also appear as Exhibits 11 and 12.

(3) Unreasonable Searches and Seizures:

The Fourth Amendment has been quoted above.

In countless cases agents of the Department of Justice have entered the homes, offices, or gathering places of persons suspected of radical affiliations, and, without pretense of any search warrant, have seized and removed property belonging to them for use by the Department of Justice. In many of these raids property which could not be removed or was not useful to the Department, was intentionally smashed and destroyed. Exhibit 2a is a photograph of the interior of a house raided by the Department of Justice. Exhibit 14 gives a recent opinion of the U. S. Supreme Court in a non-radical case, condemning seizure without warrant by the Department of Justice, and Exhibit 15 the opinion of the U. S. District Court in Montana in a more flagrant radical case. Other Exhibits bearing on this point are 2, 2a, 3 and 13.

(4) Provocative Agents:

We do not question the right of the Department of Justice to use its agents in the Bureau of Investigation to ascertain when the law is being violated. But the American people has never tolerated the use of undercover provocative agents or "agents provocateurs," such as have been familiar in old Russia or Spain. Such agents have been introduced by the Department of Justice into the radical movements, have reached positions of influence therein, have occupied themselves with informing upon or instigating acts which might be declared criminal, and at the express direction of Washington have brought about meetings of radicals in order to make possible wholesale arrests at such meetings. Attention is specially called to Exhibits 10 and 11, which are the secret instructions issued from Washington, Exhibit 13 containing an abstract of the testimony in the Colyer case in this regard, and to Exhibits 6, 7 and 8.

(5) Compelling Persons to be Witnesses against Themselves:

The Fifth Amendment provides as follows:

> "No person * * * shall be compelled in any criminal case to be a witness against himself, nor be deprived of life, liberty, or property, without due process of law."

It has been the practice of the Department of Justice and its agents, after making illegal arrests without warrant, to question the accused person and to force admissions from him by terrorism, which admissions were subsequently to be used against him in deportation proceedings. Instances of this sort appear in various Exhibits numbers 1, 1b, and 2b-2f. Attention is also called to the Cannone case, Exhibit 9, in which Department agents committed assault, forgery and perjury.

(6) Propaganda by the Department of Justice:

The legal functions of the Attorney General are: to advise the Government on questions of law, and to prosecute persons who have violated federal statutes. For the Attorney General to go into the field of propaganda against radicals is a deliberate misuse of his office and a deliberate squandering of funds entrusted to him by Congress. Annexed, as Exhibit 17, is a copy of a form letter sent out by the Attorney General under date of January 27, 1920, to many magazines and editors throughout the country, deliberately intended to prejudice them in favor of his actions. Exhibit 18 is a description of an illustrated page offered free to country newspapers at the expense of the Department of Justice, patently designed to affect public opinion in advance of court decision and prepared in the manner of an advertising campaign in favor of repression. These documents speak for themselves.

The Exhibits attached are only a small part of the evidence which may be presented of the continued violation of law by the Attorney General's Department. These Exhibits are, to the best of our knowledge and belief (based upon careful investigation), truthful both in substance and detail. Drawn mainly from the four centers of New York City, Boston, Mass., Detroit, Mich., and Hartford, Conn., we know them to be typical of conditions which have prevailed in many parts of the country.

Since these illegal acts have been committed by the highest legal powers in the United States, there is no final appeal from them except to the conscience and condemnation of the American people. American institutions have not in fact been protected by the Attorney General's ruthless suppression. On the contrary, those institutions have been seriously undermined, and revolutionary unrest has been vastly intensified. No organizations of radicals acting through propaganda over the last six months could have created as much revolutionary sentiment in America as has been created by the acts of the Department of Justice itself.

Even were one to admit that there existed any serious "Red menace" before the Attorney General started his "unflinching war" against it, his campaign has been singularly fruitless. Out of the many thousands suspected by the Attorney General (he had already listed 60,000 by name and history on November 14, 1919, aliens and citizens) what do the figures show of net results? Prior to January 1, 1920, there were actually deported 263 persons. Since January 1 there have been actually deported 18 persons. Since January 1 there have been ordered deported an additional 529 persons, and warrants for 1,547 have been cancelled (after full hearings and consideration of the evidence) by Assistant Secretary of Labor Louis F. Post, to whose courageous reestablishment of American Constitutional Law in deportation proceedings (see Exhibit 16) are due the attacks that have been made upon him. The Attorney General has consequently got rid of 810 alien suspects, which, on his own showing, leaves him at least 59,160 persons (aliens and citizens) still to cope with.

It has always been the proud boast of America that this is a government of laws and not of men. Our Constitution and laws have been based on the simple elements of human nature. Free men cannot be driven and repressed; they must be led. Free men respect justice and follow truth, but arbitrary power they will oppose until the end of time. There is no danger of revolution so great as that created by suppression, by ruthlessness, and by deliberate violation of the simple rules of American law and American decency.

It is a fallacy to suppose that, any more than in the past, any servant of the people can safely arrogate to himself unlimited authority. To proceed upon such a supposition is to deny the fundamental American theory of the consent of the governed. Here is no question of a vague and threatened menace, but a present assault upon the most sacred principles of our Constitutional liberty.

The foregoing report has been prepared May, 1920, under the auspices of the National Popular Government League, Washington, D. C.

R. G. BROWN,
Memphis, Tenn.

ZECHARIAH CHAFEE, JR.,
Cambridge, Mass.

FELIX FRANKFURTER,
Cambridge, Mass.

ERNST FREUND,
Chicago, Ill.

SWINBURNE HALE,
New York City.

FRANCIS FISHER KANE,
Philadelphia, Pa.

ALFRED S. NILES,
Baltimore, Md.

ROSCOE POUND,
Cambridge, Mass.

JACKSON H. RALSTON,
Washington, D. C.

DAVID WALLERSTEIN,
Philadelphia, Pa.

FRANK P. WALSH,
New York City.

TYRRELL WILLIAMS,
St. Louis, Mo.

Index